# Failure and Success
# in America

# Martha Banta

◆

# FAILURE &
# SUCCESS
# in America,

◆

## A Literary
## Debate

PRINCETON
UNIVERSITY PRESS

78·51156

For A.O.
and J.S.
*who were* success
*and did not know it*

# ACKNOWLEDGMENTS

This book was pretty much a one-woman project from the start. I can, therefore, provide no impressive listing of typists, librarians, off spring, or research assistants to single out for gratitude. There were, of course, the good true friends who, without laying eyes on the manuscript, gave me what I needed when I needed it. And there were four—Robert Jacobs, Donald Kartiganer, Terence Martin, and Richard Roth—who happened upon my work in various of its stages. Their reactions and suggestions—whether acerbic, soothing, amusing, or provoking—were always intelligent and useful; they acted as the necessary carrot in front and goad at the rear to keep me moving forward through a long and difficult process. My thanks to them all.

## Copyright Acknowledgments

The Belknap Press of Harvard University Press
> Emily Dickinson. Reprinted by permission of the publishers and the Trustees of Amherst College from *The Poems of Emily Dickinson*, edited by Thomas H. Johnson, Cambridge, Mass.: The Belknap Press of Harvard University Press, Copyright © 1951, 1955 by the President and Fellows of Harvard College.

The University of California Press
> *Mark Twain's Fables of Man*, edited by John S. Tuckey. Copyright © 1972 by The Mark Twain Company; reprinted by permission of the University of California Press.
>
> Mark Twain's *Which Was the Dream? and Other Symbolic Writings of the Later Years*, edited by John S. Tuckey. Copyright © 1966 by The Mark Twain Company; reprinted by permission of the University of California Press.

Samuel L. Clemens
> Letter to William Dean Howells, and "Jim Wolf and the Tom-Cats": both used by arrangement with Thomas G. Chamberlain and Manufacturers Hanover Trust Company as Trustees under the Will of Clara Clemens Samossoud.

Condé Nast Publications, Inc.
> Caroline Seebohm. "*How to Change Your Point of View*." Courtesy *House & Garden*, Copyright © 1974 by The Condé Nast Publications, Inc.

John Dewey
> *Reconstruction in Philosophy*. Reprinted with the permission of the Center for Dewey Studies, Southern Illinois University at Carbondale.

E. P. Dutton Company, Inc.
   *Darwin on Man: A Psychological Study of Scientific Creativity* by Howard E. Gruber,
   together with Darwin's Early and Unpublished Notebooks, transcribed and annotated by Paul H. Barrett. Copyright © 1974 by Howard E. Gruber and Paul
   H. Barrett. Reprinted by permission of the publishers, E. P. Dutton.

Farrar, Straus & Giroux, Inc.
   Excerpted with the permission of Farrar, Straus & Giroux, Inc. from *Notebook*,
   Revised Edition, by Robert Lowell. Copyright © 1967, 1968, 1969, 1970 by
   Robert Lowell. From *Life Studies* by Robert Lowell, Copyright © 1956, 1959 by
   Robert Lowell.

William Heinemann Ltd
   D. H. Lawrence. "The Evening Land." From *The Complete Poems of D. H. Lawrence*. Published in London by William Heinemann Ltd. Reprinted by permission of Laurence Pollinger Ltd. and the Estate of the late Mrs. Frieda Lawrence.

Hill and Wang
   Excerpted with the permission of Hill and Wang (now a division of Farrar,
   Straus & Giroux, Inc.) from *The Narrative of Arthur Gordon Pym* by Edgar Allan
   Poe, Introduction by Sidney Kaplan, Copyright © 1960 by Hill and Wang.

Norman Mailer
   Reprinted by permission of the author and the author's agents, Scott Meredith
   Literary Agency, Inc., 845 Third Avenue, New York, N.Y. 10022.

McGraw-Hill Book Company
   Eldridge Cleaver, *Soul on Ice*. Copyright © 1968. Used with permission of
   McGraw-Hill Book Company.

Scarecrow Press
   Reprinted by permission from *Theodore Parker: American Transcendentalist*: A
   Critical Essay and a Collection of His Writings by Robert E. Collins. (Metuchen,
   N.J.: Scarecrow Press, 1973). Copyright © 1973 by Robert E. Collins.

Simon & Schuster Inc.
   Justin Kaplan, *Mr. Clemens and Mark Twain*. Permission granted by Simon &
   Schuster, a Division of Gulf & Western Corporation. Copyright © 1966.

Calvin Tomkins
   *Living Well is the Best Revenge*. Copyright © 1962, 1971 by Calvin Tomkins. First
   appeared, in somewhat different form, in *The New Yorker*. Reprinted by permission of the author and the author's agents, Robert Lescher, Literary Agency,
   155 East 71st Street, New York, N.Y., 10021.

The Viking Press
   Gaston Bachelard. *The Poetics of Space*. Copyright © 1964 by The Orion Press, a
   publication of Grossman Publishers, Inc. D. H. Lawrence. "The Evening
   Land." From *The Complete Poems of D. H. Lawrence* edited by Vivian de Sola Pinto
   and F. Warren Roberts. Copyright © 1964, 1971 by Angelo Ravagli and C. M.
   Weekley, Executors of The Estate of Frieda Lawrence Ravagli. Reprinted by
   permission of The Viking Press.

   Thomas Pynchon. From *Gravity's Rainbow* by Thomas Pynchon. Copyright ©
   1973 by Thomas Pynchon. Reprinted by permission of The Viking Press.

# TABLE OF CONTENTS

PART VI   The Economics of Going On

# Failure and Success
in America

I do not wish to live to wear out my boots.
—Ralph Waldo Emerson, "Immortality"

And after all who will be the really guilty? Those most certainly who fail of success.
—J. Hector St. John de Crèvecœur,
*Letters from an American Farmer*

It's a bad country to be stupid in—none on the whole so bad. If one doesn't know *how* to look and to see, one should keep out of it altogether.
—Henry James, *The American Scene*

We all enjoy the failure.
—Henry Adams, letter of March 12, 1909

# INTRODUCTION

This book examines the still-continuing debate over the nature of winning and losing in the American context—what it feels like for an American to succeed or to fail in a country which is often defined in terms of its own success or failure as an idea and as an experience. There is little chance of coming to a triumphant halt before the definitive answer to such issues. The many arguments given breathing space here will not settle matters; rather, they will serve to complicate, not to simplify, and to extend the debate past the last page, not to cut it off.

The focus is upon the varying effects which ideas about success and failure have had upon that personal and national narrative developed by any mind which asks, "What has been the purpose of America from the start? What am I doing to further its future meaning and my own? Are we together—self and nation—succeeding or have we already failed?" Whatever cast such questions take, what matters most is winning and losing as a series of concepts, not what the world might designate as an achieved fact. In the following pages much attention is given to the mind that tosses and turns over the flawed efforts to do well and to be good which living in America exacts, and to the emotions felt by the American who senses the pressure to gain certain great ends—the emotions of contentment or chagrin, pride or shame, which rise from his need to fulfill the grand scheme of his own life and of America's destiny.

The book is divided into six parts which are, in turn, developed through a series of short chapters. The opening section sets forth the fundamental questions raised by the book's implied admonition: *more than survival*. It asks whether mind and heart are satisfied with bodily survival or whether something else is demanded before success is acknowledged. It also begins to consider this book's other concern—*less than perfection*—by questioning whether the one true criterion for success is to have reached that point past which there is nowhere better to go.

Part II examines a number of responses to America viewed as the ultimate geographical place and imaginative context for human efforts, achievements, and lapses. Part III looks at several types of the successful American. Part IV considers what Americans do when facing the fact that they have failed—what manner of gestures toward themselves, their fellows, and their country they might make, urged by shame or guilt. Part v drives to its extreme the question of how the failed American may react to defeated hopes; it surveys certain apocalyptic visions which American imaginations have offered as a way out of personal and national failure by forcing a conclusion to all human action. The section that closes the book is entitled "The Economics of Going On"; it suggests a synthesis of the many ideas that have emerged from the preceding pages and proposes a possible resolution of a mental situation which remains dangerous as long as the absence of success agitates violent reactions, vindictive or despairing.

There are dangers when men cannot stand the fact of having failed; there are dangers as well in trying to gauge the possible meanings of failure and success. Therefore, certain decisions have been made about the kinds of book this one is *not*, together with the particular kind it is, in order to bring the subject and its presentation into compatibility.

This book does not deal alone with what any one person has decided success or failure conveys to him or to her. Nor does it follow the strict development of the history of an idea, curbed by the dictates of chronological progression. It is not a review of what one closely knit group has had to say on the subject during a specifically limited period of American life. Instead, *Failure and Success in America: a Literary Debate* moves over a span of three hundred and fifty years of discussion; it chooses to shift back and forth, seeking out conceptual bedfellows no matter where they lie; it listens to a number of Americans as they aggressively appropriate the subject of winning and losing to their own imaginative needs.

The representative writers whose voices are attended to with the greatest constancy are Emerson, Thoreau, Mark Twain, Henry Adams, William and Henry James, Gertrude Stein, and Norman Mailer. They—and others who, like Franklin, Poe, Melville, Hawthorne, Faulkner, and Fitzgerald, appear less frequently but with some regularity—were selected for the advantages that are gained when such a book is committed to a number of contending (although not unpleasantly contentious) arguments. From these detailed debates we can watch an edifice of meaning in the process of being built. This house of argument may have many rooms, but each has a door that connects it to the others. These Americans hold different opinions, but their views keep converging, each acting to sharpen the edges of the others' concerns. It is a round-robin narrative we encounter here, one that is continually revised by the participating consciousnesses into a fiction that contains its own reality about success because also intent upon recording what failure is like. This narrative returns again and again to the central sensitive spot, often for the same perverse reasons our tongue seeks out an aching tooth. But always the crucial motive for such returns is to dislodge us from false delusions about what America is, as when Henry James as a child went to see *Uncle Tom's Cabin* once, then twice: first, in order to be wholly beguiled by it; next, with the conscious intent of *not* being beguiled.

The main speakers here are big names. As representative types, they are hardly substitutes for all "the little people" who care just as much whether they have experienced success and evaded defeat; nor can these selected spokesmen be said to know it all. For every wise saying offered up by Emerson there is the comment (included in Emerson's *Works*) by a fellow-townsman who said of Concord's sage, "Well, I suppose there's a good many things that he knows that I don't know anything about, and I *know* there's a lot o' things that I know a damn' sight more about than he does" (VII, 427). Indeed, and so the voice of this nameless Yankee and his like will not be entirely absent. He will be freely granted entrance into the discussion as long as he matches the type Emerson himself hailed as "the speculative man," "the right hero"—the person who is "not there to defend himself but to deliver his message . . . if broken, he can at least scream; gag him, he can still write it; bruise, mutilate him, cut off his hands and feet, he can still crawl towards his object on his stumps." That was the one Emerson, in an oration of 1876, labeled "The Scholar"; but, as we know, "scholar" for Emerson was a term he freely applied to all who devote themselves—succeeding or failing—to the life of profound winning through.

This book views America by the dawn's early light (Thoreau), by the high noon of common day (Howells), and by lurid moonshine (Poe). Crèvecœur's Farmer James and Hawthorne's Ethan Brand are quite different, but both are Americans to the core, recording experiences and defining reality in ways neither of which we dare deny. Nathaniel Ward of *The Simple Cobler of Aggawam* would rage over letting such a multiplicity of opinions gain sway against the single truth he knew was possessed by New England Congregationalists alone. For Ward and the Puritans, success and failure were synonyms for salvation and damnation, heaven and hell, God and Satan; the issue had been fixed from the beginning of time and admitted to no swervings from the revealed truth. But be-

fore contemporary scholarship and literary criticism can feel free
to come within touching distance of any manner of conclusion it
has to confront the kind of argumentative, opinionated, complicating evidence which ever infuriated Ward and his kind.

If, as seen from the point of view of an absolutist like Ward, this
book represents the heresy of resisting predetermined conclusions,
it also abides by a statement of Emerson's that helps to ground the
lightning flashes that come from writers like Norman Mailer, William James, Gertrude Stein, and Mark Twain. In the sermon
"Calamities" of 1831 Emerson pronounced, "What seems success to
many may be the worst of failures in the eye of God." This Emersonian belief is in no way limited to his early frocked-priest period.
Ten years later, in "The Method of Nature," he proclaimed that
"there is success or there is not." It is this absolute of achievement
lying somehow beyond the immediate range of fluctuating circumstances which provides the granite base and indicates the quicksand
surface of this book, if only because it is so clear as a theoretical
norm and so impossible as a worldly definition.

If we take success as an absolute state of being, success—paired
with failure—takes its place beside unequivocal words such as perfection and corruption, virginal and pregnant, unique and usual,
conclusion and continuations. Still there is, to paraphrase Henry
James, everything still to be said. Even if we could declare that
achieved states of success and failure are kinds of Pure Forms, the
various means Americans have taken to mount the Platonic ladder
in search of these universals are as relative as the historical particulars through which men think and act.

This book's "everything still to be said" works with relative conceptual means as they are applied to absolute conceptual ends. It
deals with ideas about what success is and what its opposite is not. It
concentrates on the imagination of fulfillment and frustration, not
on economic and sociological data. To go with data rather than
ideas would place the book's emphasis exactly in areas it seeks to
avoid. By seeming to limit the meaning of success and failure to
facts of material achievement and tangible social position, it would
tend to imply that success in America is measured alone by how
much one owns, how many votes one controls, or how many attend
to the call of one's written words.

The three main foci are the thoughts, the feelings, and the language of Americans caught in the press between winning and losing. Certain philosophers, psychologists, and historians furnish
supplementary material, using the expository prose forms native to

their professions. The major arguments are provided, however, by the poets of the imagination, who are apt to approach meaning through metaphors. As a result, there are times when the seams of the argument are jagged, as when the language of a philosopher like William James is laid next to that of a novelist like Henry James. An adjustment must be made between the statement set down by the one and the image built up by the other (that is, when William himself is not dealing zestfully with figurative speech). But the ideas of both men and the particular written forms they use are to be granted equal worth—at least at the start.

Another constant that steadies the book's dialectic is the concern most of these writers show over what may be called the psychological economics of success: such evaluations as too much, too little, or just enough. Related to this is their insistence that succeeding and failing are moral issues. There is guilt over that success which the recipient cannot honestly consider truly earned and shame over the failure to get enough of what is well and good. There is the consequent temptation to despair which arises from the inability *to have* whatever it takes to succeed. Finally, there is the paradox of that demand which equates success with perfection—the ultimate total amount—yet which places one's humanity in jeopardy if ever one should get just that.

According to some of the voices listened to here, success finds its manifestation only in the realm of the phenomenal. For others this knuckle-bruising world must make a finer extension by means of various modes of transcendent thought (orthodox or not) so that the noumenal is included within the final ground for success. In either instance, emphasis remains upon the enactment of the *ideas* of success and failure (which is not the same as "real-life" stories) in terms of *the world as it is* (which does without the deferred enjoyment of treasures laid up in heaven). Concepts of success defined as Pure Form attainable only "elsewhere" are hardly the main concern, any more than the fact of success defined as hard, graspable cash. Little attention is paid the premise that success is solely possible either as a mental act projected upon Lubberland, or as getting goods in Los Angeles. The passionate nature of these writers' considerations arises from their belief that success takes place—if and whenever it does—with one point of its golden compass fixed in the realm of the phenomenal. The question that tugs their debate to and fro is whether or not the other leg of that compass locates itself to any extent in the noumenal.

References to phenomenal and noumenal imply *place*. Place is important in yet another way in this book since it most frequently lodges the sources of its arguments in the minds of American writers, thereby suggesting that the work of art provides the strongest position from which the American artist can present ideas of success crucial to us all.

Place is defined alternately as an historical, psychological, metaphysical, as well as geographical fact. It tells us where we are in relation to past mistakes, to the continuing need for success, and to the possibilities for making it or failure come about. Look at it from Emerson's point of view, for instance. In his journal of 1838 he records that he told Thoreau that we are artists because we are unsuccessful people living in an unsuccessfully realized world:

> I acceded & confessed that this was the tragedy of Art that the Artist was at the expense of the Man; & hence, in the first age, as they tell, the Sons of God printed no epics, carved no stone, painted no picture, built no railroad; for the sculpture, the poetry, the music, & architecture were in the Man. (vii, 144)

According to Emerson, once the success of self and of society is fully attained, art will no longer be required. His observation provides a revealing sidelight to his assertion that success is an absolute, characterized by the unchanging fact of fulfilled perfection. In Emerson's mandate, art is that *place*, that stage, in human affairs marked by less than perfection; once the farther place of full achievement is reached, art as the fact of a lesser state of existence is ended. In direct response to Emerson's belief, this book chooses to stay with art, taking America as the time-place (not merely the space-place) in which art and artists play such important roles precisely *because* theirs is less than perfection.

What counts here is an American existence in which art is part of the reality and the proof of failure. We shall constantly deal with those works which are successful as "good art" because they effectively express the idea of the "good life" that we do not possess in America. With the exception of Part v and its look at American apocalypses, the greater portion of this book is given over to the place here and the time now: where art has not yet negated itself since, at its best, it lives side by side with the *imagination* of success, not with its actuality. For after all, it was not a tale of despair which Emerson told to Thoreau. Artists have a sane and necessary need to do away with the worth to society of their own activities; they must continually apply the pressure of art to whatever keeps men *from* success and *in* "the state of art," even as they (in Henry Adams' words) "all enjoy the failure." It is this two-way relationship which constitutes the artists' reality and reveals to us all the true presence of the America in which they and we live.

Having or not having success is a matter of practical concern for no other reason than the long tradition in America that insists on taking into account the whole being of the American and the entire swath of the country's history. At the onset the New England Puritans viewed achievement as a question of how well the soul rose in response to the urgent occasion of God's plan. By the eighteenth and nineteenth centuries, the shift was made from soul to self, just as emphasis on the cosmic destiny emanating from the City on the Hill passed to the national destiny making manifest the pronouncements flowing from Capitol Hill. Whether the definition of the terms of achievement is religious or secular, success in America seems a matter of all we do and are. Failure is thereby the betrayal of the total space we inhabit, whether it is defined as God's universe joined with the innermost regions of the soul, or as the American continent interlaid with the multiple layers of the self.

Norman Mailer likes to make grand connective sweeps between past, present, and future acts. He suggests one kind of imaginative unity-in-multiplicity which this book in its own way also attempts. A good example of Mailer's working over the question, "How successful are we?" is found at the end of *Of a Fire on the Moon* (p. 461f.). In his role as Aquarius, Mailer gives himself over to the meaning of American missions, carried out on levels both intellectually analytical and sensually impressionistic. He tries to judge the kind of success the Wasps of the NASA group have accomplished; he wonders, Why them? Why not such types as the blacks, the flower-children, and himself? Like a latter-day Gibbon or Adams, Mailer takes his seat upon a strategic viewing place. For him it is the dunes of Provincetown—"the beginning of America for Americans." There he muses about this edge of the continent "where the Pilgrims had first sailed around the point, anchored, and rowed an explorer's boat to shore"—where they confronted the land-mass which had earlier interposed its bulk between Columbus and the success of reaching India. Mailer also busies his mind over the breaking up of his marriage to his fourth wife, Beverly, a woman he has been careful to connect with the meaning of America. He further records the sad ceremony of interment for a defunct Ford whose physical collapse Mailer associates with the general moral and aesthetic failures he witnesses all around. As he draws together his report about the achievement of Mission Control in Houston in launching Apollo 11, he suggests that his own success—as a man, a writer, and an American—is somehow interwoven with the events of this, the most recent exploration into the unknowns of space, as well as the consequences of that earlier thrust across the Atlantic to Provincetown. At the end of his meditations, we as readers are left with several Mailerian questions concerning the quality of spirit it takes to get to the New World of the moon from the Old World of the earth; questions, too, whether this accomplishment is commensurate with the truest meaning of mission and the fulfillment of a proper destiny; whether it is the highest success or the deepest failure to have gone so far and done so little of all there is to do.

Like Mailer at Provincetown, like Nick Carraway on the shores of Long Island, we keep reaching out to take hold of the fabled green breast of America's meaning—grasping with that imagination whose very possession sets us as humans apart from all other created things and which lets us know, at least, what we have not got which we very, very much wish we had. Whatever meaning emerges through this book's act of grasping comes, must come, by the end of the next six sections, but not too soon, else the natural fluency of the ideas rigidifies past recognition.

We cannot take too much care to avoid fixing America in any one image: as the "Virgin Land" or the "World Elsewhere"; as the "No in Thunder" or the "Light of Common Day"; as the "Destructive Element" or "The New Heaven and New Earth." Eventually perhaps, but not yet.

In his study of E. M. Forster, Lionel Trilling chided Forster for being a critic "with no drive to consistency, no desire to find an architectonic for his impressions. We might say of him that he is a critic without any desire of *success*. In short, he is an impressionistic critic" (p. 165). So be it, but this book wants to win by moving *through* impressionism to architectonics. In this it represents that prevailing American hope of success which goes nowhere without an ingrained awareness of potential failure.

## ON FINDING THE SOURCES

A book which does without footnotes must find a way to guide its readers toward the sources of the material it uses, while avoiding eye-stopping parenthetical paraphernalia. In an attempt to meet these requirements information has been blended into the text to

make it relatively easy to get at the sources through consultation
with the listings given in the Selected Bibliography.

References and quotations taken from book-length material are
followed by page numbers. Citations from poems, essays, dated letters, and journal entries do without pagination. The understanding is that, in most cases, the original item is sufficiently short or
identifiable to allow searchers to track down the exact locations on
their own without too much difficulty.

However, when—as is sometimes the case with Emerson and
Thoreau—the journal entries are undated, pagination is given.
And—as in the cases of Henry Adams and William James, for
instance—where several sources for cited letters are likely, information is provided concerning the edition from which the quotations are taken.

Finally, as a look through the Selected Bibliography will show,
convenient anthologies are listed after certain titles (generally essays or extracts from lengthy works) as being convenient places to
find the required passages. The system used here is by no means
flawless. It does not guarantee pin-point precision in every instance. But it does provide most of the information needed for the
moment, and clues for further successful consultation of the basic
documents.

PART I

# The More
# or Less
# of Success

# CHAPTER 1

# The Insufficiency
# of Survival

In 1878 William James examined the issue of survival in the essay
"Remarks on Spencer's Definition of Mind as Correspondence." As
James phrases it, Spencer in his *Principles of Psychology* of 1855 had
decreed that if survival were to be named the highest good:

> We should then have, as the embodiment of the highest ideal
> perfection of mental development, a creature of superb cog-
> nitive endowments, from whose piercing perceptions no fact
> was too minute or too remote to escape; whose all-embracing
> foresight no contingency could find unprepared; whose invin-
> cible flexibility of resource no array of outward onslaught
> could overpower; but in whom all these gifts were swayed by
> the single passion of love of life, of survival at any price.

Having stated his version of Spencer's position, James then
thrusts forth his own observations:

> There can be no doubt that, if such an incarnation of earthly
> prudence existed, a race of beings in whom this monotonously
> narrow passion for self-preservation were aided by every cog-
> nitive gift, they would soon be kings of all the earth.

Even so, James speculates, Spencer would be unable to "hail with
hearty joy their advent . . . while the common sense of mankind
would stand aghast at the thought of them."

Years earlier, William's father, the senior Henry James, had included in certain autobiographical fragments (made available in
Matthiessen's *The James Family*) a statement of his own opposition to
"the lack of any idea of action but that of self-preservation." Devoted as he was to spiritual fineness and social rejuvenation, the
elder James abhorred what he called "the worldly mind." Wherever he found its taint in political or religious arenas of action, he
named such self-interestedness "their curse, because they thus
conflict with the principles of universal justice, or God's providen-

tial order in the earth, which rigidly enjoins that *each particular thing exist for all, and that all things in general exist for each*" (pp. 20-21).

The generation of which William James was an eminent representative was more complicated in its responses to the self and society than the generation his father chastised. Social complicity gained in merit, while bold self-aggrandizement became increasingly suspect. But William had more on his mind when he placed Spencer's views under attack than the good of the community set off against prizes seized for the self alone. If the notion, prompted by the Spencerian drive to survive, of total adjustment of mind and body to the environment is contemplated with horror by men of common sense, what were they to make of the desire not to adjust at all? May violent failure to stay alive be justified over mere survival? If so, one's ability to keep in line with biological realities no longer has much to do with ideas of success.

Three young men, boys actually—Arthur, Tom, and Sam—recount their hearts' desire:

> My visions were of shipwreck and famine; of death or captivity among barbarian hordes; of a lifetime dragged out in sorrow and tears, upon some gray and desolate rock, in an ocean unapproachable and unknown. Such visions or desires—for they amounted to desires—are common. . . . (p. 15)

> The Marquesas! What strange visions of outlandish things does the very name spirit up! Naked houris—cannibal banquets—groves of coconut—coral reefs—tattooed chiefs— and bamboo temples; sunny valleys planted with breadfruit trees—carved canoes dancing on the flashing blue waters— savage woodlands guarded by horrible idols—*heathenish rites and human sacrifices*.
>
> Such were the strangely jumbled anticipations that haunted me during our passage from the cruising ground. I felt an irresistible curiosity to see those islands. . . . (p. 5)

> Pretty soon he would be hundreds and hundreds of miles away on the great plains and deserts, and among the mountains of the Far West, and would see buffaloes and Indians, and prairie dogs, and antelopes, and have all kinds of adventures, and maybe get hanged or scalped, and have ever such a fine time, and write home and tell us all about it, and be a hero. (VII, 15-16)

These "boys" (projected by Poe, Melville, and Mark Twain in the opening pages respectively of *The Narrative of Arthur Gordon Pym*, *Typee*, and *Roughing It*) seem uninterested in living long enough to become "men." They demonstrate the possible truth of the theory put forward as well by the narrator of Poe's "The Imp of the Perverse." By favoring thrills that lead toward destruction, the "boys" deny that self-preservation is the urgent fact dominating human existence. Like the "sports" of Darwinian conjecture, they exist as excrescences which nature might cut away for refusing to conform to the basic requirement for survival: desiring it over all.

It is argued by some observers of the American scene that the boy-heart and the perverse imagination are all too characteristic of the national type. But let us return to William James—no boy—to determine whether he is able to sustain his advocacy of gaudy adventure and to justify deviations from nature's norms that fly in the face of prudential adjustment to the way things are. And to see whether he can yet pluck survival from his argument for "more than" that.

It is telling that, in his essay on Spencer, James says he speaks for common sense. Asking why "common opinion" craves "greater 'richness' of nature in its mental ideal," he quickly offers his own answer:

> . . . survival is only one out of many interests. . . . Most men would reply that they are all that make survival worth securing. The social affections, all the various forms of play, the thrilling intimations of art, the delights of philosophical contemplation, the rest of religious emotion, the joy of moral self-approbation, the charm of fancy and of wit—some or all of these are absolutely required to make the notion of mere existence tolerable. . . .

Those persons who help satisfy such impractical desires—the story-teller, the musician, the theologian, the actor, the mere charmer—are given the world's approval, James insists. Even if they themselves are weakly adjusted to life, such non-survivors are valuable because they speak to more than the externalities of existence. Through them James makes clear his belief that ideal wants must be taken into account in any argument touching the nature and value of survival.

James particularly honors qualities incompatible with survival— self-imperiling generosity, recklessness, heroism: "Even if headlong courage, pride, and martyr-spirit do ruin the individual, they benefit the community as a whole whenever they are displayed by

one of its members against a competing tribe." Sounding the note
heard in his father's autobiographical comment, he adds a remarkable new edge: " 'It is death to you, but fun for us.' Our interest in
having the hero as he is, plays indirectly into the hands of our survival, though not of his."

Our fun, your death, a good covenant, for the one side of the
bargain, at least. Was this perhaps the position taken by the Lord
God in binding the first settlers contractually to His pleasure when
He offered them America in return? That this is so is implied by
Caroline Sturgis when, upon addressing the "conversation group"
of 1841 recalled in Margaret Fuller's *Memoirs*, she specified the reasons for God's motives in creating the earth: "God creates from the
fulness of life, and cannot but create; he created us to overflow,
without being exhausted, because what he created, necessitated
new creation. It is not to make us happy, but creation is his happiness and ours." From this we might conclude that whoever "invents" a place rather than merely discovering it (as Henry James's
pert French Noémie Nioche comments about Columbus in *The
American*) gives far more weight to the self-gratifications of creation
than to sound survival. What this implies in general about the need
for the imaginative act in America will be a constant motif from
here on. But first to revisit William James's debate with Herbert
Spencer.

James wished men to resist Spencerian pressures to devote themselves to a formula marked by "unity and simplicity" which, in turn,
equated success with self-preservation. (In this James was consistent since he also denied his father's methods of "unity and simplicity," even though he, like the elder James, argued against taking
self-survival as the sole human good.) In his essay on Spencer,
James asks instead for multiplicity and extravagance. He gives his
consent to that "luxuriant foliage of ideal interests" which "co-exist
along with that of survival." Extra appendages like the tail and the
appendix give human animals no direct aid in their bumbling
along, but they are interesting to James for that very reason. He
believed that even Spencer might allow practical consideration to
the "secondary consequences and corollaries" of the law of
survival—qualities such as "Conscience, thoroughness, purity, love
of truth, susceptibility to discipline, eager delight in fresh impressions. . . ." Although these qualities were not "traits of Intelligence *in se*," they "may thus be marks of a general mental energy,
without which victory over nature and over other human com-
petitors would be impossible."

At this point in his essay (in ways typical of his method of literary argument) James stops leaning over backward to give Spencer the chance to look clever and even profound; he now straightens up with a snap and demands that we face the main issue.

But here it is decidedly time to take our stand and refuse our aid in propping up Mr. Spencer's definition by any further good-natured translations and supplementary contributions of our own. It is palpable at a glance that a mind whose survival interest could only be adequately secured by such a wasteful array of energy squandered on side issues would be immeasurably inferior to one like that . . . in which the monomania of tribal preservation should be the one all-devouring passion.

Here we come to the center of James's argument. Is the human intelligence that spins past prudential concerns a digression from, perhaps the perversion of, the human need to survive? Or is the intelligence the means by which we succeed best, since it enables us to live in possession of more than biological life? In this essay of 1878, James is speaking in generalized terms about the nature of all human existence. Yet his observations serve us in a more particularized examination of what life in America has to offer. It lets us ask whether America, specifically, gives men the best of first chances, or the hope of a second chance when the original try fails, or only the final nudge toward failure and death.

The economics of existence (which meant so much, as we shall see, to both Franklin and Thoreau) concerns William James greatly. Before moving in to demolish the advocates of Spencerian unity, simplicity, and frugality, James candidly admits, "If ministry to survival be the sole criterion of mental excellence, then luxury and amusement, Shakespeare, Beethoven, Plato, and Marcus Aurelius, stellar spectroscopy, diatom markings, and nebular hypotheses are by-products on too wasteful a scale." Such excesses, indeed, accumulate into a slag-heap that "abstracts more energy than it contributes to the ends of the machine." Therefore, "every serious evolutionist" must consider the need to reduce the "number and amount of these outlying interests, and the diversion of energy they absorb into purely prudential channels."

If such "economics" is a crucial matter in determining the weight and worth of our existence, where are we to find the "Greenwich Mean"—the sound standards—for our evaluations? "Here, then, is our dilemma," James says:

One man may say that the law of mental development is dominated solely by the principle of conservation; another, that
richness is the criterion of mental evolution; a third, that pure
cognition of the actual is the essence of worthy thinking—but
who shall pretend to decide which is right? The umpire would
have to bring a standard of his own upon the scene, which
would be just as subjective and personal as the standards used
by the contestants. And yet some standard there must be, if we
are to attempt to define in any way the worth of different mental manifestations.

Characteristically, James takes for granted that all human standards have a subjective source; he assumes that no one can ever
know who is right, once the debate has wound to its end. No matter
how vital absolute answers might be to our comprehension of why
we exist and how well we do at it, he declares against the fundamental dishonesty of believing in the existence of such absolutes.
Still, other commentators on the American scene have not joined
with James in his stand on the essential tentativeness of standards
of evaluation. The Puritans, Thoreau—and even Mark Twain in
certain moods—are among those who maintain that they are able
to make out certain laws which are eternal, universal, and ultimately verifiable to the minds of men. Obviously it makes a difference whether a lasting formula for the economy of success is recur-
rently revealed to successive generations, or whether each man in
his own time must fabricate mathematical metaphors to express a
personal ratio of expended mental energy to the yielded quality of
survival.

There is yet a further complication in the relation of human intelligence to physical survival viewed as both quantity and quality.
Many fathers are unable to forgive the wastefulness of their prodigal sons, certainly those fathers who decree that success goes to
whoever learns that "Penny wise is pound foolish" and "Early to
bed and early to rise, makes a man healthy, wealthy, and wise." But
although such fathers—and they are legion—frown upon fleshly
extravagances and ill-kept books, some adhere to an even higher
economy which urges, to use William James's words, "the
reinstatement of the vague and inarticulate to its proper place in
our mental life." To such, the wasteful, the relative, and the vague
replace the frugal, the absolute, and the concrete as elements of the
successful try at getting more than survival.

This statement by James of his resistance to an economics that gives value only to what can be marketed in measured, packaged units comes in the midst of his chapter, "The Stream of Thought," contained in the original 1890 edition of *Principles of Psychology*. If a thought-stream is intended to represent the life we possess by means of our consciousness, James seems to prefer rivers with great sprawl and diverse natures. He likes, as it were, the dangerous, fascinating Mississippi (with its sand-bottom, shifting banks, two-toned muddy/clear waters, and capacity for destroying men's fortunes and lives); he prefers the Mississippi-mind to one likened to the tidy, rock-bottomed European rivers upon whose readily charted waters commercial success comes more easily:

The traditional psychology talks like one who should say a river consists of nothing but pailsful, spoonsful, quartpotsful, barrelsful, and other moulded forms of water. Even were the pails and the pots all actually standing in the stream, still between them the free water would continue to flow. It is just this free water of consciousness that psychologists resolutely overlook.

But James, no traditionalist, states his own fascination with the unmoulded:

Every definite image in the mind is steeped and dyed in the free water that flows round it. With it goes the sense of its relations, near and remote, the dying echo of whence it came to us, the dawning sense of whither it is to lead. The significance, the value, of the image is all in this halo or penumbra that surrounds and escorts it . . . leaving it, it is true, an image of the same *thing* it was before, but making it an image of that thing newly taken and freshly understood.
*Let us call the consciousness of this halo of relations around the image by the name of "psychic overtone" or "fringe."*

For William James the trick was to survive in the midst of the destructive element, while being other than the flotsam on the flood; to be of the world, and yet more than it; to be both the object and the halo-glow surrounding it; to be in serious relation with the thing and also to become its playful extension.

# ◣ CHAPTER 2 ◥

# The Sum Total
# of Possibility

We turn from William James's halo that eradiates and enriches—
and confusingly complicates—objects by extending them far beyond their original compact, utilitarian, readily comprehensible
core. Now to hear from Josiah Royce, contemporary and philosophical adversary of James. In his 1897 work, *The Conception of
God*, Royce set down his position as neo-absolutist and idealist (the
stance James rebuked with friendly lack of rancor when he told
Royce, "Damn the Absolute!" and smiled as he said it, the two men
facing one another, astraddle a fence in a famous photograph). Listen to Royce's actual words before his phrases and James's are put
to work on the question of how our minds become conscious of
America. For if James insists that success is a matter of consciousness, not merely of physical self-preservation, and if Royce also locates value in the mind's possession of an object, then we have the
basis for proposing that the essential issue of success or failure in
America takes direction from the ways in which America is perceived, conceived, or manages to deceive.

Royce starts off with the crucial statement and the necessary
question:

> But now, in us, our ideas, our thoughts, our questions, not
> merely concern what experienced facts might come to us
> through our senses, but also concern the value, the worth, the
> relations, the whole significance, ethical or aesthetic, of our
> particular experiences themselves. We ask: Shall I win success?
> And the question implies the idea of an experience of success
> which we now have not. . . . Misfortune comes to us, and we
> ask? What means this horror of my fragmentary experience?
> . . . The question involves the idea of an experience that, if
> present, would answer the questions. Now such an experience,
> if it were present to us, would be an experience of a certain
> passing through pain to peace, of a certain winning of triumph
> through partial defeat, of a certain far more exceeding weight

of glory that would give even this fragmentary horror its place
in an experience of triumph and of self-possession.

Royce next asserts that, although individual experiences do not
present us with an organized whole, "the fact of the consensus of
the various experiences of men . . . suggests to our conception an
ideal—the ideal of an experience which should be not only man-
ifold but united, not only possessed of chance agreements but reduced to an all-embracing connectedness." This is a premise he
knows he needs to test. But how to do it?

Royce's foremost example of unity is God. God is what the
human consciousness often fights to work past, not surprisingly,
since consciousness distrusts "a conceived ideal" of the "significant,
whole, and connected experience" which it continually fails to
reach as direct experience. Frustrated, men query, "Is this conception a mere ideal? Or does it stand for a genuine sort of concrete
experience?" Frustrated, since the experience of unity is "always
sought, never present."

> . . . we have come to appeal from what the various men do ex-
> perience to what they all ought to experience, or would expe-
> rience if their experiences were in unity; that is, if all their
> moments were linked expressions of one universal meaning
> which was present to one Universal Subject, of whose insight
> their own experiences were but fragments. Such an ideally
> united experience, if it could but absolutely define its own
> contents, would know reality.

A number of the Puritans who came to the New England shores
believed that their mission was to reveal, in America, the "one Universal Subject" of God and God's plan for mankind. Later inhabitants of the continent converted the land and the nation itself into
their deity; still others came to see America as a limb of Satan or the
land of the social tyrant. This series of shifts through history drastically affected what "the consensus of the various experiences of
men" took to be the united experience. The ideal-made-reality has
shifted from God to America, and from America as a place partak-
ing in the success of heaven to that place which makes vivid to some
men the failure they feel as hell.

The basic process, however, by which the consciousness strains to
come at this unifying consensus has not altered all that much.
Minds filled with bewildered, splintered perceptions of America
still yearn to draw those perceptions together into a triumphant,

united state of consciousness; the yearning continues because the promise of success remains. From the first, whether the consciousness devoted itself to gaining greater glory for God or for the independent self, consciousness in America has acted as if all things were possible—even the power to transform the ideal into the real.

Royce summed up the essential American situation when he stated, "A possibility is a truth expressed in terms of a proposition beginning with *if*, or a hypothetical proposition,—an *is* expressed in terms of an *if*." "Every *if* implies an *is*," he concluded. Charles Sanders Peirce, although frequently a philosophical antagonist of Royce, leaned toward Royce on this point: leaned across the example of the father of William James to do so when in a letter of January 23, 1903 to William he cited the elder James's book *Substance and Shadow* in order to agree that "The real is composed of the potential and actual *together*" (*James Family*, p. 138).

When a reality linked to its ideal centers around our consciousness of that state of being, or soul, we call America, we have a strong case in point concerning the potency of that union. We are also provided with special terms by which success and failure might be judged. *Is* as the value and meaning of unity prompts dissatisfaction with *is* as purposeless circumstances. The latter denies *if*; the former is defined by possibilities that could come true. Succeeding fully, rather than surviving partially, can come thereby to depend on the *is* that America provides for every *if*.

Pilgrims and Puritans voyaged to America not merely to survive, a trick they might possibly have brought off in the Old World. They expected to do far more than to endure. Their mission was to make God's kingdom of spiritual light prevail in that darksome wilderness which, so one story went at the time, God had carefully withheld from view until 1492, the eve of the Reformation. Once Luther's hammer tapped the Theses to the church door at Wittenberg, it was safe for history to lead the purified protesters against the Whore of Babylon to the New World—that moral *tabula rasa* upon which men's cleansed consciences and corrected consciousnesses might impress the triumphant seal of God's grace for all nations to see and be saved by.

One word which nicely approximates the total confidence required to drive toward success that is possessed by any settlers of a howling wilderness is *chutzpah*. Roughly translated as outrageously nervy assertiveness, American *chutzpah* is a legacy from that other Chosen People in the Wilderness, also adept at survival, and more, during their own flight from Whorish Babylon. The Pilgrims and Puritans had, and needed, *chutzpah* in abundance. This word—one which may imply comic arrogance to us—would have meant to them an iron-strong humbleness before God and the itch to do great things in His name.

True, in the first months and years of the seventeenth century, survival in America seems to have fitted Herbert Spencer's simple formula: staying alive through mastery of and adjustment to the facts of the physical environment. In *Of Plymouth Plantation* William Bradford describes the emotions elicited by New England's unappealing shoreline, an early expression (to use Royce's phrase) of the "genuine sort of concrete experience" which comes when one steps off the deep-end of the known world into the great American void:

> . . . for which way soever they turnd their eys (save upward to the heavens) they could have little solace or content in respecte of any outward objects. For summer being done, all things stand upon them with a wetherbeaten face, and the whole country, full of woods and thickets, represented a wild and savage heiw. If they looked behind them, ther was the mighty ocean which they had passed and was now as a maine barr and goulfe to separate them from all the civill parts of the world. . . . What could now sustaine them but the spirite of God and his grace?

Note the peculiar quality of this statement: it is what a community of consciousnesses feels together. It is not yet time for Thoreau to write the introduction to his Walden experiences, where he declares he cannot express anything other than his own particular reactions to the woods. Together, the Pilgrims were menaced; together, they looked up to the only power that lay—sustainingly—outside themselves. Together, they agreed that only in God's pleasure (even as Caroline Sturgis would restate it two hundred years later) would they possess the joy that could ring their worldly actions with a sacred halo (as William James phrased it after two hundred and sixty years). Together, they would gain value beyond that of bodily survival.

Still, the Spencerian need for physical endurance remained foremost in the face of what Emerson afterwards came to recognize as the "lords of life." The settlers accorded to the brute facts of the material and social worlds the power of actuality; they acknowledged these facts as the blunt will of that foe they called the Devil out of their dramatic sense of the cosmic struggle which encircled them, since they knew that the halos surrounding earthly objects might be satanic as well as divine.

This was the nature of the contest the early settlers set themselves to win: their Roycean hope for a sanctified *if* placed against the unruly *is* of storm-time and starving-time. They possessed both the facts of *is* and the hope of *if*, but, also, their hearts' sorrowful awareness that they as fallen beings were constituted the enemies of God. What *chutzpah* it would take to expect saving grace after this! Jonathan Edwards repeated this terrible truth in the following century. In the next century after Edwards, Melville's Father Mapple of *Moby-Dick* declares that man, in obeying God, disobeys himself. In our own century Norman Mailer's D. J. Jethroe of *Why Are We in Vietnam?* swears that "God has always wanted more from man than man has wished to give him" (p. 9). Thus governed by the lords of life and his own ignoble nature, a man falls short of the full achievement of the Lord's delight. Still he stubbornly, almost arrogantly, desires the *if* to come true. Human missions fail, whether they are the will projected by the *Arbella* upon the New World or upon the new colony of the moon by the *Apollo*. In either instance, the question remains whether the *chutzpah* that demands salvation can stand off the *hubris* that assures damnation; whether it can challenge the outer, unknown spaces of *if* in the name of a special destiny that intends more than mere survival in the land of *is*.

The terms which made physical survival difficult along the eastern coast of America eased somewhat by the late eighteenth century. At least, up to the final letter written by Crèvecœur's Farmer James, it seemed a man might put his trust in a simple formula for success that called on the freeman's virtues of industry, common sense, and adaptability. Only when revolution loomed did the New American feel threatened by waves of history over which he had no control. However, the Revolution was successfully brought to its close by a distinctive American deity (the name *George* replacing that of *God* beside the letter *G* in new editions of *The New England Primer*), and problems appeared to be solved for the most part. Still, more complex ways to fail pushed back to the surface during the first half of the nineteenth century. Not only physical but also metaphysical and psychological stresses emerged on the frontier.

"Frontier": Thoreau defined the word in *A Week on the Concord and Merrimack Rivers* as that place "wherever a man *fronts* a fact. . . ." "Let him build himself a log-house with the bark on where he is," Thoreau continued, "*fronting* IT, and wage there an Old French war . . . and save his scalp if he can" (pp. 323-324). Only on such "frontiers" could Americans learn the meaning of successes and defeats and come to know what America actually was as "a genuine sort of concrete experience."

Nineteenth-century acts of physical confrontation demonstrated that, by and large, Americans had won the immediate battles of material survival in ways incomprehensible to the still struggling masses of Europe. However, the continuing battle of consciousness was yet to be won. This fight of the spirit captured the concern of many throughout the period of American springtime. Then came the Civil War, which was hardly civil in the sense of a courtesy that is attentive to the human decencies, but truly civil in that it tore apart the country's inward being as well as its physical body. In addition, questions of basic material survival that had disturbed the first settlers were again raised as a consequence of the war's bedlam. Further, there was a new set of landscapes to master: prairies, mountains, and cities in embryo; there was also a jungle of asocial cravings and a wilderness of newly released supersensual forces that might blot out the halos of human and divine values. Once again, as at the very start, there was the double burden of having to stand off defeats of both body and mind. What had been the familiar experience at the time of the original settling was now faced without the orthodox God that had sustained the American Puritan soul. By the late nineteenth century it seemed as if the self alone had to survive the pressure of the American frontier-facts of *is*; the self alone had to decide whether it was willing to try to find that other, gracious, but perhaps foolish *is* which Roycean idealism insisted is implied by every *if*.

There was indeed truth in the "seeming so" of this concentrated emphasis upon the self in the secular society. But it was by no means the whole truth—certainly not for America. Alas! that this is so for all those students of American life who express indifference or irritation over the long dragged-out "religious" years of the initial settling-in. In proportion to their own distaste for the Puritan obsession with God is their relief at the thought that all that supra-worldly nonsense came to its deserved end by the mid-nineteenth century, and their expectations at having a clear-cut "modern" America to deal with thereafter, predicated upon the good hard facts of life invincibly social, economic, political.

That relief, and those expectations, are unsoundly based. Religious obligations continued in America through the tradition of higher morality, with the transmundane God of the Puritan pulpit

replaced by the divine force of America itself. Strict Calvinist theology may have crumbled into dust together with the One-Hoss
Shay. The Methodists, Quakers, Congregationalists, Baptists,
Roman Catholics, and Lutherans may have been limited to the "just
personal" concern of hearts which go on worshipping a proper
God when even the mainstream of modern secularism sweeps past.
Granted that church-religion (certainly not absent from American
community life) lost that particular importance assigned to centers
of real power. But *America*—the beauteous, sacred, eternal nation-
under-God—became the God that rules with powers of the kind
Henry Adams knew had once belonged to the Archangel of
Mont-Saint-Michel and the Virgin of Chartres.

Unitarianism may have subverted the Christian Trinity and
thereby weakened orthodoxy itself, but the *idea of the Union* as a sacred force gladdened Whitman because he knew it would endure
forever as long as Americans were obedient servants and happy
parishioners to its democratic principles. The rest of the western
world may have forgotten the purpose for which mankind exists,
but Americans had not; and they knew how to feel within and to
say aloud their sense of mission before the idolators. The language
Whitman used to celebrate Lincoln as captain and crucified; the
language Lincoln himself used to inspire the nation and its devoted
followers; the language used by Thoreau to extol John Brown martyr for the holy cause of American principle—this was the language
of the sacred, cast with sacred intent upon a profane world still reluctant to be saved.

Consciousness had indeed become the most important modern
discovery of the years after the Civil War, and William and Henry
James were among its leading prophets. But American conciousness remained the container of the American conscience. The
moral vision of the early settlement years had not disappeared or
gone underground. Like Poe's purloined letter, it was always there,
before one's eyes—so apparent it could neither be missed nor fully
seen.

Of course those Americans given to self-congratulation and to
little thinking followed the new religion without noticing the ambiguities, contradictions, and basic *terribleness* of their situation (a
mistake no proper Puritan had ever made). They forgot to realize
the impossible fact of their position as human beings and Americans who live naturally, profanely, in what they smugly took to be a
sacred, therefore safe, place.

Failing in this fundamental way to know their peculiar plight,

Americans were hardly able to respond fully to yet another essential element of their state: the nineteenth- and twentieth-century fact that America as the good deity was engaged in almost Manichean conflict with the powers of the sensual and suprasensual universe—cruel at worst, callous at best to matters of human consciousness and conscience. The American Puritans had had only themselves (flawed) and their God (perfect) to worry about, assured as they were that the world around them was a created thing, an underling to their mutual Lord. In contrast, the thoughtful modern American religious (whether he was Huck Finn or Christopher Newman) had to contend with his sense of self, his America, and his unruly universe—all three.

The Pilgrims and Puritans had had a strong sense of making-do in the wilderness, committed as they were to the fulfillment of God's age-old plot. But think of Frank Norris' McTeague—handcuffed to a corpse of a man who was his enemy even in death, his water-canteen split open and dry, and no way out of the alkali desert where the sun overhead burns down its madness. Norris' bewildered characters had followed an errand into the wilderness of Death Valley; they ended there, dead, defeated for no purpose other than to fulfill the author's plot and to affirm the author's truth that it is greed, not grace, that greases the sun's axle. Henry Adams—a good man with a metaphor, particularly when it helped vivify his sense of catastrophe—also sensed that mankind was handcuffed to a corpse. For Adams this hunk of matter was the dying universe—not a universe blistered by the sun's heat, but one frozen to glacial stillness by the sun's wasteful diffusion of energy—all to satisfy the only plot-rules Adams knew of, the Second Law of Thermodynamics. Can you envision the little band of Pilgrims falling on their knees to pray to *that* destructive element rather than, as Bradford recounts it, to bless "the God of heaven who had brought them over the vast and furious ocean, and delivered them from all the periles and miseries thereof, again to set their feete on the firme and stable earth, their proper elemente"?

We have moved from America imaged as the howling wilderness of the Massachusetts Bay coast, attended by a watchful, coercively benevolent Sovereign, past McTeague's death in the desert afternoon, toward Henry Adams's elegantly witty contemplation of a tired world running down and fading away. But there are more than corpses of faded hopes on view, or the death of the familiar God of the Bible, or the end of a glorious American *if* that has been relegated to the concrete squalor of *is*. Instead, we move from vivid consciousness to vivid consciousness—each with a conscience responsive to what is worst, better, and best. We move from the halos of the Puritan Saints in the wilderness to the aureole which Thoreau saw playing around his shadow as he walked abroad in holiness through the woods—walking toward the "fringes of value" that continue to hover over the recalcitrant, disunified materials of American existence.

# CHAPTER 3

# The Greater Tyranny
# of Thought

Many of the experiences described in this book seem to support the famous thesis proposed by Richard Chase's introduction to *The American Novel and Its Tradition* of 1957, a thesis upheld and embellished (and, to some lights, debased) by Leslie Fiedler's *Love and Death in the American Novel* of 1960. Chase and Fiedler locate authentic American literature in the romance tradition. Such literature is, they insist, mystical, clairvoyant, individualistic to the point of social anarchy, and given to darksome fantasies of anguish and destruction. Set against the frenetic fervor of their arguments, Edwin Cady's book of 1971 is therapeutic, although not as exciting (which is much of his point). *The Light of Common Day* asserts that the most representative American literature is daytime, commonsensical, domesticated, and given to the support of basic social forms; it insists on ethical decency and humanistic concern for the needs of our fellows; it is signed over not to raging Ahabian self-isolation but to the quiet shouldering of burdens in the community. We are our brother's keeper, not his adversary. Whatever we do best takes place in the light of the everyday, not while lightning flashes across a blood-red moon. Apollonian virtues are considered more valuable to sane survival than Dionysian over-reachings.

But any discussion that involves halo-dimensions, by necessity, eventually tends to stress matters that are *extra*ordinary. Fringes of value may radiate around persons or events that are ordinary; nowhere else are they better seen. But wherever they appear, a transformation takes place—one we need not call transcendent—which would bear the transformed object beyond those planes where diurnal struggles devoted singlemindedly to survival go on. Persons or events that flame up into points of success or of failure tend to cluster at the extremities. It is not that the persons must be heros or villains, nor must the events be designated as rare moments of great gain or great loss; they are not to be set apart from the commonplace in kind. They *are* the commonplace carried as far as human possibility can go.

If common sense characterizes the commonplace, what then is the quality of the human mind that goes best with the extraordinary event?

In his essay *Walking*, first printed in 1862, Thoreau defines genius as "a light which makes the darkness visible, like the lightning's flash, which perchance shatters the temple of knowledge itself— and not a taper lighted at the hearthstone of the race, which pales before the light of common day." From the thrust of his words we know where Thoreau's strong sympathies often lie: with lightning.

In the 1872 essay "Poetry and Imagination," Emerson also proposes distinctions between imagination and common sense, but he is more ready than Thoreau to mediate between the two. Imagination is the possession of the genius, whereas common sense is held by all men. Emerson praises common sense as "the cradle, the go-cart" of our infancy. "We must learn the homely laws of fire and water; we must feed, wash, plant, and build." Common sense is man's best response to those laws of existence which are tyrannical in their necessity. The mark of valid minds is "common-sense which does not meddle with the absolute, but takes things at their word—things as they appear. . . ." Common sense is "the house of health and life." By the pungency of his next statement Emerson reveals why he ought to be associated with Franklin as an able strategist of sanity. "In spite of all the joys of poets and the joys of saints, the most imaginative and abstracted person never makes with impunity the least mistake in this particular—never tries to kindle his oven with water, nor carries a torch into a powder-mill, nor seizes his wild charger by the tail."

Having adroitly praised common sense and the world of necessity it controls so well, Emerson then reminds us that common sense concerns itself entirely with the material, the finite, the limiting. There is another, a higher "tyranny" than necessity, he announces, that we must answer to as well:

> But whilst the man is startled by this closer inspection of the laws of matter, his attention is called to the independent action of the mind; its strange suggestions and laws; a certain tyranny which springs up in his own thoughts, which have an order, method, and beliefs of their own, very different from the order which this common-sense uses.

The Emersonian poet willingly obeys a tyranny that coerces him with the reality of the infinite and the limitless. "Poetry must first be good sense, though it is something better." It is while he is in the pursuit of this "something better" that the poet "contemplates the central identity." His mind "delights in measuring itself thus with matter, with history, and flouting both." Both rebel and servant, the poet "observes higher laws than he transgresses." That *more than* common sense, Emerson declares, is *thought*:

> . . . the beholding and co-energizing mind sees the same refining and ascent to the third, the seventh, or the tenth power of the daily accidents which the senses report, and which makes the raw material of knowledge. It was sensation; when memory came, it was experience; when mind acted, it was knowledge; when mind acted on it as knowledge, it was thought.

Emerson notes the progression from sensation to experience to knowledge; at the end of this proud sequence stands *thought*, which extends beyond knowledge itself. Thoreau had concurred when he maintained that the temple of knowledge may be shattered by the lightning flash of genius. Let us take this notion of the force and flash of thought—characteristically located by these Transcendentalists within the imagination, or "genius," of the poet. Take it up for whatever it can suggest about success founded on more than common sense; take over the metaphors used by Emerson and Thoreau to explain how the mind perceives and creates the meaning and value of America.

Admittedly men of idealism, Emerson and Thoreau still believed they were dealing straightforwardly with reality, as did Josiah Royce, who, in the service of the ideal, placed hope in the possibility of leaping beyond the limits of a marred, incomplete actual world; as did William James, who, in the name of pragmatism, gave emphasis to haloed value and "more than" self-preservation. Through Emerson, Thoreau, Royce, and James we see the desire expressed for *something better* that originates in, but moves beyond, common-sense adjustments to what we have. The question is whether the desire for reality and value can ever come together with a method for working out the full experience of success in America. Somehow, these men believed, the solution had to come by means of *thought*—itself the reality, the value, and the method: all three.

That entity called America may be defined as the physical facts of the place, or as the ideas men have about it. By either criteria we try to determine the exact dimensions of its reality. For unless we decide whether or not America is real, our reality as Americans hangs in abeyance. A sense of being real in a real place seems to be the bedrock necessity for saying, "There is success." If there is no reality, failure is what we have in its place.

Edgar Allan Poe, the supposed master of terror, is a cheery writer of success stories when compared with the aging Mark Twain. According to the sprawl of Mark Twain's late manuscripts, if America is but a trifle of our fancy; if we are only a fancy in the consciousness of God; and if God Himself does not exist, there is not much sense in playing out the ridiculous game of failure. Unlike Mark Twain, Poe did not cripple his imagination by keeping to half (the "bad" half) of an inherited theology; he made up his own metaphysics out of snippets of contemporary science and random notions about the powers of the mind. He could cry "Eureka!" as he contemplated our consciousnesses whirling back to primal nothingness because God's perfect plot for the universe was being played out in time. If Poe's imagination was unable to find pleasure in this world of putrefying matter and this America of frayed democratic hopes, then it could create success by envisioning a solidly real solar system placed far beyond America. In turn, it could dissolve that cosmos, leaving behind the one true reality and lasting success—the poet's consciousness.

Charles Sanders Peirce had another method for defining reality that is less endangered by solipsism (although admittedly less fun). When that method is joined with suggestions by William James and Josiah Royce, we are provided a way of testing the reality of both the self and America—the only practical context these men saw success could have. In his essay of 1878, "How To Make Our Ideas Clear," Peirce said that reality is the potential and the possible, not merely the realized achievement. The reality of a diamond, for instance, does not depend on what it actually does. Rather, this is determined by what its latent qualities are capable of if ever allowed full expression in an action. A diamond bedded-down permanently on cotton in a box it never leaves, or consumed by intense fire, will be given no chance to scratch marks on glass—one special, distinguishing talent of diamonds. But just because it is never used or ever possessed does not mean it is valueless and without reality. Value and reality lie in an object's *being*, not in its *doing*. The *actual* fact of diamondness may never be witnessed to; the *real* fact remains of its potential to scratch.

Peirce's figure suggests one way we may consider America's reality—especially if we recall the words of Royce, a man who sat on the opposite side of the philosophical fence from Peirce and William James while repeating that *is* is ever obligated to extend itself to include *if*. We can also beckon to Edward Taylor, asking him to declare himself on the matter. In the "Prologue" to *Gods Determinations Touching His Elect*, Taylor asserted, "I am this Crumb of Dust"—a crumb "which is design'd/To make my Pen unto Thy praise alone." Taylor's crumb of *is*—a "dull Phancy" inadequate to praise God's greatness—still provides the necessary particle of reality the poet would convert by means of the sacred promise of *if* into the immense fact of salvation's success. The flawed soul of the poet wishes to seize the Peircian diamond in order to

> . . . gladly grinde
> Unto an Edge of Zions Pretious Stone.
> And Write in Liquid Gold upon Thy Name
> My Letters till thy glory forth doth flame.

If the self is an *is* straining to fulfill its diamond-possibility, the idea of America's potential is a diamond as big as the Ritz. Its *real* facts may not always be revealed in the hearth-fire of the *actual* facts of historical events viewed by Emerson's man of common sense; but its being—its lightning flashes—is no less true even if discerned alone by the Emersonian man of poetic genius.

Peirce as philosophical pragmatist and Royce as philosophical idealist are alike in affirming that reality is contained within an object, even when that reality remains latent and is not fully realized. William James went even further; he suggested that the reality of an object is, yes, *in* it, but that the reality *we* experience comes from what most *interests* us about that object. James denied giving over the full weight of reality to whatever can be measured by objective, testable data about an object remote from our minds. To James, reality is not just facts (an assertion the Puritan theologians, Jonathan Edwards, and the Transcendentalists would have supported with equal fervor). Reality is *something other than* what laboratories can test or the eye can detect; it also involves our act of *choosing among* an object's characteristics in order to select those which most concern us.

In "The Stream of Thought" James gives an example (one easily extended to an American context) of a group of men who went to Europe, each returning from his journey with a different report since each saw that place in light of what he most cared about. In the same essay James tries to make even clearer what he means about the selections that go into our sense of reality. He recognizes the sound of a clock as a matter of the total number of ticks and tocks it emits, yet he observes that that "monotonous succession of sonorous strokes is broken up into rhythms, now of one sort, now of another, by the different accent which we place on different strokes." Ticks and tocks are like dots on a surface selectively arranged into rows and groups to satisfy our own sense of what is *really* going on.

If we *confront* America actively, as Thoreau bade us, as a *frontier*-fact, our consciousnesses are besieged by the totality of America's reality—all the sounding fury of its ticks and tocks; the noisy *actual* facts, and the *real* facts—silent in their latency and potentiality. Royce as idealist would hope that America's full reality might be contained within our full embrace of experience. In contrast, James the pragmatist would insist that our sense of America will ever be partial; we select only what interests us, composing those units into rhythms, weaving everything into personal and limited designs. As James wrote in "The Stream of Thought": "Out of what is in itself an undistinguishable, swarming *continuum*, devoid of distinction or emphasis, our senses make for us, by attending to this motion and ignoring that, a world full of contrasts, of sharp accents, or abrupt changes, of picturesque light and shade." For Royce the pattern of America is already out there, waiting to be perceived and embraced, if only we can draw the threads together and, by doing so, locate our own reality. For James it is the force of our thought that creates the figure in the carpet we call the reality of our experience of America.

Consider the prodigious problems facing anyone actively involved in making some sense out of America's reality and our own. America is *actual* facts; it is the total of all the ticks and tocks that sound upon our sensible ear. America is also *real* facts, its potential for sounds not yet heard, the silence pregnant with value. Perhaps America is what is solidly out there that is not particularly *interested in us*. Or it may be only what *interests us* as we each, selectively, respond to experiences of direct concern.

The mind in America confronts a mass of aggressively actual facts, overwhelming enough in themselves; but the mind must also deal with the buried facts that lie hidden as potential—sensed only as legend, rumor, or myths of anticipation which the self may or may not choose to grasp subjectively and privately. Surrounded by this welter, we might well become nervous over whether what we grasp is the full *idea* of America, or whether we get at only those parts which manage to come to concrete *manifestation*. There is always the chance we might be destroyed if unable to match *actual* with *real*, the accomplished fact with potential force. At stake is not merely whether we can ever come to know America. It is whether we can comprehend our own essential reality. Upon that knowledge, in turn, rests our ability to judge our value (our success) or to assess our lack (our failure).

Some insist on asking whether there is an encompassing reality that would correct the solipsism of America-as-self. The Puritans steadied things by linking the reality of the American continent, of their souls, and of their worldly achievements with the unassailable fact of God's presence. For the Transcendentalists the Universal Law was the scratch from which they could start to measure success. For Henry Adams supersensual lines of force pushed upon him the testing fact of his failure. For still others it has been a matter of culture or community action or cash-in-the-bank. But how have such differing ideas gained authority as the cutting edge of reality itself?

Listen to Josiah Royce in further passages drawn from *The Conception of God*. Here Royce is at work attempting to convince his audience in 1897 that God is the one reality that counts. As you listen, make two mental acts: take Royce's argument and consider it as a kind of latter-day Puritan sermon devoted precisely to the subject he proposes—the reality of God. But also consider his argument as being concerned, not with God, but with America.

Realize that Royce's immediate subject (*God is real*) is enclosed within the larger argument of his book, which seeks to demonstrate a method appropriate to its philosophical end: to show us how we know. True, the sequence of his emphasis might actually be the other way around; by showing us how we know, he gains the means to drive us toward his main end—the mind's realization of an absolute, eternal truth that lies outside both man's subjective nature and the objective, transient world of nature. How we choose to flip the Roycean coin is analogous to whether we handle the epistemological method as means or ends: we may choose to stress what we have come to know about, or the process by which we know; we can decide that we are most absorbed by the fact *out there*—God/America—which we have discovered, or by how we continue to experience that fact as we draw it *in here* to us.

Royce maintains that the fact—that which is "something experienced"—is only one element of knowing. There is yet another important matter: "mere idea, or pure thought about actual or possible experience":

Divorce those two elements of knowledge, let the experienced fact, actual or possible, be remote from the idea or thought about it, and then the being who merely thinks, questions, and, so far, can only question. His state is such that he wonders: Is my idea true? But let the divorce be completely overcome, and the being who fully knows answers questions, in so far as he simply sees his ideas fulfilled in the facts of his experience, and beholds his experiences as the fulfillment of his ideas.

For Royce only God can completely overcome the divorcing tendency that prevents the perfect marriage of idea and fact. "Only—herein lies the essence of his conceived Omniscience,—in him and for him these facts would not be, as they often are in us, merely felt, but they would be seen as fulfilling his ideas; as answering what, were he not omniscient, would be his mere questions."

Fifty-six years earlier Emerson in "The Method of Nature" wrote as a spiritual marriage counselor: "It is the office, I doubt not, of this age to annul that adulterous divorce which the superstition of many ages has effected between the intellect and holiness." Man, Emerson avowed

> should know himself for a necessary actor. A link was wanting between two craving parts of nature, and he was hurled into being as the bridge over that yawning need, the mediator betwixt two else unmarriageable facts. His two parents held each of them one of the wants, and the union of foreign constitutions in his enables him to do gladly and gracefully what the assembled human race could not have sufficed to do. He knows his materials; he applies himself to his work; he cannot read, or think, or look, but he unites the hitherto separated strands into a perfect cord.

This passage reveals one difference between the man who is an Idealist in 1841 and he who attempts it in 1897. The earlier type is one who is himself the *incarnation* (the word Emerson uses in his next sentence) of the idea's fulfillment in the *actuality* of life; he can do for himself what Royce says only God can do. A god-incarnate from whom "all things are illuminated to their centre," he gains that paradise in which all facts match all desires because whatever he "sees" is made visible.

For the moment we can borrow terms which Sigmund Freud believed to be fundamentally in opposition: the reality principle (that tells us of our death) and the pleasure principle (that formalizes our heart's desire). In contradistinction to Freud's pessimism in this matter, Emerson's "necessary actor" makes the mental leap that joins these two hitherto estranged forces. It would seem that only under Emerson's aegis, not Freud's, can that act of leaping be made by which America is achieved simultaneously as reality and as pleasure.

Maxim Gorki, who was no Idealist or American, made a statement before the 1934 All-Union Congress of Soviet Writers which indicates how men who attempt literal revolutions in society may view the "useful" relation between the actual and the potential:

> To invent means to extract from the totality of real existence its basic idea and to incarnate this in an image; thus we obtain realism. But if to the idea extracted from the real is added the desirable, the potential, and the image is supplemented by this, we obtain that romanticism which lies at the basis of myth and is highly useful in that it facilitates the arousing of a revolutionary attitude toward reality, an attitude of practically changing the world.

The Roycean Idealist in 1897 presents a far more qualified notion of the powers of the mind than that of the man of Concord or of the Soviet aesthetician. In *The Conception of God* Royce agrees that "the sort of direct knower that you are" is limited to one "who can of himself verify only fragments." "But you can," he points out, "conceive infinitely more than you can directly verify":

> In thought you therefore construct conceptions which start, indeed, in your fragmentary experience, but which transcend it infinitely, and which so do inevitably run into danger of becoming mere shadows—pure Platonic ideas.

Thought alone is not enough. Alone, it does not grant success:

> But you don't mean your conceptions to remain thus shadowy. By the devices of hypothesis, prediction, and verification, you seek to link anew the concept and the presentation, the ideal order and the stubborn chaos, the conceived truth and the immediate datum, the contents of the organised experience and the fragments of your momentary flight of sensations.

Experiments in the experience of thought are necessary, but there is no guarantee even then:

> In so far as you succeed in this effort, you say that you have science. In so far as you are always, in presented experience, limited to your chaos, you admit that your sensations are of subjective moment and often delude you.

Win a few, lose a few—this is the plight that America as observable object presents to the roving, yearning consciousness of that

supernumerary prompted only by the "tyrannic necessity" of common sense. A consciousness which is incapable of becoming "the
necessary actor" (one in possession of both concept and verification, both intellect and holiness, both reality and pleasure) will always prove inadequate to America. This, because it is unwilling or
unable to yield itself to the greater tyranny of thought.

# CHAPTER 4

# The Economics of Want

Josiah Royce suggests a strategy for breaking away from vistas that are narrow, limiting, and fragmenting. With his aid we can come to a position which gives a clear overview of America, that territory whose mapped extent—geographical and psychological— is crucial to the question of how far we may succeed or by how much we are lacking. When we say that the sun rises and sets, Royce observes in *The Conception of God*, this is because we are captives of a cramped perspective. "A wider experience, say an experience defined from an extra-terrestrial point of view," would correct this fault. Our realization that a notion, formerly held as true, is actually false comes about when we correct it "from some higher point of view, to which a larger whole of experience is considered as present."

Poe wrote in *Eureka* of the being who views the universe "angelically" (totally) by "a mental gyration on the heel" while poised above and beyond the earth. Emerson believed we would all experience the earth as round if we could only stand far enough away from it to see the flat line of the horizon start to curve and bend into a complete circle. Thoreau sought out every summit he could find in his saunterings in order to get the expanded view of the world that short-sighted men, valley-rooted as they are, can never possess.

Yes, if we could stand high enough—say at the top of the Hill of Zion, as the Puritans longed to do—we would see reality as only God, Poesque angels, and prophet-poets know it. We could also— as the Puritans and the Transcendentalists hoped—transform America itself into that summit of reality from which true curves and life's wholeness are recognizable. A large part of those writings which have tried to define *being* and *knowing* in America involve this search for the right summit. But the highest ground we generally get to is Hawthorne's Merry-Mount. Our choices tend to be restricted to the either/or of stifling jollity or enervating gloom, airy fantasy or stern historical inevitability. In contrast, the perfect summit would give us the further alternative of true joy. But where

this preeminent point of view lies and how to arrive there is unknown to us; we only barely recall that such a place ever existed.

William James was fascinated by the human actions that are initiated when just such lack is linked with a vague memory of what
would provide its satisfaction. "Suppose we try to recall a forgotten
name," he wrote in "The Stream of Thought." "The state of our
consciousness is peculiar. There is a gap therein; but no mere gap.
It is a gap that is intensely active. A sort of wraith of the name is in
it, beckoning us in a given direction, making us at moments tingle
with the sense of our closeness, and then letting us sink back without the longed-for term."

Poe also repeatedly spoke about that madness which comes from
the perverse, ever-frustrated need to recall a tantalizingly forgotten word. To Poe words are the agent by which the mind creates
reality, or reveals it to whoever cracks the code that governs the
world. If that one true word could be found; if the mystery of
Ligeia's expression could be defined; if the hieroglyphics Pym finds
in the island cave of Tsalal might be deciphered—*then* the master
code of existence and all its secrets would be disclosed. But what we
are left with—the plight emphasized by both Poe and William
James—is contained in James's phrase, the "innumerable consciousness of *want*."

A great deal has been said about America as Eden, that lost garden, the longed-for but forever unattainable Paradise, the perfect
place we recall but can never get back to. We seem to be able to
know only both the desire and the lack. Josiah Royce admits in *The
Conception of God*, "If what I ought to experience, and should experience were I not ignorant, remains only a possibility, then there
is no absolute reality, but only possibility, in the universe, apart
from your passing feelings and mine." Having confessed to this
subjective stalemate, Royce then proceeds with intricate logic to
"prove" that the very fact we have such desires—desires curbed
from fulfillment by the preposition *if*—affirms that what would
satisfy those desires must truly exist. We cannot want what does not
have reality somewhere. Paradise as garden and Zion as summit are
*there* precisely because we are *here*. What we require is what John
Fiske described in *Outlines of Cosmic Philosophy*: our desires brought
into "proximate equilibrium with the means of satisfying them"
(III, 334). For this to come about we must become the "necessary
actor" of whom Emerson spoke—the one who is able to bridge the
difference between *there* and *here* in a leap that keeps the balance,
holds "proximate equilibrium," and does not end at the bottom of
the ravine.

In an essay aptly named "Philosophical Conceptions and Practical Results," first presented as an address in 1898, William James speaks of the benefits of *trying to get there*, even though we never do. Significantly, he specifically names America as one of the obstacles to getting to the desired-for place. "Columbus, dreaming of the ancient East, is stopped by poor pristine simple America, and gets no farther on that day. . . ." What a contrast to Whitman's "Passage to India"! Whitman's poem tells, as it were, of the happy sequel to Columbus' failure described by James thirty years later. To Whitman mankind picks up the divine journey left off in discouragement at America's shores and completes the circle; by "sailing to India" past the North American continent we fulfill the dreamed-of-desire of "going to America"—the original paradise whose memory we have never forgotten even while detained upon the trivial shores of the North American continent. The Jamesian philosopher is the frustrated Columbus who must remember the reality that lies at the unreachable center and at the far end of the circlesweep. "So I feel," writes James in "Philosophical Conceptions and Practical Results"

> that there is a center in truth's forest where I have never been . . . at moments I almost strike into the final valley, there is a gleam of the end, a sense of certainty, but always there comes still another ridge, so my blazes merely circle towards the true direction; and although now, if ever, would be the fit occasion, yet I cannot take you to the wondrous hidden spot to-day. To-morrow it must be, or to-morrow, or to-morrow, and pretty surely death will overtake me ere the promise is fulfilled.

The following statements from *The Conception of God* would be Royce's contribution to both James's and Whitman's representations of the act of taking passages to everywhere and nowhere:

> But you may here say: "This aim, this will, is all. As a fact, you and I aim at the absolute experience; that is what we mean by wanting to know absolute truth; but the absolute experience," so you may insist, "is just a mere ideal. There need be no such experience as a concrete actuality. The aim, the intent, is the known fact. The rest is silence,—perhaps error. Perhaps there is no absolute truth, no ideally united and unfragmentary experience."

"This aim, this will, is all": surely this is an adequate response to a frustrating situation, and as far as most are willing to go. But Royce is not satisfied to rest with the act of aiming, just as no Puritan or Edwards or Emerson or Thoreau would stay in such a position of defeat, however reasonable and comfortable. In a tightly argued series of assertions Royce proceeds to challenge the prevailing notion that subjective experience—with its stress on the attempt in lieu of the achievement—is all we have, and that it alone provides the pleasures and the urgencies of our existence. For Royce, as for Edwards, only God has the ability to be totally subjective; only He has the panache to say (as Royce has Him say), "with assurance, 'Beyond my world there is no further experience actual.'" "Hence," testifies Royce, "—and here, indeed, is the conclusion of the whole matter,—the very effort hypothetically to assert that the whole world of experience is a world of fragmentary and finite experience is an effort involving a contradiction. Experience must constitute, in its entirety, one self-determined and consequently absolute and organised whole."

According to Royce, where we are is somewhere within the experience of God; we are the object of His subjectivity, the facts of His reality. Our failures and God's success, our potentiality and His actuality, our remembrance of past paradise and His realized present: this is the Roycean "absolute and organised whole." Or if we insert "America" in place of "God," we can repeat the configuration in this way: Where we are is somewhere within the experience of America; we are the objects of America's subjectivity, the facts of its reality—our failures and America's success, our potentiality and America's actuality, our remembrance of paradise and its realized present. By following the sequence of this suggestion, the human mind possesses whichever entity it most desires—God or America—as the real ground for its existence and for its continuing struggle to become a greater part of that all-inclusive whole.

Design-makers by birth, we like to impose a plot upon that corner of existence which shapes for us what we feel we are. Such a plot could be characterized by formless, purposeless bits of chaos and flux. It might be a plan as tight, neat, and well-carpentered as Calvinist Covenant theology. Or it could possess a design as ramshackled and devil-may-care as the layout of one of Mark Twain's Nevada mining camps. If the setting for this piecemeal drama is America, then the several Americas that we possess subjectively join with the America that appears objectively to us—the America that is, to use Royce's terms, God's total experience, His single, absolute, subjective plot.

George Santayana's famous essay of 1911, "The Genteel Tradi-

tion in American Philosophy," characterizes the original settler as
having from the start those plans for an America that would carry
out God's *a priori* conceptions. "The country was new, but the race
was tried, chastened, and full of solemn memories. It was an old
wine in new bottles; and America did not have to wait . . . to have a
distinct vision of the Universe and definite convictions about
human destiny." In speaking of such designs, Santayana remarks:

> A system may contain an account of many things which, in de-
> tail, are true enough; but as a system, covering infinite pos-
> sibilities that neither our experience nor our logic can pre-
> judge, it must be a word of imagination and a piece of human
> soliloquy. It may be expressive of human experience, it may be
> poetical; but how should any one who really coveted truth
> suppose that it was trúe?

There have always been those in America who would disagree
with Santayana that a system which is poetically expressive of
human experience is to be judged, out of hand, as untrue. Royce,
for one, could have suggested that by happy coincidence the
subjective-objective elements of a man-made system might fit into
that "one self-determined and consequently absolute and organised whole." It would not *be* the whole, since it takes far more
than one human plot to equal the scope of God's design. But it
could be expressive of human experience, poetical and true. In the
overall debate concerning the relation between the "poetry" of
America and/or God and the actuality, Royce is obviously the exception: yet an exception significant because of the stubborn, sustaining power of the belief that an idea held to grand scale might,
just perhaps, prove true. This was the kind of idea Henry Adams
looked for endlessly, and the idea Poe speculated in *Eureka* that he
had found; the idea Theodore Parker insisted had formed the
American republic; and the idea F. Scott Fitzgerald maintained
that America (in ways unlike any other country in the world) *is*.

To be sure, the details of the various plans concerning America
have changed: from the placement of the City of God in the wilderness to the construction of the City of Man in the tamed gar-
dens of post-revolutionary America. And from time to time any
such systems become altogether suspect. Emerson and Thoreau
rebuked petty systematizers; they believed new schemes are unnecessary in a world already vibrating to the higher laws of that
perfect plot for which men may take credit only as co-authors.
Later writers rejected systems because they were seen as impos-

sibilities in a world that moves according to laws over which none have control. By now one of the few system-makers given sufferance is the private mind that works outward from its own center of intelligence. As a result, the main concern has become the quality of that mind and of the design for America it makes for itself. Design might be the means to save the country in the future, just as it aided survival in the earliest years of settlement to have God's plan to rely on. Even so, we tend to see more clearly now the mind's power to take America to the edge of disaster, destroying the same American idea-reality it once created.

In "The Genteel Tradition in American Philosophy" Santayana states:

> The truth is that one-half of the American mind, that not occupied intensely in practical affairs, has remained, I will not say high-and-dry, but slightly becalmed; it has floated gently in the back-water, while, alongside, in invention and industry and social organisation, the other half of the mind was leaping down a sort of Niagara Rapids.

Santayana then speaks directly of Emerson's decision to side with the greater tyranny of thought:

> Our dignity is not in what we do, but in what we understand. The whole world is doing things. We are turning in that vortex; yet within us is silent observation, the speculative eye before which all passes, which bridges the distances and compares the combatants. On this side of his genius Emerson broke away from all conditions of age or country and represented nothing except intelligence itself.

Poe's "Descent into the Maelström" has a narrator who saves himself from Santayana's vortex because he resists it and does not perversely acquiesce to it. In this act of thinking he is the Emersonian Poetic Genius (although his intellect is far more apparent than his holiness). He saves himself from death by moving rapidly beyond the common-sense cluster of sensation-experience-knowledge; he strives by means of imagination to reach thought. All this, while his brother, paralyzed by fear over the onslaught of just those elements of sensation-experience-knowledge, perishes in the whirlpool because he never got past imagination. Thus, whether one is "turning in that vortex" or "leaping down a sort of Niagara Rapids," the special form of thought that Emerson and Poe designated as the finest form of imagining can prove useful for survival.

Still, these questions remain: whether the imagination best serves itself and America by devoting itself single-mindedly to design-making, or whether such imposed forms lead more surely to destruction, and thought ought therefore keep itself innocent of design.

"What is all history but the work of ideas, a record of incomputable energy which his infinite aspirations infuse into man?" Emerson said this in "The Method of Nature," and more:

> Has anything grand and lasting been done? Who did it? Plainly not any man, but all men; it was the prevalence and inundation of an idea. What brought the pilgrims here? One man says, civil liberty; another, the desire of founding a church; and a third discovers that the motive force was plantation and trade. But if the Puritans could rise from the dust they could not answer. It is to be seen in what they were, and not in what they designed; it was the growth and expansion of the human race.

Characteristically, Emerson impresses the distinction between idea and design. To him *idea* signifies what men experience, thus what they are, whereas *design* is what they carry into or out of that experience. Designs function on the level of common sense and knowledge (Emerson's plane of Understanding); ideas soar to the realms of imagination and thought (Emerson's Reason). Design involves men with what they understand and results in the tangible things they build. Ideas are prompted by experiences men suddenly front in any new, unknown territory; they result in *knowing* and *being* that contain both achieved act and potential ideal.

In an essay collected for publication in 1846 by Evert Duyckinck, Margaret Fuller wished to say something important about American literature and, as her title indicates, "Its Position in the Present Time, and Prospects for the Future." She begins by announcing that she writes about what does not yet exist. America has as yet no literature and will not until "an original idea" animates "this nation and fresh currents of life" call "into life fresh thoughts along its shores." Americans can have no literature until they have ideas, thoughts other than those borrowed from the English character. English writing, like England itself, is "reminiscent of walls and ceilings"—insular, closed-in, neither frank nor expansive enough to be able to respond fully to the American scene.

Three years before Margaret Fuller's article and the same year as Emerson's "The Method of Nature" addressed itself to the idea of

America as an act of "expansion" of the soul, Theodore Parker presented his influentia' sermon of 1843, "A Discourse of the Transient and Permanent in Christianity," in which he distinguished between theological theories that are transient and religious truths that never perish. In 1872 Emerson again reminded his discipleship in "Poetry and Imagination" that poetry is the highest form of literature because it deals directly with thought; he again asserted that thought attains truth—the single, eternal fact—and thereby avoids the perils of transient theory and the ineffectuality of opinion.

According to what we may make of the collective statements offered by Emerson, Fuller, and Parker, this is the situation and the problem America represents: the Puritans had an *idea* by means of which the human race *permanently expanded* its horizons. Yet the language of their theology and the particulars of their earth-bound *designs* (civil liberty, a churchly society, mercantile prosperity) vanished like all *transient theories*, collapsing into a heap of dust like Oliver Wendell Holmes' One-Hoss Shay. By the 1840s New Englanders were still waiting for the one true word and revelation—a *poetry* which would express *that truth which lasts forever* because it expanded the mind beyond narrow, insular limits and mundane, petty designs. By contrast, what the Puritans *thought* and *were* has lasted in the best sense. They introduced a permanent fact into American existence which has grown like the living leaves of grass of Whitman's joyous vision, not like the insidious cancers of Norman Mailer's nightmares. The Puritans beheld America as that land of destiny which they had been chosen to transform from the potentiality of concept into the verification of reality. Their legacy to us is not the particular *design* they expressed—a rigid theory of a collective destiny tied to an exclusive political and theological structure of the kind that is inevitably brought to its end by the push of history. What we possess from them is rather the general *idea about* destiny that has continued to act for us as an inclusive and individualistic structure by means of which we can each, continually, create our extra-historical being.

The philosophy of history developed by Hegel is also a philosophy of destiny. His theories, especially as they are cited and expounded by Burleigh Taylor Wilkins in *Hegel's Philosophy of History*, are applicable in special ways to the question of the idea of America and the discovery of reality.

Hegel wrote in his Preface to *The Phenomenology of Mind* that truth must contain its own negations—the false and the evanescent, all that "does not come to be or pass away," all, therefore, that is failure as contrasted to the success of the true and the permanent. Because this truth includes all things, real and unreal, even the unreal participates in "the actuality and the movement of the life of the truth. The true is the bacchanalian whirl in which no member is not drunken" (p. 102). This whirl of truth (which seems to share in the "bright confusion" which Frank Kermode in *The Sense of An Ending* ascribes to poetry and not to philosophy) precedes philosophical thought. Such thought deals with the truth but is its later, less successful, manifestation. Philosophy sometimes gives itself over to formal possibilities which may not be necessary to the larger effort. Truth is *real necessity* and *real possibility*, two facts which are already identical and wait only to be revealed as such to be believed by all. Philosophy considers what it would *prefer* to see as an actuality; truth knows that it *will* become what, in Wilkins' words, "cannot be otherwise" (p. 152).

Hegel's faith as expressed in his *Science of Logic* is that Concept (the truth) will one day move as effect into the concrete; for him Concept already exists as cause. Because of the necessity of the connection between the Concept and the concrete, "only what already exists comes into existence" (p. 110). The teleological process is one, therefore, of *translation*. We currently read the world as dead or unknown language because it is veiled to us by chance and the finite; but the eternal design—the truth lying behind the coded message—is already there, to be disclosed in good time as the infinite (the best time).

Up to this point there are several striking similarities between Hegel's position and notions held individually and in concurrence by Emerson, Margaret Fuller, and Parker: the stress on truth as being more than that kind of knowledge with which philosophy is usually concerned—stress on thinking as involving more than thought; the belief in the eternal life of truth and its immanent being; the insistence upon the necessity of the fulfillment of possibility; the hope that mankind will witness the burst of reality upon the not-quite-real existence which clogs human progress. Hegelian destiny was the law Emerson, Parker, and Fuller could accept with pleasure; although repudiating restricting formulas, they submitted to the liberating laws of nature, which in turn promised the laws of thought.

The Americans diverge from Hegel over the role America is to play in the historical process leading to truth's triumphant revelation. As Wilkins stresses in his discussion of *The Philosophy of History*,

Hegel liked to characterize America as "a Land of the Future" (p. 75). In Hegel's words it was decided that the only events taking place in the New World are "an echo of the Old World." America "has no interest for us here, for as regards History, our concern must be with that which has been and that which is" (p. 75). Hegel waves America away as an area of interest to philosophy or to history. If history requires a country with past and present, philosophy deals with what "is neither past nor future, but with that which *is*, which has an eternal existence—with Reason. . . . Dismissing, then, the New World, and the dreams to which it may give rise, we pass over to the Old World—the scene of the World's History" (p. 75). America as Land of the Future is inconsequential because it has no past or present (no proper historical *time*) and is unimportant as philosophy (no eternal present). America is *dreams* (a future of continuing unreality); it is not *truth* (a continuous reality). It is ahistorical; only mere events will ever take place there—events that simply repeat the dull tyranny of contingency. America will have no part in bringing about the consciousness of freedom, the victory of spirit, and the ability to be completely "at home" in the universe—the three elements which form the nature and purpose of true history.

But precisely what Hegel thought history is meant to achieve was what the Transcendentalists believed the American spirit would make manifest in America. Rather than America being completely out of it—divorced from the single vital purpose of human destiny; rather than America being located in the wrong time (the future)—driven by the wrong needs (the unreality of dream), and committed to the wrong traits (the ephemeral and contingent); rather than America being just another place where ordinary, ineffectual history happens (causeless historicism); rather than denying the fundamental principle of truth's inclusivity of its own negations: rather than the land possessing all these faults, the Transcendentalists, flying in the face of Hegel, believed that America is the true land for truth. To them America is the land where the Cause will at last be discovered and the longed-for Effect—"the progress of the consciousness of freedom"—will find its destined fulfillment.

In reiterating the sequence of mental events that leads to the victory defined by the Transcendentalists, we find a three-fold process: *to have an idea* is to think; *to think* is to make poetry; *to make poetry* is *to expand into the truth* which is the mind's immortality and glory. To seize idea, thought, poetry, and truth is the task taken up by those who envision America as a stage in mankind's westward passage to holiness, as Thoreau does in *Walking*:

> The Atlantic is a Lethean stream, in our passage over which we have had an opportunity to forget the Old World and its institutions. If we do not succeed this time, there is perhaps one more chance for the race left before it arrives on the banks of the Styx; and that is the Lethe of the Pacific, which is three times as wide. . . .

Here is the glorious hope, and the dangerous temptation, laid out all too clearly: the self-indulgent notion that, if the "opportunity" provided by crossing the Atlantic to America is missed, there is always the "Pacific"—the "beyond America"—to explore.

In *A Week on the Concord and Merrimack Rivers* of 1849 Thoreau wrote that Columbus had come no closer to the blessed isles than had Plato. He himself toys with the vision of just such a place of blessedness that lies past the edges of America in "the OTHER WORLD which the instinct of mankind so long predicted" (p. 412). He goes even further than Columbus, who had limited his yearnings to the actual westward curve of the globe. Thoreau raises his eyes from the surface of the earth to the "immaterial starry system" to ask whether we are not "provided with senses as well fitted to penetrate the spaces of the real, the substantial, the eternal, as these outward are to penetrate the material universe" (p. 412). But to do as Thoreau does in this passage is to think past "the shores of America." It is to admit the possibility of failure in solving the economics of our immediate want within this land and this time.

"If other nations wonder at our achievements," wrote Theodore Parker in "The Political Destination of America and the Signs of the Times" (in 1848, the year before the publication of Thoreau's *A Week*), "we are a disappointment to ourselves, and wonder we have not done more. Our national idea out-travels our experience, and all experience" (p. 155). The great need is to let that "national idea" go wide, expanding as far as the human spirit, yet to keep it within the reaches of "our experience, and all experience." Out of our "disappointment to ourselves" we might be tempted toward an even greater failure: to move altogether into the "immaterial starry system," where *is* may get lost entirely in the dream of *if*.

Let us now swing full circle—back through all we have encountered in Part I, back to William James's objection to the Spencerian notion of physical survival at all costs. We have been told that if we truly desire to do more than survive, then we shall prevail, even if only by the skin of our teeth. Because of our desire for *more*, we shall have that "fringe" of rich consciousness—that expanding, bridging leap of thought; that further drive to possess a destiny; that added feeling of the purpose of life. But are we wise to believe men like Emerson and James, even when they seem to solve the problems of our basic sense of destitution? Would it be better for us to pay more heed to that twentieth-century cautionary tale by Scott Fitzgerald in which the Son of God, Jay Gatsby, becomes the poor Son of a Bitch? Are we to find America's pattern for success in the type of Thoreau, the ascetic of great spiritual wealth, or in that of Gatsby, excited as he was by the enriching idea of going about "his father's business"? Thoreau found some reality at least at Walden Pond; Gatsby came to his fantastic end in a West Egg swimming pool a few hundred yards inward from the green-breasted shores which Dutch sailors once hungered after with contemplative lust. The actual results of Thoreau's quest are vague; Gatsby's "destiny" fairly clearly images a nation where no man has yet found the link between "two craving parts of nature" or a lasting bridge "over that yawning need."

The introduction to Emerson's *Nature* speaks of the need to find the one true theory that "will explain all phenomena. Now many are thought not only unexplained but inexplicable; as language, sleep, madness, dreams, beasts, sex." If many early New Englanders once viewed Calvinist theology as the one true theory, Oliver Wendell Holmes's poem about the One-Hoss Shay describes the collapse of that theory in America; it had failed (or so Holmes asserts) because it could not explain such phenomena as the Lisbon earthquake or General Braddock's defeat in the American wilderness. (Actually, it could, but not in ways to please the humanistic common sense of a man like Holmes.) In constructing theories, Holmes, like Emerson, preferred to substitute an organic form for the man-made structure of the shay. To both men the Chambered Nautilus (vivid metaphor for continuing growth) was the more appropriate image for that theory which might yet explain everything in ways which the delicately balanced, perfectly crafted, but ultimately inflexible structure of the shay could not. Whatever its future form, such a theory will have to satisfy us as to why Thoreau and Gatsby failed; it will also need to provide the success of a "national idea" with which "all experience" can keep up—made possible because idea and experience would at last be one, even for such as Henry David and Jay.

The sense of loss and failure that pervades any narrative of the quest to find the all-inclusive idea about America is by its nature "religious." Josiah Royce made much of the fact that we know what we have, and *the more* it is that we desire, by the fact of feeling great lack. Ralph Harper—author of *Nostalgia*, with its sub-title, *an existential exploration of longing and fulfillment in the modern age*—agrees. According to Harper's argument, we know home is real by our sense of homelessness; we confirm the fact of authentic being by our sense of our fraudulence. By analogy, American journeys into the wilderness—imagined or actual—are essentially religious since, almost from the first, so much stress has been laid upon false routes taken and dead-ends reached. That central and radiant truth the Puritans envisioned is given reality by their failure to gain it; the perfect and perfecting laws claimed by Thoreau and Emerson are what the responsive mind cannot deny as genuine so long as its own poor experience is unable to encompass them; the pain of inconsequence felt by Norman Mailer is validation of the relationship of power with God he feels is rightfully his.

If Ralph Harper observes that the twentieth-century world is increasingly conscious of what it ought to have accomplished (a realization that only increases its sense of failure), Perry Miller, Sacvan Bercovitch, and Emory Elliott have demonstrated that many Puritans responded to spiritual goods made vivid by their absence. Then and now, we are like Faulkner's idiot Jim Bond of *Absalom, Absalom!* "the scion, the last of his race, seeing it too now and howling with human reason since now even he could have known what he was howling about" (p. 376). From William Bradford's "howling wilderness" to Jim Bond's "howl in the wilderness"—full-circle in just three hundred years, just as deprived, sooner and late, of the manna that fills our need. But perhaps not. Perhaps we are simply more *experienced* in our *idea* of what America might yet offer to assuage our hunger.

# PART II

# Ideas
# of
# the Land

# ◣ CHAPTER 5 ◢

# America as the Woman
# Who Waits

We have learned our lessons of cynicism well in the American school for success; our teachers have been good ones. The business of America is "well-being" (*Tocqueville*). Money-grabbing and getting ahead is the characteristic trait of the American (*Frances Trollope*). A man realizes he is a failure the day he sees he is incapable of commanding five dollars on the job market (*Henry Adams*). Although warned that America is not the *Pays de Cocagne* and its streets not paved with wheaten loaves (*Franklin*), men still devour the ground out from under their own feet (*just about everyone*).

If there has been a growing severance between doing well and being good, and a blurring of distinctions between good-living and well-being, and if ironies heap up as we compare the fates of those who are too good to live with those who are good enough to succeed, is this all there is to say about the American *facts* of failure and success? Perhaps it is. We must turn instead to an examination of *ideas* about success and failure in America. Eventually we will return to those disillusioning facts in order to reassess the possibility of whether this or any age has the power "to annul that adulterous divorce which the superstition has effected between the intellect and holiness" of which Emerson spoke. We will also reconsider Josiah Royce's one-time hope that "the divorce be completely overcome" so that a man may see "his ideas fulfilled in the facts of his experience, and [behold] his experiences as the fulfillment of his ideas."

The idea-data presented here may finally serve to support the commonly held contentions that the only hope one has to be a good person is to be a bad American and that the true American Way is the way of corruption, darkness, and defeat. But, as Henry James remarks in *The American Scene*, the "restless analyst" must forego "measurements" that are "premature" and "conclusions" that are "solemn"; he must patiently accept "abeyance of judgment"; he will be quick to recognize that in America traditional values will undergo "permeation" into "values of a new order." At this point James adds, "Of *what* order we must wait to see" (p. 382).

Restless analysts do well to jolt past the ruts of the responses we have grown up in. One such is the assertion that the only work we Americans care about is the vast and meretricious business of our Father. Kenneth Burke says we pay too much attention to fathers anyway and not enough to mothers; Henry Adams knew the truth of this and at what cost to his life.

In 1901 Adams addressed a prayer-poem to the Virgin of Chartres in an attempt to express why he had stumbled toward failure:

> If then I left you, it was not my crime,
>     Or if a crime, it was not mine alone.
> All children wander with the truant Time.
>     Pardon me too! You pardoned once your Son!
>
> For He said to you:—"Wist ye not that I
>     Must be about my Father's business?" So,
> Seeking his Father he pursued his way
>     Straight to the Cross towards which we all must go.
>
> So I too wandered off among the host
>     That racked the earth to find the father's clue.
> I did not find the Father, but I lost
>     What now I value more, the Mother,—You!
>
> I thought the fault was yours that foiled my search;
>     I turned and broke your image on its throne,
> Cast down my idol, and resumed my march
>     To claim the father's empire for my own.

In this poem Adams locates the terrain of his misspent journey within his inner life; he does not specifically name America as the arena of his failure or make his defeat a particularly American plight. But other sons of America the Beautiful have directly connected their successful homecomings or their unhappy wanderings to this country by imaging it as the mother, or mistress, of us all. Copious documentation on the subject fills the pages of the recent study by Annette Kolodny, *The Lay of the Land*, whose title really means what it says and suggests. Kolodny's approach to the female-imagery applied to men's ideas of America is different from my own; but there is no quarrel here with what her book has to say about the "oldest and most cherished fantasy" about America:

> . . . a daily reality of harmony between man and nature based on an experience of the land as essentially feminine—that is, not simply the land as mother, but the land as woman, the total

female principle of gratification—enclosing the individual in an environment of receptivity, repose, and painless and integral satisfaction. (p. 4)

At the least, this habit of thinking of the self and of the land imaged in ways that speak to the most primal of contacts strongly indicates that *relationship* is the first of considerations. Before the American can know what he has gained or can measure what he has lost, he must feel his way toward some expression of inscape and landscape as they mutually define one another.

Here follow several examples of the land imaged as the woman, taken from the fiction of William Faulkner. Long associated with tales about lost causes and victors who fall prey to self-defeat, Faulkner is also known as a man much given to the rhetoric of honor and glory, prevailing, enduring, and triumphing. It may seem ironic to call upon Faulkner for aid in assessing the ironies of victory and defeat in terms of America as woman, particularly if he hates women as much as certain of his critics say he does. But let us give him his head for the time being, tracing his leads as they take us toward that combined image of land-and-woman which, by promising total satisfaction of all desires, acts to frustrate those same desires.

In "the old days" there were two brave men: the Indian, Ikkemotubbe, and the white man, David Hogganbeck. Both loved the sister of Herman Basket—unnamed, since one who "walked in beauty" is unneedful of a name, unneedful of having to *do* anything or *possess* anything. She need not even walk about; she has only to sit in her beauty, at most casually shelling peas into a silver wine pitcher while resting on the open gallery.

The young men of the Mississippi territory are wild for the girl, stirred into lunges of activity by the very passivity of her being. But only Ikkemotubbe and David Hogganbeck are worthy of the contest of strengths, talents, and wills the men of this region consider necessary to "A Courtship." These are mythic men in mythic combat. Proper to this blessed stage of the legendary history which Faulkner is proposing for America, the two contenders for victory each wishes to achieve a true and honorable success over that rival each loves and respects. "But if I am to win," the Indian tells the white man, "I do not wish you to be hurt good. If I am to truly win, it will be necessary for you to be there to see it" (p. 371).

The men are true lovers because they love one another, even as they dream they love the unnamed, almost unseen but always sensed, presence of Herman Basket's sister. As the final test they set for themselves, they decide to run day and night for one hundred and thirty miles to a cave whose roof is reputed to lose its fragile equilibrium at any shock of noise. In their running their mutual compassion is fully demonstrated. On their arrival at the cave, where the two men throw themselves into the black pit whose sides tremble as if to engulf them, each man wins a victory which is simultaneously a victory for himself and for both.

Indian and white—perfect types like Cooper's *beau-idéal*, achieving perfect victory—settle to their hearts' satisfaction who is to possess Herman Basket's sister. Meanwhile she—passive, never moving—has chosen Log-in-the-Creek, a nonentity incapable of holding his whiskey, given to lying on his back upon the gallery floor and blowing into his harmonica. "Aihee," Ikkemotubbe says at the news, "At least, for all men one same heart-break" (p. 380). Even in the old time—in a good land where there was "always something to be found to eat"; where "there were men in those days"; where among such men no one was defeated and everyone won (pp. 362, 373)—the male dream of possessing the thing of great beauty is shattered by a woman's whim that defeats male patterns of honorable action and male faith in the logic of cause and effect.

Several times during this tale of 1948 Faulkner tells us it all took place while the Indian was "still just Ikkemotubbe, one of the young men, the best one, who rode the hardest and fastest and danced the longest and got the drunkest and was loved the best, by the young men and the girls and the older women too who should have had other things to think about" (p. 363). Later in time Ikkemotubbe goes away, returns with a new white friend, eight slaves, and a murderous, wily plan to become the Man in the territory—named *d'Homme* because he is Doom, the strongest and the cleverest; the one who lives by the "possessive"; but no longer the most loved, never again the honorable man generous in true victory.

In "A Courtship" we see Ikkemotubbe as lover and victor, even if only "another of the young men who loved and was not loved in return and could hear the words and see the fact, yet who, like the young men who had been before him and the ones who would come after him, still could not understand it"(p. 379). In "The Old People" included in *Go Down, Moses* we realize what Ikkemotubbe becomes in time—a winner, using treachery, threats, and murder to gain power over that land which, Faulkner insists, any man is a fool to think he can possess or trade to other power-hungry men. Ikkemotubbe finally has a woman, the black slave whom he later casually sells, together with his unborn son, in order to possess yet more land, more power. The more the Man acquires in the years subsequent to "the old days" the more he loses; the more he reaches out to seize, the more rapidly the land recedes from his claims. Herman Basket's sister and her chosen one—Log-in-the-Creek, the Thoreauvian idler and harmonica-player—vanish from the scene, but the land remains, imaged as she who sits in beauty and will not be had.

According to Faulkner's historico-poetical view, what has altered within the life-span of Ikkemotubbe is the quality of the community of men (transmuted into the rule of the Man) and their definitions of success (from victory willingly shared with their brothers, to the seizure of power for the self alone). That much of Faulkner's fiction deals with the dire effects of just such changes from "the old days" and "a good land" supports J.R.R. Tolkien's view that "It is a strange thing, but things that are good to have and days that are good to spend are soon told about and not much to listen to." In Faulkner's imagination the idea of success, coupled with the facts of failure, is more conducive to good literature, even if it gives a halt to the happy life.

After the historical period depicted by "The Courtship," generations flow on through the time-reach of Faulkner's imagination. The land has come to be known as Yoknapatawpha County. Those who were once men are now merely males. In the last decades of the nineteenth century another woman sits under the ravenous gaze of the gallery-sitters, but she at least still retains the old power Herman Basket's sister had had. Eula Varner of *The Hamlet* suggests "some symbology out of the old Dionysic times—honey in sunlight and bursting grapes, the writhen bleeding of the crushed fecundated vine beneath the hard rapacious trampling goat-hoof." She exists "in a teeming vacuum in which her days followed one another as though behind sound-proof glass, where she seemed to listen in sullen bemusement, with a weary wisdom heired of all mammalian maturity, to the enlarging of her own organs" (p. 107).

Like Basket's sister, Eula also chooses not to move. Her idleness—not unlike the *vis inertiae* studied by an aghast Henry Adams—is characterized as "an actual force impregnable and ever ruthless" (p. 107). Like "a moist blast of spring's liquorish corruption," her presence is the catastrophe which defeats any civilization founded on theories of order, work, and concerted goals; it is "the supreme primal uterus" (p. 129)—that which destroys the confidence of Labove, the man who once thought himself above love and empowered by his will to take the straight road toward the governor's mansion and success.

Eula Varner of *The Hamlet* is "a kaleidoscopic convolution of mammalian elipses" which outraged men must transport "across the embracing proscenium of the entire inhabited world like the sun itself" (p. 113). Like the sun, "she was the serene and usually steadily and constantly eating axis, center" (p. 145). She is the center first to a crowd of girls, then of boys, finally of men—each galaxy increasingly violent in its desire to possess Eula as the hub and meaning of desire.

One man among them, McCarron, wins the prize away from the men who have tirelessly carried out ruthless military campaigns by day and night. Though his rivals break his arm in the melée, McCarron is Eula's choice. She exerts the physical strength to brace up her wounded lover while he triumphantly possesses, for the night, her teeming vacuum. It is for Labove, however, the fierce monk, to foretell Eula's future, and for Ratliff, the cheerful celibate, to locate her origins. First, Labove:

> He could almost see the husband which she would someday have. He would be a dwarf, a gnome, without glands or desire, who would be no more a physical factor in her life than the owner's name on the fly-leaf of a book . . . the crippled Vulcan to that Venus, who would not possess her but merely own her by the single strength which power gave, the dead power of money, wealth, gewgaws, baubles, as he might own, not a picture, statue: a field, say (pp. 134-135).

At this point in Labove's vision, Eula is transformed from a goddess-woman into the divine but violated land itself:

> He saw it: the fine land rich and fecund and foul and eternal and impervious to him who claimed title to it, oblivious, drawing to itself tenfold the quantity of living seed its owner's whole life could have secreted and compounded, producing a thousandfold the harvest he could ever hope to gather and save (p. 135).

By the rich intuitive knowledge that is his, Ratliff senses that the hamlet of Frenchman's Bend had been chosen by the gods as the natal place of an incarnate dream of victory and defeat:

. . . a little lost village, nameless, without grace, forsaken, yet
which wombed once by chance and accident one blind seed of
the spendthrift Olympian ejaculation and did not even know
it, without tumescence conceived, and bore— . . . a word, a
single will to believe born of envy and old deathless regret . . .
the word, the dream and wish of all males under sun capable
of harm . . . —the word, with its implications of lost triumphs
and defeats of unimaginable splendor—and which best: to
have that word, that dream and hope for future, or to have
had need to flee that word and dream, for past (p. 169).

Woman—land—word—dream: all blurred together by the lull-
ing, yet compelling, rhythm of Faulkner's language, itself an
example of the danger, as well as the good, of any attempt to impose reality defined by means of myth-sustaining style upon reality
defined as myth-denying fact.

Flem Snopes, with the surprise of a hawk's nose, minute dot of
bow tie, and eyes like stagnant water, takes Eula (who is metaphorically the land) and the Frenchman's Place (which is literally land as
dowry—money, power, and respectability; also, figuratively, land
as mystery, treasure, dream). But Flem is defeated because he
merely owns; he does not *have* Eula any more than he has the
Frenchman's garden—defeated, of course, only metaphorically
and figuratively; victorious in any obvious literal sense. But dreams
are powerful in *The Hamlet*; dreams by moonlight of buried
treasure—whether of Eula or of the gold in the Frenchman's
garden—which can turn sane men into mad dogs in Faulkner's version of the essential Ovidian myth of metamorphoses; dreams
which also transform men who know they are losers into those who
live in the hope they might yet gain their heart's desire. Eula as
just-woman remains the still center of the frenetic action, a force
both literal and figurative, but the land-as-Eula is even more powerful. Eula may exude "scent" from her "supreme primal uterus"
and transform men like Labove past self-recognition, yet the earth
is the Circe-force that most drastically maddens men with dreams
of ripping gold from its yielding softness.

Faulkner's women characters are sometimes active, aggressive,
masculine types, stung by the sexual wasps of nymphomania and
the urge to command: Charlotte Rittenmeyer, Joanna Burden-
by-night, Mink Snopes's wife. But his females are also passive, im-
perturbable *vis inertiae*, a force which sits and dreams, even while
driving men wild with the hope of possessing that dream and that

dreamer. War-clashes marked by the general absence of honorable behavior toward one's rivals fill the air of Yoknapatawpha—the noise of outrage and frustration; but the earth-women remain enveloped within the still vacuum of their musings.

A final example—drawn from "The Jail," one of the prose sections encasing the drama *Requiem for a Nun*—indicates the basic paradigm for the relations between defeat, victory, land, and the mother, spun out of Faulkner's vision of the history of mankind. But first a brief reference to an observation made by Hawthorne, another poetic historian of America.

By the last pages of Hawthorne's "The Maypole of Merry-Mount" the contest between iron and silk, gloom and jollity, has already been worked out and played out, with the ambiguous victory going to the Puritans. Then, at the very conclusion of that tale, Hawthorne diffidently suggests a third alternative to the action; it is introduced in the shape of the circlet (domesticated roses of stock brought from England entwined with wild, indigenous American blooms) thrown by the stern hand of Endicott over the heads of the two lovers, Edith and Edgar. If Hawthorne's tale represents the beginning of the English-speaking experience in America, then it is a kind of historical inevitability that takes us from Merry-Mount to Hester Prynne, standing in the doorway of the Salem jailhouse beside a rosebush. That bush was perhaps planted by the rebellious hand of Anne Hutchinson; it was certainly planted there by Hawthorne to remind us of the kinds of hurtful victory that are won by the individual heart at the cost of tearing itself loose from the will of society.

Faulkner, like Hawthorne, attempted to write the history of a particular region of the American continent in order to record the civil wars that have altered the land and its people. He, too, stressed the central position held in Jefferson, Mississippi, by the jailhouse. Without the jail there cannot be a courthouse; without a courthouse there can be no town, no human habitation possible in the midst of the wilderness. (The jail, perhaps, is the Frostian tennis-net kept as momentary stay against confusion.) But no dark-haired, richly voluptuous Hester Prynne stands defiantly, an unholy madonna of the future, at the portal of Jefferson's jail. Rather it is a

> frail blonde girl not only incapable of (or at least excused from) helping her mother cook, but even of drying the dishes after her mother (or father perhaps) washed them—musing, not even waiting for anyone or anything, as far as the town knew, not even pensive, as far as the town knew; just musing

amid her blonde hair in the window facing the country town street, day after day and month after month and—as the town remembered it—year after year for what must have been three or four of them, inscribing at some moment the fragile and indelible signature of her meditation in one of the panes of it (the window): her frail and workless name, scratched by a diamond ring in her frail and workless hand, and the date: *Cecilia Farmer April 16th 1861....* (p. 229)

Hester Prynne (who helps us to trace Hawthorne's historical progression from Puritan Salem to Zenobia's nineteenth-century Blithedale) has been prepared for imaginatively in *The Scarlet Letter* by his account of the rebellion and counter-rebellion at Merry-Mount. Cecilia Farmer (meagerly occupying the niche that will, in later Mississippi times, be filled more amply by Eula Varner) has herself been historically prepared for within *Requiem for a Nun* by the figure of Mohataha, the Indian queen, mother of Ikkemotubbe of "the old days." Dressed in the cast-off purple silk of a French queen, Mohataha rides into the town to ask, "Where is this Indian territory?" Once she has the west pointed out to her—the direction which will comprise the historical future of her exiled people and of America—she sets her x "on the paper which ratified the dispossession of her people forever." Then Mohataha

vanished so across that summer afternoon to that terrific and infinitesimal creak and creep of ungreased wheels, herself immobile beneath the rigid parasol, grotesque and regal, bizarre and moribund, like obsolescence's self riding off the stage enthroned on its own obsolete catafalque, looking not once back, not once back toward home.... (p. 217)

The Indian queen and mother silently gives over the land of the People to the Men. She disappears from the sight of conventional historical records, although not from the story of history as told by Faulkner. For Faulkner the result of Mohataha's act—silent, invisible, a mere "inked cross at the foot of a sheet of paper"—is as momentous in its consequences as lighting "the train of a mine set beneath a dam, a dyke, a barrier already straining, bulging, bellying, not only towering over the land but leaning, looming, imminent with collapse . . . " (p. 221). The mother of Ikkemotubbe (*d'Homme*—Doom) is banished by the symbolic betrayal perpetrated by all such sons. The wagon of the queen, pulled forever westward as if on a Grecian urn, does not just vanish "but was swept, hurled, flung not only out of Yoknapatawpha County and Mississippi but the United States too, immobile and intact—the wagons, the mules, the rigid shapeless old Indian woman . . ." (pp. 221-222). The mother is sent into exile, and the land she both represents and has had seized from her continues to live out its history, as explosive as a powder-train and as vulnerable to collapse as a dam.

Faulkner's sense of history, not dissimilar to that of Henry Adams, gives an account of the accelerating forces by which "the time, the land, the nation, the American earth, whirled faster and faster toward the plunging precipice of its destiny . . ." (p. 226). In the midst of Whirl, "musing, not even waiting for anyone or anything," stands Cecilia Farmer in 1861 (p. 229). Three years later "the frail and useless girl musing in the blonde mist of her hair beside the window-pane" upon which she has cut her name (*Farmer*—ironic since her father, a failure at tilling the earth, can only tend the jail) looks up at a soldier who suddenly appears on the street by the jail—"gaunt and tattered, battle-grimed and fleeing and undefeated"—the two of them "looking at one another for that moment across the fury and pell mell of battle" (p. 232).

A year later, 1865, the soldier who had vanished from the town "firing a pistol backward at a Yankee army" reappears, "still gaunt and tattered and dirty and still undefeated and not fleeing now but instead making or at least planning a single-handed assault against what any rational man would have considered insurmountable odds. . . ." The girl watches him dismount at the door to the jail, he not taking the time to look at her "since she was not his immediate object now, he was not really concerned with her at the moment, because he had so little time, he had none, really . . . " (p. 235). Full of "weary and indomitable outrage" that he must expend three precious days getting society's permission to take the musing girl off to Alabama as his bride, the undefeated soldier knows he must hurry home to thrust a sockful of corn into the war-depleted earth before it is too late.

The girl, just barely named, had stood at the window the day she scratched her name on the pane; had stood, still, the day the soldier glanced at her before the battle whirled him out of town; stood still the day he returns: "a year, and still not even waiting: meditant, not even unimpatient; just patienceless, in the sense that blindness and zenith are colorless . . ." (p 256). Hers is the power of "the impregnable, that invincible, that incredible, that terrifying passivity" which had the force to draw the soldier down from Virginia—a man "who had swapped his charger for a mule and the sabre of his rank and his defeatless pride for a stocking full of seed corn" (pp.

256, 257). Drawn "by that virgin inevictable passivity more inescapable than lodestar," the man pauses, outraged, just long enough to seek sanction to bear her with him into a new life "which was not even simple frontier, engaged only with wilderness and shoeless savages and the tender hand of God, but one which had been rendered into a desert . . . by the iron and fire of civilization" (pp. 260, 257).

Cecilia Farmer's fate is to become "the farmless mother of farmers (she would bear a dozen, all boys, herself no older, still fragile, still workless among the churns and stoves and brooms and stacks of wood which even a woman could split into kindling; unchanged), bequeathing to them in their matronymic the heritage of that invisible inviolable ineptitude . . ." (p. 258). Those are the mere events of her life, but *what* she means is the thing which "yourself the stranger, the outlander . . . passing through Jefferson by chance or accident on the way to somewhere else" must try to find out (p. 260). Further, her meaning comprehended by means of the mind's logic is less important than what one feels in the presence of her memory.

Faulkner foresees that you, the passerby, and the local fellow who has rarely been out of the county, will be drawn together by that name faintly scratched on the pane; all of you united as one person, affected by the force of a girl who was "not *might* have been, nor even *could* have been, but *was*: so vast, so limitless in capacity is man's imagination to disperse and burn away the rubble-dross of fact and probability, leaving only truth and dream . . ." (p. 261).

As Henry James is wont to say, "And there we are!" But just as James's characters must thereafter inquire—as they attempt to assess how far they have indeed traveled through perilous regions of consciousness—exactly *where* is that? Well, at a beginning at least. Without implying that Faulkner planned to fix an allegorical relationship between these female characters and men's responses to the American landscape, we may take his poetic representations of women and land, extracting them briefly from their place in the tales for our use, neither mutilating the original narratives nor doing hurt to this corner of the American experience in our effort to get at some part of its meaning.

It is not Faulkner alone who made use of the figure of the woman who waits by which we come better to learn "where we are" as Americans. Early on in *The Golden Bowl* (XXIII, 49-50), Henry James has Prince Amerigo—the Old Roman whose process of education will take him into the terrain of the New Woman of

America—characterize American-born Charlotte Stant as the typical woman of his European experience. He thinks that Charlotte is one who will always do the thing "that gave her away. She did it, ever, inevitably, infallibly—she couldn't possibly not do it. It was her nature, it was her life, and the man could always expect it without lifting a finger." Amerigo rests comfortably in his knowledge that his was the advantage—the "position and strength"—because "he only had to wait." By using his patience, the Old Roman feels assured he will get the benefit of the woman's active doing—which was "her weakness and her deep misfortune—not less, no doubt, than her beauty."

Notwithstanding Amerigo's complacent belief that he knows what Charlotte is, we are led to ask whether Charlotte, indeed, represents a true American girl in James's view, or whether she is not rather quite "other" than America. Perhaps she has become entirely European because of her *doing* set off by the man's *waiting*. Certainly, the several roles played by Maggie Verver in the same novel serve to complicate the answer. Maggie is continually presented in *The Golden Bowl* as more typical of her nation than her compatriot Charlotte. James first shows us the experienced Charlotte, who has learned to act to get the man who waits on what he wants. He then gives us Maggie, who in her naïveté simply waits. But he also offers Maggie as the woman who comes through painful wisdom to the point where she knows how to stay very, very still, at last getting what she wants from the man who now must move to come to where she stands. In the end Maggie more truly represents the Muse of American City, even as she prepares the way for Charlotte's journey of exile to that place, whereas Charlotte has yet to benefit from what the American Maggie has discovered about the relation between waiting and winning.

Filled with expectation, Theodore Dreiser's heroine Sister Carrie "came fresh from the air of the village, the light of the country still in her eye" (p. 91). First seduced by the city of Chicago, she finds the act of submission consummated when she accepts "two soft, green, handsome ten-dollar bills" from Charlie Drouet, the "salesman"—the bills more sensuously fascinating to Carrie than the man (p. 47). Carrie is later driven out to "an open grassy prairie" to be seduced by the enticing words of Hurstwood (p. 94). But George Hurstwood, the "manager," soon loses his own grip on the world of moth-luring gas-lights and shining saloon mirrors he once solidly possessed. The one person who will come out ahead in

this story of gain and loss is Carrie, the "star" who comes to dominate every situation even though she seems to remain passive, pli-
able, the quintessential victim who waits to be taken.

Norman Mailer—who tries to be like Drouet around women,
even while re-enacting the ultimately pathetic bumblings of a
Hurstwood—likes to define the great power women have as their
possession of inner space. For Mailer this inborn structural fact enables them to create the future while allowing them to dominate
the present moment. Women have what men desire but can never
own. The male is condemned eternally to be "The Prisoner of Sex."
He moves anxiously to discover that space the female ovum in-
habits, calmly, in perfect freedom.

Mailer continually acts to merge his image of the woman with his
imagination of America. The poor male as American thus lives in
double jeopardy, since he is under the power of female forces
whichever way he turns. Perhaps such quirky notions are merely
Mailer's private fantasies. But if they are shared by others, is it still
merely a collective fantasy insidiously at work? Or is there good
reason to hope that we can apply with profit the image of the
woman who waits to America as a *place* with certain actual conditions for success and failure?

Looping his way through an involved sentence in *The Armies of the
Night* (p. 114), Mailer describes the emotions he feels toward the
Pentagon—"chalice and anus of corporation land"—in his attempt
to penetrate "some dim unawakened knowledge of the mysteries of
America . . ." as female. He responds with love to a nation that is
both "Awful deadening programmatic inhuman dowager of a nation, corporation, and press" *and* "tender mysterious bitch whom
no one would ever know, not even her future unfeeling Com-
munist doctors if she died of the disease of her dowager, deadly
pompous dowager who had trapped the sweet bitch."

America to Mailer is a symbol compounded of several types of
women. In turn, his fourth wife Beverly is that woman who best
symbolizes his relation with his country. If he loses Beverly, "why
then he would finally lose some part of his love affair with America"
(p. 171). Ironically, he sees he will indeed lose Beverly if he treats
her as a symbol, not a person. By implication, America also eludes
the mind that tries to fix it into symbols that are too self-containing:

We will remember that Mailer had a complex mind of sorts.
He would have considered it irretrievably heavy-handed to
have made any direct correspondence between his feelings for

his wife, and the change in his feeling toward America . . . but he would also have thought it cowardly to ignore the relation, and dishonest to assume that none of his wife's attractiveness (and unattractiveness) came from her presence so quintessentially American.

It was after all natural that he should have a love affair with America—how much worse if the grandsons of the immigrants did not. No, the trick was merely to never lose sight of his fourth wife's absolutely unquenchable even unendurable individuality. Let him treat her as a symbol, and he was out of it—which is why perhaps she was so American (pp. 171-172).

Mailer forewarned is not necessarily Mailer forearmed. He moves on recklessly to assign other qualities of femaleness to the country, as in *Of A Fire on the Moon*. America is "our redneck Molly abloom"—"witch and bitch on a holiday"; capable of putting a curse on the rocket into space, she can just as readily pray for its success in the name of the country which has "served to replace the tender sense of the Virgin in Protestant hearts" (pp. 63, 61). The one who prays, the one prayed to (America), and the purpose of the prayer (the moon-mission): all three are female to Mailer. As in *The Armies of the Night*, he is still "not able to decide if her final nature was good or evil" (p. 171). In this sentence "her" refers specifically to Beverly, but as always his feelings for his wife and America are "damnably parallel." Mailer does not really want to find out the mysteries of America or of the woman: he wishes to keep America mysterious by calling it *woman*, its meaning the fact of its mystery. His success as an artist depends on providing the best metaphor for the female unknowableness of the land. At the conclusion of *The Armies of the Night*, in "The Metaphor Delivered," Mailer exhorts all to do as he does:

> Brood on that country who expresses our will. She is America, once a beauty of magnificence unparalleled, now a beauty with a leprous skin. She is heavy with child—no one knows if legitimate—and languishes in a dungeon whose walls are never seen. . . . [She] will probably give birth, and to what?—the most fearsome totalitarianism the world has ever known? Or can she, poor giant, tormented lovely girl, deliver a babe of a new world brave and tender, artful and wild? (p. 288)

Mailer's view of the writer's task is that of a man who wants the success of power. Power is what women already have. Through his often brutal contact with them, Mailer struggles to gain some mastery for himself. In his book on Mailer, Richard Poirier recognizes that for Mailer to succeed as a writer he must condemn buggery ("sexual entrances that lead not to the centers of creations but to the center of waste"); he must celebrate completed heterosexual penetrations, the winning thrust into the waiting space so that he may "dominate worlds" (p. 152). He must be female as well as male; androgyny of the imagination is the final, difficult solution to the necessity for merging the meaning of sex, art, and country into one elaborate image that affords a man some control over the America of his own nature.

Here are four brief views of what the female means to the male imagination that seeks to gain domination over personal worlds of power. They test whether the idea yields to further expansion or remains limited to the private fixations of Mailer, the Brooklyn boy who naïvely believes in "sympathetic magic."

(1) Paul Ricoeur in *the Symbolism of Evil* does not see woman as "the second sex." Woman represents a certain quality that lies within each individual—restless instability that resents curbs and finitude and that seeks freedom from possession. (2) Gaston Bachelard also defines the feminine as a floating element contained within both male and female; it is the quality of an idea—what "the masculine" sets up as "the Other" by means of reveries that idealize both the dreamer and the contemplated object. For Bachelard (as for Keats) Eve was created with great beauty because of Adam's dream; the dream through which he was to possess her had of necessity to come true. (3) According to William Faulkner, to be the Man is to be fated (Doom) to repeat acts that fulfill the genitive case of possession (*d'Homme*)—the main objects of male possession most likely to be women and the land. (4) As Ernest Hemingway sits writing a story in a Paris café in the 1920s, an incident recalled in *A Moveable Feast*, he sees a beautiful girl. She disturbs and excites Hemingway; he wishes he could put her into a story. But he keeps working at his present task—pausing now and then to look over at her, where she sits waiting for a man. Within his heart he addresses himself to her:

> I've seen you, beauty, and you belong to me now, whoever you are waiting for and if I never see you again, I thought. You belong to me and all Paris belongs to me and I belong to this notebook and this pencil.

Then I went back to writing and I entered far into the story and was lost in it. I was writing it now and it was not writing itself. . . . (p. 6)

The story finished, the girl gone, Hemingway is "empty and both sad and happy, as though I had made love" (p. 6).

These four views lead toward dreams of seizure and fulfillment. But what if the dreamers consciously hold to the idea of America as the mother? Those guilts pertaining to incestuous desires aside, what dangers come to the imaginations that seek to possess but end by finding themselves *possessed by* the mother who would have them forever?

There is Thoreau's mother-theory, which he wrote into his journal of February 1857: "America is the she wolf to-day, and the children of exhausted Europe exposed by her uninhabited and savage shores are the Romulus and Remus who, having derived new life and vigor from her breast, have founded a new Rome in the West" (VIII, 151). Even more playfully, Thoreau, in *A Week on the Concord and Merrimack Rivers*, figures all human history an old wives' tale: "From Adam and Eve at one leap sheer down to the deluge," past countless events, "down through Odin and Christ—to America":

> It is a wearisome while. And yet the lives of but sixty old women, such as live under the hill, say of a century each, strung together, are sufficient to reach over the whole ground. Taking hold of hands they would span the interval from Eve to my own mother. A respectable tea-party merely,—whose gossip would be Universal History. The fourth old woman from myself suckled Columbus . . . the nineteenth was the Virgin Mary . . .—the sixtieth was Eve the mother of mankind. . . . It will not take a very great-granddaughter of hers to be in at the death of Time. (pp. 346-347).

Such mother-images of America do not remain unqualified for long. Mark Twain's unpublished work "The Secret History of Eddypus, the World-Empire" is an elaborate spoof on the takeover of humankind by "Our Mother"—Mary Baker Eddy, his exemplary type of the American female opportunist and financial success. But the comic horror described by Mark Twain in this piece included in *Fables of Man* is expressed with more authenticity of fright by Norman Mailer. In "An Impolite Interview," included in *The Presidential Papers*, Mailer places the end of freedom in America at "the moment we start mothering mankind and decide that one truth is good for them to hear and another is not so good . . ." (pp. 136-137). Mailer believes that men may never attain that knowledge which women are born knowing, but they must be permitted the right to struggle to attain the knowledge which the "mothers" wrongly forbid.

The destructive movement away from "mothers" is crucial to many of Melville's narrative structures. Pierre Glendinning, compelled by the idea he creates concerning his father's guilt, uproots himself from the locked embrace of both his mother and mothering earth and starts on his career as wanderer—only one of the Melvillien males who must flee the feminine succor of the land. As *Moby-Dick* declares, ". . . in the port is safety, comfort, hearthstone, supper, warm blankets, friends, all that's kind to our mortalities." In opposition to solace is the type of Bulkington, the man who heeds "that mortally intolerable truth, that all deep, earnest thinking is but the intrepid effort of the soul to keep the open independence of her sea; while the wildest winds of heaven and earth conspire to cast her on the treacherous, slavish shore" (p. 97).

Just as Joe Christmas in Faulkner's *Light in August* instinctively repudiates the "treacherous, slavish shore" of Mrs. McEachern's maternity and Joanna Burden's mothering desire to pray over his soul, American males discover that the aspiring soul (paradoxically designated as "her") must escape the mothering of the lee shore (the "she"). Rose of Sharon, the sister-mother of John Steinbeck's *The Grapes of Wrath*, will press a starving man's mouth against her over-flowing breast as a momentary stay against disaster. Hers is an act that affirms Steinbeck's hope that the wrathful grapes of the land will be trod into the wine of human communion by the Family—the saving mother-core of America. But still the Bulkingtons, portrayed by Melville, Faulkner, and Mailer among others, tear themselves away from the comforting breasts of the lee shore so that they may perhaps be better able to contemplate from afar the green breasts of their world-wonder.

Whatever the historical facts, images persist of America as woman. Often they have had to persist in opposition to earlier American timidities about the female form. Over in Europe, Bachelard in *Water and Dreams* complicates the original image of mothering nature by introducing the milky water substance celebrated by Novalis. Water projects the female upon the visible world as "*dissolving girl*, as a *liquid essence of girl*" (p. 62). When Mark

Twain drifts on a raft along the Neckar River in *A Tramp Abroad*, he
tells of a lovely girl standing partially naked at water's edge, but he
did not let us see such a maiden on the shores of Huck's Mississippi.
True, Walt Whitman dared to place naked bodies at play beside an
American river, but they are the bodies of men—like those of an
Eakins painting, seen and longed after by a woman waiting at the
window.

According to Bachelard in the passages included in the Gaudin
collection, "Feminine forms will rise out of the very substance of
water, at the contact of the man's breast, apparently when the
man's desire takes a precise form." Dreams of this type "exist only
when one touches them: water becomes woman only against the
breast. . . ." "The water has taken on the property of the dissolved
feminine substance. If you want immaculate water, dissolve virgins
in it. If you want the seas of Melanesia, dissolve Negresses in it"
(pp. 62-64). But the young Melville had to go to Polynesia in order
to dissolve his image of Fayaway in the waters of the Edenic lagoon;
his dream could not materialize in America, for him the land of the
restricting mothers.

Dream needs touch—the substance of matter—to come true.
"But the voluptuous substance," Bachelard continues, "exists before the forms of voluptuousness . . ." (p. 62). Matter and dreams:
this is like comparing Titian's *Flora* with Botticelli's *Primavera*—
matter (painterly) compared with form (linear). If the essential,
most deeply American type of painting is indeed luminism, as will
be discussed further on, then linear form has the means by which it
can merge with the radiance of solid matter. Flora touches Primavera; Fayaway's shy glance meets Hester Prynne's proud gaze; Rose
of Sharon tips mother's milk into a stranger's mouth so that life's
manna will not be wasted; Sister Carrie offers her dreaming face to
an eagerly receptive audience of inarticulate men. Innocence,
knowledge, suffering, hope; "as dissolved girl, as a liquid essence of
girl."

Dreams must be "about something," as Henry James puts it.
When in Faulkner's *The Hamlet* Ike Snopes' beloved, the Olympian
heifer, is taken from him, his cousin Eck in compassion gives the
idiot the carved effigy of a cow. "Yes. I felt sorry for him. I thought
maybe anytime he would happen to start thinking, that ere toy one
would give him something to think about" (p. 306). If ever we
think, we must have something *to think about*, whether what we possess is actually America or its toy-surrogate. But we must also take
care that the ideas we think and dream about for the sake of their

power do not make us vulnerable to the facts of that America already in our possession.

In Fitzgerald's *Tender Is the Night* Dick Diver muses that a nation of men was given "the illusions of eternal strength and health, and of the essential goodness of people; illusions of a nation, the lies of generations of frontier mothers who had to croon falsely, that there were no wolves outside the cabin door" (p. 117). The ability to persuade the American male that there are no wolves out there in the night is a masterful one, especially when it is done as much out of love and knowledge as out of ignorance and evasion. Just the same, it is necessary to realize exactly what one is being given to think about. "America is the she wolf to-day," Thoreau said, meaning it as a compliment to the country that gives exhausted races "new life and vigor" and establishes "a new Rome in the West." But to persuade oneself that such a land and such women have no bite is not wise.

Love's desire produces fine images, as Bachelard maintains. But whether the effects will be injurious or not depends on the kind of desires—whether America will act as "the intense inane" that grinds one to powder in the mills of the conventional, or whether she serves the mind as "a liquid essence" of strengthening wonder and hope.

In the beginning there was not only the wonder experienced by those who gazed upon the green-breasted shores of America. America itself seemed to be waiting in wonder, like Shakespeare's Miranda, for that world elsewhere to discover her. The land seemed to greet all its suitors named "Smith" with the ebullience of Robert Penn Warren's country gal in *Brother to Dragons*.

> He had a right to hope, that fellow Smith,
> In that heyday of hope and heart's extravagance
> When Grab was watchword and earth spread her legs
> Wide as she could, like any jolly trollope
> Or bouncing girl back in the bushes after
> The preaching or the husking bee, and said,
> "Come git it, boy, hit's yourn, but git it deep."
>
> And every dawn sang, "Glory, glory be!"
> Sang, "Glory be to Grab, come git it, boy!"
> Sang, "Git it, boy, hit's yourn, but git it deep!" (p. 16)

Yet it is Warren who warns that in America "The beast waits" within the labyrinth of the human heart. "He is/Our brother, our darling brother." The mother of the beast (she who is also our mother) is "Pasiphaë, huddled and hutched in the cow's hide,/ Laced, latched, thonged up, and humped for joy . . ." (pp. 7-8). We—the brothers to dragons—must try to comprehend what dream of beast and beauty drives the "mother" of our destinies.

> In your mind you saw some meadow grass, or some grove,
> Some childhood haven, water and birdsong, and you a child.
> The bull plunged. You screamed like a girl; and strove. (p. 8)

Warren tells us we must forgive our fathers for the rape of America's ideals; he also urges us to say to our mothers, "We have not loved you less, poor Pasiphaë" for being the maddened victim of perverse desires (p. 8).

When the green breasts of Miranda and the lusty country gal have a scarlet *A* placed upon them; when Olympian, bovine Eula Varner is handed over to the frog-like Flem Snopes; when only the idiot Ike can experience true love on the Homeric greensward with his love, the heifer: then men's need for wonder is frustrated, or—having become completely sane like the Snopeses—they no longer seek wonder. The mother and the mistress alike are ravaged by the violent bull or blighted by the eunuch steer. Once upon a time Europa's rape led to the successful establishment of a new continent during the movement westward from the cradle of the race in Asia Minor; today America's own deflowering seems to follow with failure the discovery of yet another virgin world.

Henry Adams is largely known by college students for his images of the Virgin and the Dynamo, one famous variant on the machine-in-the-garden complex. As a young man he set himself to the task of analyzing the evolution of yet another feminine image, one of particular significance to the settlement of the American wilderness by the force of an idea.

In a review-article written in 1867 for *The North American Review* Adams carefully moved through the scholarly labyrinth caused by the changing legend of Pocahontas. The problems which Adams faced in the conflict between historical scholarship and personal myth-making are briefly these: Captain John Smith's account of 1624 contained in *The Generall Historie* tells of his capture by the Indians and the saving of his life by the young Pocahontas, "the Kings dearest daughter." As Adams noted, the story given in that year by Smith had been granted almost total confidence for over two hundred years:

In the enthusiasm which her act has called out, language, and perhaps common sense, have been a little strained to cover her with attributes of perfection. Her beauty and wild grace, her compassion and disinterestedness, her Christian life and pure character, have been dwelt upon with warm affection, which is the more natural as the childhood of the nation has furnished little latitude to the imagination.

The odd fact Adams uncovered was that both "A Discourse of Virginia" of 1607-1608 and "A True Relation of Virginia" of 1608 (the former written by Edward Maria Wingfield, the latter by John Smith) laid doubts upon the veracity of Smith's famous story of 1624—"familiar," says Adams (making early use of one of his favorite phrases), "to every school-boy." Both Wingfield and the Smith account of 1608 left out any mention of the dramatic scene in which the Indian maid throws herself protectively between the brave Englishman and his savage executioners. Thus the only immediate information provided during the first years of the Virginia settlement omits all reference to the girl or the heart-stirring incident.

In order to gain alternative perspectives upon the matter of Pocahontas' true character, Adams set himself to survey the accounts written within five to ten years after Smith's capture. Reports of 1615 by Raphe Hamor and William Strachey, and the famous letter by John Rolfe in which he tries to justify his marriage to an Indian and non-Christian, speak of the girl as she is seen just before her baptism as Rebecca Rolfe and her removal to England in 1616. Hamor and Rolfe were obviously intent upon creating sympathy for Pocahontas; yet neither man alluded to Smith's exciting tale. Samuel Purchas' third edition of his "Pilgrimage" in 1617 was also silent concerning the girl who was currently causing a great stir in court circles. By the time Rebecca Rolfe died in England in 1617, there had been several printed references to her life's history, but no such scenes as the one John Smith suddenly mentioned in "New England's Trials" in 1622, and then fully developed in the 1624 *Historie*.

"God made Pocahontas the means to deliver me," Smith finally wrote. Adams is especially struck by this phrase; he takes it to be one made by a man who is lying, whether or not he fully realizes that fact. Commenting upon the "degree of quaint dignity" to which "the men of this time could rise, even in falsehood," Adams further notes that, upon Pocahontas' arrival in England, imagina-

tions immediately began to work up Mrs. John Rolfe into the subject for a stage drama. Adams conjectures that Smith "may have
merely accepted" the additions to his original story "after they had
obtained a strong and general hold on the minds of the contemporaries." By 1624, when Smith had need to increase his own reputation by a new telling of his Virginia adventures, "Pocahontas was
made to appear in it as a kind of stage deity on every possible occasion, and his own share in the affairs of the Colony is magnified at
the expense of all his companions."

Through Adam's résumés, the Indian girl gives us fine examples
of the several types which still others saw her as representing before Smith's 1624 account swept in to blot them out. (This, over
three hundred years prior to John Barth, who has taken his turn at
her legend in *The Sot-Weed Factor* in which Pocahontas, like Warren's country gal, entreats the man named "Smith" to "git it deep.")
To King James, to whose court she came as Rebecca Rolfe,
Pocahontas was truly the daughter of a king, endowed by her "imperial blood" with divine rights. Rolfe, the simple gentleman who
had married her, required chastisement for his presumption in
marrying so far above his rank. To William Strachey, who wrote of
her around 1615, she was "a well featured but wanton young girle
. . . of the age then of eleven or twelve yeares." She was wont,
Strachey reports, to "get the boyes forth with her into the markett
place, and make them wheele, falling on their hands, turning up
their heeles upwards, whome she would followe and wheele so her
self, naked as she was, all the fort over." Imperial lady and wanton
girl, Rebecca Rolfe and Pocahontas: this female had the power to
make men submit to her image. In later generations, members of
the FFV would speak with pride of having descended from her
body. In George Bancroft's *History of the United States*, the earnest
historian would cite her compassion and Smith's courage with the
highest praise. Each succeeding century embellished the original
imaginative creation until, in Henry Adams's words, "The lights
are intensified; the shadows are deepened; the gradations are sof-
tened; the copy surpasses its model."

However debunked—or at least deflated—the Pocahontas story
may be by now, the image-value of the original American Girl
overwhelms the demonstrably more useful contributions to white
exploration and settlement by that other Indian heroine, Sacajawea, the Bird Woman. Sacajawea also intervened at a crucial
moment between her warrior brother and the American explorers,
Lewis and Clark, and she helped further the opening up of the

continent westward in the name of Thomas Jefferson. But does she serve as well as Pocahontas for the carved toy that sits upon the idiot's knee? Would Hart Crane for one have found in the wife-mother-sister image of Sacajawea what he found so wondrously in Pocahontas?

We can still make use of Pocahontas just as we do James Fenimore Cooper's dusky beauty, Cora Munroe. Because Cora threatened to merge three races (white, black, and Indian), thereby preventing the historically "necessary" termination of the Mohicans—Cora had to die for the sake of the success of Cooper's narrative comment upon historical inevitability. It is her blonde, racially pure half-sister Alice who gets to win the west that is made safe for America once "the last of the Mohicans" are out of the way. But dark Cora's fictional annihilation has assured her continued life in the American literary imagination, while sweet Alice now fades from mind and sight. Cora is useful to us; Alice is not. And so we possess the one and not the other.

Out there, waiting as if they would yet be possessed, are still other images of America as the woman who can make or break those who pursue, or try to flee from, her ambiguous power.

# CHAPTER 6

# America
# as Wonder

It is with a start, the heart's lurch of sudden discovery, that the three young men in Faulkner's stories cited in the last chaper first gaze upon the females who are to shape their imaginative life. Although he has known her since childhood, Ikkemotubbe still has the experience of *suddenly* seeing Herman Basket's sister. The young lieutenant, flung by battle down the street of Jefferson, glances quickly across at the jail and just as suddenly glimpses the lodestar that will pull him back through the currents of war. Labove feels the cold touch of fate as he looks up to see Eula Varner enter the schoolhouse door. It is significant that in each of these three instances the initial emotion is one of *wonder*, followed almost at once by feelings of frustration, heartbreak, or outrage.

The suggestions that flow out of Faulkner's scenes reoccur in other writings, other times, to amplify the implications of the shock upon men's minds of the discovery of America.

You set out to look for something else and stumble onto America. By failure have you arrived at success? Is what you find worth the loss of what you had originally sought? Or can you transform what is found into the sought-after thing? In his journal of 1834 Emerson asked just as rhetorically, "Why not a moral Education as well as a discovery of America" (IV, 324). In turn, we might counter, "Cannot discovery be the moral education?"

"Expeditions for the discovery of El Dorado, and also of the Fountain of Youth," Thoreau wrote in an undated journal entry of 1850, "led to real, though perhaps not compensatory discoveries" (VIII, 11). One such discovery was Walden Pond; it had been waiting, Thoreau declared in *Walden*, on "that spring morning when Adam and Eve were driven out of Eden" (p. 179). By Thoreau's words we see America as the good place needed by *history* for success, the New World sanctuary ready to receive exiles from the failed chances of the oldest of the Old Worlds.

The English, the French, and the Spanish sailed westward for many reasons—economic, political, religious. But, tellingly, the great expeditions that followed upon the initial touching in upon the shores of a new continent came in those years when, as Marjorie Hope Nicolson phrases it, the universal circle was being broken. Later, Whitman announced that the Passage to India had one purpose only—to disclose the full global, historical, and spiritual curve to men's imaginations, thereby enabling them to complete the 360° of the world's destiny. However, the first hundred years or so of settlement made it appear as though the curve was little more than a moderately arched bridge between homeland and colony; to the literal-minded the differences between there and here seemed largely those of degree, not of kind. Even after the Revolution, America to Coleridge was merely England in "a state of glorious magnification"—a place "viewed through a solar microscope," as Emerson commented while noting down Coleridge's *Table Talk* in his journal of 1835 (v, 36n). The miserliness of such disparities irked minds like Emerson's, just as it bothered Ellen Olenska of Edith Wharton's *The Age of Innocence*, who says, "It seems stupid to have discovered America only to make it into a copy of another country" (p. 242).

Simply to shape America into a larger England was a waste of human energy; it was no better if America simply offered new ground upon which men could spill out their ancient vices—a place where Pavel and Peter of the Old World (whose fates are portrayed in Willa Cather's *My Ántonia*) come to die in failure, living out in America the mental penalty exacted of guilts incurred in Russia. In line with this notion, Mark Twain sets up the moral of *Roughing It* (a fact that warns us to be on guard against swallowing it whole): "If you are of any account, stay at home and make your way by faithful diligence; but if you are 'no account,' go away from home, and then you will *have* to work, whether you want to or not" (VIII, 339). Perhaps only fools, idlers, and scoundrels keep moving, like Sam Clemens on the run from a war he decided he did not want to fail at any longer. Or perhaps the best settlers are men like the three whom Faulkner tells about in *Requiem for a Nun*, sent out in 1820 by the legislature on a trip down the river to find a proper site for the capitol of the State of Mississippi: "soldier to cope with the reality, engineer to cope with the aspiration, patriot to hold fast to the dream" (p. 105). There is no guarantee that the men of "account" will fare better than those of "no account," but still they go.

Beguiled travelers searching for novelty like those on the first tourist cruise to North American waters in 1536 came to their end cannibalized. In 1610 The Virginia Company assured its stockholders in *A True Declaration of the Estate of the Colonie in Virginia* (in a passage cited in Miller's *Errand into the Wilderness*, p. 112) that America was no different from the rest of the world when it came to weal and woe. "It is but a golden slumber, that dream of any humane felicity, which is not sauced with some contingent miserie. . . . Griefe and pleasure are the crosse sailes of the worlds euer-turning windmill." But come they would, urged on by news, to use a phrase of C. S. Lewis', "from a country we have never yet visited," harkening to "something we have overheard." They came, excited by the promotional writings of the early years of the seventeenth century—accounts of America that were hardly more accurate, although fully as lively, as those given in "The Secret History of Eddypus," where we are informed by Bishop Mark Twain of New Jersey that George III's grandson, Peter the Hermit, also known as the Black Prince, sponsored the settlement of Plymouth Rock by Sir Walter Raleigh, who was finally driven away by the attacks of "the Puritans and other Indians" to that territory he named Pennsylvania after himself.

No stranger to extravagance and paradox, Thoreau was hardly more restrained than the good Bishop of New Jersey when it came to assessing the quality of surprise afforded by America. On April 2, 1852 he noted in his journal, "How novel and original must be each man's view of the universe! for though the world is so old, and so many books have been written, each object appears wholly unexplored. The whole world is an America, a *New World*." Thoreau was of the same mind as John Josselyn, who wrote of America in 1639 (in a piece included in R. M. Dorson's *America Begins*) that "there are many stranger things in the world than are to be seen between London and Stanes." What Thoreau most wished was that one day all men would discover that "American wonder" extends throughout the entire universe.

It has been suggested that American writers stubbornly insist on rediscovering for themselves what has already been discovered by others. They take it as their task, endlessly, to start all over again, repeating and repeating their discoveries. But if one runs through the single tale of America over and over, will its *wonder*—the point of it all—not wear out? The first time we hear the rhyme told by the Ancient Mariner, we stand transfixed by wonder, but what might *he* feel by now about the value of that tale he stands condemned to repeat for eternity? Are we also inflicted by a failure of the imagination as we plod past the all too familiar landmarks of the American Dream one more time? Or are these oft-told tales rather discovered anew to us each time, as well as that wondrous land which elicits them? The ideas that form America—that discover it—may be the same from generation to generation, but each return to the primal home seems ever new since experienced by each man for the first time. As Newland Archer of *The Age of Innocence* says of Ellen Olenska (the true American woman, discovered by him only on her return from Europe), *"Each time you happen to me, all over again"* (p. 289).

Man finds his home near whatever gives him a sense of the presence of God, argues T. S. Eliot in "Little Gidding":

> We shall not cease from exploration
> And the end of all our exploring
> Will be to arrive where we started
> And to know the place for the first time
> Through the unknown, remembered gate
> When the last of earth felt to discover
> Is that which was the beginning. . . .

This theme, used so brilliantly by Eliot in 1943, had earlier renditions which apply it directly to the matter of America—one by Alexis de Tocqueville in 1833, and others by Emerson throughout his lifetime.

Tocqueville chose the form of the extended prose essay to report that only in America has mankind seen itself clearly. Having been drawn together in its entirety for the first time in America, mankind is at last able to offer itself as "a fertile theme for poetry" (p. 486). However, Tocqueville decided, this chance at full manifestation of the poetry of the self is marred. The revelation of self to the self is only partial, even in America. Although "the nature of man is sufficiently revealed for him to know something of himself," enough still remains "sufficiently veiled to leave much in impenetrable darkness, a darkness in which he ever gropes, forever in vain, trying to understand himself" (p. 487). It is not that men find themselves out in America; they find themselves *in* America—this partial discovery made possible by the place that forever veils its own true nature. When Emerson told the men of Williams College in 1854 that the American geography was sublime, while Americans were not, he was reaffirming what sublimity and America are: the traditional attributes of "God"—the wonder, mystery, and power which men seek but can never fully know, and thus, not knowing, can only misunderstand their own greatness.

Others also came to the conclusion that "to know God" would be fully to know America and the self. To such imaginations the first journeys away from the worn-out mental terrain of Europe enjoyed the success of "justification"—that influx of grace which reveals the force of America's mystery while keeping its own nature hidden. The initial sense of failure in America came when the settlers realized that "justification" was not leading them on to "sanctification"—the fact of authentic acts of good-doing. It is this sense of wonder sought and lost sight of that makes many of the accounts of the early comings into the new continent deeply religious. Tales told of failure are most memorable when the doomed, perhaps damned, travelers are reminded of the triumphs exacted by the God who provided them with the place in which to find Him. And if "God" serves to express whatever it is that charges the mind with wonder, then it is this god and his relation to America and the self which instructs alike the authors of *Wonder-working Providence of Sion's Savior*, *Walden*, and *The Great Gatsby*. This is the god which sets the goals of success and marks the boundaries of the failure. Wonder is here, and it is real. It is not that it does not exist or that it exists only in worlds created out of fantasy. But wonder can remain so deeply buried it is not found, or—found—it is misunderstood or misused. It is not that the god is dead or absent from his world; he is waiting—often within the woman who waits and the land which waits—for the man who stops short in wonder before them both.

Comments made about America's failure to sustain the hopes that aided in her discovery frequently center around the issue of freedom of the inner spirit. Be the wind that bends the grass, not the grass itself, entreats Thoreau in *Walden*, as he tries to join his own being with the force that stirs and soothes the surface of the pond during that decade in America when winds of change were building up to dispossess later generations of any sense of home. In the same years as Thoreau's discovery at Walden of liberating wonder, Tocqueville concluded that "literary genius cannot exist without freedom of the spirit, and there is no freedom of spirit in America" (p. 256).

Richard Poirier agrees in essence with the Frenchman's conclusion. To Poirier, America's finest writers are doomed never to find freedom in the world of systems and society—in the "real world" of America. The only flexibility they can ever have, one gained at great cost to them, derives from the imagination that forces them to discover "a world elsewhere" placed far beyond the America which has betrayed men's hope to be free here and now.

If America never gave, or all too quickly lost, the original power to offer freedom of consciousness to those who came to these shores in hope, this may signal the end of all useful discussion of the possibilities for success. If the human spirit has never had a chance in this country; if material acquisition has been the single conceivable kind of success (one limited to a special few); then defeat in, through, and of the American experience is the only reality. If this is the way it is, the attempt to talk of human victory can be done only by means of the mythic past-tense and in tones of the ironic, the bitter, and the futile. If so, the talk is purely academic as it traces the record of how early in America's history defeat came to lay men low; we are left with lists of the sullen forms failure has taken over the years. If a realistic assessment of the things hoped for are matched one-to-one with all the things not achieved, then the facts of loss and absence become the whole story.

We may, however, note the ways in which both the creating imagination and the analyzing mind continue to extract satisfaction from thoughts of what has been desired, even though denied. Frustration of the heart's hope might possibly have led to actual victories of the pen. Successful works of literature may have resulted from the accounting they take of the failure of men's lives and the defeat of a country's intended meaning; these successes are surely not imaginary. But if it can also be shown that success is not limited to a sheet of paper and the telling of a good story about terrible loss; if the success we can enjoy has its existence in the world we have—then well and good.

In the three stories by Faulkner examined earlier, the sense of sudden discovery of the silent, still, and musing woman is joined with the sense of astonishment that such a person can be. Wonder is the essential element in the emotions that cluster around the woman in whose name a straining attempt for victory is made. With this in mind we can glance at the final page of *The Great Gatsby*. It is that passage we all probably know by heart, but it is still possible to rediscover the force of Fitzgerald's famous lines as they image the Dutch sailor's first recognition of America's "presence"—that "something commensurate to his capacity for wonder"—a presence that forces him "into an aesthetic contemplation he neither understood nor desired."

Fitzgerald's Dutchman and Faulkner's Labove have much in common, as do Ikkemotubbe and the lieutenant fleeing through Jefferson, Mississippi. For all these men—Dutchman, Indian, and the two Southerners—theirs is not a pleasant fate. The wonder that catches them up will be replaced by strain, heartache, and frustration. But if they could, would they deny the chance to undergo that particular fate and, by doing so, give up the experience of "aesthetic contemplation"? From what we can make out about the later lives of the Dutch sailor-as-type, Ikkemotubbe, and the lieutenant (Labove alone sinks forever out of sight), the three men exchange the aesthetic for the practical. Each man forsakes wonder for those concerns the real world thrives on. But, at least once in his life, each man strove to possess something known as "America."

Perhaps there are *two* Americas—the America of initial wonder and subsequent loss, sorrow, and the workings of the unresting imagination; and the America of facts, attainments, and the straightforward responses of common sense. The America of Poe, let us say, and the America of Franklin, each one finding the success appropriate to its place. This duality is not one that simply sets up "a real America" and its opposite, "a world elsewhere." Each America exists here and now; but the one is like a Peircean diamond that has experienced the act of scratching glass, while the other is that diamond that lies in cotton or has had its potential diamondness withheld while it hangs like a spoil around the neck of a kept woman—its rarest qualities yet to be recognized by being "used" for "aesthetic contemplation" and more.

In *Nostalgia* Ralph Harper refers at length to the French philosopher and playwright Gabriel Marcel, who has said much of what Harper wishes to recount about "presence":

> Marcel's "passionate longing for the unknown," for "a universality not of the conceptual order," his opposition to philosophers who "ignore the personal, ignore the tragic, ignore the transcendent," and who "end by ignoring presence," set him apart from the man who has a corner of life taped off by categories and routines that he no longer questions. This is the most durable habit of the bourgeois mind . . . and its only passion, the disposition to conserve its ego by denying what it cannot understand or feel. Marcel . . . makes much of this disposition to *refuse*, and he opposes this refusal by *invoking* reality. (p. 36)

If Marcel in part defines the possession of presence as having one's self wholly at one's disposal—as not being prey to life's circumstances—then we see him as kin to Emerson. The American affirmed that "reality" is an inner mental and spiritual conviction, while "unreality" stalks anyone (whether of "bourgeois mind" or of "genius") who takes the world of objective phenomena too seriously. "Genius is very well," Emerson wrote in his journal of November 10, 1841, "but it is enveloped & undermined by Wonder. The last fact is still Astonishment, mute, bottomless, boundless, endless Wonder."

By pressing the leads of Marcel and Emerson to the extreme (putting aside for the moment Emerson's comment that even if the "last fact" is wonder, other important facts still precede it), it can be argued that there is only one true America, not a dualism of subject/object set in endless civil strife. The America of wonder exists within the acutely perceiving mind; it also exists within the world of facts, not elsewhere or nowhere.

This is Harper commenting on Marcel: "The mysterious is not, for him, the unknowable. It is within the realm of the intuitively known—or what Pascal calls the 'esprit de finesse' or order of charity. Mystery is essentially shareable. . . . For Marcel mystery is that which is inexhaustible yet somehow comprehensible. Presence and mystery are the same thing" (p. 42). It was the Dutch sailor's inability to move from wonder toward an understanding of what he wondered about that drove him and his kind to become the "bourgeois mind" devoted, as Marcel believes, to "its only passion, the disposition to conserve its ego by denying what it cannot understand or feel" (p. 42).

Proust is another of the mind-types Harper draws upon to aid in his definition of that homeland all men strive to return to, for Proust insisted that Paradise—the place of fullness—exists and is not merely dreamed about. Proust also stressed that it is by a gift that we have been given a glimpse of Paradise, not by the consequence of our own actions. If his contention has any validity, then America considered as a place that waits to fill men with a gracious sense of completion would be a place to stir both joy and frustration.

These two emotions tremble throughout a journal entry of May 20, 1890 written by Alice James (included in Perry's study of William James). Here is her nostalgia for the homeland she fears she will never again see:

> What a tide of homesickness swept me under for the moment! What a longing to see a shaft of sunshine shimmering, through the pines, breathe in the resinous air, and throw my withered body down upon my mother earth, bury my face in the coarse grass, worshipping all that the ugly, raw emptiness

of the blessed land stands for,—the embodiment of a huge chance for hemmed-in humanity; its flexible conditions stretching and lending themselves to all sizes of man. . . . (pp. 179-180)

Alice's brother Henry had left America to find his home elsewhere. In *The American Scene* (p. 321), on his return visit, he remarks upon the same "ugly, raw emptiness" extolled by Alice; he comments on America's "flexible conditions" as well. In fact, he compliments the country on being made of material that is "elastic" in "the manner of some huge india-rubber cloth fashioned for 'field' use and warranted to bear inordinate stretching." James's account of his recognition of the capacity of "the American material" to adjust lacks the deep sentiment of longing brought to it by Alice's language, but, like her, he sees how America can help "hemmed-in humanity." In James's own words, "everything and every one, all objects and elements, all systems, arrangements, institutions, functions, persons, reputations, give the sense of their pulling hard at the india-rubber. . . ." Although unable to become lyrical over what seems to be a vast continential mackintosh, James points to two other traits he considers admirable: the American material provides both "tension" and "resistance," and it stretches far but "almost always, wonderfully, without breaking it off. . . ."

Having given of his praise, however edgy, James then singles out the area of his deeper concern. By the very fact that "the American material" can be stretched, it never quite manages "to lie thick." It cannot cover up for him "the ugly, raw emptiness" which Alice is able to love and he is not. He is willing to concede that America's "thinness should so generally—in some cases, to all intents and purposes, so richly—suffice." Henry James, as much as Alice, as much as Proust or Marcel, desires the "presence" which is one's true "home." He has not the snob's objections against finding it in the land of his birth. But what is sufficiency for most Americans, even for Alice, is insufficiency for him. What it is precisely that stretches so well is the vaunted chance in America for material and social success, but at the cost of the loss of wonder and of presence—of the kind of imaginative and moral *thickness* that brings the mind the only kind of success James could ever call his "home."

Ralph Harper says that Gabriel Marcel sees the contraries posed by the two worlds of the measurable and the mysterious. His contraries "fit like Chinese boxes," Harper states:

Life is compounded of what one can measure, deal with—what
Marcel calls problems, functions, techniques, what we might
call jobs, position, comfort, security, success, and what one
cannot measure or deal with—what he calls mystery, what we
might call adventure, flirtation, surprise, exploration. The
land of the measurable is that Apollonian world of light,
health, and prophecy that Nietzsche wrote of in *The Birth of
Tragedy*. The land of the immeasurable is the land of "presence." The former is the world of history, as those historians
Tolstoy quarreled with in *War and Peace* thought of history.
The latter is the world of drama, of persons, where the only
measure comes from the dramatic form itself. . . . (p. 38)

Harper concludes this part of his argument by commenting, "It
is not possible to choose either one or the other of the sides of Marcel's antinomies. Both are real and in some way necessary. But
there are people who would attempt to ignore one side altogether,
and it is against this exclusion that Marcel has always fought" (p.
38).

Gaston Bachelard, like Gabriel Marcel, has also fought against
shutting out the world of wonder from its existence beside, or
within, the world of the measurable. Bachelard's resistance to the
austerely objective stance (by means of what Northrop Frye calls
the Frenchman's "subversive wit") is characterized by a remark
from *The Psychoanalysis of Fire*: "Man is a creation of desire, not a
creation of need" (p. 16). (This remark, quite inadvertently, recalls
the terms of Caroline Sturgis' belief in God's creation of the universe for the purpose of His pleasure.) Psychological discoveries of
the kind common to the primitive mind interest Bachelard far
more than do the findings of modern scientific rationalism, since to
him desire is the earliest human motive and precedes need; and
Bachelardian desire is what we have been referring to as the wonder that waits.

Emerson may have stated in his 1838 journal that all inquiry into
the past is "simply & at last the desire to do away with this wild,
savage, preposterous *Then*, & introduce in its place the *Now*; it is to
banish the *Not Me* & supply the *Me* . . ." (VIII, 111). But we know
that Emerson's beloved Now was filled, like Bachelard's, with the
wonder and exaggeration common to that universal primitive intuition (the "wild, savage, preposterous *Then*") he always honored
in whatever form.

Bachelard asks that we be freed from the sin of the utilitarian explanation; he wishes us to arrive at a more profound recognition of purpose. Fire is desired, he reminds us, not for mere warmth, cooking, and protection, but for the pleasures and impressions of well-being it gives. Analogously, he argues that poets and dreamers rank higher than the psychoanalyst. For Bachelard scientific psychology is normative, socializing, and general; it remains fixed upon the unchanging objective properties it attaches to nature. In contrast, his preference is for the poetic psychology that is personal, able to contradict nature through the changing values that adhere to qualities constantly altering within men's imaginations.

Obviously Bachelard's stress is upon the unconscious, the exception, and the contradiction. Through exaggeration, Bachelard writes in *The Poetics of Space*, we gain the first sign of wonder. Saved from falsity by the "fact" of the imagination's inability to invent what is not already true, we can indulge that exaggeration which takes us on farther toward the boundaries of the real—as Thoreau, for one, would have agreed; and Poe, for another, since his own aesthetic insisted that the wondering mind discovers, does not create, previously existing reality.

If we take up the several leads offered by Marcel and Bachelard, together with the particulars of its relation to the discovery of America and the ways in which writers have tried to represent its wondrous qualities through female images, then the question of wonder goes well beyond the level suggested by Tony Tanner's *The Reign of Wonder, Naïveté, and Reality*. We shall turn to Tanner's arguments in a moment, but first we shall test (sometimes ironically, sometimes subversively, but usually with sympathy) a few reports of wondrous encounters in America that provide us with suggestive examples of exaggeration, contradiction, and surprise.

In 1953 at Harvard E. E. Cummings delivered six of what he called non-lectures. He excused his insertion of certain autobiographical remarks by saying that he could not tell what he knew until he told who he was, and that that was something he could determine only by rediscovery of the nature of his parentage and of the places of his growing up. Like the child Henry Adams, who had experienced the polarities of Quincy and Boston, Cummings grew up in Cambridge, Massachusetts, hearing about the differences between it and Somerville. In between those two places lived Charles Eliot Norton and wooded nature. It was there in "Norton's Woods," between the poles, that Cummings reports he discovered wonder:

Here, as a very little child, I first encountered that mystery who is Nature; here my enormous smallness entered Her illimitable being; and here someone actually infinite or impossibly alive—someone who might almost (but not quite) have been myself—wonderingly wandered the mortally immortal complexities of Her beyond imagining imagination. (p. 32)

What Cummings found in the Woods is somewhat atypical of the American response; his poetic vision of nature takes no account of the narrow fellow in the grass, and his emotional responses to wonder are devoid of the sense of zero at the bone realized by Emily Dickinson; for his is wonder without *terribilità*.

George Santayana has said that to turn to the landscape at all is to attempt to evade unhappiness. In "The Genteel Tradition in American Philosophy" of 1911, Santayana stated that whereas serious poetry and profound religion are "the joys of an unhappiness that confesses itself," the genteel imagination is driven for comfort away from experience toward the abstract arts of music and landscape painting. In order to avoid such accusations against ourselves (one that would cut to the quick of what Henry James has called every American's right to be unhappy), we must seek out what else "Norton's Woods" has to offer. We have to know whether its wonder has more to it than the mere pleasure of the picturesque.

A score of years or so before Emily Dickinson discovered *terribilità* in her own backyard, Frances Trollope had had a similar experience. A far less sympathetic America-watcher than Cummings, Mrs. Trollope gained an impression of the Potomac Falls in 1831 which stirred her with the sense of wonder the vacuous American society had been unable to provide. However carefully her eye had been tutored by the norms of the picturesque, it still responded with impulsive, primitive, almost Bachelardian pleasure to conflicting images of beauty and treachery:

Despite this uproar, the slenderest, loveliest shrubs peep forth from among these hideous rocks, like children smiling in the midst of danger. As we stood looking at this tremendous scene, one of our friends made us remark, that the poison alder, and the poison vine, threw their graceful, but perfidious branches, over every rock, and assured us also that innumerable tribes of snakes found their dark dwellings among them. (p. 238)

Cummings, Mrs. Trollope—our third observer is Thoreau, a

good man to ask for responses to the "Norton's Woods" of his experience. Our special need is to know how well Thoreau did with snakes and other creatures of "Potomac Falls." That is, we know he usually found the joy of wonder, but did he note its potential *terribilità* as well?

Like Bachelard, whose own first memories were of forests—what the Frenchman calls the "before-me"—Thoreau in his dying words went back to the primal images of moose and Indian. "We want the Indian's report," he had also jotted down on August 18, 1841. "Wordsworth is too tame for the Chippeway." If too tame, also too controlled in expression, too precise in detail, ever to suggest the inchoate mass of America. Wordsworth's own landscape possessed "a reminiscence of walls and ceilings, a tendency to the arbitrary and conventional"—that which Margaret Fuller remarked upon in rebuke in her essay on the differences between British and American literature. During his trip to the Maine woods in 1857 Thoreau noted, "An Indian tells such a story as if he thought it deserved to have a good deal said about it, only he has not got it to say, and so he makes up for the deficiency by a drawling tone, long-windedness, and a dumb wonder which he hopes will be contagious" (p. 172). Some critics of Wordsworth would say that the style of the Indian's speech describes that poet's own manner all too clearly; others might locate its verbal tics in the worst of Walt Whitman's attempts to portray the exaggerated grandeur of America. All the same, Thoreau realized that to say what America is really like requires a special way of expressing its *mooseness* and its *Indianness* that is neither too tame nor too dumb in its treatment of wonder.

The Lake Poets could not handily deal with the wonders of Chippeway territory; the nightingale had to be replaced by the thrush. "I doubt if they have anything so richly wild in Europe," Thoreau wrote of the thrush in his journal of July 27, 1852. "So long a civilization must have banished it. It will only be heard in America, perchance, while our star is the ascendent. I should be very much surprised if I were to hear in the strain of the nightingale such unexplored wildness and fertility, reaching to sundown, inciting to the imagination."

The first Englishmen who came to America needed words to match the challenge of the new "reaching to sundown, inciting to" emigration as well as "to imagination." Thoreau wrote in praise of the men who had found the right language in his 1855 journal, on January 9th:

What a strong and hearty but reckless, hit-or-miss style had some of the early writers of New England, like Josselyn and William Wood and others elsewhere in those days; as if they spoke with a relish, smacking their lips like a coach-whip, caring more to speak heartily than scientifically true. They are not to be caught napping by the wonders of Nature in a new country, and perhaps are often more ready to appreciate them than she is to exhibit them.

The last sentence suggests a tendency on the part of early settlers to invent what they could not discover; or it might simply mean (as Bachelard suggests) that the mind does not need to use its energy to create what is actually there, even though hidden. If many things in the New World *seem* larger, more plentiful, more rare, is it not *actually* so? And ought not men's actions follow the lead of these verifiable wonders? "If the moon looks larger here than in Europe, probably the sun looks larger also," Thoreau observed in *Walking*. "If the heavens of America appear infinitely higher, and the stars brighter, I trust that these facts are symbolical of the height to which the philosophy and poetry and religion of her inhabitants may one day soar. . . ."

Thoreau was aware of yet another peculiarity of wonder—"the pregnant fact." He noted on October 1, 1856 that sometimes the fact is given and seems merely that: "it does not surprise us." Only later, after an interval, its "pregnancy" gives birth to "the poetic and dramatic capabilities of an anecdote or story." Wolfgang Born, a contemporary critic in the field of American painting, has observed that American art during the nineteenth century was more beholden for its effects to the influence of curiosity than to obedience to tradition—the latter source more characteristic of European artists of the same period. Wandering, rather than going straight down the road, is also the mark of American art. Wandering, curiosity, surprise: these elements, in this sequence, are crucial for America. Certainly strange images constantly drop from the womb of "pregnant facts" as Thoreau wanders in the sacred woods near Walden.

Sometimes I rambled to pine groves, standing like temples, or like fleets at sea, full-rigged, with wavy boughs, and rippling with light, so soft and green and shady that the Druids would have forsaken their oaks to worship in them; or to the cedar wood beyond Flints' Pond, where the trees, covered with hoary

blue berries, spiring higher and higher, are fit to stand before
Valhalla. . . . (*Walden*, p. 201)

Mental shrines of belief and beauty are erected when one *saunters*
forth (according to Thoreau's conceit from his journal of January
10, 1851) upon the *Sainte-Terre*. The edifices Thoreau adds to the
actual scene described above share a likeness with the dream-
visions used by two other American writers—Robert Penn Warren
and William Styron. These visions are attributed by Warren and
Styron to two men drawn from history, turned by them into fictional characters in order to articulate their own troubled sense of
America's capacity to stir wonder in sometimes fearsome ways. The
first is the remembered temple at Nîmes, which "Thomas Jefferson" of *Brother to Dragons* mentally erects as the paradigm for
the wondrous American Republic—sacred and pure—he once
envisioned:

> I stood in the *place*, and saw it. There is no way
> For words to put that authoritative reserve and
>           glorious frugality.
> I stood there, and I saw the law of Rome and the
>           eternal
> Light of just proportion and the heart's harmony,
> And I said: "Here is a shape that shines, and here is
> A rooftop so wrought and innocent of imprecision
> That a man who hoped to be a man, and be free,
> Might enter in. . . ." (pp. 39-40)

The second dream-vision is given to Styron's Nat Turner as he
drifts effortlessly toward the sea down a river beneath a high cliff,
his little boat moving through air that is "almost seasonless—benign
and neutral, windless, devoid of heat or cold" (p. 3):

In the sunlight the building stands white—stark white and
serene against a blue and cloudless sky. It is a square and
formed of marble, like a temple, and is simply designed, possessing no columns or windows but rather, in place of them,
recesses whose purpose I cannot imagine. . . . The building has
no door, at least there is no door that I can see. Likewise, just
as the building possesses neither doors nor windows, it seems
to have no purpose, resembling, as I say, a temple—yet a temple in which no one worships, or a sarcophagus in which no
one lies buried, or a monument to something mysterious, in-
effable, and without name. But as is my custom whenever I

have this dream or vision, I don't dwell upon the meaning of
the strange building standing so lonely and remote upon its
ocean promontory, for it seems by its very purposelessness to
be endowed with a profound mystery which to explore would
yield only a profusion of darker and perhaps more troubling
mysteries, as in a maze. (p. 4)

Nat's white temple is perhaps the same doorless, "purposeless"
temple which Warren's Thomas Jefferson in his first innocence believes will offer access to all men, and succor to their lives once it is
entered. After the brutal, irrational, but deeply comprehensible
murder of a black slave by Jefferson's nephew, Jefferson comes to
see the temple at Nîmes as a mockery of his hopes for America. Lil-
burn Lewis' butchery of the slave George rising out of an imagined
insult to the memory of his mother, who, because she died, proved
she did not love him enough, is matched in poetic counterpoint by
Styron's version of Nat Turner's murder of the white woman who
also did not love him sufficiently and so had to die along with his
dream of entrance into the temple on the bluff.

The "facts" of Thoreau's vision of sacred places in the woods remain unshaken by events because he is able to sustain the force of
his own will to wonder. Jefferson's memory of the temple at Nîmes
and Nat Turner's wistful dream of the unassailable shrine of white
liberty lead quickly to frustration, violence, and despair, then to a
kind of resignation past hope once the dream-facts are drastically
readjusted to the world-facts.

Man-made monuments are easily besmirched. Flaubert found
this on his visit to Egypt, where the barren stone temples of once
great kings were stained white by the excrement of vultures. "It is
as though Nature said to the monuments of Egypt," Flaubert
wrote, " 'You will have none of me? You will not now wish the seed
of the lichen? *Eh bien, merde!'* " (p. 200). Public buildings in America
are particularly vulnerable to the droppings of the Bald Eagle. The
White House is whitened even further when both institutions and
natural forces struggle over the primacy of their sacrosanctity and
men's visions of wonder are bleached of hope. But there are still
those who insist on having both wonder and hope. They keep to
their idea of the place that is good because it contains the "presence" of the unmeasurable which *merde* cannot sully.

The Indian burial mounds that rise above the insane floodtide of
the Mississippi River in Faulkner's story "Old Man" become the
meeting place for fleeing beasts, writhing snakes, and outraged

human beings on the run; they provide the stable point where a child can be born, as well as a burial trough for washed-up carcasses. In a world flooded with war, Hemingway came to believe that places where men live and die are the truly sacred plots of earth. Both "place" and "God" share the same word, *Mahom*. American sculptor Barnett Newman discovered this in his search for the wondrous noumenal acts of human existence, just as he learned that *Adamah* means both "earth" and "Adam." How can we, Newman asked, fail to link the observable facts of "place" and "earth" with the intangible realities of "God" and "Adam"—each entity connected by the Michelangelesque fingertip of the creator that touches the fingertips of the created, sparking life with the urgency of curiosity, surprise, wonder?

# CHAPTER 7

# Luminism and
## *Terribilità*

If the wonder stirred by America's landscape participates in the sacred which even the profane acts of history cannot deny, this same
quality of the sacerdotal and the wondrous combines into what
Michelangelo termed *terribilità*. According to Barbara Novak in
*American Painting of the Nineteenth Century, terribilità* lies well within
the American way of looking at its terrain. Mrs. Trollope's pleased
shivers of fear over the falls of the Potomac are somewhat pret-
tied-up versions of the more extensive anxiety with "its pleasures of
risk, its throttled fear like the sensuous tremorings of a fall in a
dream" which Norman Mailer calls for in *Of a Fire on the Moon* (p.
365). In Mailer's book the search for wonder and *terribilità* lifts the
imagination up from America's flats toward that farther female
"presence"—the moon. If the moon is larger when seen in
America, as Thoreau maintained, it looms larger yet—more fearsome and fascinating, more exaggerated and contradictory, more
strange and more factual—when seen by Americans en route to a
still newer world of exploration.

Wonder causes and expresses *terribilità* and also luminism. In her
book on American painting, Barbara Novak argues for what she
names "An Alternative Tradition" for nineteenth-century art. By
means of luminism artists could respond to America in another
way than the pictorial realism devoted to solid confidence in what
Emerson named as common sense. Luminism as a specific trend in
painting is the mode of seeing found in the work of Fitz Hugh
Lane, John Frederick Kensett, and Martin Johnson Heade, and
—on occasion—Frederic Edwin Church, William Sidney Mount,
and Alfred Bierstadt, with traces detectable as late as Charles
Sheeler. A style that commingled, in Novak's words, "primitivism,
realism, classicism, and an idealism that took full cognizance of the
spiritual," luminism was bred from two impulses native to mid-century America: the mysticism present in Emersonian Transcendentalism and the interest in the accuracy of scientific notation (p. 164).

Atmosphere in a painting is luministic when the hazy distance of
the background and the sharply focused foreground are simulta-

neously read in terms both metaphysical and physical. Luminism is a vision, Novak writes, an idea that originates ". . . from the core of the artist's sensibility"—out of which "ideal core [the] real took shape." "Actuality quietly encysted a nucleus of abstract idea." By using both these means (the inner vision, the external detail), "luminism was the most genuine answer to the demands of the age for a synthesis of the real and the ideal . . ." (p. 117).

Melville and Mailer each seek the qualities characteristic of luminist art. By the mid-1800's the Yankees depicted by Melville had already begun to give themselves to what Mailer believes is the Wasp avidity for projections into space, whether launched in the name of society and facts or in the hidden cause of wonder. Melville's characters used the whaler and the long-boat, not the space-ship, but they drove just as deep into the midst of the armadas of mystery. As Ishmael observes with awe, joy and woe alternate in the consecutive rings of great whales. But the true center of all such circles—"deep down and deep inland"—is pervaded by "mute calm" and the "eternal mildness of joy" (p. 326). Whether Mailer writes about thrusts by the astronauts away from America toward the Sea of Tranquility (where dread assures that moments of peace will be sacred, not bland) or Melville describes the voyage by the *Pequod* toward the Ocean of the Pacific (where calm counterbalances sharkish turbulence), both men tell of outward journeys into centers of luminist wonder that parallel the way the keenly observing eye drives into the midst of America's own "synthesis of the real and the ideal."

That eye which wonders rightly is capable of endowing what it looks upon with "a precious element of dignity." This is what Henry James said in his Preface to *What Maisie Knew* (included in *The Art of the Novel*, pp. 147, 149-150). It is "by her 'freshness' " that Maisie adds "the stuff of poetry and tragedy and art" to "appearances in themselves vulgar and empty enough." The child has "simply to wonder, as I say, about them, and they begin to have meanings, aspects, solidities, connexions—connexions with the 'universal!'—that they could scarce have hoped for." James wishes wonder to be "about something"; he also saw that the act of wondering gave "aboutness"—the needed meaning—to the object under contemplation. Wonder is often about terrible, dangerous things (such as the events which beset Maisie's own young life), but in turn the wonderer is "guarded and preserved" (somewhat like Melville's whalers in the midst of the great armada) by the "active, contributive close-circling wonder." Even while looking reveals the menace, a protective magic ring is drawn around the one who looks—not always, of course; no guarantees about that.

Men are "condemned to meaning," Ralph Harper quotes in *Nostalgia* (p. 9). Their present facticity is not sufficient to end the act of the quest. They must endlessly search for orgins, faintly but piercingly remembered, that would take them beyond facts alone. Yet rather than feel fear in the face of the mysterious area that lies beyond the known—Schlegel's area of "absolute chaos and infinite association and meaning"—Harper believes that those who actively work in league with wonder are not struck into dumb passivity (p. 8). Such minds find joy at the center (Novak's "nucleus of abstract idea") of the endless circles of the whale-stirred vortex (that encysting "actuality").

So hardily won, if even through a glance, meaning ought to be kept clear, whatever its complexity. This is especially true if the contemplated meaning emerges from a public monument in the form of the American Girl and the American General. Henry James, who wants both wonder and wonder "about something," shows his unease over the Saint-Gaudens statuary group in honor of General Sherman placed in a New York City plaza. The general, portrayed both as "the Destroyer" and as "the messenger of peace," is escorted by "a beautiful American girl, attending his business." In the passage from *The American Scene* (p. 174) in which James troubles over the ambiguity of the relationship between the girl and the general, he records "a lapse of satisfaction in the presence of this interweaving—the result doubtless of a sharp suspicion of all attempts, however glittering and golden, to confound destroyers with benefactors." James concludes his musing over the sculptor's handling of the complex relations between the man of war-as-hell and the charming girl whose smile-is-heaven—both heralded as representative of uniquely American triumphs—with the words, "And monuments should always have a clean, clear meaning"— especially when exposed to public views and made vulnerable to the droppings of irreverent birds. This suggests that if luminism hopes to keep company in America with *terribilità* (as it must if the full wonders of "Norton's Woods" are to remain believable), then the artist must make as good use of fear as of calm. He must feel it, recognize its full implications, and join it to "that ideal core" out of which "the real took shape" under the pressure of the wondering eye.

"It is evident that all this ado does not proceed from fear," Thoreau wrote of a red squirrel he found whipping about in a tree one October day in 1857:

There is at the bottom, no doubt, an excess of inquisitiveness and caution, but the greater part is make-believe and a love of the marvellous. He can hardly keep it up till I am gone, however, but takes out his nut and tastes it in the midst of his agitation. "*See there, see there*," says he, "who's that? O dear, what shall I do?" and makes believe run off, but doesn't get along an inch—lets it all pass off by flashes through his tail, while he clings to the bark as if he were holding in a race-horse. He gets down the trunk at last onto a projecting knot, head downward, within a rod of you, and chirrups and chatters louder than ever. Tries to work himself into a fright. (xvi, 65)

Leaving this squirrel to flex its tail, let us look at the central argument of Tony Tanner's *The Reign of Wonder, Naïveté, and Reality*. Tanner outlines the shift from Rousseauistic analysis to those Wordsworthian and Emersonian modes of wonder which largely reject logical thought and analytical observation. Tanner cites William James's definition of the child's actual world—"the buzzing, booming chaos"—as the perception that moves closer to reality than the gentle notions of wholeness ascribed to the nineteenth-century child in response to the natural world. Passively beholding—and beholden to outside stimuli—this child's innocent vision lives in a safe and beautiful place, shielded from the terrifying and destructive world assigned to the adult mind. The dangers of such a state of innocence are obvious: once the naïve and wondering eye encounters terror, that terror and whatever joy manages to survive cannot be fully controlled by the mind of a child unpracticed at the art that organizes experience by means of thought.

Tanner concludes that wonder as it is expressed in American literature tends toward passive assimilation of data that stops short of the mastered, conscious possession of phenomena. One thinks here of the poem by Emily Dickinson, "Before I got my eye put out." If there is risk in attempting to take possession of the world by means of sight (since such total seizure could blind), better the partial possession gained

> . . . with just my soul
> Upon the Window pane—
> Where other Creatures put their eyes—
> Incautious—of the Sun—(i, 259)

Therefore, if Tanner's contention concerning passive innocence is correct (and he certainly mounts up evidence to sustain it as far as he goes), and if the moderation suggested by this particular Dickinson poem is to be emulated, *then* there is little room in their

America of timid, childlike souls for either Thoreau's squirrel or Norman Mailer.

As Thoreau describes the red squirrel's action, it is hardly "naïve" or "innocent." Artful; using its energy with calculation, however expensively; playing with fear in order to gain immediate pleasure: Thoreau's squirrel responds to the wonder it finds within by seeking to elaborate upon it through outward gesticulations of fright. As for Mailer, if it is commonly thought that naïveté is marked by the unawareness of fear, then Norman Mailer is not naïve. He requires dread as part of the process for feeling fully alive. Both Mailer and the red squirrel of Thoreau appear as believers in the value of an imaginative creation of dread; they are quite different from the oft-proclaimed American naif who cannot even recognize the abyss over which he dangles.

Furthermore, Mailer is not like the leaves of that grass observed by Emily Dickinson which "does not appear afraid." Mailer is more like the "Emily-eye" in the poem "What mystery pervades a well?" who is moved to remark of the grass.

> I often wonder he
> Can stand so close and look so bold
> At what is awe to me. (III, 970)

Of course, Mailer is not *the* American, redskin or paleface, just as Thoreau's red squirrel is not the all-purpose American squirrel. (In any more extensive squirrel-survey of American letters, we would have to include the one which terrifies that innocent, Henry Fleming, in the midst of the battle-forest of *The Red Badge of Courage* or those which spin around the agitated head of the Faulknerian naif, Boon Hogganbeck in "The Bear.") But Mailer, together with Thoreau's squirrel, represents possible triumphant reactions to the wonder which embraces luminism's serenity and the dread which gives force to *terribilità*. Such reigns of wonder that desire fright and can create and control it on the spot offset any overly simplified description of the American as naif. They also serve to complicate the definitions of the success toward which such Americans urge themselves with every flash of their tails.

In an article of 1935 for the *New York Herald Tribune*, "American Food and American Houses," Gertrude Stein maintained that the American character is marked by both trustfulness and suspicion. This duality of response sets it off from other national types colored by one or the other. But perhaps there was that time in American life—the time cited by Tanner as the Concord Period—

when some Americans were trusting wonderers in the full Tanner sense. In *Notes of a Son and Brother* Henry James describes the trustfulness in Concord during the years just before the Civil War introduced suspicion as one of the ground-rules for survival. The age was known by

> the range of high spirits in the light heart of communities more aware on the whole of the size and number of their opportunity, of the boundless spaces, the possible undertakings, the uncritical minds and the absent standards about them, than of matters to be closely and preparedly reckoned with. They have been, comparatively speaking, experiments in the void—the great void that spread so smilingly between wide natural borders before complications have begun to grow. (p. 217)

Yet complications have always existed in America alongside "the great void"; they did not just appear after Bull Run. Take the eagle, for a long time America's emblem of power and dignity. In 1671 Arnoldus Montanus' "Description of New Netherland" was published, an account filled with the wonders of the New World observed at first-hand by this Dutchman (a type like the one to whom Scott Fitzgerald gave over the concluding vision of *The Great Gatsby*). It contains this fine portrait (included in Dorson's *America Begins*, pp. 95-96) of the eagles abounding (although not with Grace) in the skies over America:

> All have a strong body, bones without marrow, claws as long as a man's finger, the bill strong and crooked, the brains dry, the eyes small and hollow, the feathers hard, the right foot bigger than the left (both ill-looking), the blood gross, the excrements highly offensive. . . . Yea, when ahungered, they attack each other. . . . They fall like lightning on the game they pursue, as the blood of animals serves them for drink. They are exceedingly lascivious, so they go together more than thirty times a day, not only with their own kind, but even with the female hawks and she-wolves. . . .
>
>     Their sharp-sightedness is most remarkable, for lifted up in the clouds far beyond the eye of man, they perceive the smallest fish in the river and a skulking hare in the stubble. Their breath stinks badly, wherefore the carcasses on which they feed rot rapidly. Though lascivious, they are long-lived; they die mostly of hunger, as the bill becomes by age so crooked that they cannot open anything. Thereupon they finally fly to

the highest regions towards the sun, tumble down into the coldest stream, pluck out their feathers, clammy with sweat, and thus breathe their last.

In the 1881-1882 edition of *Leaves of Grass* Walt Whitman's inclusion of a brief description of two great eagles coming together in mid-air to copulate raised the ire of the Society for the Prevention of Vice. One asks whether the Society's disgust was over the fact of copulation or because the character of eagles was defamed. It is not known whether the eagle of Montanus or of Whitman was of the species *American Bald*. But either writer's image suggests the ambiguous power, together with the ability to cause wonder, characteristic of this emblem of America. Benjamin Franklin stated that he much preferred the turkey to the eagle as the American symbol because "the Turkey is a much more respectable bird." Norman Mailer could hardly be mistaken for Franklin in his general responses to the unrespectable, but in Mailer's apocalyptic novel of dread and delight, *Why Are We In Vietnam?* he sees to it that D. J. and his daddy will concur on at least one matter:

> Terrible creature the eagle. I've heard they even pull the intestine out of a carcass like a sailor pulling rope with his mouth. It got me so upset to recognize that E Pluribus Unum is in the hands of an eagle that I almost wrote an open letter to the Congress of America. . . . But I think it's a secret crime that America, which is the greatest nation ever lived . . . is nonetheless represented, indeed even symbolized by an eagle, the most miserable of the scavengers, worse than crow. (pp. 132-133)

During the 1840's the Jacksonian encouragement of local banks led to a potpourri of currency issued by each. At that time, Asher Durand (later a well-known painter) designed a bill depicting a girl naked to the waist who holds out a tankard to the American eagle. Henry James would probably have been as unhappy over the juxtaposition contained in Durand's engraving as he was over the Girl and the General. If designs for our currency were allowed such free flights of fancy today, we might be tempted to replace the sign of the eagle altogether with E. W. Kemble's illustration of Huckleberry Finn, thereby enhancing America's image before the world. This act would not, however, bring to an end questions concerning the nature of those qualities of wonder most representative of America.

The "innocent eye" of Huck and the "small and hollow eye" of the eagle as described by Montanus; the boy's warm heart and the bird's "brains dry"; the sweet-smelling odor of Huck's unwashed decency and the "excrements highly offensive" of the scavenger eagle: all are facts illustrative of the pluralities of wonder and the varieties of responsiveness to wonder that America contains. Montanus and Mark Twain are both excellent examples of the teller of tall-tales in America: both wish to cause wonder; both work with facts (however fabricated) that possess the raw edge of dread.

The eagle in the air and the boy on the river are vulnerable as literary types to conflicting interpretations, as is the tradition of writing tales that created them. But Gaston Bachelard has said in *The Poetics of Space*, "All values must remain vulnerable, and those that do not are dead" (p. 59). If we insist on giving value to writing about wonder, and to living with wonder, then American writers must continue to edge near the brink of the Potomac Falls deep in the midst of Norton's Woods. They must discover and rediscover the continent, ever surprised by secrets located at the center of the circles of great whales. They must be actively conscious, rather than passively receptive, in their wondering. They must recognize both the vicious eagle and the innocent boy, the general and the girl, even while giving such associations the "clean, clear meaning" that Henry James demanded. And they must be willing to remain vulnerable to defeat in order not to be dead—the final failure.

The need for a testy balance between vulnerability and an unnaïve consciousness—between a wondering that is open to surprise and a flexibility that can withstand the shocks—leads to yet another consideration. Is the average, normative, *usual* man more an American (perhaps a better one) than the person who crowds in upon the particular and the peculiar? In a society generally devoted to utilitarian crop-plants, Hawthorne saw himself as a nosegay, Thoreau was likened by Emerson to the rare eidelweiss, and Adams merrily admitted he was only a begonia. Were such frivolous flowers to be made use of, after all, as Endicott had used the wreath of roses at Merry-Mount, looping them around the necks of young lovers in order to bind them to the stern community of work and duty?

In one of the many reprises of the themes of Royall Tyler's "The Contrast," Senator Albert J. Beveridge in *Americans of To-Day and To-Morrow* of 1908 praised true Americans for being "plodders"— "And thank Heaven that this is so" (pp. 130-131). For Beveridge American plodding is better than being an effete and clever European *boulevardier*. (The Thoreauvian saunterer would probably have been beneath Beveridge's contempt.) Emerson had no such thing in mind, however, when he admonished his American audiences "to wonder at the usual." Beveridge's mind depicts the America of the unwondering, wonderless, ordinary man; Emerson's imagination centers upon the America of the wondrous usual and the wonderfully ordinary. Each type in turn invites the possibility of certain kinds of success while resisting others.

After considering Beveridge and Emerson's notions of the admirable American, we are led in due course to judge Richard Poirier's observation concerning literary success in America. Success is assured by the writer's failure to stress the realities of society (what Poirier calls in *A World Elsewhere* "the rest of life") and by his ability to devote himself to uncommon dreams of liberation by means of inward expansions of the consciousness. We must listen to Poirier; we should also attend to Edwin Cady's insistence in *The Light of Common Day* on the success by which this light rises from its source deep within the imagination of the writer—whether a Howells or a James—in order to radiate the realm of "Poor, foolish Reality" and "clumsy Life again at her stupid work."

We ought also to move with the suggestion made by Barbara Novak that a significant segment of the best American painting of the nineteenth century placed partial claim to the thick and suggestive atmosphere of Rembrandt, at the same time its meticulousness ran counter to those American paintings which drew from the Dutch genre tradition. Sharp foreground, hazy background: that is one way the Luminists had to capture American wonder. Galumphing about in that same foreground all the while are Senator Beveridge's plodders, to whom the aesthetic contemplation of the green breasts of America sounds like something obscene. But the good Senator from Indiana cannot be denied, nor can Thomas Flexner's counter-argument to Barbara Novak's emphasis on luminism, when he insists in *That Wilder Image* that the true American vision in nineteenth-century painting was not that of the prophet's vision or the mystic's revelation, but the clear-sighted reportage of the populist.

Still, wonder insists on itself. How can it be avoided in a continent where so many reactions are possible to all that space;—where the land is too big for the ideas to be small? Thoreau records in the journal of May 5, 1859 that the

> wilderness, in the eyes of our forefathers, was a vast and howling place or *space*, where a man might roam naked of house and most other defense, exposed to wild beasts and wilder men. They who went to war with the Indians and French were said to have been "out," and the wounded and missing who at

length returned after a fight were said to have "got in." . . .

Eleven years earlier, Theodore Parker remarked about America's size in "The Political Destination of America and the Signs of the Times" in words that had even by 1848 become a commonplace. He described America as a big country that requires "ideas as vast as the Mississippi, strong as the Alleghenies, and awful as Niagara" (p. 169). Almost sixty years after this cliché had started to harden into America's bedrock, Henry James had had time to think differently about the same facts in *The American Scene*:

> Extent and reduplication, the multiplication of cognate items and the continuity of motion, are elements that count, there, in general, for fatigue and satiety, prompting the earnest observer . . . to the reflection that the country is too large for any human convenience, that it can scarce in the name of Providence, have been meant to be dealt with. . . . (p. 122)

And there had been that war in the 1860's which irrevocably separated all the space into what Faulkner marks in *Requiem for a Nun* as the division between the South and the Others, between We and Them. He records the *before* of history, when there was once "one last irreconcilable fastness of stronghold from which to enter the United States," and the *after*, when there is "No more into the United States, but into the *rest* of the United States" (pp. 246, 239). Even so, the South is alien to "the stranger, the outsider," who, having by accident stumbled into Yoknapatawpha's wonderland, must "unfumble among the road signs and filling stations to get back onto a highway you know, back into the United States . . ." (p. 261). Having carefully made these distinctions in historical time and between geographical places, Faulkner dismisses their claim to being the way things are: "not that it matters, since you know again now that there is no time: no space: no distance . . ." (p. 261). How could there be when a frail, hair-veiled girl once scratched her name "almost depthless in a sheet of old barely transparent glass . . ."? Historical artificialities of time and place dissolve before the wonder we feel at the silent sound suspended "across the vast instantaneous intervention, from the long, long ago: '*Listen, stranger: this was myself: this was I*'" (pp. 261-262). At such moments there is no "out" and no "in," no too large or too small, no then or now; there is only the submersion in the luminism and the *terribilità* of the experience of that land and that girl by means of which we might yet discover ourselves.

# CHAPTER 8

# America
# as "Eventing"

Before the sense of human presence and its mystery, the continent evaporates, yet also coalesces, regroups into places and times felt, seen, realized—the land itself a presence, a mystery. Faulkner's imaginative relation to space is much like that of the Hopi Indians defined by Benjamin Lee Whorf in his essay "Time, Space, and Language." To the Hopis reality is viewed in terms of events (or "eventing"), both objective and subjective. They know no imaginary space, only the actuality, in contrast with the space-concepts of the "English" mind.

"We see things with our eyes," states Whorf, "in the same space form as the Hopi but our idea of space has also the property of acting as a surrogate of non-spatial relationships like time, intensity, tendency, and as a void to be filled with imagined formless items, one of which may even be called 'space' " (p. 165). If the "English" mind works with abstraction, the Hopi mind deals with the world as we directly experience it. Time is "early" or "later"—nothing else is needed. Space is what is materially there; what is forced upon our experience by things that happen to us.

"Wonder" survives in either Hopi or English time and space patterns, just as "America" survives either as an imagined abstraction or an experienced actuality. "For if we inspect consciousness," Whorf urges non-Hopis, "we find no past, present, but a unity embracing complexity; *everything* is in consciousness, and everything in consciousness *is*, and is together" (p. 161).

In a letter she wrote around 1880, Emily Dickinson recalls meeting an Indian woman. "Her little boy 'once died,' she said, death to her dispelling him." This anecdote makes one ask, is whatever *has* happened—like that child's death—the same as its never having taken place? Or is it *still* true, still going on, as in the incident Henry James tells about in *The American Scene*? Late in the century James knew an old lady for whom all time was now. " 'You know William Hazlett has fallen in love with such a very odd woman.' Her facts were perfectly correct; only death had beautifully passed out of her world . . ." (p. 259). James himself, standing in Concord near the river bridge, "fairly caught on the breeze, the mitigated perfect tense. 'You know there has been a fight between our men and the King's . . .' " (p. 260).

As a fact of time America is both what we experience in the present and what we imagine. Faulkner frequently associates the actual experience of the South with its imaginative sense of Then and Since Then. In *Requiem for a Nun* he marks the sequence of the Old People replaced by the Tall Men, the latter in turn supplanted by the Snopeses. But Faulkner also imagines "the might-have-been" that moves the heart with more force than "was" set next to "is" ever can. The boy in *Intruder in the Dust* is told and retold the events of the fateful charge by Pickett's men (that "event" which decisively ended Then and led to the South's history of failure Since Then). But the boy still has hope—a hope he unravels in one long sentence that presses back and holds down time-as-history so that he can replace it by time-as-wish where victory is yet possible:

> "It's all *now* you see . . . and it's all in the balance, it hasn't happened yet, it hasn't even begun yet, it not only hasn't begun yet but there is still time for it not to begin against that position and those circumstances which made more men than Garnett and Kemper and Armstead and Wilcox look grave yet it's going to begin, we all know that, we have come too far with too much at stake and that moment doesn't need even a fourteen-year-old-boy to think *This time, Maybe this time. . . .*" (pp. 194-195)

*This time. Maybe this time*: such a phrase, echoing with poignancy and power in the mind, might be said to be both a eulogy for all our lost "American" hopes and the impetus that gives them continued life.

Rather than take on events which systems of society or the push of history seem to control, we desire moments when—to use Richard Poirier's phrase—"there is less a tendency to criticize existing environments . . . than an effort to displace them [with] a world elsewhere" (p. 6). Poirier also speaks of "the expansion of national consciousness into the vast spaces of a continent and the absorption of those spaces into ourselves" (p. 3). His rightly famous argument promises to displace those environments which resist one's longing to possess them in total mastery (which means just about all of America) with a finicky pick-and-choose method: first, to reject what would push you away; then, to assimilate only what passively acquiesces to your imaginative act of domination.

This way of dealing with America's riches works in modes analogous to certain sexual fantasies in which the male, mocked by a woman of wide worldly experience, dreams that he takes her as easily as if she were an untried ingenue. Given over to images which fix America's *reality* as the Bitch Goddess Success and its *dream-being* as the Virgin Land, ideas of possession become obsessive, and confused. They also lead toward a falsification of the larger truth about America which we discover when we let our fantasies keep their uncurbed validity *within* the more inclusive reality.

Gaston Bachelard has a point in *Air and Songs*: "*A stable and completed image* clips the wings of imagination." In this sense, to fix America, once and for all as the virgin waiting to be penetrated by means of forceful possession is as wing-clipping as to limit America to the unpossessable bitch that forces one to slink off, humiliated, to spaces "elsewhere."

In *The Wings of the Dove* Henry James's American "heiress of all the ages" has to put up with the way her English acquaintances keep fixing her as a particular type. Milly Theale is recognized by the crowd only as Merton Densher's "little" American girl, the one he is given credit for having "invented." Such schematizations—which read Milly as being very sweet, very wealthy, very simple, and very easy to handle—serve at first to limit the flights of the American dove. But in the end even Kate Croy must acknowledge that the shadow cast by Milly's soaring wings is far greater in power and complexity than the original clipped, stable, completed images allotted to Milly had implied.

In "Does Consciousness Exist?"—one of the posthumously published *Essays in Radical Empiricism*—William James recognizes that our thoughts tend to stop and fix an image even though "pure experience" is larger than limiting thoughts. Pure experience (which for William is the central fact of our reality) exists before, and is greater than, consciousness and self; it is that neutral state which has no personal pronoun. But once one exchanges the immense area of experience for the bounded region of everyday thought, then personal pronouns, personal distinctions—the "sticky" accouterments of what we tend to call real life—take over. But perhaps (and this is a matter neither of the James brothers fully decided upon) what takes place in the untrammeled region of pure consciousness is *even more real* than the self-centering thought-images we most commonly make use of. The Jameses did not believe that solidly fixed facts are the whole of reality; neither did they think that the usual way we shape ideas about people is useless. But for Henry, to be interested in someone causes one to care;

and caring creates the desire to know. For William, faith in a fact helps to reveal that fact's deepest significance, since how we feel must supplement what we think. If we move the Jameses' epistemology over to the problem of America, we see that whereas clipped, stable images are inadequate "inventions," those created images and disclosed facts which rise out of *caring* and *faith* are the best way in to the "discovered" reality of an ever "eventing" entity.

An "eventing" America is here and now, as well as elsewhere. "Each new poetic world is not a pure invention, it is a possibility of nature." This comment (p. xxvii, *Of Poetic Imagination and Reverie*) is by Colette Gaudin, translator and glosser of Bachelard's essays; it suggests that we do not need to be inventors to succeed at getting our hearts' desire. Whatever we dream, we shall find realized once we awake. The American continent, by analogy, already contains as many dreams of itself as it has possibilities of nature. Still and all, there is one fact (among many) that forbids success to an image, in turn denying success to its possessor: an image does not always adapt to the space that lies in wait to receive it. "The images invented by men evolve slowly, laboriously," Bachelard observes in *Water and Dreams* in a passage included in Gaudin's collection:

> and we understand the profound observation of Jacques Bousquet: "An image costs as much labor to humanity as a new characteristic to a plant." Many attempted images cannot live because they are but formal play, because they are not really adapted to the matter they are to adorn (p. 12).

In the American environment "English" abstraction requires interaction with "Hopi" actuality for proper development and adaptation. Imaginative Darwinism assures survival to the fittest, with failure accorded those images not indigenous to the American context. This is a failure that comes to more than images, since failure of the imagination is tantamount to a failure of the people. If the world of America ever comes to a bitter end, that "eventing" will be the result (so says an old Zuni prophecy translated by Alvina Quam in her book on this American Indian tribe) of the self-frustrating acts of its people:

> Maybe when the people have outdone themselves, then, maybe the stars will fall upon the land, or drops of hot water will rain upon the earth. Or the land will turn under. Or our father, the sun, will not rise to start the day. . . . But the people themselves will bring upon themselves what they receive. (p. 3)

Gaston Bachelard contends in *The Psychoanalysis of Fire* that imagination "delineates the furthest confines of our mind" (p. 110). This suggests that the "land boundaries" of the mind are governed by the mind's ability to project, not necessarily by the facts of America's soil-content or geography. But in his work *Lautréamont* (cited in Gaudin's edition) Bachelard also recognizes the importance of the adjustment of mind to the environment—which he sets down in images of metamorphosis: ". . . it is by studying the deformation of images that we shall find the measure of the poetic imagination. We shall see that metaphors are naturally linked to metamorphoses and that in the realm of imagination the metamorphosis of a being is already an adjustment to the imagined environment" (p. 34).

To support his contention Bachelard refers in the same essay on Lautréamont to the poetry of Paul Éluard, in which the object rushes to fill the shape of its environment, even as that environment gloves the object. Environment and being are made "coherent" via the transformation of one function into another, each perfectly matched. Bachelard concludes by contrasting *"Eluardian correspondence*, clearly formal" with *"Baudelarian correspondences*, so strongly material." He declares the usefulness of "classifying poets in two large groups: those who live in a vertical, intimate, internal time" and those who stay with "a frankly metamorphosing time, swift as an arrow flying toward the limits of the horizon . . . ," each poet "translating in his own way the life of the metamorphosis" (p. 35).

Art critic Harold Rosenberg is interested in a particular phenomenon taking place in the contemporary American art world which he terms "the artist-as-porter." This type is one who participates in "Earthworks Art." His task is not to contemplate the world, but to alter its shape by moving its parts from place to place. As a result, no new earth is created and none is destroyed; the land is both displaced and possessed. But what about those all too empty spaces America provides which can hardly be nudged by Caterpillar tractors into new places and new forms?

The American "caricature" (a word preferred because of its rightly one-dimensional connotations by Thomas L. Hartshorne in *The Distorted Image, Changing Conceptions of the American Character Since Turner*) has been "formed" by confrontations with an empty continent. But what does it take to shape three-dimensional character? And is that necessary ingredient readily available in the America of immense space? Or does America either reduce men to flat caricatures or annihilate their identity altogether? What are we given by America: something material to fill the original inner emptiness, or emptiness itself?

Bachelard can speak of "the life of the metamorphosis" possible to the poets of France, but "the artist-as-porter" in America does not seem to make much headway against voids. Since a great deal is at stake in the matter of whether the American imagination can work well with the right kind of images, it might appear that Americans are at a permanent disadvantage. All there is is space, not the rich stuff of Europe to fill and alter the land and our minds. What kind of "metamorphosis of being"—dependent on "adjustment to the imagined environment"—is possible when our environment is essentially emptiness?

Bachelard has one solution to our fear that all we have is space and no filler. He believes in "the purest sort of phenomenology—a phenomenology without phenomena . . . one that, in order to know the productive flow of images, need not wait for the phenomena of the imagination to take form and become stabilized in completed images." For Bachelard "works of art are the *by-products* of this existentialism of the imagining being," while "the real *product* is consciousness of enlargement." These remarks taken from his book *The Poetics of Space* (p. 184) explain themselves even further as Bachelard delves into Baudelaire, one who believed that "man's poetic fate is to be the mirror of immensity; or even more exactly, immensity becomes conscious of itself, through man" (p. 196).

Now, if there is even more immensity in the New World than the French have had to work with, there is also *more fate* here for men to bear. As Faulkner says in *Requiem for a Nun*, there is "one universe, one cosmos: contained in one America":

> . . . one towering frantic edifice poised like a card-house over the abyss of the mortgaged generations; one boom, one peace: one swirling rocket-roar filling the glittering zenith as with golden feathers, until the vast hollow sphere of his air, the vast and terrible burden beneath which he tries to stand erect and lift his battered and indomitable head—the very substance in which he lives and, lacking which, he would vanish in a matter of seconds—is murmurous with his fears and terrors and disclaimers and repudiations and his aspirations and dreams and his baseless hopes, bouncing back at him in radar waves from the constellations;
> And still—the old jail—. . . . (p. 247)

Faulkner's quick shift back from cosmos to jail serves to deflate whatever easy rhetoric might have acted to bloat the preceding passage; it grounds the power let loose by images of soaring. The jail is the architectural form and the metaphorical inner core of Faulkner's America. It is obviously ominous in terms of the invoked sense of imprisonment, yet tenderly commemorative of all human desires that are both limited and released by the jail-shape of nature in ways reminiscent of Paul Éluard's glowing correspondences, as well as of Wallace Stevens's jar placed in Tennessee or Robert Frost's tennis-net hung in the wild world.

In speaking of the handling of space in the paintings of Winslow Homer and Edward Hopper, Barbara Novak reminds us that

> the use of space as an emotional vehicle suggestive of imminent danger or simply to arouse vague fears of the unknown enters sporadically into America's art, as part of a romanticism that is frequently tied to some form of realism. Less bizarre than orthodox Surrealism, less obvious than more overt romanticism, it gains its power through the *fact* of the real, often requiring just a slight shift of focus from thing (tree, person, house) to space, which then becomes the implicit theme of the picture. (pp. 175-176)

This relationship of object (the man) to the containing space (America) gives meaning to both. Barnett Newman is cited by Harold Rosenberg as the artist who

> worked with emptiness as if it were a medium. His works divide it, measure it, shape it, color it; it is the substance out of which his paintings and sculptures are made. To invoke emptiness is, however, by no means the same as being empty. . . . (pp. 16-17)

Barnett Newman's response was affirmative to the questions posed above concerning success for an American imagination of emptiness. Newman's method is the same one Henry James also used to pour meaning out of his mind into the voids he found lying in wait to destroy the artist in America. Such acts of containment are partial, however, and peculiar to a few men. If "the old jail" is not close to hand to shore up the void, we are left with Faulkner's image of "the abyss of the mortgaged generations" and "the vast hollow sphere of [the] air." Space that is more terrible than illuminating appears as the blanks in the American scene, with the power to defeat the mind. Some strategy for control is necessary in order that Americans can go far enough to make friends with the medium of emptiness, stopping short of being coerced into destruction by all that space.

There is fear of space as absent things, and the hope of space as container for concepts of material and movement. There is gothic anxiety over the imagination of voids, and security offered by the common sense that stuffs space with the actualities of trees, soil, rivers, and persons. There is Thoreau, who, without taking pause over problems of literal space, wrote in his journal of February 12, 1851, "I am thankful we have yet so much room in America." And there is Frances Trollope, always ready to tell Americans what they ought to know about the reality of things, who states in *Domestic Manners of the Americans*:

> . . . I think no one will be disappointed who visits the country, expecting to find no more than common sense might teach him to look for, namely, a vast continent, by far the greater part of which is still in the state in which nature left it, and a busy, bustling, industrious population, hacking and hewing their way through it. (p. 303)

Faulkner could get as impatient as Mrs. Trollope over such affairs. An expert in the observation of what happens to the land when the people go "hacking and hewing their way through it," Faulkner also cautioned in *The Hamlet* that one

> cannot escape either past or future with nothing better than geography . . . (Geography: that paucity of imagination, that fatuous faith in distance of man, who can invent no better means than geography for escaping . . .). (p. 242)

But even Mrs. Trollope could respond in Faulknerian ways to paradoxes concerning time and space in America. She remarked in the rough draft for *Domestic Manners*, "Since we had left New Orleans, I used to think when hearing of the 'eternal' forests of A[merica] that people spoke as looking backward to the eternity of time they had endured, now I began to suspect that it was in looking forward to the eternity of space they covered" (p. 35). As Faulkner knew all along and Mrs. Trollope did at moments, common sense maps and geography-book scalings of the miles that separate arbitrary points must contend with those acts of mental expansion that project the self out past America's material format into the infinite cosmos, or that focus inward, as through a magnifying glass, upon minutiae.

Gaston Bachelard finds immensity in the world of the miniature. He maintains in *The Poetics of Space* that by looking through a magnifying glass he discovers "this nucleizing nucleus is a world in itself. The miniature deploys to the dimensions of a universe. Once more, large is contained in small" (p. 157). For Bachelard (as for Thoreau when miniaturizing the cosmos in a thawing railroad bank), this is a powerful strategy for keeping control, while retaining the full impact of wonder. "Too often the world designated by philosophy is merely a non-I," Bachelard complains:

> its vastness an accumulation of negativities. But the philosopher proceeds too quickly to what is positive, and appropriates for himself the World, a World that is unique of its kind. Such formulas as: being-in-the-world and world-being are too majestic for me and I do not succeed in experiencing them. In fact, I feel more at home in miniature worlds, which, for me, are dominated worlds. (p. 161)

Thoreau was a miniaturist like the medieval artist whom Bachelard locates in that earlier "great age of solitary patience," leisure, and peace. Both Thoreau and the artist-monk needed just those elements for the enjoyment of deeply loved space. But Thoreau was also a nineteenth-century expansionist—of a special kind, since he detested political imperialism. Thoreau jibed at the way the sciences were politicizing the stars. As he drifted along the Concord and Merrimack Rivers he asked questions similar to those which Mailer would press later at Cape Kennedy. "I know that there are many stars," Thoreau stated. "I know that they are far enough off, bright enough, steady enough in their orbits,—but what are they all worth? They are more waste land in the West,— star territory—to be made slave States, perchance, if we colonize them" (p. 413). For Thoreau true expansionism involves an "unaccountable transition" from

> a comparatively narrow and partial, what is called commonsense view of things, to an infinitely expanded and liberating one, from seeing things as men describe them, to seeing them as men cannot describe them. . . .

The roving mind impatiently bursts the fetters of astronomical orbits, like cobwebs in a corner of its universe, and launches itself to where distance fails to follow, and law, such as science has discovered, grows weak and weary. The mind knows a distance and a space of which all those sums combined do not make a unit of measure,—the interval between that which *appears*, and which *is*. (p. 413)

Excellent. We know that America eyed by the transparent Transcendental eye-mind leaps from leaves of grass toward cosmic passages to India. Full of wonder, delight, and the facts of idealism, it is a bit short of matter. How might we supplement the Romantic view of America-as-spirit with some flesh? It is understandable that the appetites of phenomenologists like Bachelard and naturalists like Thoreau can, paradoxically, gorge to their satisfaction on miniature mind-worlds. Inebriates of air are often made uneasy by large land masses that do not promise ready domination by the imagination. But if America is to be successfully *had* (so that we can escape *being had* and can avoid *having* the land to the point of destroying it and ourselves), then other methods of possession with some bite—and much tenderness—are needed.

# CHAPTER 9

# The American Claimant

In 1829 Thomas Skidmore denounced out of hand the entire conception of heirs and contracts between generations. He felt no property should be thought of as transferable; no father ought to hand on *in absentia* land or money to his sons. Mark Twain also rebuked the burden imposed upon him by the charge his father had given him on his death-bed, "Cling to the land and wait; let nothing beguile it away from you." As he records it in his *Autobiography*, the Tennessee Claim was for the Clemens family both unattained dream and solid land that contained coal, iron, copper, timber, grapes, and oil; it was both irritant to action and the excuse for inertia. (Why go out and take hold elsewhere when you've all that land in Tennessee?) The promised gift was a curse to be renounced by Samuel Clemens the son and the spur for the half-joking comment of Mark Twain the writer: "I wish I owned a couple of acres of the land now, in which case I would not be writing autobiographies for a living" (p. 19).

As "the Tennessee claimant" who remained unsuccessful in taking possession of the wealth that would free him from the labors of his profession, Mark Twain wrote a great deal in a variety of literary forms, but he never turned his land to the lucrative peddling of pornography. That was a type of writing better left to the corrupt European mind. Now, *The Story of O* is an exercise in literary pornography by the Frenchman Georges Bataille for which Susan Sontag, for one, has strong praise. This novel concludes with the heroine led to a party in chains, direly mutilated, and costumed as an owl. No longer recognizable as a human being, she has gained what she sought for—the *O* of void, nothingness, the obliteration of self's power and liberty. Playing out the possibilities of the metaphor established by so many American authors—among them Mark Twain in certain of his later, darker, more nihilistic tales—we can ask whether *O* is the Omega-ending of the quest for success (the heart's desire) which is best gained by means of failure (the self's voiding). Before answering, we must look deeper into the matter of "possession" as perhaps the one most crucial to winning and losing in America.

It is significant that *The Story of O* is a European novel, and that the favored women of Hemingway's fiction—whose creator takes rough possession of their independence—are almost never Americans. Marjorie, the American girl in "The End of Something," is exactly the kind Nick Adams must give up if he is to protect his own freedom to roam, and the American girls who walk by in "Soldier's Home" are the complicating type Krebs knows it is nice to look at but never to move in to take.

Hemingway insisted upon the maleness of his artistic heritage; his imagination was fathered, he said, by Mark Twain. Gertrude Stein claimed, however, that she had given birth to Hemingway, and that she and Sherwood Anderson (as the "Father," perhaps) were both proud and ashamed of their work. But Ernest the son had to slay the mother who looked, he wrote in *A Moveable Feast*, like a Roman Emperor—"and that was fine if you liked your women to look like Roman emperors" (p. 119). Hemingway's gambit for freedom was to repudiate American mothers and mistresses alike; theirs were the possessive natures, difficult for a man *to convert to* the satisfaction of his own needs.

Hemingway was unable to make the imaginative leap across the gap of sexual differences. "Yet whoever believes that such a leap is not possible across the gap," writes Norman Mailer, in his role as the well-fettered Prisoner of Sex; and whoever believes "that a man cannot write of a woman's soul, or a white man of a black man, does not believe in literature itself" (p. 152). This may be one of the tests in defining success in general: the ability of the imagination to leap gaps. The success of literature in America or one's success as an American seems to depend on the three-fold ability *to know*, *to possess*, and *to convert*—and not to get killed while doing any of these things.

One might think that the ultimate contradiction of Hemingway and Mailer would be Thoreau and Henry James—men who appear to confirm Richard Poirier's reminder in *A World Elsewhere* that in America the word "continent" refers not only to the land-mass but also to the relinquishment of "normal" satisfactions enjoyed through the sexual possession of matter. Listen, though, to James's spilling out from a "vast succulent cornucopia" of metaphors the child's sensual pleasure in the American scene imaged as a New York produce market:

> What did the stacked boxes and baskets of our youth represent
> but the boundless fruitage of that more buccolic age of the
> American world, and what was after all of so strong an assault

as the rankness of such a harvest? Where is that fruitage now, where in particular are the peaches *d'antan*? where the mounds of Isabella grapes and Seckel pears in the sticky sweetness of which our childhood seems to have been steeped? ... We ate everything in those days by the bushel and barrel, as from stores that were infinite; we handled watermelons as freely as cocoanuts, and the amount of stomach-ache involved was negligible in the general Eden-like consciousness. (pp. 70-71)

James's memory, caught here in *A Small Boy and Others*, was later impressed in Europe by the imaginative significance of the women of Boulogne, who stood in marked contrast to "the artless mid-Victorian desert" of the town's English colony:

I speak of course in particular of the tanned and trussed and kerchiefed, the active and productive women, all so short-skirted and free-limbed under stress. . . . To hit that happy means of rightness amid the mixed occupations of a home-mother and a fishwife, to be in especial both so bravely stripped below and so perfectly enveloped above as the deep-wading, far-striding, shrimp-netting, crab-gathering matrons or maidens who played, waist-high, with the tides and racily quickened the market, was to make grace thoroughly practical and discretion thoroughly vivid. (p. 409)

Only in Europe were "homemother" and "fishwife" able to combine sexual attractiveness with "the sense of the suitable, of the charmingly and harmoniously right"—pleasing the senses of the small boy with their abundance, as had nature's fruits in Manhattan. The women of Boulogne appear on James's pages as a variation of the bird-girl who is imaged in Stephen Daedalus' imagination as the fine alternative to the sexual repressions of the Irish national conscience. But to return from Boulogne to America is to restrict the fecundity of the country to descriptions of a boy's rapture over "peaches big and peaches small, peaches white and peaches yellow . . . 'cut-up' and eaten with cream at every meal . . . and when ice-cream was added, or they were added *to* it, they formed the highest revel we knew" (p. 71).

Whether it is downy peaches or fishwives that are exposed to the appetitive eyes and mind, some form of eager imaginative possession takes place. David Bakan in his study of the links between Protestantism, Darwinism, and Freud (*The Duality of Human Existence, Isolation and Communion in Western Man*) comments:

Implicit in Darwinism is the notion that the sins of sex, aggression, and avarice are meaningful and essential to survival; and
survival was, in the Darwinian framework, an ultimate. . . .
Darwin's whole scheme of survival is based precisely on characteristics which had previously been regarded as sins. . . . Somehow, in Darwin's thought, sin turned out to be associated with
the very survival of the species. . . . (p. 31)

As a child Henry James decided that a stomachache was little
enough to suffer in exchange for the lush fruit consumed by "the
general Eden-like consciousness." One asks whether James's boy-
Eden was comparable to the earliest stage of paradisical existence
when fruit was not *thought of* as forbidden and there was no imagination of sinning; when survival was assured by the absence of the
deadly consequences of *taking* since all was freely given; or whether
James's childhood was marked as that later stage of Eden with its
conscious—"fallen"—urgency to take possession of whatever
pleases one's appetite, no matter the result.

Bakan's own thoughts on the subject are colored by his
acceptance—however qualified—of the Weber-Tawney theories of
seizure. "Prerogative and possession are both aspects of *property*,"
he writes (p. 137). Further, aggressiveness is the male trait; passivity, the female role. When a woman is aggressive, she is "more masculine," thus "more sexy" to the male view.

Eula Varner is not sexy; she is sex—to be seized aggressively as
property. If Eula is a Faulknerian image for the American land,
her fate is the paradigm for what the male force—even when sexu-
ally impotent, as in Flem's case—does to the femaleness of the
earth's sexual core.

America's national disease is cancer, Norman Mailer insists.
America is female, he states repeatedly. If this notion serves as a
temporarily useful metaphor (*pace*, Susan Sontag), then Bakan's
interpretation of recent medical and psychological studies is also
suggestive in like ways. According to research carried out during
the 1950s and 1960s, women who suffer from cancer of the breast
often have histories of unsatisfactory sexual relations with husband
or lover. Even if not true facts from a medical standpoint, they help
give validity to those "facts" which writers of American literature
keep proposing: from Melville's *Moby-Dick*, the great phallus which
Ahab assaults as his special fate; to Philip Roth's *The Breast*, in
which the hero accepts as his fate his metamorphosis into that
female source of plentitude; from cancer of the prostate to cancer
of the green breasts; from the Biblical sin of fornication that pre-

vents men from entering the Promised Land to that sin Mailer dwells on obsessively in *Why Are We in Vietnam?*—buggery that leads (in Poirier's words) "not to the centers of creation but to the center of waste" (p. 152).

Sexual force (the woman-image) used perversely results in cancerous waste and death. Does not the Venus-principle of life itself demand death? Kermode tells us in *The Sense of An Ending* that in Spenser's "Garden of Adonis" section Venus assumes a "pandemic form" in order to ensure "the immortality of the kinds." She chooses to leave "her heavenly house" so that lower forms might be invested with matter, life, and decay; she has given to humankind the enjoyment of sexual bliss but affords no guarantee of survival for the individual. Both delighted and distraught by the double edge of her endowment, we keep asking about the necessity for a birth into matter which in turn requires its own death. We ought also to ask about the kind of feeling—love or malice—that lies behind this ambigious gift, offered by what kind of ambiguous force.

Spenser's Venus is the goddess turned woman who sacrificially seeks out incarnation for the general good of mankind. The Darwinian Venus is nature which aggressively destroys the individual. Both forces sustain the *type* in the world of brute matter at the cost of the individual. What is hugely different is the way the earlier force inspired the imagination of Spenser and the ways in which the later force has driven writers of the post-Darwin era to picture it. Portraits of tenderness and self-sacrifice have tended to yield to images of ruthlessness and the self-aggrandizing sacrifice of others.

As for the American Venus: she has been depicted as the beneficent force of nature that kills so that the ever-renewing soil may receive further acts of procreation; as "the killing" made in the name of the Bitch Goddess that controls success on Wall Street; and as the killer of the heart's desires that drags men's hope down into the cancerous void where all things are consummated as the story of *O*.

In *The American Scene* Henry James gazes at "a certain little wasted and dim-eyed head of Aphrodite" in the Boston Museum of Art. He wonders if she will remain interested in the power she has. "She has lost her background, the divine creature," James writes of the goddess, who is as much an exile in Boston as Eula Varner was a stranger to Frenchman's Bend and Jefferson, Mississippi. Aphrodite has:

> lost her company . . . but so far from having lost an iota of her
> power, she has gained unspeakably more, since what she es-

sentially stands for she here stands for alone, rising ineffably to
the occasion. She has in short, by her single presence, as yet,
annexed an empire, and there are strange glimmers of moments when, as I have spoken of her consciousness, the very
knowledge of this seems to lurk in the depth of her beauty.
(p. 253)

Keep the Aphrodite happy by maintaining her interest in empire
and sovereignty; then, even though exiled in Boston, her power
will be benign. James's Venus is a cultural, not a biological, force.
She has the potential to charge the imagination, not the soil or the
flesh; but even that particular power is a possible good only if her
existence is acknowledged.

The Venus of Jefferson, Mississippi, is not unlike Boston's. Since
Eula Varner Snopes has no soul she is susceptible, like James's
Aphrodite, to the boredom which eventually shapes her desire for
death and an acceptance of her doom. Perhaps this is a warning. If
we can keep our resident goddesses from becoming bored, we
could save them from extinction and ourselves from the death of
the sacred force they embody and the havoc they cause. But first we
must say we know who they are.

Henry Adams also realized that Americans generally distrust the
Venus of art and of sex, however much they may worship her
under the asexual guise of Dame Nature. Whenever his country-
men are confronted with the varied meanings of her power,
Adams declared, they decide that the only good Venus is a Venus
ignored. Rejecting her, they risk falling under her wrath.

Scott Fitzgerald's Nick Carraway has a dream-fantasy which he
likens to "a night scene by El Greco" (p. 212). In it "four solemn
men in dress suits are walking along the sidewalk with a stretcher
on which lies a drunken woman in a white evening dress. Her
hand, which dangles over the side, sparkles cold with jewels.
Gravely the men turn in at a house—the wrong house. But no one
knows the woman's name, and no one cares" (pp. 212-213). For
Nick this dream-woman represents the East—the original shore of
America, whose once green breasts now sag, the siren who formerly could lure men over the ocean now a mute drunk; the one-
time goddess Aphrodite now an unknown woman of the streets.

Twenty-four years before *The Great Gatsby* was published, Mark
Twain worked on an unfinished allegory called "The Stupendous
Procession" (included in *Fables of Man*). In that procession the lead
figure is "The Twentieth Century"—a "fair young creature, drunk
and disorderly, borne in the arms of *Satan*. Banner with motto, 'Get

what you can, keep what you get' " (p. 405). This is America as seduced and ruined Clarissa in the arms of Lovelace, with the Bitch Goddess Success, the procuress, lurking in the wings. Even earlier, on the first centenary birthday of the Republic, Ungar, one of Melville's characters in *Clarel*, speaks of his country as the "Arch strumpet of an impious age." At their most stringently moralistic, Melville and Mark Twain alternate early praise with the later curses of their disillusionment. Henry James, in *The American Scene* of 1907 (contemporaneous to Mark Twain's allegorical piece), is much more generous as he elaborates his metaphor for New York, the quintessential American city. The city is imaged by James as a "strident, battered, questionable beauty, truly some 'bold bad' charmer . . ." (p. 108). He rather likes her, since "she is one of those to whom everything is always forgiven"; after all, "there must indeed be something about" this "Poor dear bad bold beauty" (p. 109). But James seems to be one of the few men able, up until Fitzgerald, Faulkner, and Mailer, to feel lasting though troubled affection and concern for the Goddess-Whore of America: affection for all she has to give the "good" possessor in beauty, audacity, satisfaction, and hope; concern over the fact that, in revenge against her "bad" possessors or self-blinded repudiators, she can both "take" them and give them the ultimate "social disease" that would make them become impotent and go mad.

In 1584 Captain Arthur Barlow anticipated both Henry James's boyish glee over the marketplaces of Manhattan and the Warrenesque hope held by "that man named Smith" as he dove into the bushes to "git it deep." Barlow saw Virginia as a place

> so full of grapes, as the very beating and surge of the Sea overflowed them, of which we found such plentie, as well there as in all places else, both on the sand and on the greene soile on the hils . . . that I thinke in all the world the like abundance is not to be found. . . .

Two hundred years later, in 1799, Dr. Benjamin Rush delivered three *Lectures upon Animal Life*. In the third he offered, as scientist and man of medicine, these congratulatory observations on the moral vigor of America and its natural plentitude, the two intertwined in his mind:

> There is an indissoluble union between moral, political, and physical happiness; and if it be true, that elective and representative governments are most favourable to individual, as

well as national prosperity, it follows of course, that they are most favourable to animal life. But this opinion does not rest upon an induction derived from the relation, which truths upon all subjects bear to each other. Many facts prove, animal life to exist in a large quantity and for a longer time, in the enlightened and happy state of Connecticut, in which republican liberty has existed above one hundred and fifty years, than in any other country upon the surface of the globe. (p. 168)

When in *Walking* Thoreau asks what it implied for America's soul that the moon looks larger here than in Europe, he gives an answer in effect when he speaks of his trust that the people of the nation might "grow to greater perfection intellectually as well as physically under these influences." Thomas Jefferson had once hoped just that, and *Notes on the State of Virginia* affirms his faith in a country inhabited by the virtuous beasts of Benjamin Rush, shone upon by the vaster sun and moon of Thoreau, and possessed of and by and for a noble yeomanry.

What, then, caused the slaughter of nature's innocents which John James Audubon recorded in the 1820's and 1830's? Had virtue drained out of the land because its simple farmers had been betrayed by the "canker" and "degeneracy" of the new industrialism Jefferson warned against by which the "mobs of great cities" learned to grab, not to cultivate? Or were the farmers destroying their own prosperity by regression to the uncivilized hunter-state? Was America a people enacting the history of the "future" or of the "past," either one a history of self-defeat?

Cultural and historical relations of cause to effect are seldom as clearly etched as Jefferson and Thoreau would wish them to be. What we do have in abundance is the record of the physical consequences. Through documents that let us glimpse the earlier *mille-fleurs* tapestry effect of America, we can today take note of all the absent things. The relative emptiness of our present sky, pond, and thicket indicates the loss of once plenteous quantities of passenger pigeons, wild turkeys, golden plover, heath and prairie hens, snipe, blue-winged teal, and woodcocks, together with salmon, sturgeon, eels, sea trout, herring, cod, mackerel, flounder, lobster, crab, clams, mussels, and oysters. Alas, for all the lost *things!* But have the bountiful *ideas* of America been stripped back as well, or do they still contain a saving abundance which offer possibilities of good possessing still to come?

Jonathan Edwards, God's historian of cause and effect, wrote in *A Treatise Concerning Religious Affections* that we dare not judge the value of the tree by the sweet-smelling, vividly colored flowers it wears in the spring; only by the true fruit it yields at the harvest may we know it. Edwards would have a ready explanation for the fruit—bitter and sweet—which has already come from the flowering of New England and the birth of the Republic. It indicates that man has failed God in his haste to succeed on his own terms. But Edwards would caution that all the harvest has yet to be gathered; that the true fruit is not fully known; that only by means of the final consequences shall we one day experience the real nature of what we now have and its true cause.

Singling out a precise cause for the state of secular affairs she found in the 1840's Frances Trollope criticized the American mania for making "improvements" on a piece of land by the act of putting up placards and buildings that lay claim to its ownership. By the end of the nineteenth century the hero of William Dean Howells' *The Rise of Silas Lapham* splashes advertisements across coastal rocks near Boston to promote Persis Paints. It is as if Americans cannot believe that the land is theirs until they have carved their names upon its surface; until they have—to pursue one of the recurring metaphors of this section—turned pimp for their sister, their wife, and their mother.

In *Life on the Mississippi* Mark Twain points out that De Soto found America's heart in 1542, but not until 1672 did La Salle find an *idea* for its use; once La Salle did this, the great slumbering river was transformed into something useful. Mark Twain personally experienced a similar situation and met it in an analogous way. Involved in an argument over the question of international copyright, he was told that ideas are not property and thereby are worth no money. Repudiating this view, Mark Twain offers in his *Autobiography* a parable concerning the force of the idea as profit. It is one which we, in turn, may use to suggest the development of America as a remunerative product: a movement from an early stage of sparsely used natural plentitude and no ideas, to later times when the cultivation of ideas concerning that plentitude as a source for cash becomes a major activity:

> I said that if by chance there were a company of twenty white men camping in the middle of Africa, it could easily happen that while all of the twenty realized that there was not an acre of ground in the whole vast landscape in view at the time that possessed even the value of a discarded oyster can, it could also happen that there could be one man in that company equipped with ideas, a far-seeing man who could perceive that

at some distant day a railway would pass through this region
and that this camping ground would infallibly become the site
of a prosperous city, of flourishing industries. It could easily
happen that that man would be bright enough to gather together the black chiefs of the tribes of that region and buy that
whole district for a dozen rifles and a barrel of whiskey, and go
home and lay the deeds away for the eventual vast profit of his
children. It could easily come true that in time that city would
be built and that land made valuable beyond imagination and
the man's children rich beyond their wildest dreams, *and that
this shining result would proceed from that man's idea and from no
other source*. . . . (Italics mine.) (p. 283)

Jefferson appropriated John Locke's phrase "the pursuit of life,
liberty, and property" and transformed it into the famous "pursuit
of happiness." But what men pursue as an *idea* in America becomes
a matter of *property*; in turn, that pursuit promises them *happiness*.
Whether the fact of that pursuit (joining idea with property) will
indeed gain them happiness is the nagging question; but at least it
cautions us not to rest with the notion that property means material
possession alone.

In *A World Elsewhere* Richard Poirier's concern is with "the so-
called hero-poet [who] turns his gaze away from the American
landscape and becomes an imperialist of the inner lives of other
people" (p. 94). At this point in the grand debate about the meaning of America we need to stress the possession that takes place in
the world of America—here, not elsewhere—through the act of
looking and of thinking about the land. Possession through the
creation of ideas about how to use America becomes an extension,
therefore, of Poirier's observation concerning the act of imaginative imperialism.

When one attempts the conversion of natural goods into commercially profitable products, mistakes can be made. Raw material
taken by itself is seldom the true test of its value; it is how it is
thought about that counts. Samuel Eliot Morison provides an excellent example illustrative of the crucial difference between thing
and idea. In his book *The European Discovery of America, the Northern Voyages* (p. 321), he tells that Captain Estévan Gomez was instructed by Charles V not to return to Spain with an empty ship.
Dutifully, Gomez came back in 1525 with the hold filled with Indian slaves. The word *clavos* flew back by messenger to the court,
and excitement grew over the great profit this expedition would
bring its royal sponsor until it was learned that Gomez had only

*esclavos* with him. The Indians were released and Gomez treated with scorn. Cloves would have been the profitable cargo, since Europe had learned to desire them, but of what use were Indian slaves? Once the original semantic errors were corrected—and once both *esclavos* and *clavos* found their market—America was proved a success (of sorts) because made fuller use of, both by way of actual goods and of canny ideas about taking profit from its raw materials.

In "The Method of Nature" of 1841 Emerson wrote about the need for essential distinctions between the Not Me and the Me. It was the viewing mind that made the difference to him between the immediate scene and its potential value:

> The universal does not attract us until housed in an individual. Who heeds the waste abyss of possibility? The ocean is everywhere the same, but it has no character until seen with the shore or the ship. Who could value any number of miles of Atlantic brine bounded by lines of latitude and longitude? Confine it by granite rocks, let it wash a shore where wise men dwell, and it is filled with expression; and the point of greatest interest is where the land and water meet.

In his journal of April 2, 1852 Thoreau stated that he did not always require a human figure in the landscape to make the world real or important. "I do not value any view of the universe into which man and the institutions of man enter very largely and absorb much of the attention. Man is but the place where I stand, and the prospect hence is infinite." But by no means does this imply that Thoreau did not require a mind, a Me, to be on the scene to bring it to usefulness through mental possession; it was just that he did not need a congregation of minds or bodies to sanctify his solitary act of creation.

In marked contrast to these nineteenth-century men of Concord, the Puritans were no romantic lovers of the landscape; but, like Emerson and Thoreau, they viewed the American terrain as the solid stage for the great drama of the relation of mind and soul to the divine principle, by means of which their own human value was to be created. Christian doctrine forbade the Puritans from ever locating the source of their sufficiency within the self or outside in the sensible world. Nevertheless, as Christian *thinkers*, they were deeply concerned with discovering within the self and the world manifestations of that forever separate Being they called God in order that they might adore Him. From the first days of settlement the continental fact of America held importance for the Puritans. America was part of their awareness of being caught up in world and body—both permeated by invisible forces they must try to comprehend through thought before assigning value to their human acts under a divine plan.

The Puritans had faced the raw material of the land and the need to convert it to sanctified use, and also some reasonable worldly profit. But it seemed to come only to what is depicted in the following scene of failure:

> A flat morass, bestrewn with fallen timber; a marsh on which the good growth of the earth seemed to have been wrecked and cast away, that from its decomposing ashes vile and ugly things might rise; where the very trees took the aspect of huge weeds, begotten of the slime from which they sprang, by the hot sun that burnt them up . . . this was the realm of hope through which they moved.
>
> At last they stopped. At Eden too. The waters of the Deluge might have left it but a week before: so choked with slime and matted growth was the hideous swamp which bore that name. (p. 360)

This passage, taken from Charles Dickens' *Martin Chuzzlewit*, describes the first disheartening glimpse gained by the gulled settlers of the real-estate project—spuriously named by its promoters "The Valley of Eden"—that has pulled them halfway across America. The idea which led these innocents to the false Eden was a betrayed ideal; the idea used by the promoters to lead the dreamers resulted in their own success. Both the dreamers and the con men have had to live with the consequences—the America brought about by betrayal on the one hand and by success on the other.

But trustful men and true dreamers still try to get to that special place where ideal and reality match, not just con and cash. We may never know what would have happened to Dickens' characters if they had actually arrived at Eden instead of at "Eden," but Henry James suggests what it is like to possess the ideal-reality of Florida. "You may live there serenely, no doubt," James wrote in *The American Scene*, "as in a void furnished at the most with velvet air; you may in fact live there with an idea, if you are content that your idea shall consist of grapefruit and oranges" (p. 411).

James would today be fascinated by a state's economy that rests on profits gained from peddling velvet air, fruit, and Disneyworld. But then James's mind responded favorably to paradoxes that tell

of payment from unlikely sources. Florida paying its way with lim-
pid air is not really unlike what James had noted in a New England
Shaker community. There "grimness," "active, operative death,"
"the final hush of passions, desires, dangers," and the "savagely
clean" had been converted into "a monstrous comb for raking in
profit"; it was a place where "the oddest appearance of mortifica-
tion [was] made to 'pay' " (p. 49). If the travelers Dickens described
lost out because their idea did not jibe with what they got, others in
America have been able to take what they are given—reality and
idea—and to turn a profitable penny from it.

Such manipulations between fact and notion can prove a
dangerous business. Mark Twain intended "The Fable of the Yellow Terror" (written around 1905) to be a parable about the dire
effects of America's commercialization of ideas sent in export to the
Far East. His tale argues that a people can be destroyed by the very
hunger it invents and then imposes upon others who have never
before felt that hunger. Destruction and self-destruction by the
Something created out of nothing—the idea of a new need—
becomes, in turn, an act of blasphemy that returns one to nothingness, all because "you have done what was never done before, save
by the Creator of all things" (p. 429).

Norman Mailer is also deeply concerned over the return to nothingness he envisions as America's possible future. Trying to determine why this slide toward the ultimate *O* might take place, in *Of a
Fire on the Moon* he characterizes the shift from the old-time im-
moral type of rapscallion user and usurer to the new amoral power
of the American corporation:

> Where the old capitalist had a rock glint, "I'm a crazy old bas-
> tard," he would confide to any reporter, thinking of his ability
> to water the stock of widows and head the drive to distribute
> Christmas packages to the poor, proud of every paradox in
> him, as if in the boil of his contradictions were the soups and
> nutrients of his strength, so his son was a dull-eyed presence, a
> servant of reason—contradictions as odious to him as words of
> filth before a table of the immaculate. (pp. 183-184)

The evils of grab embodied by a scoundrel who is still recognizably someone human provokes less dread in Mailer than the
economics of possession master-minded by a clean-living, clear-
thinking machine. This is not a highly original idea these days,
although Mailer manages to give the notion the vitality of paradox
he shares with his old-time capitalist. Like Jonathan Swift before

him, Mailer has to find ways to make his animosity toward "projectors" and "projects" come alive in his language; he is helped by the fact that he can not only take on the problem of possession in America and the world, but can move the dread fact of projections away from this globe toward far planets in space. Mailer benefits, too, from his audacious condemnation of America's Faustian impulse that sees possession of the entire universe as the only possible success story for the American mind.

Others, though sticking to questions of strictly terrestrial imperialism, have had enough to keep their minds busy. The railroads of America have offered excellent symbols for the ambiguity of thrust, as Leo Marx has explained so well in *The Machine in the Garden*. Gertrude Stein praised the railroads for the making of America when, in *Everybody's Autobiography*, she wrote that the "railroad did not follow the towns made by the road but it made a road followed by the towns and the country, there were no towns and no road therefore no country until the railroad came along . . ." (p. 286). In contrast to Stein's optimistic acceptance of the relation between the creation of America and the laying of the rails, Henry James puts "the last question" to these same trains in *The American Scene*. To James's ears the trains with "great monotonous rumble" seem "forever to say to you: 'See what I'm making of all this—see what I'm making, what I'm making!'" James's reply is this:

> "I see what you are *not* making, oh, what you are ever so vividly not. . . . If I were one of the painted savages you have dispossessed, or even some tough reactionary trying to emulate him, what you are making would doubtless impress me more than what you are leaving unmade. . . . Beauty and charm would be for me in the solitude you have ravaged, and I should owe you my grudge for every disfigurement and every violence, for every wound with which you have caused the face of the land to bleed." (p. 463)

It is characteristic of James that he fears those seizures that result in *less*, in acts that negate, in creations that destroy, in sums that tote up to zero. The economics of possession that ignore the meagerness actually there to be made use of is an economics filled with the dread of running out.

Henry James's brother William said in a letter of October 5, 1899 (cited by Perry), that what he loved best about America was "her youth, her greenness, her plasticity, innocence, good intentions . . ." (p. 249). But Henry pressed on with his chastisement of the railroad-force, the new Snopesism, the nascent NASA thrust. "No," he continues to argue in *The American Scene*,

> since I accept your ravage, what strikes me is the long list of the arrears of your undone; and so constantly, right and left, that your pretended message of civilization is but a colossal recipe for the creation of *arrears*, and of such as can but remain forever out of hand. (p. 463)

Creation of nothing out of something: we can match Mark Twain's notion of "The Yellow Terror" with James's words in *The American Scene*:

> You touch the great lonely land—as one feels it still to be— only to plant upon it some ugliness about which, never dreaming of the grace of apology or contrition, you then proceed to brag with a cynicism all your own. You convert the large and noble sanities that I see around me, you convert them one after the other to crudities, to invalidities, hideous and unashamed. . . . (p. 464)

James has just likened the railroads in their effect upon America to that force that grinds his American lady, Isabel Archer, in the mills of the conventional. The threat of her destruction will not come by the dilettante's hand of Gilbert Osmond, but from the iron-hard grasp of Casper Goodwood. Goodwood as surely as Osmond seizes Isabel's mind against her will, but he does it through the force for success which both James and Mailer place under suspicion—the American tycoon acting as the "servant of reason— contradiction as odious to him as words of filth before a table of the immaculate."

In an earlier passage from *The American Scene* James characterized the New England landscape as commercially valueless. Speculating upon the fate of land that offers the practical mind no expectations of profit, he casts the situation into a monologue spoken by the place imaged as "feminine from head to foot, in expression, tone and touch, mistress throughout of the feminine attitude and effect" (p. 19). This personification of "the poor dear land itself" seems to James "to plead, the pathetic presence, to be liked, to be loved, to be stayed with, lived with, handled with some kindness, shown even some courtesy of admiration. What was that but the feminine attitude?" (p. 20). James is quick to add, "not the actual, current, impeachable, but the old ideal and classic: *the air of meeting you everywhere, standing in wait everywhere*, yet always without con-

scious defiance, *only in mild submission to your doing what you would
with it.*" (Italics mine, p. 20.) Next, James reminds us about the obvious: to say we *may* do what we wish with this wistful ingenue is
absurd because of "the notorious fact that nothing useful, nothing
directly economic, *could* be done at all" (p. 21). New England has
been deserted by the users and takers who have long since shoved
westward, but James lingers behind to listen compassionately to the
voice of the deserted land. She pleads that men ought not to demand money of her, but something else. "Live upon me and thrive
by me," is the promise the land knows she *cannot* offer. Instead, her
best suggestion is "Live *with* me, somehow, and let us make out together what we may do for each other—something that is not
merely estimable in more or less greasy greenbacks" (p. 21).

At one point in *The American Scene* James suggests that there is a
similarity between the power of the machine and the mother-force,
when he likens the railroad to "some monstrous unnatural mother"
who strews "unanswerable questions" like "a family of unfathered
infants on doorsteps or in waiting-rooms" (p. 464). He strives to
keep distinctions clear, however, among the many female metaphors that have been accumulating throughout his book. For James
the image of the young woman is essentially associated with America's natural landscape (just as the slightly blowzy courtesan is for
him the American city). On the other hand, it is "the American social order" that appears "in the guise of a great blank unnatural
mother" (p. 432). James means the plight of the American girl as
shown in *The American Scene* to be taken literally (as with a Daisy
Miller) or to be pressed into symbolic service as representative of
the land's neglect and the faulty economics that end in the possession of *O*. He intends his condemnation of the American mother to
be taken seriously, whether he presents her factually or as a symbol
of the pervading force of ugly social pressures and blind ignorance.

James's conclusions concerning America as woman make an interesting reversal of Thoreau's favorite formula for success. To
Thoreau one wins by being in a *true* position and *in* the nick of
time; to James the American Girl has been forced into "a *false* position," out of the nick—placed where she can only know failure
—through a series of betrayals, of which those of the "monstrous
unnatural mother" are foremost (p. 464).

The machine-mother of James's imagery shares traits with the
promiscuous bitch to which Mailer refers at the conclusion of *The
Armies of the Night*, cited earlier in this section. But in James's world
"nobody cares or notices or suffers" that this American mother

abandons the children born of her misused fecundity. Her act is even worse than if she acted as a procuress to sell her daughters for profit. This is the terrible augury for the future upon which James rests: ". . . in that fact itself, that fact of the vast general unconsciousness and indifference, looms, for any restless analyst who may come along, the accumulation, on your hands, of the unretrieved and the irretrievable" (p. 464).

In 1867, almost forty years before Henry James brought *The American Scene* to its anxious conclusion with his assessment of America's future, he wrote his friend Thomas Sergeant Perry (in a letter included in Edel's edition) of his pleasure over the thought that "we young Americans are (without cant) men of the future" (I, 77). James admitted that, because their country had lacked a clearly defined culture, Americans had previously been at a disadvantage. But now James felt differently: ". . . it seems to me that we are ahead of the European races in that fact that more than either of them we can deal freely with forms of civilization of our own, can pick and choose and assimilate and in short aesthetically &c *claim our property wherever we find it.*" (Italics mine, p. 285.)

Not only were Americans learning through aesthetic means to possess the best of other countries, James continued; he and his compatriots also had "something of our own—something distinctive & homogeneous—& I take it that we shall find it in our moral consciousness, our unprecedented spiritual lightness and vigour. In this sense at least we shall have a national cachet . . ." (p. 285).

Possessions, aesthetic and moral: good. Possessions, tangible and material: bad. Are we to adhere to so simple a set of formulas? How can this be when the land gives us our moral consciousness and aesthetic pleasure, and then tempts us to profane the sacred and ravage the beauty?

Thomas Jefferson linked the country he admired to the quality of its people's morality. So did Mr. Coldfield of Faulkner's *Absalom, Absalom!* but this fact made him hate

> his conscience and the land, the country which had created his conscience and then offered the opportunity to have made all that money to the conscience which it had created, which could do nothing but decline; hated that country so much that he was even glad when he saw it drifting closer and closer to a doomed and fatal war. (p. 260)

We ask whether it is possible to use the land rightly; to shape it with the mind so that it remains maiden and mother, sister and lover; to prevent the nation from being transformed into that old sow which devours her American young. One seemingly obvious solution to the problem is for the land to be possessed first and last by the imagination and held as poetry alone; not to be possessed as idea only so that it may be seized as material plunder or become fixed within a fervid nightmare or daydream. The first, more positive, act is what Walt Whitman did in his poetic marketing of America. But even this mode of poetic possession can pass over into the type of seizure that despoils.

In *A World Elsewhere* Richard Poirier realizes the conflict set up between those poets who seek to possess and those who wish to relinquish. He cites Emerson's distaste for America's subservience to Europe and its devotion to property (p. 70). By Emerson's implication, to be truly "American" one must be free both of being owned by European culture and of owning land in America. To own is somehow connected with being owned by, even though the first act deals with the material (the *here* in America) and the second with the cultural (the *there* in Europe). What would Emerson have made of Gertrude Stein's pleased sense of familiarity with the American landscape during her first airplane flight over the midwest? The farmland she saw from above made the same patterns as the French cubist paintings she owned. Her imagination (tutored by European art) already felt cozily at home with the radical visual shapes of the new art from abroad. During the flight she was able to place the designs traced out by the native soil side by side in her imagination with the paintings on her walls back in Paris. Thus she turned the terms of Emerson's dictum and his warning around. By owning objects of European culture, she thereby possessed imaginatively the American landscape—gaining, not destroying.

It seems as if some Americans can turn the trick of being judicious claimants of the land they do not reduce to naught in the process, but this depends on the kind of mind that seizes upon the "vast succulent cornucopia" of America. It depends upon whether "the amount of stomach-ache involved" in indulging one's desire to gorge negates the joy of the idea, or whether all can be converted by the American claimant into "the general Eden-like consciousness."

# CHAPTER 10

# The Payment of
# Ego-Pacts

For wide-eyed individualists the city has been seen as the place where success is to be found, seized, and enjoyed. To Edith Wharton's returned American in *The Age of Innocence*, New York also appears safe enough, its cross-streets gridded and evenly numbered On the other hand, Henry James's restless analyst in *The American Scene* finds havens of comfort from the dizzying press on the streets only in the big hotels. But both grids and havens are risky when they impose uniformity of spirit upon those who enter the city's boundaries.

Returning in 1918 from the excremental togetherness of the Enormous Room, the French concentration camp of his recent experience, E. E. Cummings comes upon the New York harbor as a vision of hard-edged light and hope:

> The tall, impossibly tall, incomparably tall, city shouldering upward into hard sunlight leaned a little through the octaves of its parallel edges, leaningly strode upward into firm, hard, snowy sunlight; the noises of America nearingly throbbed with smokes and hurrying dots which are men and which are women and which are things new and curious and hard and strange and vibrant and immense, lifting with a great ondulous stride firmly into immortal sunlight. . . . (p. 271)

Some fourteen years earlier, both Henry Adams and Henry James viewed that same "hard" harbor with mixed excitement and apprehension. The more familiar description, given in *The Education of Henry Adams*, is an account of Adams' response of November 5th, 1904. He found the harbor frantic, hysteric, full of things exploded, marked by speed, power, and everything that was "irritable, nervous, querulous and afraid" (p. 499). James's description from *The American Scene* of the same city-fact in late August of the same year is less well-known but equal to Adams in its portrait of the new forces that would demand new kinds of men to control them:

There is the beauty of light and air, the great scale of space, and, seen far away to the west, the open gates of the Hudson, majestic in their degree, even at a distance, and announcing still nobler things. But the real appeal, unmistakably, is in that note of vehemence in the local life of which I have spoken, for it is the appeal of a particular type of dauntless power. (p. 74)

After this description, almost "luminist" in its sense of air and space and splendid joy, James drops into an intensifying series of verbs and nouns in collision. That "note of vehemence" he wishes to mark out as "the real appeal" of New York comes to us as a *danse macabre* that has nothing to do with earlier, older traditions of the celestial dance of the spheres formed in harmonious, holy delight:

The aspect the power wears then is indescribable; it is the power of the most extravagant of cities, rejoicing, as with the voice of the morning, in its might, its fortune, its unsurpassable conditions, and imparting to every object and element, to the motion and expression of every floating, hurrying, panting thing, to the throb of ferries and tugs, to the plash of waves and the play of winds and the glint of lights and the shrill of whistles and the quality and authority of breeze-born cries— all, practically, of a diffused, wasted clamour of *detonations*. . . . The universal *applied* passion struck me as shining unprecedently out of the composition; in the bigness and bravery and insolence, especially, of everything that rushed and shrieked; in the air as of a great intricate frenzied dance, half merry, half desperate, or at least half defiant, performed on the huge watery floor. (pp. 74-75)

The vision projected in *The Enormous Room* was written by the man who would become one of his generation's merriest experimenters with language, but this passage has a strange rigidity; it is as if the city transfixed Cummings and took over his imagination. In contrast, the city seen by James (a writer whose prose style was already being rebuked by its critics for its encrusted refinements) is a force that is countered by a verbal imagination just as active as it is. James seems more aware than Cummings of the meaning New York has for the people caught in the maw of the monster of energy. "One has the sense that the monster grows and grows," James continues: ". . . the future complexity of the web, all under the sky and over the sea, becoming thus that of some colossal set of clockworks, some steel-souled machine-room of brandished arms and hammering fists and opening and closing jaws" (p. 75).

There is more here than conventional unease over a city viewed as a Deist's mechanical pride and joy which has been transformed into one of Dr. Frankenstein's monsters. James's real fear (one source of the strength of his assessment of the city that is lacking in Cummings' passage) rises from his awareness of New York as a human being in the violent process of undergoing a moral crisis. The city is not merely a machine without soul or consciousness. New York "doesn't believe in itself" (p. 110). How, then, can it ever help those living there to believe in their own worth? What will happen to those existing in the midst of a sense of *terribilità* whose terror has no discernible meaning for the place or the population?

Thoreau rejected all cities. His 1851 visit to New York stirred him to ask on July 25th, "What right have parents to beget, to bring up, and attempt to *educate* children in a city?" In this he anticipated James's later remark in *The American Scene* that universities situated in the city suffer the fate of Rappaccini's Garden—virtue surrounded by "the poison-plant of the money-passion" (p. 57). But since James was that marked American type—the city-boy—he would never deny the city entirely. Other American writers of the late nineteenth and early twentieth centuries also found it difficult to turn their faces from the "tall, impossibly tall, incomparably tall, city shouldering upward into hard sunlight. . . ," however much they continued to be disturbed about the kind of success the city appears to offer.

Henry Adams characterized New York in terms of its doubled energy. Energy was something Adams always honored, however ambiguous and alien an environmental context it provides for human action, personal or collective. But Mark Twain sallied forth with hope from the West to New York to seek his fortune, while Chicago excited the imagination of Theodore Dreiser. Dreiser thought it nice when the city lets you inside its gates to get at its money and power; it is not nice only when the city seals off its gleams of gaslight behind high walls that mock aspirants like Sister Carrie for their failure to breach those walls.

Dreiser's walled city contrasts with the metaphors James provided for that open city where the young Benjamin Franklin went to seek his fortune and found it. James describes Philadelphia in *The American Scene* as "The very goodliest" of villages, "the very largest, and flattest, and smoothest, the most rounded and complete," "the vast firm chess-board" (pp. 279, 283). It was obviously the perfect terrain for Franklin, that famous eighteenth-century winner at chess, or for anyone who prefers to move unobstructed over the surface of unwalled flatness toward a city's centers of power. But if Franklin assured his worldly success by making multiple chess-moves along the slick, gridded surface of the relative and the expedient, he also went below the surface to find the kind of private victories promised (according to Emerson and Thoreau) to the genius who dives deep into unity and principle.

Philadelphia has other points in its favor. If New York seems to Norman Mailer to be that pestilent city deserved by a schizoid society, Philadelphia for Henry James is the corrupt city with a perfect society in residence. James stresses this paradox: in this city the Happy Family lives next to the Infernal Machine of rotten politics. Philadelphia is therefore one of the better American places because it reveals a nucleus of perfection in the midst of the expected corruption.

But what most impressed James about Philadelphia is its bounty of history. James argues in *The American Scene* that there can never be too much history in American places. Yet cities can swallow plains and swamps and still achieve no history; they can remain little more than extensions of the American Margin, that great blank which devours any real possibility of success.

Always to Thoreau, and at times to James, it seemed that an America envisioned by means of metaphors of the city contained only the dire fact of nothingness. Long before either James or Thoreau rediscovered America and the potential terror of the void, Chateaubriand stated, "*Il n'y a de vieux en Amérique que les bois.*" Are Chateaubriand's trees, then, the solution to finding the needed context for human success in counter-force to the ambiguous city?

In his poem celebrating the cutting down of great trees, Walt Whitman forced words of hope upon the felled redwood; the tree itself projects his vision of a glorious westward future for America as the consequence of the slaughter of the forests. Frederick Jackson Turner came to the opposite conclusion in his retrospective survey of the irrevocable loss of the wilderness. We who wish to avoid the romanticism of either Whitman's hopes or Turner's unease can still learn from the questions put to us by the trees, which have for so long acted as metaphors for writers in contemplation of the original American scene, its plentitude, and its vulnerability.

Are our chances for success done with once the verticals of trees are replaced by the verticals of the city? Whitman looked into the future and found the felling of trees to be good, but what was the bright future to him is already part of our marred past. We tend to say that his poetic vision was inadequate in its simplicity, powerless to fend off the complexities for which his misreading of America's destiny is partially responsible. But our own future lies beyond. The success or failure of the poem our own minds are now writing about America has still to be tested; we have yet to see whether our imaginations can move around the obstacles to success with more surety than Whitman's. Will our poem contain trees at all, or will it have to make do with "the tall, impossibly tall, incomparably tall, city . . ."? Will there also be room in that poem for images of the waiting land, of the fecund woman, of the eager claimant—all of those elements which, until recently, insisted on their centrality to the American scene? Or will those images, together with the toppled redwoods of Whitman's misguided poem-idea, go the way of failed dreams and botched ideas? If so, what will replace them in our new poem of America so that our minds will not starve in the midst of the "universal *applied* passion"—driven by appetites unsatisfied by what "doesn't believe in itself"?

Henry Adams and John La Farge in Tahiti in 1891 quipped about the cannibals who gained land-rights by eating the former owners. "Give us this day our daily hunger," Gaston Bachelard prays to the god of books, who gives us ideas about things that feed us. "Need" is the word Sartre applies to our existence, and "poverty" is Wallace Stevens' tag. Whether we are poets or the readers of poetry, we have no wish to fast while milk and honey flow in America. We will eat in America, even at the risk of eating it all up or of being eaten.

Thoreau also wondered how we may eat well, caught as we are in locales in between Mount Ktaadn (the primitive wilderness of raw matter) and Concord (the village green). As an ascetic of the flesh, Thoreau gladly feasted on huckleberries and pure spring water, but there was also the wilder woodchuck appetite of his mind to assuage. Neither self could be—ought to be—wholly denied. In worlds elsewhere, diets may consist of Olympian ambrosia; in America red meat must be furnished as well. But how to get it without going too far into acts of eating that end in self-devouring?

Eating and ownership go together, and so does the act of creating "poems" about America. On October 23, 1855 Thoreau commented in his journal that he was against the stoning of trees in order to shake down their nuts. "It is not innocent, it is not just, so to maltreat the tree that feeds us." To hurt the trees that feed is to raise a hand against one's parents. "These gifts should be accepted, not merely with gentleness, but with a certain humble gratitude." The next year, on March 23 of 1856, Thoreau further probed the consequence of men's misuse of the land: "I cannot but feel as if I lived in a tamed land, and, as it were, emasculated country."

Thoreau's images are characteristically masculine. Even in speaking of America he turns aside from the feminine principle. To lose one's innocence is to strike the father, to emasculate the male spirit of the land. Yet the land must have a hand run over it to "smooth" it, even while assuring that it is "varied"; land needs the poetry of meaning, which is more than can be suggested by the masculine "savage" alone. In this Thoreau touched the note common to Henry James's later review of the New England landscape cited above. He decided in the 1853 "Chesuncook" section of *The Maine Woods* that an unfingered wilderness is "simple, almost to barrenness." The "raw material of all our civilization" must be "partially cultivated" so it might "continue to inspire, the strains of poets, such as compose the mass of any literature" (p. 155). Before poets can possess the land, the land must be to some extent possessed by the hand that "alters" the primal masculinity. What may result, if we follow Thoreau's language strictly, is a movement from the barren to the gelded; yet, according to Thoreau, the celibate poet, this seems the paradoxical process necessary to generate the poetry that grants the right kind of ownership.

Thoreau reveals his own sense of the ambiguous goods involved in acts of possession and alteration. In his journal of April 8, 1859 he attests to the fact that white men attempted to Christianize the savages (*salvages*—simple men of the woods) before exterminating them in the name of "a vast rat-catching society." Twenty years before in a conversation with Emerson, Thoreau made bitter comment that the American poet had had the globe snatched out from under his feet, leaving him no place to stand. Thoreau's remark drew the reply by Emerson cited earlier in the Introduction; crucial as it is to the arguments contained within this section and to the entire book, it is forthwith repeated at this point. "I acceded," Emerson noted in his journal of 1838,

> & confessed that this was the tragedy of Art that the Artist was at the expense of the Man; & hence, in the first age, as they tell, the Sons of God printed no epics, carved no stones, painted no picture, built no railroad; for the sculpture, the poetry, the music & architecture, were in the Man. (VII, 144)

Art is the mark of the "fallen man." We are all artists if only because we have been dispossessed from our true country. The act of imaginative possession—as much as any material seizure—merely continues to remind us of the present state of man's imperfect success. It was what Emerson knew as the fact of our being but "ruined gods." There is in America or elsewhere no innocent act of possession possible, by the poet or anyone. But since *this* is the world where we exist, the acts of the artist promise both the greatest success and threaten the greatest failure. The artist is both the one who is innocent and the recorder of acts against innocence that result from the fact of our present condition, itself most accurately expressed by the genitive case: Possessor = *d'Homme* = Doom.

Yet another problem. The artist—however fallen, however much he senses the earth being pulled out from under his feet—strives to fix his place in the world of time and of matter. He attempts to set up a center of force or light around which he can gravitate. Norman Mailer carefully examines what has happened to the age-old assurance of spatial stability. During the Renaissance, Mailer reminds us in *Of a Fire on the Moon* (p. 300), "Western civilization arrived at a materiality of forms where every surface was recognizable in its own right." If a canvas by an Old Master had been painted, say to look like lace, then to snip away an inch-square from the canvas would not leave the viewer bereft of the sense of what that canvas represents. "Cézanne, however, had looked to destroy the surface" (p. 301).

Within the new world of Cézanne's paintings tablecloths could be mountains, apples be transformed into rocks, and skies become seas. Cézanne was the explorer who cast us loose in space because he succeeded in banishing "the orders of magnitude"; he showed "the similarities between surfaces now [to be] more profound than the differences." By a stroke of his brush "Art had embarked on an entrance into the long tunnel where aesthetics met technology." As a result, Mailer concludes, artists and astronauts "would go out to explore the dissolution of all orders of magnitude and so begin a search into the secrets and unwindings of death" (p. 301).

These ponderings by Mailer come at that point in *Of a Fire on the Moon*, where he is trying to decide the possible consequences of further explorations by Americans out past the earth's dissolving surface—on into outer space toward "the dimensionless dimensions of the moon on its far side" (p. 301). For Mailer this topic, vital in itself, merges with a further, even more urgent, query: if surfaces are leveled, if magnitude and differences blur and vanish, and if we arrive by such a process at the gravity-less moon, what will this do to the human ego cut loose from its ancient center?

Perhaps ego will dissolve at the touch of NASA's new technology, just as the apple was transformed by Cézanne's new technique. According to the myth of Eden, the apple led to the discovery of ego in the garden; according to Voltaire's pretty tale about Newton, the apple gave the scientist proof by which the law of gravity could be disclosed; according to Mailer, ego traveling beyond gravity's hold results in the discovery of the moon at the loss of ego. Men are now like Cézanne's apple—without magnitude. Indeed, what Mailer fears is not the unbridled ego which follows upon the accursed exile from the garden, but rather the loss of ego through the colonization of the gravity-less moon sanctified by technology.

Quite early in the history of the American Republic, Alexis de Tocqueville voiced his concern over the possibility that Americans might flatten out into the grey blur of uniformity. The argument in Mailer's book about future-loss jolts forward through images intended to fill us with dread over the end of differences, consequent upon our loss of that primary measure of spatial magnitude—the human ego—through America's inordinate devotion to technology and the world of matter. But Tocqueville turned the problem around. The Americans' first failure came when they ceased giving proper homage to the soil, "which in their eyes is just inanimate earth"; second, by their denial of the customs and religions of their ancestors. Lacking possible centers outside themselves—repudiating the land, social values, and the past—Americans "find their country nowhere . . . and they retreat into a narrow and unenlightened egosim" (p. 236).

Tocqueville defines the rise of egoism in America as part of the process of uniformitarianism; in contrast, Mailer believes that a nation predicated on sameness will in fact abolish the ego. Without this one true center by which each man knows where he is and what he possesses, all America will have left is the void appropriately represented by the NASA Space Center.

Tocqueville implies that if the self would only absorb itself in the land Americans might gain a saving center around which their values could rotate. In *The Poetics of Space* Bachelard also suggests that such an act of placement might provide one with the meanings toward which the ego-world can gravitate. It seems that the ego is strongest when it is distinct from the surface upon which it stands, yet gives honor to that surface—that other-than-self. Whether this necessary distinctiveness is best sustained by active interpenetration of the ego with the land's surface or advanced by passive acquiescence to the land, it may be too late to have a choice between these two responses. If Mailer speaks truly, that surface and that center have already been taken from us. Men's egos can "find their country nowhere" in America; they can only move on into spaces beyond this globe. Furthermore, the new explorers may merely repeat the situation Tocqueville warned against; they may become like those earlier Americans who, cutting loose from all ties to a living land, a vital past, and universal law, remained exiles pulled down by the gravitational drag of their lonely selves, eventually to lose even that sense of ego.

Failure: ego lost first in America; ego regained by the movement toward "worlds elsewhere"; ego lost again once and for all in empty spaces beyond gravity, self, and measure's meaning. Failure: arrival at that place beyond the possibility for success which requires all three of these elements. There is sufficient record that we have had enough trouble in "reaching for America." In its deepest metaphorical sense, "reaching for the moon" may prove to be too much even for the hungriest American appetite.

Josiah Royce wrote William James in 1888 (in a letter included by R. B. Perry), "I teach at Harvard that the world and the heavens, and the stars are *real*, but not so *damned* real . . ." (p. 164). The blasphemous ego projecting itself into space declares that only it is real, not the cosmic structure. The orthodox give reply that this notion is the subjective reality known by the damned—the terrible lie perpetrated by the devil. "Will it not be dreadful," Emerson wrote in a letter of July 3, 1822, "to discover that this experiment made by America, to ascertain if men can govern themselves—does not succeed? that too much knowledge, & too much liberty makes them mad."

In a section originally intended as part of "The Great Dark" (included in *Which Was the Dream?*) Mark Twain introduces a character called "The Mad Passenger"—known as M. P. This man is an exile searching for his lost country, one which he describes as the place where there are no words like "modesty, immodesty, decency, indecency, right, wrong, sin." There, his true home, he would encounter no "Religions," or any "curious system of government," or "odd code of morals" (p. 566). *There* would be the real world set well away from the nightmare "normal" world which possesses too many forms of the idea of *no*.

Freud has said that in the world of our dreams there are no *no's*. Perhaps America is meant to be that place where, enjoying total freedom from restrictions, we would appear mad to those who do not share our dreams. It could be defined as the country where ego (the power to desire all things) is truly at home, divorced from the rest of a world that is governed by the need to adjust to earthly limitations (the denial of our desires). If so, then America is what Emerson was afraid it would become—the devil's lie, the ego's reality, the solipsist's dream of endless *yesses*. But we cannot disregard Mailer's countering fear that the devil, the ego, and the boundless yes are forfeited at the cost of all chance for human success.

Somehow a balance of the ego and of the realities independent of that ego must be maintained. If one could only cultivate the ability to keep one's poise in the midst of the temptation to make self-assertive leaps into what might prove to be "not so *damned* real." Sam Patch jumped for public edification and personal profit over the Passaic Falls and the Niagara in 1827. In 1829 he informed his audience at the Genessee Falls that, although Napoleon and Wellington had been great men, neither could jump the falls as he was about to do. He jumped; his body, losing its accustomed poise as it fell, did not rise from the engulfing waters. George Washington, in contrast, seems to have found the proper method; he stood beside the Potomac Falls, feet solidly on the ground, and flipped a coin across the falls with perfect coordination and self-assurance. Such successful acts are what make good Fathers of the Country.

Americans tend to be swayed between liking bravado leaps like Sam Patch's or careful, winning ways like Washington's; they would like to be able to choose one over the other—the uncurbed yes or the qualifying no; ego or idea. Melville's Ishmael notes, of course, that some men try to steady sea-rocked ship-keels by making use of both Locke and Kant—profiting by the two philosophical systems symbolized by the balanced heads of the right and the sperm whales. But Ishmael's own suggestion—to throw "all these thunderheads overboard, and then you will float light and right"—indicates a desire to do without ego and idea altogether (p. 277).

But as much as they abhor the overly neat symmetry of perfectly balanced systems, both the world of *Moby-Dick* the novel and the action that takes place within the novel repudiates the vacuum left by the voiding of ego or of idea. Ahab's weight of egomania paradoxically springs from his idea about the possible vacancy of meaning behind the white brow of the whale and the universe—a vacuum that would say no to the ego's limitless expectations. His ego rushes in to fill the space left open by the crew's submission of its individuality to his greater force. He absorbs the men of the *Pequod*, and the novel, too, by his will. The *Pequod*, and perhaps the novel, is pulled off balance by that ego which ends by annihilating all but one man in the vortex. The only ego which remains is the one required by the author to tell his tale, to embody *his idea*— sufficient guarantee, in terms of the imperfect whole of art described by Emerson, against the temptation to do away with egos altogether. But the aloneness of Ishmael's ego at the novel's conclusion is also an illustration of Tocqueville's America, where the people survive at the cost of finding "their country nowhere."

In *Of a Fire on the Moon* Mailer looks at the Americans he likes to generalize about so much. Suddenly his mind—Aquarius' mind—

> was brought up short with the radically new idea that perhaps some instinct in American life had been working all these decades to keep the country innocent, keep it raw, keep it crude as a lout . . . for then, virgin ore, steadfastly undeveloped in all the hinterworld of the national psyche, a single idea could still electrify the land. Culture was insulation against a single idea, and America was like a rawboned lover gangling into a middle age, still looking for his mission. (p. 70)

According to Mailer/Aquarius, ideas are not necessarily at odds with the ego's desire to possess all things. If ideas know about the facts of *no*, they can be used to find a way around limitations; they can transform adjustments into extensions, and sanity and experience into astonishing accomplishments. Ego needs ideas, and ideas require mission in order to move forth from untested innocence into the act that is necessarily "not innocent." Only culture, which is complexity, can guard against the single idea characterized by the simplicity of egomania and the mission compelled forward by the fanatic. Culture needs to be able to work over the "virgin ore" of an idea like the one Mailer has just had about ideas in America.

Can anything end this maddening whirl which upsets the poise required to keep ego and culture, yes and no, innocence and knowledge, in some sort of workable balance? Saint Augustine stopped the spinning of the wheel of ego's relativism when he asked two essential questions: Whose is the earth? Who is the Lord? When Earth replied that *it* was not the source of reality, Augustine discovered that he also was not the Lord. Once firmly located in the ranks of the created things, Augustine experienced gravity by becoming that self whose value and joy orginates from its pull toward the center which is its God.

One thousand years before the American settlements, Saint Augustine resolved the debate between the ego which calls itself its own world and the Revealed Idea which defines ego as what longs to return to the True Center. Augustine's solution (however affirmed as part of doctrinal truth by English Protestantism) was insufficient to the time and the place provided by sixteenth-century America. This was not Augustine's age, and the geographical wilderness of North America was different from the heretical darkness of North Africa. Furthermore, the settlers brought with them from Europe two contradictory ideas that lost them their innocence even as these ideas helped to sustain their survival: first, the Puritan idea that the people were meant to act as stewards to God's kingdom, and, second, the English idea that they must cultivate the land in order to make its possessors thrive in earthly terms. Ego found its way over to America after all, and once again the new colonists became exiles in re-enactment of the original sin in the garden.

Or so goes one version of this continually retold tale. It is the version with which William Faulkner's imagination did so much. As an artist (that man who, according to Emerson, re-establishes the fact of the Fall each time he strives to express what once required no further expression than the possession of consummate being), Faulkner made literary success out of his depiction of the dramas which arise when the perhaps accursed ego is set against itself by the force of the idea of its peculiar mission to remove that curse.

There are other ways of viewing the consequences to America of the two ideas brought along in the holds of the *Arbella* and the *Mayflower*: the idea of mission and the idea of profit. For one, it is possible to define the first idea (mission) as a good and the latter (profit) as an evil. In turn, this situation may be read as moving in one of two directions: either the evil drives out the good when profit starts to triumph; or the good outweighs the evil because the American energy for mission has the talent to save more than greed destroys. However, some critics of America reverse these values completely. They assign evil to the fanatical idea of mission, and good to the realistic need to cultivate the land for the benefit of the community. When this particular line of argument is taken, the debaters still have to decide whether the "good" realism of land-use can succeed in driving out the "evil" fantasies of self-righteous saviorism, or whether both—the wracking sense of mission and the intensive use of the land—are perverted by the human ego which lies behind either idea.

One more approach is possible to what have been essentially moral evaluations: the view that notions of sin and moral judgment—depicted by words like *evil, ego, pride, self-assertiveness, desire, possession*—must themselves be put to the question and perhaps to the axe. If the suggestions made by Darwin, Freud, Nietzsche, and Sartre can be trusted and their implications applied to America, then a nation whose gravity is centered in the aggressive ego has all the health needed to assure survival. "The growth of the ego is intrinsic to the growth of the individual," David Bakan argues out of Freud in *The Duality of Human Existence*. "Unless the ego develops within the individual, he remains as he was originally, dependent and inept in the conduct of life. If the growth of the ego is related to sin, then it is certainly 'original' sin, in the sense that the growth of the ego is intrinsic to human development" (p. 55).

Freud taught that the Christian culture that defines ego as the strategy of the devil is now the obstacle which men must overcome in order to succeed. Belief in one's sinfulness is no longer the means by which control is kept over one's humanity; it is an anxiety debilitating to human existence. Bakan quotes the statement Freud made to his associates, "Do you not know that I am the Devil? All my life I have had to play the Devil. . . ." Bakan comments, "To 'play the Devil' means to allow thought to go as it will . . . means to enter into the realm of the Devil, and to understand that realm . . . means to try to behold that which is 'behind' . . ." (p. 91, Surely such a beguiling journey ought to be taken, even at the risk of an anal projection of the Devil-ego, as Mailer would put it; even at the risk—as Emerson said it—"that too much knowledge, & too much liberty makes [men] mad."

Nietzsche argued that man through his ego can be happy by himself; he has no need for others, no need for love or any projections beyond the self. Sartre takes a different angle by suggesting that ego-isolation is what shields one from a weakening dependence upon others and love. To Nietzsche or Sartre ego could be the sin that saves. The ego seizes what it can and must, not in the orthodox sense of sinning, but in fulfillment of the true faith that only through total, creative possession of the material world is the life-principle able to renew itself.

Thus viewed, America as ego is one long victorious act perpetrated by the rapine life-force upon the fecund land. Neither Nietzsche nor Sartre were American in their views of the self, and they are hardly the best direct source for the sense the god-self has concerning its divine right to ravish the Ledas of the land, to seize the Europas of the new continent, and to commandeer Mirandas like any Caliban. We are closer to home with Walt Whitman, the

poet who did what he could to banish ideas of sin and guilt and to
herald the uncurbed sexual interaction of mind and body upon the
continent. But John Woolman, the Quaker, and Henry Thoreau,
the Transcendentalist, are also true Americans. If Whitman
worked out of ego alone, Woolman and Thoreau were men of ego
combined with idea. Extravagant in their ideas and self-sufficient in
their actions, their aims did not lead them to "play the Devil." They
fought to subsume the proud forces of self-sufficiency to laws
higher than the ego and to apply extravagance to the end of conserving the land.

We seem to be left once again with unreconcilable views about
which idea ought to take precedence in shaping our own use of
America. It would be odd, but not improbable, if a possible solution
came to us by way of D. H. Lawrence. Not the Lawrence of *Studies
in Classic American Literature*, but of the poem "The Evening Land":

> Oh, America,
> The sun sets in you.
> Are you the grave of our day?

With these lines Lawrence commences his examination of what it
is about America that both repels him and draws him to it—either
emotion a fact to frighten his soul. "I confess I am afraid of you."
The cause of that fear is quickly defined:

> The catastrophe of your exaggerate love,
> You who never find yourself in love
> But only lose yourself further, decomposing.
> . . . . . . . . . . . . . . . . . . . . . . . . .
> You who in loving break down
> And break further and further down
> Your bounds of isolation
> But who never rise resurrected, from this grave of mingling,
> In a new proud singleness, America.

His fear is of America's habit of mingling that might contaminate
his own individualism; fear also of "Your more-than-European
idealism" and "your single resurrection/Into machine-uprisen perfect man." Here we have an interesting readjustment of the terms
we have been dealing with. For Lawrence exaggeration of self is
loss of being. Ego is diffusion and the end of personal singleness;
self is absorption, is decay, and the fall into the abstracting idea.
But it is one thing to fear what one has no desire for; it is another to
be afraid of finding in America what is literally entrancing:

> Yet, America,
> Your elvishness,
> Your New England uncanniness,
> Your western brutal faery quality.

> My soul is half-cajoled, half-cajoled.

The poet is able to fend off the "two spectres" of "Your horrible, skeleton, aureoled ideal/Your weird bright motor-productive mechanism," but not what is "Glimpsed now and then"—the flash of wonder, of mystery, of "presence." For he cannot tell whether they are glimpses of things *really* there or only illusions:

> What am I in love with?
> My own imaginings?
> Say it is not so.

Lawrence pleads with America to be able to tell him truly that he can yet discover

> . . . in the sound of all your machines
> And white words, white-wash America,
> Deep pulsing of a strange heart
> New throb, like a stirring under the false
>     dawn that precedes the real.

As much as Thoreau ever did, Lawrence desires to witness a true dawn in America. Unlike Thoreau, he cannot be certain he will not be tricked by a delusive light. Still he pleads on:

> Dark, elvish,
> Modern, unissued, uncanny America,
> Your nascent demon people lurking
>     among the deeps of your industrial thicket
> Allure me till I am beside myself.

Lawrence wants an idea that is an instinct that can entice, not logically coerce, him toward the real; he desires the idea with the power to draw him out of the self-absorbing ego that is devoted to killing seizures and depletions. He wants an America that is the state of being "beside myself." His deity is not the orthodox Lord of Saint Augustine or of the Puritans; nor is it the devil of the solipsist's dream. It is the demon-presence which has long been in hiding in the American landscape, waiting to lead men toward the ultimate failure or the ultimate success, depending on how well it is confronted, accepted, and used.

This section has been an introduction to some of the fertile image-ideas that have emerged from the minds of several explorers of America. These thinkers have been intent on knowing what kind of a *place* it is they possess or are possessed by, and what manner of relationship there is among the ego, the idea, and the land. At this stage it is not so much a question of whose ideas are correct; it is more important to follow up on those images which have the greatest intrinsic power to instruct our imaginations. Now that the context—*ideas of the land*—has been offered, we can move on to ideas concerning the human types best suited for defeat or for survival, or for more than survival, in America.

PART III

# Winning
# and
# Losing

# CHAPTER 11

# "Presence" and "Pittsburgh"

If it is difficult enough to succeed; it is even more difficult to know what success is and what it means, truly, to fail. Yet however much the writers to whom we are listening realized that the worlds of words they create are unlike the object-hard universe they live in, they continued to attempt to define "winning" and "losing" as active terms in the immediate reality.

In 1624 Christopher Levett stated the essentials of that view which places the blame of failure squarely upon the men, not the country:

> They say the country is good for nothing but to starve so many people as come in it.
>
> It is granted that some have been starved to death and others have hardly escaped, but where was the fault, in the country or in themselves? That the country is as I have said, I can bring one hundred men to justify it; but if men be neither industrious nor provident, they may starve in the best place in the world.

But what would Levett have made of Sir Humfry Gilbert, who made two trans-Atlantic voyages in 1578 and 1583 in order to establish colonies for Elizabeth? Samuel Eliot Morison in *The European Discovery of America* insists that Gilbert (whose family motto was *Why not?*) was one of the few early English explorers with a sound *idea* about what he was doing. In Morison's words, Gilbert "regarded a colony, not as a place to exploit the natives and get rich, but as a social experiment to cure unemployment at home and realize the Utopian dream outlined" in Thomas More's book. "Long did he entertain these ideas, never did he give them up. . . . But the Queen sized him up correctly as a man of 'no good happe at sea' " (p. 578). Gilbert was lost off the coast of America during the second voyage—a failure, it would seem, even if he appears personally to have possessed what we may call "presence."

There have been many Americans who acknowledge personal responsibility for the required "good happe," even as they point to those devastating outer circumstances termed "Pittsburgh" (for reasons that will be explained later on in this chapter). "Pittsburgh" are the facts which simultaneously keep admirable persons from achieving what they want and get them blamed for having failed. Tocqueville was chillingly accurate in his observation that Americans who dwell in what is intended to be the perfect democracy are asked *to be intelligent every day*. Now it seems that a large part of that intelligence has to be given over to asking, "Why failure and not success?" Or, "Why are certain kinds of winning called losing?" And, "What is the use of having 'presence' if 'Pittsburgh' gets you every time?"

Some argue that to be great one must fail in the eyes of the world. By this roundabout means success is assured through the private value one appropriates to oneself. In his sermon "Christian Calling" of 1641, John Cotton asserts the belief embraced by those elected to be greater in kind than the unregenerate will ever know: "We have done most there, where we are least accepted; that is the happiness of a Christian. . . ." Emerson, whom Cotton would doubtlessly have judged a heretic, observed of Osman, the special self he studies in his journal of 1841, that Osman "was never interrupted by success," a not un-Cottonian sentiment. Emily Dickinson, yet another heretical soul from New England, implies the similar thrill of victory she feels in being set apart from those who command the world:

> I'm Nobody! Who are you?
> Are you—Nobody—too?
> Then there's a pair of us!
> Don't tell! they'd banish us—you know! (1, 206)

Like Norman Mailer, who considers it no fun to succeed conventionally and less boring to fail, Emily Dickinson concludes:

> How dreary—to be—Somebody!
> How public—like a Frog
> To tell your name—the livelong June—
> To an admiring Bog! (1, 206-207)

But more often she focuses upon the person who by failing more fully measures what he does not have:

> Success is counted sweetest
> By those who ne'er succeed.
> To comprehend a nectar
> Requires sorest need. (1, 53)

Or she refers to those who cull a morsel of value by dealing with
the fact of public failure through silent courage:

> To fight aloud, is very brave—
> But *gallanter*, I know
> Who charge within the bosom
> The Cavalry of Wo— (1, 90)

In these poems (whose simplicity of method verges on the
simplistic of thought) Emily Dickinson sets up certain questions
basic to the task of defining success, and gives some of her answers.
Is the norm of success declared by them or by you? By you, she
decides. But much tougher issues remain. Nothing is solved by letting the self go on a romp of deciding for itself when it has had a
splendid, if self-defined, triumph. If success is an absolute, as
Emerson implied, all depends upon determining the laws of victory: laws equally out of reach of the world's tampering and free
from the mind's self-interested creation of wishes and fulfillments.

Absolutes involve measurements of right amounts and accuracy
of placement. If the laws of success do not act to distinguish between *enough* and *not enough*, or to mark what is *in place* from what
is *out of place*, success can have no perfect sense of itself. Odd as it
seems to say that there is more than one kind of absolute, we need
to acknowledge that we are dealing here with a type of absolute
more special than the convention of the one and the uniform. This
absolute follows laws of a kind that are complex rather than simple
and that vary in nuances according to the different contexts out of
which it is defined.

In *Miami and the Siege of Chicago* Norman Mailer views the Wasp
supporters of Eugene McCarthy at the Democratic Convention of
1968 as both forward-strivers and antediluvians. McCarthy himself
obviously upsets Mailer, for how possibly could such a man ever
win with such losers as his disciples? With: "academics with horn-
rimmed glasses in seersucker suits or pale generally lean politicians
with hard bitten integrity on their lips, and the women for the most
part too wholesome, some looked as if they had not worn lipstick in
years." Indeed, "the cynical wonder intruded itself how they would
celebrate a victory. Defeat was built into the integrity of their characters. Vinegar was the aphrodisiac of their diet" (p. 182).

In *Moby-Dick*, called by some Melville's "democratic epic,"
Ishmael broods upon the inability of "intellectual superiority" to
"assume the practical, available supremacy over other men":

This it is, that for ever keeps God's true princes of the Empire

from the world's hustings; and leaves the highest honors that
this air can give, to those men who become famous more
through their infinite inferiority to the choice hidden handful
of the Divine Inert, than through their undoubted superiority
over the dead level of the mass. (p. 129)

The morally superior people assessed by Mailer at Chicago lack
joy and are driven by the sour, stinging wasps of defeat; Melville's
"true princes" possess the inert power of intellectual superiority
but lack the "practical" expression of such power that would assure
them success in the world. In McCarthy and his followers and in
Melville's special men something of importance is lacking: the ability to bring one's *amount* and one's *placement* into alignment with the
changing needs of the world and the external exactions of the laws
of success.

Thoreau generally chose not to think anything was lacking in his
life. He worked to avoid the position which pushes Mailer to com-
plain (in *The Armies of the Night*) that there was "probably no impotence in all the world like knowing you were right and the wave of
the world was wrong . . ." (p. 176). Thoreau might know he was
right but he sought to escape the impotence of being entirely unlike the world. To do this he often fell back upon sharpening his
own self-esteem. In 1847 the Harvard class secretary sent him a
query about his activities (translate: his success) and Thoreau reported that he had been "A Surveyor, a Gardener, a Farmer, a
Painter (I mean a Housepainter), a Carpenter, a Mason, a Day-
laborer, a Pencil-maker, a etc." The class secretary might do what
he would with that information. On October 18, 1856 Thoreau
noted in his journal, "Joy and sorrow, success and failure, grandeur and meanness, and indeed most words in the English language do not mean for me what they do for my neighbors." He
often seems to do little more than insist that the criteria for success
lies wholly within the consciousness. It is not a matter of what one
does or the labels one applies, but what is daily revealed of the
inner self by means of the spiritual daguerreotype imprinted by
staring into Walden Pond or into the face of the sun.

"How do you like what you have," Gertrude Stein asks in "Portraits and Repetition," one of her *Lectures in America*. "This is a
question that anybody can ask anybody. Ask it." Just as Thoreau
made a regime out of thinking about what lies deep within the
pond-self and the sun-being, Stein muses out loud about peoples'
portraits:

If they are themselves inside them what are they and what
has it to do with what they do.

And does it make any difference what they do or how they
do it, does it make any difference what they say or how they say
it. Must they be in relation with any one or with anything in
order to be one of whom one can make a portrait. I began to
think a great deal about all these things. (pp. 171-172)

Characteristically, Stein's sentences act both as questions and
statements concerning the success that lies within—*the right having*
of what is known as "presence."

Anybody can be interested in what anybody does but does
that make any difference, is it at all important.

Anybody can be interested in what anybody says, but does
that make any difference, is it at all important. (p. 172)

Portraits or still lives: they are almost the same since they involve
the stillness of being inside, not the doing that goes on outside.

I wonder now if it is necessary to stand still to live if it is not
necessary to stand still to live. . . . I wonder if you know what I
mean. I do not quite know whether I do myself. . . .

I have just tried to begin in writing Four in America because
I am certain that what makes American success is American
failure. (p. 172)

In early 1840's Thoreau offered the historical example of Sir
Walter Raleigh to prove the correctness of Gertrude Stein's hy-
pothesis ninety years before she made it. Thoreau typically laid ad-
ditional stress upon the *free* core of the one who sits still—or
stands—for his life-portrait. "Such a life is useful for us to contemplate as suggesting that a man is not to be measured by the virtue of his described actions, or the wisdom of his expressed
thoughts merely, but by the free character he is, and is felt to be,
under all circumstances" (p. 216).

Emerson in turn used Thoreau in "Historic Notes of Life and
Letters in New England" as the portrait of a free man of presence
in his argument against the second-rate quality of the Fourierists:

Thoreau was in his own person a practical answer, almost a
refutation, to the theories of the socialists. He required no
Phalanx, no Government, no society, almost no memory. He
lived extempore from hour to hour, like the birds and the
angels . . . the only man of leisure in his town; and his independence made all others look like slaves.

In "Thoreau," the elegiac address read over the new grave, Emerson described Thoreau's dinner-manner: "When asked at table what dish he preferred, he answered, 'The nearest.' " Does Thoreau's retort indicate greed and grab on his part, or indifference to petty distinctions like "better" or "worse," in his confidence that anything found on the outside can satisfy the man already complete (like the birds and the angels) on the inside? No doubt Emerson meant the story to signify the latter, but questions hover in the air of Concord concerning the wider uses of "presence": whether Thoreau actually wanted simply *to be*; if to be, thereby to serve, or to dominate? That is, to be *presence* (standing still to live), to be *christian* (to hand out), or to be *cannibal* (to suck in)? Let it rest for the moment that, whatever most moved Thoreau's will, the means he used to gain his end-game of success was the free-wheeling, free-standing consciousness.

But if it looks as if Thoreau believed that his being sprang entirely out of himself, this is not so. If his means (his middle) and his ends are self-directed, the beginnings of presence come from the solitary self in alignment with the universal laws which came before him and would continue after him. It was as Emerson phrased it in "Immortality": "We live by desire to live; we live by choice: by will, by thought, by virtue, by the vivacity of the laws which we obey, and obeying share their life— . . ." Here Emerson reiterates the conditions for failure laid down by Levett in 1624: ". . . we die by sloth, by disobedience, by losing hold of life, which ebbs out of us."

Emerson and Thoreau on the issue of presence share points with Ralph Harper in *Nostalgia*. Amplifying his readings of Gabriel Marcel, Harper locates presence in *being*, distinguishing that from mundane definitions of success which demand *having*. Being is Dionysian—unmeasurable, mysterious; having is Apollonian—measurable, functional. The one resides in drama, the other in history; the one is inexhaustible, the other eventually comes to an end.

If having is different from being, as Harper and Marcel see it, they require one another. Neither "cannibal" having, nor pure "standing still to live," presence is the "christian" reaction of self with world—being with having. We see examples of this, negative and positive, in Bernard Malamud's *The Assistant*. Morris Bober is committed to virtue in obedience to the Law of the Torah. But because he does not possess the energy of presence, he is a failure. The Bober grocery-store functions in the greyish, bad-luck world of unpaid bills, attacks of pneumonia, and freakish spring snowstorms, while the cannibal world of good luck, fluorescent lights, new enameled display-cases, and success exists only for others down the block. But the grocery-store world in which insistent creditors demand every penny on account is suddenly, mysteriously, penetrated by "presence"—that gift of Christian Grace infiltrating a Jewish novel, perhaps. By the end of the narrative Morris Bober is dead in his exhaustion, but his "son" Frank Alpine is on the spot to receive the strange gift that transforms his *gonif*-acts, self-deceptions, and repetitious failures into an active state of obedience to the Law. However much the rest of us may brood upon Frank's possible future entombment in the grocer's coffin, Thoreau would read the concluding sentences of Malamud's novel in terms of energizing dawn, hope, life, and success.

There is something similar going on in Henry James's assessment of Milly Theale, his American princess, the dove of great presence which drops down to surprise us all: ". . . and this was what it was to be a success: it always happened before one could know it" (xix, 157). Where it happens, it is hauntingly felt—to use the phrase James applied in *Notes of a Son and Brother* to his own father's "presence"—as "something perpetually fine going on" (p. 163). James found presence, too, in his elder brother; it was what he described in William as "all his vivacity and Williamcy of mind undimmed" (*James Family*, p. 325).

Fine, going on, perpetually, vivacity, undimmed. Marked by these special traits, *presence* comes with suddenness and surprise. And presence keeps on acting (even when *doing* is not involved). It is the necessary requirement for the absolute success that exceeds all understanding. This, at least, is that lustrous idea of success held by some Americans.

Still lives stand or run deep through layers of existence. They also require breadth, span, duration, *time*. This fact complicates any definition of success sought alone as a thing of quality, as being defined as *the right amount* set to active use in *the best place*. Throughout his writings Emerson acknowledged the insistencies of time in general; he noted this in particular when he came to Thoreau's graveside to ponder over the dead man's life of success or failure:

> Had his genius been only contemplative, he had been fitted to his life, but with his energy and practical ability he seemed born for great enterprise and for command; and I so much regret the loss of his rare powers of action, that I cannot help

counting it a fault in him that he had no ambition. Wanting this, instead of engineering for all America, he was the captain of a huckleberry party. Pounding beans is good to the end of pounding empires one of these days; but if, at the end of years, it is still only beans!

However well intended, these remarks from the eulogy-essay "Thoreau" are rather standard stuff. They appear to limit successful action to the juggling of the market value of beans and empires. More interesting is the finger Emerson places upon a deeper failure on Thoreau's part. "The scale on which his studies proceeded was so large as to require longevity. . . ." But Thoreau died before his time. Even if he did not fail himself by stopping short of the completion of his explorations into the inner life, he failed us. In an undated journal of 1850 Thoreau himself acknowledged the necessity for time. "Regard not your failures nor successes. All the past is equally a failure and a success; it is a success in as much as it offers you the present opportunity" (VIII, 44). But opportunity only works when there is *at least a moment left* to seize what it holds out; dying wipes out that moment and denies that success.

Almost twenty years before Emerson gave public voice to the fact of Thoreau's failure through dying so young, he noted in his journal of 1843: "Young men like H. T. owe us a new world & they have not acquitted the debt: for the most part, such die young, & so dodge the fulfillment" (VIII, 375). Thomas Jefferson once suggested that it was a pity Jesus died too soon to make his ideas count. Lambert Strether of *The Ambassadors* retorts to the glib remark "Better late than never!" with "Better early than late!" since "What one loses one loses; make no mistake about that" (XXI, 216). And in the sonnet "For John Berryman" from *Notebook*, Robert Lowell speaks of "Herbert, Thoreau, Pascal/born to die like athletes in their forties . . ."—losses even at the moment of victory. The basic fact of human fate (as David Bakan puts it) is that we all survive until we die. This fact is as potent in America as elsewhere. Herbert and Pascal may represent the decadent stock of the Old World whose weakness Thoreau scorned, but Lowell's poetic line wedges the name of the New Englander between the Englishman and the Frenchman; he is placed in fatal conjunction with everyman's morality. Even Walden offers no escape from that.

Time does not merely promise the fact of dying; it has the power to inflict havoc upon the circumstances of living. Time drives many to say with Theodore Dreiser, "I had seen Pittsburgh!" That is, you may have a vision of the eternal laws of the City of God and possess the potency of "presence" within, and suddenly be plunged into full experience of the City of Man, the external forces of history and defeat. In Thoreau's terms, you could experience Walden and then see Manhattan—the defeating force of the latter closing off the expanding idea of the former.

In a letter of 1894 Dreiser wrote out his ambivalent feelings about the American midwest: "The very soil smacked of American idealism and faith, a fixedness in sentimental and purely imaginative American tradition, in which, I alas! could not share. I was enraptured . . . but I could not believe that it was more than a frail flower of romance. I had seen Pittsburgh!" In this letter (included in McAleer's study of Dreiser, pp. 29-30), Dreiser makes it clear that "Pittsburgh" was for him what Henry James meant when he spoke in *The American Scene* (p. 53) of "the hungry, triumphant actual" that cancels the values of the past by turning them into "the superseded things." Yet if the Pittsburgh-pressures of contingency and time make it the doom of someone like Milly Theale of *The Wings of the Dove* "to live fast," and if hers is "a question of the short run and the consciousness proportionately crowded," James and Milly also believe that "idealists, in the long run, I think, *don't* feel that they lose" (XIX, 159, 161). The crucial embellishment added by James is faith in the *idea* of success. Next to his portrayal of the harsh ways in which life acts to deny idealism, James places a glimpse at the power of the idea of succeeding. Having this idea, and the fact of "presence," may not assure his losers extravagant wins, but if "presence" without such ideas is not enough for success—defined as the extra amount—"presence" joined with "idea" at least lets them break even.

Henry James believed that one cannot resist the facts that impose failure upon human life unless one is able to comprehend the meaning of success. Because of this belief he tried to provide his writings with brief penetrations of the ideal—the basis for all ideas about winning well. In his preface to Volume XII of the New York Edition (included in *The Art of the Novel*) James discusses "the high and helpful public and, as it were, civic use of the imagination" (p. 223). He asks, "How can one consent to make a picture of the preponderant futilities and vulgarities and miseries of life without the impulse to exhibit as well from time to time, in its place, some fine example of the reaction, the opposition or the escape?" (p. 223.) It was in the cause of the "civic use" of the imagination that James continued to state that the artist must provide (to refer to Dreiser's words) visions of "American idealism and faith," as well as of "Pittsburgh."

In his study of early nineteenth-century Romanticism, *Natural Supernaturalism*, Meyer Abrams comments that post-Kantian philosophy located "the justification for the ordeal of human experience . . . in experience itself" (p. 187). When experience in a fallen world is elevated in importance, consciousness rises in value as well. The unconsciousness characteristic of an original innocence that requires no experience recedes in worth, but it does not disappear as a fact. It remains, still able to undercut the prestige of consciousness. Further, consciousness (the equipment needed to record experience in an imperfect world) in turn depends on "the noumenal ego, or moral will, which assumes absolute freedom" (p. 200). At the same time, the imperfect world asserts "the inescapable limitations of the phenomenal ego, or man as a part of nature"; it makes that ego "subject both to [man's ] instinctual and sensual drives and to the laws of strict causal necessity" (p. 200).

The terms by which one is meant to gain success—the force of free will set going by conscious manipulation of the experiences offered by life in a blemished world—become maddeningly entangled in the terms that trip one up: mental subservience to unconsciousness and instincts and bodily obedience to dictatorial phenomenal necessities. Under such conditions how can the success-ideal overcome the Pittsburgh-fact?

Abrams calls upon both Kant and Milton's Adam to provide an alternative to the dead-ends that face us as we stand in history and in nature—in "Pittsburgh." Abrams interprets Kant as saying, "It is both gain and loss, depending on the perspective one assumes" (p. 205). Kant grants the possibility of looking from the Mount of Hope out over the head of history. But Milton's Adam is skeptical about the Kantian solicitude offered by the Archangel Michael. Adam is poised in uncertainty between the experience he has just undergone (the eating of the forbidden fruit) and the experience that lies ahead in the world beyond Eden. His painful memories of lost bliss seem to have no value for him; he hardly knows if he can rely on the future bliss promised him by Michael as they look down from the Mount into history and beyond toward a strange new paradise regained. Therefore, Adam must say, "Full of doubt I stand. . . ."

Gabriel Marcel would have Adam trust in what lies beyond Pittsburgh, even while existing within the experiences of the world. Marcel gives his reasons (included in Harper's *Nostalgia*):

Hope, which is not merely desire, consists in asserting that there is at the heart of being, beyond all data, beyond all inventories and all calculations, a mysterious principle which is in connivance with me, which cannot but will that which I will, if what I will deserves to be willed, and is in fact willed by the whole of my being. (p. 99)

Kant, Adam and the Angel, and Marcel: the argument circles back to the power ascribed by Meyer Abrams to "the noumenal ego, or moral will, which assumes absolute freedom." It is this ego—however thwarted by the "phenomenal ego," by history, and by nature—that is expected to be the victor, Pittsburgh or not. One is, as it were, doomed to the obligation to keep hope going while it concerns itself with experience, even if one must—because one lives with experience—doubt.

Born with an austere inheritance of hope, Henry Adams (the self-appointed heir of Adam the skeptic) soon recognizes himself as an extravagant creature of doubts. A man who, according to Justice Holmes, wished the world handed to him on a silver platter, Adams discovered that history was the muck that formed and fixed his feet of clay. Brother Brooks wrote in his introduction to *The Degradation of the Democratic Dogma* that Henry had posed

as having been a failure and a disappointed man. He was neither the one nor the other, as he knew well. He was not a failure, for he succeeded, and succeeded brilliantly, in whatever he undertook, where success was possible; and he was not disappointed, for the world gave him everything he would take. (p. 6)

If we choose to believe Brooks Adams, a characteristic Adamsian irony is in play. According to Brooks, Henry succeeded in the world "where success was possible" and he took from the world what he wanted. Let us use terms shared by Kant and Harper/ Marcel: whatever success Henry Adams had took place in the world of history and the phenomenal ego; yet it was in the realm of presence and the noumenal self that victory turned into dust and ashes (the same which Holmes said resulted from Adam's own blighting touch). Judged relatively, in the world's view (the world of his own circle, of course, since who else among the American populace knew what he was like *absolutely*?), Henry Adams was a success. Assessing himself in just such final terms, Adams could decide he was "the champion failure of all."

The recognition of oneself as "the champion failure" contains its own ambiguity. If you are the best of a kind, you still possess a sort of success. In *The Education of Henry Adams* the manikin-Adams is set up by his author for judgment as a failure, not for the proving of the greatness of "Henry Adams." That book's persona cannot see itself as a champion at anything. It is the same with Lambert Strether of James's novel *The Ambassadors*, that fictional character who plays out a number of Adamsian responses to a baffling Paris that breaks his "historical neck" almost as surely as it did Adams's. Strether says to Madame de Vionnet, "Everything's comparative. You're better than *that*." She replies, "You are better than anything" (xxii, 120). But Strether and the manikin-Adams will never see their own success. James will see it for Strether; Adams will see it, perhaps, for his own self. What remains is to decide whether James and Adams as observers worked out of comparative or absolute knowledge of the facts of triumph and of failure.

There is still another question. In the somewhat later literary version Edith Wharton gave the type of Strether/Adams-manikin in *The Age of Innocence*, we are asked to consider whether it is better to take it forgranted that you will not get what you want (which is what Wharton's Newland Archer does), or whether it is smarter to be like Archer's son who takes it forgranted that you will. One thing seems sure: Dallas Archer will never write (either because he cannot or because he would not bother) a champion book about championship failure, nor will he figure as the hero of important books like *The Age of Innocence*, *The Ambassadors*, or *The Education of Henry Adams*. As the man of obvious success, he remains merely a figure glanced at in passing.

Norman Mailer would agree that that kind of success—Dallas' kind—is boring to read about. The essays of Emerson and the writings of Thoreau constantly had to resist devoting themselves to the Dallas-idea that says, "Of course I'll succeed, how can I not?" In their own endeavors to celebrate success they had to bypass the boringness of complete self-confidence in the power of "the noumenal ego" to triumph. Henry James, no philosophical optimist, learned how to use the idea of success by placing it in contexts of doubt and defeat; the philosophical optimists Emerson and Thoreau failed in their efforts whenever their ideas of success left out "Pittsburgh" and stayed too long with "Dallas."

In reviewing those who believe that the idea and the fact (and the contradictions set up between them) constitute the basis for whatever engagement men have with success or failure, we have stretched past the rather simple (although not ignorant) conviction of Christopher Levett that the fault for losing in America lies in the man rather than in the land. We have seen some of the ways Thoreau and Adams dealt with the facts of failure that come from outside while continuing to concentrate on the state of affairs within themselves. Now we turn to those (Adams included) who acknowledge history as a brutality they must study. For some, history is what they must challenge; for others, it is cannier to accept history's primary power than to resist it. Either way, history becomes the good alibi for failure that gets a man out of the box of self-recrimination. If you cannot blame it "on the country," then accuse history of dragging you down.

Adams' keen sense of the reality of history led him to his particular method for defining success and failure: the method of the ever-watchful schoolboy whose location in the classroom in no way protects him from what it is he studies. And how carefully Adams, while a student at Harvard, counted up the merit points by which the university thought to fix his value. He once accumulated 18,580 points as a scholar, only to have the amount nullified for appearing in class without a collar. Consequently he graduated forty-fourth in a class of eighty-nine, although his academic record placed him much higher. What did Adams make of this? Did he accept the way the university ranked him at the end of his senior year? Or did he stubbornly want to be known by the fact of his earlier successes? Or did he insist his worth was equal to the whole spread of his endeavors? Of the various ways history and mankind can be judged—by piece-meal conclusions, by beginnings, or by entireties—Adams (devoted student of causes and effects as he was) chose inclusivity.

Tagged as an inconsequential "begonia" by his critics, Adams refused to be limited by the implication of Thoreau's journal notation of July 13, 1857 which rebuked men "not serious enough either for success or failure." Adams could hardly be *seriously* serious about himself since he felt so keenly the joke of the contradictions of his situation—historical, social, and personal. In *The Education of Henry Adams* this champion of failure and scholar of paradox admitted that "the faculty of ignoring" contradictions is the mark of "the practical man." Indeed, ". . . any attempt to deal with them seriously as education is fatal" (p. 48). He had discovered the secret that brings success to those who turn aside from the contradictory facts and live with the illusions of the logical. But Adams refused to use that secret. He refused to deny any situation, however paradoxical.

Say that he was fated not to win by an historical displacement which put him out of his proper century. Adams would keep on trying (freely willing to do so), aware that by this act he thereby condemned himself to the perpetration of his failures. Say that historical events determined that men who had been successful soldiers during the Civil War could well be failures their first day as civilians. Adams would gaily disregard his own warning when he set out "to deal with them seriously" (p. 48). He chose to think about the contradictory facts and to confirm the failures; he did this rather than to will ignorance of contradictions and to guarantee a certain kind of success. Defeated by history, Adams' strategy was *to think about history* and to shape books out of what he thought. Such books in themselves are, of course, no token of success—quite the contrary. As he wrote a friend on March 12, 1909 (in a letter included in Cater's collection), "My favorite figure of the American author is that of a man who breeds a favorite dog, which he throws into the Mississippi River for the pleasure of making a splash. The river does not splash, but it drowns the dog" (pp. 664-665). Still and all, although the dog is dead, the writer, who stands apart on the solid ground of the river bank of his skepticism and his amusement, is not.

In *Of a Fire on the Moon* Mailer acknowledges the force of history's contradictions to turn values upside down. He says, ". . . History often used the best of men for the worst of purposes and discarded them when the machines of new intent were ready. As often History had used the worst of men to convert an unhealthy era to a new clime" (p. 90). Mailer also insists in *The Armies of the Night* that history's judgment is what human success ultimately depends upon (p. 6), and, as he reports in *Miami and the Siege of Chicago*, the dream is for a man "to show the center of history that he was not without greatness" (p. 62). That the man he cites as a point in fact is Richard Nixon does not disprove his rule, but rather defines the nature of the failure Mailer is out to understand as well as the success.

Still, if history is the only exhibition hall a man has, what if the acoustics are all wrong and the view of the stage is obscured—as it was for Mailer at the Ambassador Theatre in Washington D.C., in October 1967? Under such ill-favored conditions the actual greatness of the man will neither be rightly heard nor seen. The resulting "judgments" (as announced and sanctified by the press) may be so uncertain that we cannot know whether Mailer was stupid-drunk that night or crazy-great. Even if we could get to the truth of that particular October night, what about all the other days and nights of all the existential years of Mailer's life? Is it what he did or did not do on that single night which tells us he has had success in historical terms; or must *all* his deeds be totaled before we can know this—as Adams believed they had to be? Mailer sees himself presenting the same kind of puzzle we feel concerning the historical placement of U. S. Grant. What was that man, after all? "Unconditional Surrender" Grant the great general, or "Useless" Grant the inept president? Are we supposed to give more value to the middle of his life, or to the faltering start and ending? And is the decency of Grant's dying well to be forgotten altogether? How *are* we to arrive at the *mean* when the parts appear to contradict one another?

The questions that agitate the sleep of historians like Adams and Mailer did not bother Henry James. Adams and Mailer believe they have to move back and forth between historical judgments imposed from without and the highly ambiguous nature of the inner man. In contrast, James makes it clear in *The American Scene* that history is not all that distinct an entity from ourselves. History is what our own consciousnesses choose to read into it, not necessarily what others make of it in an objective, external sense.

James's assertion brings us back to history-subjective, not history-absolute. The mind is the absolute creator of the truth, implies the Adams who toys as a philosopher with epistemology; but the Adams of *The Education* says the historian "must not try to know what is truth"—not "if he values his honesty; for, if he cares for his truths, he is certain to falsify his facts" (p. 457). Unlike the Jamesian pseudo-historian, the Adamsian archivist of history merely records changes in the world; he does not create them or search them out. But even Adams at times, and Mailer quite often, go beyond the mild subjectivism of Henry James. They have moments when they desire to transform the world to fit the conception of perfection held fast in their minds. Only by such means can they possess a world refined enough to reveal to history their own greatness. Theirs is not the silly solipsism of those who dream their way into success; it is the crucial engagement of the world with the mind's idea of itself.

In *Advertisements for Myself* Mailer feels depressed by the betrayal which Hemingway's suicide represents to him; he rebukes his mentor for having left us all "marooned in the nervous boredom of a world which finally he didn't try hard enough to change." On his good days Mailer sees himself as capable of influencing history

first-hand by his words, his deeds, or his presence; or at the least
becoming the instrument through which another—say "The Patron Saint of Macdougal Alley"—saves the world. In *The Degradation of the Democratic Dogma* Brooks Adams reports that John
Quincy Adams was once convinced he could alter America for the
better through his writings, but that Henry Adams finally lost confidence in his power to do the same. Yet both grandfather and
grandson had had the hope of *being history* which they share with
Mailer. It makes little difference what stock one comes from—the
*humilitas-sublimitas* of Mailer's neo-Romantic imagination or the
stuff of classicism the Adamses were made of; they both experienced the excitement of the faith in a personal act of alteration that
would save America—and the anxious conviction they might be
held accountable if they failed to bring about a shift in history itself.

What else might be done to placate the contempt of history:
change the Not Me to match the Me, or transform the Me into material which the world is willing to judge as meritorious? Saint
John de Crèvecœur held tight to the latter formula within his
"novel" about the eighteenth-century American yeoman. His
Farmer James writes of such a miraculous metamorphosis taking
place in America. In a secularized version of the Calvinist scheme
of salvation, King George replaces the Lord as god-father and
law-maker on the throne ruling over a happy earthly colony of
good men:

> Every thing has tended to regenerate them; new laws, a new
> mode of living, a new social system; here they are become men.
> . . . By what invisible power hath this surprising metamor-
> phosis been performed? By that of the laws and that of their
> industry. . . . From whence proceed these laws? From our gov-
> ernment. Whence the government? It is derived from the orig-
> inal genius and strong desire of the people ratified and con-
> firmed by the crown. (p. 42)

With these words Crèvecœur hands over to America one of its
favorite ideas about itself. He (or his Farmer James) believes for the
moment that one stunning alteration is all that is needed; occurring
once and for all time, this historical shift will fix America in the unchanging bliss of c. 1770. To place stress on *always changing*, as does
Gertrude Stein, would baffle the man possessed of this one great
idea. No wonder that Farmer James, dispossessed of his land, has
become by the end of his account a man bewildered by the moving

lines of revolutionary force he can neither comprehend nor control.

In *The Making of Americans* Gertrude Stein writes that "always and always it is more exciting the knowing in one completely the character of them, the whole repeating in them, the whole range of being in them and yet not then being completely certain of them whether they will be succeeding or failing in living" (p. 275). She remarks of one of these Americans in the making, Mrs. Redfern:

> . . . it came very nearly being certain that she would not be suc-
> ceeding in living but she might have been succeeding in living.
> It was not a certain thing, not completely a certain thing, and it
> was not a certain thing that she was not succeeding in living not
> succeeding in living before the ending of her living. (p. 275)

In place of the straightforward sentences employed by Farmer James in his explicit insistence upon success coming once and for all time in America, Stein's prose works by implication to suggest the slow, repetitious, problematic nature of success—based as it is upon living which is always changing, ever beginning, never complete until the final full stop is conclusively reached. As a novelist—a person who is traditionally expected to provide happy endings with demonstrably successful outcomes—Stein can only say that "sometimes perhaps everything will come to be showing something and that will be then a happy ending of all this beginning" (p. 290). Only after such long delays, only after "all this beginning" could a man like Mailer, for instance, be able to evaluate the importance of his appearance at the Ambassador Theatre that October night in 1967.

Gertrude Stein suggests that for Americans to stay in the running for success they need time for a series of constant transformations; they require all the span that history can give them to unfold the processes of their being. But in those plummy days before the murmurous drone of success was shattered by the cacophony of rebellion, Crèvecœur's eighteenth-century persona thought it unlikely that a man could attain success today and fail tomorrow. All ends and beginnings would be the same. But the equilibrium once promised to Farmer James before the Revolution was betrayed by what Henry Adams notes as a commonplace in his review of the after-years of the Jefferson and Madison administrations. More than Pennsylvania farmers toppled when the original balances did not hold. There were the Puritans of Massachusetts who had, even earlier, hoped to fulfill "a higher destiny" in the name of the forces of unity. Their type was transformed by the push of disintegration; ignominiously, they became "the best people of Boston," whose "want of moral sense was more proof that the moral instinct had little to do with social distinctions" (this reproof recorded in Adams' *History of the United States* and cited by Samuels' *The Middle Years*, p. 378). Farmer James had extolled the eternal glories of unceasing mediocrity. Adams, wittily, deflates the meaninglessness of being *merely* the best in an imperfect world. During the state of equilibrium, the level can be that of success. With flux, even peaks can count as failure if they lie below the level-best of that heightened, ordered society required by the true eighteenth-century man, whether Crèvecœur or Adams.

Perry Miller liked to point out, and Sacvan Bercovitch still does, that the progeny of the first Puritan settlers possessed a special knowledge of a kind denied to secularists like Crèvecœur. They knew—and were reminded in public accusations—that they had fallen below the original plane of rightness. Deep within what Miller called "The Marrow of Puritan Divinity" lay the hurtful realization that the more one learns, the less "innocence" one has and the heavier responsibility for failure one must assume. Always, on the Calvinist scale, there was failure to be measured. The "natural knowledge of natural law" serves "to make men know they have fallen short of something which they cannot even conceive" (*Errand*, p. 78n).

In certain significant ways Emory Elliott's *The Power and the Pulpit* qualifies Miller's essay and Bercovitch's *The Puritan Origins of the American Self* in terms of which generation was most active at rebuking whom. But even Elliott's revision of the tensions set up between fathers and sons over the profound central question of success before God supports this general truth: that to be a Puritan in the New World entailed a painful knowledge about that better life one could never have and the obligation to strive for it just the same.

Here is Gertrude Stein in *The Making of Americans* on the matter of just such an effort:

> In between those first and last are many little times of tired, many ways of being very tired, but never any like the first hot tired when you begin to learn how to press through it and never any like the last dead tired with no beyond ever to it. (p. 46)

Stein's meaning is not unlike the Puritans'; surely this at least can be agreed to. They share the same insistence that men make the most of the "many little times of tired" which is all they have to redeem since they cannot control the coming of "the first hot tired" of birth or "the last dead tired" of death. Neither Stein nor the Puritans could consider *not* caring about what they have done *before* they arrive at the time "with no beyond to it."

Freud might say that whenever self-tormenting persons mark how far they have slid away from perfection, it is only presumptuous hubris that tells them they began with a higher estate; it is wiser, he suggested, to realize human failures are as petty as the original state of our biological being. But Americans often refuse such sensible balm. It is their special pride to insist upon having fallen far. Alone of all the nations, theirs is the truly catastrophic failure in not having fully altered the world-self as they were chosen by history to do. Such Americans consciously choose to emulate a vision of an earlier, better age or of some time yet more perfect in the future. They would rather struggle with great losses and self-chastisements than to give in without a struggle to the present state of triviality and self-complacency.

In the "General Introduction" to *Magnalia Christi Americana* of 1702, Cotton Mather cites Peter Ramus' retort to those who urged him to remain a Roman Catholic (here given in translation from the original Latin): ". . . of the fifteen centuries since Christ, the first is truly golden and . . . the rest, the further they are removed the more they are wretched and degenerate; therefore when I had free choice, I preferred the golden age." In case his readers were slow at catching his gist, Mather moved to clarify what particular act such a choice must lead to. "In short, The *First Age* was the Golden Age: To return unto *That*, will make a Man a *Protestant*, and I may add, a *Puritan*."

In Mather's eyes, of course, to be a "Puritan" is equivalent to participating in the victory of "presence" (possessed by both men and by God) over "Pittsburgh" (the place of Pandemonium, not the City on the Hill). Perhaps defeat seems fated because history has moved one away from golden beginnings, but—according to Ramus and to Mather, perhaps even to Adams and to Stein—that same defeat will be revealed as voided once it is transformed by the rightly chosen effort into a true conquest over the "many little times of tired."

# ◤ CHAPTER 12 ◢

# Getting Goods, Being Good,
# Good Getting,
# and Well-Being

Up to this point the various definitions that circle around success and failure have largely dealt with "presence," and presence has been taken as a finer state of being which is highly ethical at the least and of rare moral quality at best. The emphasis has been upon the chances for *being good* in America. Definitions of success that invoke *getting goods* are more straightforward and the examples more numerous. By 1913 Theodore Dreiser (in a passage from *A Traveler at Forty* included in McAleer's study) tentatively suggested the piquant hope that there is

> the existence of a force or forces that, possibly ordered in some noble way, maintain a mathematical, chemical, and mechanical parity and order in visible things. I have always felt, in spite of all my carpings, that somehow in a large way there is a rude justice done under the sun, and that a balance for, I will not say right, but for happiness, is maintained. (p. 49)

*Being right* and *being happy* seem to be two separate matters in Dreiser's eyes. An American democrat and a democratic American are also different, which further compounds the problem of being right and happy and democratic and *having*, all at once. In 1848 Theodore Parker reported, in his essay "The Political Destination of America and the Signs of the Times," that Americans of two types fought over the right to claim the word "democracy." "The motto of one is, 'You are as good as I, and let us help one another.' That represents the democracy of the Declaration of Independence, and of the New Testament. . . . The other has for its motto, 'I am as good as you, so get out of my way' " (p. 154).

"It's good to be shifty in a new country" was the kind of "good" expediency Simon Suggs, Melville's Confidence Man, and Poe's Diddler had in mind during the same years Thoreau devoted himself to failing in the eyes of his neighbors so that he might enjoy the private good of being principled. In 1849, in *A Week on the Concord and Merrimack Rivers*, Thoreau insisted that we must all study those "modes by which a man may put bread into his mouth which will not prejudice him as a companion and neighbor" (p. 136). In 1854 *Walden*, Thoreau's revised unstandard version of the Scriptures, named man's chief aim as "a simple and irrepressible satisfaction with the gift of life . . ." (p. 78). Compare Mark Twain's "Revised Catechism" of 1871 (included in Justin Kaplan's book) which asked and answered:

> What is the chief end of man?—to get rich. In what way?— dishonestly if we can; honestly if we must. Who is God, the one only and true? Money is God. Gold and Greenbacks and Stock—father, son, and the ghost of same—three persons in one; these are the true and only God, mighty and supreme: and William Tweed is his prophet. (p. 96)

When in 1924 Bruce Barton wrote down his *R.S.V.*, he proudly introduced American society to "The Man Nobody Knows." He revealed that Jesus Himself "had somehow somewhere" awakened to "the inner consciousness of power. . . . Somewhere, at some unforgettable hour, the daring filled His heart. He knew that he was bigger than Nazareth. . . ." During the same decade as Jesus's apotheosis on Madison Avenue (noted in Cawelti's book on the self-made man, p. 198), the boy Robert Lowell looked at the portrait of his great-great-grandfather and found in Mordecai Myers's complacent eye neither allegory nor the *Mayflower*, just the ability to gain money and enjoy worldly prestige.

In such a milieu, where wealth and power preempted the good life and even Jesus would soon be discovered to have joined "their side," Henry Adams was only stating the blunt truth when he reflected about his brother Brooks's failures: "He is like Clarence King, Richardson, LaFarge and all my crowd whom cleverer and richer men exploit and rob. It is the law of God! It is also the law of common-sense." This law to which Adams alluded in a letter (see Ford, II, 367) was not the law of success to which "presence" was rightly obedient; it was a law by which stubborn adherence to presence, ideals, and the absolute could only bring loss.

According to the version of evolutionary doctrine that teaches how to get good at getting goods, the "development" of Chadwick Newsome of *The Ambassadors* might be considered "hideous" by the impractical, but it can only be judged as "fortunate" by the astute (XXII, 205). As a scientist of practical forces, Adams would have to agree that Chad was in touch with contemporary modes for success. "Advertising scientifically worked presented itself thus as the great new force," Lambert Strether observes, as he listens to Chad declare the code of action by which the younger man will bring his own "magnificence" into play: " 'It really does the thing, you know' " (xxii, 315). Bruce Barton's Jesus Christ and Henry James's Chad Newsome have alike discovered the "scientifically worked" means which make ends (absolute or otherwise) unnecessary.

In *The Mansion*, the final novel in Faulkner's trilogy about the "new men" of business, Mink Snopes moves toward the murder of another Snopes because of his belief in the basic principles of energy: *"A man can get through anything if he can jest keep on walking"* (p. 270).

Whether men strive for better goods or to be better, economic evaluations are involved. It is an economics that strives to account for the right kind and amount of energy for the job. By the latter half of the nineteenth century, energy was frequently the acknowledged goal of life whose successful attainment made it possible to accumulate other strengths—whether goodness, happiness, wealth, or power. Our consciousness exists only to continue, William James said in the *Principles of Psychology* of 1880; it will hardly move on without being recharged by pulsations of energy. Henry Adams decided that Jews had the required energy, while his kind—"the best people"—had wasted whatever force they once had. But the science of economics must also study what the Snopeses signify. Snopes-energy does not always appear as visible activity. But even static energy—when provided in great quantities, in highly concentrated forms, moving as glaciers move—can divide and conquer the morally good who lack the right kind of energy.

Furthermore, it takes the energy of one Snopes to do in another Snopes. Flem Snopes just keeps on chewing the invisible stuff of his insatiable appetite for respectability and power. Mink Snopes just keeps on walking until he comes to the satisfaction of his unquenched hunger for revenge and justice. Those who are "out of it"—the good presences of V. K. Ratliff and Gavin Stevens—can for the most part only look on, unable either to aid in the act of murder or to prevent it. "Economy of energy is a kind of power," as Adams remarked in 1901 concerning the *vis inertiae* of Russia and Asia, pausing in *The Education* to prophesy that those countries—which might be seen as "Snopes" countries—would crush all in their paths (pp. 439-440).

Whatever its varying forms, energy plays no moral favorites. It *could* even support the righteous. Neutral in its own amorality, it brings success to the artist—the man, Faulkner insisted, who would willingly push his aged mother down the stairs for a chance to write the "Ode on a Grecian Urn." Nothing can stop him to whom, as Faulkner noted further in the Foreword to *The Faulkner Reader*, ". . . the blood and glands and flesh still remained strong and potent, the heart and the imagination still remained undulled to follies and lusts and heroisms of men and women . . ." (p. x).

Notwithstanding these remarks by William James, Henry Adams, and William Faulkner, we are not necessarily back with Herbert Spencer's survival-at-any-cost. Nor are we at full stop before the notion that it hardly matters whether we are cannibals or christians as long as we hold fast. It does matter whether we are "sane crooks" or "mad saints," as Nicole Warren Diver observes in Scott Fitzgerald's *Tender Is the Night*. Out of her experience of being both victimized "christian" and victorious "cannibal," Nicole chooses to be the crook. Better to sleep with a sober cannibal than a drunken Christian, Ishmael also notes in *Moby-Dick*, and Thoreau and Emerson both proclaimed that it is sounder to be that pagan who finds life's triumphs in this world than to be a Christian preaching success for the next world only. But probably best of all is to be the cannibal who is actually the christian, not the Christian who is really a cannibal. This is Mailer's sage suggestion, though he then unsettles useful distinctions by defining "cannibal" as one who believes "that survival and health of the species comes from consuming one's own, not one's near-own, but one's own species" (p. 4).

We have come again to the economics of energy: the amounts consumed, conserved, or wasted; the purpose and the results that go beyond the survival levels of keeping body (cannibal) and soul (christian) together. As you might expect, Norman Mailer swivels from pole to pole on the matter. The pleasure Mailer takes over the gyroscope in *Of a Fire on the Moon* comes from perceiving that it devotes its energy "to being precisely where it is" (p. 426). If he—the artist advertising his work on, say, *The Deer Park*—could only share without impediment in the world's supply of "the energy of new success," he would be infused with new blood. In *Advertisements for Myself* Mailer says that that man who most approximates the gyroscope's success of being well placed is the hipster ("Faustian," "strong on his will"). The opposite type, and failure, is the beatnik who either does not know where he is or is in the wrong place. The beatnik "contemplates eternity, finds it beautiful, likes to believe it waiting to receive him. He wants to get out of reality more than he wants to change it, and at the end of the alley is a mental hospital" (p. 374).

This seems a useful new distinction to add to our list of the traits that let a man be as successful as he is meant to be; but actually the gyroscope-reference only introduces an arresting variation on the ideas presented by Thoreau, Adams, and others in Chapter 11 on the need to be in the right place at the right time and on having enough of what it takes. The main point Mailer contributes is that the gyroscope not only wins because of its sufficient energy and perfect aplomb; it enjoys the amorality of its force. But if it is a thing more of good-getting than of being good, it is not completely *that*. When Mailer holds the gyroscope in his hand to examine it for its meaning, in ways reminiscent of Hamlet looking upon Yorick's skull, he finds that his meditations about amoral power are wrenched about into consideration of the forces of that good which goes beyond the mere "to be" and the basic "to get."

Mailer likes energy when it challenges him to a fight, *mano a mano*. He believes that if you are really good—successful, with the goods—you push close to death without dying. That is being good: being successful with goodness. On the other hand, to die is to have tried too hard or not well enough. Placed in a false position and out of contact with energy, you are a failure. For Mailer, failure means fear and fear means sin because you have lived and died without making sufficient contribution to the cosmic economy. But we will come back later to Mailer and energy, success and sin, after we have practiced more at keeping up with his dialectic dances.

To survive creatively, thus economically, even while mortally limited, is the solution to the crisis of energy suggested by Mailer and Melville. Ishmael (who in Mailer's terms has moments as both hipster and beatnik) survives the suicidal vortex and is spewed up out of the void of death. One can hardly say his survival is the result of his will. Perhaps, though, Ishmael returns to his nick of time in possession of what Meyer Abrams, when referring to just such Ishmaelean experiences, calls the knowledge of our tragic destiny. If this is what happens to Ishmael, he will have acquired salvation as well as physical survival: *good*, as well as *goods*.

"You know so, at least, where you are!" (xxii, 283.) This is to apply the hope voiced by Marie de Vionnet in James's *The Ambassadors*. Henry Adams was of like mind when he explained that if he could ever puzzle out how the currents of history and universe ran, he might be able to move through the corridors of chaos even though he had no hope of mastering them.

To survive creatively, economically, perceptively, and morally— all together—may be too much for anyone to manage. Certainly this is the terrible impossibility for the girl without a nose who writes to "Miss Lonelyhearts" (in Nathanael West's novel of the same name) to ask why she cannot be happy; certainly this is the insurmountable task for Miss Lonelyhearts himself who dies trying to find out why everything fails except uncreative suffering and amoral energy. Certainly the knowledge of the tragic destiny possessed by that girl and that man gives them no saving grace—the extra, unexpected surge of energy that settles all accounts for the good. The *facts* asserted by West's novel are enough to put an end to the value or moral sanction of drawing upon *ideas* about success or failure. The entire matter is closed here and now for those of like mind. But others than West continue to ask whether ideas may not decently share the same world with such facts, and perhaps even come to have dominance over them.

Still another aspect of the discussion concerning getting goods, being good, and good-getting serves both to validate ideas of success and failure that liberate energy and to deny potency to those same ideas when one is assaulted by "the lords of life." This is the relation between the ideas men have on the subject of winning and the Ideas which God may have about the success He enacts of their lives.

Success can provide the tangible something one is able to touch. It is also the intangible feeling that takes possession of one's mind. Mythically viewed, America is the land where streets are cobbled with wheaten loaves or bricks of gold, the place where men know the world applauds their visible value. By habit many Americans have come to assess with disgruntlement their success or failure in terms of a myth they no longer believe has any truth to it. Others prefer to make less skeptical and more satisfactory use of myth even in a demythologized world; they argue that—because our limited experience rarely lets us know the nature of our heart's desire—myth offers a totality of vision which tells us what we are by the image it provides of that desire.

For instance, when we read Lévi-Strauss's words, "The Universe signified long before man began to know what it signified," we can substitute "America" for "Universe" and gain some assurance that America contains the truth of how far we have come in filling out a destiny that is still hidden from our comprehension. Lévi-Strauss says, ". . . it signified from the beginning the totality of what humanity might expect to know about it." We might move even closer to the value of myth if we incorporate Paul Ricoeur's elaboration in *The Symbolism of Evil* upon Lévi-Strauss's argument (cited on p. 168):

This totality, thus signified but so little experienced, becomes available only when it is condensed in sacred beings and objects which become the privileged signs of the significant whole. . . . The Sacred takes contingent forms precisely because it is "floating"; and so it cannot be divined except through the indefinite diversity of mythologies and rituals. (pp. 168-169)

Myths for Ricoeur make clear "the discrepancy between the purely symbolic plentitude and the finiteness of the experience that furnishes man with 'analogues' of that which is signified." Ricoeur reminds us, "If the plentitude were experienced, it would be everywhere in space and time," but since it is only intimated, it requires myth to guard "the finite contours of the signs." These signs in turn "refer to the plentitude that man aims at rather than experiences" (p. 169).

One of the most potent myth-types concerning success is the one which designates a certain country (whether Italy, England, or America) as destined to manifest the gods' success in history. For that place and its people to fail the gods is blasphemy; to attain victory is simple obedience. Under such urgencies myth is used to separate evil (man's failure) from *virtue* (divine acts of creation which supply this word with its original meaning of "power" and its later meaning of "goodness"). Myth is what justifies the ways of gods to man and admonishes men to do the divine will. This is why the special meanings given by the Puritans to "justification" and "sanctification" are also applicable to the mythic stance. Success in America is evidence of God's giving of justification to mankind through Christ's virtue, as well as proof of men's sanctification of that gift through their virtuous thoughts and deeds. If this predestined process can be carried through completely, God, the country, and the people will all fulfill their intent, and "plentitude" is indeed "experienced" "everywhere in space and time."

No doubt Larzer Ziff is correct to emphasize in *Puritanism in America: New Culture in a New World*, his study of the social facts of the New England settlement, that the first group of Puritans did not come to America with many "mythic intentions" in mind. But take an imagination like Ricoeur's (or that of Perry Miller and Sacvan Bercovitch)—one strong on the ordering principles of hindsight and a dramatic sense of affairs. This imagination easily detects the meaning of America, and the beauty of such meaning, in the design which reveals itself in that special kind of history expressed by rhetorical and literary forms. Perhaps the very first group of Puritans did not give excessive thought to fulfilling God's plot concerning their "peculiar" success in America, but later spokesmen did. It is hardly perverse to continue to take up the imaginative lead they thrust upon us instead of feeling limited to the "facts" of the Puritan settlement. Even Ziff acknowledges the weight given to the sense of sacred purpose by the second-generation Puritans. There is a delay in time before the myth of design and destiny gains momentum in America, but once it takes hold it is as if it has always been there to shape what we think of success and failure. Under the terms of this myth America is seen as a *planned* experience; its significance becomes infinite and sacred, though the contingent forms continue to be finite and usually profane. Americans may have come slowly at first to the belief that what they have done and might yet do is exacted by mission. Their motives for coming to this faith may also be highly questionable. Still, the force of that idea—for better or for worse—remains.

Myths of mission have taken many forms in America, proliferating especially during the latter decades of the seventeenth century and the early days of the Republic. Sometimes made upon the spot to explain recent occurrences, they show their haphazard origins and lack of historical logic. They have had to contend with other myths in the process of emerging into favor, all of them jockeying for primacy in the public imagination. The Puritan myth of the sacred mission of theocracy had to be qualified drastically when it ran head-on into subsequent myths of happy colonials and achieved democratic principles. Distinctions insisted upon by the Puritans as the necessary means to the sacred ends become blurred in late eighteenth-century versions of mission committed to mundane ends of politics and economics. In Tocqueville's words, both the elect and everyman were caught in the pull of historical inevitability; moral sheep and goats "have been driven pell-mell along the same road, and all have worked together, some against their will and some unconsciously, blind instruments in the hands of God" (pp. 11-12). The Frenchman defined early nineteenth-century equality as "the sacred character of the will of the Sovereign Master"—that is, the will of the people. In contrast, the Puritans had defended social hierarchies in the name of obedience by all servants to the will of all masters. Shifting the meaning of "master" away from Puritan definitions, Tocqueville's American viewed any "effort to halt democracy . . . as a fight against God Himself." His belief was firm that "nations have no alternative but to acquiesce in the social state imposed by Providence" (p. 12).

In all this it appears to be God (but is it actually?) who commands the voyage and leads the mission. As America moved past earlier myths into new, more modish ones, the single constant was the need to follow a supreme leader, whoever he is—God, the People, the Single Solitary Self. It is as if we were all aboard Melville's *San Dominick* (set within the tale "Benito Cereno"), as beguiled as the good Yankee captain before the ambiguities of who is the sovereign master there—Providence, the Spaniard, or the Negro. It is the same dilemma that shakes the initial calm on the *Pequod* and on Captain Vere's warship: which is the mission and who the leader, and what are the chances for success?

The American—whether seventeenth-century Puritan or nineteenth-century democrat—could envision himself as successful insofar as he fulfilled the general role assigned him by his "Sovereign Master." That he was also a success as a private individual remained unclear. In "The Marrow of Puritan Divinity" Perry Miller rephrases the notion advanced in John Cotton's "Covenant of God's Free Grace" of 1645: ". . . there need be very little difference between the performances of a saint and the acts of a sinner; the difference will be in the aims and aspirations of the saint and in the sincerity of his effort. The proof of election will be in the trying, not the achieving" (p. 83). Only the Master would ever know who was successful, but men of this mind could consider themselves participants in the scheme that brought *Him* success, however uncertain they had to remain about the nature of their own achievements or what benefit they themselves might gain.

Ricoeur's view of myth involves the notion that the sacred design floats abroad in the world awaiting its fulfillment in the finite experience of men. The Puritans were of a generation which lived and acted strongly in response to the sacred purpose that floats just out of reach, in order to make it come solidly into being on God's earth. William James's was a much later generation, far more given to agnostic doubts, but in a letter of 1868 (included in *The James Family*) he makes a remark applicable to the question of how America might go about achieving its missions:

> I have been growing lately to feel that a great mistake of my past life . . . is an impatience of *results*. Inexperience of life is the cause of it, and I imagine it is generally an American characteristic. . . . Results should not be too voluntarily aimed at or too busily thought of. They are *sure* to float up of their own accord. . . . (p. 216)

The Puritans acted to bring "floating" and "results" together, to conjoin "plentitude" and "experience." William James came to ap-

preciate those who accomplished *floating up* through the practice of
the secular virtue of "a long enough daily work at a given matter"
(p. 216). This seemed better to James than that *floating down* which
comes about through providential plans beyond men's power to
control at will. By the end of the nineteenth century the sovereign
master whose mission is to be obeyed was generally located within
a man's mind; the means by which one could give obedience to that
mission were less often willed than stumbled upon. But the sense of
urgency and the obligation to do something well was and is not yet
lost, not as long as success floats forever just ahead—like the green
light at the end of the Buchanan pier that beckons Gatsby toward
his destiny.

In *Moby-Dick* Father Mapple reminds us, "And if we obey God,
we must disobey ourselves; and it is in this disobeying ourselves,
wherein the hardness of obeying God consists" (p. 45). Ahab, who
makes a tragic career of hurtling himself against this hardness,
cries out, "Why this strife of the chase? why weary . . . ?" He laments, "I feel deadly faint, bowed, and humped, as though I were
Adam, staggering beneath the piled centuries since Paradise. God!
God! God!—crack my heart!" (p. 444.) It is indeed bitter to wish to
succeed as oneself—to follow out the narrative of one's own private
myth—and then to be dashed against the myth of God's willed destiny for our lives.

The dilemma of being caught between contending masters
makes finding success a doubtful feat. Perhaps it can be resolved
only by transformations such as Thoreau pictures in a journal
entry of February 1851. There he writes of the primal failure converted into the ultimate success through the recognition that success lies in matching one's idea with God's. Proposing a new variation on the old rhyme from *The New England Primer*, Thoreau adds
magic potion to Calvinist doctrine.

> In Adam's fall
> We sinned all.
> In the new Adam's rise
> We shall all reach the skies.

An infusion of hemlock in our tea, if we must drink tea,—
not the poison hemlock, but the hemlock spruce, I mean,—or
perchance the Arbor-Vitae, the tree of life,—is what we want.
(VIII, 153)

Thoreau continues to suggest the heresies that uptilt old
priorities by transforming the will of the Sovereign Master into the

self's will: America can be viewed as the land promised to us all, not
only as the Land that God promised Himself in order to justify His
purposes and to sanctify His actions; America is the place where
the crucial gap between wills may be closed, not exacerbated, because here what man most desires coincides with the holy will of the
universe, and the efforts required to arrive at cosmic success simultaneously satisfy men's craving for personal triumph.

If all these things could come about, what a difference it would
make in the country's literature! It would be transformed from a
bitter history of contention and failure to a joyous account of reconciliation and success. It would be transformed from the agonistic
to the irenic—from the less-than-perfect form to the best of all possible shapes. But so far we have an *if* which in no way matches the
*is*. As a result, we also have Thoreau's *Walden*.

Literature successfully based on a sense of destiny possesses a
strong sense of form. Henry Adams pointed this out when contrasting the failure of his own account of an aimless education with
the literary excellence of Saint Augustine's record of the movement
from unregenerate self-will to compliance with God's will. Augustine was not only able to use God's plan as the model for the
structure of his own life; in writing out his story he also discovered
the forms needed for the personal narrative of his life's meaning.
But when he came to write the story of man's design for "a better
country" in *The City of God* he concluded that that country and its
capital "whose builder and maker is God" could be found only in
heaven, and that it can be entered alone by those who have dis-
obeyed themselves in this life by keeping fast to their covenants
with God.

In strong secular contrast to Augustine's literary endeavors we
have *Roughing It* by Mark Twain. Throughout this personal narrative we follow the Clever Young Man, frequently on his uppers, as
he journeys deeper into the land of speculation, promises, and
blind-leads. Mark Twain quickly discovers that contracts made out
west are generally worthless; men keep no covenants—with God or
man. It is hardly by coincidence that the frontier world of will-I-
nill-I contributes to the ramshackle structure of Mark Twain's tale
of wandering which is markedly different from the form lent Augustine's prose by the sense of sacred destination. But both men
were writers of confessions and both were bent under the weight of
the meaning of human experience. Augustine could write as he did
because he had had revealed to him absolutely the reality of God's
will for men's lives. Mark Twain wrote as he did because he was

groping for the meaning of success and failure in that area of floating and imagination which is called mythic.

The Adam in America who staggers "beneath the piled centuries" of an idea of victory that damns him if he succeeds on his
own terms and not on God's, and yet damns him if he does not, has
found only two finite forms to fit his purpose. They are the land
and the narrative. But, ironically, these forms are most frequently
used to express the failure of that idea which would, if it could,
transform "floating" plentitude into something grasped solidly by
the hand. These forms give the exiled Adam a strong sense of the
promise and an equally sharp experience of its non-fulfillment.
Augustine's narratives contained the reality of the revealed Truth
of the City of God, while showing how the City of Man responds to
that reality as if it were mere fantasy. But the narratives of Mark
Twain, set in the Territory which entices men with promises of success, countenance neither the Truth nor the myth; they insist upon
the truths of loss and disappointment. Yet both the land and the
narrative form as practiced in America perpetrate what Ahab,
moaning, calls "This strife of the chase." The finite, contingent *facts*
about the American experience which ought to put an end to the
self-destructive nonsense of hope act instead to enhance that which
floats just on the other side of realization—the *idea* that success is a
reality. Thus land and narrative are coerced into bringing that reality into conjunction with the facts of space and time, even though
both land and narrative know better—or think they do.

" 'What have they done?' growls Smelfungas, tired of the subject"—as weary of America as was Thomas Carlyle, the literary
creator of this spokesman in *Latter-Day Pamphlets* of 1850. " 'They
have doubled their population every twenty years. They have be-
gotten, with a rapidity beyond recorded example, of Eighteen
Millions of the greatest *bores* ever seen in this world before,—that
hitherto is their feat in History!' " (p. 21.) By 1850 Herman Melville
was also on occasion peckish about the notion that Americans were
providentially chosen people. He saw that America's soul was still
trying to complete the global circle which whales easily accomplish;
but whales worship the King of Cannibals—Yojo, O Joy!—not
stern Christian fathers, whether called God or George by *The New
England Primer*.

Fantasies and fanaticisms of success satisfied many people in the
early nineteenth century and dismayed a few. Norman Mailer
reads that period as a time when the facts that encouraged move-

ments outward were diverted into inward-turning fantasies; the solid selfhood promised by external achievements splintered into the hero-hallucinations indulged in by the introspective. The next step was to go from fantasy to fanaticism. Men who evolve victory-fantasies in personal terms tend to keep the scope of their images modest. Men who move toward public fantaticism force large bodies of men and acres of land into line with their expanding dreams. Mailer, as much an expert on fanaticism as on fantasy, locates the fanatic's ideal outside himself; it is a projection imaged alternately as God or Devil. Mailer's notion coincides with Melville's definition of the fanatic as one who testifies that he has God's will to fulfill. In a loud voice that carries over the land, the fanatic asserts this conviction even though it may be his own petty will the Devil persuades him to follow.

The religious belief that compelled the Puritans to glorify God as the chief end of man was expressed in the strong, sane logic of the public pulpit. The private assurance that moved the poets of Concord to rephrase the Westminster Catechism in heretical ways was uttered in oracular but still civil language. Even the secular version of the original catechism that preached, "Young man, get rich, go west!" was limited in its shrillness to the 18-point type on posters selling frontier destinies. But there was always the danger that the voices might come from the wrong source to counsel evil plans. Even John Woolman, most modulated of Quaker voices, was troubled at times by his mandate to bring God's concerns in America to a successful conclusion. He was intended, he knew, to be the trumpet through which God speaks His truth, but he sensed that he frequently said more than God asked him to. Those superfluous words—rising unbidden out of his own heart—might well bring about achievements in areas which God forbade.

Whose voice do we follow when we act to bring visions to fruition? Charles Brockden Brown's Wieland thought the voice he heard was God's, but the butchered family that lay in blood at his feet, murdered by his hand, did not make him a blessed parallel to Abraham standing over an Isaac spared. Norman Mailer says we can never be certain whom we follow (though *he* acts at times as if he knew he was God's chosen tongue). Whenever the strong voice of the master of the *Pequod* speaks out about missions to be followed—whether in the name of God, Mammon, or the Devil—it is the subservient citizen from the Isle of Man who heeds the call to destiny and destruction.

Those obedient to the will of fanatics are acted upon by the ideas of those who, in turn, believe they obey higher wills. But (to paraphrase Paul Ricoeur in *The Symbolism of Evil*, p. 212) if we take the tragic view of such a relationship, we see that men are bound to the *spectacle* of certain *facts*, not relieved through *speculations* about certain *thoughts*. An Ahab may be right in his *ideas*, thus noble in his endeavors to gain the successful conclusion of his imagined mission. But no matter his thoughts; as their consequence, the *facts* are tragic: the ship goes down and lives are carried to their senseless end. This is the lesson of life which Ricoeur asserts is brought us by the tragic dramatists and the actors who perform their spectacles: there is no way out of the tragic since all the facts are set against men's chances of winning.

In contrast to the writers and actors of the tragic mode, philosophers and talkers urge us—says Ricoeur—to choose to be saved by ideas that are sacred and to avoid words that are evil. Their way is tricky since the evidence is profoundly ambiguous, but it is a way that could free men from the tragic hedging-around of contingencies. Wieland's terrible fate as told by Brockden Brown is unlike that of Sophocles' Oedipus, if we believe there *is* a God and a Devil to distinguish between, as well as a Carwin. If we believe this, then we can think and choose for ourselves to our own good-getting. But if God is none other than the devilment of tragic fate, or if Carwin's is the one real voice contained within a completely secularized drama, then all we can do is watch the bloody spectacle of facts unfold along the banks of the Schenectady River. The "Wieland dilemma" is only that—a resolvable argument between ideas—when viewed under Ricoeur's terms as open *speculation*. In contrast, there is no dilemma, since no choices are allowed, when the drama insists on being closed and fated *spectacle*.

In the twentieth century Norman Mailer, latter-day Carwin (itinerant ventriloquist, voyeur, and meddler), likes to act as an authority on matters of America's mission. In his writing he works both with modes of speculation and with spectacle; he darts with the speed of dialectic flashes of lightning between free will and fatality. He acknowledges his admiration for the hyped-up Renaissance Man and reluctantly gives respect to the curbed-in American Wasp, both types which he sees as possessed of an invincible sense of destiny. Mailer would himself like to be a man providentially selected to do great things and to say memorable ones. As he projects himself into "the captain" of "A Calculus at Heaven" (the story written when he was twenty, later included in *Advertisements for Myself*), he images a man daily caught up in a personal "Wieland dilemma." As the fictional captain or as "Norman Mailer," Mailer views with mixed emotions of alarm and pleasure the American talent for mission-mongering. He most commonly attacks America as an out-sider would—one who calls himself free of America's own vice of devil-fanaticism. At the same time he knows that by such detach-ment he may lose the benefits of victories apportioned to fanatics. Mailer also realizes he might be denying the trait inborn in him that makes him, if acknowledged, an insider to America's ener-gies, both ugly and fine. To attack America's worst is perhaps to attack himself; to try to save America by staying with its commit-ment (and his) to high mission and dramatic success is to stay with both its best and its worst. A sharp risk surely, but just what he pre-fers since it promises him the dread that adds much to living well.

When Texas-based technicians set up Mission Control to go to the moon, Mailer asked whether their journey of exploration and settlement was more or less noble than that of their New England ancestors. Throughout *Of a Fire on the Moon* Mailer has been argu-ing that only through the force of a sense of mission can successful leaps be made to the stars, as such a leap was once made from the Old World to the New. He also knows that Wasps are bred to serve destiny. The very thing he is arguing both excites and disturbs him. In contrast, the chaplain who contemplates the success of Apollo 11 experiences no such agitation. The sense of dread that is part of the commitment to purpose is found rather in the language which William Bradford once used to meditate upon the meaning of ar-rival at distant places. Here, first, are the words of the chaplain from *Of a Fire on the Moon*, then Bradford's description of the com-ing of the Pilgrims in *Of Plymouth Plantation*:

> Our minds are staggered and our spirits exultant with the magnitude and precision of this entire Apollo 11 mission. We have spent the past week in communal anxiety and hope as our astronauts sped through the glories and dangers of the heavens. As we try to understand and analyze the scope of this achievement for human life, our reason is overwhelmed with abounding gratitude and joy, even as we realize the increasing challenges of the future. This magnificent event illustrates anew what man can accomplish when purpose is firm and in-tent corporate. . . . From our inmost beings, we sing humble, yet exuberant praise. May the great effort and commitment seen in this project, Apollo, inspire our lives, to move similarly in other areas of need. May we the people by our enthusiasm and devotion and insight move to new landings in brother-hood, human concern and mutual respect. May our country, afire with inventive leadership and backed by a committed fol-

lowership, blaze new trails into all areas of human cares. (p. 453)

But hear I cannot but stay and make a pause, and stand half amased at this poore peoples present condition; and so I thinke will the reader, too, when he well considers the same. . . . They had now no friends to wellcome them, nor inns to entertaine or refresh their weatherbeaten bodys, no houses or much less townes to repaire to, to seeke for succoure. . . . And for the season it was winter, and they that know the winters of that cuntrie know them to be sharp and violent, and subject to cruell and feirce stormes, deangerous to travill to known places, much more to serch an unknown coast. Besides, what could they see but a hidious and desolate wildernes, full of wild beasts and willd men—and what multitudes ther might be of them they knew not. . . .

What could now sustain them but the spirit of God and His grace?

In the former passage we have the confidence that supports a well-planned United Way campaign; in the latter, dread—that essential element for the successful experience of life as defined by Mailer and as expounded by the American Calvinist theology; dread—its energy creating finer hopes as well as possibilities of total failure.

Mailer's Provincetown—a stone's throw from the Pilgrims' landing place—is still a place of dread. But the hope is lacking; only the failures are real. Mailer sees it as the unhallowed spot where drugs and divorce are the rule of the summer's day, and where even the great god Ford has to be laid away in burial with solemn but somewhat senseless rituals. Someone failed somewhere in bringing about the true destiny of the land. If only one could now know *which* destiny had been intended and *whose* voice ought to have been heeded! Perhaps the task of defining future missions for America must now be taken over—at the risk of initiating equal follies and fanaticisms in the future—by the non-Wasps, Jews and Blacks; the task put into the care of those currently more capable of expressing dread and ambiguity than is the good chaplain who expounds upon Apollo 11. So Mailer broods by the Pilgrims' rock. Mailer's America is at least still the land where the "Wieland dilemma" makes choices possible—both terrible and saving ones—and provides thoughts that are more valuable than are spectacles.

However much he faces up to his dilemmas (or perversely creates them), Mailer continues to hold faith in a destined future that Americans are meant to choose for themselves. Like Melville, he attends to Lucifer's acceptance of a world of woe; he repudiates the orthodoxy of optimism which would deny the reality of such a world. But Mailer also chooses to believe that the world where the Lucifer of failure reigns also contains a God of success, and that he, Mailer, must act as a double agent to both their causes, threading his way perilously like Stephen Rojack along the parapet of *An American Dream* between getting goods, being good, and good-getting.

Tocqueville concluded that the only enemies Americans had were themselves; they merely needed to will happiness and their successful destiny as a democracy would be achieved. But Henry Adams believed that Americans had to ask the same question put by the early Christians as they wended their anxious way among the lions: "Quo vadis?" Melville disguised as Tommo in Typee Valley or as Ishmael on the *Pequod* could never be certain whose will he ought to accept as his own: the ways of the Cannibal King (O Joy!—or murder) or the ways of the Christian Lord (wrath—or sweetness). Where two opposing dreams meet, crack-ups take place. The counter-currents of Mark Twain's Mississippi—muddy and clear—suggest this, as well as the wish-polarities held in intellectual tension by the men who could be successful (so Scott Fitzgerald said) if they do not first go mad. Well, then, if on the first time through America we pick the wrong way to go or the false voice to heed, why not a second chance?

Archibald MacLeish was berated in 1971 by Walter Kerr of *The New York Times* for "Scratch," his adaptation of Stephen Vincent Benét's *The Devil and Daniel Webster*. Kerr was upset by the naïveté of MacLeish's belief that America is the land of second chances. Such romantic nonsense was one target Mark Twain aimed at in *Innocents Abroad* (the Second Advent to take place in mangy, modern Palestine?) and in several pieces contained in *Fables of Man* (the Second Coming to be manifested anywhere in America?). Henry Adams—the man who inherited idealism and grew up with realism—mixed skepticism about the new America with the vestiges of his romanticism. Fresh opportunities for action constantly keep opening up, Adams noticed jauntily; there are more ways to fail than one's father ever knew about. But however assailed by witty jibes, American romantics have held fast to the faith and assiduously rework imagery of second comings and further chances. Thoreau is only one of the breed which awaits the upspring of hope that wells from Walden, the sacred center of the earth, and from America, the soul of the future.

Urian Oakes's sermon "The Sovereign Efficacy of Divine Providence," delivered in 1677, speaks of God as first cause and all subsequent events as second causes. If we can momentarily assume that America is one of God's created things, Oakes's words may be taken as suggestive of the potential the country contains to fulfill God's purpose:

> That he doth by a previous influx excite and stir up and actuate the active power of the creature, and set all the wheels going. For the most operative, active created virtue is not a pure act, but hath some potentiality mixed in it; and therefore cannot put forth itself into action unless it be set going by the first cause.

America, then, is not the oldest fact in time; it is not so ancient as the chaos and old night out of which it was created by the Ancient of Days. But next in age to the Prime Mover (He whom Oakes designated as "the Lord of time") was the earth, the first *idea* God had—the original creation, the shaped context for human success enacted for His greater glory. Oakes did not wish the minds of his congregation to focus upon America, secondary cause as it was; but eventually, as Perry Miller has shown in "Nature and the National Ego," and Sacvan Bercovitch in his study of the orgins of the American self, this is what American ideas about God's idea came to.

Chances (first or second) in a land viewed as Primary or Secondary Cause require time. America's age must be taken into account. The discovery of the North American continent is of relatively recent calendar date if one compares it to the length of European civilization. This brief span of chronological time is shortened even more when one subtracts the years it took to achieve English settlement and takes into account the further delay before colony became nation. So computed, America has known merely two hundred years of adolescence. But there are other ways than calendars to judge age. In *Miami and the Siege of Chicago* Mailer asks that the question of America's age be gauged in terms of achieved power. If America is ever to "grow up," it has to seize more power, not less. One half of America is a Johnny-come-lately, a greedy Lawrentian infant in bawling contention with the other half—the Wasps who were born old, parsimonious, and "refined

away from the source of much power—infantile violence . . ."
(p. 91).

Gertrude Stein also looks to definitions of power in order to
place America within the world's range of success. Columbus may
have "invented" America in a way that makes the Old World seem
the ancestor to the child, but America has "created" the twentieth
century which Europe is just now inheriting from its parent.
Europe adhered to the narrative form of the Old Testament's "Be-
gat" chapter, which insists that the child obey parental law;
America is the New Testament, which rejects repetition of the Old
Law. This alone does not make Europe "old" and America
"young," but it does make America the first to possess the world as
it now exists. Europe lagging behind the new dispensation is
forever retarded in intelligence, imagination, and power. Nonetheless, Stein decided that if America is mother of the twentieth
century—the best age *to be born into*, this century is not the right age
*to live in*. In "Why Do Americans Live in Europe" of 1928 she explained that she chose the long childhood of France, with its de-
layed entry into modern times. Stein carefully cultivated success
wherever she lived, but it is significant that she felt she could do
better with her chances in an infantile Europe than in an aging
America.

As long as America deals in destinies, it deals with the future
tense. Destiny is what is about to be; it is not yet, not finished. Once
destiny is achieved—all chances (the first and the last)—are gone.
Completeness is the end of chances. The past tense is death. Even
the present tense risks moving too near the edge of what is over
and done with.

It is not surprising that a writer like Stein, who was actively concerned with the grammar of time, should run her remarks concerning verb tenses through a gloss on American success set up in
comparison with English success and the English language. England is the island-nation of daily living, Stein states in "What Is English Literature." At first, with the Elizabethans, words were lively.
Words involved choice about the ways they were to be used: to
serve God through directness and completeness, or to serve mammon when used indirectly, as parts. By the eighteenth century
there was no sharp separation between words viewed as direct or
indirect; where the earlier time *chose* its words, the eighteenth century *had* them. By the nineteenth century the people—given almost
wholly to mammon—*owned* everything, including their words. By
then the English were only interested in *explaining* through literature the separate parts of what they possessed; they were indiffer-

ent to those affirmations which are possible to the people of God who, having completed something, have attained wholeness.

American literature, Stein continues, might superficially seem like nineteenth-century English literature. But it does not live the daily island life; it has no daily telling to contend with. Besides, there is the continued American reliance on *chosen* words: chosen to lie next to one another in order to make clear the separation of the Me from the Not Me. True, American writing is more like the literature of the people of mammon than of the people of God in that it deals with parts, not wholes; but at least the parts are chosen, as they are by the God-people, not owned. The real differences in the literature of America, however, lies in its *future feeling* (the lack of the sense of an ending; the insistence upon continuity) and *the floating paragraph*. What Stein says here reminds one of Ricoeur's likening of myths to what floats the presence of the sacred whole into the midst of lesser contingencies. What Stein suggests gives us an America which is both the "oldest" country and one which, ever floating with future feeling, has yet to use up its first fully chosen chance—the only chance America may ever get. But first it must rid itself of that taint of the "English" desire *to have* and *to own*. Then alone will it rightly possess its entire destiny.

America characterized as future feeling set in motion within a floating paragraph leads one to ask, Will victory go to the tortoise or to the hare—the serene "walker" like Thoreau or a nervous "runner" like Mailer? To ask this is to return to the earlier issue of the relationship between being good and getting goods.

Mark Twain, who contained the personalities of both loafer and climber, was drawn toward the serenity of the Old World in his 1867 trek with the Innocents Abroad; he was also fascinated by the restless get-up-and-go of Yankees like Hank Morgan, though he realized worlds could be blown up as a result. Just as he sensed that the two routes the American could take were those of strife or contemplation, so did Henry Adams. This issue informed the letters exchanged between Adams and his brother Charles in 1869 (included in the Ford edition). Here, Henry's focus centered on America's inability to accommodate the man of thought—contemplative tortoise or banal begonia:

In America there is no such class, and the tendency is incessant to draw everyone into the main current. I have told you before that I mean to be unpopular, and do it because I must do it, or do as other people do and give up the path I chose for myself

years ago. Your ideas and mine don't agree, but they never
have agreed. You like the strife of the world. I detest it and
despise it. You work for power. I work for my own satisfaction.
You like roughness and strength; I like taste and dexterity. For
God's sake, let us go our ways and not try to be like each other.
(1, 160)

By 1889 Henry Adams found American society content with its
economic successes. This observation served to confirm what he believed had become fixed in the American character as early as Jefferson's administration. In his chapter "American Ideals," placed
in the first volume of *History of the United States of America during the
Administrations of Thomas Jefferson and James Madison*, Adams stated
that the American type had achieved exceptional uniformity by
1815. It was the same type Tocqueville singled out when discussing
the American success-idol. The American had but one wish—to
give himself to *well-being* to the exclusion of all else in the name of
"this mother of all desires" (p. 448). Between 1800 (viewed through
Adams's retrospective glance) and 1835 (assessed by Tocqueville
on the spot) nothing had changed the American fervor for the
comfortable life gained largely through careers in trade. "I fear,"
Tocqueville commented, "that the mind may keep folding itself up
in a narrower compass forever without producing new ideas; that
men will wear themselves out in trivial, lonely, futile activity, and
that for all its constant agitation humanity will make no advance"
(p. 645).

Fifteen years later and still no real change. In an address given
on July 4, 1849, entitled "Socialism and Civilization" (included in
*The James Family*), Henry James, Senior remarked, "But suppose
the battle to have been never so successful in a material point of
view, suppose me to have realized any amount of superfluous
potatoes, yet after all how mere a potato-cask do I remain, destitute
of inward pith and riches!" (p. 55.) Potato-cask or folded-up piece
of goods: how impoverished the American; how far forward he
was not surging; how *mere* his rewards for staying put with the
"mother"!

In the generation before the emergence of the Jeffersonian
American, and two generations before the American observed by
Tocqueville and the elder James, John Woolman as a young man
might have seemed your average man of business acumen. But he
was unusual on at least one count. He was troubled over having too
much commercial success. He was that unsettling hybrid: a natural
businessman who is also a man of God—one who is constantly

driven to ask himself if business could be done in the name of love
and service, not out of pride and for profit.

There is, however, one intriguing divergence between the traits
of the successful American noted by Woolman and the type that
Tocqueville defined. Woolman's Quakerism was especially sensitive
to manifestations of "the fierce spirit." He insisted that the man of
business was liable to the wickedness of prideful power, the masculine aggressiveness Tawney and Weber later came to associate
with the competitive capitalist. In contrast, Tocqueville was struck
by the American's blandness, notwithstanding his real devotion to
the competition of the marketplace. No council of humility was
necessary in America, he concluded. "Moreover, I know nothing
more opposed to revolutionary morality than the moral standards
of traders. Trade is the natural enemy of all violent passions. Trade
loves moderation, delights in compromise, and is most careful to
avoid anger" (p. 637). As Tocqueville pictures her, well-being—
"this mother of all desires"—is the calming spirit which sees to it
that her children's wants are satisfied and their aggressions soothed
out of existence. But Tocqueville also remarked, "They are much
more in love with success than with glory. What they especially ask
from men is obedience. What they most desire is power" (p. 631).
Did he detect that the child of well-being demands a strong father
as well as a placid mother?

Henry Adams counseled the readers of his history of Jeffersonian America that Europeans have never understood the New
World mentality. Foreigners tend to notice only the contentious-
ness of men on their way up or the complacency of those who have
made it; they overlook the idealism and sense of mission which
Adams argued had prompted more Americans to action than had
money. But even with Adams's careful reminders that the American urge for well-being is as much of the soul as of the pocketbook,
we, like the Europeans, like to believe that the truth lies nearer to
hand in the examples offered in John G. Cawelti's *Apostles of the
Self-Made Man*.

Cawelti's exegesis of a New Testament devoted to the Bitch
Goddess Success stresses what John Woolman had warned against:
the double pulls of business methods and religious ethics. Cawelti
concludes, as had Woolman, that such pulls continually fail to join
in a common principle of good-getting. The type of American resulting from this unseemly split often seems more stupid than
venal, more bemused than cynical. Still, the self-made American
who has created himself *ex nihilo* forces us to deal with complicating
factors such as luck and Divine Providence, will-pride and compla-

cent conformity, aggressive individualism and political conser-
vatism. Along with social theories drawn unthinkingly from
Franklin, Emerson, Darwin, and Christ, he asks that we admire in
him his likeness to both Simon Suggs and Ragged Dick. We are
made witness to Theodore Dreiser in the act of writing critically in
his novels of the social pressures that destroyed George Hurstwood
and Clyde Griffiths *and* in serving as consulting editor for *Success*,
whose motto declared, "Unceasing struggle in adversity brings ultimate triumph." The self-made man—whose whole-cloth is a
patch of self-contradictions—becomes more than a figment of
Norman Mailer's paranoid fears about the schizoid splits in America's soul; he is the actuality we have to live with.

When Mailer, that exemplary over-achiever, reconsiders David
Reisman's thesis, he states in *Advertisements for Myself* that it is men's
deeds that count, not their moral intentions. Hugh Kenner has
slyly suggested in *The Counterfeiters* that in any society dominated by
fakery, there is no value in effort, only in intention. (It is not
whether a dollar bill is real, but whether it intends to look so that
counts.) But Benjamin Franklin on the frontier of Pennsylvania
during the Indian Wars concurs with Dreiser, Bruce Barton, and
Mailer on the necessity of an ethic of work. Do it first, then pray. Or
at least get the prayers over with before providing the workers
their rum-dole. What matters is to test the immediate situation, to
decide the most difficult thing to be gotten done, then do it before
passing out the pleasures.

Endlessly set up as an example to self-making Americans,
Franklin is better than his reputation; he tried to be good, to do
good, and to get goods; to possess both good-being and well-being.
But sometimes we fall into doubts concerning this secular saint and
the validity of his miracles. We fail to have the faith that one man
might achieve success in the two worlds of providence and mammon at once. Together with Mark Twain (who wittily lists in his little piece "The Late Benjamin Franklin" the reasons "bad boys" detest "good boys" like Franklin), we tend to resent Franklin's almost
arrogant attempt to be so totally a winner. We may even fear that
his attempt actually worked. If we fear this it is because we know
that if ever *one* person in America could do it all, then that success
marks the failure of the Mark Twains among us who can never
manage such wholeness of effort and achievement. And so we turn
in relief away from Franklin toward other more representative
Americans: those who have chosen either to be fully in the world of
getting goods or those who have stayed out of the world in order to
be good.

"I think I would not have put things on quite such a lofty level," George McGovern said after his resounding loss in the presidential race of 1972. In considering what his strategy might be if given a second chance, he concluded, "I would have tried to combine morally sound positions with a greater emphasis on appeals to self-interest." Once, Euclid indulged his contempt for a man who requested a practical use for mathematics. "He wants to profit from learning—give him a penny." But the milieu of the idealist in 300-B.C. Greece is not the same as the one provided the idealist in America, even if Euclid's remark sounds essentially like the stress Franklin placed on self-integrity over self-interest. But would even Franklin be able to make it now? Perhaps Franklin's belief in the success gained through American wholeness is just as anachronistic as that inept idealism concerned with only half of life (with a transmundane City of God set out of time and space—out of America altogether). Unlike Fitzgerald's Jay Gatsby (a self-birthed man who also devised the causes of his own death), Chad Newsome—"Woollett's finest"—sprang out of the Platonic conception of perfection held for him by another: by Marie de Vionnet, both his creator and his victim. Chad is more like Fitzgerald's Dick Diver. Like Dick, Chad "suggested, invented, abounded"; like Dick he is an impresario who gives marvelous parties by seizing occasions "as an opportunity for amusement," leaving "but scant margin as an opportunity for anything else" (xxii, 161). Ultimately both of Fitzgerald's heroes—Jay and Dick—fall low from the heights of well-being. But this is because they are so much a part of the evolving complications of the twentieth century. In 1903 Chad Newsome still enjoys the best of his new century, unconcerned as he is by either Franklin's older ethical standards or Fitzgerald's later existential anxieties. Chad is *in place*; he cannot be dislodged from the embrace of that well-being which is truer mother to him than Mrs. Abel Newsome—fixed fast as *she* is in her tiresome "eighteenth-century" moralities and her ambiguous "nineteenth-century" responses to much money illy gotten.

Chad Newsome will never be "had," as so many American heroes are. He is the supreme type of the man who "has" because he knows exactly where he is—or thinks he does according to his own terms. That Henry James, his commentator, suggests that Chad ultimately has "had it" (because unable to give the correct answer to *where* in relation to the mandate, "And there we are!") may be beside the point. Much depends upon *which* point along the scale a man must be to be a success.

# CHAPTER 13

# In The Nick and Out of It

There have always been Americans—just as "American" as those who pull at the motherly breasts of well-being or who strive to emulate the father in power—who are actively in pursuit of *thought*. Henry Thoreau, Henry Adams, and Henry James are such men.

Henry James grew up (as he put it in *Small Boy*, p. 49), knowing there were three kinds of adult you could become in America: the tipsy, the businessman, or Daniel Webster. Henry and William —the two of their family most put on the line—had lost all business sense (at least in the way of "trade") somewhere between their grandfather (the highly successful "William of Albany") and themselves. They felt exposed in America because set apart from the uniform society built up by inventors, manufacturers, and bankers. Since Henry and William were as little tipsy or Websterian as they were mercantile types, they could hardly claim an American existence in the conventional sense; they were "out of it."

Henry James knew that he and his brothers had fallen from the heights of the grandfather, an Irish immigrant who left a fortune of thirteen millions to descendants who promptly converted their inheritance into leisure and culture, those diversions businessmen in America were not much interested in at that time. In 1870, in *Portraits of Places*, James described the Yankee tycoons of the postwar period, uneasy in their idleness, lean and hard as nuts, chewing tobacco and scanning newspapers on the veranda of the big hotel at Saratoga Springs. In 1904 he found the same type riding to and fro on the trains as salesmen or in closed ranks downtown on Wall Street—still invincibly banal, still impervious to those areas of life where yet another kind of man finds his only success in the ability to use ideas for their own sake, for their own good—not as a means to getting goods.

One of Henry Adams' less admiring observers remarked of him that he thought success meant being given all the consideration due an Adams. But what respect would a business society accord a writer who severely assessed the same system by whose terms he was a failure? Edith Wharton's Newland Archer—who nicely fits into Adams' notion of the helplessness of his own once innocent generation—is told he ought either get down into the muck and work for power or else emigrate. Archer eventually has a brief try at public office under Theodore Roosevelt's direct urging, then is pushed aside into the quiet sponsorship of cultural enterprises while the world of practical force whirls past. What Newland Archer's mother once called, in horror, "trends," make a crack in the old house of her hitherto secure world; Henry Adams saw just such lines of force casting the House of Adams, like that of Roderick Usher, into the dark tarn of historical obsolescence.

The third Henry of this group of out-of-it Americans spoke with characteristic acerbity against the lives of quiet desperation given over to the attainment of well-being. Thoreau even detested the sound of words devoted to rapacity with their Latinate -cious endings. On September 1, 1851 he wrote in his journal that words like *tenacious*, *voracious*, *luscious*, *audacious*, and *avaricious* express:

> the greediness, as it were, and tenacity of purpose with which the husbandman and house-holder is required to be a seller and not a buyer,—with a mastiff-like tenacity,—these *lipped* words, which, like the lips of moose and browsing creatures, gather in the herbage and twigs with a certain greed.

Himself a skilled jack-of-several-trades, Thoreau worried over the paradox that one is forced to give up living in order to get a living. Work brings money and money inculcates habits that, in turn, require a man to use up more time to get more money. America's economic soul could be saved, just as the political soul could "win," only through "losing"—either its western territories, thereby beating the slave-state issue, or all worldly gain, thereby breaking free from time and work.

In his journal of October 22, 1853 Thoreau further condemned the lack of simplicity of lives devoted to commerce, and intimated that to him *they* were "out of it," not he. "No *trade* is simple, but artificial and complex. It postpones life and substitutes death. It goes against the grain." Take ice and the huckleberry as cases in point for life lived with the grain, naturally, uncommercially. The huckleberry can only be gathered freely for immediate eating. Ice is unmarketable. Men break their backs cutting and hauling it from the place of supply toward the place of demand. But they often stop short of getting the slabs into Boston, and the ice molders, then melts—a loss to everyone.

Thoreau once found himself in the unpleasant position of realizing he could become a successful tradesman in cranberries. Just in time, he drew back from the spiritual ruin of getting and spending. Emerson was unhappy that Thoreau had been a failure because merely the captain of berrying parties; Thoreau was uneasy whenever he sensed that he might be too successful as a berry-tycoon. Thoreau never voted; finally did pay his poll-tax so the state could go off and pester someone else; wrote *Walden* while Karl Marx and Friedrich Engels were proclaiming the new dawn of an economics quite different from his. By each of Thoreau's chosen failures to act—those holes he punched in the time-being—he announced his own economy of independence from success inhibited by the temporal and the mundane. To go the way of trade or politics did not signify being in place; it meant being put into place. Going his way promised he might be in the nick, moving on the straight route toward the one destiny intended for him alone. As he confided in his journal of December 5, 1856, "I have never got over my surprise that I should have been born into the most estimable place in all the world, and in the very nick of time too." Time-references for Thoreau included, but went well beyond, the historical moment. He sought the true center in the personal destiny that cuts across all time and space in order to fulfill a fate preordained by the universal laws of success.

Samuel F. B. Morse did not succeed as a "pure" painter devoted to composing historical scenes; he acquired more money as a popular portraitist; he got even more wealth and fame when he became the type of hero America much prefers to the artist—the inventor. The inventor is the kind of American whom Henry Adams depends upon in his history of the early Republic to support his contention that Americans do take some interest in ideas, not merely in money. Yet Adams would have had to admit that such idea-men usually converted their conceptions into cash, unlike Franklin, who frequently gave away his inventions and the unclaimed money his ideas could have brought him. In a variation on Franklin's reluctance to gain materially from his own cleverness, Adams tried to avoid the temptation of allowing his talents to be rewarded by cash. Since the only value ever conceded him by his generation came from academicians, his gestures of refusal were limited to turning down various honorariums from Harvard and Columbia; the American public at large did not even know he was doing a noble thing by those refusals.

Adams' idealism (backed as it was by a private income) constantly had to contend with the realities of money around him. The Wall Street sharks and the gold-bugs seemed to him to win every time, while his own friends dropped, according to his hyperbole, like swatted flies. The equation Adams came to goes this way: usurers (men of cunning) who take will flourish. You know who the usurers are by the fact that they win, and who the intelligent but decent men are by their losing.

Norman Mailer (one of the gold-bug race, Adams might comment contemptuously) says it could possibly go the other way, as when he argues that the genius of Charles Eitel of *The Deer Park* is proved by the making of millions. It looks like the old theological debate between Faith and Works all over again—the particular Puritan version of the chicken-egg controversy that keeps easy conclusions concerning the Protestant Work Ethic off balance by asking which comes first and what is of most value: being or doing. This question prompts the further one: whether the one quality *needs* to be set before the other, either in terms of time-sequence or in the ranking of a man's virtues. Perhaps the impulse to split *being* and *doing* apart is an ignorant and unnecessary act, comparable to saying that the City of Man can never coincide with the City of God, or that the "presence" that floats will never be realized as the "fact" which remains. Since these are precisely the matters crucial to the problem of winning and losing in America, we ought to hear out what has been said by those who always tried to avoid thinking in ignorant and unnecessary terms, even when making observations about an American scene that continually tempts one to do both.

Henry James came to certain conclusions while standing at the top of a hill, looking down through the streets of Old Boston at the new city beyond. In *The American Scene* (pp. 236-237) James found himself viewing the results of the shift from the Puritan passion (which had certainly included in part a passion for virtue) to the single-minded money-passion of his contemporaries. Where once the New Englander placed God's glory first among Matters of Concern, with getting goods relegated to Matters of Indifference, now "active pecuniary gain" was the prime mover of Boston life. So James read the meaning of the early twentieth century: only make "the conditions so triumphantly pay" and all else in life is reassessed as mere scratches "directly treatable with the wash of gold."

In *A Small Boy and Others* (p. 355) James vividly recalled a play he saw as a child. In the plot the young man was led to his downfall by

"the money-monster"—"Le Diable d'Argent." As a boy he had also
overheard the remark that women will do "anything" for jewels,
though he did not know what "anything" might mean (p. 383). One
could say, then, that the Boston James surveyed in 1904 was like
the Whore of Babylon, who had departed from the True Faith in
order to do "anything" and "everything" for money and for power.

It is necessary to take care when moving an observation made by
James in one context across the board into another space. In his
reference to the childhood anecdote given above, he implies the
naïveté of the adults who passed on the gossip about "such women"
as much as he stresses the innocence of the small boy's unawareness
of "anything." Nor does the stage-melodrama about the evil effects
of the "money-monster" on susceptible young men itself escape
sharing in the childish simplicity of the audience. James's remarks
addressed from the Boston hilltop in *The American Scene* about the
decline from virtue to greed are delivered in a tone altogether different from that used to heighten the tidbits from *A Small Boy and
Others*. But we have to ask whether James stands tarred by his own
brush in *The American Scene*—guilty there too of a naïve response to
those who *do*, and who do for motives of money; guilty of responses
of the kind he had chided "children" for holding in his other book.
Or is not James, as he stands overlooking Boston and its past, indicating that a relatively simple distinction can be made between
being (virtue) and doing (acts that do not necessarily follow the line
of the virtuous)?—a distinction that is yet free of the simplistic approach to absolute good and evil characteristic of the childlike and
the childish?

In *The Education of Henry Adams* the author-spectator observes
that Americans do not know how to "worship" money. Unable to
hoard it as Europeans do, they only waste money out of an
"atheism" which makes it impossible for them to believe in money
as the Prime Mover of existence. Adams seems to suggest, through
his complex definitions, the basic split (the same one James and
Mailer recognize) which makes Americans both money-mad and
mad for the ideal. America's dollar bills do, after all, contain the
ambiguous Messianic message, *Novus Ordo Seclorum*.

The common response is to remark how fine if the two halves of
the American character might be rejoined, but isn't it a pity they
never do? That depends upon what is meant by joining the breach.
In *The Age of Energy* Howard Mumford Jones furnishes evidence
for the American possibility of being two kinds of person lodged
in one body. During the late nineteenth century, Jones argues, the

dominant trend in the business world was a movement away from
the predatory acquisition of money and toward the thoughtful use
of it for public service. Mailer speaks to this same phenomenon
somewhat more cynically in *Of a Fire on the Moon* when he characterizes the turn-of-the-century capitalist as a mass of contradictions
held in balance within one self-satisfied mind. Beneficence and
rapacity *do* go together (as anyone can testify who has grown up
with the Mason Glass Jar and is aided by direct experience of what
it meant to live in "Middletown"—rather than having to rely on
Robert and Helen Lynd's sociological data about that almost mythic
place deep in the heart-land of Indiana). Duality will always be
Mailer's thrust, as it was Adams', just as ambiguity is the darling
explanation of Henry James for similar phenomena. The Jamesian
ambiguity or the Mailerian duality is different from the polarities
described by Cawelti in *Apostles of the Self-Made Man*. To Mailer the
human contradictions that urged the blunt-faced Andrew Carnegie to give libraries and take steelers' blood have been replaced
by blandly faceless corporations that neither smack their lips over
Thoreauvian *-cious* words nor succor widows and orphans. Splits
(healthy to the extent that they signal a *human* being, however
diseased) are replaced by the unity of zero (impervious to sickness
because a machine, not a body). Splits bring lively dread along with
their flux; fixed polarities tend to establish apathy and inertia.

In "What Is English Literature" Gertrude Stein continued to
work out what it means to serve god or mammon. Those who *read*
(one form of "religious" observance) do not need to *run* (a ritual of
mammon-worship) toward what is outside themselves. The reader
and the thinker is filled; is complete inside. When the inside is kept
separate from what is outside, there is no confusion between god
and mammon. The Elizabethans managed this saving separation,
this divinely ordained dualism, but by the nineteenth century
people had become confused between inside and outside. But not,
Stein says, Henry James. James is the type she singles out (among
those treated in *Four in America*) as the man who avoided serving
mammon because he did not live by what someone else has earned
and thus he was not bewildered over what he himself could do well
as a reader and a thinker.

It was because he was an American, not an Englishman, that
James knew what he was up to. Stein states in her "portrait" of
"Henry James" that with James she has the fine example of a man
who does what he does willingly, freed from being harassed into

earning or giving in to bribes. Her view of James acts as a rephras-
ing of Thoreau's question, "How do you like what you have?" Stein
praises James as the man of genius, the true American, possessed
of movements lively enough to be a thing-in-itself-moving—so
lively, in fact, she notes James did not even need to move *against*
something. With this special ability, "the American" does not have
to run to find completion outside himself as do mammon-idolators;
he is a self-sufficient prime-mover—himself god-centered.

Actual Americans—in contrast with the "real Americans" described by Stein, Adams, Thoreau, or James—are often runners,
hot on the trail of well-being, money, and, especially, power. Power
as Emerson defined it is being able to land on your feet like a cat.
But power defined as reaching forth and grabbing things out there
in the world was beyond Emerson. A college friend fingered Emerson's skull, looking for "the bump of ambition"; when the right
bump was located it was found to be "very very small." Without the
bump you may land cat-like, but you tend to come down where you
began; with ambition, landing moves you several strides up the
road toward your goal.

Like Emerson, Adams also lacked the right omens for power. As
a young man his handwriting was analyzed for clues to his character; it was pronounced to be markedly detached. To be detached
means not to be at the center of energy; it is to be "out of it." This
fact hurt Adams deeply. In a letter of July 9, 1880 to Henry Cabot
Lodge (cited in Ford's collection) Adams insisted that men ought to
seek "occupation," not "objects" if they wish happiness, but he
knew that Washington, D.C.—the City of Man for which he had
been "educated"—was the object of his craving. He wanted to be at
the controlling center of its power, but he was not the man able to
go for "openings" (1, 324). Penetration (almost sexual in Adams'
phrasing) could send, Adams said, a man to hell as easily as it had
Blaine and Butler.

Adams' contemporary, Theodore Roosevelt, had the bump of
ambition, the proper handwriting, and the ability to land ahead on
down the road that portends success. Roosevelt also encircled his
solid talents with a magic talisman. Grasping a ring that contained a
strand of hair taken from the head of the assassinated Lincoln, he
went forth with confidence to his inaugural ceremonies. Looking
out over Washington, D.C. from the powerless periphery where *his*
writing-hand had placed him, Adams could have noted that really
strong types like U. S. Grant need no tokens like the hair of dead
men; Grant was so self-contained he was able to go to a costume

ball dressed as himself. But, then, as Adams recognized—reeling back in dismay at such a thought—Grant was so special a man because he was already extinct.

Mailer, like Adams, believes that the effect of moving into central positions of force can drain one of all energy. Adams watched John Hay die of the strain of having to give too much of himself; he realized that if power corrupts, it also depletes. But Mailer and Adams both crave the thing whose getting they fear. Particularly in his early writings, Mailer dotes on power-at-the-top as he plays out various summit-fantasies concerning presidents and leaders of the Soviet, even though, like Adams, he often images himself as the Court Fool. At least that role moves him nearer the throne. If Mailer wants the salvation which having power might deny him, he will work for power while he is waiting for that salvation.

The Puritan desires both the precious crumb dropped from the Communion Table and the good things sent by Mammon. Thoreau rebukes the hunger that lips at life with words ending with -cious; he is also the man Emerson said asks for whatever is the "nearest" at the dinner-table. Mailer admires the fact that only hungry fighters win knockouts, and it is difficult for Adams to conceal his appetite for power. At times it looks as if Americans only get two choices—"cannibalism" that consumes things of the world, and the "christian" asceticism that feeds on spirit alone. But mightn't they be ravenous enough to win at having both?

Failure is not merely the lack of success. Failure possesses traits particularly its own and calls down judgments more drastic than the praise accorded to victory.

Henry Adams, self-styled connoisseur of failure, remarked to Elizabeth Cameron on December 28, 1891 (a letter included in part in Samuels' *The Major Phase*, p. 79) that he remained reverently on his knees before achieved perfection. He acted as a judge of "only what is not good." Such judgments carry with them the duty of assigning a "right cause." The judge cannot merely describe the failure; he must make an effort to account for it.

Failure becomes a moral issue the moment it entails both an objective study of cause and the judgment of consequences. Why, for instance, was one of the men in Mark Twain's unfinished tale "The Refuge of the Derelicts" (included in *Fables of Man*) a failure in all he set out to do? "Governor" Garney is described as an Emersonian type who first tried to be like Benjamin Franklin, then like Mary Baker Eddy. Perhaps his failure lay in his not being what he was

meant to be, in his failure to find his own "nick"—the true placement of his character.

Adams had a different reason for his failure. He knew what he
was meant to be—an Adams, but he had come into this privileged
place out of the nick of time. When you are "of age," Adams wrote
his brother Charles on February 20, 1863 (letter found in Ford, 1,
94), you can do whatever you please; or so your father, the Chief,
always tells you. By implication if you do not fit the era you live in,
the world will do with you what it pleases.

In yet a third instance, a letter of 1868 by William James (from
*The James Family*, p. 215) suggests a way to be well in place and in
time. James declared that he intended to make "my *nick*, however
small a one, in the raw stuff the race has got to shape, and so assert
my reality."

We have just seen three examples—two failures and one possible
success: to reach out fumblingly for the wrong destiny (Mark
Twain's Garney); to accept the bad luck of not having one's true
character coincide with the times (Adams); to make, shape, assert
one's destiny on the spot, thus assuring a proper fit (James).

Thoreau would seem to be like William James in such matters;
he obviously valued the asserted life. A crucial distinction separates
the two men, however. Whereas James stressed the *creation* of one's
nick, implying an *ex nihilo* event, Thoreau's acts were based on the
self's demand for the personal fate that already lies in waiting as
one of the laws of the universe it is each man's duty to discover and
to obey.

But if the two men differed in the cause, the source, of successful
destiny, Thoreau and William James had much in common in the
way they viewed the failed man as the one "ill-at-ease" with the
world. On April 4, 1839 Thoreau wrote in his journal, "The atmosphere of morning gives a healthy hue to our prospects. Disease is a sluggard that overtakes, never encounters us." For
Thoreau, as for James, health is associated with efficient doing,
with good getting, while sickness is a falling away, the failure to do
the good thing at the best moment.

> We have to start each day, and may fairly distance him
> [disease] before the dew is off; but if we recline in the bowers
> of noon, he will come up with us after all. . . . In the morning
> we do not believe in expediency; we will start afresh, and have
> no patching, no temporary fixtures. The afternoon man has
> an interest in the past; his eye is divided, and he sees indiffer-
> ently well either way.

The failure is the afternoon man who does not use the "right" time; lagging behind, he finally falls back to where the "wrong" time lies in ambush.

Frank Kermode says success is a matter of consequences—what happens as the aftermath to our present acts. Angels, he writes in *The Sense of an Ending* (p. 86), have no heed for success, since they exist out of time, in *aevum*. Human success (or failure) results from choices made now and results enjoyed (or suffered) later in the "hurly" and the "burly"—those two elements which make up the complex facticity of our lives. However much he was the idealist, Thoreau refined on Kermode's definition and did not seek to deny it. The 1839 journal entry cited above is not a record of the intention to escape time in order to live angelically in *aevum*; it was Thoreau's insistence on the need for time—the right time, the present time. Given the choice between an angel which does not know success or the man capable of either success and failure, Thoreau chose to make himself the man of dawn time.

Of course, Emerson liked to think that "Every man is an angel in disguise, a god playing the fool." In this journal entry of January 14, 1835 Emerson is stressing failure of identity, not the dilemma of whether one exists in *aevum* or the hurly-burly. Anyone in the full health that comes from knowing who one is, in time, is a divine being; there is no necessary distinction between angels and mortals. The weak are gods playing the fool; they do not fit the occasion. As Emerson wrote in his essay "Power," such minds are not "parallel with the laws of nature. . . ." For example, take Edward Everett, as Emerson does in his journal of April 1835. "He is not content to be Edward Everett, but would be Daniel Webster. This is his mortal distemper." Emerson is recounting what he had just seen at a ceremony in Lexington as Everett and Webster sat on a platform before the public gaze:

> Daniel Webster, Nature's own child sat there all day & drew all eyes. Poor Everett! for this was it that you left your own work, your exceeding great & peculiar vocation, the desire of all eyes, the gratitude of all ingenuous scholars—to stray away hither & mimic this Man, that here & everywhere in your best & unsurpassed exertions, you might still be mere secondary & satellite to him, & for him hold a candle? (v, 33)

To compound the irony, Webster—the man for whose sake Everett forsook his own true nature and failed—was also driven by the same demon to be other than he was. Emerson's journal of

1842 records the sad metamorphosis. "Pity that he was not content with being Daniel Webster, but must be a President also" (VIII, 327).

The Greeks might call this desire to be someone else *hubris*; Christians would link it to Satan's sin—the prideful craving to vacate one's destined position in the God-given scheme. Emerson and Thoreau saw the act in more appropriately American terms: when the New Adam failed to live in his rightful nick, he re-enacted the fall of the Old Adam at the insistence of the Old Nick that crouches, whispering, within the inner ear. The Old World, thereby, takes its revenge upon the envied paradise of the New World. If America has failed its chances, all else must also fall out of place.

The Jameses—father and second son—pondered the causes of failure which are similar in nature to those defined by Thoreau and Emerson. In *Notes of a Son and Brother* (pp. 277-278) Henry James remembers his father's account of an Albany man he had known in his youth. Frustrated when the girl he loved was denied him by her father, Matthew Henry W. sought revenge by marrying "a stout and blooming jade . . . absolutely nothing but flesh and blood." Although he immediately realized his error, he stuck by his commitment, escorting his new wife about while "Everybody stood aghast." Falling deep into poverty, his legs crippled, and forced to call for police protection against his wife who beat him though he refused to strike her back, Matthew Henry W. was "always superior to his circumstances, met you exactly as he had always done, impressed you always as the best-bred man you knew, and left you wondering what a heart and what a brain lay behind such a fortune." His original love died young and horribly of small-pox, but Matthew Henry W. kept his charming manners and undaunted eye until his death. "I never knew his equal," wrote the elder James with far more sympathy than rebuke, "for a manly force competent to itself in every emergency and seeking none of the ordinary subterfuges that men so often seek to hide their imbecility. I think it a good basis. . . ."

The elder James carefully noted the errors made by Matthew Henry W. and the grave consequences which resulted; but he also pointed out the special courage with which such types as Matthew bear responsibility for the failures they have urged upon themselves. His son Henry also eyed the sad waste which comes from being misused. As he enumerates in *A Small Boy and Others* the plenteous, picturesque, but pointless deaths of the young men and women within his own family circle, he acknowledges the failures

such unused lives constitute. But Henry James extended the meaning of failure from the bad (*something* wasted) to the worst (*nothing*
there to waste). "It wouldn't have been failure to be bankrupt, dis-
honoured, pilloried, hanged; it was failure not to be anything."
*That*, John Marcher finds out, is the most terrible of fates. But,
after all, the point James makes with Marcher in his tale "The Beast
in the Jungle" is that Marcher's is the unique failure. The commonplace of American failure continues to revolve around the
misuse of the something which one has got—whether the cause of
the fault lies in the self or "in the country."

In *The American Scene* James refers to those persons who have
been unable to "make it" in America and so have gone to live in
Europe. He also notes the frustrated middle-class which remains
behind, misplaced between the upper and lower classes that have
made a place for themselves. In contrast, the entire population of
the American South is in place but out of time. After the Civil War,
Mark Twain angrily maintained that the South became a crashing
failure because it continued to linger behind with dreams of
feudalism. More calmly and perhaps more perceptively, James devotes important chapters in *The American Scene* to a similar study of
the consequences of the deep-seated folly of Southern consciousness that manifested itself with the War of Rebellion.

Had all those young Southerners died, James muses ironically, so
that the survivors might suffer bad service from emancipated
Negro servants? The grievous error of living out of time in a
dream-world cast the South into a wasteful, terrible war. As a result, still more waste, more folly, more dire things to come in the
future. Failure leads to further impotence, the gyre never ending.

Failure is not merely the inability to be something in a time and
in a place that fits the person's idea of himself. The idea held by that
person and the fact lying beyond the self must also match—else the
failure is complete.

The early Puritans who wrote biographies of their illustrious
men delighted in recording the successes confirmed by death-bed
pronouncements (as in this instance included in Miller and
Johnson's *The Puritans*). Increase Mather told with pride what his
father Richard said "The very morning before he died." "*I see*
(saith he) *I am not able, yet I have not been in my Study several dayes, and
is it not a lamentable thing that I should lose so much time?*" Three
hundred years later all Robert Lowell can report in "Terminal
Days at Beverly Farm" about the elder Lowell is that he said at the

time of his death, "I feel awful." In "91 Revere Street" and the poem "Commander Lowell, 1887-1950," also from *Life Studies*, we get the further sad story of the father who, having come "of age" on the Yangtze River at nineteen, had nowhere to go after that. It was downhill all the way. Even the names of the family automobiles—Hudson, Buick, Packard—were a testimony to his defeat as they declined in dignity from "ascetic, stone-black" through "plump brown" to "custom-designed royal blue and mahogany," the latter car as subtle a statement of the descent into failure as the still later "little black *Chevie*"—"sensationally sober."

Failed nerve and "feeling awful" is what T. E. Hulme attributed to the Romantics in general. Their "split religion" left them crying over it, and their defeat was assured. But is there something in certain people at certain points in history that makes them lose their nerve, thus fating them to be losers? David Bakan asks this crucial question. So did Bruno Bettelheim after he witnessed millions of fellow Jews marched off to extinction in the Nazi camps in what has looked to some like the massive failure of an entire race. Others ask whether blacks are born to be victims. Robert Lowell writes a poem for *Notebook* (pp. 169-170) about the failed lives of Coleridge and Richard II, then comments:

> White glittering inertia of the iceberg—
> it was a comforting fancy that only blacks
> could cherish enslavement for two hundred years;
> most negroes in London had onward looking thoughts
> by 1800, moved farther from the jungle
> and reveries of kings, than Coleridge,
> the poet who blamed his failure on himself.

One could decide from these lines that Lowell has folded irony within irony; that he is, in part, chastising blacks for their habit of placing blame on others "out there" while that exemplary self-denigrating Anglo-Saxon, Coleridge, knew that the fault lay in him, not "in the country." If so, is this subtle attack a variation on the Wasp way of condemning whiners and bleeding hearts both, viewing the latter as the true failures since they prefer to believe that outside circumstances are what destroy the inside self? Let Gertrude Stein—who liked to demand the last word anyway—speak to this last point. If the outside puts your value upon you, she writes in *The Making of Americans*, and your inside thereby gets to be the outside, then you fail. Your fault? Perhaps, but Stein is not the sort to press home judgments. Wherever the guilt goes, the *cause* seems clear, just as it was for Thoreau, Emerson, and James: you are not *where* you are supposed to be (in this case, *inside*); you are not doing what you are meant to be doing at that special time provided only for you.

If to be *inside* is the moral crux, then to be *outside* can crucify. But even if one acts to hold true to the destiny within, the various forms of Not Me out there can still take their toll. The spiral of the self seems inevitably to move from the inside center to the farthermost reaches; from self to "the others," and from "the others" on to still greater forces of luck or fate. *Out there*, where inside gets muddled up with outside, control may be lost and Whirl becomes king.

# CHAPTER 14

# Fate, Will, and
# the Illusion of Freedom

Mediocrity can seem flat as fate. The extraordinary, in contrast, jumps about and looks like chance. In the minds of those Americans who are most actively against living on bland plateaus, the flatlands is where the real anxiety begins. But the same men who desire the extraordinary often want the benefits of cause-and-effect orderings, not an erratic world of random events.

Henry Adams would not rest until he went back behind all events to learn their purpose. In their day Emerson and Thoreau had less urgency to know why since they believed that through strong character and will men could overcome all obstacles. If one is *capable* of winning, no matter the enemy, it is not as important to know the nature of that enemy as it was for Adams, for whom success and failure were far more problematic. All paths but your own belong to fate, Thoreau said in *Walden*; to tread along the line of your own destiny makes you free. The superior man is the wind; the common man the grass. Each man has the choice either to record what *happens to* him (failure) or to mark how he has *happened to* the universe (success).

Thoreau, like Emerson, believed in the fact of fate, but wished to think he was its controller. It was the notion of luck that each man rejected—that impudent force other Americans liked to claim as their special property, thinking it would always come supported by the adjective "good." In his journal of February 1, 1852 Thoreau wrote: "Going to California. It is only three thousand miles nearer to hell. I will resign my life sooner than live by luck." In "Demonology" Emerson also decried a life lived in the "California" shadow of "Coincidences, dreams, animal magnetism, omens, sacred lots. . . ." Since all men are born equally, sharing the same universal law, it is folly to believe that some live by luck, good or bad, which singles them out in advance for special treatment. And how could the triumphant will of men whose choices amount to something exist in a world which would govern them by occult means? That world Emerson described as follows:

'T is a lawless world. We have left the geometry, the compensation, and the conscience of the daily world, and come into the realm of chaos or chance and pretty or ugly confusion; no guilt and no virtue, but a droll bedlam, where everybody believes only after his humor, and the actors and spectators have no conscience or reflection, no police, no foot-rule, no sanity,— nothing but whim and whim creative.

Chance, no; the right use of fate, yes. Emerson took up the argument in his poem "Success." He declares, "One thing is forever good;/That one thing is Success." It is success that is "Dear to the Eumenides,/And to all the heavenly brood." In the essay "Fate" Emerson wrote that though this force is everywhere, each man is equally part of it.

. . . seeing its immortality, he says, I am immortal; seeing its invincibility, he says, I am strong. It is not in us, but we are in it. It is of the maker, not of what is made.

With Emerson's words we are back with Gertrude Stein's attempt to distinguish between *inside* and *outside* and her question concerning *what* contains *whom*. Like Stein, Emerson came in time to believe that success means holding oneself inside oneself—being part of the fate that is itself held tightly within the Law.

"All successful men have agreed in one thing," Emerson wrote in "Power":

. . . —they were *causationists*. They believed that things went not by luck, but by law; that there was not a weak or a cracked link in the chains that join the first and last of things. A belief in causality, or strict connection between every pulse-beat and the principle of being, and, in consequence, belief in compensation, or that nothing is got for nothing,—characterizes all valuable minds. . . .

The earliest settlers in New England had in Emerson's view "valuable minds." They had believed in a special Providence by which God could, and did, directly show His power in the world by saving the godly and punishing the wicked. As an example of this, the year is 1666, the town is Marshfield, Massachusetts, the recorder of the remarkable event is the Reverend Samuel Danforth (and the immediate source is Dorson's collection, *America Begins*):

. . . a certain woman, sitting in her house (some neighbors being present) and hearing dreadful thunder cracks, spake to her son and said, "Boy, shut the door, for I remember this time four years we had like to have been killed by thunder and lightning." The boy answered, "Mother, it's all one with God whether the door be shut or open." The woman said again, "Boy, shut the door." At her command the boy shut the door. But immediately there came a ball of fire from heaven down the chimney and slew the old woman (whose name was Goodwife Phillips), and the boy, and an old man, a neighbor that was present, and a dog that was in the house, but a little child that was in the arms of the old man escaped. And a woman with child being present was sore amazed.

Seventeenth-century Americans might not have been as serene about living so near the reach of providential power as Emerson thought, but at least they believed that the fates imposed upon them by a transcendent God had a purpose. Eventually we arrive at the world of Herman Melville—coincident in time with Emerson's, but placed elsewhere in terms of man's vulnerability to chance occurrences. A Melvillien man may lean idly against the window-sill in "Bartleby," smoking his pipe on a lovely summer's evening, only to be struck dead by a random, whimsical bolt sent down from the demonic world Emerson rejected for being "the realms of chaos or chance and pretty or ugly confusion."

However cheerfully Henry Adams accepted the fact of his own day and world, Adams believed he had been fatefully dealt a special hand of cards at birth. "Metternich," "Patience," and "Napoleon at St. Helena" were the names of the actual card games Adams especially liked to play. In his own fated game of existence, he was meant to wait like Napoleon, to offset losing streaks by means of the diplomacy of Metternich, and to make high use of patience all around.

Even more than Adams, Mark Twain demonstrates how far one can move away from Emerson and Thoreau, not only in the terms by which a man lives in a world of fate or chance, but in his attitude toward that world. Samuel Clemens was born lucky, but this did not negate the fact that the universe seemed to be ruled by a malign force. Mark Twain eventually decided that all he had done—the "good" things, as well as the "bad," the "successes," as well as the "failures"—had been predetermined. None of it was really his own doing. He had come in with Halley's Comet and gone out with it. Truly he was a random flash in the pan, not a divine spark guided purposefully by the benevolence of Divine Providence.

The general pessimism of such conclusions characterize the end of Mark Twain's life. However, even in *Roughing It* (a young man's book), he assumes guilt for not having taken advantage of the lucky chances that kept coming his way in the mining camps. When a man, however playfully, stresses at the start his responsibility for guilt and then later emphasizes his lack of responsibility (with feelings of guilt still present), that man is defining doom as the structure of life. One is damned if one does act freely and damned if one does not, as Huck Finn knows to his own sorrow.

When we look back along America's history from settlement to the present, it is too simple to decide that in the beginning America rested in the omnipresent, omnipotent palm of the Lord, who guided its success and failure; or to state that by the early 1800's man's will had become the main force; or to conclude that—by the latter half of the nineteenth century—fate, and possibly chance, were the malign masters of America. By the same reason, it is also unjustified to insist that by 1900 most Americans clearly admitted the sad truth of Henry James's description of what had them at its beck: "the hungry triumphant actual" and "the cold Medusa-face of life." All around, relatively few were paying attention to William James's acknowledgment (mentioned by Perry, p. 171) of "the prima facie rebelliousness of the world of facts." Living cheek to jowl with the doubts and unease of Adams, Mark Twain, and the Jameses was Horatio Alger, with his devout belief in the good rewards of a good Providence. (Even Henry James had moments when he said of William in *Notes of a Son and Brother*, p. 15, what Alger believed to be the case of his Ragged Dick: "Occasions waited on him, had always done so, to my view. . . .") Many Americans of the time gladly accepted a world in which good luck and a beneficent fate handed them deserved rewards. In *The Armies of the Night* Norman Mailer sees America's middle-class still being carried along by the momentum it gains from its belief in "one such fierce element of the fantastic" (p. 223). Luck caused by virtue is less important now than it was to Alger, but luck—Lady Luck—is another of the faces of that female by which America continues to embody itself.

William James was no Horatio Alger, but by acting *with* the grain of his temperament, not against it, he came to terms with fate. A letter of January 1868 (included in *The James Family*, p. 212) gives his definition of the need to accept one's type—imposed "like the curl of your hair" from external sources. By 1907 James had learned to require more than acceptance. In *Pragmatism* (in a passage included in *The James Family*, pp. 237-238) he wrote that the forthright man *"trusts* his temperament." He recognized that the great man is one of "strong temperamental vision," one "positively marked," who seeks to make use of what is his own. Still, James always envied those "well-constructed whelps who travel on their free-will and moral responsibility. . . ." "What solidity the web of their life has," he wrote Thomas Ward in October of 1868 (the letter included in Perry's study, p. 111). "On purely materialistic principles they are the greatest success of any of us, the most susceptible of happiness. . . . To measure yourself by what you strive for and not by what you reach! They are a superb form of animal. . . ."

Like many American qualifiers of idealism, William James recognized that the animal type (whether four- or two-footed) enjoys success in ways consistently closed out to "the erect man." If Emerson said success means landing on one's feet when dropped from a height, Mark Twain knew that only cats do this really well. The cat is "the only creature in heaven or earth," he wrote in "The Refuge of the Derelicts" of 1905-1906, "that dont have to obey *somebody* or other, including the angels. . . . He is the only independent person there is." But William James, at least, preferred working out his fate as a man, even if it slew him.

In this choice William James was joined by his brother Henry. *William*: we must fight as if this were a real fight over which we have some control, even if we do not. *Henry*: (via Lambert Strether in *The Ambassadors*): ". . . for it's at the best a tin mould . . . into which, a helpless jelly, one's consciousness is poured—. . . . Still, one has the illusion of freedom . . ." (XXI, 218). There is, however, a different stress in the way the James brothers viewed the efficacy of will. William insists upon *would*; Henry upon *could*. This distinction becomes part of Milly Theale's perceptions on the day she learns for certain that she must die even though she wishes to live:

> . . . she saw once more . . . those two faces of the question between which there was so little to choose for inspiration. It was perhaps superficially more striking that one could live if one would, but it was more appealing, insinuating, irresistible, in short, that one would live if one could. (XIX, 254)

In *The Wings of the Dove* Henry James was interested in something other than the "superficial"; he wished to dramatize what is appealing and irresistible, however tragic. As a philosopher of pragmatism, William stayed closer to the superficial of *would*; his brother required the tragic "tributes to the ideal" of *could*.

Only stray from that level of popular culture where people like the thought of being lucky, or avoid the willed-hope of William and Henry James, and you come to Henry Adams and his circle, who were the self-chosen spokesmen for pessimism. Not wide-eyed luck (alert and innocent), but "blind luck" hounds Clarence King from cradle to final disaster; King—the man whom John Hay had described as the one man who had had everything in his favor, the one man whom Adams hoped might succeed at gaining great wealth without the use of corrupt means. In the narrow social and cultural corner of American life inhabited by Adams, thought was honored; but thinking is what he knew best as having little efficacy in a world of iron determinism. Popular notions might insist upon every American's free choice of his destiny, his mastery of fate, and his possession of the only luck there is—good luck, but the men of science generally conceded that choice was not free, even for Americans. The physical laws of the universe on view by the end of the nineteenth century would never be overturned to give America a miraculous waiver from obedience to the facts.

In *The American Scene* (p. 326) Henry James observed the crucial division between the stand made by the Constitution concerning equality of opportunity in America and the lie given the Constitution by the actions of both nature and technology. The American majority might be shocked by the allegations voiced by devilish eastern intellectual elite types such as James and Adams, but there they stood: the subversive notions that thought is the discovery of weakness, not the disclosure of power, and that the Constitution, the most perfect legal design set down by the mind of man, is no guarantee of protection against the patently "un-American" forces of the physical universe.

In the twentieth century arguments over fate and free will are still lively, and the tentative answers just as hard-won. History, culture, and chance rule the new century, Norman Mailer decides in *The Presidential Papers*, together with the old magic of "totem and taboo." In *The Prisoner of Sex* Mailer concludes that males are born with the luck of force their sex gives them, but because they have not earned that force guilt comes to them as a matter of course. In *The Armies of the Night* Mailer argues that we may try to will ourselves to be at important places in order to achieve our fated greatness, but accidents intervene to prevent us from being there "in the nick." We obey the shape of our character, Mailer says, and character is fate, as almost everyone agrees but especially that part of Saul Bellow who speaks through Augie March. The self which is merely mundane is caught up by circumstances, but the transcendent self wills as it chooses. For this very reason Bellow, as glossed by Helen Weinberg in *The New Novel in America*, asserts that the free self takes care not to achieve its aims; in order to gain success of being, the hero must choose to stop short of perfect action. Another observation by Bellow: in this world of fatality we struggle between two further choices—to be great or to look it. *Being great* is reality, even if you exist in the world where *looking great* seems the only evidence. In contrast, looking great when you do not yet know whether greatness is your particular fate is mere vanity.

Mailer, Bellow. Let us conclude with Gertrude Stein. She believed in fate of a whimsical, creative kind. Picasso claimed he created her by the act of painting her portrait. She might not have looked like his painting just then, but she would, he promised; and she did. If Stein believed in art as fate, and Mailer insists upon style as character, and Bellow suggests that character is fate, and all had hunches about fate as luck, where are we?—caught on the age-old wheel of which comes first: character, fate, luck, or style. Whatever the reality is, one thing remains: "Still, one has the illusion of freedom. . . ."

When whirled on such gyres it is best not to become too dizzy. As Emerson suggested during his 1862 lecture "Society and Solitude," if one finds oneself doing an equestrian act, try to "leap from horse to horse but never touch the ground," "like vaulters in a circus round." We need *to use* what might destroy—the facts of fate, chance, and circumstance. This requires great style or it will not work. But that perfect balance seems possible only in, say, the silent films of Buster Keaton. In *Outlines of Cosmic Philosophy* (III, 334) John Fiske said that when men's desires come into "proximate equilibrium with the means of satisfying them," their best dream will be realized. Perhaps it is only in *true dreams* that we can teeter without fear on high places, not needing to call upon devil or angels to steady us. As things now are, we tremble with dread like Stephen Rojack in Mailer's *An American Dream*, perhaps because it is a threatening tale about dreams, not the saving dream itself.

Successful balancing acts come off in dreams; or in paintings like the still-lives executed by William Harnett. In *American Painting of the Nineteenth Century* when Barbara Novack gives her appraisal of Harnett's paintings, she notes the precarious placement of the objects on the canvas. They look as if they would tip out onto the floor, but they never do. As actual objects they would fall; as painted things, although insecure, they contain a stabilizing center.

Because the painter has included them within a formal system, they indicate the perfections that are possible in the realm of abstractions. More importantly, when speaking humanly (this side of abstraction), objects receive attention within a painting as things that *could* teeter, even if they do not. They express the reality of disaster, even as they are saved by art; they exist on the canvas as actuality as well as fictions; they preserve success but suggest and define failure.

In *The American Scene* Henry James examined the landscape-with-figures which appeared to his eye. He looked for signs of serenity and balance—not the kind characterized by stasis, but those which live and tremble on the edges of things. He believed that it takes history, tradition, and taste—that is, art—to arrive at such saving poise. Yet he feared that America would not expend the time necessary to achieve the grace arrived at after years of disciplined development. Henry Adams also prized a functional style for writing and for living; a style as "impersonal as fate" in Ernest Samuels's words, as trimmed down as a runner or prizefighter. Emerson and Thoreau, Hemingway and Mailer, are other Americans who describe the artist's effective opposition to fate by means of analogues taken from the world of professional athletics that go beyond Teddy Roosevelt's simplicities about the strenuous life.

Poise through art, and art as balance poised upon a mastered center of gravity: this is necessary in a country where events move so quickly that they slide the hub of the continent out from under. Boston is the heart of that hub, Adams wrote; he had been born just there in 1838, and its center was fatefully his own. Whatever happened to it happened to him. Long before Adams' death in 1918 Boston had lost its original stability. When Robert Lowell viewed Boston during his childhood in the 1920's he found it a topsy-turvy place poised precariously on the outer rim of the hub of a universe which itself had long since been knocked off-center.

In the 1850's the young Adams had relied on more than Boston to give him the stable world from which to work toward greatness; he had believed the study of law's logic would assure the needed firmness in the world of shifting circumstance. But by 1881 his friend Oliver Wendell Holmes, Junior, had this to say as his introductory remarks to *The Common Law*: "The life of the law has not been logic: it has been experience" (noted in Samuels, *The Middle Years*, p. 179). If even the law had capitulated to instability, what was left to stand on? Not, surely, the Universal Law which Emerson and Thoreau had always counted on rather than civil legalisms.

The conclusion Adams finally came to was what Melville's Ishmael had already discovered during the time the young Adams and the men of Concord were still looking in the direction of the law, secular and sacred, that lay protectively behind the individual. Ishmael realized a man has to provide his own balance. When rushing through life in a whaling boat, pulled by the power of the world's largest creature, when surrounded by coils of rope that Adams might well have called "lines of force"—man has to keep himself steady, even as the flooring of the boat leaps out from under his feet.

In *The Education of Henry Adams*, near the conclusion of the chapter aptly named "The Abyss of Ignorance," Adams takes on the same question of balance which Emerson had so finely likened, in "Society and Solitude," to a circus act:

> To his mind, the compound ψυχή took at once the form of a bicycle-rider, mechanically balancing himself by inhibiting all his inferior personalities, and sure to fall into the sub-conscious chaos below, if one of his inferior personalities got on top. The only absolute truth was the sub-conscious chaos below, which everyone could feel when he sought it. (p. 433)

For Adams, ψυχή (soul or mind) careens along, trying not to fall off the high-wire into the abyss of ignorance of the lesser self. The fact that the mind must be observed intently as it both rushes from the center and draws near to it only increases the vertigo:

> On him, the effect was surprising. He woke up with a shudder as though he had himself fallen off his bicycle. If his mind were really this sort of magnet, mechanically dispersing its lines of force when it went to sleep, and mechanically orienting them when it woke up—which was normal, the dispersion or orientation? (p. 434)

Adams does not need to debate this question overlong. He knows

> that his normal condition was idiocy, or want of balance, and that his sanity was unstable artifice. His normal thought was dispersion, sleep, dream, inconsequence; the simultaneous action of different thought-centres without central control. His artificial balance was acquired habit. He was an acrobat, with a dwarf on his back, crossing a chasm on a slackrope, and commonly breaking his neck. (p. 434)

To believe in the stability of the external world or to declare that balance can only be found within: these two notions create essential differences between men who test possibilities for success in the nineteenth century. But they all had to come to terms with the kind of mental balancing acts required by moving in between two worlds. Ishmael tells us that whales (whose eyes stare from the far sides of their vast skulls) have two points of view; the psychological consequence of this dual vision is timidity. Men, Melville cautioned, ought not remain fixed between differences, nor should they face in one direction only—glaring into fire or into darkness—else they lose all sense of balance and capsize. It is better *to move between* sunlight and demonism.

Melville's suggestion is closely paralleled by Thoreau's belief that we ought to live in rustic landscapes placed midway between wilderness and town. Henry Adams continued the practice described by both Melville and Thoreau. His pendulum-mind kept moving constantly—searching for unity, discovering multiplicity; but always in motion, perhaps in the belief that sitting ducks and static minds are too readily shot down. All three men were wary of seeing exclusively. They differ mainly in the amount of faith each had in dealing with wholes easily and in the assurance that spectrums, even when experienced in their entirety, can save you.

Movements of the mind involve one in as much risk as they serve to avoid risk. Risk is a good thing, however, according to most of the strategists consulted in this book. Without the constant possibility of danger that accompanies the urge to thrust forward, the mind might lose its resilience and sag into complacency and stasis. Thoreau noted in December of 1839, "Cowardice is unscientific, for there cannot be science of ignorance. There may be a science of war, for that advances, but a retreat is rarely well conducted; if it is, then it is an orderly advance in the face of circumstance" (vii, 98). The self must gain its pleasure in making contact with the world, not in fleeing it. Thoreau may not have always heeded his own best advice, but he knew at least what success requires.

Poe-Pym and Melville-Ishmael move out, by choice, from Nantucket Island to make acquaintance with horrors and pleasure. These are brash young men who speak somewhat perversely of the pleasures of risk and rush. But even Mrs. Trollope appreciated the thrill she felt when poised over the Niagara, though she hedged a bit by defining "the pleasure felt" as "real safety and apparent danger" (p. 384). Gertrude Stein—who frequently strikes us as being eminently cautious and sensible—also spoke in *The Making of*

*Americans* of the need for those passions that "rise and plunge" (p. 18). Hemingway (whom Stein called yellow) was a major devotée of danger. He praised danger with discipline, however. The bull-fighter is fine when he risks his life within the rules given for his protection; he is foolish when he moves outside that magic circle. The best men—matadors or writers—work close up, with eyes open, where they can see the danger clearly.

Erik Erikson, the psychologist, says we all live swinging in between. Saul Bellow, the novelist, defines a like situation: a world out there barely holding itself together, and ourselves balancing on its razor's edge by means of tension, poise, and coordination. Bellow seems to agree with Thoreau and Melville about taking in *everything* by endless moves between fire and darkness, the objective and the subjective, the facts and the fictions. But Bellow is said by Helen Weinberg to urge more conclusive moments. Advance resolutely to the outside caught up in one piece; don't linger inside among the pieces. Inside is the hideous dream that destroys and makes failure a lasting fact. On the other hand, Emerson and Stein suggest that we seize success by pulling the outside inside in order to get at the true reality. Who is right? Who of all these theorists about winning and losing is correct? Or do the many—often contradictory, frequently confusing—definitions of success and failure set forth within Part III, when taken all together comprise the only reality we have; give us the fundamental context out of which we experience "the complex fate" of being an American, so complex it involves the American's right to pursue failure and to deny his destiny as he chooses? At least let us pay attention to Gertrude Stein's report that the children in her family liked to toss coins for heads or tails in order to do the opposite of whatever the coin demanded of them—since they felt free (or fated, if you will) to reverse the chancy pattern of things.

Gertrude Stein preferred to make use of the eye and the conscious mind, not the ear and the unconscious. In *The Autobiography of Alice B. Toklas*, noting the difference between the force of the hysteric, who scatters meaning, and the force of the saint, who creates ideas, she chooses the saint. Furthermore, she believes that intelligent people also manage to keep two kinds of time going at once. In "Portraits and Repetition" Stein speaks of the time of remembering and the time of telling, the latter being the time for actual creation. When the mind remembers, it says what it is not creating. You cannot remember yourself and be truly you, Stein states in "What Are Master-Pieces and Why Are There So Few of Them."

You are ever a newly created self; when doing, you cannot be knowing, because that entails a completed, remembered act.

Let us say, then, that if the remembered present-time is Eden—the place of shelter where one does not even need to dream of flying free—there is where the mind is content with what has been created for it; it rests willingly with the repetition of what already exists. In contrast, the mind that has left Eden behind is excited about creating new things for itself and moving beyond repetition. Eden is comparable to Shakespeare's sonnets as they are defined by Stein in "Henry James": both Eden and the sonnets are the type of *going to be written*. Beyond Eden lies Shakespeare's plays, described in the same essay as the type of *being written*. Going to be written lacks the force of being written, Stein says. The state of Eden possesses greater clarity, but to Stein, "It is not clarity that is desirable but force" (p. 127).

Adams, student of force, was aware that men might possess it by the fact of their ignorance. Witness what he described in *The Education of Henry Adams* (pp. 333-334) as "the Cameron type": "The strongest American in America"—practical, simple, narrow, coarse, unaware. Look at that force in comparison with the New England (Adams) type: weak because refined, idealistic, complex, abstract. "Cameron types" are forceful because ignorant. Further on in *The Education* (pp. 485-486) Adams notes persons of yet another type who are forceful by accident. Since force is not actually contained within them, they are merely lucky enough to be its channel. Franklin, for example, did not "face the stream of thought," Adams argued; Franklin was simply the man of his age in America who chanced to be an "electric conductor" of the "new forces from nature to man, down to the year 1800. . . ."

> Certain men merely held out their hands—like Newton, watched an apple; like Franklin, flew a kite; like Watt, played with a tea-kettle—and great forces of nature stuck to them as though she were playing ball.

Adams much preferred the man who has force—not through ignorance or accident—but because he knows what he has and controls it. Adams usually placed a premium on thought as the source of this kind of force, though—as in "The Role of Phase Applied to History"—he also worried about thought which becomes forceless. Adams wanted thought to will the course its force takes. Thought and choice, not ignorance and chance, were Adams' lines of power translated into the terms of human action and the elements for success.

Others agree that force may come from choice but argue that choices do not necessarily result from clarity of thought. In *Of a Fire on the Moon* Mailer states that psychology is a study of the *style* of choices we face and make. Emerson would have been in agreement that style is determined by character, not by brain. Character is force, style, the result of choice and also its cause. The name given to what links result and cause is structure. Structure is the sum of what lies within the mind and outside of it; it is a matter of relations. Relations are forceful when they reflect a constant outward movement that involves hazard and risk—what makes the heaves of the mind different from the smooth progress of machines. The mind moves out from its "heavy" inner world of memory, ignorance, and self-satisfaction to engage itself actively with all that might destroy it—fearing, loving, and needing hazard.

Like Whitman before him, Saul Bellow is fond of Columbus. This is not just because the Genoan explored areas that took him away from safe successes; what counts is that he *cared about* transcending limits of maps and commercial aspirations. The mind that leaps to circumnavigate the globe goes so far from stable centers it enters the *Terra Incognita*; there it finds force in the act of examining ignorance, not peace through acceptance of unknowns. But if the mind wills to be greater than the boundary-tight circumstances of maps and trading interests, the mind also wills to be more than mind. It tries to transcend itself in order to become spirit. But if ever the process of Columbian exploration succeeds—if it manages to push past the obstacles of the North American continent and continue on to India—the result might prove to be the deepest failure. Rather than having gone far enough, it will have gone too far. It will have overshot its goal of the successful life and arrived at the dubious success of death. Here, anyway, is where Saul Bellow (with Gertrude Stein) parts company with Walt Whitman in dislike of completions. With the final circling of the globe the mind would return to memory, to shelter, to peace—to the end of being and of will. It might arrive at clarity, but its force would be lost.

The mind goes outside or inside at great risk whenever its movement presses to extreme lengths. Risk is gain as long as it is not pushed over the line of danger into achievement and safety. Here follow three examples of the American mind placed in jeopardy, all taken from experiences recorded soon after World War I. In each instance there is an attempt, with varying degrees of success, by that mind to set its own style, to refuse to accept narrow limits, to insist that it is character and fate, and to demonstrate the artistry that creates force.

E. E. Cummings refuses to name the Enormous Room of the French concentration camp as his "prison"; he calls it an ever-expanding space in which his mind is free to rove. But once his friend *B.* goes away, the necessary movement between his mind and other minds ceases, and he falls into a tranced state he later recognizes as having taken him near madness. He has only his self, and he feels locked into it, separated from any space but that of his mind. When Cummings is released by presidential action from the camp, released in effect from the enclosures of his mind, he experiences a sense of being reborn as a complete man. He is transformed back into himself. It is significant that shortly after he likens himself to a city (Paris). Upon his return to America his mind converts the idea of the city (now imaged as New York) into a new dream of the future. The enormous spaces of America (the country whose government had restored him to liberty) are joyfully possessed as a dream, just as the cramped hell of the French prison had previously been transformed by his mind into a space filled by Delectable Mountains. The unanswered question raised earlier in Cummings' book remains, however, even to the end. Although it is not voiced by him, it is a question felt by us. Is he not still vulnerable to being trapped inside a tranced subjectivity, just as when he had no *B.* to tether him to the world outside? How can he escape future immersions in the origin of all things—that place where he found terror and no power?

Gerald Murphy held off circumstances by calling them peripheries and accidents, not the core and essence of existence. He did this by inventing a better life within his mind that contradicted the outside world. In a letter included in Calvin Tomkins's *Living Well Is The Best Revenge*, he told Scott Fitzgerald that

> for me, only the invented part of life was satisfying, only the unrealistic part. Things happened to you—sickness, death, Zelda in Prangins, Patrick in the sanatorium, Father Wiborg's death—these things were realistic, and you couldn't do anything about them. "Do you mean you don't accept those things?" Scott asked. I replied that of course I accepted them, but that I didn't feel they were the important things really. It's not what we do but what we do with our minds that counts, and for me only the *invented* parts of our life had any real meaning. (p. 138)

One could propose that Zelda Fitzgerald, one of Murphy's unimportant realistic things, is an excellent example of what happens when the mind goes too far in the direction of inventing a better

life. It did not work for Zelda; one doubts if it worked perfectly for
Murphy. But perhaps Sherwood Anderson was more successful in
using the same approach tried by both Cummings and Murphy, yet
controlling it. This is what William Faulkner recalled (in an essay
included in James Meriwether's collection). One day in New Orleans, Anderson told Faulkner of a dream, laughing in his pleasure
over what he had gained from it:

> he had dreamed the night before that he was walking for miles
> along country roads, leading a horse which he was trying to
> swap for a night's sleep—not for a simple bed for the night,
> but for the sleep itself; and with me to listen now, went on
> from there, elaborating it, building it into a work of art with
> the same tedious (it had the appearance of fumbling but ac-
> tually it wasn't; it was seeking, hunting) almost excruciating pa-
> tience and humility with which he did all his writing, me listen-
> ing and believing no word of it: that is, that it had been any
> dream dreamed in sleep. Because I knew better. I knew that
> he had invented it, made it; he had made most of it or at least
> some of it while I was there watching and listening to him.
> (pp. 3-4)

The telling, the listening, and the inventing of

> his whole biography into an anecdote or perhaps a parable:
> the horse . . . representing the vast rich strong docile sweep of
> the Mississippi Valley, his own America, which he in his bright
> blue racetrack shirt and vermilion-mottled Bohemian Windsor
> tie, was offering with humor and patience and humility, but
> mostly with patience and humility, to swap for his own dream
> of purity and integrity and hard and unremitting work and ac-
> complishment. . . . (p. 4)

It seems as if Sherwood Anderson had, in *telling his story* (Stein-
like, not just *remembering a dream*) found at last what Thoreau had
once sought and never found: horse, dove, and hound; found
them because he converted the dream into art and the art gave him
America in swap for virtue and work—an America forcefully invented and created, not an America merely dreamed upon in
futility.

# CHAPTER 15

# Principles, Things, People, and Mass

It is uncanny the way the American mind is able to *think* its way into strength. But it is misguided to believe that foes simply melt before the burning glance of the idea of victory. The obstacles are many, and possibilities for failure continually rough up the texture of the imagination of *virtus*—the inner power that is goodness and the central good that acts with force. If idea attempts to transcend contingency, it must live with the fact that *principles* (iron-bound ideas and unbending ideals) are often at the mercy of *things* with the thrust to crack open the inflexible. This is the source of the pity we feel when we hear Mrs. Doc Hines in Faulkner's *Light in August* say she wishes that her grandson Joe Christmas be "Decently hung by a Force, a principle: not burned or hacked or dragged dead by a Thing" (p. 421). To be "hung by a Force, a principle" is the failure exacted by death, but at least it is failure qualified by the event finding its place, its time, and its particle of meaning. It is a kind of success; but success qualified by its desire to be *unlike life*—thereby doubling back toward failure.

In "The Heritage of Henry Adams" Brooks Adams alleged that the America of principles was defeated by 1828, replaced in the saddle by the triumph of Jacksonian *things*. By 1853 Thoreau acknowledged that things are indeed the usual winners in the world. For himself, he was more interested in lecturing than in surveying, but he seldom got to lecture, while the business of measuring the space-things possessed by landowners paid well and frequently. "All the while that they use only your humbler faculties," he wrote in his journal of December 22, 1853, "your higher unemployed faculties, like an invisible cimetar, are cutting them in twain."

In *The Duality of Human Existence* David Bakan speaks at length (pp. 1-15) about the killing effect upon the person who rejects the life of "ultimate concerns" (what is unmeasurable) for a life given over to "idolatry" (absorption into what is "manifest"). In turn, even those who are not unprincipled idolators get nervous when excessive worth is given to the ideal at the cost of the actual. Mailer, for one, sees the possibility of principles denying the right of instincts; in the resulting stalemate, things come in and take over. American democracy, he writes in *Cannibals and Christians*, is eager to make "the best" available to everyone, now. In contrast, life "tends to make what is best in itself most inaccessible." Thereby, democracy "endangers life in the name of a noble ideal"—"a logical impasse!" (p. 279.) However, others think with confidence of America as the place that fosters modes of perception which synthesize such hostile elements. Gertrude Stein declared in *The Making of Americans* (p. 261) that instincts can be as pure as ideals; she proposed that we link *idea*, *instinct*, and *ideals*. If this consubstantial trinity could by means of the *word* be joined with *thing*, then everyone would be happy in a good world.

The Transcendentalists are usually criticized for their support of "ultimate concerns" to the exclusion of life's immediacies. But at their best they did not wish to reject the "manifest" altogether. Even airy Bronson Alcott was praised by Emerson for his verbal ability to make the Ideal "as solid as Massachusetts." The Transcendentalists attempted a kind of communion of spirit and matter; they strove to convert principle into almost tangible forms of thought. If Elizabeth Peabody tended to walk headlong into trees, it was because, although she saw them, she did not always "realize" them. But trees were clearly realized by Thoreau at most times of the day and night. His *ideas* about the victory of life over the annual defeat of death found its *manifest form* in the organic and excrementitious mud-bank beside the pond; his *ideas* provided the necessary *words* for the writing of *Walden*.

Henry James was attentive to things in ways Thoreau might have considered idolatrous, but when in *The American Scene* he viewed the "progress" made at Harvard he concentrated in Thoreauvian ways upon the lack of synthesis between the manifest of the buildings and the educational ideal. He was not merely interested in the architectural embellishments of an affluent society; nor was he sensitive only to the abstractions of education. He was too aware of the need for both a "physical plant" and "sensitive plants." What he decried was the fact of the former and the absence of the latter when once in the early years of Harvard it had been—just as hurtfully—the other way around:

> This process almost always takes the form, primarily, of more lands and houses and halls and rooms, more swimming-baths and football-fields and gymnasia, a greater luxury of brick and mortar, a greater ingenuity, the most artful conceivable, of

accommodation and installation. Such is the magic, such the presences, that end, more than any other, to figure *as* the Institution, thereby perverting not a little, as need scarce be remarked, the finer collegiate idea: the theory being, doubtless, and again most characteristically, that with all the wrought stone and oak and painted glass, the immense provision, the multiplied marbles and tiles and cloisters and acres, "people will come," that is, individuals of value will, and in some manner work some miracle. In the early American time, doubtless, individuals of value had to wait too much for things; but that is now made up by the way things are waiting for individuals of value. (p. 254)

If simplifications are possible when speaking of either Thoreau or James, it comes down alike for them to a matter of ends and means: not the cynic's stress on ends; not the idealist's uncompromising insistence on means; but an inseparable bond between the two. "Value and effort are as much coincident as weight and a tendency to fall," Thoreau jotted down on June 30, 1840. "In a very wide but true sense, effort is the deed itself. . . ." One could as well say that it was not the apple alone that mattered to Newton, but what it was *doing* as it fell. Yet without the apple the pure principle of nature would have no value for the minds of men who wish to join the fact of matter to the beauty of God's ideas.

"I hear an irresistible voice," Thoreau wrote on January 5, 1851, "the voice of my destiny, which invites me away from all that [the voice of conventional morality]." What counts is a life of sacred vocation, not that of occupation. Men do not have *everything* to do, Thoreau argued in *Civil Disobedience*, but certainly they have *something*. Occupation that tries to deal with everything leads to an existence in which men are possessed by a power outside themselves. Like Faulkner's Joe Christmas, they are easily "burned or hacked or dragged dead by a Thing." Vocation, by concentrating on *something*, gives men what is theirs—a sacred *thing* that is more than idol because endowed with intangible value, the needed *principle* that is more than abstraction because it is value made manifest. It gives men the apple, the act of motion, and the law of gravitation.

With vocation there is no split between principle and thing; with occupation there is only thing. Continually Thoreau tried to balance the belief that he was Apollo, the poet-god, with the fact that he was also servant to King Admetus, mentor of the business world. This is where the worrisome division came in. Could the split between Apollo's vocation and his occupation in King Admetus' court be healed, and could this come about in America, of all places?

Howard Mumford Jones picks up on America's fatal insistence upon the divided life in *The Age of Energy*; he comments (pp. 433-434) that by the late nineteenth century things were no longer—as they had been for Jonathan Edwards, Emerson, and Thoreau—windows to the ideal. Nor were things, as they had generally been up to that time, facts drawn from the immediate world of actuality; things were by then often the excuse for private, in-drawing musings. Things from the outside taken inside in this way did not liberate men's minds or bring them success. How different from the way American minds had once been able to keep touch on things out there while somehow uniting them with the centering principle within!

Thoreau rejected the New Testament on the same grounds for which Jay Gatsby would have also denied it: it was "just personal." (To Thoreau's disgust, Christ might actually have been concerned about news transmitted by transatlantic cable of Princess Adelaide's fever.) True to his philosophical stance, he was the great generalist, for all his emphasis upon proud individualism. He concentrated the all-encompassing energy of "ultimate concerns" upon one self—his own (that self offered up, of course, as a paradigm for those selves all men have it as their vocation to save). "In the society of many men, or in the midst of what is called success, I find my life of no account, and my spirits rapidly fall," he wrote in his journal on February 8, 1857:

> By poverty, *i.e.* simplicity of life and fewness of incidents, I am solidified and crystallized, as a vapor or liquid by cold. It is a singular concentration of strength and energy and flavor. . . .
> By simplicity, commonly called poverty, my life is concentrated and so becomes organized, or a κόσμος which before was inorganic and lumpish.

"Good" poverty is quite the opposite of impoverished living; it is as expansive as it is concentrated. "How meanly and miserably we live for the most part!" Thoreau wrote in the same year on August 10th: ". . . we should have some spare capital and superfluous vigor, have some margin and leeway in which to move."

Mark Twain advised others—especially his brother Orion—to concentrate, to stay put. It was an admonition whose importance he understood clearly, since his own tendency was to spread himself

out. Wilky James, younger brother of two famous men, was part
Mark Twain, part Orion Clemens, while Henry James pictured
himself as standing between William (who seemed to succeed at
anything out of sheer will-power and concentration on essences)
and Wilky (who failed because he had no power to make distinctions, a man for whom "all cats are grey"). Henry early learned the
value of being in the middle, compact, self-contained, more his
own man. Here is how he expressed it in *A Small Boy and Others*:

> There was the difference and the opposition . . . that one way
> of taking life was to go in for everything and everyone, which
> kept you abundantly occupied, and the other way was to be as
> occupied, quite as occupied, just with the sense and the image
> of it all, and on only a fifth of the actual immersion. . . . Life
> was taken almost equally both ways—that, I mean, seemed the
> strangeness; brute quantity and number being so much less in
> one case than the other. (p. 290)

Henry James believed that privacy of consciousness gives one "a
standpoint in the universe which it is probably good not to for-
sake." "Only, don't, I beseech you," he wrote in a letter of 1883 to
Grace Norton (included in the Edel edition), "*generalize* too much
in these sympathies and tendernesses—remember that every life is
a special problem which is not yours but another's, and content
yourself with the terrible algebra of your own" (II, 423). If self-
isolating egotism is a danger in James's world, it is also a dire fate to
be the person who has pleased so many others that he or she must
cry out, like one of James's characters, "What a brute then I must
be!"

Throughout *The Adventures of Augie March* Saul Bellow tries to
trace the question of everywhere being nowhere. Augie dreams at
times of settling in upon a life of Walden simplicity, but Augie is
simultaneously enticed to go everywhere. Thoreau could have told
Augie he would fail at the pond-experiment. Augie burns hot with
love in all its various forms and feels he has "everything to do";
Thoreau burns cold with his vision of the something he alone must
be. In the passage given above, from Thoreau's entry in the journal
of February 8, 1857—the one about his need to concentrate,
solidify, and crystallize—Thoreau added a note concerning the
need for chill: "Chastity is perpetual acquaintance with the All." If
Thoreau is often reluctant servant to Admetus, Augie is unweary-
ing servant to Love. Augie is made painfully aware that loving
keeps him vulnerable to others' plans for his destiny. Self-fulfilling

vocation for Augie seems hardly possible, only devotion to the self-annihilating voice of love.

Mailer's Stephen Rojack of *An American Dream* also yearns to be both free bachelor and lover. But Rojack concludes that though it takes courage to love, love is an obstacle to courage. Is not God courage/power, rather than love/weakness? The nature of one's service to God is itself ambiguous; it might entail satanic devices or diffusion (sexual, as well as spiritual); it could lead to extravagant waste, not divine concentration.

Love and death are frequently cited as the major tiger-trap in the American success story. Augie March and Stephen Rojack believe they must choose between power (life) or love (death); they must elect to be free agents or love's servants. It is greatness they want— that special kind of power that lets a man *invent* his fate. To love and to be loved involves the *creation* of a destiny. Through them we are asked again whether America is still being invented out of the urge for greatness and whether it has ever been created out of love.

In *The Ambassadors* Chad Newsome is "created" by Madame de Vionnet in Paris, but he wishes to "invent" a Woollett, Massachusetts, fate for himself. Chad's American future means movement away from the life of the European dilettante; he will switch from the *amateur* who loves and enjoys what he desires to the *professional*, specialist in the art of advertising which acts to create desires in others. In contrast to Chad, Augie March wants to remain the amateur; like Whitman, Augie would spread himself out to include, and to be, everything. Augie as lover tries to keep the inside and yet bring in the outside; he resists being merely the loved one (the person whose inside is drawn outward to appease another) or the inventor (one who holds himself separate from the object he controls).

Augie March's way of balancing opposites is risky, since love may be the failure that brings diffusion and death. But he might manage to achieve what Meyer Abrams said the great Romantics attempted: recognition of the contraries leading to love which act redemptively as imagination to convert debilitating pain into the strong energy of joy.

The speaker in Emily Dickinson's poem "Our lives are Swiss" ponders what it would mean to give up a life under control; she considers "going across" into dangerous areas of love, where power is dissipated. Milly Theale in *The Wings of the Dove* "comes down" from the Alps to re-enter the world as love's potential victim; she finally gains the power of the princess who, dying, leaves her passion's mark upon others. In *The Diaries of Adam and Eve* Mark Twain's Eve "comes out" from Eden. "The Garden is lost, but I have found *him*," she declares of Adam (not of the God Who remains behind), "and am content" (p. 59). These three instances—of "going across," "coming down," and "coming out"—stress the need to love a particular person in an imperfect world. They turn aside from self-isolation or the expending of charm in wholesale lots. They suggest that one ought to be love's amateur like Augie, Emily, Milly, and Eve—not a specialist in selling desire like Chad Newsome.

Would it were always so simple. How nice if all one needed for success was the courage to will more than courage, and the daring to plunge into the wild world of love, away from stabilized worlds of controllable power. But it may have been in some part the fear of failing this most important test which caused Thoreau to settle for the diminished state of bachelorhood. Thoreau admits that marriage is the crucial proof of a man's ability to succeed. "To be married at least should be the one poetical act of a man's life," he wrote in his journal of August 11, 1853. "If you fail in this respect, in what respect will you succeed?"

If marriage is the perfect expression of the fulfilled spiritual life, Thoreau indicted it as it exists in the present state of human affairs. In the same journal entry he noted that that union was now "but little better than the marriage of the beasts." Henry James, Senior, also viewed marriage—the "great disillusioning"—as the mark of an imperfect society in which men delude themselves that they love a particular person. When the Great Society comes about, he argued, all men will wake from their illusions to love the divinity common to all persons. This is being the amateur with a vengeance, in ways similar to those extolled by Emerson in "Love" from *Essays, First Series*. If the English Romantics examined by Meyer Abrams believed love to be the means toward the perfect existence, the Americans Thoreau, Emerson, and the elder James viewed "personal" love as an obstacle to the life of the spirit. As one could expect, Mailer (in whichever of his fictional manifestations) and Bellow's Augie March are pulled both ways. They give priority to succeeding in this imperfect world of beasts, illusions, and drained powers; they also honor—albeit cautiously—the idea of love's perfection.

Concurrently with the return of the NASA rocket from the moon, Mailer's marriage fails with Beverly—his "America." It is as if he can now only hope that the moon will receive him as an Endymion from Brooklyn; if so, perhaps this newest American colony in space will have warm love as its motivating force, not merely cold NASA power. But what really counts for victory, Mailer continues to suspect, is the courage that concentrates on itself alone.

If the love of a man for a woman confounds easy formulas for success, the question of friendship is no less complex in its implications for failure. "Absolutely speaking," Emerson stated in "Natural History of the Intellect," "I can only work for myself."

In both *The Duality of Human Existence* and *Disease, Pain, and Sacrifice* David Bakan examines recent medical research to determine whether one survives best as a single, solitary self or as the member of a cohesive group—the basic question any successful democracy must solve, as Whitman knew when trying to wrangle a truce between the potential antagonists. Bakan ponders the data which indicates that repression of the communion impulse leads to cancer. He attempts to connect these medical findings with a flow of theological teachings and psychological theories. He emerges from all this with the highly metaphoric argument that the ego is the Satan which separates itself totally from God and the human community in an obsessive desire for mastery—what Bakan calls "agency." This essentially male principle attacks the "enemy"—the female principle of healing communion. Bakan's linking of ego, Satan, and agency with the force of Protestanism suggests that the male force has usurped nature's power in order to found a society in its own image; yet agency has not mastered death. Death—the cancer of separation which multiplies from within, cannibalizing all in its path—itself originates in agency.

Bakan's thesis sounds very like Mailer on America, quirks, brilliance, and all. Mailer dreads cancer, and he blames its birth and its spread upon the Wasp stress on agency expressed as satanic hatred, envy, narcissism, and separateness. Yet Mailer's celebration of the individual ego in *Of a Fire on the Moon* lives side by side with his uneasiness about NASA. The original Protestant ego—individualistic, contradictory, cantankerous, ruthless, and creative—has been taken over by the genderless corporation which devours America by means of its conglomerates of ego-destroying cancers. Nonetheless, the astronauts' need to repress their separate egos in order to arrive safely at the new world of outer-space is a latter-day extension of John Winthrop's declaration on board the *Arbella* that we must work together or die. In this, the Saints of New England or Houston, Texas, would hardly find themselves among the "aristocrats" described by Emerson in his 1848 lecture of that name. "The Golden Table never lacks members," Emerson affirmed as he played with metaphors suggested by King Arthur's legendary brotherhood; "all its seats are kept full; but with this strange provision, that the members are carefully withdrawn into deep niches, so that no one of them can see any other of them, and each believes himself alone."

The earliest settlers in New England were cautious types, relying of necessity upon horizontal community and vertical authority. Thoreau phrases it nicely in a passage from *A Week on the Concord and Merrimack Rivers*: "The white man comes, pale as the dawn." This earlier vision is quite different from the future dawn that vibrates through the conclusion of *Walden*. As described in *A Week* the new American arrives

> with a load of thought, with a slumbering intelligence as a fire raked up, knowing well what he knows, not guessing but calculating; strong in community, yielding obedience to authority; of experienced race; of wonderful, wonderful common sense; dull but capable, slow but persevering, severe but just, of little humor but genuine; a laboring man, despising game and sport; building a house that endures, a framed house. (pp. 52-53)

The notion that America (female) is discovered, explored, and exploited by the ego (the male working in corporate teams or as satanic polarities) continues to beg the question whether all this is done in the name of freedom for the sublime individual or for the satisfaction of the larger social whole. And what about friendship? Does this particular form of human relationship seal the private pact of communion between two individuals or does it impose a block-community? Is it working on the *Pequod* to weld the crew collectively under Ahab's "sultanic" eye or to pull Ishmael and his strange bedfellow together? One of the answers to this intricate question is provided by Thoreau's *Walden*; in turn, that answer becomes clearer when set in contrast to the ending of that other famous manual for personal worth, *The Courtier* by Castiglione.

*The Courtier* counter-balances Machiavelli's study in the power of Renaissance agency, *The Prince*. The final pages of the gentler work by Castiglione leave behind two main images. Peter Bembo's long disquisition comes to its close with the ladder that mounts away from the earth toward the ideal abstraction of love found in the stars. This image of pure self-concentration (which anticipates

Gatsby's ladder that leads "to a secret place above the trees" that he could possess "if he climbed alone") dissolves in the last paragraphs into a new image. The members of Prince Ludovico's court—true friends for all their witty jibes—gather together in hope to watch the new dawn break over the Umbrian hills. They look out on a particular landscape in this world and this time; it is no Neo-Platonic abstraction thrown above and beyond into eternity.

Thoreau's *Walden* also moves toward its conclusion with a hymn to Aurora. Thoreau has been serving as an American Bembo, his words lifting him up and away from friends and earth in a magnificent effort to be a free and solitary spirit. But the New Englander's book does not provide what the Italian Castiglione did: final paragraphs which follow *after* Bembo's vision to make dawn-viewing a matter of communion and friendship. We the readers of *Walden* are self-isolated by the individualistic vision we are given by Thoreau. All of us are meant to be blessed by this saving American dawn; but it must come to each of us in our privacy.

Thoreau included a lengthy essay on "Friendship" in *A Week on the Concord and Merrimack Rivers*. Reading it, one wonders if Sara Murphy would have found it necessary to rebuke Thoreau, as she did Scott Fitzgerald, for theorizing too much. "You can't expect anyone," Sara wrote Scott (in a letter included in Tomkins' book),

> to like or stand a continual feeling of analysis, & sub-analysis & criticism—on the whole unfriendly—such as we have felt for quite a while. It is definitely in the air—& quite unpleasant. . . .
> If you don't know what people are like it's *your* loss. . . . But *you ought to know at your age* that *you can't have Theories about friends.* If you can't take friends largely, & without suspicion—then they are not friends at all. (p. 114)

Thoreau would doubtless have been unconcerned over what a woman like Sara Murphy might have to say, but he answers her charge in part through making a fine analogy of the friend with the New World. In *A Week* he proposes that a friend is something *found* (not merely sought out through that analysis which pries but does not really probe well). Friendship is where "perfect equality" is forever enjoyed; it is that place Thoreau always searched for, where "All things are as I am" (p. 310). It is where one progresses through the deadlocks of *complaint* and *plaint* to the release of *love*—that expression that needs no words and ends all distrust and grief. It is the place where friends are by nature "taken largely" since love-feeling fills all space.

The tragedy and secret of the universe, Thoreau decided in *A Week* is that while we call for community with cries of "Sweet Friends!" the echo returns, "Damn your eyes!" (p. 281.) Even Thoreau's New World of friendship inevitably dissolves into universal rancor. Pressure mounts within Thoreau's mind to avoid the failure which follows the botched marriage of true souls. Better to be the one person more important, more valuable (or more alone) than the rest of the world's populace. He realizes that to concentrate on the self is a surer success, and also a lesser one—a situation potentially cancerous, satanic. But Thoreau's God is a solitary, whereas his Devil is legion, ever-present, to be bumped into constantly unless a man keeps a saving distance from the Devil's smiles and arm-clutchings.

In 1852, on January 16, Thoreau wrote in his journal:

> I see that to some men their relation to mankind is all-important. It is fatal in their eyes to outrage the opinions and customs of their fellow-men. Failure and success, therefore, never proved by them by absolute and universal tests. I feel myself not so vitally related to my fellow-men. I impinge on them but by a point on one side. It is not a Siamese-twin ligature that binds me to them.

One has cause to ask, in assessing Thoreau's remarks in justification of aloneness, whether his is the simple case of man who—by accident of the type—is incapable of communion. We want to know whether he had to evolve a theory of life that justified his failure as a man by commending his success as an ideal American, or whether his is the more complex instance of someone who comes at his faith positively, not merely as negative self-compensation. It is fashionable to say that whenever men have psychic weaknesses they seek to talk it into a general strength. Perhaps it is closer to the particular essence of Thoreau to read his declared ideas as abstract strengths matching whatever strengths he actually contained as a man. At any rate, his flaws as lover and friend receive no public notice in his writings; they are like Princess Adelaide's fever—not to be telegraphed to the world in any form.

Crèvecœur's Farmer James watched the advance of the American Revolution with horror since it threatened the very principle of the family. Political revolt weakened the future hope of relation between himself and his sons, and of his sons' relation to the Fatherland—this dissolution brought about for the sake of the perfect, perfectly free individual. When Farmer James asked, "What is an American?" the self-government of rebellious sons was not what he had in mind as the right answer.

In her own way Gertrude Stein also believed that the effect of freedom on the new American could make him eccentric, separate, a god inside himself. For Stein, where there is true progress in America it is the progress of the family. Individuals die, but as long as the family remains, America continues. One sometimes wishes, when reading *The Making of Americans*, that all of Stein's people were orphans. We might then be spared the endless details of "begatting" which delay the entrance of characters with sufficient power to act on their own. One wonders, what if it had been she, not Faulkner, who had attempted to write the story of Thomas Sutpen's dynasty. We are saved, however, from such a disturbing fate, for that is one story which Stein—intrepid and conservative as she was—would never choose to write. Only for her the *making* of Americans, not the undoing. Thoreau, the bachelor, believed that the best way for Americans to keep alive is to avoid the Devil, and this is to be done by touching no one but oneself. Stein, the matriarch, felt that the best method is to spin webs (solid, almost granite-like) of words that throw a protective veil over the Ark of the family, which must not be rent, else the Tabernacle fall. Walden hut or the commodious Oakland, California, residence of the Steins: either home is more lasting than Sutpen's Hundred.

At one end of the spectrum is the single, solitary self. In the middle is the family, altering individual identity into something it uses to span more moments than the intensely personal now. At the farther end, we find the group—called "community" by its friends, "mob" by its adversaries, and "mass" by those who cannot decide whether America is more quick to give success to the one or the many.

"Don't melt too much into the Universe, but be as solid and dense and fixed as you can," Henry James wrote Grace Norton in his letter of 1883, the same in which he urged the sensitive consciousness not to "*generalize* too much" (II, 424). As early as 1865 James was at work criticizing types like Whitman for blurring those precise edges which keep one man from merging too completely into another's consciousness. In 1904 James, acting as the restless analyst of *The American Scene*, credited the family with bringing aid to the individual; but he quivered at the sight of "the monstrous form of Democracy"—"the huge democratic broom" that sweeps the sky empty—the "democratic consistency" with "its hard light" that has "everything else at its mercy" (pp. 54-55). Early and late, James identified a common threat to America and to the individual consciousness: the tendency to *level off* which comes up from the mass and serves to pull distinctions down.

In his novels and tales Henry James actively worked to recount the strong lives of special persons, at least to deal with people who tried to be special and strong. In contrast, Gertrude Stein argued in *The Making of Americans* that honor is due Everyman by the telling of his story. The writer is a potential failure unless telling "a history of every one of every kind of them" in America (p. 123). The task of the American artist is, indeed, Benjamin Franklin's task of affirming "happy mediocrity." In her novel Stein theorizes that the writer finds success in accepting the fact that we are what we most are at the *bottom* of our selves. This basic self, not the heights of the soul, is the reality. It is "the one thing always human, vital, and worthy it—worthy that all monotonously shall repeat it—and from which has always sprung . . . the very best the world can ever know, and everywhere we always need it" (p. 123).

In Ernest Samuels' words (from *Henry Adams: The Middle Years*, p. 12), what John Quincy Adams (Brooks Adams' ideal of the great man) lacked most was "the one thing needful for success, the common touch." Certainly he was no crowd-pleaser like Franklin, our prime American monument to winning, but Paul Conner in *Poor Richard's Politicks* reminds us that Franklin derived his own notion of mediocrity not from Everyman, but from Plutarch—himself a collector of the model lives of monumental men. Recall, too, that Franklin detested the mob as much as Thoreau did when the latter wrote in his 1838 lecture "Society," "The mass never comes up to the standard of its best member, but on the contrary degrades itself to a level with the lowest. As the reformers say, it is a levelling down, not up. Hence the mass is only another name for the mob."

Whether Franklin automatically defined the mob as the mass is open to question. Mrs. Trollope said so, but she ought not be consulted for the final answer to anything, however often she may be regularly checked out for first impressions. Franklin seems to have found the mass to be sound and sober men amenable to moral behavior; he disliked the mob for breaking rules of common sense and rejecting the temperate action that assures success. Franklin may well have disliked the mob because it could only fail, whereas the mass in America had an obligation to succeed and could. But we continue to ask, At what does it succeed?

In 1912 the Director of the Y.M.C.A. commented:

> When a typical American town is visited, we come face to face
> with what America means to civilization. The streets are clean,
> the homes are well kept, the yards and lawns are cared for, the
> gardens are full of flowers. The church and school are centers
> of light, the public library is well patronized, literature comes
> to the homes, and the children are trained in the ways of virtue
> and decency. That is the character of towns which are true to
> the American type.

It is devilishly easy to ridicule such a view of success (cited in
Hartshorne's book, p. 64), especially if one hews to Mark Twain's
belief that such a place is too close for comfort to God's Heaven
which, together with the Mississippi, possesses all

> the monotony of the blank, watery solitude; and so the day
> goes, the night comes, and again the day—and still the same,
> night after night and day after day,—majestic, unchanging
> sameness of serenity, repose, tranquillity, lethargy, vacancy,—
> symbolic of eternity, realization of the heaven pictured by
> priest and prophet, and longed for by the good and thought-
> less!

If this passage from *Life on the Mississippi* (p. 213) seems to describe both Gertrude Stein's theory of communality and her prose
style, Stein herself would have hastened slowly to explain that, after
all, it was the variety and the incompleteness of "basic being" that
most intrigued her. In "Portraits and Repetition," "Henry James,"
"What Are Master-Pieces and Why Are There So Few," *The Making
of Americans*, and elsewhere, she repeated the fact, forever interesting to her because repeating did not pull it forward toward fixed
conclusions. Here is how Stein puts it in *Everybody's Autobiography*:

> To me when a thing is really interesting it is when there is no
> question and no answer, if there is then already the subject is
> not interesting and it is so, that is the reason that anything for
> which there is a solution is not interesting, that is the trouble
> with governments and Utopias and teaching. . . . (p. 213)

"Basic being" for Stein was not the same as leveling off. She had
sharp words for that process as she saw it taking place in America
by the 1930's. According to the theory of American history she expressed in *Brewsie and Willie*, thinking—that act which makes each
person different from the others—has been given up by too many

Americans. In their anxiety, men have started to talk alike and to care only for looking for jobs—that urge which most pulls men into comformity. Better by far to suffer, to think, and to be different, as good Americans had once done.

One century before the Depression—the decade Stein named as doing havoc to American individualism—Tocqueville in the 1830's believed that the American mind had already lost its ability to think exploratively. "I fear that the mind may keep folding itself up in a narrower compass forever without producing new ideas, that men will wear themselves out in trivial, lonely, futile activity, and that for all its constant agitation humanity will make no advance" (p. 645). Early in what we could call the happy "Y.M.C.A. years," men were monotonously alike. Tocqueville acknowledged it was true that at times of peril "great characters stand out in relief like monuments at night illuminated by the sudden glare of a conflagration" (p. 199). But once the great men have subdued the crisis and put out the flames, they disappear as forces because no longer needed by the community and perhaps even feared.

Tocqueville anticipates the argument of Brooks and Henry Adams that individual greatness marked the initial crisis years of the American settlement, but that such stature has been on the decline ever since. In his journal of 1841 (contemporaneous with Tocqueville), Emerson took the opposite tack:

> What business have Washington or Jefferson in this age? You must be a very dull or a very false man if you have not a better & more advanced policy to offer than they had. They lived in the greenness & timidity of the political experiment. The kitten's eyes were not yet opened. They shocked their contemporaries with their wisdom: have you not something which would have shocked *them*? (VIII, 58)

"Our American lives are somewhat poor & pallid," Emerson continued in his journal of 1843. "Franklins & Washingtons [,] no fiery grain. Staid men like our pale & timid Flora. We have too much freedom, need an austerity, need some iron girth. Sunday Schools not friendly to heroism" (VIII, 398). But although he reversed certain of Tocqueville's assessments, Emerson, too, feared leveling off.

Leveling takes place most readily through what we now call "stock responses." Angus Fletcher describes the process in *Allegory, The Theory of a Symbolic Mode* as "the fixation of a normally labile response, and this fixation requires activity to be stilled into inactivity, emotion which is ongoing to be stopped, and replaced by the fixed idea." Fletcher continues, "Any monument likewise stills the flow of time at a specific historical moment" (p. 363). In this way great men like Washington and Jefferson (and Emerson) become monuments by the fact of their success of character. In turn, they threaten the future successes of other men by seeming to freeze the motion of character into stillness.

Henry Adams wished the Saint-Gaudens' monument for his wife at Rock Creek Cemetery to represent quite vaguely the ideal of peace; he was irritated that the populace tried to fix onto the figure their stock responses as to its sex and its didactic message. "Every magazine writer wants to label it as some American patent medicine for popular consumption," he complained in a letter of January 24, 1908 to the sculptor's son (included in Cater)—"Grief, Despair, Pear's Soap, or Macy's Suits Made to Measure. Your father meant it to ask a question, not to give an answer; and the man who answers will be damned to eternity like the men who answered the Sphinx" (p. 89).

Ideal Americans like Washington and Jefferson are in danger of becoming monuments that hint at answers as inadequate to the problems of a dirty world as Pear's Soap. It is better to place emphasis upon the riddling effect of their lives as men. Then their presences—by embodying the difficult pleasures of human variety and uniqueness—can put an end to stock responses to the ideals of unity and universality they too easily represent.

Emerson was a gadfly against the American tendency to melt and to fix. In 1841 he wrote in his journal, "We are a puny & fickle folk. Hesitations & following are our diseases . . . America is therefore the country of small adventures, of short plans, of daring risks, not of patience, not of great combinations, not of long, persistent, close woven schemes, demanding the utmost fortitude, temper, faith, & poverty" (VII, 431). A generation later the populace was still given up to conformity. " 'Tis a wild democracy," Emerson stated after the Civil War in "The Fortune of the Republic"—"the riot of mediocrity and dishonesties and fudges"; it was also "the age of the omnibus." The omnibus happened to be the communal vehicle in which Henry James, Senior, took great pleasure; to him it was a truly "celestial" mode of transportation quite unlike Hawthorne's pawky, reprobate railroad; it was the sign that America might hope for a perfected society. But for Emerson it symbolized "the third person plural, of Tammany Hall" that caused him to ask, "Is it that

Nature has only so much vital force, and must dilute it if it is to multiply into millions?"

A cosmic and social conservationist, Emerson feared the diffusion that defeats the greatness which comes about from concentration, not waste. Furthermore, the rules of simplicity, austerity, and virtue being advanced in America were those suggested by the model life of Franklin; they were not the same as the simplicity, austerity, and virtue sanctioned by Emersonianism. There is often only a hair's-breadth of difference between these two master models for success in America, but Franklin's camel of visible gain would never be able to pass through the eye of the Transcendentalist needle into the heaven of invisible value.

Freud, himself an arch conservationist, seems more the champion of Franklin, not of Emerson. In the words of Philip Rieff in *Freud: The Mind of the Moralist* (p. 278), "Freud shows us not the rebel individual of our democratic affections, feeling his erotic unity with all mankind and yet his splendid isolation, but the self-conscious prudent man whose mind has freed itself inwardly from authority, and who therefore no longer pays the price of conflict and neurosis." But Rieff also adds that Freud realized that the humdrum is not uninteresting; it is not a bore, not a world of mere social adjustment. "To find the humdrum behavior of everyday life psychopathological, as Freud did, is to move nearer that excitement of the wholly interesting life that characterizes the nineteenth-century Romantics' attempt to escape precisely the humdrum in experience" (p. 334). What Rieff is referring to is nicely shown by Norman Mailer—who is as much an enemy of boredom as of the ordinary—in *The Armies of the Night*, when he demonstrates the *frisson* gained by the commonplace gesture of picking up a telephone.

The possibilities for man's heroic destiny might seem limited to three: life that is satisfying (not necessarily heroic), marked by "happy mediocrity" which licks everything into sameness; life as melancholy ordinariness which makes one neurotic, jumpy, and interested; life as unique, assertive, tragic, an existence which insists, in Tocqueville's words, that "nobody has the right to force his fellow men to be happy" when what one really wishes is to be extraordinary at any cost (p. 374).

There is yet a fourth side to be heard from—the world of "the grey and preterite souls" loyally supported by Thomas Pynchon in *Gravity's Rainbow*. Speaking on behalf of those who are mediocre

but neither especially happy nor neurotic, and certainly not assertive or exceptional, Pynchon would have us all pause to bow our
heads in a moment of homage:

> Those whom the old Puritan sermons denounced as "the gloz-
> ing neuters of the world" have no easy road to haul down.
> Wear-the-Pantsers, just cause you can't see it doesn't mean it's
> not there! Energy inside is just as real, just as binding and ines-
> capable, as energy that shows. When's the last time you felt *in-
> tensely lukewarm?* eh? Glozing neuters are just as human as
> heroes and villains. In many ways they have the most grief to
> put up with, don't they? Why don't you, right now, wherever
> you are, city folks or out in the country, snuggled in quilts or
> riding the bus, just turn to the Glozing Neuter nearest you,
> even your own reflection in the mirror, and . . . just . . . sing,
>
>> How-dy neighbor, how-dy pard!
>> Ain't it lone-ly, say ain't it hard,
>> Passin' by so silent, day-after-day, with-out,
>>     even a smile-or, a friendly word to say? Oh, let me
>> Tell ya bud-dy, tell ya ace,
>> Things're fal-lin', on their face—
>> Maybe we should stick together part o' the way, and
>> Skies'll be bright-er some day!
>> Now *ev*'rybody— (p. 677)

The discussion which engages the whole of *Failure and Success in
America: a Literary Debate* is not devoted merely to "heroes" or
to "villains"—to those bright extremists who add flash to any debate. But admittedly its concerns over the nature of losing and
winning seem to preclude dealing in the depth they deserve with
the good grey preterite souls whose only achievement is that they
are demonstrably "human." Those who attain the absolute of success can hardly be gauged by halfway means, however intense their
"lukewarmness" might prove to be. Even the losers cited in this
book are generally those who lose resoundingly. The *extraordinary
common man* is the norm here, and whenever he feels terror it is the
kind that comes over him as he confronts the mills of the conventional built by the "glozing neuters" who follow the bouncing ball of
the communal song-fest into oblivion.
Benjamin Franklin cared about what might provide the best life
in America for the artisan, the small businessman, and the farmer.
He gave little thought to what an artist in America might require

for success. To Franklin, if imagination is that which jams the wheels of the mills of the conventional, then the mills must triumph. To types like the Transcendentalists, if Freud's hum-drumming neurotic is unable to move toward the madness of the artist, then madness must take over to provide the necessary sanity. The one side argues that if there are such things as miracles they must shine forth in daylight by Greenwich Mean Time; the other asks that the poet (read: any man who stretches beyond the mean) convey both the ordinariness of life and its moonstruck epiphanies.

On November 16, 1850 Thoreau affirmed that "In literature it is only the wild that attracts us. Dulness is only another name for tameness. It is the untamed, uncivilized, free, and wild thinking in Hamlet, in the Iliad, and in all the scriptures and mythologies that delights us. . . ." Thoreau wanted an America of scamps, muskrats, and skunk-cabbage. Gentled-down town-types in black suits were too bland for his prodigal appetites. He, like John Woolman, the young Richard Henry Dana, Junior, and Melville's Ishmael, also re-jected the isolating experience of shipping out into life with the aristocrats and the officers. "But no, I do not wish . . . to take a cabin passage," Thoreau wrote on January 22, 1852. "I will rather go before the mast and on the deck of the world." It was *perfect* equality Thoreau wished, placing his stress on the descriptive ad-jective. He craved that ideal democratic existence in which "All things are as I am."

Accordingly, the best America is a plural-situation comprised of infinite numbers of splendid individuals—what Henry Adams called the "real people"—going it alone in perfect harmony. That this seems an impossibility is what cankers the American heart. As viewed by Henry James in *The American Scene* the United States Constitution promised us likeness, but "Nature and industry keep producing differences as fast as constitutions keep proclaiming equality . . ." (p. 326). Whether one argues against a life of similar-ity and for difference, or whether one wishes to reverse that order, the process James detected seems inevitable: society and govern-ment go in one direction; the individual and nature go in the other. The result: countless failures of spirit. If Isabel Archer was ground fine in the mills of the conventional in Europe, James discovered more such mills in America than the Lowell factory-system ever dreamed of.

Private citizens can be hedged in by the petty. It may be even worse for the public artist who believes that "the thing is not worth doing at all unless something big and strong is got out of it," as

James wrote on November 8, 1894 (in an entry from his *Notebooks*). The editors at Harper hampered a man just as much as did the bland structures of society and government. "They want, ever, the smaller, the slighter, the safer, the inferior thing . . ." (p. 177). "Variety of imagination," James decided in his assessment of Adam Verver in *The Golden Bowl*, "—what is that but fatal, in the world of affairs, unless so disciplined as not to be distinguished from monotony?" (xxiii, 128).

James's wit tended to be devastating whenever the subject of mediocrity came up (a fact that does not necessarily make him a mandarin). In his 1910 essay "Is There A Life After Death?" (included in *The James Family*) he suddenly introduces the matter in the midst of his consideration of personal immortality:

> . . . what we dimly discern as waste the wisdom of the universe may know as a very different matter. We don't think of slugs and jellyfish as the waste, but rather as the amusement, the attestation of wealth and variety, of gardens and sea-beaches; so why should we, under stress, in respect to the human scene and its discussable sequel, think differently of dull people? (p. 603)

In his next sentences James concedes that the universe might conceivably entertain the Whitmanian over-view; it might accord success immediately to all creatures, whether interesting or boring in his own eyes. But James admits he can look at the subject only from the limits of his personal human perspective. He is, thereby, baffled as to why "the universe should be at the expense of a new start for those on whom the old start appears . . . so to be wasted" (p. 603). One must earn a go at a second chance in James's scheme of election. By implication (one made explicit throughout *The American Scene*), America may also forfeit its right to more chances: not through being too prodigal, but by being *too mere*.

As might be expected, Henry James did not settle upon any one set of responses to the American scene. He disliked sameness with all the fervor his mild manner could muster; still, he marked in *The American Scene* (p. 196) the failure of the Anglo-Saxon type before the onslaught of Irish, Italian, and Jew and the resulting loss in American society of comforting homogeneity. James sensed that he was losing his own country—that place where "everyone" once shared the same kind of "English" background which encouraged each person to be himself within a common context. In turn, "the inconceivable alien" who kept arriving on American shores rapidly stopped being what he had uniquely been back in his native land; he got leveled off into a new type with whom James (third-generation Irish) had "nothing 'in common.' "

In the 1770's Crèvecœur's Farmer James had taken joy in this metamorphosis of the Old World type of non-entity. By coming to America a man became what he was ideally meant to be—a full-sized integer, and American. But by 1904 Henry James was uneasy over the failure of the original European—the one who, by coming over and having "disembarked," loses what he once had, while gaining something of dubious value in return.

Variety, distinction, and thickness are prime Jamesian virtues, but banality pervaded the nation wherever the restless analyst glanced in 1904. It seemed to James as if "the sum of its passions" were "the cash-register, the ice-cream freezer, the lightning-elevator, the 'boys' paper,' and other such overflows . . ." (p. 312). America looked covered over by a "neutrality of respectability," likened to "a great grey wash of some charged moist brush causing colour and outline . . . effectively to run together" (p. 455). This was the legacy, D. H. Lawrence would argue later in *Studies in Classic American Literature*, of that snuff-colored gentleman, Benjamin Franklin, who had turned America into "the country of small adventures" of which Emerson was so contemptuous, diminishing all conceptions of success and of failure by his imposition of the norm of "happy mediocrity."

Someone with a principle may think himself invincible, but things, persons, and the mass can do him in on any city street in broad daylight. If he should make it alive past those perils, he has still to find whether his idea of destiny can withstand the cheats of change, whether his idea of succcess can stand off the preordained strictures of fate, and whether his bottom being can deny the weight of all that "levels off."

# CHAPTER 16

# Bottom Being

The man of character cannot fail at anything he does since he has chosen to fulfill his natural birthright of joy. "I am *Defeated* all the time," Emerson assures himself in his journal of 1842, "yet to Victory I am born" (VIII, 228). Life is a battle that mankind is meant to win, Thoreau writes on March 21, 1853. "Despair and postponement are cowardice and defeat. Men were born to succeed, not to fail." Of course, various moods may run through the same man, as Thoreau notes on November 4, 1851. He may contain "dark and muddy pools," but higher up lies his true source—the pure water of the trout stream, what Gertrude Stein would call in *The Making of Americans* a person's vital, essential "bottom being"—that being which is devoted to success (p. 318).

Character defined as spine is more important than brains, suggests Ishmael. Character announces its presence by the sound of great booms; the "natural phenomenon" noted both by Thoreau at Walden in the springtime and by Gertrude Stein in *The Making of Americans*. (As Stein phrases it, "the bottom being" strikes the ear as "a louder and louder pounding.") Character enables a man to be what Thoreau called the true American: the man who is free—the man like Emerson's Osman, who is able to seize the apple at the center of the cosmos and to eat it in a great gulp without choking over the loss of either paradise or power.

But what is character, and what are its powers which promise such victory? Character is known by several traits, chief among them *discipline, work, friction, concerns, style*, and *health*. On the need for these traits such disparate types as Thoreau, Emerson, Adams, Stein, and Mailer agree. "Character" is, indeed, not a New Englander's fate alone; although the voice of the Wasp predominates, others also make reports on the matter. Stein and Mailer serve to indicate the ways in which character possesses dimensions unthought of by the men of Boston and Concord. But for them all, "bottom being" is fundamental to the ability to win.

Mailer says enviously in *Of a Fire on the Moon* that discipline is what the Wasp has working for him. The flower children may have sweetness, but they lack fiber; the blacks have the style, but not the power to sustain. The moon—the dream-kingdom for all three groups—was lost to those who only dreamed about getting there and failed to hone their efforts to the knife-edge to make it happen. Think how sick of heart Mailer would be, therefore, to have heard Emerson's oration of 1876, "The Scholar," in which the "speculative man," praised as "the right hero," is described as one who "is not there to defend himself but to deliver his message." Even "if broken, he can at least scream; gag him, he can still write it; bruise, mutilate him, cut off his hands and feet, he can still crawl towards his object on his stumps." However much Mailer would like to go paunchy and be lazy without regret, he agrees with Emerson that one must take the hard way.

Mailer's appreciation of work as a prime American trait is shared, perhaps surprisingly, by that most leisurely of novels by Henry James, *The Golden Bowl*. Charlotte Stant is American-born but so assimilated into a European pattern of life she hardly thinks of herself as an American; she believes she is like Prince Amerigo. Fanny Assingham, however, makes the cogent observation that whereas the Prince acts like a Prince—that is, he "plays" like the Old World Roman he is—"Charlotte works like a horse," a true American, in this at least (XXIII, 398). Far more than Charlotte, Maggie Verver offers an instructive portrait of the American with both an "idea" and the readiness to achieve it that is missionary in its intensity. In the scene in which she waits out the crisis of the cracked bowl with which she must confront the Prince. Maggie is

> *found* ready, without loose ends or exposed accessories or un-removed superfluities; a suggestion of the swept and garnished . . . that reflected her small still passion for order and symmetry, for objects with their backs to the walls, and spoke even of some probable reference, in her American blood, to dusting and polishing New England grandmothers. (XXIV, 152-153)

James makes clear throughout *The Golden Bowl* that several dangers menace Americans filled with a passion for mission and order, and that these Americans, in turn, menace those upon whom they impose their ideas. But if Maggie will force Prince Amerigo to discover what lies behind "the great white curtain" (the means by which he images, via reference to Poe's *Pym*, the American moral consciousness), she, too, will have to make a leap away from order into the dark. "*Found* ready," Maggie may yet face disillusionment and despair at the new mission-stations. She may perhaps inflict pain on others out of frustration if she is unable to get past that darkness. Perhaps she may—if able to surmount the failures of resentment and anger—carry her spirit to a good conclusion. At the point pictured in the particular scene just cited we are not able to decide what the outcome will be, but we are shown the *type* of the American of character born out of a tradition of successful missions.

In *A Week on the Concord and Merrimack Rivers* Thoreau defines character as that devotion to a sacred mission which gives a man a sense of abrasive presence: with it he stands out like a pillar in a desert (p. 45). Alas! Faulkner's Joe Christmas in *Light in August*—a man of character but no identity—has a mission that exposes him like "a lone telephone pole in the middle of a desert" (p. 106). Mission makes him a target for killing; but, after all, self-exposure is part of Joe's mission. Character comes from friction, Stein says in *The Making of Americans*: contrast, contact, and relationships of surface, since character will not exist inside a vacuum. When Joe Christmas stands in the midst of his desert—insistent upon being *seen* by the others—his presence sets up the relationships that result both in his death and in the tenacity with which his memory will adhere to the walls of the townspeople's minds.

To have specific "concerns," John Woolman said, makes all the difference between the men with mission and those who lack it. If character springs from the possession of mission-strong discipline, character requires continuing work to keep it from becoming wasted power; "concern" makes this possible. Mark Twain commented in his autobiography that his mother had character but no career; in a sense she had character without public power—a contradiction in terms. Not a contradiction to Thoreau, however; he believed that the greatest power was pure character freed from the limitations exacted by doing something in particular. But Thoreau defined *being* as *doing*; merely to do things was dissipation of being. Giving himself to a lifetime of "concerns," he dismissed the more literal-minded focus of Woolman on the details comprising mission. He would have welcomed Mrs. Clemens into the circle of persons of true and potent character.

Discipline, work, friction, and "concerns" are relatively observable elements in any person of character. Health will be too (although there is more to say in a moment on that matter). But *style* seems to be the trait that falls outside the Wasp experience. To possess an aesthetic is an attribute Mailer admires greatly, even though

defining its nature and its results baffles him at times. Mailer willingly picks style over content, yet he constantly sees content moving
other people ahead. Contemplating the possible outcome of the
march on the Pentagon in *Armies of the Night*, he decides he wants to
win or lose "with boom! and baroque in the style," but he realizes
that even under such "stylish" circumstances he has just as great a
chance of losing as winning (p. 8). He is especially unhappy that
most of the Wasps who win goals of value lack style. They all seem
to drive beige VWs, give beige parties in beige living-rooms, and
have beige-clothed wives. But they are full of ideas. Quite lacking
in style, they are strong on content. In contrast, the flower children, the hipsters, and the blacks have more than enough style.
Theirs is an aesthetic without ideas—and so they seldom win.

Henry James remembered vividly the impression made upon
him as a boy on a visit to Sing Sing Prison by a suave gentleman in
an impeccable white suit. As described in *A Small Boy and Others*
(p. 174), the man lounged grandly in one of the prison corridors,
the epitome of style and wit. What is more, he seemed to know just
who he was—usually a good sign of a man of character. According
to the somewhat playful theory which James proposes in *The American Scene* (pp. 300-301), those who turn up in prison are persons
who, unlike most of us, have fully disclosed their true selves to the
eyes of society. By implication, they are losers because they have
been caught out, in contrast to those "outside" who are winners in
the true sense or by the fact of concealing their losses. The man in
the white suit at Sing Sing had not learned one fundamental lesson
of success: that crime does not *pay in* to a man, and that even the
stylishness of the criminal type cannot alter the fact of his *lack of
content*.

The child-persona of *A Small Boy and Others* may be accused
of moral platitudes about the failure of crime to pay in terms of
character, but when James writes about Chad Newsome in *The Ambassadors* the same point is being pressed with even more sophistication. One glance at the quality of Chad's life and we see how aesthetically striking it is. Further observations reveal how "beautifully" Chad has put off upon others the burden of making crucial
choices. The crime of being a man of style without content brings
Chad success on precisely those levels about which the young man
is most knowledgeable and self-complacent.

But to James and to Strether this aesthetic man of high-style has
evaded the chance to choose character. He has stopped short with a
beauty that lacks the sustaining idea of success. That idea depends

as much on the possession of the attributes of discipline, work, friction, and "concerns" as it does on style, but Chad Newsome certainly does not have them. Returning home to the prison of Woollett society, Chad will end like the suave man in the white suit whom James once saw at Sing Sing, hosting a perpetual party in the corridors of society, revealing to the perceptive the fact of his deep failure.

Fortunately for Mailer (who dislikes seeing his pet arguments about style contradicted by events) and for James (who revered the aesthetic quality of life), there appear from time to time examples of Wasps who have both style and content. For instance, to the rescue of Mailer's theory in *Armies of the Night*, in the midst of the generally dingy march on the Pentagon, come William Sloane Coffin, Junior, Chaplain of Yale, and Robert Lowell of Boston, two men who—with himself, Mailer hopes—are shaped to suit "the aristocracy of achieved quality" (p. 14). James might have agreed with Mailer on this, though he would have still other questions to put to these three men before deciding upon the quality of their success. But before we turn James loose to pose these questions, there is the crucial matter of sickness and of health to take up.

F. Scott Fitzgerald appreciated the life of style, but he knew something else was needed to gain and to sustain victory. In *The Great Gatsby* he has Nick Carraway look at Wilson and then at Tom Buchanan and decide "there was no difference between men, in intelligence or race, so profound as the difference between the sick and the well" (p. 148). Tom is a winner and Wilson a loser—the latter "so sick that he looked guilty" (pp. 148-149). We would probably rather not call Tom a true success since he has health without character, but according to some students of the subject character is, above all, health.

"If I am well, then I see well," wrote Thoreau, a prime believer in character-as-health, on August 6, 1841. That same year, on December 31, he noted that society as a whole was gravely ailing; even the best men had sickened. The city is the society, and Thoreau in 1843 encountered that City of Man known locally to its residents as Manhattan. As he mentioned in a letter home on October 18th, he knew that a man must begin "from that grain of health which he has left. . . . I have the jaundice myself; but I also know what it is to be well" (VI, 118).

1850 and 1851 inspired Thoreau to many jottings on the question of health (VIII, 45, 160, 449, 471). One dare not, he warned, take excessive alarm from the diseases of society, else the contagion spread. "As for health, consider yourself well, and mind your business. Who knows but you are dead already? Do not stop to be scared yet; there are more terrible things to come and ever to come. Men die of fright and live of confidence."

Physical elasticity is vital, Thoreau believed: "Health is the free use and command of all our faculties, and equal development." Indeed, "only the healthiest man in the world is sensible to the finest influence; he who is affected by more or less of electricity in the air." Thoreau admitted that "disease is, in fact, the *rule* of our terrestrial life and the prophecy of a *celestial* life." "Disease is not the accident of the individual, nor even of the generation, but of life itself." Having conceded the unlikelihood of full health (total self-possession) in this world, Thoreau counter-attacks this position in the same entry of September 3, 1851: "It is, nevertheless, a cheering fact that men affirm health unanimously, and esteem themselves miserable failures."

The man of character must *choose* health to avoid defeat. "Be of good cheer," Thoreau wrote on September 7, 1851. "Those Jews were too sad; to another people a still deeper revelation may suggest only joy." (According to Thoreau, if we respond to Malamud's *The Assistant*, we must decide not to be like dying Morris Bober but like Frank Alpine ever asking for "the better life.") "Don't I know what gladness is?" Thoreau continued. "Is it but the reflex of sadness, its back side?" (According to Thoreau, Mailer's route of dread in *Why Are We in Vietnam?* indeed takes one into the dark satanic passages of disease and buggery.) "In the Hebrew gladness, I hear but too distinctly still the sound of sadness retreating. Give me a gladness which has never given place to sadness." (As if by an act of will, Thoreau chooses not to be Mailer, who, in so many other ways, is his brooding cousin; yet by an act of will Mailer also tries to keep out of Morris Bober's coffin, although he, too, at times dances on its lid like Frank Alpine.)

Energetic choice of one's destiny: always that with Thoreau. Choice of health through never remitting discipline of will. "A little relaxation in your exertion, a little idleness, will let in sickness and earth into your own body. . . ," he wrote on April 27, 1854. (Mailer often lets in "sickness and earth," even as he fights to keep back the cancers spreading inward from "out there" in society.) "Every human being is the artificer of his own fate in these respects. The well have no time to be sick."

"I have noticed," Thoreau wrote on May 26, 1857

that notional invalids, who report to the community the exact condition of their heads and stomachs every morning, as if they alone were blessed or cursed with these parts; who are old betties and quiddles, if men: who can't eat their breakfasts when they are ready, but play with their spoons, and hanker after an ice-cream at irregular hours; who go more than half-way to meet any invalidity, and go to bed to be sick on the slightest occasion. . . . I observe that such are self-indulgent persons, without any regular and absorbing employment. . . . They come to you stroking their wens, manipulating their ulcers, and expect you to do the same for them. Their religion and humanity stick. They spend the day manipulating their bodies and doing no work; can never get their nails clean.

Spiritual Portnoys are the kind of masturbators Mailer also detests, but he, as the primal city boy, cannot find ready restorative powers in nature. For Thoreau, "in sickness all is deranged," as he notes of himself in his journal of November 18, 1857: "I lost for the time my *rapport* or relation to nature." For Mailer, madness comes when society loses rapport with men, but both Mailer and Thoreau celebrate that joyful moment when the mind is in union with the body. "Suddenly our condition is ameliorated," Thoreau wrote in 1857, on December 27th, "and even the barking of a dog is a pleasure to us. So closely is our happiness bound up with our physical condition, and one reacts on the other." Thoreau and Mailer surely would agree on the point taken in *A Week on the Concord and Merrimack Rivers* (p. 272) that quackery is the attempt to cure only the body that leaves the mind in a suspended state of malaise. Yet if melancholy is a dire disease, Mailer actively enjoys it. To feel melancholy is proof that he is right to denounce the sickness of the American social imagination. If America were actually healthy he would have no justification for his own aches. One suspects at times, however, that Mailer's melancholia is more constitutional than Constitutional. Like Carlyle, perhaps Mailer "could have been the merriest of men, *had I not* been the sickliest and saddest."

Thoreau has the Wasp aversion to whining which Mailer both agrees with and chafes under. Thoreau does not publish his despairs, while Mailer rushes his into print. Thoreau can say in *A Week* that men "cry better than they speak" and that those who cry while they speak are the ones setting themselves up as reformers of society (p. 111). Faulty bowels and bad indigestion are the seat of much philanthropy, he insists in *Walden* (p. 77). (Mailer sometimes chooses to image society's ills as constipation; he would probably

agree with Thoreau that such ills are treated best by men not suffering the same complaint.) *Walden* proliferates with Thoreauvian
slurs against hypochondria: Hebe, not Hygeia, is his muse;
America is a nation of the sick-minded; the Fourth of July has become a day of canker-rash; Americans ought to work out of
strength, not illness; one cannot build on ruins or live inside
mausoleums; robins of hope are birds indigenous to American
woodlands, not the melancholy nightingales of tubercular English
vales.

Emerson stood behind Thoreau on matters of success defined as
health and of society's failures viewed as self-indulgent hypochondria. With a head-start of ten years to make many of these same
metaphors work for his meaning, by 1841 Emerson had several entries in the journals on the subject:

> The Whig party in the Universe concedes that the radical
> enunciates the primal law but makes no allowance for friction
> and this omission makes their whole doctrine impertinent.
> The Whig assumes sickness, and his social frame is a hospital.
> His total legislation is for the present distress,—a universe in
> slippers & flannels, with bib & pap-spoon, swallowing pills &
> herb-tea, whig preaching, whig poetry, whig philosophy, whig
> marriages. (VIII, 87)

> And now that sickness has got such a foothold, leprosy has
> grown cunning, has got into the ballot box, the lepers outvote
> the clean, society has resolved itself into a Hospital Committee
> and all its laws are quarantine. (VIII, 89)

In describing the person of success in "Aristocracy," Emerson
wrote in 1848:

> Certainly, the origin of most of the perversities and absurdities
> that disgust us is, primarily, the want of health. Genius is
> health and Beauty is health and Virtue is health. . . . Temper-
> ament is fortune, and we must say it so often. In a thousand
> cups of life, only one is the right mixture—*a fine adjustment to
> the existing elements*. (Italics mine.)

Henry Adams was another American attentive to the hypochondria of spirit and body suffered by society and himself. Characteristically, he diagnosed the seed of this illness as restlessness (in
letters included in Vol. 1, 476, 523, of the Ford edition). "Alack, it is
disease!" he wrote on March 16, 1891 from the South Seas. On
September 10th from Ceylon: "Another Paradise opens its arms to

another son of Adam, but the devil of restlessness, who led my ancestor to the loss of his estate, leads me." The craving for motion
was an appropriate symptom of an age of acceleration, but the illness was an ancient one. Adams continued to distinguish between
the calm motion that saves and the hectic motion that harms, just as
he noted distinctions between the heat of the sun that sustains life
and the hot fevers that weaken. He reported on the childhood
fever that had altered him, leaving him smaller in frame than his
brothers, equipped with doubts and hesitations; its after-effects,
which let loose a "malaise" in the blood-stream, had led him toward
the choice of failure as his true destiny.

As a child Henry James also underwent a soul-changing siege
with fever which he records in *A Small Boy and Others* (pp. 281-285;
399-400). His case, however, was unlike Adams' in its effects. His
illness acted upon him like those redemptive brain-fevers that inflict characters in the novels of Dickens and Dostoevsky, and he
rose from the sick-bed with a renewed consciousness, alert to new
possibilities for response. Since, for James, such alertness is a major
element of success, he started out well ahead of Adams, who said
*his* illness cut him down and put him off-balance. Yet Adams did
not slide all the way back. If he (although no more than Henry
James) was "out of it" as far as the world of doing-as-getting is concerned, Adams was not "out of" the particular world of doing-as-
giving which he shared with James. Yet they were not really well,
either of them, and they knew it.

Genius is akin to childhood and convalescence, both Poe and
Baudelaire agreed. An edge of fever, a touch of maladjustment,
saves one from detested normalcy of temperature and outlook.
"There are certain kinds of success which are indistinguishable
from panic," Degas once said, and William James believed that
"mere sanity is the most philistine and (at bottom) unessential of
man's attributes." In "Our Country and Our Culture" from *Advertisements for Myself* Mailer states his resentment of the "healthy
manifestoes" that coerce the American writer into being mature,
realistic, and integrated (p. 188). Mailer prefers to define true
health as Jewish *ego* (somewhat damp-palmed) rather than as Wasp
*character* (cool and 98.6°). Mailer believes that ego lives in ignorance
and feeds on pain, but it can still get you authority, certainty, and
the ability to win out. Emerson may have had character, for instance, but he closed his eyes in embarrassment whenever he
smiled; inhibited in his ego, he could never truly win greatness.

Character is, briefly, that Steinian quality which is so strong and self-sufficient that it never needs to go outside its god-self for any kind of medication. Ego is what makes mammon-men run; run also because of nervous susceptibility to criticism and self-doubts; run in constant response to other forces that try to keep the ego from succeeding on its own. Character, which is success, keeps you in success. Ego, often uncongenial to successfulness, grants greatness whether or not you win. Expressed in various ways, the code of ego is upheld in common by such non-Wasps as Anna Freud, David Bakan, and Norman Mailer. It is supported, too, by Erik Erikson (half Jew, half Kierkegaardian Dane), and by Herman Melville (all too much, at times, the blue-eyed Anglo-Protestant), who noted that morbidity and disease are the significant traits of great men.

Why success anyway? In *Apostles of the Self-Made Man* John Cawelti ponders this as he runs through the methods for winning offered by Norman Vincent Peale and Dale Carnegie. If in order to command success one must first become confident, serene, and happy—that is, successful in and through one's healthy ego disguised as character—why bother with the goal itself? Mailer could ask a further question: Why bother with success if one can make use of the itch of ego to run after greatness? Mailer is his own best answer to this. Ironically, it is his insatiable ego which both urges him to grab at greatness and to want the success of character. William James was right when he noted the artificiality of making categories of difference between men. In a comment from *Pragmatism* (quoted in *The James Family*, p. 240) James pointed to the truth that "few of us are tender-footed Bostonians, pure and simple, and few of us are typical Rocky Mountain toughs, in philosophy. Most of us have a hankering for the good things on both sides of the line." So, too, Mailer.

Character is the necessity of virtue and the acceptance of the self as less than virtuous. The figure of Thomas Jefferson in *Brother to Dragons* learns this at the insistence of his creator, Robert Penn Warren. Once this lesson is possessed, the Jefferson-type is able to pull his dream of hope concerning man and America past the impasse of nightmare despair. But Jefferson is also taught by R.P.W., the poet-figure in the poem, that greatness rises above the necessity for virtue. Thoreau agreed that the best thoughts have no morality. "The moral aspect of nature is a jaundice reflected from man," he wrote in his journal of August 1, 1841. "To the innocent there are no cherubim nor angels." Accordingly, we ought to rise into the morning light, where there is no need to choose between right and wrong; once saved, we recognize only the need "to live right on" the life that is "the very vitality of *vita*."

In Thoreau we have a man who can argue both for virtue and character, for ego and greatness. That another kind of power lies beyond chastity and purity is an idea he willingly concedes in a journal entry of 1850. Picking up a hog-jaw with white, sound teeth and tusks, Thoreau is reminded "that there was an animal health and vigor distinct from the spiritual health. This animal succeeded by other means than temperance and purity" (VIII, 36). Of course, Thoreau did not want to win at life as a hog does. He wished to rise by means of purity above the need to name purity at all. But if it required that he call upon both ego and character to gain the realm where the self no longer exists and success is but a name, this man of high principle was ready to use any expedient to get there.

Thoreau watched the moon conquering the clouds that tried to master it and he knew its greatness, but he acknowledged that men are not the moon. Several of Faulkner's characters also learn that they are different from the high, cold, perfect, indifferent stars. They must, whether frontally or obliquely, deal with virtue insofar as it helps to define the self—that sole basis for character or for ego—but they must eventually move past virtue. Mailer is also reluctant to climb "moral ladders," even while admitting the need in the Virginia jail to experience a troubling rite of passage that takes one past morality. The armies of the night must somehow try to reach the dawn-time.

Character or ego will always be defeated in the world Thoreau observes in *A Week on the Concord and Merrimack Rivers*. It is the place where God may indeed know when each sparrow falls to its death, but where sparrows fall just the same. In such a universe, the red squirrel that delights in scaring itself over what may never take place is matched by the sparrow that knows the sorrow of certain death. Men ruled by such laws are unable to take success or greatness in all areas at once. It is a world of difficulties, no doubt about that. Some holding action is necessary to tide one over the gaps, some aggressive plan as well, since virtue alone will not do it. Will it be accomplished by character or by ego? Perhaps a third force is needed with qualities that supplement virtue and edginess, and that promise the particular kind of success and/or greatness which a sparrow-falling world requires.

Long after the event, Alice James recalled an unpleasant summer's afternoon in 1856 spent as a child on an outing with Henry, Wilky, and Bob. (William, typically, was absent; he had not had to put up with the terms of failure which plagued his sibling inferiors that day and so many other days.) "We were turned into the garden to play," Alice writes (in an anecdote included in *The James Family*, pp. 84-85), "—a sandy, or rather dusty expanse, with nothing in it, as I remember, but two or three scrubby apple trees from one of which hung a swing." In the midst of this wasted Eden, Henry (thirteen years of age) and Alice (eight years) sat together "as the sun began to slant over the desolate expanse, as the dreary hours . . . passed." (Typically, the ever-blurred brothers Bob and Wilky have faded from the scene of Alice's memory, leaving only herself and that *distinct* brother, Henry.) Then "Harry suddenly exclaimed, 'This might certainly be called pleasure under difficulties!'"

Alice records how her "whole being" stirred responsively "to the exquisite, original form of his remark. . . ." It came to her "in a flash—the higher nature of this appeal to the mind." She experienced for the first time "the sense of self-satisfaction" that comes when facts lacking in value are changed by "wit" into "a new sense, a sense whereby to measure intellectual things"—finding them converted into gold. This is an act of the mind that is "moral" in that it requires courage, discipline, and fineness of being (the central element of character). But it also rises above morality in that its mode is that of wit and its goal is satisfaction (in ways that remind one of the ego's favorite qualities). It is *mind* that takes the laws of limits, endurance, and duty and transforms them into human triumphs, even while sparrows and men fall like rain all about and you know you may very well be the next.

Henry James, together with Thoreau, shows us the kind of American in the nineteenth century who needed to know how to fail in order that he could win: how to work skillfully with discipline, style, health, character, some ego, and much mind. The sorrow the sparrow feels as he falls cannot save him from death. A man's sorrow can bring him pleasure if he will only convert it through some kind of idea about "tributes to the ideal" in the midst of an achingly actual world. He must (as he remembered Minny Temple doing, in a passage from *Notes of a Son and Brother*, p. 492) play at the "old hobby of the 'remote possibility of the best thing' "—"better than a clear certainty of the second best."

The news of Hawthorne's death in 1864 (also recalled in *Notes of a Son and Brother*, p. 411) moved James to consider the uses to which

> American matter could be put by an American hand: a consummation involving, it appeared, the happiest moral. For the moral was that an American could be an artist, one of the finest, without "going outside" about it, as I liked to say; quite in fact as if Hawthorne had become one just by being American *enough*. . . .

Hawthorne may have died believing he had failed. It may well be that, because James saw what Hawthorne had accomplished and Hawthorne did not, it is only James who succeeded by having provided this tribute; but the tribute was James's way of putting it on record that Hawthorne had done something of value. Either way, some might think the amount of "success" gained in this artistic transaction is negligible. Still, James in his life-long references to what the living can do for the memory of the dead shows that he, for one, considered that an actual conversion from nullity to value was taking place.

If James learned how to turn the trick of converting difficulty into pleasure for himself by the age of thirteen, in 1895 he was still at it. In his notebooks he urged himself to take the fact of the plays he had so miserably failed at and to make use of that experience in developing the dramatic technique of his novels. "IF, I say, I have crept round through long apparent barrenness, through suffering and sadness intolerable, to that rare perception—why my infinite little loss is converted into an almost infinite little gain" (p. 188).

James testified about the success he felt that Hawthorne snatched from the dull coals of the American experience; he hoped he could do the same with the losses of his own years as a failed playwright. It was also necessary for Thoreau to discover success in his life where his contemporaries could not. Thoreau once carelessly set fire to the woods. After the event he devised a larky plan by which future conflagrations could be handled by a company of firefighters, complete with music to regulate, refresh, and celebrate the work. But the citizens of Concord knew only about a man who was unable to tie his shoelaces properly by the age of thirty-six; a man who did not know when to come in out of the cold or to dress suitably for protection against bronchitis; a man they called "a damned rascal" because of the woods-fire incident. They could not *see* him, so he had to see himself.

Thoreau noted on July 6, 1851 that there were advantages to being "the humblest, cheapest, least dignified man in the village, so that the very stable boys shall damn you." What did that matter since Thoreau, like the bound-servant to Admetus, knew he was Apollo in disguise? Cellini, humiliated before society and in prison, had had a dream that his head was haloed with light; by reminding himself of Cellini's self-confidence, Thoreau affirmed his own worth when he, too, remarked the halo that shone around his shadow as he walked home through the moonlight.

Perhaps the most notorious converter of pain into cheer in American letters is Pollyanna. There are times when Thoreau seems to best her at a game they played in common. In 1853, on November 12, he told himself he was grateful that, because of lack of money, he had been "nailed down to this my native region so long and steadily, and made to study and love this spot of earth more and more." On September 19, 1854 he wrote, "Ah, how I have thriven on solitude and poverty!"He asked rhetorically, "If I go abroad lecturing, how shall I ever recover the lost winter?" By January of 1857 he congratulated himself that he could count on getting only one to three annual invitations to give lectures, and sometimes none at all. Better to be like a bear in a trunk in winter, he concluded, sucking its paws, than running around to no use. Through the means Thoreau adopted in viewing his worldly set-backs he made his failures "tragical" and thereby a stroke of high success; this was far better than the mundane dullness of winning out. Thoreau is that "aristocrat" about whom Emerson lectured in 1848. This breed knows "a hero's, a man's success is made up of failures, because he experiments and ventures every day, and 'the more falls he gets, moves faster on.' . . . ." At this point in Emerson's public address, he tipped in that favorite entry from his journal: "defeated all the time, and yet to victory born." To Emerson and Thoreau alike, failure is very much an essential of success. Success is not just the *better* thing that follows after and is contrasted with failure. Success *contains* the failure it converts; it never removes— or wishes to—the fact of that bitter ingredient.

Henry James, Senior, contemporary of Thoreau and friend of Emerson, was another advocate of victory as trial, error, suffering, and gains; he believed that by extravagant experimentation, waste would be converted to fertility, hell subsumed by heaven. Out of such a parental background his son Henry learned during the Civil War to deal with the shame of "an obscure wound," possessed instead of a public badge of courage. In *Notes of a Son and Brother* Henry James tells what it meant to be "only" an "obscure, a deeply hushed failure" at school (p. 4). His brother William was a splendid success as a student; Henry was not even a brilliant failure. But the back injury that kept Henry from military service in the war was converted from a source of private shame into a method for the cultivation of the imagination which brought him the only kind of deep success he was ever to know.

The results of James's efforts have little to do with the theory of compensation Emerson talked about when he was being less than perceptive about the nature of *important* victory. James did not merely have something nice balance out something bad. The bad retained its reality, its sting, since this was a real world in which such calamities continued *to happen to* James. Rather, the bad was simultaneously coerced into becoming the occasion for gain and the source for value. Further, the conversion took place not because James lived in a decently run universe, but because his mind—the "wit" Alice praised when they were still children—made it take place.

The surgeon whom James consulted about his wrenched back said nothing was wrong. With this statement James was provided no medical justification for lying prone for hours in order to relieve the intense pain he felt. In *Notes of a Son and Brother* he writes, "There were a hundred ways to behave . . . and I think of the second half of that summer of '62 as my attempt at selection of the best" (p. 301). He realized he had to provide the critical country at war with some reason for his languor while others marched erectly off to battle. So he took up a book to make it appear as if it were study he were committed to, not indolence. To have a book in hand gave the "cynicism" of his prone position (physical and moral) "a certain fine plausibility." This was at least "a negative of combat," James recalled, "an organized, not a loose and empty one, something definitely and firmly parallel to action in the tented field" (p. 301).

There was more to the act than this gambit which, after all, only served to placate the outside world and to hold its petty criticisms at bay. Just as Benjamin Franklin had worked two ways with the facts so that he could give the appearance of being a diligent businessman at the same time he actually was busy, James set up the appearance of study and also went about supplying his mind with material for later use as a writer. Through the books James read during this time of war, through the sheer act of *reading*, the Man of Imagination—never considered the hero of the conventional American success-story—hoarded his wealth and began the process of converting shame and vagueness of purpose into something of value; the shame and the vagueness remained, but he would not settle for that.

It is telling that this mild and somewhat tentative young man *converted something out of* pain and shame by an act of will and wit, while his brother William—generally considered to be the stronger of the two brothers—had first to be *converted to* health, and to movements away from severe soul-sickness, through his readings in Renouvier and Wordsworth on the power of the will. And there was Henry's decision to grow a beard in his fifties. It made him feel younger, he said; even more useful (in fine Franklinian argument) was the fact that the time he saved from daily shaving could be given over to his writing. James's conversion strategies did not always work, of course. He admitted in a letter (included in *The James Family*, p. 262) that the sentences he spun in response to the death of Minny Temple could not alter the truth that "she is *dead*." He knew that that act of his was a "fruitless attempt to transmute [her death] from a hard fact into a soft idea." Even so, James was "willing to leave life to answer for life." Such "tributes to the ideal" could not change the real or balance out death with life's weight; but they gave to the fact of death a liveliness that was nearly as vital as actual living.

Henry Adams was another American who played constantly at making strength out of melancholy and disaster. On April 25, 1895 he wrote Charles Milnes Gaskell (in a letter included in the Ford edition, II, 66): "As I grow old, I become more and more Carlylean, Palgravian, Woolnerian and anarchian; and my pessimism has served me well, in the contrary sense, for, among the Jews, I should be admired as almost the only known Gentile who had managed to get richer in the lap of ruin."

Adams would certainly have given Gertrude Stein her due as a Jew who knows how to succeed. Stein seems to be referring in turn to Adams with her comment in *Everybody's Autobiography* that "Most of the great men in America had a long life of early failure and a long life of later failure" (p. 86). Intermediate success bracketed by failures is implied, even if it is the quality of start and finish that catches the eye and undercuts the myth of America as "a land of success" for the sons of Adam. Norman Mailer also senses himself as one of the chosen people who insist on their own continuing worth in the face of the fact of having an erratic career in the sight of the onlookers. The heritage Mailer chooses for himself, however, in *The Armies of the Night* is that of the Romantics rather than of the Hebrews. The Romantics' true act, he tells himself, drunken, at the Ambassador Theatre, is to convert defeat into victory and not to bother being quiet about it.

One way to bring off this conversion (and to avoid having to be subtle and a gentleman) is to take credit for having caused the defeat of big events. Mailer cheers himself with the idea that if the march on the Pentagon collapses, it will be his doing. This is a singular method for asserting the authority of one's presence, but it is better than being shut out of Dwight MacDonald's mind altogether. In the end, that October night's noisy, outrageous, and obscene speech did not really bring Mailer a satisfactory sense of himself as someone to be reckoned with. Even being arrested before the Pentagon proved him to be just barely important enough to be marked out by the police for punishment. This helps, but to be able *to imagine the creation* of the success or failure of a major event in history— that *is* something because it changes everything.

To be overlooked altogether is a true defeat. Henry Adams knew this by bitterness of fact, as much as Mailer does. The young Adams, mere secretary attached to his father's ministerial post during the American Civil War, writes an article in London critical of the British. There is momentary consternation in the Minister's household over the adverse effects such an article might have on the delicate relations between the American North and Great Britain. Would a diplomatic break result from the son's indiscretion, and an alliance be announced with the American South? No, thank heavens, crisis is adverted because the Minister's son is such a nonentity no one notices what he has written. The Union is saved, and another American tastes the bitter dust of failure because of his lack of power and presence. But that failure is eventually crafted into an anecdote for *The Education of Henry Adams*. There is some conversion, away from the impotence demonstrated by the original event, toward the later success, however slight, got by the telling of the tale.

This conversion is somewhat different from Mailer's experience during the Pentagon march, but hardly different from Henry James's during the Civil War. The distinction is this: in their war experiences Adams and James were immediate failures in any conventional sense of the word. Of course, Adams was comparatively even more a failure than James because the lesson he learned convinced him of his utter lack of worldly influence, while James was learning on his war-time couch how to draw positive force from a negative fact. It was different with Mailer. While his escapades were somewhat ludicrous (in actuality as well as in the comic way he reports them), Mailer made his point *at the time* that he was there in the "war." His actions were not wholly dismissible even then. Aside from these minor distinctions, however, what counts is what the three men took from the occasion. As writers each eventually got more power (in Adams' instance—the only *real* power) out of the telling of his experiences. The original events and the subsequent artistic embellishments are distinct matters; the former and the latter involve different kinds of patterns of success and failure, but together they add up to something that helped all three men "to get richer in the lap of ruin."

The American who is also an artist has a way *into* success denied the American who is just that and no more. No one is quicker than the artist to note the handicaps he suffers in his attempts to be a winner; but he experiences winning whenever he moves an event out of the fixed meaning of historical or purely personal time into the expanded meaning of the narrated art-fact. As it *had happened*, it may have simply been failure. As it *comes to happen* in his shaping of it after the fact, it can contain both that failure and more than failure.

*Thoreau* (journal of November 5, 1855): "Thus men invite the devil in at every angle and then prate about the garden of Eden and the fall of man."

*Martha L. Smith* (from *Going to God's Country* in which she records a life of travel from Missouri to Texas to Oklahoma to Oregon and back to Oklahoma at the turn of the nineteenth century): "We had spent 48 years together hunting for God's Country. Before he [her husband] died we learned that God's Country isn't in the country. It is in the mind. As we looked back we knew that all the time we was hunting for God's Country, we had it. We worked hard. We was loyal. Honest. We was happy. For 48 years we lived together in God's Country" (pp. 184-186).

It is not surprising to recognize that the mind can destroy itself, or recreate itself, out of pride in its own powers. But since the word "dream" is so frequently connected with the many facts of the American experience, yet one more brief examination of the force which dreaming has upon the life of the imagination in America is in order, and inevitable. And necessary, since "dream" is different from "idea" and "vision"—the two matters of more concern to this book even than dream.

Here follows a statement of certain distinctions between the mind that dreams and the one that does not, with the presence or absence of force that results.

That action succeeds which moves forward through a continual present marked by awareness (both of self and the contingencies surrounding that self), by assertiveness, and by calm to arrive at that sense of control which is its prime goal. Control, in turn, means an idea has been fully realized. The actor here is the non-dreamer, one who is pragmatic and non-poetic, if not anti-poetic. The victor is the fully realized self, whereas the community may be either the victim or the beneficiary of his concentrated energy of purpose. The materials used to tell his tale of triumph are usually exclusive in nature, drawn consciously from the prose of history. The reader-witness of the life of the non-dreamer gains his pleasure from witnessing an affirmation of individual possibilities.

That action fails which lapses back into the far past in search of the lost Eden (fulfillment of remembered desires) or pushes forward into the far future (in anticipation of the New Jerusalem of attained perfection). The fact that the actor is the dreamer—idealistic and poetic—determines that the self can never attain complete control over either identity or circumstance. The victors in the tale are the natural environment or the community which stands apart from or in antagonism to the dreamer-victim. The materials used to tell the victim's tale are inclusive and mythic, tragic (even if sometimes comic in detail) in their recognition of the waste of powers, and nostalgic or Utopian in emotional tonality; they are dream-materials whose intrinsic beauty is the one positive reward gained by the dreamer and by the reader-witness of that dream which is doomed by definition to failure.

These distinctions (abstract and severely reduced to their outlines in order to withstand the blurring which usually characterizes actual events) place stress upon success as concept and the presence of control—what one gets by means of a realized idea; and upon failure as concept and the absence of control—what happens through insistence upon unfulfillable dreams. But more than control and concept must be taken into account if we would move past the dryness of such formulas. *Wonder* is that other element which reaches beyond the concept, often dictating the termination of control once its splendid, and frightening, force explodes upon the scene.

In 1946 Albert Einstein wrote in his *Autobiographical Notes*:

> What, precisely, is "thinking"? When, at the reception of
> sense-impressions, memory-pictures emerge, this is not yet
> "thinking." . . . I think that the transition from free association
> or "dreaming" to thinking is characterized by the more or less
> dominating rôle which the "concept" plays in it. . . . (1, 7)

Einstein then examines the relation between thought and
wonder:

> For me it is not dubious that our thinking goes on for the
> most part without use of signs (words) and beyond that to a
> considerable degree unconsciously. For how, otherwise,
> should it happen that sometimes we "wonder" quite spontane-
> ously about some experience? This "wondering" seems to
> occur when an experience comes into conflict with a world of
> concerns which is already sufficiently fixed in us. Whenever
> such a conflict is experienced hard and intensively it reacts
> back upon our thought world in a decisive way. The develop-
> ment of this thought world is in a certain sense a continuous
> flight from "wonder." (1, 9)

The immense question is whether wonder is a flight away from
the thought that succeeds and toward the dream that defeats, or
whether wonder may provide both the way to success and a definition of the visionary victory it wins.

Frank Kermode's argument in *The Sense Of An Ending* (pp. 80-
81) is useful here: first, for what it implies about the problem set up
by Einstein and the position taken in America toward thought as it
appears in philosophy and differently, in poetry; second, for the
attitudes taken toward the dream and the vision.

This is the difference between what Kermode would like to see
going on within poetry and what he believes ought not to seep out
of the poem into the outside world: What takes place *in* the poetry
is good in Kermode's eyes; it is a helpful vision which knows it is not
true. What goes on *outside* poetry is reality, not fiction. If you go on
speaking as if poetry were still the fact *out there*, then the situation is
very bad: poetry and vision are hardening into a dream and a myth
that believe they are true.

The difference between philosophy and poetry is this: philosophy is thought devoted to order and the end of confusion. Poetry,
in Kermode's words, "must in some measure imitate what is extreme and scattering bright, or else lose touch with that feeling of

bright confusion." Furthermore, because it deals with thought, philosophy is complex, whereas poetry, because it deals with what is "more sensuous and more passionate" than thought, is simple. What is "simple" comes to philosophers only when, in discussing the rankings of universal being, they struggle to realize "a pure idea of simplicity" for God or for an angel—that being which is "less simple" than God but "simpler than man." Out of its own simplicity, poetry can suggest "pure being" more strikingly than can philosophy, perhaps because it also works with "what is extreme and scattering bright."

Now, if poetry can handle the world with *wonder* (for what else is the "bright confusion" and the "extreme and scattering bright"?) in ways that philosophy's ordered conceptual systems cannot, one asks why poetry must be kept as closely locked in as Kermode argues that it must? Perhaps this is because he unhesitatingly defines the reality that resides outside the poem as dark chaos and impure complexity. If "bright confusion" and "pure being" are indeed only charming fictions, then it would be dangerous to let them leak out upon the world. However, let us consider what it would be like if the vision of wonder that takes place inside the poem could win the right to live outside the poem because it helps to qualify and to surmount man-made "fictions" about the world's chaos and impurity, and the artificial constructs of philosophical systems. If this act of opening up could take place, the poet would be released from the bondage to "reality" Kermode imposes upon the poet and his creations. He would no longer be hedged about by our own "continuous flight from 'wonder'" because of fear of beauty in the name of obedience to realism. He could then help us all find and nurture our "bottom being"—the source of our success.

Ralph Barton Perry speaks of William James's resistance to "any *reduction* of the ideal to the real. The ideal is the preferred form of life—something *to be made real* through the energy of the will" (p. 252). The ideal illustrated by Edgar Allan Poe and the real summed up by Benjamin Franklin offer useful examples of the complexity attending the need to gain control and wonder, both, in America. These two American types are chosen to illustrate the extremes of the real and the ideal; it would not be easy to find value in Poe if "real" is one's highest good, or to abide Franklin if "ideal" is one's prime reason for living. The question is whether "the energy of the will" can reconcile the world *in* the poem (Poe) with the world *outside* the poem (Franklin).

Franklin stands for the man who has made a success of his life, knows it, and pretty much how it came about. That particular American fable realized by his life and shaped by his description of its components (optimism, affirmation of human abilities, experimentation, utilitarian pleasures, and public service) concerns the social man who is able to control the destructive qualities of his own nature and those of the world that press in around him. It is not money or social rank that urge the Franklinian type onward; it is the attainment of the power to be what one wills. Matching art with nature, appearance with reality, he who is his own man can assume any number of roles—can *be* all the roles any one person potentially contains—as he enters upon a public life "that required a whole man to execute." Only the letter by Benjamin Vaughn —enclosed within the essentially dreamless record of the *Autobiography*—defines, and yearns for, that particular dream which will be sought by future generations of Americans. Franklin does not himself need to dream, since a dream attained is a dream ended, but those who come after him have his model-life to consult in order to know best how to be—and to be wholly and successfully—within the fabled American democratic mold.

In contrast to Franklin, Edgar Allan Poe's life (whether expressed by himself, the Reverend Griswold, Baudelaire, or Allen Tate) seems to be largely composed of dream elements. Dreaming dreams which never end, because never fulfilled, the Poe-figure is unable to find a place of power's leverage outside the dream in order, like Archimedes, to move his world. Whereas Franklin is ever the complete franklin—forger of the consciousness of his race, recognized and admired as the model democratic man—Poe is the partial poet, the man of imagination who exists outside society in resistance to everything which brings success in society to a man of common sense. The Poe-world is the other half of the American world; it is the realm which remains unclarified by Franklinian common sense; that which repudiates the ordinary and the democratic; and that which cannot be kept in line by a conscience demanding seriousness of effort in turn for the guarantee that there are clear-cut motives for everything—failure and success.

The Poe-esque dream stands opposite the Franklinian desire which not only can be, but is meant to be, attainable. The Poe-esque dream is of an unattainable Eden of the past or the unattainable supernal of the future; it is not of this mundane world seized, through common sense, in this democratic moment. The Poe-poet takes arms against the logic of an absurd universe ruled by the tyrannical patronage of the Imp of the Perverse, and is thereby assured of plunging toward self-destruction while loving it—this, in opposition to marching forward calmly to the democratic fifes and drums of self-survival and success.

There are points where the Franklinian man and the Poe-figure seem to converge. "I felt a calm but inquisitive interest in every thing," states the narrator of "The Man of the Crowd," as he moves from "an abstract and generalizing turn" to an avid examination of "details." But the poet who observes makes use of qualities ignored by the scientist—such as Dupinesque intuitions which seem almost preternatural; his powers are lavished upon the solving "of enigmas, of conundrums, of hieroglyphics" approached for their own sake with no thought after their future social usefulness. When Poe wrote "The Philosophy of Composition" that exposes the program he used to create the emotional effects of "The Raven," one suspects he was speaking as slyly as Franklin did when he revealed his ivory-tablet program for moral behavior. But however similar the two programs in their calculation, their aims are characteristically different. Poe wants to achieve the pleasures of beauty, thrill, irrationality, and a life doomed to Nevermore. Franklin desires to inculcate the pleasures of truth, calmness, and rational virtues for the sake of accomplished success. By foregoing soul, music, poetry, and the human aspirations for supernal beauty and the ideal, the Franklinian man appropriates to himself only that part of the imagination which, working with clear mind and controlled heart, can reach out and attain the rewards of reason and passion. Thus self-limited, he can be assured of full triumph and a sound night's sleep.

Franklin cheerfully lives without Poe, while the Poe-figure has to suffer in, and play with, Franklin's world—and much more. This "much more" is what causes the excitement and sorrow which agitate the Poe-esque dream. The dreamer recognizes the pull of the real (the place of imperfection where success takes place) and yearns for the ideal (the perfect, the measure of one's necessary failures). The dreamer dangles over maelströms of science (law) and imagination (chance); of the ordinary and the extraordinary; of the democratic group (which obeys whatever heals) and the aristocratic individual (who pursues the destructive).

If we ourselves can imaginatively and simultaneously encompass these two contending traditions, drawn from our sense of what Franklin and Poe represent as symbolic shorthand, we possess an important part of the American Dream. But that dream is not made up solely of the original forces which animated Franklin in the eighteenth century and Poe in the early nineteenth century. It contains those forces, yes, but also their corruptions in the years of history that followed. The dream that starts out in the Franklinian mode can deteriorate to a demeaning search after wealth and respectability; such possibilities were always latent in the parent-dream, even though they were initially checked by Franklin's own emphasis upon creative self-awareness and the integrity of power. And how easily the Poe-esque version of the dream can disregard its potentialities for playful flights of imaginative powers; it can keep to the bogs of self-destructive cravings for perfection or self-flaunting abnormality and become one of the worst kinds of failure—the one that bores.

This is what really counts: pure or debased, the Franklin-mind and the Poe-imagination are stirred by wonder. It is a wonder passed through the imagination, assimilated into the self-created man, and brought out again into the reality of his self-fulfillment.

Scott Fitzgerald's Dutch sailor intuited, almost with dread, that it was left to the American continent to provide "something commensurate to his capacity for wonder." Consider the fact that that sailor's contemporary was Thomas Pynchon's fictional character, William Slothrop, the first of the hopeful, paranoid Slothrops to push on to America. Slothrop's descendant Tyrone will be pursued throughout the length and breadth of *Gravity's Rainbow*, at last torn literally to pieces by the destructive forces of the twentieth century. But in William's day seventeenth-century America was a miracle meant to be enjoyed by men like himself. " 'That's what Jesus meant,' whispers the ghost of Slothrop's first American ancestor William, 'venturing out on the Sea of Galilee' " (p. 554.) But William finally came not to like what he found in America. "He saw it from the lemming point of view. Without the millions who had plunged and drowned, there could have been no miracle. The successful loner was only the other part of it: the last piece to the jig-saw puzzle, whose shape had already been created by the Preterite, like the last blank space on the table" (p. 554).

Since even Jesus had been unable to make America safe for the lemmings, wonder or no, William finally

sailed back to Old England, not in disgrace so much as despondency, and that's where he died, among memories of the blue hills, green maizefields, get-togethers over hemp and tobacco with the Indians, young women in upper rooms with their aprons lifted, pretty faces, hair spilling on the wood floors while underneath in the stables horses kicked and drunks hollered, the stars in the very early mornings when the backs of his herd glowed like pearl, the long, stony and surprising road to Boston, the rain on the Connecticut River, the snuffling good-nights of a hundred pigs among the new stars and long grass still warm from the sun, settling down to sleep. . . .

Could he have been the fork in the road America never took, the singular point she jumped the wrong way from? (p. 556)

Christopher Levett would have disagreed. In the face of "the Slothropian heresy," Levett (one of the types William sailed away from) would keep on stating and restating his rhetorical, loaded query: "but where was the fault, in the country or in themselves?" Yet even now we cannot name precisely the fork in the road that we as Americans ought to have taken to avoid all the faults that lay in ourselves. We would rather resist being forced to choose absolutely between Benjamin and Edgar, control and slippage, the real and the ideal. Another William (James) speaks for us when he offers an alternative way—"the Jamesian heresy"—which insists on having the ideal as "something *to be made real* through the energy of the will." Anything to keep us balanced by wonder between the worlds of reason and of dream.

In 1838 Charles Darwin put together several notebooks concerning what his editors, Howard Gruber and Paul Barrett, call "Man, Mind, and Materialism." Two excerpts from the M and N notebooks show Darwin worrying over certain distinctions between dream, will, reason, and action. Having noted that dreams violate the rules and relations of time, identity, and place, Darwin comments that they seem to exert little "influence on our conduct":

Sir J. Franklin when *starved*, all party dreamt of feasts of good food.—The mind wills to do this, & hears that, but yet scarcely really moves.—the willing therefore is ideal, as all the other perceptions. (p. 285)

Further on, Darwin quotes from James Mackintosh's *A General View of the Progress of Ethical Philosophy Chiefly During the Seventeenth and Eighteenth Centuries*:

Reason, as reason, can never be a motive to action. It is only when we superadd to such a being . . . sensibility, or the capacity of emotion or sentiment . . . of desire and aversion, that we introduce him to the world of action. (p. 359)

To these remarks of Mackintosh Darwin responded, "there is some great puzzle in what Sir J. M. says of pure reason not leading to action, & yet our emotions being only bodily actions associated with ideas" (p. 347).

By the close of the century William James (a psychologist with much to say about the sequential relations between body, emotions, and idea) was at work with several of the same questions that Darwin had placed in his notebooks a generation earlier: *Dreams*—the mind's desire for the ideal that has no power to initiate action, since even "the willing therefore is ideal." *Ideas*—so reasoned out they give no "motive to action." *Desires*—capable, when added to idea, of bringing a man "to the world of action." By conflating James's thoughts with Darwin's, we may perhaps tentatively conclude that the ideal can be made real—made an active force in life—"through the energy of the will." But it would take the idea together with emotion to do it, not diffused dream or idea alone. Perhaps we can push even beyond Darwin and James to suggest that the idea, instructed by dreams of wonder, might move Americans of whatever persuasion (Franklinian or Poe-esque) toward the realized ideal of wonder—the "something *to be made real*," that "bottom being" of both the land and ourselves.

# PART IV

# Renewal
## or
# Revenge

# ⟡ CHAPTER 17 ⟡

# Making Scenes

"Correspondence" interested William James as it did Emerson. In his essay of 1878, "Remarks on Spencer's Definition of Mind as Correspondence," James examines the implications for men's lives drawn from Spencer's term, then rejects what he finds. Spencer's synonyms for correspondence—"adjusted," "conformed," "fitted," "related," "meets," "concord," and "harmony"—lead James to this biting observation:

> The fox is most beautifully "adjusted" to the hounds and huntsmen who pursue him, the limestone "meets" molecule by molecule the acid which corrodes it; the man is exquisitely "conformed" to the *trichina* which invades him, or to the typhus poison which consumes him; and the forests "harmonize" incomparably with the fires that lay them low.

James proceeds to tear asunder Spencer's uncertain distinctions between "action pure and simple and *right* mental action." Unless the moth can detect differences between the pleasure given by a candle's flame and the death caused by fire's searing, that moth will fly toward the candle, "failing" to survive, rather than moving "successfully" away from annihilation. Spencer may have believed that correspondence brings mental action into line with outward relations in ways that favor survival, but James insists that such an attitude, largely deterministic in its preconceptions, is far less useful than spontaneous responses to experience that would invite the choice between flame's pleasure and flaming death.

James's essay continues the argument against Spencerian theories of survival on two levels: against their faulty advice about how to survive, and against their stress on physical survival as the only matter of human concern. James wants effective survival strategies, with top honors given to what he considered the most important elements of human existence—ideals, values, and hopes. The question left begging by James's attack—apparent to us after the smoke of his sentence lifts—is how such extra-physical goods can encourage human effort when everything in a man's environment seems set against him, body as well as soul.

What is one to do, for example, when America proves not to be the promised green breast, but rather the wasteland of one's endeavors? What reactions to defeat does one take? Does the weary fox flee before his pursuers with his heart uplifted at the thought that he is part of a universal scheme of correspondence, Emersonian or Spencerian? Does the moth, unable to seize the pleasure of the candle's light without being crisped by its heat, rush headlong into the flame in suicidal ecstasy, or in despair? If mental action cannot produce right choices for action, fatefully caught up as mind is by predetermined strictures, what will the mind's response be to failure?

Quietism, passivity, and submission make up one possible set of reactions to defeat. Aggrieved and bitter violence is another. But if Freud is correct, the rush into battle, however catastrophic, is no more negative than the sinking back into the ditch's dark warmth. Freud realized that the merely good person, in his passive avoidance of the risks of doing wrong, is neither clever nor strong. The quest for The Peaceable Kingdom in America may have failed, but the greater failure could be the peace which comes when that quest is altogether abandoned in full acquiescence to death.

E. E. Cummings saw security as negative; Saul Bellow warns against any relaxation of effort; Henry Adams disliked the jars of revolution and reform and sought amusement and quiet, yet he throve on the fun of catastrophe while others dropped like flies during the Panic of 1883; Henry James found it significant that one of the few places of serenity in all of loud and bristling New York City were the still, white wards of Presbyterian Hospital. Perhaps, then, an existence marked in contrast by the restless activity of violence is blest.

Here is a single example drawn from William Faulkner, a writer adept at portraying worlds marked by silent corners of peace and rough surfaces of noisy turbulence; it is an example taken from *The Mansion* (p. 34), which serves to open up questions, not to resolve them.

Deep in Yoknapatawpha County Mink Snopes moves toward his fated rendezvous with his cousin Flem and murder—a voluntary act of violence that arises from Mink's despair over a world that once exacted of him one dollar too many. He passes through "a section of all Negro homes, even with electric lights too, peaceful, with no worries, no need to fight and strive single-handed, not to gain right and justice because they were already lost. . . ." But Mink is going forth "just to defend the principle of them, his rights to them" after everything but the sense of that principle and those rights has been stripped from him.

Mink's earlier killing of Houston had not gotten him back his dollar. That act of murder brought him years of prison, where his only strength was his belief in justice and his unswerving desire for revenge against Flem, the personification of earthly injustice. Mink's faith in such abstractions (stirred by his experience of their human embodiment) has sustained him through great hardships. Only when his task is finished and Flem is dead is Mink able and willing to relax back upon the earth, pulled toward the peace and serenity of death.

Mink Snopes's stern progress through the County on his pilgrimage of vengeful murder is unsettling. We see what he is doing and what drives him to do it, and we are deeply moved by it all; but are we to agree *to live by* such principles of implacable hatred and purity of violence? Is this what Thoreau's diatribe against expedient men has led to: the celebration of men of principle like John Brown and Mink Snopes devoted to selfless morality of killing? Is the queasiness we experience the result of our acknowledgment that such men successfully defend our right to rights in ways we are too weak to attempt? Erik Erikson says that animals and women know how to survive without the need to slay, but that the male is forced to choose between the virtue and vulnerability of the non-killer or the guilt and power of the murderer. With Mink, then, we are left exposed to one man's outrageous desire to be at once plaintiff, judge, and executioner.

Those who are defeated by the world at large, and by American society in particular, can decide to gain a greater success by adjusting fully (giving in to) the way things are; or they can try to resist the facts at the risk of compounding their initial failure. Since the fine alternatives—adjustment by a joyous fitting into the social and natural spaces; dismissal of inadequacies by reshaping them into sufficiencies—seem lost to us, we are led to see resistance (violence) as preferable to adjustment (passivity). Norman Mailer and Frederick Crews certainly indicate their preference in the matter as they brood over the effects of psychoanalysis and positivism that pull men into shapes acceptable to the outer world. These critics of American society would rather have the wild, irrepressible instincts revolt from below. They want to underwrite Poe's tale "Dr. Tarr and Prof. Fether" in which the instincts burst from their basement cells to seize power from the oppressors upstairs—the logical, rational consensus-consciousness.

Justification of violence can be negated in the name of pragmatism. After all, rebellious assertions of men's rights, even when
pushed into deeds, are often unable to affect any lasting change.
From the cynic's view Mink Snopes's act of revenge is useless. In
the short run the dollar unjustly exacted by Jack Houston is unre-
turnable; in the long run the murder of Flem Snopes gives no assurance that the forces of Snopesism will not continue to crush
down justice. We also recall that the asylum inmates who revolted
against the authority of Dr. Tarr and Prof. Fether were herded
back into their cells, the *ancien régime* of rationality firmly
reinstated.

A countering rebuke to *that* counter-charge comes in the name of
Henry Adams. As cynical in his idealism as possible, Adams be-
lieved that his "outlaw" railings against the bad things of the world
had no value as long as no one listened to his violent words. Active
in the denunciation of the ills of society, he suspected that his pro-
tests struck others' ears as the mere "squeakings" of a "begonia."
Indeed, when he launches into his diatribes against the Jew and the
Broker, Adams seems no more amusing and instructive than Jason
Compson with his throbbing headache, ineffectually lashing out in
*The Sound and the Fury* against the same targets, as well as the world
in general in which carnival men with red ties offer the final outrage to the frustrated and the impotent. Yet Adams furnishes the
reader with the sense that he is doing more than lobbing ignoble
squeaks at the heads of our common enemies; nor is he merely
running away to bury his patrician head in the sands of time.
Whether talking or running, he gives the effect of someone on the
move who is for that reason harder to hit with history's fatal bullets.
He makes his presence known to the world, even as he makes it
difficult for others to corner and squash his gadfly-self. The world
may not be altered by Adams' verbal violence, but the world finds it
has to adjust itself to *him*, even if only by a particle.

Matters of the ego, then, are involved, as well as character. Character intends to change the world; ego is pleased to annoy it. Just
the same, "outlaw" attacks are wearing on the "squeakers," and it
still must be asked whether the ego does better to accept the facts
and to leave off resisting defeat. But in this section emphasis is
being placed on those Americans who, having failed at winning,
have gone on to respond to failure as the last chance at success they
will ever know.

But, first, brief portraits of those who set out from the American
context with the belief that their egos will handily win the game

from the outset, getting them victory without the stain of either shame or guilt. To many the fact that a man possesses an ego is what dooms him to failure by leaving him open to remorse over the sins of having succeeded too well or not enough; but for others a sturdy ego brings its own assurance of unblemished success.

Both Emerson and Thoreau derived confidence from their belief that the self is essentially in harmony with nature, not its antagonist. But Emerson had occasion to visualize the ego as an aggressively healthy infant that strikes out with its fists and heels to assert its will, its angers useful to its growth as an independent personality. In *Natural Supernaturalism* Meyer Abrams also points to that strain of Romanticism embodied by Fichte which had previously underlined the fact of the mind in hostile conflict with the universe. Later, William James—no German Idealist or American Transcendentalist—defined life in similar terms as the voluntary resistance of the ego to the world. Contemporaneous to James, Freud was describing narcissism as an active, assertive, loving state of being which replaces the old peace-craving ego with a new ego that demands its rights to win at all its desires.

How different from Fichte, Freud, and William James is this image proffered by Gaston Bachelard: the innermost self housed in dreams, lying happily amidst the fixations of a motionless childhood. As described in *The Poetics of Reverie* Bachelard's baby-ego possesses no aggressions that seek to kick down the doors holding it back from its destiny *out there* in the world. It wishes only to stay home, forever. This snugness is not the result of its having to crawl back within the enclosures of its defeat; rather, it comes from never having to incur defeat because it has always located its peace *inside*.

Thoreau is an excellent example of the American writer who alternated Bachelardian impulses with the feistiness cited by Fichte, Freud, and James. *Thoreau*: against the easy life, but for living on the stretch; for lazing in a drifting boat and reclining on "the cushion of necessity," but also for heaven imaged as an armed camp; for the luxury of standing all day in a swamp without stirring, yet reveling in the combativeness of war which he defined by the boy pleasures of friction, excitement, and companionship; for taking holidays from the pressure of public events by going berrying; for knowing the right time to go to jail and the best time to play.

Freud said that those who refuse to suffer think they are somehow "special" and beyond human fate. Indeed, Thoreau believed himself to be the uncommon man; he often sought to separate himself from others—to be the ego-as-spectator, not an active participant in the world's war-games. But Thoreau did not forget to remind himself that this world is the sole arena the ego has in which to test its ability to succeed. To Thoreau, a reformer like Jesus failed because he taught preparation for the next world and set his sights too high, while a reformer like J. A. Etzler, author of *The Paradise Within the Reach of All Men*, pitched his view too low by limiting his actions to the world of materiality. The ego's proper task, Thoreau argued, is to take on the here and now at the highest point of spirit this world allows, thus winning the crucial battles of both the inner and outer realms of being. The one sin Thoreau acknowledged, the only guilt possible, is for the self to deny its godlike worth; the only shame is not to succeed at being the common man disclosed at his most extraordinary.

In the chapter entitled "Protestantism, Science, and Agency" from *The Duality of Human Existence*, David Bakan retells the story of Adam's fall in light of the meanings associated with the apple (as famous as Eve's) that fell (according to Voltaire's tale) into the garden where Isaac Newton sat. "This is a marked shift in myth," Bakan suggests:

> The fruit is not plucked from the tree as a result of the agency of man, but falls because of the law of gravity. The separation of the fruit from the tree is not man's sin, but the result of an inexorable law which God himself had created. With the kind of knowledge that the law of gravity provides, mankind was in a position to exert his agency with less sin or guilt. (p. 28)

First Newton, then Freud, supply Bakan with references he can use concerning the effects of psychoanalysis in releasing the ego from conscience. So freed, the ego goes forth in power to conquer new territories. If Bakan reads the law of gravity as the excuse that allows the ego to be whole and free from its eternal enemy—the super-ego or conscience that would frustrate it in its desires—then we are meant to define gravity as the necessary condition for ego's success and lack of gravity as the fundamental cause for failure. Gravity represents the beneficial outer world and its natural laws that offset the inner rules of guilt and remorse that might weaken men's actions. Whatever restricts the ego acts as an agent of failure whose most telling weapon is the infliction of shame and guilt.

Bakan proceeds to argue that Protestantism both encourages "gravity" in the possessor of an active ego and inculcates the sense of sin. John Woolman, that vigorous Quaker, is but one American who has directly placed the blame for the world's evil upon that "fierce spirit" within men's hearts which tears away at the world's natural harmonies. "Making scenes"—demanding one's own way—is the visible and outward sign of sinful pride. Later writers, however, move toward quietism, not out of any sense of the Christian need to contain pride and to reject sin. For them to keep quiet becomes increasingly a matter of self-protection against public humiliation over their failures. Henry Adams would have made scenes if he could, thereby assuring that his mark be imprinted upon the public memory, but he carefully veiled his natural arrogance and desire for success (defined by him as the possession of self-respect) with an assumed humility, even as he proudly played the role of a loser.

In *A Small Boy and Others* (pp. 184-186) Henry James, one of the least egotistical of men, cherished the importance of "making scenes," a lesson he learned from a spoiled cousin with the habit of commandeering situations by means of the violent assertion of her will. Characterizing himself as a failure in the world because he lacked the needed battle-garb of jealousy and competitiveness, James admired those who could fling their egos into the world's face; but he continually acknowledged his own quietism. A Bachelardian type in some ways, he seems to have found ease in the acceptance of his limits; he seems to have been content to stay *inside*—"a small boy" who was not given over to attention-getting temper tantrums like "the others."

In *The Poetics of Space* Bachelard further praises quietism through his belief that the unconscious in its normal state is safely "at home." But he suggests that we also possess an exiled unconsciousness that needs to be set in motion; it must try to go to its other home out there. The vast spaces provided by the world beyond the ego offer room for the exterior destiny which the interior being, even though essentially a home-body, requires. Not to leave home at all means one is not engaging one's destiny. This would make one be like those pilots of Hudson River boats who are chary of sleeping ashore at Manhattan since they do not trust the little they glimpse of that ego-devouring city. The few short blocks that lie just beyond Pier 81—between 8th and 42nd Streets—present unfamiliar territory, a threat to their inner being, so they gladly stay close by that river where egos receive no shocks nor offer any. The pilots' way follows the strategy of concealment about which Adams wrote William James in 1907 concerning *The Education* (in a letter included in Ford 1, 485). Adams confided he had written his "study of the twentieth century" as a place "where I could hide" in its pages. "No one would take the smallest interest in these. I knew they were safe. So was I."

Although Thoreau was touchy on his own account about his ideas that were lost to view in unread books, he would have argued that those Hudson River pilots are doing the sensible thing by sticking to their proper place. He willingly returned home to Concord from New York City, where he had intensely felt defeat. The woods and meadows around the Massachusetts village were for him the reality that sustained his ego's sense of success, as the alien terrain of the city never could. To make scenes in the wrong place was to project a false actor's image, to incur bad faith, and to fall into the sin of living according to another's definition of one's ego and one's destiny.

Notwithstanding Thoreau's mettlesome insistence upon his right to remain at home and to stay inside, we continue to question the whole tale of Walden Pond and to wonder if it is not just a beautifully expressed account of an essential failure. The leading questioner in this matter has been Perry Miller in his assessment of Thoreau's "lost journal" of 1840-1841 in *Consciousness in Concord*. As Miller bends his skeptical eye upon the mass of thawing mud at Walden Pond, he states, "Anticipation is the cause for living, and for beating the game, but also the assurance of failure." To Miller, Thoreau could live only by waiting for success, since success—life, love, springtime—requires the "filthy" "afterbirth of mud and clay." This is Thoreau, as Miller reads him: ". . . circumventing death, evading women, discounting friendship, he anticipated the impossible, so as never to be seduced by the moments he loved so passionately" (p. 127).

In contrast, the strong go forth from the garden and the pond, free from scruples that weaken, forcefully armed by the law of gravity, ready to live with what is. The ineffectual and the quiet stay home or return there quickly out of fear of the defeats which virtue meets at the hands of corruption and compromise, and out of belief that they would have to learn to kill in order to survive out there—especially to murder the hope of a higher joy. This at least is the image we get of the idealists, when viewed by those who prefer to forego anticipation and who want to commit themselves to "making scenes" now.

# ◣ CHAPTER 18 ◢

# Guilt, Shame, and Laughter

In Hawthorne's *The Marble Faun* Hilda trembles at the threat she feels when it is suggested that original sin might be the useful means to a higher joy. She is frightened to have it said that we may need to murder before we can move on to a finer destiny. Particularly frightening to Hilda, and to us, is the hint that it is God's will that we commit our sins. Shamed over our required dependence upon God and guilty over what He demands us to do, we may need to defy God altogether, as Frederick J. Hoffman argues in *The Mortal No*. Lionel Trilling, interpreting the human situation in *Freud and the Crisis of Our Culture*, slips "culture" in place of "God"; but he is talking about the same thing in our need to *oppose*. Both Hoffman and Trilling's books advance the question of patricide and infanticide. In *Disease, Pain, and Sacrifice* David Bakan flatly states the same impossible choice: the child must either slay the father or let itself be slain by him.

America may be a place just like the others on this earth where the only way a man can feel good when he sins is not to give a damn for soul's damnation, and yet a place where he will probably feel guilt for doing so. But America might be, the story goes, the one country where questions of shame and guilt have been conveniently erased. Perhaps America has been singled out by the bold commandment to succeed by means of the strongly assertive ego that takes what it needs, not only with impunity, but without remorse. Alas, it appears that America is really just like any other country, unless it has the misfortune to be distinguished by the very hopes that make the man who fails feel even worse than the citizens of countries which have always accepted their inadequacies.

Brutal acts of self-preservation, not virtue, are the law of the world. Crèvecœur's Farmer James is forced to concede this fact in direct reversal of his original confidence in the sweet reasonableness of virtue as the one clear route to success in the American colonies. But if many men are aggressive and successful without feeling guilt, more pressing is the problem of those who choose to be good. It is they who are certain to be defeated by the ruthlessness of others, yet coerced into feeling shame over that defeat. Farmer James asks in bewilderment:

> What can an insignificant man do in the midst of these jarring contradictory parties, equally hostile to persons situated as I am? And after all who will be the really guilty?—Those most certainly who fail of success. (p. 203)

The greatest shame in America is to be guilty of failure. Mark Twain's name leaps almost too readily to mind as the figure of the American of guilt. He is both the superb achiever and the stunning self-accuser, with Farmer James's question the thorn at the heart of Mark Twain the writer and the man.

Mark Twain tried to avoid the sense of guilt and shame that came to him on many occasions. Out of his efforts he eventually constructed a part-time philosophy that shakily assuaged personal guilt by making men's lives be largely determined by the fatal forces of heredity and environment. He also had periods of railing against the evils of American democracy. Not the stars above but the fools in Washington were to blame for the fool things Americans can do. In 1876 he celebrated the centennial of America's nationhood as a citizen "overwhelmed with shame and confusion" who wished, a friend observed, that "he were not an American." Justin Kaplan points out in *Mr. Clemens and Mark Twain* that a trip of escape to England and the passage of time helped temper both Mark Twain's loathing for American society and for himself as its blameworthy citizen; but a lasting imprint had been made on this man of good humor. By 1879 he remarked to William Dean Howells, "I don't ever seem to be in a good enough humor with ANYthing to *satirize* it; no, I want to stand up before it and curse it, and foam at the mouth—or take a club and pound it to rags and pulp" (p. 169).

In Mark Twain we watch a working out of the ambivalent feelings vividly described by Alexis de Tocqueville a generation earlier when the Frenchman set down what it means to be the raging witness of another's success in a democracy:

> In democracies private citizens see men rising from their ranks and attaining wealth and power in a few years; that spectacle excites their astonishment and envy; they wonder how he who was their equal yesterday has today won the right to command them. To attribute his rise to his talents or his virtue is inconvenient, for it means admitting that they are less virtu-

ous or capable than he. They therefore regard some of his vices as the main cause thereof, and often they are correct in this view. In this way there comes about an odious mingling of the conceptions of baseness and power, of unworthiness and success, and of profit and dishonor. (p. 221)

Mark Twain demonstrates in brief one clear pattern of reaction to the essential problem of being an American. First he shows us the pleasure of feeling there are no limits to what one may enjoy and can do. Then comes anger against the fact of others' succeeding—a fact it is "inconvenient" to take as proof of one's own lacks. Or there might be a stage marked by doubts over why one has succeeded so ostentatiously while others do not. Last, there is the growing sense of shame (over failing or succeeding) and futile attempts to dissociate the self from guilt either by flight or by attack. But Mark Twain found he could not simply rid himself of unpleasant emotions by denying or denouncing his identity as an American. Beyond his nationality he felt he carried a greater burden. Just to be a human being was to be doomed to blushing and the need to blush, doomed to ridicule as well.

In the M Notebooks of 1838 (from the collection edited by Gruber and Barrett), Charles Darwin asked himself, "What is the Philosophy of Shame & Blushing? Does Elephant know shame— dog know triumph—" (pp. 293-294). With some smugness, Mark Twain could have replied that he knew all about such matters. It was an affliction to which humans alone were susceptible. Even in death persons were open to ridicule. The corpse of the girl hung in the Missouri cave where sightseers could gawk at her dead face was proof of this. As one reads over the array of his writing as it unfolds throughout this career, then through his reminiscences in the *Autobiography* and the later pieces collected in *Fables of Man* and *Which Was the Dream?*, one wonders when Mark Twain was *not* ashamed.

As a boy Sam Clemens performed a "Royal Nonesuch" routine only to realize suddenly that, like Noah drunken, he had been viewed in his nakedness by some giggling girls. Other pranks follow in his memoirs that involve the humiliations attendant upon *exposure* of the kinds considered indecent by society, and by himself, that most socially conditioned of persons. Then there was the time he became a public sensation by responding gorgeously to a mind-reading act; a gaudy success, he had to live with the private guilt of having cheated to bring off his success. (In contrast, Henry James, himself exceedingly vulnerable to humiliation, tells in *A Small Boy and Others* [pp. 115-116] how he also underwent "my great public exposure" on stage on Broadway during a similar mind-reading act guided by a Signor Blitz. He felt no guilt, however, since he had not cheated his way to fame and adulation. Unlike Mark Twain's guilt-ridden success, James's appearance had been an honest flop, the "plunge . . . into the shame of my sad failure . . .").

If Mark Twain was gripped at times by the cosmic guilt of being a son of Adam, he more specifically located his shame as the consequence of failing to make it in America. As reported by Kaplan, when Mark Twain went into bankruptcy in 1894 he was told by John Mackay not to be upset since "we all have to do it at one time or another, it's nothing to be ashamed of" (p. 329). Not in a society marked by large sums of money quickly gotten and quickly lost. But it is hard not to feel a fool for having failed one's wits, or—as Kaplan puts it—for having failed one's manhood. To be shamed of one's virility by the Virgin Land or the Bitch Goddess is indeed a blow. Orion Clemens, comic archetype of failure, could achieve fame if he would only write The Autobiography of a Fool, as his exasperated brother urged. But was being a fool like Orion any worse than being Sam Clemens who must write out the autobiography of shame? Fools escape knowing shame; clever, sensitive men know only too well what opportunities America offers them which they have failed to take. Shame, at least, is the decent response to one's failure. According to Mark Twain's *Autobiography* Bret Harte had many causes for shame, but felt none. Mark Twain was enraged over this greater sin, for how dare a man not know shame over his guilts of failure unless "the sense of shame was left out of Harte's constitution" (p. 300)?

The story of the greenhorn who is both fool in the face of America's possibilities and aware of the shame of his failure gives us the success of *Roughing It*—the gold of literary popularity. But to write amusingly about what it feels like to learn that you are very young and very gullible in the new lands out West hardly mitigates the pain sensed by the reader. Pain, yet great fun. We also experience this mixture of emotions in the writings of Henry Adams and Norman Mailer, two other of America's more sensitive plants. On January 30, 1908, Adams wrote to Margaret Chanler (a letter included in Cater's collection, p. 611) concerning what he felt about *The Education*:

> It is meant only for revision, suggestion, correction, and general condemnation. It undertakes to offer itself for blame, contempt, and refusal. It hobbles on its knees, asking to be raised

and educated. . . . I am ashamed of it and sent it out into the world only to be whipped.

If we follow the imperatives of this letter, then Adams' book is an idiot child that ought to be ashamed of itself. As we read *The Education of Henry Adams* we are encouraged to share Adams' view of the book to the point of our whipping it and blushing for it alike. Mailer not unsurprisingly also emphasizes his fear of shame and of accumulating further guilt that could interfere with his rites of passage. In *Miami and the Siege of Chicago* (p. 185) he says he knows he must grow past the shame of fear by taking "a step into his fear," so as to be free of it, but one wonders whether his susceptibility to fear-shame is not a necessary element in the kind of success he achieves as a writer, however devastating it may be to him as a man. Like Mark Twain and Adams, Mailer gains in power by passing himself off as a comic figure, constantly meeting defeats in an America where to fail is somehow (as treated in their narratives at least) more laughable than tragic. If true, this fact makes it even harder on the men who write out of rage over the ridicule they must act out in order to bring their readers the benefits of both fun and pain.

What distinctions can be made between a man like Henry Adams, who portrays himself as the patrician American failure, and a man like Benjamin Franklin, who stands as the common man who escaped the ravages of ridicule?

However much mild self-mockery entered into its writing, Franklin's *Autobiography* serves as a handbook for self-satisfied success; it is Franklin's gift to the America which provided him with the right context for exhibiting the native abilities he worked diligently to perfect. Adams' *Education* is ostensibly a handbook for self-chastising failure, and a warning to America about what happens when one of the "best" people gets his feet tangled in the wrong time and place. But perhaps Adams' narrative extracts its own Way to Wealth from its record of humiliations and inadequacy. Compare Adams with Melville. In the introductory remarks to his edition of Melville's poems, Robert Penn Warren says that Melville was no Machiavelli—the man of failure who can write persuasively about how to succeed. Warren reads Melville as trapped by a more painful irony and a more profound role. Melville is the failure who, like the fox in the fable of sour grapes, repudiates the world in disdain and sorrow. Perhaps Adams goes beyond both

Machiavelli and Melville and manages to meet Franklin on the ground of American success, however unsure that footing may have seemed to him.

Lord Morley remarked that if Henry Adams had ever looked at himself "naked in a glass" he might have lost some of his arrogance; but it is difficult to see how Adams could have been more severe with himself. Self-depreciation may have cloaked arrogance, but it might be that the arrogance disguises the essential sadness he felt for his historical expendability and his general human failure. Just as *Roughing It* records the talent which an innocent from Missouri has for stumbling across occasions for humiliation, *The Education of Henry Adams* lists the public shames of a proper Bostonian set in an improper world. Here are two examples:

> No one knew him—not even the lackeys. The last Saturday evening he ever attended, he gave his name as usual at the foot of the staircase, and was rather disturbed to hear it shouted up as "Mr. Handrew Hadams!" He tried to correct it, and the footman shouted more loudly; "Mr. Hanthony Hadams!" With some temper he repeated the correction, and under this name made his bow for the last time to Lord Palmerston who certainly knew no better. (p. 134)

> His little mistake in etiquette or address made him writhe with torture. . . . Still another nightmare he suffered at a dance given by the old Duchess Dowager of Somerset, a terrible vision in castanets, who seized him and forced him to perform a Highland fling before the assembled nobility and gentry, with the daughter of the Turkish Ambassador for partner. This might seem humorous to some, but to him the world turned to ashes. (p. 118)

Henry Adams forced into doing the fling with the Turkish Ambassador's daughter at a London ball is Mark Twain laughed into littleness by the boys at Jim Blaine's *soirée*. But Adams seems able to do what Franklin did and Mark Twain did not: be amused over the fact of defeat in ways superior (as Adams phrases it in *The Education*, p. 272) to society's "vacant and meaningless derision of its own failure."

By the time he reached twenty-five Adams knew that once a man who is "cool, witty, unaffected and high-toned" moves away from his "skin defences," he is open to humiliation. As he wrote his brother Charles in 1863 (the letter included in Ford's edition, I, 111), he would do all he could to avoid losing just those protective shields.

Such self-defense took various forms. Abusive language cast against himself and others worked at times; so did avoidance of depleting passions—whether angry quarrels, tender family attachments, or grief over Marian's suicide. He also recognized that the detached exercise of passion (anger, tenderness, or tears) carried out as if it were a game could defend him against the fear of failure; as would the cultivation of the stoic mode. But self-manipulated passions of rage, sentimentality, or escape into calm impersonality are only temporary aids. The ability to laugh provides more lasting defense, though not the final solution, if solution there is.

Adams very early began to study the different uses society makes of laughter. It could be a strategy for deceit, as in the instance of Palmerston's hyena-laugh described in *The Education of Henry Adams*:

> The laugh was singular, mechanical, wooden, and did not seem to disturb his features. "Ha! . . . Ha! . . . Ha!" Each was a slow, deliberate ejaculation, and all were in the same tone, as though he meant to say: "Yes! . . . Yes! . . .Yes!" by way of assurance. It was a laugh of 1810 and the Congress of Vienna.
> (p. 135)

Adams found he could use laughter as an instrument of ridicule for his own attacks or, by anticipating the enemy's derision, as the way to save honor in the midst of disaster. But once he stopped believing in its power to fulfill any special purpose, he seems finally to have used it for its own sake. He became an *amateur* of wit, instead of a professional (like Chad Newsome) out for "the money in it."

D. H. Lawrence reads America as melodrama, and despises Franklin's role in this particular stage-work. In a world-drama which Lawrence prefers to describe as a rage of passions, the sly snuff-colored hypocrite plays a farcical and falsifying part. With Franklin around, it is like having Rossini's Don Basilio sidle on stage in the midst of the *Oresteia*. But Lawrence's view may be off the mark concerning the genre most appropriate for presenting the drama of American life. Franklin might be more correctly credited as having made America a little safer for high social comedy, not melodrama or farce. If so, then laughter—not the rage or the sentimentality of despair—is the proper gesture for the man of success. High comedy of the "restoration" mode (a word to be taken in reference both to a literary type of a particular period and to its figurative, psychological sense) certainly proved the genre best suited to Henry Adams since he winced at the thought of tearing up the scenery with rantings or getting trounced on stage by a burlesque-comic's bladder. It has to be seen whether Adams' talent "for the jugular" made him an even greater authority on comedies of revenge in the style, say, of John Webster.

That Benjamin Franklin learned the tricks of the dead-pan comedian is suggested by Robert Sayre in his study of American autobiography, *The Examined Self*. Men of the eighteenth century were proud of their skill at cruel verbal attacks, but Franklin soon decided to play, and win, by foregoing self-indulgent rages that gain only Pyrrhic victories. Indeed, when writing the widowed Madame Helvétius in 1778 about a dream he had had that his wife had been appropriated by the dead Helvétius, Franklin urged the lady, "let us revenge ourselves." The occasion for the letter is said to be the actual spurning of his suit by the Frenchwoman. See, then, how he manages to contain whatever hurt he felt. He presents his outcry in playful words; he sheathes even his toy knife by transforming the occasion into a dream-incident; he speaks of rejection and revenge, but not by and against Madame Helvétius— only in terms of the absent Mrs. Franklin, who was not the woman who had most immediately caused him his pain and possible humiliation.

When Franklin made mistakes he sought to correct them, either by converting them into a bagatelle of the imagination or by dealing with them directly in actuality. He could do these things because he viewed mistakes as human *errata*, not as irrevocable sins. Errors come from lapses of common sense. Possessed of common sense in abundance, Franklin could usually catch up on his deficits in ways that it is difficult to do with the unredeemable debits of sin. He was unable to make up for the lack of the innoculation that caused his son's death, but he could give back what he owed Miss Reed and his brother James for his absences from their service. He showed no shame whenever he closed off past events by taking present actions. The past could be largely rejected with whatever it contained, failure and all, since it is the present that seals success.

As for the famous ivory tablets: In the *Autobiography* Franklin moves to a new stance in this sequence, away from his earlier strategy of telling the facts of his life simply and without apology. Here he becomes the wise older man who looks back upon the relatively innocent young man who had hoped to arrive at perfection by means of the proper plan and the right amount of will. Mark

Twain looking back at his younger self often writhes in humiliation over greenness. Franklin, in looking back over the naif's failure to keep up the fast moral pace demanded by thirteen ivory columns devoted to virtue, converts that passing incident into the present success of the relaxed self. Franklin wills us into accepting his own sense of ease over his recollection of the very young man glimpsed far away in the midst of failing to pull away from his imperfections. If we are persuaded that Franklin can now assess with amused good sense the comic juxtaposition of such youthful self-admonitions as "Rise, wash and address Powerful Goodness!" how can we deny his sense of not having failed? Samuel Pepys, William Byrd, and James Gatz are lovable at best and, at worst, are not to be mocked for making similar exclamations in their secret diaries. How then can we resist the forthrightness of Franklin's advice "Night—Sleep," which he places at the conclusion of his New Gospel for the soul's salvation? As the wise old man reviewing the young man's follies of hopefulness, his own sleep will surely be the sound repose enjoyed by the successful man.

Franklin learned that to act with sufficient humility was to present a seamless surface to the world. He made himself useful in ways impossible for men who close themselves up within the needle-points of their pride (rolled up like that porcupine Adams was playfully likened to by his friends). The look of humility makes a man difficult to attack on grounds of one's own jealousy, whereas the arrogant man is vulnerable to constant assault because he presents a broad front and back and a large chip on his shoulder. Franklin does not deal in false modesty since that would be a denial of the self-esteem that was his strongest suit. He makes it clear to his son that he is handing on this account of his life precisely because he has little to be ashamed of. But he includes two fan letters from Abel James and Benjamin Vaughn in his autobiography, letting them make clear his importance to future generations of young Americans who need to be instructed in the way to success.

Humility for Franklin has nothing to do with shame. As Vaughn phrases it in his letter of praise, Franklin has pride in himself and in his stock ("you are ashamed of no origin"). Franklin also has control over his life. Vaughn notes Franklin's ability to frame plans ("by which you became considerable") that indicate "the propriety" of a man "waiting for his time for appearing upon the stage of the world"—a man who knows how to "arrange his conduct so as to suit the whole of life" (p. 177).

Self-control marks the entire *Autobiography*. Having allowed himself to be named colonel of the Philadelphia regiment, Franklin comments that the firing of several rounds of ammunition in front of his house in public homage caused the breakage of some of his experimental apparatus. His honor "proved not much less brittle" than his glassware since the English quickly moved to strip colonials of their military rank (p. 286). Franklin understood "the poverty of glory" and thereby gave it little attention (p. 178). Intelligent humility was worth more to the public man than glass-shattering glory, and he valued it accordingly.

America exacts success of her populace, yet offers plentiful opportunities for failure and the consequences of guilt and shame. It becomes a crucial issue whether the good citizen tries to alleviate his shame by meeting it with humor or by rage. Once one admits the guilt of having proved inadequate to the high demands of a country in which anything is possible (both the climb to the top and the slide to the bottom), does the placement of that guilt within a controlled perspective of *comedy* save one from self-destructive loathing? Perhaps it is more efficient to refuse to admit the guilt and to try to escape the shame by projecting the cause of one's failure upon another, thereby setting up a *melodrama* enacted between virtuous victim and evil agents.

Here are a few examples of those who face the deepest shame and their immediate reactions.

Mark Twain out of work in San Francisco:

> I became a very adept at "slinking." I slunk from back street to back street. I slunk away from approaching faces that looked familiar, I slunk to my meals, ate them humbly and with a mute apology for every mouthful I robbed my generous landlady of, and at midnight, after wanderings that were but slinkings away from cheerfulness and light, I slunk to my bed. I felt meaner and lowlier, and more despicable than the worms. (VIII, 172)

Mark Twain (also in *Roughing It*) recalling "a former crisis" when he had "taken an aristocratic young lady out driving, behind a horse that had just retired from a long and honorable career as the moving impulse of a milk wagon . . .":

> I remembered how helpless I was that day, and how humiliated; how ashamed I was of having intimated to the girl that I had always owned the horse and was accustomed to grandeur; how hard I tried to appear easy, and even vivacious, under suf-

fering that was consuming my vitals; how placidly and malici-
ously the girl smiled, and kept on smiling, while my hot
blushes baked themselves into a permanent blood pudding in
my face . . . (VIII, 308-309)

Flem Snopes in Faulkner's *The Town*, caught up for the first time
in having money, and the need to protect it, in Jefferson, Mississippi:

> when he first really tasted that which he had never tasted
> before—the humility of not knowing, of never having had any
> chance to learn the rules and methods of the deadly game in
> which he had gauged his life; whose fate was to have the
> dreadful need and the will and the ruthlessness, and then to
> have the opportunity thrust upon him before he had had any
> chance to learn how to use it. (p. 266)

In which of these instances could humor save the man from his
terrible sense of helplessness and shame? Samuel Clemens eventually decided that *to know* is to be unable to laugh, while Faulkner's
country men continue to experience the slow shame of *not knowing*.
It sounds sensible to insist upon laughter as the way out of adversity; but suicide as an escape from shame, or murder as the means
to get at the enemy, might be a more practical, and far more emotionally satisfying, response. Humor is high intelligence, but melodrama fills basic needs which humor leaves unfulfilled.

Ernest Hemingway is a writer who wished to conserve energy
even while gaining satisfaction, and a man who seldom seems to
have really laughed. He proves an expert on methods other than
humor to win victories. In *Death in the Afternoon* he tells the story of
a gypsy, killed by a fighting bull, whose brother and sister implaca-
bly track down that bull in order to assassinate it in a solemn ritual
of revenge. Further on in the same work, Hemingway makes the
remark that any great artist must love to kill. Still later, he begins an
extended attack upon other writers by means of sexual slander.
Hemingway makes no direct connection between the anecdote
about the gypsy and the comments that follow, but the links are
there. To Hemingway "killing" is a ritual of revenge against "the
bull"—one's enemies, whoever they may be. Killing is necessary to
sustain one's sense of power and to escape anticipated shame.
Hemingway's world is the melodrama of Them or Me. His techniques are those of thrust and stab. The laughter appropriate to
high comedy has a difficult time breaking through the iron ring of
such grave ceremonies of killing and being killed.

What would Franklin have done? The *Autobiography* shows us the young man handling a series of events that might have disconcerted someone with less self-esteem. We learn how *entertainingly* he gets his own back from petty tyrants who impose humiliations or restraints upon his plans for success.

While still serving as his brother's apprentice, Franklin disguises his handwriting, composes an anonymous paper, and puts it "in at night under the door of the printing-house" where it is found the next morning and shown to the brother's friends. "They read it, commented on it in my hearing, and I had the exquisite pleasure of finding it met with their approbation . . ." (pp. 56-57). Franklin found in his older brother James one who "considered himself as my master. . . . I thought he demean'd me too much. . . ." The brother was "passionate, and had often beaten me, which I took extremely amiss . . ." (p. 57). Soon Franklin finds himself "the rather inclined to leave Boston when I reflected that I had already made myself a little obnoxious to the governing party . . . it was likely I might, if I stayed, soon bring myself into scrapes. . . ." In order to escape from foes actual and potential, the young hero strikes out for himself, "sensible that, if I attempted to go openly, means would be used to prevent me" (pp. 59-60).

A disguised identity is called for, and he boards a sloop under pretense of being a young fellow "that had got a naughty girl with child, whose friends would compel me to marry her . . ." (p. 60). On the run himself, he pretends to be in flight for reasons linked to the shame and guilt he does *not* feel for his own circumstances. Then he makes his now-famous entry into Philadelphia, his progress through the streets accompanied by the titters of a young girl at the sight of the rustic who seems of "a most awkward, ridiculous appearance" (p. 65). We can easily guess the pleasure with which the aged Franklin reports, as Mark Twain rarely could of his own shamed young men, on that teasing girl's future role as the hero's wife.

Franklin makes his way upward by what appears to be merely a neat series of lucky strokes, but all along he is busy transforming luck by means of pluck and prudence into certainties. A letter of his comes into the hand of the governor, who reads it, is surprised upon learning the age of the writer, and declares of him that he "appeared a young man of promising parts, and therefore should be encouraged . . ." (p. 70). This mighty man comes to the shop where Franklin works as a lowly helper to a man named Keimer and "would have me away with him to the tavern, where he was

going . . . to taste . . . some excellent Madeira. I was not a little surprised, and Keimer stared like a pig poison'd" (p. 70).

Soon after, Franklin makes a quick visit to Boston, where

> my unexpected appearance surpriz'd the family; all were,
> however, very glad to see me, and made me welcome, except
> my brother. . . . I was better dress'd than ever while in his serv-
> ice, having a genteel new suit from head to foot, a watch, and
> my pockets lin'd with near five pounds sterling in silver (p. 72).

The young man is not beyond playing up these tokens of his
wordly rise before going off again to Philadelphia with his brother's
envy ("grum and sullen"—"offended"—"insulted") and "some
small gifts as tokens" of his parents' love, "their approbation and
their blessing" (pp. 72, 74).

In all these incidents Franklin keeps careful control over *appearances*. Appearances let him demonstrate his rise in the world in
ways that needle his adversaries (Keimer and brother James), while
protecting him from any open act of wrath on their part. Franklin
plays his part well. He has it both ways—subtle little revenges concealed by the general approval of the public. The sober demeanor
he often assumes is the one used by men who know how to *play off*
their appearances against the needs of their feelings, while keeping
such feelings under sufficient control to prevent them being turned
into self-destructive rage or malice.

At times Franklin follows the tradition of the jokester-apprentice
who tests how far he can go. Once, he promised himself "some
diversion in half starving" Keimer, who was known as a "great glut-
ton" for flesh. For three months Franklin held Keimer to a bargain
to eat "neither fish, flesh, nor fowl; and the whim suited me the better at this time from the cheapness of it. . . ." Simultaneously
pocketing money and watching Keimer twitch, "I went on pleas-
antly, but poor Keimer suffered grievously, tired of the project,
long'd for the flesh-pots of Egypt, and ordered a roast pig" for a
general feast. Unable to "resist the temptation," Keimer "ate the
whole before we came" (pp. 81-82). This turn to the little plot did
not cast Franklin's joke back upon him; he lost no money by it,
cared not that much for pig, and got to see Keimer make a public
fool of himself.

The successful campaign against Keimer shows Franklin's joking
self-assertion in the face of whatever strikes him as impetuous and
foolhardy. Especially telling is the practicality of the joke (what
practical jokes seldom are). He gets away with it because he never

goes too far or lets himself become too exasperated; he stops short before the duller Keimer can catch on and turn against him. His sense of the economics of humor would have won the sanction of Sigmund Freud; his knack for comic timing would have forced the envy of Mark Twain; his wily ability to enjoy superiority while acting out humility would have engaged the approval of Henry Adams. Melodrama is avoided and the public pleasantries preserved.

*The Education of Henry Adams* is a repository of comic attacks and counter-attacks—Joe Miller's Joke Book for the artistocratic circuit. Adams notes Dickens' use of satire, Matthew Arnold's rebellious ridicule, and Gibbon's darting glances of contempt. Adams says that he himself cannot tell funny stories, but he likes John Hay's ability to laugh at the presidents he helped make and then at himself for laughing. Realizing that the comic egotism of politicians could be met with either rage or tact, he tries for tact. But if Adams is generally able to deal with people through laughter, the special problem that was his and not Franklin's was how to handle the world in the same way.

The world, Adams notes in *The Education* is good-natured to whoever amuses it, but he feels the strain of laughing in acceptance of the world's frictions (p. 327). There are times, however, as during the financial panic of 1893, when the "economic" situation is in his favor: ". . . he had the banks in his power; he could afford to laugh" since "he had nothing to lose that he cared about, but the banks stood to lose their existence" (p. 337). The result of the Panic for them is decline and death; for him it is increased vigor and life: ". . . Boston grew suddenly old, haggard, and thin. Adams alone waxed fat and was happy, for at last he had got hold of his world and could finish his education. . . . He cared not whether it were worth finishing, if only it amused. . . ." (p. 338).

Change is amusing, Darwinism is fun. Leisure and torpor are also fun. But the world can use change or torpor to destroy the men it calls bores. Adams tries to strike a bargain that would give him an edge in a touchy situation. He will try to amuse others as amusement is done unto him. In danger whenever he becomes in the view of the universe an expendable yawn, he in turn hands his challenge to the world: if once it ceases either to amuse or to educate him, it "has even less right to exist than he" (p. 357). This threat holds the world in covenant to his own wit; with the power of his laughter he is united to the world, whose force no man can successfully flee or fight.

Melodrama was the characteristic drama-form played out by the medieval mind. In a world structured according to dualisms of good and evil in combat, goodness was guaranteed the victory by God's will—on paper, at least, and in the long run. The Middle Ages was neither amused nor amusing in the "modern" sense since its people lived, in Adams's words, with "the illusion of Truth which did not amuse . . . and which had never changed" (p. 231). This remark from *The Education* sets off Adams' contrasting view of the contemporary mind, caught up as it is by multiplicity and change, yet still desirous of reconciling unity. Adams—a fiend for change and pursued by the furies of complexity—could not rest with the platitude "Laugh and the world laughs with you." The Sino-Japanese War, for instance, was comic, but it was a war of chaos just the same. Adams realized that Clarence King's death amused Life, but it was no less tragic. Still, Adams held to laughter as the strongest chance that weak men have to improve their shaky position in a tyrannical world and the best way to lessen melo-dramatic divisions between victim and victimizer.

*Silence*, Franklin recorded on the ivory of his Platonic tablets, is more useful a habit than "prattling, punning, and joking, which only made me acceptable to trifling company" (p. 191). Franklin even places silence in importance ahead of *Order*, perhaps because it is order's context. In *The Education* Adams ranks silence ahead of rage because rage acts chaotically and cannot order chaos. In a world of acceleration "dispute was idle, discussion was futile, and silence, next to good-temper, was the mark of sense" (p. 501). True, but Adams and Franklin (not unlike Mark Twain and Nor-man Mailer) are men given over to talk, talk, talk.

" 'Come, Dan!' cried a crony," in John S. Robb's tale of 1847, "Fun with a 'Bar' " from *Streaks of Squatter Life*; " 'give us something to laugh at, and let us break this silence, which seems to breed a spirit of melancholy—stir us up, old fellow, do!' " (p. 104.) The words of this appeal lead us toward fun, but where do the countless words of others like Adams, Mark Twain, and Mailer take us? To-ward peace or war, confessions of shame or self-justification for wrath's revenge?

Many writers have set their minds to the task of determining the relations between shame, guilt, and comedy; and between comedy as a way to assuage humiliation's pain and comedy as a mode of revenge. The famous theories of Bergson, Meredith, and Freud have been supplemented by Wylie Sypher, Boris Sidis, and Helen Lynd; by Ernst Kris, Morris Brody, Gerhart Piers, Milton B. Singer, Paul Schilder, and Kurt Goldstein, among many others.

They provide arguments to prove that shame and guilt are polarities, or are interchangeable; or that certain cultures cause persons to feel shame, while quite different cultures load on the guilt. Other theories proliferate about the uses of humor, wit, and the joke. The ways into the pluralisms of comedy seem endless. Questions are asked whether forms of humor are essentially mechanistic or transcendentally dream-like, rational or irrational, what lock us in or set us free. The drift of one of the major arguments, taken up by several advocates, concerns the compensatory nature of the comic impulse—the ways it attempts to make up what has been lost through humiliation by means of seizures of another's esteem; and whether it is, by doing so, additive, creative, and purposeful, or depleting, destructive, and random.

Among the many arguments concerning comedy (often stated without a sign of humor on the part of the theorists), one point gains general agreement: laughter helps to placate deep feelings of humiliation; by humor the original victim is enabled to take revenge upon the agent of his shame. But even this commonly shared position hardly covers the possible human variations, the differing capacity for attack, and the vulnerability to shame possessed by individual races, nations, or cultures. Certainly it cannot formalize specifically American responses to failure.

In *The Armies of the Night*, for instance, Mailer likes to speculate that Wasps are particularly apt to act from a sense of failure in their moves toward hatred and revenge. In *Advertisements for Myself* he admits that Jews like himself also try to divert hatred away from themselves onto others by expressing useful rage through "good style." But Mailer is better as a moral universalist of human emotions than he is as a sociological particularist. At least his arguments sound more his own when he has Rojack remark in *An American Dream* that shame, guilt, and revenge are common to all men, and that perhaps God has also failed; that perhaps part of the guilt he feels is over God's humiliation.

John Quincy Adams suffered from the old-fashioned notion that if anyone is meant to feel guilt, it is man, not God or the universe. In "The Heritage of Henry Adams" Brooks Adams explains that his grandfather believed it was better to admit personal guilt for having somehow failed in America (thereby failing God's plan) than to hold doubts of the goodness and potency of God or America. One of the views Mark Twain finally edged toward—that God's is the guilt alone, while man is freed from self-accusation by the fact of his essentially determined state—is yet another old-fashioned idea. To say in contrast that God and men have alike been "sold" by America and fate is to take the more contemporary slant (even though it does make use of the Hawthornian notion of the brotherhood of shame and guilt experienced by Goodman Brown in the dark forest and by Robin in the nighttime city).

One can join in the universal demonic laughter that mocks one's futile attempts to escape shame and guilt; or one may isolate one-self within private bursts of laughter in the desire to take revenge on the rest of the community or cosmos. Either way merely pro-longs the nightmare. But American writing also provides other, perhaps more positive suggestions—certainly more diverting ones—for escaping the shame of failure and for converting guilt into a new kind of success.

Jonathan Edwards' loud weeping over his sense of sin and vile-ness led him out of the soul's forest, where Hawthorne's Goodman Brown was doomed to remain among the self-damned. Freed by his confession, Edwards moved toward a share in the "sweetness" of God's presence, away from the bitterness of man's failure before God's will. A member of the generation contemporaneous with Goodman Brown, Samuel Sewall stood up in church while the words of his confession of guilt over his participation in the Salem witchcraft trials fell around his ears. Edwards and Sewall gained strength from private and public admissions of their essential sin-fulness. Like Saint Augustine centuries before them, they were able to benefit through faith in the purpose of guilt; they were capable of moving past shame; they could suffer and still create value out of suffering. They did not yet know what it is to be Poe's Roderick Usher, for whom the suffering of guilt is the end of creativity.

In between the Neo-Augustinians and the Romantic Roderick Usher comes Benjamin Franklin. This man of America's Augustan Age avoided the plight of Poe's hero, but not in the ways taken by Edwards or Sewall. Paul Ricoeur in *The Symbolism of Evil* defines guilt as an advanced stage of a highly individualized and inte-riorized experience that locates the problem within the self. Franklin's talk of *errata* seems to place him within a more archaic stage than this, that which Ricoeur calls the sense of fault—mere defilement or stain infecting a man from without which can be re-moved by adequate social acts. If Ricoeur's definitions are accurate, Franklin is representative of a moral period that predates both Au-gustine and Sewall and Edwards. Freed from any loss of personal power by his belief that he cannot be deeply marred, Franklin erases his faults from the ivory tablet with no real harm done if he attends to them promptly and sensibly.

Augustine, Sewall, and Edwards are types who are released from psychic paralysis through the act of confession; sins lying deep within their hearts are cast outward by words addressed to the God Who has the sole power to remove all sin. In contrast, Roderick Usher's guilt pervades his whole nature like a birthmark; it is doubled in intensity by his twinship with Madeline. Casting out sin involves exorcism that brings death breathlessly anticipated because personally exacted, but death nonetheless.

Henry Adams realized he no longer enjoyed the special advantages of either Augustine or Franklin; he was fated to experience the fall of the house of Adams without the elaborate compensatory histrionics of Usher's fall. Adams could not have listened to the story of the "Mad Trist" of Sir Lancelot Canning without smiling over its vulgar pastiches of the medieval imagination. Adams knew, like Usher, the benefits of confession, but he also (according to Vern Wagner in *The Suspension of Henry Adams*) had a flair for *Ecclesiastes* read with humor. If Usher found his pleasure in hysterics that pulled him down into the tarn, Adams used the comic mode to keep himself suspended halfway between satisfaction and despair. Roderick Usher fits Freud's description of "the pale criminal" who desires punishment; Adams does not. Usher plays at the prolongation of his suffering, just as the sexual adept attempts to savor fore-pleasure; Adams does not. Adams found himself in the Usher-situation of the tumble into the tarn of multiplicity, but he adapted both the modes of the confessional and of flippancy as a means—at least in part—out of the embarrassment of his existence.

Adams was no greater a fool than Rousseau and as witty a citizen as Franklin, as sensitive a poetic imagination as Usher, and as cosmically determined as Edwards; but as a complex man adrift in a complex world, he had to shape his methods to suit the times. Borrowing approaches used by his illustrious predecessors, he transformed them to fit the particular needs of the occasion. Sometimes he affected the stoic pose of silence; sometimes howls of rage let him play at games of revenge; sometimes it was wit practiced by one of the best stand-up comics of his generation; often it was talk, talk, talk—that comforting form of penance used by either Ancient Mariner or Norman Mailer. A thoroughgoing Protestant for all his mariolatry, Adams managed without the aid of priest or analyst. He placed himself—or rather his stand-in, the manikin "Henry Adams"—in the confessional box of *The Education*. Adams valued self-knowledge. Adams busily knowing himself was a man hard at work grasping at what it is to be an Adam and an American—one who carries in his blood that guilt Freud says comes even before the crime.

On board the *Pequod*, Stubb and Ahab, however different in other ways, alike manage to avoid self-knowledge, guilt, and shame. If one cannot face guilt and surmount it like Adams, it is perhaps better to go the way of Stubb's nonchalant self-approval or Ahab's violent self-justification. If afraid to examine the Waldens within, it is wise to stay away from men like Thoreau and Emerson, who force self-confrontation with the facts of one's capacity to fail. But Emerson also knew that most men enjoy a bit of self-accusation—what we see in Thoreau when he records his excitement over the curses the villagers leveled at him for carelessly setting the woods afire. The self-admitted criminal often profits from the enormity of his confessions. This is as true for Sewall and Edwards, Thoreau and Adams, as for the more blatantly professional confessors like Mailer. And can we say that Robert Lowell believed he had failed more than Franklin succeeded because of the detailed recitations of guilt in *Notebook*, *Life Studies*, and *History*, whereas Franklin had only petty *errata* to concede to the *Autobiography*? Lowell's pleasure comes from the exquisiteness of his suffering (as well as from its sordidness); Franklin's comes from his moral indifference to the specific matters involved, however much he retains his general sense of ethical responsibility.

Robert Lowell kept fondling the personal wounds of guilt and shame caused by his mother's psychic murder of the father. E. E. Cummings has informed us, without a wince, in *I: Six Nonlectures*, that his mother cut his father in two in a car accident; then, in a brilliant non-sequitur, he proceeded to praise her extravagantly. Whether we decide that Cummings' was the healthier response to an unhappy family event, or insist that his was a more perverse reaction than Lowell's, this comparison does not solve the problem which rises from the consensus that Lowell was a better poet. Nor can we easily say that Franklin's *Autobiography* is more "useful" or more aesthetically attractive than the self-analyses of Adams (or of Lowell, Cummings, and Mailer) simply on the basis of *how* each man confesses himself or *what* he confesses. If we are unable to decide with certainty about the comparative value of art written out of pleasure or rent from recollections of pain, we cannot know whether Gertrude Stein has the whole truth about life when she writes in *Everybody's Autobiography*, "About an unhappy childhood well I never had an unhappy anything. What is the use of having an unhappy anything" (p. 75).

In the remarks and examples given in this section, there is no pretense of solving the mystery of the ways in which personal suffering from guilt can act to slay or to revive the heart. They can, however, suggest that guilt and shame are possessed in amplitude by many American writers who have had to find ways *past failure* toward some manner of success, however marred. They indicate that one such way has been to claim the guilt and to confess the shame—to make sound coinage, as it were, out of wooden nickels so as not to be "sold."

Years after an event which could have been mercifully put aside, or at least left untold, Henry James—failed student of the Law— carefully

> kept to the hour a black little memory of my having attempted
> to argue one afternoon, by way of exercise and under what
> seemed to me a perfect glare of publicity, the fierce light of a
> "moot-court," some case proposed to me by a fellow student—
> [here, a note of the melodramatic and the paranoiac playfully
> slips in]—who can only have been one of the most benign of
> men unless he was darkly the designingest, and to whom I was
> at any rate to owe it that I figured my shame for years much in
> the image of my having stood forth before an audience with a
> fiddle and bow and trusted myself to rub them together des-
> perately enough (after the fashion of Rousseau in a passage of
> the Confessions,) to make some appearance of music.

Like Adams' autobiographical reminiscences, James's *Notes of a Son and Brother* (from which this passage was drawn, p. 340) takes in part as its patron-saint Jean-Jacques the Confessor. Rousseau the blusher, not Franklin the cool, is the model-life James's remembrances follow, perhaps with the same hope of recouping gain out of publicly acknowledged losses.

A man like Scott Fitzgerald writes into *his* notebook, *The Crack-Up*, "I talk with the authority of failure—Ernest with the authority of success. We could never sit across the same table again" (p. 181). Fitzgerald tended to be as remorselessly serious about his guilts as Roderick Usher. In contrast, Norman Mailer in *Cannibals and Christians* tells an interviewer (which is himself posing as father-confessor) that telling all is good for the bowels (pp. 281-282). In this bizarre remark Mailer is both outrageous and slyly perceptive. For are not the bowels the traditional seat of mercy? When Mailer places "A Public Notice" in *The Village Voice* to publicize his guilt over a mistaken evaluation of a production of *Waiting for Godot* (included in *Advertisements for Myself*), he is following the tradition of Samuel Sewall's declaration in church about the part he took in the Salem witchcraft persecutions. *The Village Voice* is today's Congregational Church, and each age must seek out its arena for confession.

Whenever Mailer launches into his carefully itemized lists of the historical and cultural debacles for which he feels personally responsible—from the assassinations of the Kennedys to the Patterson knock-out—he is simply being less pretentious than Arthur Miller when the playwright solemnly reminds us how guilty we ought all to feel over every sparrow that has fallen and every Jew who was gassed. Perhaps Mailer makes himself liable to even more guilt for appearing to turn real tragedies into play when their burden of sorrow should never be allowed relief. Our task here, however, is not the assigning of guilt to one or another of these American experts on sin; it is rather our need to discover how well they each have handled the weight of guilt they possess as men and as Americans.

# CHAPTER 19

# Strain and Relaxation

We should test those strange occasions when a man's guilt becomes an actively useful fact. Mailer, Adams, and Henry James's Lambert Strether provide instructive cases in point for the value of strain when it is set in contrast to the too easeful man freed from any sense of guilt at all.

The metal tips of Norman Mailer's whip of self-flagellation are essentially the same felt by those who came to listen to the words of Emerson and Thoreau. To sit and to accept such statements—*you are not good enough or brave enough or great enough*; or *you have failed yourself and that country which can be no better than the inner fiber of you, its people*—is to force oneself to bear the pain of admitted guilt and shame. When Mailer bears down on his obsessions concerning sexual shame (chastising Paul Goodman for not feeling guilty over feeling no guilt about sex), and when he berates himself for having failed to deliver the Great American Novel to the world, he appears more quirky and trivial than he actually is. His notions about failures as male or as writer are only part of his unflinching conviction that America—and we who are the country—have simply not done what both were created to do.

Mailer is not necessarily challenging us to be *more than* we are, only to be *what we are, fully*. This is a reiteration of the Emersonian belief that we are but ruined gods obliged to feel shame until we can fill up the entire sphere allotted us by our particular destiny. What Mailer desires to expose, using himself as his own best example, are the compromises we are continually making, the mismanaged economics, and the halfway measures of our lives. His hope is that all this talk, all these words of confession, may yet help to bring us up to the full amount we need to be *right*.

In a blood-sense perhaps even more complicated than Mailer's visceral needs, Henry Adams lived with the fact that he, grandson of the originator of the Standard of Weights and Measures of the United States of America, did not fill out all the corners of his destiny (familial, national, personal) or prove more than a lightweight on the scales of public influence. Like Mailer, Adams sensed that our aggressive attempts to be good, brave, and large enough can very well cause hurt to others. As Ernest Samuels' biography points out, Adams' letters suggest that he came alive when his wife Marian died, but he also had to work out the guilt that resulted from questions of why he had not been able to give enough for her to want to keep on living, and the guilt that came from being somehow released by her death from a life of marking illy used time. As Adams lingered on and on into the twentieth century, he carefully noted the Harvard classmates who failed by dying first. Perhaps the letters of condolence he sent out after each man's death were as much a form of confession to guilt over his audacious holding on to the world as was the annual "death" he observed in memorial of Marian's suicide. Between November and December of each year after 1885 he shrank into a dying sense of guilt; each new New Year's Day he was free to take yet another stab at living the full life he felt morally obliged to pursue.

Adams said he was disgusted by the confessions that overflowed from John Quincy Adams' diaries, but his own were no less in the family tradition, even if more wittily phrased. It is significant, though, that Adams failed to respond in kind to the muted confessional undertones in Henry James's memoirs. In Adams' mind James glorified and falsified the earlier years both had shared. Adams did not notice those passages in which James had to face humiliations and guilts as deeply disturbing to him as any recorded by Adams or Mark Twain. Escaping active participation in the Civil War, James found in his memories private pleasures mingled with the "ache" brought on by the "obscure wound" that stirred whatever uneasiness he had in not having gone out to die with all the others. But men who feel guilt over not having been killed are hardly in a class with those filled by the shame of not having fully lived.

Because he is a character in a novel (and of a James novel at that, with its large amount of artfully controlled meaning), Lambert Strether and his adventures may serve to make clearer the autobiographical musings of actual men over what guilt of the highest kind involves, how it might rightly be met, and what it means to lack a sense of guilt altogether.

Simply for a man to live past the age of fifty, Mark Twain wrote in "The Recurrent Major and Minor Compliment" (included in *Fables of Man*), is to know "shame, insult, self-contempt for guilty conduct, and the scorching humiliation of exposure." Lambert Strether at fifty-five experiences these same unpleasant truths, but he is better equipped than Mark Twain to counter the paralysis of self-loathing with feelings that quicken him back into life, even as they keep active the sense of responsibility for his own actions.

There is Strether, and there is Chad Newsome. The younger man has a strong and vigorous body and a mind untouched by thoughts of guilt. He is free even from those potentially weakening ethical concerns of Benjamin Franklin concerning the need to make up for personally incurred debts. Chad is thus described in the first chapter of Book VIII of *The Ambassadors*:

> He was waiting cheerfully and handsomely, but also inscruta-
> bly and with a slight increase perhaps of the hardness origi-
> nally involved in his acquired high polish. He was neither ex-
> cited nor depressed; was easy and acute and deliberate—
> unhurried unflurried unworried, only at most a little less
> amused than usual. (xxii, 65)

In William James's "Gospel of Relaxation" included in the 1899 *Talks to Teachers and Students*, William seems to write in celebration of the Chad-type, chiding those who deal in moral tension of Strether's kind:

> It is your relaxed and easy worker, who is in no hurry, and
> quite thoughtless most of the while of consequences, who is
> your efficient worker; and tension and anxiety and present
> and future, all mixed up together, in our mind at once, are
> the surest drags upon steady progress and hindrance to our
> success.

What Chad "so beautifully" lacks is the strain and intensity which the citizens of Woollett and Milrose alike share. But theirs is an intensity that gives them the *capacity* to move past false moralism of conscience and failures of the imagination. However inept they are at well-being, they at least contain qualities needed for that authentic consciousness which Chad—hollow at the core—will never know.

In Chapter II of Book Ten of *The Ambassadors* we are shown the somewhat comic diminishment of Waymarsh. He appears before Strether, sporting a flower in his buttonhole and a wide white planter's hat, but his new suavity comes at the cost of the "old intensity" now gone "feeble and flat" (xxii, 194). Waymarsh is now a man at long last "having a good time," but he is, unfortunately, doing so by placing himself "in a false position" (xxii, 190).

One of the functions of this little scene—funny, and obviously not meant to be one of the novel's "big" events—is to impress upon us that, for James, his best people are free but they are not easy. They must continue to maintain the burden of moral strain even after they have won through to a precious new liberation of the imagination. James strives to represent by means of his dramatic argument (not merely by rhetorical statement) that those who continue to pay tributes to the ideal will at last come into their inheritance of moral fineness, however questionable a legacy in terms of worldly success or happiness. Such types protect their newly attained fineness by means of paying with strain, whereas Chad Newsome—whether the original American version or the newly shaped Parisian form—and the new Waymarsh gain social polish and habits of relaxation at the cost of an accompanying moral coarseness.

Chad's world has the "mellowest lamplight and the easiest chair" and the "subtlest of servants" (xxii, 228). He, indeed, has learned the secret of "knowing how to live" successfully (xxii, 231). From the night of the first shock of recognition at the theater box, on to the Sunday afternoon in Gloriani's garden, and further through the rest of the events of that sun-dappled Parisian summer, Strether continues to envy mightily the way Chad demonstrates an extraordinary knack for turning the most demanding of situations from the potentially "hurried and feverish" into "one of the largest, loosest and easiest . . ." (xxii, 230). Chad is adept at the "pleasant backward glance over his possibilities of motives"; he is able to reduce his "personal friction" and his "personal offence" down "to almost nothing" (xxii, 233). It is left for Strether, during the river encounter, to deal with a situation sensed by him as "really stiff." Marie and Strether together suffer the strain, while Chad, then as always, "habitually left things to others"—which was "such vivid illustration of his famous knowing how to live" (xxii, 264).

The day after the moral shock that results when the scene shifts on the river from a carefully framed Lambinet painting to an open-ended *human* situation, Strether goes to see Marie de Vionnet. He feels the necessity for "sternness" and "discipline." He knows there is

some awkwardness they would suffer from, some danger, or at least some grave inconvenience, they would incur. This would give a sense—which the spirit required, rather ached and sighed in the absence of—that somebody was paying something somewhere and somehow, that they were at least not all floating together on the silver stream of impunity. (xxii, 272)

The language of the penultimate clause may remind us of H. L. Mencken's definition of the American puritan as one who fears that someone somewhere might be enjoying himself. But for James the truly terrible life comes as the consequence of a man who is so casual he feels indifference for what is happening to others. Just as it was for the original Puritans, for Strether and for James our lives are shaped by Matters of Indifference and Matters of Concern. To be indifferent to things not of indifferent value is a sin; morality is the acknowledgment that we must take concern whenever realities of the heart are involved.

It may seem odd to say "Chad Newsome" and "Daniel Webster" in one breath, but Emerson's itemization in his 1843 journal of the "*three rules* of living" adhered to by Webster coincide with Chad's:

> 1. Never to pay any debt that can by any possibility be avoided.
>
> 2. Never to do anything today that can be put off till tomorrow.
>
> 3. Never to do anything himself which he can get anybody else to do for him. (VIII, 324-325)

Chad hardly strikes us as a Fallen Ichabod, but he joins Webster as a man who chose to concern himself only with himself.

Chad likes to "get off," to do what he is perfectly "free to do." It is important to notice that he becomes increasingly "restless" over the course of the narrative. By the end of his Parisian adventure, he is still morally easy but beginning to fidget mentally over which of several "ideas" for increased personal success he ought to follow up in order to take advantage of "the money in it." Strether, as morally tense as ever, is now mentally serene. He has but one idea to move with as a basic rule of behavior: "Not, out of the whole affair, to have got anything for myself" (XXII, 326). Strether—and we surely—must envy Chad his freedom from care (because incapable of caring very much about anything but himself), and liberation from shame and guilt (because dissociated from those human connections that might exact responsible actions and the accompanying sense of falling short in those commitments). Ease and strain: Chad and Strether. As James imprints this tale upon the reader's moral imagination, we come to honor strain, even as we continue to envy ease.

In *Notes of a Son and Brother* Henry James wrote that the precious commodity of "serenity" is gained by the artist not in spite of strain, but because of it. Perhaps, though, all those American types from "Woollett" are wrong. Perhaps the guilt, shame, and "old intensity" shared alike by James and Adams, Edwards and Emerson, Mark Twain and Mailer, are proof of exactly how *not* to live in America. What if Chad Newsome's way of "knowing how to live" is the better one because his is the raft of the free, easy, and comfortable that floats down the "silver stream of impunity"? What if Chad's portrait ought to be purged even of the restlessness that marks the final scenes of James's novel since those jitters are a sign of the author's overly moralistic conviction of Chad's damnation—an erroneous exaction of punishment on James's part? What if America's special gift to mankind *is* the promise that here indeed we need never again feel guilt or know shame?

Any discussion of the issue of success yields at least two basic definitions. The one rests upon success as the attainment of prosperity and worldly power; the other insists that the true triumphs take place within the moral man. The materialists call members of the opposition fools, while the moralists fling back the epithet, "Scoundrels!" But perhaps there is an alternative to *doing well* or *being good*—success gained simply and superbly by *feeling good*.

Appropriately, it is Henry James in *The Golden Bowl* who gives an amusing view of what it is like *not* to be allowed to relax:

> ". . . it's 'sort of' soothing; as if we were sitting about on divans, with pigtails, smoking opium and seeing visions. 'Let us then be up and doing'—what is it Longfellow says? That seems sometimes to ring out; like the police breaking in—into our opium den—to give us a shake." (XXIV, 92)

This is Adam Verver voicing his pleasure in indolence. Yet he seems to suggest the greater pleasure that comes when torpor is broken by the shrill police-whistle—the signal by which we are alerted to our duty, the duty (what Freud calls the Super-Ego) by which we are told that our leisure is also our work:

> "But the beauty of it is at the same time that we *are* doing; we're doing, that is, after all, what we went in for. . . . We *have* worked it, and what more can you do than that?" (XXIV, 92)

It is possible that this dual celebration of idleness and duty—coming as it does from Adam Verver, that gentleman of questionable morality—only merits our skepticism. It is William James who indicates better ways to stay put with impunity in the opium den, effacing present trouble with oblivion. In his discussion of the soul in the first volume of *Principles of Psychology* James compares orthodox belief in the soul's "forensic responsibility before God" with Locke's assertion "that God would not, in the great day, make a person answer for what he remembers nothing of." James agrees that "those who demand a plentitude of retribution" will insist upon the soul's keeping track of its lapses from perfection, but he observes that "modern readers, however, who are less insatiate for retribution than their grandfathers," will prefer the "mere stream of consciousness, with its lapses of memory [which] cannot possibly be as 'responsible' as a Soul which *is* at the judgment day all that it ever was."

If America and Americans could only flow lazily along the great Lethean stream of forgetful consciousness, as indifferent to the moral sense as is the Mississippi, perhaps even the Hucks and the Strethers—the Souls—could let themselves be swept along its surface, freed from "raspy" memories of the links between human acts and moral consequences.

In *A Small Boy and Others* Henry James equated sophistication with growing and with knowing, and knowing with fear (p. 235). Always strong on memory's associative links, he recalled how disturbed he had felt as a boy in 1858 when faced with Holman Hunt's painting, "The Scapegoat." It was a fear that had no direct tie to anything *he* had done; it was nourished only by a general sense of human guilt (p. 316). Augustine, Wordsworth, and Woolman all suffered feelings of sinfulness as boys when, respectively, they stole pears, a boat, and birds' eggs. William Faulkner has also endlessly imaged the communal fear that falls alike upon all Americans who inherit the guilt of theft of that land and that race which is no man's to possess.

If, however, the historical sense—prized so highly by both Faulkner and Henry James—could break down, men would be freed from a weight as heavy as the Moral Sense lamented by Mark Twain, freed from the recollection of what they or their fathers have ever done to America, freed, too, from regret, penance, and the endless climb up the moral ladder that Norman Mailer is so critical of.

Freud said that guilt does not come from the transgression of any actual moral fact but is a matter of psychological response; when we feel *un*worthy—feel we are *less* than what the circumstances seem to call for—we suffer from a dire sense of economic poverty. But America is supposed to make us all be *more* than we are, or at least to make us *as much as* we once were. We were promised by Crèvecœur and Emerson that we would reach full stature in this land, and John Quincy Adams busied himself to provide an official Standard of Weights and Measures, both moral and commercial, that would set the accurate mark for that fullness. But conscience on its own is merely frugal, not fulfilling. Thoreau stated as much in *A Week on the Concord and Merrimack Rivers* in his review of the teachings of Menu in the "Monday" section. Conservation of conscience only acts to preserve the dead, while Thoreau wished men to have more than that. Men's consciences are analogous to the human appendix or tail-bone—once useful in ruder stages of our growth, but now distracting, valueless, and often painful. It would be better to discard conscience altogether in order to be free to float forward and to seize life lived up to the mark.

The need to get loose from remorse was one of Thoreau's main arguments. The intense man from Concord was hardly Chad Newsome at ease in Paris, yet Thoreau (in his journal of September 24, 1859) actively denounced the stockholders of "Repentance & Co." Melancholy can slay, and Thoreau was that killer's foe. He constantly tried to free himself from having *to think about* virtue. How blessed he felt when he forgot to be good, since forgetfulness proves the surest way out of attendant guilt. It is better to cease seriousness and "to cut capers," Thoreau wrote on January 24, 1841; best still, he added on August 1st, to stop living in "a Jewish gloom" by becoming so innocent one need not know "cherubim nor angels."

Emerson also rebuked the Byronisms of guilt. Both he and Thoreau spoke out against the orthodox tradition which William James later described as a cast of mind eager for the unceasing memory of sin. What James called "chronic anxiety" and what Gaston Bachelard calls the artificial creation of anguish is also attacked by Mark Twain in "The Refuge of the Derelicts." In this piece (included in *Fables of Man*) he states that "teaching" ignorantly defines repentance as applicable only to wrong-doing. Actually, it is "experience" which shows you that all acts, good or bad, bring remorse because conscience (the heart's enemy) smites you whatever you do, since you are completely controlled by inherited temperament and the circumstances imposed by life.

In order to gain relief from the oppressive weight of guilt, it hardly helps to work out from Mark Twain's theory that we are unable to keep from doing wrong or that we will suffer whatever we do, even if it is right. Nor are we given instant aid if we follow through with Thoreau and Emerson in their attacks on the orthodox habit of arraigning guilt before the judgment seat. Turning men's faces away from heaven, they tried to make them confess to the sin of being false to themselves. But what benefit do we get in escaping one brand of guilt only to fall heir to another?

Under the gaze of Mark Twain on one of his moodier days, we are forced to concede guilt under the laws of nature, with no appeal to conscience or to conciousness. According to the orthodox, on the other hand, we who daily break the divine law have its ideal of godly perfection laid upon our conscience. For the Transcendentalists, our guilt comes from having denied our personal obligation to be perfect under the law of our own consciousness. The one way out and past all three of these assignments of mortal failure is to throw over notions of right and wrong action together. But such total repudiation seems beyond the ability of many Americans. Their sense of morality (an even greater task-master than the Moral Sense) will not let them go free to consider pleasure as being the primary value. It would seem that every satisfaction demands a moral basis in America, else it is of no good.

James Wilson, signer of both the Declaration of Independence and the Constitution, wrote about a law of nature quite different from the one later testified to by Mark Twain. In *Lectures on Law*, first delivered during 1790-1791, Wilson insisted that men love virtue because it brings them pleasure and welcome morality because it sharpens enjoyment of the natural beauty of goodness. A generation or so later, the essay "Transcendentalism" by Theodore Parker accused the Sensationalists of stressing pleasure whether or not it was united with virtue. Where Wilson had insisted that to be good was the greatest pleasure, Sensationalists like William Paley (according to Parker) said that pleasure was the only good.

> In politics might makes right, so in morals. Success is the touchstone; the might of obtaining the reward the right of doing the deed. Bentham represents the sensational morals of politics; Paley of ethics. Both are Epicureans. The sensationalist and the Epicurean agree in this—enjoyment is the touchstone of virtue and determines what is good, what bad, what indifferent. . . . In either case virtue ceases to be virtue, for it is only a bargain. (p. 59)

But if Thoreau was one of the men whom Parker sought to place in opposition to the Sensationalists, there are times when it sounds as if Thoreau would have us be merry with impunity. Gladness, he says, is more important than learning the laws; idleness is true virtue, since it lets one stretch and grow. And if Mailer-the-moralist cautions us not to gain pleasure through an avoidance of pain, else we end with compromise and cancer, even he wishes he could get at joy by giving great parties that would entirely change our lives. Henry James raised the question in *A Small Boy and Others* whether an American people ought to be so innocent that dancing becomes its only care, but he also declared that life is the gaining of pleasure under difficulties. Still—for all their winning talk of idling on the pond, going to parties, and savoring the peculiar enjoyment wrung from dealing with the Woollett terror of "ought not"—as long as we stay within range of the voices of Thoreau, Mailer, and James, we are apt to be coerced into believing in that virtue which is good primarily because it is goodness, not because it promises us pleasure in reward for its pursuit. Thoreau may urge us to saunter, not to run, but his goal is still *la Sainte Terre*. Mailer is a sensual man, but not a Sensationalist. And Henry James still finds his most lasting pleasures in strain, not away from it.

Unrepentantly, many of us continue to yearn to hear able arguments for the other side. We like to listen to blandishments from the un-American mouths of Paley or Bachelard, who (like Kingsley Amis's Lucky Jim) insist that nice things are nicer than things that are not nice and that the agreeable is more valuable than the merely useful or the necessary.

The Lawrentian baby-ego feels good because it is aggressive, selfish, and angry, able to exploit its erotic and anal needs, to resist the demands of the mothers, and to trust to its senses. If only Huck Finn had been more like that, and Maisie Farange—those novelistic children of all too American fathers—they might have been able to show us an America devoted to revelry rather than to dismaying Hawthornian choices between Merry-Mount's phantoms and Puritan rigor, neither of which we want. As we read our way through American letters we keep getting transitory glimpses of Quincy, Massachusetts, and St. Petersburg, Missouri, awash with light in the sensual summertime; but then we are admonished by our betters that maturity and moral responsibility forbid us continued enjoyment of Massachusetts and Mississippi River holidays, even if the world could be persuaded to give them to us. Benjamin Franklin twits us for dreaming of the *Pays de Cocagne*, and Richard Poirier for seeking a World Elsewhere. Only Walt Whitman seems to be wholly on our side. But even with Whitman there are those

doubts which D. H. Lawrence imbeds within us when he tells us
that following the Whitmanian road of the free and easy down
which the Good Grey Poet beckons us may lead to our death.

In American writing the men of pleasure frequently come across
as "boys," while the children haunt us with the painful wisdom they
wring out of experiences far in excess of their years. Ishmael and
Queequeg luxuriate in being sociable, tucked free and easy in a
warm Bachelardian bed away from the night's chill, even as Huck
Finn shivers from more than the damp, while he meditates upon
the demands imposed by the voices within that tell him what he
must do about Nigger Jim. In the instances provided by Melville
and Mark Twain, the fact of the characters' consciousnesses remains
strong. But in the former case the "boys" keep dreamily to bed; in
Huck's case, consciousness keeps him tensely awake, anxiously
"working it out."

In "What The Will Effects" of 1888 William James says the only
way we ever get out of bed on a freezing morning is to do it

> without any struggle or decision at all. We suddenly find that
> we *have* got up. . . . It was our acute consciousness of both the
> warmth and the cold during the period of struggle, which
> paralyzed our activity then and kept our idea of rising in the
> condition of *wish*, and not of will.

Melville's "boys" remain serenely *in* the pleasurable area of *soft
wish and indifference*; Mark Twain's worried little man is propelled
against his will *out* of the free and easy realm of wish into *hard
thought and concern*.

At times it seems that in all American letters only William James
gets to enjoy the advantage of living to his great pleasure in the
world of personal will. But even he stresses that this world and its
success cannot be directly put to the use of gaining pleasure.
"Pleasure is apt to be throughout a secondary complication to the
drama of stimulation and desire," he wrote in "What The Will
Effects."

> And when the idea of it does propel, and becomes itself the
> motive, it is only as one among many ideas which have the
> privilege coequally. If one idea, such as that of pleasure, may
> let loose the springs of action, surely other ideas may. . . . In-
> numerable objects of desire and passion innervate our limbs
> just as they light up a fever in our breasts. . . . Blind reactive

impulse at the beginning, ideational coercion of some sort at
the end, such are the poles between which the evolution of
human conduct swings.

We live mainly within that area of "involuntary life" from which
the voluntary life darts out to assert its choices. To James, in *choice*
lies pleasure. This does not mean that pleasure is merely *what* one
chooses. His views tend away from Freud's premise that locates
pleasure in the passivity which tries to avoid demonic activity.
James also differs from Bachelard's belief that will brutalizes our
reveries of leisure. The American way represented by William
James stands opposed to these two Continental theories in its (quite
secular) suggestion that "in our will is our peace." But it also resists
the equally American urgency to gain pleasure through yielding up
the individual to the all-feeling.

When George Santayana sought to trace what had happened to
the original Puritan morality (based on the will to virtue), he
thought he detected two separate traits—one that honors the "passive sensorium," the other that reads the human will as pleasure.
Here is Santayana speaking in "The Genteel Tradition in American Philosophy" of 1911:

> Whitman became a pantheist; but his pantheism, unlike that of
> the Stoics and of Spinoza, was unintellectual, lazy, and self-
> indulgent; for he simply felt jovially that everything real was
> good enough, and that he was good enough. In him Bohemia
> rebelled against the genteel tradition; but the reconstruction
> that alone can justify the revolution did not ensue. His at-
> titude, in principle, was utterly disintegrating. . . . He reduced
> his imagination to a passive sensorium for the registering of
> impressions. No element of construction remained in it, and
> therefore no element of penetration. But his scope was wide;
> and his lazy, desultory apprehension was poetical. His work,
> for the very reason that it is so rudimentary, contains a begin-
> ning, or rather many beginnings, that might possibly grow into
> a noble moral imagination, a worthy filling for the human
> mind. An American in the nineteenth century who completely
> disregarded the genteel tradition could hardly have done
> more.
>
> But there is another distinguished man . . . who has given
> some rude shocks to this tradition and who, as much as Whit-
> man, may be regarded as representing the genuine, the long
> silent American mind—I mean William James.

At first glance, Whitmanian pleasure through the loss of the individual personality, through return to the abstraction out of which
it has arisen, seems atypical of America. It looks more native to the
meadows and forests of "Bohemia." Yet it, as much as the I-am-Will
method of William James, is part of "the genuine, the long silent
American mind. . . ."

When we move to Part v of this book—the one which speaks of
certain central American visions of catastrophe—we can decide
whether it is Whitman or William James who suggests the most
useful *final* way out of failure. We will also hear more about the
kind of pleasure some Americans like best: the intense fun that
comes about when the angry imagination sets its will-to-disaster
against the idea-of-America that has so severely disappointed its
expectations; when relaxation that believes "that everything real
was good enough" is pushed aside by strain whose sole faith is in
the reality of what is too bad to bear because not enough like perfection.

# CHAPTER 20

# Eyeless in Hate;
# Killing in Style

To keep for a while to questions of strain and relaxation: melo-dramas are built upon tensions, broken only when evil is destroyed and virtue is released from enslavement. The life of humor, how-ever relaxed in many of its manners, also undergoes its tensions be-fore it can fully succeed. The only guaranteed way out of strain of whatever kind is to run from it. Escape suggests an end to failure, since it tries to avoid those conditions wherein failure may be en-countered. American writing provides a fine array of materials for manuals on escape-techniques: escape into nature, into emotional detachment and through geographical distancing, into mindless-ness, drowsiness, and reverie, evasive movements into childhood, nostalgia for the past, and dreams of Utopian futures. All these modes of escape have had distinguished advocates who present their arguments for ducking altogether occasions to fail. But in this section we will examine responses to the fact of failures *already* suf-fered. We have just looked at various ways that Americans, through their acceptance of guilt, have faced up to the shame of having failed. Now we shall see what happens when the American angrily refuses to accept the scent of failure that the rest of society lays upon him, and what he does in his revenge upon those who have tried to humiliate him.

Robert Eisler in *Man Into Wolf: An Anthropological Interpretation of Sadism, Masochism, and Lycanthropy* tried to locate in time the origins of masochistic feelings of guilt and acts of egotism; he concluded that it was not until the late "civilized" stages of man's history that individuals were no longer able to contain the rages caused by their life in society. In *The Poetics of Space* Bachelard remarks that wolves leaping from boxes are more frightening than those which lope toward one across open space. By analogy, the man taught by soci-ety that he is guilty of failure, yet held back by its restraints from expressing his anger at what it has made him do, will finally leap out of tidy social boxes to take his wolfish revenge.

When Freud placed Michelangelo's marble Moses under analysis, he proposed that that statue represents a man of justice filled with wrath, but one who carefully keeps it in control because of the demands of his larger social commitment. In contrast, we recognize that Michelangelo's Christ in "The Last Judgment" releases His rage in order to punish all the failures of mankind which have been loaded upon Him in the name of His father's will. Americans unable to contain themselves within the marble posture of the restrained Mosaic law-giver sometimes prefer to think of themselves as righteous Messianic judges. They allot themselves the right to kill, thereby escaping self-judgment as brothers to dragons or wolves who slay without moral justification.

Self-righteous explanations for rage given by Americans barely keep pace with the theories concocted by psychologists and sociologists to reveal why Americans are such a violent people. Thomas Hartshorne in *The Distorted Image* places such theories about righteous wrath in the context of the tensions that resulted from an uneasy mix of materialism and idealism, pioneer and puritan, ethical confusions and moral schemata. Like Hartshorne, Norman Mailer locates the violence he finds in the Wasp heart in the paradoxes that split the American into warring halves that strike out, killing whoever gets in the way. And, according to Howard Mumford Jones, abusive language was just as characteristic of the late nineteenth-century Age of Energy as was its more publicized tradition of gentility and controlled emotions.

Eyeless in Gaza, Samson drags down part of the world in his wrath against false gods. Shelley's Prometheus lies "eyeless in hate," gnawed by rage against the cosmic tyranny of Zeus. Blake, assisted by the Fourfold Vision that clarifies the nature of the outrageousness it is his mission to attack, excels at insulting idiots and deities. There are many Americans who similarly hate in God's name or who hate God; the former are willing servants, the latter rebellious sons: both are potential killers.

The German Romantic strain (which poured part of its emotional juices into the American philosophic bloodstream) tended to stress the "striving and struggle" which insists on battle and victory as the one way to truth. Meyer Abrams, who provides this insight in *Natural Supernaturalism* about Hölderlin and his kind (p. 238), traces in ways not unlike Mailer's the plot of the hero who defies both nature and God out of his enraged response to what Hölderlin describes in *Hyperion* as "the dissonances of the world." The Romantic impulse furnished the literary imagination with the type who justifies acts of rebellious estrangement in the name of the ills done to himself; he envisions himself as the punishing son who strikes at the sins perpetrated by the antagonistic mother (Nature) and the brutal father (Nation).

We can hardly line up all Americans with the Romantics in general or the enraged in particular; but, however varied the emotional and intellectual archetypes upon which the national imagination draws, it is certain that America has not been settled by peace-lovers. Captain John Smith selected for his personal emblem the head of the Turk he claimed to have slain in holy wars against the infidel. Smith's emblem was the visible sign of the equally militant doctrinal spirit asserted by the Puritans against the legions of sin, whether Indians or Quakers. In turn, the eighteenth-century Quaker John Woolman spoke in the name of quietism against men who act in the name of hatred at the same time he vigorously attacked easeful relations with the ungodly. It is difficult to be both quiet and resolute. Woolman had to caution himself continually to put down within his own heart the "fierce proud spirit of war" that possessed American society by the mid-1700's. Some nineteenth-century Americans, like Ishmael, shipped their angry coffin-moods out to sea, but most stayed at home ready to turn their hand against the next person to show himself. Father Mapple's sermon instructs the people to hate and to destroy evil for God's sake; he is hardly unlike Ahab or Colonel John Morelock of *The Confidence Man* in this. Melville's own concluding remarks concerning Oberlus in "*The Encantadas*"—"a creature whom it is religion to detest, since it is philanthropy to hate a misanthrope" (p. 202)—also suggest the tradition of Edward Johnson and Nathaniel Ward which makes it a Christian's duty to act in righteous wrath against the ungodly and inhumane.

Man is born into outrage. Melville and Faulkner show us this. Every moment of breathing reminds a person of the incredible things being done to him by the very universe he is told to honor. For long years Mink Snopes contains his rage against life in general and Jack Houston in particular until the time comes for him to strike out. And so filled with rage is that part of *Moby-Dick* which is not drenched in brotherly love that we tend to believe that Starbuck is at fault because, like Michelangelo's Moses, he contains himself and follows the Lord's commandment not to kill, even the God-defiers. What would have happened if Starbuck, abiding by the spirit of God's will and not the letter of His law, had slain the rebellious Ahab? Would the community of the *Pequod* have been saved, and is this peace-maker to blame that it was not? And as the readers of *Moby-Dick*, we become so tutored in rage that we, like Ahab, feel the need to rebuke even the blacksmith. Numbed as he is to feelings of wrath and of joy, how *small* a man he seems in contrast to Ahab! Stubb laughs and Starbuck glooms; they are the reverse side of the common man. But Ahab acts; he stands as the extraordinary man apart from those he uses to further his self-righteous wrath, even while he ignores the reasons God might have for calling upon the white whale to be agent for *His* rage against the world's failure to succeed.

If Ahab rises above the commonplace in his all too common rebellion against the divine principle of a malevolent universe, Emerson and Thoreau provide portraits of the extraordinary man who, on the proper occasion, makes use of the language of violence to affirm his own godhood within the benevolent laws of the world. In Mark Twain and Henry Adams, we also see the close relations between wrath, language, and style.

Emerson mildly criticized Carlyle's Ahabian desire to insult and to kill. His low vitality for revenge made it easy for him to spot irritable types like Carlyle and John Quincy Adams. When he was upset he would go into his garden and putter out his angers in the soil. Yet Emerson was aware that writing can be an aggressive act—so aware, that Jonathan Bishop in *Emerson on the Soul* concludes that Emerson sought to undermine the power of this weapon by assuring readers that his essays could not harm them. In "Self-Reliance" Emerson makes it clear he would not have sided with the S.L.A., the Black Panthers, or Jewish mothers—those who victimize whom they wish to control and to be revenged upon by inflicting an oppressive sense of guilt. Yet the weapon hidden in the weight and sharpness of Emerson's own prose has the same effect, however much he denies its presence.

Like Franklin, Emerson argues against the use of a controversial, antagonizing style; but even more frequently than we find in Franklin, his statements march out upon the neutral ground of the lecture hall or the printed page to punish those who have sinned against truth's circles and nature's spirals. Emerson's eyes were mild, but the words of his early essays cause us to judge ourselves harshly. Only when his words soften somewhat in the last essays are we able to forgive him—not because he has shown us the way to be stronger, but because we are eased away from our fear of his chastisement.

Always on the search for patterns of cause and effect that would unify all events, Emerson was once disturbed to read of a violent murder. At first it seemed meaningless, he reported to his journal of 1838; but soon after he was cheered to learn there had been a reason for the slaying. It had been occasioned by the murderer's desire to revenge an ill which had been done to him. Such an emotion gave Emerson an understandable cause and confirmed that the world is ringed around by "scientific laws" of the kind which later led Freud to believe there are reasons for all our acts. Perhaps violence "that is dreary and repels" is the absence of true power, as Emerson wrote in "Character"; but violence motivated directly by passionate hatred at least links otherwise uncomprehensible events. After all, as Emerson wrote in his essay "Fate," fate is a tiger, marked by rapacity and violence. As Blakean in this as in other aspects of his dancer-and-the-dance theory of compensation, he held that universal law is tiger as well as lamb. In his own confidence in a perfecting process that would change basic types, the reformer Robert Owen said he could even educate tigers. However much a fellow-believer in melioration, Emerson saw such changes as unnecessary; he was willing to live with tigers as they are. He was neither interested in becoming a tiger nor having tigers become like him. Rather, as Emerson suggested while musing on solitude, "the Lonely society which forms so fast in these days" might take as its seal "Two porcupines meeting, with all their spines erect, and the motto, 'We converse at the quills' end!'" (*Works*, VII, 346n.) Emerson had confidence that he could share his sheets with whatever strange and prickly bedfellows might happen along.

Emerson disliked argument, but he could be ignited. He was a peaceful man, but he praised the cleansing qualities of lightning and war. But of the little band of Concordians, it is Thoreau who was the best hater, the man whom Emerson described in his 1862 eulogy as having had "such terrible eyes," and the one whose prose style prompted Margaret Fuller to remark that reading in his essays was like walking under a cliff that threatens to give way at any moment in an avalanche. Thoreau's words are effective, and they can be chilling. His is *wit* as Emerson defines it in "The Comic": "... like ice, on which no beauty of form, no majesty of carriage can plead any immunity,—they must walk gingerly, according to the laws of ice, or down they must go, dignity and all."

Thoreau believed that the moon in its serenity is the highest good; but the moon lies outside civilization. War is valuable because it exposes men to themselves as they are within society, as the moon cannot. When Thoreau delivered his address in homage to John

Brown, he stated he could foresee that right "nick" when he himself would kill or be killed in violent action against society's evils.
He held murderous thoughts against the state and phrased them
openly. He urged passive resistance, but knew that that method
carried on too long might itself lead to unuseful violence. The
blacks of Thoreau's time were too docile to gain his praise because
they danced, while the Indians had given over their fine energies to
war. He said he smiled when he was locked into jail, but the jailer
later reported on Thoreau's fury. During the Fourth of July the village militia paraded about in Concord in comic seriousness, a
parody of true militancy, while Thoreau, in earnest play, beheaded
the weeds in his beanfield. He wrote Emerson from New York of
the advantages gained through the hating of the city. He said he
preferred being dealt a blow to getting the wet kiss of comradeship
offered by that greasy reformer A. D. Foss. He noted that when
crows rebuke and owls screech, they are expressing nature's accusations against men's sins. Anything would be better, he wrote on
the 26th of August of 1854, than the "dull rage" for the universe
that glazes the eye of the snapping turtle in a sluggish version of
the general outrage of all created things against "the trials of this
world. . . ." There were times, indeed—as when "Massa-chooses-it"
let the boss-men uphold the Fugitive Slave Acts—when Thoreau
would have liked to destroy the world with his anger. He stated this
vehement wish quite clearly in his journal of May 29, 1854: "Rather
than thus consent to establish hell upon earth,—to be a party to this
establishment,—I would touch a match to blow up earth and hell
together."

If Thoreau was a splendid hater, there was something equivocal
about his rages. He made distinctions between the serene moon
and snappish civilization, between himself and other men. He was
able to make such distinctions because he believed that the ultimate
reality is peace and joy. Unrelieved by such faith, Mark Twain is
the best all-round hater of our band. He finally learned to feel
anger for almost everything and everyone because he felt he had
discovered that reality itself is formed of malice and fright.

Mark Twain's education on the river included lessons in rage
and revenge that for a long time were kept under control or released harmlessly by his playful imagination. One of the traits the
cub pilot noted and admired in Captain Bixby was the older man's
ability to be filled by fury at the dangerous incompetence of under-
lings, yet to hold it in during a tight spot until the immediate crisis
to the steamboat was past. By this delaying action the explosion of

Bixby's emotions did not adversely effect his rational command of the situation. The young apprentice liked this in Bixby, but in *Life on the Mississippi* far more narrative stress is placed on those occasions of magnificent lettings-go.

If Bixby contained his rage so that the safety of the boat and passengers might not be jeopardized by the self-indulgent gaining of his own pleasure, the cub pilot had to control his wrath against such men as Captain Brown for his own sake. His inferior position on the steamboat permitted him no rights for expressing himself with violence in public. Bixby gained personal glory from the onlookers by the splendor and variety of his invectives; the cub had to "kill" Brown in private, and whatever creativity he managed through these imaginary verbal murders had to remain part of a secret ceremony of release. In either case language was the weapon. Bixby and the cub slew their foes by the extravagance and concentrated force of their cursings—public or private. In addition, in one glorious instance, Clemens got to lay low the hated Brown by pointing out to him his faulty grasp of grammar. By words and syntax "the best man" could create weapons to destroy.

"Revenge is wicked, and unchristian and in every way unbecoming," Samuel Clemens told Livy in 1870 (as Justin Kaplan reports). "But it is powerful sweet anyway" (p. 109). Life was sweet as long as language had the power to delight by letting him talk out his rage against human cruelties and divine injustice. The terrible fate yet to come was to feel nothing, as after his daughter Suzy's death: to feel indifference where before he had actively, creatively, hated or loved life. Still later on, he was able to work himself up into feeling again, but the work-ethic involved in this strenuous effort to move from numbness back towards intensity resulted in the straining of the imagination that weakened his beloved grand effects. This strain is revealed by his endless fiddling with words during the last ten years of his writing and talking career. Originally wrath had been a source of spontaneous pleasure; it had powerfully focused itself on particular individuals and events and exploded through language into effective force. Eventually his rage and his words spread themselves out over a wider and wider area until they came to be all-inclusive and largely self-defeating.

As one's bile rises over the times one has been sold by life, the desire to kill the culprit closest to hand, even an innocent stand-in, increases. One can tell a story about rage and make it amusing, especially if the story is told about someone else. Mark Twain's companion innocent abroad, Jack, is the fellow who wants to kill the next turtle he comes upon in Palestine. The Bible had spoken of "the voice of the turtle," but Palestinian turtles do not talk, so they ought to be exposed as frauds and destroyed. Mark Twain can stand by during all this and look humorously at Jack's being a bit of a fool because of his angry desire to kill out of ignorance. In after years Mark Twain's wrath shows itself more clearly as being his own, not that of someone handy like Jack. Because it is *his* rage it is not so amusing anymore. Further, he has turned away from the punishment of surrogate "turtles" to get down to attacks on the true culprit. Not turtles, but the Bible itself must be exposed for its lies. Then (having struck through the cardboard mask of that particular "Moby Dick"), Mark Twain next acts to unmask God as the supreme universal fraud. By words he began to attack the prime enemy—the Word which has "sold" men by gulling them with hopes that have no basis in reality.

Mark Twain noticed that there were men like U. S. Grant who remained as impassive under provocation as Indians enduring torture, but he himself finally came to the point where his choices appeared to be limited to cursing or to weeping, with cursing the more satisfying of the two. There were no *good* answers to the bitter questions he asked about life, even about trivial matters. Why had not Oxford offered him an honorary degree much earlier? Why couldn't Mrs. Thomas Aldrich be set adrift with him on a raft as his sole source of provisions? Some of the questions he asked were not so minor. Why was it that Slade, the outlaw of the Nevada Territory, got to "kill his man" on the slightest pretext, while the rest of us have to try to stay in control? And why had Slade the enviable power to shoot men down in *anticipation* of an outrageous insult before the event took place? The morality of Mark Twain's angry attack against the ignorant vindictiveness of the jury system in *Roughing It* is put into doubt by his statement that if there were no courts a man would be free to take personal revenge—as Slade did; as the mob finally did against Slade; as Mark Twain wished to do, at least through language, if not with the outlaw's gun or the law's hanging rope.

Henry Adams, as Conservative Christian Anarchist, was another man who liked to smash things. There was a touch of wrath in his cool Bostonian blood that he realized could go out of control. Anger filled the Adams family whenever Quincy's principles had to face the effrontery of State Street's expediency. And when the mood of rebellion was in ascendance, bother the cause. Henry Adams' brother Charles attacked him openly in his letters and in an anonymous review of one of his books, while Henry's 1882 biography of John Randolph (a man who was himself given to insults) took revenge on the statesman for what he had done to the family. Brooks Adams cautioned Henry to remove expressions of petty irritation from *The Education* in order to keep its tone Olympian. Henry, who had in turn urged Brooks to strike out offensive passages from *Law of Civilization and Decay*, said he would like to go along with Brooks's warning about his own book but found it almost impossible to do. Henry told himself that he ought to curb his angers since a man's private suffering is no excuse for public bad temper. However, the editor of *The Nation* remarked in 1870 (in material included in Samuels' *The Young Henry Adams*, p. 194) that Henry was a true Adams like his grandfather. Incorporating a characterization of John Quincy Adams by Rufus Choate, he agreed that Henry Adams had " 'peculiar powers as an assailant . . . an instinct for the jugular and cartoid artery as unerring as that of any carnivorous animal. . . .' " As they had been for Mark Twain, words were the best weapon a man like Adams, who felt he had lost all other powers, could use.

Adams early decided on certain types to dislike actively. He boxed the ears of a Jewish boy at school, then wrote home about this interesting event. In Adams' eye the Semitic gold-bugs were causing America's economic decline; they continued to get their ears boxed by his prose. But Adams tended to be a generous bigot (if there is such a thing). Eager for a good fight, argument for its own sake was what he sought in the main and his opponents need not be Jews to qualify. Franklin, who had made a policy of not going crazy, commented that John Adams went out of his senses at times over the way America was being handled by the idiots in power. The Adams grandson also viewed John Quincy as essentially humorless and preachy, and as a man who became interesting only when he was really fighting. This observation by Henry Adams is characteristic. Anger for him was primarily a stave against boredom. He preferred that use rather than to justify anger as a weapon in the sacred cause of righteousness. Since a pervading decency and kindliness had made the general social scene in America so colorless, and detached it from Adams' own feelings about life, only the cultivated violence of rage could possibly jolt him back into being *in it*.

In *Henry Adams: The Major Phase* Ernest Samuels speaks of the Calvinist contempt that mixed itself in with Adams' urbane tolerance of others' flaws and with his liking for courteous silences and relaxed good-humor. But Adams was concerned about more than moral reasons against anger; it was what it did to one's *force* that mattered most. Curbing excessive rage had immediate advantages for one's emotional state since Adams knew the debilitating effects of anger indulged in for private pleasure. Such emotions were essentially futile. He would like to grin and tear, he said, against the whole world, but to what practical purpose were any of his words if the sky were made of steel? Why not become as hard as the sky? The cryptic lines written on the back of a drawing, perhaps by Raphael, which Adams once purchased, have been translated by Professor Joseph Fucilla to include these final phrases:

> You see and you no longer believe in your valor.
> All jealousies have already passed:
> You are of stone: and you no longer suffer pain.

Wrath or silence, witty life or embittered death, Quincy ease or Boston hardness were the pulls felt throughout Henry Adams' life. Why think and form theories when theories only shake us awake from the slumber that soothes? But *not* to think, though thinking involves a fair amount of rage, is not to live. Worse than rage with thought are the entropic consequences of thoughtless anger. This was one of the few lessons Adams learned while at Harvard, and he learned it from Roony Lee. To have an uncontrolled temper without any mind behind it like that young Southerner was dangerous—both for Roony's opponents and for the man of rage himself. Look at what happened to the South, of whose type Roony was, all-consumed by anger in the war. The feud between Sumner and the Adams family made a great impression upon the young Henry even before his encounter at college with Southern rages; so did the public vituperations and canings of the years before the war. Much later Adams wrote in *The Education* about yet another public man, Theodore Roosevelt, who made a point of showing his angers. With thought, anger might prove of practical value; without thought, it was only bared teeth and a big stick.

The main curb Adams continued to place upon his self-acknowledged tendency to wrath was the emphasis he gave to education. After the end of a war that was dehumanizing alike to the North and to the South, he did not demand revenge; he wished instead to educate and to humanize the South. But it was difficult for him not to attack since it was a deep part of his nature to do so. Known to his friends as *Porcupinus Angelicus*, Adams tried to keep his violent language down to those moments when he was alone.

Yet as he wrote his brother Charles in November of 1910 (in a letter included in Ford, II, 554), if he tried to keep his tongue still for too long he was in danger of suffocation.

Adams believed the true silence of contentment comes when there is nothing left to say because a man has received a complete education and known the essential goodness and purpose of all things. But his world forbade such contentment. In such a place, bad temper and good-humor were, simultaneously, possible means of exploration, useful in the unending process of getting an education. Adams felt he had to keep on testing the uses of rage as well as of silence, hot wrath as well as cool self-control. If any of these methods could help him in getting an education—the single human activity that surmounts the sense of human futility—both bad temper and good-humor were worth the costs each imposed upon the human psyche.

In *Disease, Pain, and Sacrifice* (pp. 74-78) David Bakan discusses how we project the blame for our pain outside ourselves; we need to believe that "it" is the cause and we are "its" innocent victims. There are victims who keep silent to their graves over the wrong that has been done to them; there are victims who yell out a revolution of rage. Each type has its justifiers, but the cohorts of rebellion often get fancier rhetorical backing than the legion of the resigned. In an article of 1967 for *The Partisan Review*—"Love in the Western World"—Frederick Crews wrote that when we speak of a man's anger "getting the upper hand" or "getting the best of him," these phrases characterize the values of civilization; it fears that its hierarchies of authority (with the super-ego at the top) would be threatened if the lower-classes (the libido) break out of control. According to aristocrats of rationality, success comes from the control of our angers; failure means being defeated by the anarchism of the instincts. But to the *demi-monde* of feelings, failure is suppression and success is revolt.

At his best, Adams—simultaneously a conservative and an anarchist of the feelings, and aware of this inner dualism—was able to gain force from both rationality and impulse. Through style he could keep down and let loose. Those not as versatile as Adams tend to act as Hemingway said Gertrude Stein did: first to feel hate for Ezra Pound, then to invent plausible reasons for her feelings later on. (This is the way it gets told in *A Moveable Feast* by Hemingway, whose own ability to hate frequently follows through the same sequence of feelings-then-reasons for which he criticizes

Stein.) But perhaps Stein was as alert as Adams as to why and how she hated. She believed that artists needed to be at war with themselves and to cause anger in others. Whatever they did they must not encourage disciples. To be surrounded by lovers is bad for the artist, who must protect his own freedom to agitate. Quarrelling, attacking, winning: these are the interrelated acts by which success is achieved. Success—not victimization—is what interests Gertrude Stein, and she says so in *The Making of Americans*.

> Quarrelling is to me very interesting. Beginning and ending is to me very interesting.
> Quarrelling is not letting those having attacking be winning by attacking, those having resisting being be winning by resisting, those having dependent being be winning by depending being, those having engulfing being be winning by engulfing being. This is quarrelling in living, not letting each one by some one be winning by the being in them. (p. 332)

Although he seldom works up a style as confident as Gertrude Stein's, Norman Mailer would like to use the language of anger as affirmation of success, not as confession of failure. In *Miami and the Siege of Chicago* he reports he is not so much afraid of the physical violence the police could use against him as he is of what he might do to them if once he let himself go. Self-mockery is certainly (we hope) partly at work in such a remark, but that same mockery is part of the anger Mailer constantly turns against himself for not having discovered a way by which, with style, he might successfully be an American whose powerful presence alters events by threatening those in control.

Just living in America can make Mailer's "cyst of the weak, the unreal, and the needy" break open and release rage. It is then that he fancies himself as "an outlaw, a psychic outlaw" whose mind-bullets kill more effectively and with more style than those of a Nevada desperado like Slade (*Advertisements for Myself*, p. 217). Like Mark Twain, Mailer makes lists in order to focus his angers. Unlike Mark Twain, when moody over the futility of rage, he seeks to justify the use of violence by dwelling on its potency. He distrusts men like Eugene McCarthy who do not show their anger; such men are more dangerous in their potential as hanging judges than are the outlaws they would sentence to death. Mailer believes that the suppression of one's latent rage starts cancers and that this is one of the main reasons America has failed: by being eaten from within by anger. When he urges Americans to explode in a single, great, and final gust of anger as a cure for the cancer, it is the conservative in him that says it—that self in kinship with the cancer-ridden Wasp of Middle America which he has named as society's most violent force; he is certainly not speaking out of that self-as-hipster who circumvents cancer by daily playing with rages.

As much as Thoreau did in Concord, Mailer needs confrontation in Chicago in order to feel success and power. He is not sure he can love what he wants to kill, which makes him different from those— like Melville, Hemingway, and Faulkner—who have ritualized aggressive confrontations in their fictions into acts of communion. Perhaps Mailer may one day join that august inner circle. True communion involves absorption, and he likes the idea of cannibalism. If he could only push cannibals and christians together, a love-feast might result that honors the enemy with blood and dignifies the act of anger with style.

Morally, of course, it is suspect to cultivate the delusion that honor and dignity are involved with acts of wrath, however stylishly they are brought off. Mink Snopes going forth to get his revenge on Flem Snopes is made dangerous for the reader by the language with which Faulkner appears to clothe in beauty what is just plain murder. Faulkner's style seeks to bring grace to blood-sports in the dark corners of the wilderness; it also tends to elevate violent men into the stature of heroes. Perhaps American literature takes this moral risk whenever the method of the telling places its psychic outlaws at the imaginative center of attention. Probably Mark Twain meant to expose Slade and Colonel Sherburn's authoritative brutality, but his writing style serves to enhance them at the same time he tries, morally, to defrock them.

*Living with style*: this definition has inserted itself several times into our discussion of the success native to the American experience. Is it actually success we have when presented with rituals marked by high style and rage—rituals carried past the point of ceremonial play to the point of *killing with style*? How seductive to believe that perhaps there are ideal situations, even for murder. If one could kill with the splendor rituals are meant to provide, the beauty of the act might offset the ugly fact that death is required for birth to come about. So one can theorize, but dare one put this idea to the test? It worked for the ancient Sumerians, we are told by Paul Ricoeur, and it set the cosmic combats of Marduk aglow; but will it work in America and through indigenous types of narrative? Perhaps the *childish* quality continually associated with American responses to life is what could gain creative killing an approved access into our society.

In Mark Twain's "Little Nell Tells a Story Out of Her Own Head" (included in *Fables of Man*), the child prattles before an audience of adults about having babies. The grown-ups almost strangle with suppressed laughter, but no one dies because the laughter is finally released. Just as important, there is no anger involved on the part of the unknowing child or the entranced members of the audience. It was a "killing" occasion kept at the level of innocence and of fun. How enticing to the adult mind is the idea that one could continue to make use of the child's pleasures and effective action while letting them pass over the line between just-pretend and for-sure. Mark Twain once intended to dedicate *Roughing It* to Cain; he well knew that each man out West has "his man" to kill by gun or by word. Perhaps he left out that revealing dedication because he realized how hard it is for grown-ups to get away with such candid statements; better to let *Roughing It* seem to be merely a lark.

Some types live lives of Cain with impunity. Stubb urges his oarsmen forward over the water with words of fun and fury. Moby Dick is good-natured and playfully cruel. Both figures are endearing, dangerous, and able to get away with it. Harlem basketball players win by their athletic skills, but also by the stylish way they inflict massive amounts of shame upon their opponents. They look like youngish men messing around in a boy's game; the fact of the real slaying power they possess with ball and manner is partially disguised, fully accepted, and very effective.

Writers are particulary adept at using the look of games to get away with violence. Norman Mailer takes revenge on political and literary enemies by means of books that attempt to shoot them down, one by one. Hemingway plotted his annihilation of Sherwood Anderson's style in *The Torrents of Spring* and called it fairplay. Henry Adams knew that to honor an enemy (or friend) with a biography is to murder him. The highly amusing minstrel-shows familiar to Samuel Clemens' young manhood taught him excellent ways of wounding others with fast repartee; he learned he could move in behind his *nom de guerre* "Mark Twain" (which he said he won by ridiculing a river pilot) in the same way minstrels stood concealed behind their blackened faces to jibe at the world. In his witty encounter with U. S. Grant on November 13, 1879 on the battleground of the after-dinner speech in Chicago, Mark Twain partially cancelled all those Northern victories over the Confederacy. He attempted to reverse history on still other occasions when he presented, during a speech on October 1, 1877 and as a published piece in the December 1885 *Century*, a wild tale of the humiliation he felt as a military bumbler. "The Private History of a Campaign That Failed" brought this ex-Confederate some sense of success on his own ground; he could talk history into being what he wanted it to be when he disguised it as child's play.

Writers who view themselves as men empowered with the rights of their creativity—with the word that slays as well as causes life—are prone to that other temptation particular to artists: the desire to play a god handing down divine justice. " 'Vengeance is Mine,' saith the Lord," and the writer strives to put himself into that enviable position where he can slay with impunity in the name of both art and justice. But he may argue the fact of his outraged humanity as justification for avoiding the duty of beneficent deities to be merciful. The artist would like to make use of the best of two play-worlds by taking over *the divine right* to kill justly and *the human right* to forego granting mercy. This is the point when childish games, with the look of innocent merriment on their surface, reveal the murderousness of "the boys" at play.

It is a long way from Mark Twain's Little Nell or the Tom of *The Adventures of Tom Sawyer* to Hank Morgan's fun and sport at Camelot. Once Hank turns the tournament into a shooting match against unarmed knights, we are well on our way to Hank's blowing up thousands of men in the name of Yankee righteousness and right reason. Adults who play at being children are either appealing or a little unpleasant. Grown-ups who play at childhood while committed to the game of being gods are downright dangerous. Pretense is dropped, and the games are nakedly seen as being deadly serious. The particular reality that gets played out most often is rituals of judgment against those who have failed. Even the original stress on aesthetics—the style of the thing—gets passed over by the intensity of the interest taken in the morality—the vindictive righteousness—of it all.

# CHAPTER 21

# Some Versions
# of Melodrama

In a world where justice appears to be the most one can ask for, there is no room for forgiveness and much space for the particular cruelties practiced in the name of the war against wickedness. Significantly, those who stress justice often turn it most harshly upon themselves. According to Paul Ricoeur in *The Symbolism of Evil*, to trace the history of men's reactions to sin helps us to distinguish the stages through which mankind has moved in its reactions to the world. In the earliest stage, the force that punished the guilty lay outside men. Once conscience became consciousness, the arena of evil and judgment shifted to its present inward position. Men are now apt to see themselves as judges who have to assess their own guilt. Exactions of punishment are as severe upon the evil found within as they ever were upon the evil projected out there.

Ricoeur argues that the next possible stage of human progress would be characterized by gods imaged as the embodiment of love, not wrath; if that time ever comes about, men may be as merciful to themselves as the gods actually are. In that better future, self-forgiveness replaces self-contempt, and mercy dominates. Men live in the full glare of knowledge, but are at last able to bear what they are and to love it truly.

How different that time would be from what it has been and what it now is! Superstition once left men in darkness, thrashing about aimlessly in an attempt to know their unseen oppressor. The partial light of self-knowledge characterizing the present makes life no less strenuous; increased awareness results in an aggressive justice insistent upon stern reckonings exacted for each failing brought out into the glare. So Ricoeur argues. This same situation is projected by Dorothea Krook as she tries to explain what happens to the novel when the drive for justice dominates the world because love is too weak to command.

In Dorothea Krook's discussion of *The Golden Bowl* in *The Ordeal of Consciousness in Henry James*, she speaks of the immense difference it makes to that novel that justice and love are so terribly at odds. As she recounts it:

... though love by its nature has this power to transform and
perfect reality and therefore the power to supersede justice by
incorporating it into itself, and though in a world completely
and perfectly redeemed by love justice would, finding its occupation gone, cease to exist as a separate and distinguishable entity, love never in fact, particularly when exercised by imperfect or limited human agents upon imperfect or sinful fellow
humans, succeeds in accomplishing its redemptive task completely and perfectly. It never therefore succeeds in rendering
justice supererogatory; and in a world incompletely and im-
perfectly redeemed by love—in the actual moral world, that is,
as we know it—justice is for this reason supreme. (p. 285)

Neither justice nor love was assured in the deterministic world
Mark Twain increasingly came to live in. He felt he might be forgiven if he were bad without knowing it; he knew he could never
deserve mercy if he consciously confessed his guilts. Since God protects idiots and children, he might be loved as God's fool but not as
a wise man. Sometimes Mark Twain twisted that notion around to
declare that in an unjust world the innocents are punished together
with the wicked; a crazy God is out to get someone, even if it is a
person only tenuously connected with the guilty deed. "I knew that
Providence was not particular about the rest," he declares in the
*Autobiography*, "so that He got somebody connected with the one He
was after" (p. 123).

While he had them, such thoughts permitted Mark Twain no
way past pain, based as those thoughts are upon the notion of a
world and a god for whom neither justice nor mercy has any meaning. If there were a world where justice is God's only mode of self-
expression, a man might yet be a humorist (one who shows his own
mercy through laughter), instead of a satirist (one who punishes
through wit). But since Mark Twain's world is one in which God's
justice is a farce and where attempts on the part of society to act out
forms of justice are absurd, he could not remain a humorist. There
were stretches of writing time in which all he had left was the
preaching of justice in an effort to fill the role God had abdicated.
"Humorists of the 'mere' sort cannot survive," Mark Twain states in
his *Autobiography*. "Humor must not professedly teach and it must
not professedly preach, but it must do both if it would live forever.
By forever, I mean thirty years.... I have always preached. That is
the reason I have lasted thirty years" (p. 273). He survived, but increasingly as a satirist who judges, not as a humorist who loves.

While Mark Twain held to the chosen role of preacher, his powers as a writer ended at the edge of futility; all he had to show was that each creature is fixed by temperament to commit acts it cannot keep from doing. But however ineffectual at large, preaching can prove a necessary social act. If Providence blames you unjustly for what you cannot help, the preacher will forgive you out of the humanity you both share—at least for a while, at least until he begins to talk like the god-who-never-forgives. Then the Twainian preacher implicates all things within his own helpless sense of the inevitability of guilt, you included.

Humor seems unlikely in a world such as the one Mark Twain finally evolved in his imagination. There is wrath, or there is the sentimentality typical of the stories he prefaced by insisting that although they are not funny they still have value. But sentimentality readily turns into cruelty. Jackson the villain in "Newhouse's Jew Story" (included in *Fables of Man*) is called "cruel by nature and unforgiving." If Jackson cannot help himself, why then is such grim pleasure taken in telling the story that sees him outwitted and slain by the virtuous, unforgiving avenger of another man's honor? "Newhouse's Jew Story" is not even true melodrama. Sentimentality may act in the name of good opposed to evil, but since neither virtue nor vice has any reality in the wholly deterministic world of the tale, the sentimentality is exposed for the cruel pleasure it actually is. On such occasions melodrama and sentimentality are interchangeable; they are both concerned with the pleasure gained through the contemplation of catastrophe. One has here that strange mix which characterizes a significant part of Mark Twain's writing. Inside the world of this kind of prose, one sees that words like "justice" and "mercy" have lost meaning on a recognizably human plane. All is stripped down to the pleasure-principle of gods who admit no moral questions to disturb them at play.

The monotony of the weather in San Francisco described in the following passage from *Roughing It* is the monotony of a deterministically controlled life that craves the upheavals of melodrama. A certain moral premise is proposed. It says there is a "real fight" going on here between good and evil. But the evil is ennui, not vice; the good is variety, not virtue:

> . . . after you have listened for six or eight weeks, every night to the dismal monotony of those quiet rains, you will wish in your heart the thunder *would* leap and crash and roar along these drowsy skies once, and make everything alive—you will wish the prisoned lightning *would* cleave the dull firmament asunder and light it with a blinding glare for *one* little instant. You

would give *anything* to hear the old familiar thunder again and
see the lightning strike somebody. (VIII, 151-152)

Excitement is needed at whatever cost, so much so that

along in the summer, when you have suffered about four
months of lustrous, pitiless sunshine, you are ready to go down
on your knees and plead for rain—hail—snow—thunder and
lightning—anything to break the monotony—you will take an
earthquake, if you cannot do better. And the chances are that
you'll get it too. (VIII, 152)

The God-to-whom-Mark-Twain-prays at this point is likely to answer this one prayer, if no other; it is the kind of prayer He likes to
fulfill, just as it is certainly the kind of prayer that the god-player
likes to make. Novels analogous to the world imaged in this passage
from *Roughing It* are themselves claustrophobic and catastrophic;
their authors are like the gods of amoral melodramas, not like di-
vinities who create comedies of mercy or tragedies of justice. These
authors are not the possible artificers of the Great American Novel.
That yet unwritten fiction will contain both justice and mercy, the
fulfilled dream of the second chance, and that wondrous America
in which both Jay Gatsby's innocence and veniality gave him the
faith to believe.

Mark Twain's notes and manuscript fragments indicate he had a
continuing interest in the figure of Huckleberry Finn. Did he think
that if he gave the boy his head, Huck might accomplish what
adults are unable to do? Did he believe that by repeating Huck's life
in further sequels that life might come out better on the second or
third go-around; that it might at least break out of its deterministic
mold?

In *The Duality of Human Existence* David Bakan says adults believe
in *understanding*, and it helps them judge themselves; children,
however, believe in *grace* that ends violence, anger, and the need to
feel guilt and shame (p. 74). Mink Snopes looks like a boy, but
when in *The Mansion* he states, *"Old Moster jest punishes; He dont play
jokes,"* he is repeating one form of adult wisdom (p. 366). Theoreti-
cally, if a child like Huck could wrest free of a book written by Mr.
Mark Twain, he would dream up a whimsical, playful god who,
toppling the strict terms of justice, grants another chance to be
happy, successful, and *good enough*.

We like to think that the right kind of gods for America have
ample bowels for laughter and mercy, as well as attentiveness to

humane justice. They are the gods of the happy child, not of
dangerously playful "boys" or dark-tempered adults. They are the
gods Thoreau implied when he wrote in his journal of August 1,
1841 to repudiate "Jewish gloom." While at Walden, he noted in
his journal of 1845 (VII, 265, 391) that the orthodox God is marked
by "an inflexible justice" and "infinite" power; He has "not grace,
not humanity, nor love even—wholly masculine, with no sister
Juno, no Apollo, no Venus in him."

Rabid, vengeful virtue was repellent to Thoreau. He loved lightning as much as the citizens of Mark Twain's San Francisco, but he
responded to it in ways significantly different from the previously
cited passage from *Roughing It*. In his journal of June 27, 1852
Thoreau described the flashes he saw in the sky:

> There was displayed a Titanic force, some of that force which
> made and can unmake the world. . . . Is this of the character of
> a wild beast, or is it guided by intelligence and mercy? If we
> trust our natural impressions, it is a manifestation of brutish
> force or vengeance, more or less tempered with justice.

But Thoreau believed that the keenest observer is not limited to
"natural impressions" that restrict childlike minds like the Cana-
dian woodcutter of his Walden experience. Fully thinking men go
beyond those "melodramas" of "brutish force" which are caused as
much by allegiance to pantheism as to determinism. As he continued in the same entry, "it is our own consciousness of sin, probably, which suggests the idea of vengeance, and to a righteous man it
would be merely sublime without being awful." Men must partake
of a higher innocence in order to realize the sublime; else they become like the dangerous Twainian innocents who experience the
world as melodramas of vengeance and justice.

Now, Norman Mailer's God is enough like that of Mink Snopes
and too much like the God of "Jewish gloom" ever to please
Thoreau. Either that, or Mailer is insufficiently "righteous" ever to
detect the sublime in those titanic forces "which made and can un-
make the world." One of Mailer's favorite arguments against the
technocrats is that they deny taboos and the sins of the fathers. Better to be hauled up in guilt before a suffering judge, he says in *Of a
Fire on the Moon* than to be sentenced by a merry jurist (p. 435). We
must acknowledge that we are the sons of our fathers and subject to
their sins, but we must not allow ourselves to be merely "children."
We need to do without grace; we must make our own choices; we
may not count on outward sources of forgiveness. We have to re-

treat from the father as someone we might love—whether it is Daddy Rusty Jethroe, father of D. J. in *Why Are We in Vietnam?*, or the Lord God.

Just such questions concerning justice and mercy, melodrama and comedy, rage and humor, sons and fathers—and the various answers they elicit—help to complicate, and to clarify, the meaning of success and failure in America. They are measurements of what you are, what old burdens are laid upon you, and how well or poorly these exactions are met.

The ways that the second- and third-generation Puritans were brought to see themselves as guilty sons is one of the themes reiterated by Perry Miller in his famous accounts of the New England settlement; by the well-known essays of David Minter and Cecelia Tichi ("The Puritan Jeremiad as a Literary Form" and "Spiritual Biography and the 'Lords Remembrancers' "); and by the recent book-length studies by Sacvan Bercovitch and Emory Elliott. In "Errand Into the Wilderness," for example, Miller speaks of Cotton Mather's *Magnalia Christi Americana* as a book "full of lamentations over the declension of the children, who appear, page after page, in contrast to their mighty progenitors, about as profligate a lot as ever squandered a great inheritance."

It would seem, by implication, that if the children were unwise spenders, they did not dare place the blame for ill events upon their own fathers or the God Father. To be the child, then, is to be perpetually in the act of receiving. To be a good child is to do well by that gift; to be bad is to have fallen into the ways of faulty economics, the misuse of bright new gifts. But the child is vulnerable to declension in ways other than those of extravagance. We see this better when we look at the special privileges fathers have and sons may not have that deny the possibility of success to the young altogether.

In his essay on "Humour" written in 1928 Freud likened the prime humorist to the man who acts as the father. The adult figure who reduces others to the level of children, he also mocks at his own participation in childish matters. Freud believed this was an instance of the force of the super-ego agreeing voluntarily to contract its vast power into the smallest force of ego. The super-ego says, "Look here, the world is merely child's play." By reducing the world's capacity to hurt, the father-humorist comforts us even as he retains the superiority of his larger perspective. To be a father, therefore, is linked with knowing; in turn, it is associated with the sin of the child who attempts to know too much. If success has much to do with how much we know, it merges with the issue of how much we have the right to know, as well as what we do with that knowing, all of this involving the relations between father and son, judge and humorist and defendant.

Elsewhere in Freud's writings (as in those of the Puritans), we find the psychic image of the God who declares that He alone has the right to forgive or to seek vengeance, the one Being freely allowed to act in both humor and wrath. In such instances men benefit only when humor is allotted to them and punishment is given to others. But men sin if they usurp God's favorite roles, moving in rebellion against their condition by being first to laugh or to kill. They sin if they seek to spend lavishly and to know extravagantly. Laughing, killing, spending, and knowing *to that extent* are the prerogatives of God alone. But as Freud read the history of the human heart, men continually re-enact the primal crime of the overthrow of the father by their insistence that they are superior to him in power and in privilege. They choose to commit this sin rather than to live as the father's victim and as shamed failures in his sight.

Life in America makes it difficult *to go beyond* our fathers without incurring guilt. At first Crèvecœur's Farmer James saw America as the perfect place for both fathers and sons—the land finely possessed in order that it might be handed down as a gracious gift through posterity. Then the Revolution (rebellious sons against fatherland and king) upset Farmer James's original bright hope. Americans were cast into that world which young Robin discovers during the strange night in the city depicted by Hawthorne in "My Kinsman, Major Molineux." Robin can neither go home again to his actual father, nor find support from the worldly "father," his kinsman. He becomes a son without a father, one perhaps who helps to "slay" the Major by the laughter and the knowingness he extravagantly adds to the general hilarity and violence of rebellion and revenge. Later on in the new society that resulted from the Revolution and was compounded by the Civil War, Henry Adams spent his own life searching for a father. To be amused, he said, by what he might find—whether *Pteraspis* or lemur—but also to be able to forgive that primal father for making the son seem such a failure to himself.

Not unsurprisingly, Mark Twain felt guilty for being a "bad father" (somehow the cause of the deaths of his brother Henry, his own son, and of Suzy); he also worked up feelings of guilt as a "son" over his touchy relations with his elder brother Orion. Now,

Leon Edel probably goes too far in insisting that Henry James felt nervously guilty toward *his* elder brother to the extent that the writing of *The Turn of the Screw* resulted mainly from his apprehension over the audaciousness of buying his own house at Rye, thereby declaring his wish to move out from under William's fraternal thumb. But F. O. Matthiessen's remark in *The James Family* is useful concerning Henry's portrait of William when both were boys. Henry, says Matthiessen, shows us the "playing off the hero against the willing dolt" (p. 74). Certainly Henry did play himself down as a failure and William up as a success, but he seems to have avoided the less happily managed irritations apparent in Samuel Clemens' relations with Orion, the brother whom Sam continually surpassed.

Wherever there is a struggle in which one person succeeds and someone placed very close to him fails, there is the chance there will be guilt of the kind that accompanies the metaphoric acts of "patricide," "fratricide," or "infanticide." If these feelings are paired with a strong belief in the force of justice, then the one who succeeds and the one who fails will alike have to work out certain expiations in order to get things back into economic balance.

If the victorious father sees his children as his victims, he may try to mitigate his guilty act. Or if the world is characterized by injustice altogether, the children can say that failure happened *to* them and they could not help it. Either way, there are advantages to being the victim—the one in the child's role. Indeed, to be the victim of a melodrama that is based on justice vs. injustice—whether sacred or secular in nature—seems one of the best ways to evade the shame of failing.

David Bakan has a great deal to say about the psychology of the victim in *The Duality of Human Existence*. He asks that whenever we examine types of religious doctrine that we notice whether the focus falls on the elder or the younger generation (e.g., is Judaism the religion of fathers, while Christianity caters to sons?). Bakan's test-question is appropriate to our study of America if we see that, while the founding fathers initiated the original flow of possibilities, America has become primarily a nation of sons.

Even so, further questions still hang in the air: do the sons of America stand guiltless and obedient before a just father who rebukes his own guilt and rewards them for whatever pain he has caused, or is their world devoid of mercy or justice, entitling them to rebellion and vengeance? Is it a boy's heaven without judges (a perfect democracy of Yes); an adolescent's hell (the tyrannous society of No) that gives him licence to revolt and set up the archetypal anarchy; or is it the paranoid's paradise that delights in the harsh determinism of Them and Me (the ultimate totalitarian state)?

Let us look at the further implications of the part paranoia has to play in any try for success.

Perpetually to be the victim of a heavily determined plot lends its own strange impression of triumph. If history is translated through the eye of the paranoic into the terms of melodrama, the victim-hero is always right, whatever happens. In one version of the basic plot, the victim's suffering is proof of virtue besieged by the wicked, yet witnessed to by the omniscient eye of Pure Justice. In another version, the victim admits to the fated sinfulness of his nature and sets out pursued by that same Pure Force upon a road that curves toward punishment and death. In either case, there is Someone who cares and the son has ample assurance that he is no orphan.

According to David Brion Davis in his *The Slave Power Conspiracy and the Paranoid Style*, a man in the 1860's could be either John Brown or John Wilkes Booth and feel neatly placed within the nick of history. Such men knew the rightness of their deeds and could count on the fame which history would accord their expert handling of the melodramatic roles of martyr and avenger. Life viewed as a tight net of conspiracies has dignity and possesses the important fact of meaning; life lived unmelodramatically catches one up in a farce full of cheap tricks and the shameful failure of never knowing what any of it is about.

Many American writers have actively fended off the tendency toward melodrama. William Dean Howells insisted that American life is best characterized by its smiling aspects and the average run of ordinary human events. Even if his tale includes a Bunyanesque array of satans and angels, E. E. Cummings begins and ends his introduction to *The Enormous Room* with the sensible caution, "Don't be afraid." But the stance of being sensible about absurdly simplistic demonic plots requires a certain simplicity in itself. Howells' mind was anything but simple; still, he maintained, to all intents and purposes, that America's mind was.

In *A Small Boy and Others* Henry James sums up the America of his childhood as unsophisticated, then says that sophistication is what one knows and that to know is to fear. Mark Twain, yet another friend of Howells, takes the suggested sequence a step farther. In his *Autobiography* he declared his belief that a man is "never quite sane at night" (p. 43). Nighttime is when you face the knowledge of failure without relief from the delusions that sunlight provides. *Sophistication* (or, in the word favored by Henry

Adams, multiplicity—the opposite of simplicity), *knowledge, fear*:
perhaps madness, most likely the end of laughter.

Thoreau desired the life of surprise for the sake of its freshness
and sense of renewal. Freud spoke of the anxieties that keep us
from cultivating surprise, but he did not know about the red squirrel of Thoreau's acquaintance that pretends fright in order to have
fun. "Ignorance is the parent of fear," says Ishmael, narrator of a
novel which purports to make us knowledgeable about whaling,
and thereby sophisticates of the world, yet carefully acts to keep us
ignorant of the mysterious meaning of Moby Dick and the universe
that creature may represent.

The Melvillien child may anxiously but safely live in his father's
world that is filled with those things he does not know and could not
bear to learn. To be made, like Pip, to face the truths of the world
propels us into that special madness, that lucid lunacy, not unlike
the piercing awareness of the cause of all things envisioned at the
close of Dante's *Paradisio*. But if the child is neither like Pip, nor
like Dante, but like Ahab—one who refuses to acknowledge the
truths he might discover about himself—then he stays sealed within
the security of the melodrama which characterizes the *Inferno*.
There is the third way: to bring everything to the surface. This is
what would happen if we experience both the *divina commedia* of
Pip and Dante and the melodrama of Ahab. It is what could lead to
the terrifying, unsettling sanity of the tragic world of *Purgatorio*—
the state of being whose outcome trembles between success and
failure.

By the end of his life (and this is admittedly a highly controversial assertion), Melville seems to have moved past the anger and
fear of melodrama to the acceptance and love found in tragedy. He
traveled from the heretic's paranoia, in which the world fits into
one seamless plot, to the Christian's dual view, which deals with
both divine paradisiacal comedy and human purgatorial tragedy.
Melville left off seeing the world as rigidly governed by Ahab's conspiratorial God; he came eventually to a more expansive (and no
less painful) sense of the universe—the one envisioned by Captain
Vere as the tragic anomaly of men's self-contradictory desires and
relativistic notions of earthly justice caught up and contained
within the controlling facts of absolutes and supra-human justice.
The particulars of this tragic universe were ones which writers
like the later Melville, and Henry James and Faulkner, could face,
but not Mark Twain. Thoreau and Emerson hedged; they named
the universe high comedy, and resisted calling it melodrama or

tragedy. They could not assign leading roles to the innocent victim or the guilty hero placed in the world by dread fatality, nor would they grant reality to the usual materials of fantasy out of which melodramas are crafted. "My idea of heaven," Emerson wrote in "Immortality," "is that there is no melodrama in it at all; that it is wholly real."

If the paranoid lives with his fear since it explains his guilt and guarantees him a kind of success within a rigidly controlled sequence of events, the Transcendentalists felt guilty only when they could not banish fear. Emerson and Thoreau would not admit the powerlessness of men to fulfill all demands. Success was to come on *their* terms and because *they* chose it, not merely because the world's will allowed it. Even failure must be a matter of choice, the prideful assertion of one's will not to take the right and destined way. Unlike Emerson and Thoreau, Melville—together with James and Faulkner—came to define fear and guilt as the tension set up between justice and mercy, the logical, painful structure of a tragic universe on whose terms alone success is to be measured and failure to be judged. The tragic hero lives fearlessly with his guilt because it expresses all he knows he ought to have been and done, and yet could not become because of the pressure of the world's circumstances.

Near the walls of the Pentagon, Jewish Norman Mailer finds himself locked into a police van with a blue-eyed Nazi; it is the paranoid's favorite dream-scene. Mailer works up fine anxieties over his own whiteness, too, when he asks in *An American Dream* whether whites don't want to be slain by blacks in order to placate their guilts. Melodrama is home-ground for him, but eventually his "on the one hand—on the other hand" imagination breaks him partially free from the sense of the cyclical which is so comforting to the paranoid. The drama of having been wronged which Mailer-as-victim likes to play is split apart when he abides by the honesty of a dialectic that projects him beyond victimization. If his "on the other hand" merely moved him from the innocence that is unjustly treated over to the companion drama of the man who is wicked and rightly punished, then Mailer would be lost for all time inside the box of melodrama—exactly where Richard Poirier fears that Mailer is now.

It is true that Mailer is enrapt by the clear-cut patterns in which his mind takes such delight, even as his mind's nervous agility urges him to escape their entrapments. It is true that we (who, like Poirier, share Huck Finn's taste in vittles—slopped-together mixtures resisting distinct categories of *this* and *that*) also become uneasy over Mailer's rhetorical habit of "one hand" and "other hand," especially when we see how easily they convert into the unyielding philosophical absolutes which dialectics often mirror. But there is a way out: by going *through* melodrama, not by avoiding it altogether.

Perhaps Eric Bentley and others can help us past the crisis caused when our appreciation of dialectics' concern with "reality" is placed at odds with our apprehension over the tendency of the dialectical method to take on the look of melodrama's "artificial" constructs. In *The Life of the Drama* Bentley sees that "The melodramatic vision is in one sense simply normal. It corresponds to an important aspect of reality. It is the spontaneous, uninhibited way of seeing things. . . . Melodrama is not a special or marginal kind of drama, let alone an eccentric or decadent one; it is the quintessence of drama" (p. 216). Then there is that man of melodramatic perception called by Leo B. Levy in *Versions of Melodrama* the possessor of "refinement of intention" and "higher ethical awareness" (pp. 11, 104). If the melodramatic view is alike appropriate for the "normal" consciousness (Bentley) and the "higher" awareness (Levy), it would seem as if those who do not have it, or who deny it, are either not responding to the general way things are or are insensitive to the inequities they encounter; they may be living below or above the realities, reacting *under* the moral threshold or *too coarsely*. With such admonitions in mind, some "good" melodrama, together with the "best" dialectics, might not be a bad way to deal with the histrionics of Mailer's universe.

Melodrama is no easy term to deal with. Observers of the genre such as Levy or Jacques Barzun (in the latter's piece on "Henry James, Melodramatist" in the *Kenyon Review* of 1943) have detected in James's fiction alone such variations as "comic melodrama" and "aesthetic melodrama." In James's 1907 preface to *The American* (included in *The Art of the Novel*) the novelist admits that, in all realism, the Bellegardes would not have let a mere trifle like family honor keep them from getting their hands on Christopher Newman's money. It was "romantic" of himself, James confesses (p. 37) to present the Bellegardes as villainous plotters excessively sensitive to a principle. In actuality they would have been grosser, been true trimmers, been willing "to haul [Newman] into their boat under cover of night perhaps, in any case as quietly and with as little bumping and splashing as possible, and there accommodate him with the very safest and most convenient seat" (p. 36).

Yes, this is "the way things are," James's basic definition for realism; but—as he cheerfully acknowledges next in his preface-confession—"it wouldn't have been the theme of 'The American' as the book stands, the theme to which I was from so early pledged" (p. 36). We catch James admitting that the plot of *The American* placed melodramatic stress on the betrayal by Evil of Goodness; we also find him insisting that this choice was right because it gave him the aesthetic and emotional effects he wanted, not because it fitted sane definitions of "real" behavior. He chose the "romantic"—the melodramatic—over the realistic since the former met, in his words, "my *requirement* that somebody or something should be 'in [Newman's] power' so delightfully . . ." (p. 36).

James wanted interest, delight, and refinement in his fictions rather than the commonplace, the dull, and the coarse. (Which is not the same as saying he was not devoted to the realism of the usual, the expected, and the grit of human affairs.) It is significant, too, to see him proceed to argue in the following paragraphs of his preface that the romantic (marked by the predetermined plot) is not *not* reality. It is *another kind* of reality. It is, as Bentley would put it, "simply normal," and, as Levy sees it, a matter of "higher ethical awareness."

In line with the terms of the melodramatic vision suggested by Bentley, James's preface to *The American* also insists that there is reality in our sense of "this rank vegetation of the 'power' of bad people that good get into or *vice versa*. It is so rarely, alas, into *our* power that any one gets!" (p. 37.) This latter occasion—someone getting into our power—*that* would provide fantasy and fiction; *there* is where few men would be able fully to recognize their human condition.

Emerson had seen this too, in part. In his essay "Immortality," based on a lecture of 1861 (the year America entered a new phase of melodrama with the Civil War), he described heaven as the place where there is "no melodrama" since "it is wholly real." He was implying that melodrama does exist in the realm of the phenomenal—the not quite real. Emerson's scheme of things, of course, contained both the noumenal (where each man's success is the sole fact) and the phenomenal (where the unreality of failure is mixed in with the reality of power). James's world provides but one plane for human events: that breeding ground for the facts of ineffectual goodness and the actuality of melodrama. For a writer who is as much committed to realism as he is stimulated by the romantic, some versions of melodrama are necessary. How else could he show what it feels like to lose and what it is like to crave to win?

# CHAPTER 22

# Huckleberry Finn /
# The American

Huckleberry Finn is devoted to common sense appraisals of reality, but the world of melodrama is imposed upon him willy-nilly by an author who liked literary messes as much as Huck prefers culinary ones. To use William James's terms, Mark Twain was both "morbid-minded" and "healthy-minded," susceptible to literary ambivalences of comedy, tragedy, farce, satire, and melodrama. But melodrama became as necessary to Mark Twain for his depiction of the truth of human affairs as it did for Henry James. The melodramatic tradition gave each writer a direct way to present dramatic, somewhat paranoid, plots of victim and oppressor; it also helped them to define possible consequences of the melodramatic situation: the victim who stalks the wicked in his righteous wrath, or the victim who falls back in silent acquiescence to his helplessness. Let us now examine Henry James's *The American* together with Mark Twain's *Adventures of Huckleberry Finn*. From them we may learn which passions rule these works (indignant revenge or resigned withdrawal) and whether we see in them the seizure of success or the infliction of failure.

The novel of 1877 by Henry James and the one of 1883 by Mark Twain represent a number of the anxieties and desires characteristic of late-nineteenth-century America; they reveal the qualified victories possible to harmless victim and to vengeful hero; most of all, they offer a nadir useful to the discussions that have engrossed this book to this point. For we are in search of the lowest mark to which the American might come and yet survive, and survive *significantly*. Finding this point in *The American* and *Adventures of Huckleberry Finn*, we can ask whether any survival which requires such responses of acquiescence or rage is truly successful, or is instead a special kind of defeat.

A glance first at Thoreau's *A Week on the Concord and Merrimack Rivers* in conjunction with *Huckleberry Finn*. Of these two books concerning hopes for release on the river, Thoreau gives us the greatest sense of holiday. Whether it is John or Henry Thoreau who load melons onto the boat in preparation for their journey, or Huck and Jim with their cache of eatables, pleasure is foremost in their minds. There are differences of motive, of course. Thoreau sees the river adventures as ennobling; he is able to meditate with conscious profundity upon what it means to float upon waters that simultaneously reflect the passing scene and intimate higher realms of spirit. Huck does not think much about nobility; as far as he knows, that is what the Duke and the King stand for. Thoreau rejects the jabbing demands of conventional conscience; committed to buoyancy and life, he repudiates the moral sense which is so conservative it serves only to preserve the dead. Everywhere Huck goes he is burdened by the conscience that itches his hide on the raft and on the shore for no other reason than to make him uncomfortable. But river life is fine in many ways (storms and ugly customers aside). Both the boy Huck and the young man Henry avidly absorb its pleasures. Dawn especially makes them feel as if the world could indeed be new and good.

The same freshness found on the Mississippi and Concord Rivers also lies over the Hudson River revisited in *The American Scene* by Henry James (pp. 29, 149). It comes from the luminism of light that acts to blur the details of shore life; it radiates in a halo of beauty around each object encountered upon the river. Now, William James said that what *really* counts for us are halos—those fringes of meaning and value. When Herbert Spencer suggested that we live only to survive—that is, that we exist for bread alone—William James countered with his notion that, as long as halos surround things as they are and do not deny reality, such signs of luminous, ideal value are as necessary as the bread of tangible success.

When Huck Finn and Henry Thoreau respond with peaceful joy to the haloed things along the river, what are they most deeply responding to: the pleasure that is analogous to Spencer's bread or the pleasure of William James's ideal values? The answer is obvious in Thoreau's case; it is not so clear in Huck's.

When Huck says he most wants a life of the free, easy, and comfortable, it is not immediately evident whether this refers only to the hedonism of bodily comforts. His may actually be the more complicated desire to have some peace in the midst of a world that seems designed solely to encourage struggles for brute survival. While disguised as Sarah Mary Williams George Elexander Peters, Huck tells Mrs. Loftus he is looking for Goshen, that oasis of peace and plenty provided the Israelites while wandering abroad in Egypt. Goshen, however, is a peaceable kingdom in a negative sense; it is a tentative place of rest for exiles in the heart of enemy territory. Its stay against confusion is momentary to the extreme. Therefore, if Huck is indeed given to Goshen-goals, all his adventures could be seen as negative ones—avoidances of pain and conflict—rather than movements toward something strong and useful.

In his *Autobiography* Mark Twain said he was "born to indolence, idleness, procrastination, indifference—the qualities that constitute a shirk" (p. 263). He wished his books would write themselves since work meant anxiety and strain for him. But he worked and worked at *Huckleberry Finn*, so hard the tale discloses this fact by the signs of fatigue it shows around its middle and by its end. Still, the book's immediate spokesman is Huck, who says he will do almost anything to keep from getting sweated up. Kemble's illustration of Huck holding up a mess of fish (probably caught with little effort while drowsing on the bank) gives Americans an alternative to the image we preserve of Benjamin Franklin diligently pushing a wheelbarrow through the streets of Philadelphia under the approving gaze of the townspeople. The relaxed Huck-image replaces the icon of Franklinian energy, and getting by with as little strain as possible bypasses getting ahead. Whereas taking trouble often means getting into trouble, surviving well is tantamount to shirking danger.

Huck is constantly thwarted in his adventures from arriving at "Goshen." Nature is dangerous; it runs expediently along Spencerian lines without asking if the humans in its midst prefer the peaceable kingdom of principle instead. If nature is risky, human nature is even worse—ironically worse, because the humans Huck meets often take the general notion of halo-values seriously; they act as if tangible survival were not as important as the intangible principles of Grangerford or Shepherdson honor; they look as if the physical hedonism of getting by were not half so ontologically exciting as stirring up fracases between dogs and sows, Sherburn and Boggs, or as existentially significant as taking the long "bookway" around to the freeing of an already manumitted slave.

In 1770 Benjamin Franklin wrote his sister that "men are devils to one another." He had discovered the truth confirmed for Huck when the boy watches the public humiliation of the King and the Duke. The Massachusetts riverside loafers whose mockery Henry Thoreau had to put down with terrible eye-glances are as potentially dangerous as the Arkansas louts who itch for the chance of violent merriment at the cost of a stranger's comfort. No wonder that the river trips taken by both Huck and Thoreau are occasionally marked by dreams of escape about moving beyond the hurtful reach of the natural and the human scene!

According to Edwin Cady, even to think about escape is a boy-response appropriate only to a boy-book context. But the desire to escape experienced by us as we read the accounts of Huck and Thoreau rises out of an adult wish, if "adult" refers to the knowledge that is sadder and wiser than that possessed by "boys." We know, and the authors know—long before we see the boy Huck and the young Henry arrive at that knowledge—that "going to Goshen" is a hope of success made impossible by both Spencerian bread-realities and Jamesian halo-values. Boy-wishes are usually nullified by the experience of having to survive in a tough and risky world, as well as by the need to have something more than survival; furthermore, boys seldom know why their wishes are frustrated. Such facts indicate the innocence of the characters *within* the narratives. The adult-wishes held by readers located *outside* the narrative are doubly frustrated: they are both denied and know why they are being denied their hearts' desire. To read about escape-dreams is certainly no escape. Reading that is also knowing can be more painful than merely living out the futility of such dreams.

It is our task here to make clear the nature of the dreams of escape in *Adventures of Huckleberry Finn*, and why they cannot work. After all, some (like Keats and Poe) have insisted that if dreams are beautiful enough they must be true. So we need to ask whether Huck's dreams are not sufficiently beautiful for a Romantic God to be willing to honor them, or whether they are denied just because they *are* beautiful and God is a Realist, and nasty to boot.

Nietzsche's *The Birth of Tragedy* of 1872 uses a phrase of Schopenhauer to depict Apollonian illusion as a "frail bark" in which "in the midst of a world of torments the individual human being sits quietly, supported by and trusting in the *principium individuationis*." Then along comes the supreme Dionysian force of the real to ram and wreck the illusions of the ideal. Huck's own "frail bark" is continually being run down by the ruthless "tragic" forces of process that never let this little Apollonian enjoy his dream of Goshen's peace.

Let us look at one example—Huck's escape from the Grangerford-Shepherdson feud. Filled with horror at the meaningless slaughter, he is "red-hot to jump aboard [the raft] and get out of that awful country" (p. 161). Together with Jim, he floats two miles downstream and well out into the middle of the river before judging "that we was free and safe once more" (pp. 161-162). The night of blood, during which five Grangerfords were murdered, including his special chum Buck, has been forgotten by means of the boy's remarkable recuperative powers (a healthy, callous egotism that can put aside another's pain and death in his own immediate pleasure at being alive). Feasting on "corn-dodgers and buttermilk, pork and cabbage and greens," Huck observes:

> . . . there ain't nothing in the world so good when it's cooked right—and whilst I eat my supper we talked and had a good time. I was powerful glad to get away from the feuds, and so was Jim to get away from the swamp. We said there warn't no home like a raft, after all. Other places do seem so cramped up and smothery, but a raft don't. You feel mighty free and easy and comfortable on a raft. (p. 162)

This is freedom to fill the belly and to relax in companionable self-congratulation for escaping the cramped and smothery place of the graves the Grangerfords will occupy, freedom from the new clothes the Grangerfords had given Huck, distasteful to him because they were "too good to be comfortable, and besides I didn't go much on clothes, nohow" (p. 165). This bodily freedom from what is "too good" and the chance to be safe and sensually at ease in flesh and mind is Huck's immediate goal, the continuing surface motive for his movements along the Mississippi and its shores.

Freedom as naked comfort is seldom accomplished on shore. But what nakedness represents—a bodily hedonism which brings equal comfort to the mind—can be found in society as well as on the river, just as many of the fears common to the shore will be experienced on the raft. Shore and river are not opposed, but share a number of like qualities. For those on the river there is the fear of being swept by storms onto snags, rammed by steamboats at night, and being too visible to would-be captors by day. The river also represents danger to those who live on shore in such a town as Boggs-Sherburn's, which "has to be always moving back, and back, and back, because the river's always gnawing at it" (p. 195).

Below Cairo the Mississippi is revealed by daylight as actually being two rivers, "the clear Ohio water inshore, sure enough, and outside was the old regular Muddy!" (pp. 129-130.) Side by side, free and slave, the streams flow whose Ohio current could take Jim to legal freedom on shore (sending him back toward the dull details of an everyday life of clothes and toil) and whose other, yellowed rush floats Jim farther into the regions of legalized bondage (as well as into a further river life of prolonged pleasure). The river has two natures, but in the fog the way of the Muddy with its own mixture of clarity and ambiguity, pleasure and fear, is elected for the drifters.

The French have a phrase—*nostalgie de la boue*. It speaks of that craving for mud felt by those who have risen socially but who look back upon the good old days before they had to be so *clean*. Huck certainly is for "mud." One of the reasons he will want to light out for the Territory at the conclusion of his tale is to escape civilization's stress on cleanliness and godliness. But mud is also the silt of thoughtlessness about which Jim has cause to shame Huck; it is the muck of cruelty with whose brush the Duke and the King are tarred (in the meanness they do to others and the meanness done to them). Mark Twain, who went in for spotlessly white suits, knew the pull of *nostalgie de la boue*, with its dual meaning of delight in the free, easy, and comfortable and of fright over the vermin-filth of man's baser instincts.

There is yet another aspect to mud. Charles Sanders Peirce wrote in his essay of 1878, "How To Make Our Ideas Clear," that self-consciousness is intended to aid comprehension of "our fundamental truths" and what is "agreeable to reason." But Peirce saw success going to nations lacking in the "rich mud of conceptions" and "excessive wealth of language," sustained instead by "meagre and restricted" ideas. Mark Twain (together with Henry James) preferred to risk success as a writer by dealing with the "rich mud of conceptions" and "excessive wealth of language." Because characters like Huck Finn (and Christopher Newman) are given complex, dual-natured self-consciousnesses, they are vulnerable to failure in the face of the concentrated power held by the "meagre and restricted" theories of the Grangerfords (and the Bellegardes).

Add to the multi-natured river the presence of a boy with two natures, and you have even more complications (and a more interesting novel). As Walter Blair has pointed out in *Mark Twain and Huck Finn* (p. 104), Huck is no Tom Blankenship, even if Mark Twain (in remembering the boy whose "liberties were totally unrestricted," the "only really independent person" in Hannibal) said Tom and Huck were one person. Others agree that Mark Twain's memory of Hannibal's "bad boy" who was "tranquilly and continually happy" yields too simple a figure to be equated with Huck. To borrow terms provided by Henry Nash Smith in *Mark Twain: The*

*Development of a Writer*, there is the Huck committed by nature to "vernacular" values and the Huck urged by environment to the values of "the dominant culture" (p. 123). Huck has crises of identity when he plays off the dualities contained within his own nature against the overt disguises he briefly assumes under certain pressing circumstances. When he tells the Phelpses he is Tom Sawyer, he thinks, "Now I was feeling pretty comfortable all down one side, and pretty uncomfortable all up the other. Being Tom Sawyer was easy and comfortable, and it stayed easy and comfortable till by and by I hear a steamboat coughing along down the river" (p. 310). Made complex from the start by his inherited nature (for which the divided River stands as apt metaphor) and by environmental nurture (represented by the Shore), Huck is affected doubly whenever conflicts are set up by the coming together of actual river and shore incidents.

Fear comes via the two-natured river to the two-natured boy on the shore, and fear comes to him while he is on the raft. Location on the river does not save him from having to set his town morality against his vernacular morality. We witness this when he apologizes to Jim (after being forced to identify himself with the silt and debris tossed up from the river by the storm), or when he fends off the slave-hunters (who float toward him upon the current), or tears up the note for Miss Watson (as he sits tensely on the raft and decides for hell).

Huck enjoys comfort on the raft, but comfort also comes on shore—at the Grangerfords' domain, the Phelps's farm, the Wilks's house. Since comfort, inner and outer, is what he most wants, he is ready to end his journeying to get it by moving back into society. Because Huck is seen as susceptible to material, shore-life comforts, he has been scorned for being a born joiner out of passivity or expediency. In contrast, other critics suggest that his ability to act for peace wherever he goes is precisely the grounds for his appeal and his strength. As Albert E. Stone, Jr. argues in *The Innocent Eye* (p. 157), Huck's decision to "compromise" with the King and the Duke when they threaten to bring dissension onto the raft comes from his "creed of social harmony," the one positive thing he learns about life and "the most sweeping generalization" he ever comes to.

Certainly, the words Huck uses to explain why he tries to get along with everyone whenever they intrude upon his river or shore comforts are those of an ease-and-satisfaction man. "It took away all the uncomfortableness and *we felt mighty good* over it, because it would 'a' been a miserable business to have any unfriendliness on the raft; *for what you want*, above all things, on a raft, *is for everybody to be satisfied, and feel right and kind towards the others*" (italics mine). Even if he suspects they are frauds, Huck is willing to go along with the King and Duke's lies: ". . . it's the best way; then you don't have no quarrels, and don't get into no trouble" (p. 174).

But trouble will come sooner or later in the Twainian world, and often it results from an earlier act of placation. For the sake of soothing the King and the Duke, Huck and Jim are forced to set aside their private enjoyment of free, easy, and comfortable companionship; as a result of making welcome the men who pushed themselves onto the raft, events are initiated that drag Jim ashore again as a slave.

A boy who desires comfort of body and freedom from uneasiness of mind, whether on the raft or ashore, has no absolute of behavior, no tested mode of escape from trouble. He must be ready to extract the best from each situation by accepting the fact that that best will be stirred in with the worst. Huck's belief in the *desirability* of mixed culinary effects is stated at the very beginning of the novel; it stands him in good stead when he finds out the *inevitability* of the mixed effects of experience. Displeased by food cooked and served in separate portions, he observes, "In a barrel of odds and ends it is different; things get mixed up, and the juice kind of swaps around, and the things go better" (p. 2). Take the shore and the river as you find them, and things go better there too.

In the "Notice" that prefaces his book, Mark Twain warns that "persons attempting to find a moral in it will be banished." Does this mean banishment *from* a society that lives by "raspy" moralities, and thus a reward, not punishment, for readers adhering to Huck's code of comfortable survival? Or does it threaten us with what we do not want because pleasure largely exists *in* the society from which we are to be expelled?

We need to review Huck's attitudes toward escape from society to see whether this movement gains him what he desires. The novel opens with his having to face the fact that the Widow Douglas "allowed she would sivilize me" (pp. 1-2). He tries out this new approach for awhile, but—as he tells it—"when I couldn't stand it no longer I lit out. I got into my old rags and my sugar-hogshead again, and was free and satisfied" (p. 2). But the lure of joining Tom's band of robbers, an enterprise tolerated (and in essence, encouraged) by the settled society of the village, proves too great.

Huck reenters the world that provides pleasures only "respectable" boys can enjoy. Back in the widow's well-intentioned hands, he admits his plight: put "in them new clothes again . . . I couldn't do nothing but sweat and sweat, and feel all cramped up" (p. 2). He also has to contend with Miss Watson's talk about heaven and hell. He soon decides that if society's heaven is the "good place," he is willing to go to the "bad place" for strictly private reasons: the pleasure of being with Tom (friendship) and of being somewhere else (novelty). "All I wanted was to go somewheres; all I wanted was a change, I warn't particular" (p. 3).

Huck learns that civilized life at the widow's itself constitutes a pleasurable variation from his old life. "So the longer I went to school the easier it got to be. I was getting sort of used to the widow's ways, too, and they warn't so raspy on me." Ever adaptable, he admits, "I liked the old ways best, but I was getting so I liked the new ones, too, a little bit" (p. 21). Then his father (the old ways) suddenly reappears on the new scene. Previously, Huck had been relieved by his father's absence ("that was comfortable for me") since he had "to take to the woods most of the time when [Pap] was around" (the woods itself a place of comforting non-constraint and refuge) (p. 16). Comfort had been wherever Pap was not, whether in town or in the woods. But Huck's attitude toward Pap now shifts from having been "scared of him all the time, he tanned me so much," to being hardly "scared of him worth bothering about" (p. 26). Taken into captivity by Pap, he is shifted from the earthly "good place" of the town to the earthly "bad place" of the shack in the woods, but rapidly comes to view the latter in terms of easeful familiarity: ". . . it warn't long after that till I was used to being where I was, and liked it—all but the cowhide part" (p. 33). The old free and easy physical comforts enjoyed in the woods offset the fact of his captivity and the physical discomfiture of beatings. Only when Huck becomes concerned that his father might drunkenly kill him does he plan to run away from both kinds of comfort—his father's woods-kind and the widow's town-kind. Holding on to life is the ultimate pleasure. For life's sake one must resist the temptations offered in the name of comfort which threaten that great good; one must light out and "so get so far away that the old man nor the widow couldn't ever find me any more" (p. 36).

Usually a lover of drift and indolence, Huck expends a great deal of energy and ingenuity upon his "escape." He goes to Jackson's Island (away from the shore, surrounded by the river, and yet on land, in the woods). There he is alone, totally free. "I laid there in the grass and the cool shade thinking about things, and feeling rested and ruther comfortable and satisfied. . . . I was powerful lazy and comfortable—didn't want to get up and cook breakfast" (p. 51). As if by the magic stroke of the Aladdin's lamp, whose efficacy he was previously too skeptical to take on faith, his wants are supplied by the natural world he has chosen as his home, but also in a small, yet significant, way by the society he has rejected. Retrieving the loaf of bread cast upon the river by the townspeople, who are trying to find their lost one (his acceptance of the loaf perhaps symbolically adumbrating his later return to the bosom of society), Huck eats well, pleased in addition by the stir he is causing back in town. Relaxing in body and mind, he "then went to bed; there ain't no better way to put in time when you are lonesome; you can't stay so, you soon get over it" (p. 54).

Lonesome, yes, but loneliness will pass. Bored, no, but aware of the possibility of boredom and thereby wanting to "know all about" the island through exploration—to "put in the time" (p. 55). Eating, sleeping, looking around: this is the initial pattern of Huck's first and only achievement of total escape. He had first turned his back upon the discomforts of Pap's way of life that made him ready to take to the widow's way. He next moved from the "sweat" of civilization back into Pap's ken. But these were only partial forays, preparatory to taking flight from the discomforts native to either way of life. Huck's movement to Jackson's Island takes him completely away from other people into a society-less place that is his alone, all alone.

Then Huck meets Jim. In the name of friendship and novelty— the same lures that had earlier caused him to join Tom's band—the central movement of the novel begins. At this point, and consequent upon the earlier explorations in and out of society, alternations of action commence between the raft and the shore, between escape and entry, between sleep and stimulation. This is the particular span of the narrative upon which we now focus our attention, but these shifts have been at work in brief from the start.

The reason for these movements finds its metaphor in *Goshen*. It is significant that Huck tells Mrs. Loftus that, although he was on his way to his good place, he first decided "to turn into the woods for my regular sleep" (p. 84). A pilgrim of comfort on his way to the land of plenty, he frequently turns off the main road to his unreachable destination in order to gain the immediate comfort of escape which sleep offers.

Sleep pervades the towns along Mark Twain's "river of life"—whether St. Petersburg, Bricksville, the Phelps's farm, or Dawson's Landing. As Henry Nash Smith observes in *Mark Twain: The Development of a Writer*, such "sleepy indolence" had for Mark Twain "two contrasting kinds of associations. On the one hand it connotes intellectual apathy, ignorance, and credulity; on the other it signifies the dreamlike peace and happiness of childhood" (p. 157). Neither the white trash nor the white elite seem to have to work. Work is taken care of by the slave system, which lets the waking life of the whites pass like a dream and permits the blacks to loaf freely only in their sleep. (This may be the reason whites said niggers were always asleep—or "dead"—on their feet.) Childish dreams and irresponsible indolence act as a perfect preservative for decaying Scottism. When Huck tells Jim about the nobility of Europe, he is also describing the Grangerfords (as well as the common loafers on the village streets). " '*They* don't do nothing! . . . They just set around . . . except, maybe, when there's a war; then they go to the war. But other times they just lazy around; or go hawking . . . ' " (p. 107).

No man can live by the pleasures of sleep alone and stay alive for long. One must come awake at times, by whatever means. " 'We was all boys, then,' " Mark Twain has Simon Wheeler explain in "Jim Wolf and the Tom-Cats" (a piece included in Edgar Branch's study, p. 269), " 'and didn't care for nothing, and didn't have no troubles, and didn't worry about nothing only how to shirk school and keep up a revivin' state of devilment all the time.' "

"Revivin' " is not accomplished by Christian resurrection that trades in the old Adam for a new. The Mississippi River loafers are full of the Old Adam and the Old Nick. They are stirred up by cruelty-as-pleasure when they start dog-fights or incendiary actions against strays, encourage Boggs to push his confrontation with Sherburn, or—getting excited over a circus and the "Royal Nonesuch" production—plan revenge upon the circus ringmaster and the King and the Duke. The "aristocrats"—Grangerfords, Shepherdsons, and Sherburn—are hardly different; they merely look to the more socially superior form of pleasureful stimulation that comes from shooting down one's victims.

The comforts civilization offers as a pleasant midway point between the stupor of sleep and the stimulation of death games entice Huck ashore for long periods of time. There is the Grangerford establishment of fond memory—"a cool, comfortable place. Nothing couldn't be better. And warn't the cooking good, and just bushels of it too!" (p. 145.) *Grange* and *Shepherd*—idyllic, pastoral, Goshen-like names—form a patch of peace Huck enjoys, whether he lounges outside in the breezeway or inside in the parlor with its unrecognized call to the more arduous demands of life and morality suggested by the tablecloth from Philadelphia with its red and blue spread-eagle pattern, and the books *Pilgrim's Progress*, the Bible, and *Friendship's Offering*.

Just as life with the widow had meant school and prayers as well as certain comforts, living with the Grangerfords' provincial luxuries necessitates dutifully going to church to listen to "pretty ornery preaching—all about brotherly love, and such-like tiresomeness" (p. 152). The Grangerfords, social creatures par excellence, enjoy the sermon and have a lot to say about it, untroubled as they are by the complicating fact of the guns leaning against their knees, but Huck makes a nice distinction, and a characteristic one, when he notes that if the Grangerfords and Shepherdsons feel they *have* to go to church, the hogs come freely, enjoying the place for the simple fact that the building is a cool and inviting resting place.

The violence latently part of the somnolence erupts at the Grangerford place, and Huck flees. Later, sucked once again back into society, he approaches the Phelps's farm, only to find the same mixture of sleep and stimulation that continually characterizes his shore-side stops. Passing through the death-like silence of the yard, he is suddenly surrounded by a pack of suspicious hounds. Scattered by servants slinging wood, the dogs come back "wagging their tails around me, and making friends with me" (p. 305). Huck adds, "There aint no harm in a hound, nohow," unconsciously implying a marked contrast with the ways of humans, who alternate helpful hospitality with harmful hostility and mean both. The Phelps family lavishes brotherly love upon Huck when he identifies himself, and soon after, when Tom Sawyer arrives, "Everybody made a rush for the front door, because, of course, a stranger don't come *every* year . . ." (p. 315). What causes momentary discomfiture to the traveler is the fact that such a rush signals either a full meal or a bloody attack.

Inside the container of civilization people respond with the cruelty or kindness their humanness is capable of. A wandering boy testing the possibilities of escape and entry can never be sure which reaction to his coming will prove his fate, but he can be pretty certain he will eventually encounter both. Huck, who starts his book by moving *within* that container, has only the briefest moment of total freedom on the *outside* when on Jackson's Island he

sleeps, eats, and puts in time all alone. Almost at once, in joining up
with Jim in a mutual search for the free, easy, and comfortable, he
is again *within* the social container and stays there for the remain-
der of his adventures. Having made his final entrance into community life with Jim, he never really escapes again; he can make
only token gestures in the name of flight.

Huck moves back and forth from shore to raft, from one kind of
thoroughly enjoyed but momentary pleasure to another; he flees
but never escapes the discomforts of mind and body which any
place *in* the world ultimately brings. His is the classic American dilemma which leads to the basic American failure. The desire to attain the bliss of *complete* freedom (possible only outside all society
and beyond all relationships) is manifested by Thoreau as he goes
forth to Walden; by Melville's alter-egos as they leap away from the
lee shore; by Whitman as he loafs as a solitary soul along the open
road. It is the desire for the perfect success, and the defeat of that
desire. Escape and entry, entry and escape, become the unending
cycle of movement which simultaneously provides the way of the
quest after success, the quest itself, and the final frustration of that
quest.

*The American*, a book of 1877, elicited from its author a preface
written in hindsight in 1907. In his preface James speaks of his
book as a romance, and of the romance as that literary form which
lifts our imagination above the world like an ascension balloon. He
also likens the romance to artless schoolboys at play, who do not
know enough to ask the questions that are posed by older, wiser,
and sadder adults set down hard within the world of realism. As it
was noted in Part IV, Chapter 21, James admits the book's melodramatic stress on victim and victimizers. But it was through just
such types as romance and melodrama—through means not usually considered available to the conventional realistic novel—that
he tried to show what it is *really* like to be The American.

By the 1870's James was just beginning to work out the sophisti-
cations of the imagination he needed to express what it signifies to
live in a drastically self-limiting world and yet to strive for halos of
value in that one and only world. His narrative *The American* was
published six years before Mark Twain completed *Adventures of
Huckleberry Finn*, and eight years after *Innocents Abroad*, in which the
Mark Twain persona in many ways appears like Christopher
Newman, himself a grown-up Huck Finn. If Christopher Newman
and Huck Finn are complementary types, the books which contain

them are also similar in their sometimes jangled mingling of literary genres and in their mutual stress on themes of revenge and rebirth. But how different they are in the responses of their heroes to the terms of their fictive worlds!

As Huck and Newman near the conclusions of their respective narratives, each reacts to the assaults of society in fairly clear-cut ways. Never very assertive at best, Huck becomes increasingly passive. After he is repudiated by the Bellegardes, Newman loses his original composure and actively demands his moral rights. Lacking the self-confidence and protective good humor that might give him the brass he needs to face up to the world, Huck allows himself to be manipulated by others while clinging to his private dream of peace. Initially the possessor of calm self-esteem and a wry sense of humor, Newman's easy confidence is distorted into harsh egotism. Huck shies away from vengeful acts; Newman takes sour pleasure in the weapons of revenge. Huck's tale moves nearer the traditional comic reconciliation of self and society; Newman's story becomes more nearly pure melodrama.

What happens to these two Americans, child and man, arises surely from their character—or rather, from their *types*. There is no cheating in the consistency of cause and consequence Mark Twain and Henry James almost instinctively uphold in the depiction of their heroes. What we get are two portrayals of mixed personalities that contain equally the possibility of flexible adjustment and the bent toward rigid resistance. What wants to be emphasized here is that—in either story—both adaptability and resistance are carried out in the name of pleasure. It is the means Huck Finn and Christopher Newman take to that end and the ways they view their failures to get it which stand them in such sharp opposition.

At the end of the Civil War, Henry James noted a two-fold reaction on the part of Northern society. In *Notes of A Son and Brother* (pp. 406-407, 426-427) he points out that at first the "black cost" of war came in the form of an increased "quantity of military life"— the flow of a monster tide. This "most masculine" emotion was accompanied by the collective inner relief that flowed from the coming of spring's softness and hope during that April of 1865. Then came the sudden shock of Lincoln's assassination. This vengeful event, together with the return of the veterans parading in uniformed force through the streets, gave the upper hand to what James calls the "masculine" factor. Through the excitement of victory and the death of the President the North discovered its capacity for revenge and hardness of heart.

In *The American Scene* (pp. 387-389) James also analyzes what defeat brought the Southern consciousness. Oddly it is hardly different from what the triumphant North experienced: desire for revenge and dedication to moralistic rigor. He tells of the pleasant young Virginian whose father had made "a desperate evasion of capture, or worse, by the lucky smashing of the skull of a Union soldier." James remarks of the young man that "it was his candid response that was charmingly suggestive. 'Oh, I should be ready to do [these things] all over again myself!' " In later pages of the book, James provides two further images for the defeated South—the figures of an invalid and of a sick lioness: the male-type stripped of "fierce and moustachioed" power by the events of history, neutered by its "defiance" and "deprecation" (pp. 377, 417). This is the same South represented by the charming, vigorous young Virginian—"a fine contemporary young American, incapable, so to speak, of hurting a Northern fly, *as* Northern, but whose consciousness would have been poor and unfurnished without this cool platonic passion" (p. 388). This son of the War was one for whom "there were things . . . that, all fair, engaging, smiling, as he stood there, he would have done to a Southern negro" (pp. 388-389). Somehow the outer look of health is mere facade for the mutilating sickness within: the energies spring from hatred, shame, and defiant self-justification.

James's observations in *The American Scene* take the form of cultural-historical reportage provided by "the restless analyst" who probes abstractions such as "North" and "South" and "War." His handling of *The American* is based on the different method of the writer of fictive tales concerned with particularities about this person and that person. But characteristic of the fine consistency that plays over the various kinds of writing to which he gave himself is the way several of the moods and motifs found in the ruminative pieces on America commenced in 1904 are also at work in the 1877 fictional narrative devoted to The American. The question of responses to shame—explored so well in Manfred Mackenzie's *Communities of Honor and Love in Henry James*—never dropped from James's mind. Early and late, he sensed that the defeated inevitably turn toward violence. The victorious ought, by contrast, to be freed of the need for such moral ugliness; the "masculine" factor ought to demonstrate itself in ways more creative than destructive. But once Newman, the hard-edged man of the North, experiences defeat, he finds himself emotionally emasculated like the defanged lion of James's *The American Scene*; like the young Virginian, he is made capable of murderous acts by the rancors in his heart.

In the war's immediate aftermath Christopher Newman is ready to emerge out of social obscurity. He has already experienced the success of physical survival. It is nothing to take pride in especially, yet he has succeeded where thousands failed. He has come out with his "legs and arms—and with satisfaction. All that seems very far away" (p. 21). War, which sanctions blood-revenge even in a democracy, has been an unpleasant fantasy to him:

> . . . his four years in the army had left him with an angry, bitter sense of the waste of precious things—life and time and money and "smartness" and the early freshness of purpose; and he had addressed himself to the pursuit of peace with passionate zest and energy. (p. 27)

But Newman will at length turn away from easy, good-natured leg-stretchings toward the strain of pitting his own "angry, bitter" righteousness against the Bellegardes' "waste of precious things." He will experience a sense of defeat previously unknown to him. For Newman the Bellegardes' wickedness is reason enough that they be made to suffer at his hands. He does not believe he is being made to suffer because of his own faults; instead, he has been terribly put upon precisely because of his goodness and good nature. These are the definitions he makes of himself—the distinctions he carefully places between himself and his foes. Unwilling to examine whether he is also to blame, he further fails to ask whether suffering is inevitably the direct consequence of *anyone's* actions. All he cares to believe is that if a man suffers it is because of his decency which others have taken advantage of, and that he is thereby free to cause suffering in the name of a judgment upon evil. Newman does not consider that this formula might be fallacious on several counts. It is enough for him to take it for the truth and to act on it.

Henry James does not try to answer in full whether the actual cause of Newman's plight lies in the opposition of Evil and Goodness set up by melodramas of betrayed innocence. He directs his attention primarily toward the effects which Newman's decision to take revenge has upon the character of an American originally marked by naïveté and decency, shrewdness and good humor.

There is one other point to be made before going on. James requested of a piece of writing that above all things it be *interesting* and contain *interesting* characters. In *The American Scene* he gives reasons why he, "the restless analyst," finds the South so absorbing a study. He comments on the value to the imagination of a defeated and defiant South exposed before the world in "the *bled* condition" (p. 414). He adds, ". . . the South is in the predicament of having to be tragic, as it were, in order to beguile" (p. 420). "It was very hard," he admits, "and very cruel and very perverse, and above all very strange; but what 'use' had the restless analyst here for a lively and the oblivious type" It has this use: it throws one back

> with renewed relish on the unforgetting and the devoted, on the resentful and even, if need might be, the vindictive[.] These things would represent certainly a bad *état d'âme*—and was one thus cold-bloodedly, critically to wish such a condition perpetrated? The answer to that seemed to be, monstrously enough, "Well, yes—for these people; since it appears the only way by which they can be interesting." (p. 420)

James's story of Newman-Agonistes is also, in part, the result of his creator's cold-blooded desire to made him interesting whatever the costs to his hero's *état d'âme*. If William Faulkner was willing to throw old ladies down the stairs as a trade for the writing of "Ode on a Grecian Urn," Henry James could hardly balk if put to the choice of making Newman nice and dull and Newman mean and fascinating—"the resentful and even, if need might be, the vindictive."

In concluding the passage in which he notes the intriguing quality of vindictiveness which defeat has given to the South, James says, "See when they try other ways! Their sadness and sorrow . . . has at least for it that it has been expensively produced. Everything else, on the other hand, anything that may pretend to be better— oh, so cheaply!" (p. 420.) In contrast, Newman was originally angry and bitter over the wastefulness of the war he had helped to win for the North but with no desire to increase the cost in exacting penalties of his former enemies. It is only later that he again becomes angry and bitter as the result of his expensive European education in defeat. The book which tells his story is enriched by the interest added, not taken away, by Newman's own changing reactions to "the *bled* condition."

When we first meet him, Christopher Newman has largely escaped Huck Finn's inborn wisdom, which acknowledges the two-fold nature of self and of life. Full of confidence in what he believes to be the strong unity of his personality, Newman turns aside as nonsense the perturbed criticisms of Babcock, the man who accuses him of appearing "to care only for the pleasures of the hour" and of holding "that if a thing amuses you for the moment, that is all you need ask for it" (p. 91). Almost at the same moment, he also encounters an Englishman who accuses him of being "too virtuous by half . . . too stern a moralist . . . cursed with a conscience." "This," Newman decides, "was rather bewildering. Which of my two critics was I to believe?" Each of them, if only he had known himself. But satisfied in his ignorance, he does the characteristic thing: "I didn't worry about it and very soon made up my mind they were both idiots" (p. 97). Newman initially maintains his self-composure by putting the rest of the world in the wrong, whereas Huck maintains his equilibrium by agreeing with the world's belief that *he* is the one out of step. Newman later supports his sense of solid superiority by wishing the Bellegardes in hell, while Huck simply sees hell as the proper place for him to be.

Huck, Newman, *and* the society which surrounds the two—all rock between alternative possibilities for the promise of pleasure, that of keeping very still and that of erupting into violence. Huck and Newman choose between these possibilities according to the ways they are pulled by their dual natures and the directions toward which society pushes them.

Before Huck's wide gaze, two dramatically contending choices are constantly posed by those whom he meets: dreaminess (what his "vernacular" side likes best when it blots out the pains caused by the interaction of world and self) and vengeful action (what his "social" side could conceivably prefer in the name of excitement and self-righteousness). Newman also witnesses, in the lives of those close to him, several attempts to avoid the unpleasant, even if he does not fully realize the significance of what he sees. For some persons, sitting "very still" works best; for others it fails. M. Nioche learns quietness in order to escape disagreeable scenes and the accusations of "bad conscience"; his strategy works so well he nearly disappears into the blank peace of idiocy. Claire de Cintré finds that being quiet *in* the world is not enough; attempting to flee pain altogether by burying herself in the "death" of the convent, she very quickly assumes "monastic rigidity" and a "lifeless" touch (p. 356). Formed "to be happy in a quiet, natural way," Claire decides that her way is not the way of the world; " '. . . we *must* give pain; that's the world,—the hateful, miserable world!' " (pp. 364-365.) She informs Newman, " 'I am going out of the world,' " then adds,

" 'It is only peace and safety. It is to be out of the world, where such troubles as this come to the innocent, to the best' " (pp. 365-366).

Newman also watches Claire's brother Valentin try to escape by refusing to face the pragmatic necessities for survival. By leaping toward honor's "satisfaction," Valentin achieves in literal death what Claire gains through renunciation of the world and what M. Nioche accomplishes by blending himself into the protective coloring of social moralities. Newman rejects the particular forms of withdrawal taken by M. Nioche's idiocy, Claire's eternal vows of monastic silence, and Valentin's grave of honor, although he, like they, retreats within the self-satisfaction of conscience. In contrast, he actively turns conscience into a weapon of attack against the world where Madame de Bellegarde and her son Urbain live out their own tough-minded desire to avoid disagreeable things, himself included.

Newman considers the Bellegardes the enemy because they keep him from getting what he wants by insisting upon their own satisfaction. It is ironic that he does not see himself becoming one of them when he discards his "American" trait of relaxed good humor that could lead him toward reconciliation and self-knowledge. But he discards it in order to nurture that other quality latent within his American nature: the propensity to seek satisfaction by means of revenge.

In the war games that follow chapter eighteen, the American and the Europeans employ the same weapon of dark ironic thrusts to the heart of the others' comfort. However, Newman is at a disadvantage from the onset. First, by placing himself on the same side of the line as the people he detests, he is thrown off balance. Second, he is playing in unfamiliar territory, with no landmarks of value to show him where he is or how well he is doing. Third, he commits himself to two rules of the game dictated by the Bellegardes: to keep from seeming the fool, make the other party the fool first; to gain the end reward of pleasure, inflict pain greater than the pain received. All Newman has on his side is his trust in the proud notion that as an American he deserves—has the right—to win. Actually, an American of conscience who is bent on revenge is both better and worse morally than the Europeans who cannot be fretted by considerations of conscience; he is certainly worse off in the practicalities of war.

Newman rapidly finds the idea of swift vengeance a new and pleasing form of self-entertainment, one soothing to the pride, whose hurt he significantly describes in terms of physical pain. But he soon prefers yet another kind of pleasure—that which comes from the anticipation of the withheld stroke. "He was nursing his thunder-bolt; he loved it; he was unwilling to part with it"—disposed as he was "to sip the cup of contemplative revenge in a leisurely fashion" (p. 408). Newman, though, is not the type to linger like Hamlet with his broodings. In keeping with the energy of character that has brought him this far into worldly success, he becomes like the hero Nietzsche praised—a man of thunderbolts and lightning, versatile at inflicting cold wounds. Newman will never prove as magnificent a figure of baffled rage as Ahab, but Ahab's crucified face is what he would like to imitate. Ahab has to take on the mystery of the universe; Newman has only Europe to fathom, yet Henry James knew how difficult it is for an American to trace what lies behind the cardboard masks of the Old World.

By actively enacting the portrait he draws of himself as all-knowing hero of Jovian justice, Newman tries to strike out the memory of having once looked like "a terrier on his hind legs" to the European aristocrats (p. 281). Thomas Jefferson had said Americans visit Europe as if it were a zoo, but it has been a shock for Newman to have Madame de Bellegarde glance over him as if it were he who were a creature of the menagerie. He must convert the image of himself as a dog doing tricks in a circus into the sense of himself as a god sitting in judgment. He does not believe there is any power in being entertaining; there is much power in being wrathful.

When Newman calls upon the Bellegardes soon after confronting them in the park with news he has proof of the murder done to the old Marquis, he "laughed the laugh in which he indulged when he was most amused—a noiseless laugh, with his lips closed" (pp. 435-436). His amusement over his threat to do what "will be very disagreeable" is somewhat checked when Urbain concurs but adds, "it will be nothing more" (p. 439). The new man (Newman) and the old man (Urbain), the democrat and the autocrat, are in outward contention. These two types are also in conflict within Newman himself, a duality that prevents him from being at peace until he can come to terms with each of these categorical forms.

"Well, I ought to begin to be satisfied now!" Newman tells himself when he leaves his confrontation with the Bellegardes (p. 439). But when he attempts to take the private pleasure he has wrung from the occasion into the public arena, two things mar it; others refuse to respond as he had imagined since they have no pleasure to gain from it; he senses he might seem the fool to society rather than the hero triumphantly revealing the Bellegardes' villainy to the world. He does not yet understand that revenge is best enjoyed within the privacy of one's own humorless, self-congratulating fantasies. The best Newman can be is a figure in a melodrama of his own devising. By using the literary mode of the melodrama James, the teller of the American's tale, aids and abets the desires of his fictional hero from his own writer's need to show the innocent "in the power" of the wicked. But James's direct contribution is *the plot* of melodrama, not the *mood*. The latter is what Newman provides in his responses to the plot's frustration of his original pleasure.

As a result of the treatment Newman receives in the presence of "the comical duchess," he takes a reviving step back toward his previous "good" nature: ". . . he stretched his legs, as usual, and even chuckled a little . . ." (pp. 440, 442). "He seemed morally to have turned a somersault, and to find things looking differently in consequence" (p. 444). However, this slight movement back into the American humorousness that detects the folly and pretentiousness of public revenge is more than countered by Newman's decision to continue to experiment with even more subtle forms of ego-gratification. He decides not to make known the paper which accuses the Marquise of murder. He does this, not because of a compassionate wish to forego hurting others, but rather to savor the power and pleasure of his own beleaguered decency. "What the paper suggested was the feeling that lay in his innermost heart and that no reviving cheerfulness could long quench—the feeling that after all and above all he was a good fellow wronged" (p. 463). When "he restored the little paper to his pocket-book very tenderly, and felt better for thinking of the suspense of the Bellegardes," Newman has merely devised a new way of tormenting his foes (p. 463). He has them in his power, he believes, as long as they are beholden for their safety to his magnanimity.

Newman has just undergone an inverted version of the decision Huck Finn makes to withhold his note to Miss Watson. Viewing himself as a bad fellow, Huck feels somewhat better for ending his own suspense concerning where he will spend eternity; since he knows it ought to be hell, he might as well place himself there. Viewing himself as a good fellow, Newman enjoys the suspense he inflicts upon the Bellegardes over their supposed realization of the ease with which he can place them in an infernal position.

Meanwhile the deadening effects of Newman's perverted approach to self-satisfaction have been making inroads upon the once vigorous spirit and healthy egotism of the American. To make this clear to us, James throws up clusters of characters around Newman who act out forms of pleasure-seeking and revenge-taking which mimic those of his hero. James also presents for our benefit the cautionary tale of Mrs. Bread, though it does the self-blinded Newman no good. Mrs. Bread's life-long desire for vengeance upon Madame de Bellegarde—as faded in intensity as the red ribbon once worn about her neck—is now reduced to a "grudge" she is unable either to end or to fulfill. Her real obsession is "respectability," another name for what some in James's story call "honor" and yet others call "comfort" or "satisfaction." Revenge taken up in the guise of righteousness, conscience, and morality has turned the once pretty young girl into an old woman likened to "an ancient tabby cat, protracting the enjoyment of a dish of milk. Even her triumph was measured and decorous; the faculty of exultation had been chilled by disuse" (p. 394). Mrs. Bread, like Newman, had once been electrified into action by thoughts of revenge, but revenge has become her route into deadening stillness. " 'Quiet I call it, but for me it was a weary quietness. It worried me terribly, and it changed me altogether' " (p. 401). Mrs. Bread joins Valentin, Claire, and M. Nioche as self-inflicted victims of silence, leaving a niche open for Newman to fill beside them.

One of the first signs of the crepuscular hold which revenge has upon Newman comes when he leaves Poitiers "feeling rather tired." He admits that "nursing a vengeance was, it must be confessed, a rather fatiguing process; it took a good deal out of one . . ." (p. 408). Taking to travel, he finds that flatness of spirit has replaced the exuberance of his earlier journeys around Europe. However, "the dullness of his days pleased him; his melancholy, which was settling into a secondary stage, like a healing wound, had in it a certain acrid, palatable sweetness" (p. 461). The wound of hurt pride is beginning to heal itself in natural stages in order that Newman might yet return to wholeness of self, but he has a way to go; he must first pass through a convalescence which is very like death.

Turning away from action and toward thought to gain his pleasure, Newman

> lived over again the happiest hours he had known . . . [which] had subtilized his good humor to a sort of spiritual intoxication. He came back to reality, after such reveries, with a somewhat muffled shock; he had begun to feel the need of ac-

cepting the unchangeable. At other times the reality became
an infamy again. . . . (p. 461)

Acceptance and resistance, reality and reverie, humor and
revenge—all these impulses still alternate within Newman. But for
a while fantasies of a future of dulled pleasure continue to rule his
thoughts. He contemplates devotion to the mariolatrous religion
(thus an "un-American" one) of doing nothing which might dis-
please the divine Claire, absent "out there" in a better world than
his.

> It would be lonely entertainment—a good deal like a man talk-
> ing to himself in the mirror for want of better company. Yet
> the idea yielded Newman several half hours' dumb exaltation
> as he sat . . . over the relics of an expensively poor dinner, in
> the undying English twilight. (pp. 461-462)

Such a life will not even possess the physical excitement of Valentin's dying with "satisfaction." Newman would only linger on like
Mrs. Bread, who moves wraith-like through the rooms of the
empty Parisian house, herself too uncomfortable to sit down and be
at ease. Concern over the Bellegardes' "treachery" has led Newman
into self-betrayal and turned him into a "hopeless, helpless loafer,
useful to no one and destestable to himself . . ." (p. 464). He is a far
cry from the alert lounger at the Louvre, atingle with possibilities,
introduced on the book's first page.

Charles Darwin made some jottings (included in the Gruber-
Barrett edition) which he called "Old and useless Notes about the
moral sense & some metaphysical points written about the year
1837 & earlier." In them he remarked that "the passion rising from
weariness leads to striking blows" (p. 403). This was not the only
time Darwin associated the emotion of anger with physical fatigue.
In his notes of 1838 concerning John Macculloch's *Proofs and Illus-
trations of the Attributes of God*, Darwin took up Macculloch on the
latter's notion that the universe shows signs of a fatigued God because of its incomplete or faulty physical structures. "[The] designs
of an omnipotent creator, exhausted & abandoned. Such is man's
philosophy, when he argues about his Creator!" (p. 417.) The tone
of Darwin's contempt aside, we can trace the line of his own notions
of the connection between fatigue and anger through his reference
to Macculloch's attention to the exhaustion occasionally detected in
God's creations. By taking hints from both Darwin and Macculloch
we arrive at the essential "philosophy" Mark Twain used "when he

argues about his Creator"—the Being tired, angry, a botcher of universal structures. In contrast, Henry James (writing in his 1910 essay "Is There a Life After Death?") preferred to think of God (if God there were) as a gentleman and skillful artist. But James is more than willing to associate that fatigue-unto-dying with human beings; he sees it as one of the crucial responses to life they can choose to take as a result of their frustration and anger over failure. Christopher Newman as the tired would-be god of wrath and justice has no chance for renewed creativity as long as he remains in the easeful dark of his melancholy.

Newman briefly returns to America, where he tells friends he has brought back no "new ideas." Indeed, he has gathered only outworn European habits of decaying energy, conscience, and the obsessive need to avenge one's honor. He has also learned to apply, with a vengeance, what Adams called in *The Education of Henry Adams* the American intellectual method by which the mind

> likes to walk straight up to its object, and assert or deny something that it takes for a fact; it has a conventional approach, a conventional analysis, and a conventional conclusion, as well as a conventional expression, all the time loudly asserting its unconventionality. (p. 369)

If ever a man needed rebirth away from overly sophisticated European ontologies and all too conventional American epistemologies, it is Christopher Newman.

"Brain-fever" was the way to rebirth for many a nineteenth-century fictional hero. Newman begins to show the flushed signs of that illness as his consciousness awaits its own recovery. His state of suspended animation becomes marked by feverish restlessness; in place of his earlier slothful self-preening, self-condemnations start to emerge which Norman Mailer would be pleased to lay to Newman's cancerous conscience. Newman senses he cannot be "content" until he returns one last time to Europe, but he does not yet know why Europe is the source of his disgust. He is still unaware that to equate revenge with righteousness and then to use both to seek pleasure through destructiveness has cost him his humor and his "life." "Not to know" these matters is what makes Newman the dangerous innocent he still is.

Newman is at last released from his spell (the *dream* of death and the *idea* of pleasure) as he stands facing the blank wall of Claire's convent on the Rue d'Enfer. "It was a strange satisfaction, and yet it was a satisfaction; the barren stillness of the place seemed to be his own release from ineffectual longing. . . . Everything was over, and he too at last could rest" (p. 468). He goes into Notre Dame to sit momentarily "out of the world." (Like Henry Adams, Newman must end his "education" concerning the effect of the Woman upon his life's quest for "amusement" in the contemplation of "Notre Dame.") There within the quiet sanctuary, "The most unpleasant thing that had ever happened to him had reached its formal conclusion, as it were . . . he felt that he was himself again" (pp. 468-469).

When Newman leaves the Cathedral, he has not gained a victory or even come to a conscious decision. He is only The American once again, "strolling soberly, like a good-natured man who is still a little ashamed" (p. 469). *Strolling soberly*: he is a man both relaxed and chastened. He has concluded that the Bellegardes "had hurt him, but such things were really not his game" (p. 469). Christopher Newman had almost lost himself, but now it seems he may yet be renewed, regained, rediscovered: a success.

"Whether it was Christian charity or unregenerate good nature—what it was, in the background of his soul—I don't pretend to say . . ." (p. 469). The author-narrator of Newman's story will not overtly disclose which of these motives triumphs, but from the start James had included the clues necessary for a general understanding of what is happening to Newman at this moment late in the story. James worked early, middle, and last to prepare us to react with educated sensibilities to what will take place on the final page of the book. Let us briefly return to an earlier passage (pp. 31-33), where Newman gives an account of a strange incident that befell him just prior to his first trip to Europe.

When troubled in mind by "a question of getting ahead of another party" in a stock-market deal, "something very curious happened." " 'This other party had once played me a very mean trick,' " Newman explains. " 'I owed him a grudge. I felt awfully savage at the time, and I vowed that, when I got a chance, I would, figuratively speaking, put his nose out of joint.' " Settling upon the motive of righteous indignation, Newman decided the other party "really deserved no quarter." He felt justified in turning to speculative combat on the stock-market (a natural way for Americans to "get their man" in a society with a strong anti-dueling bias). Primed for revenge, he had then jumped into an "immortal, historical hack" that looked as if it were normally used for Irish funerals. Once inside the cab-hearse, Newman may have dozed:

"At all events I woke up, suddenly, from a sleep or from a kind
of reverie, with the most extraordinary feeling in the world—a
mortal disgust for the thing I was going to do. . . . I couldn't tell
the meaning of it. . . . The idea of losing that sixty thousand
dollars . . . seemed the sweetest thing in the world. And all this
took place quite independently of my will, and I sat watching it
as if it were a play at the theatre. I could feel it going on inside
of me. You may depend upon it that there are things going on
inside of us that we understand mighty little about."

Meanwhile the driver feared his carriage had "turned into a
hearse" because his fare was so long silent. Indeed, Newman remembers he had felt as immobile as if he had been a corpse; he
recalls, "What I wanted to get out of was Wall Street." Wall Street
was his potential grave, not the surrogate hearse which acted instead as a lying-in cubicle for birth. A Whitmanian soul suddenly
bursting with new life, Newman told "the man to drive down to
Brooklyn ferry and to cross over." There he "spent the morning
looking at the first green leaves on Long Island. . . . I seemed to feel
a new man inside my old skin, and I longed for a new world."

Henry Adams observed, in *The Education of Henry Adams* (pp.
500-501), "The new man could be only a child born of contact between the new and the old energies"; and again, "The new American must be either the child of the new forces or a chance sport of
nature." For Newman this necessary fusion came about once he rejected that version of "old world" revenge prompted by Wall
Street, recognized that the game of speculation is a "boy's" game,
and accepted the greater value of the open green world beyond the
walled city streets. As a result of that initial metamorphosis he had
set off for Europe—in his imagination, a New World of exploration, aesthetic contemplation, and the possibility of wonder. In
Europe he had once again to repeat the same sequence of the
ordeals of consciousness: the easy-going quest for pleasure gotten
through play and humorous self-confidence; the sudden break-
down that turns one toward pleasure defined as revenge and
deadly serious self-righteousness; the rejection of all that dulls and
deadens, replaced by a new consciousness that has the force to
quicken the quester into signs of reinvigorated life.

An article by Caroline Seebohm on lateral and vertical thinking
entitled "How to Change Your Point of View" suggests a contemporary notion of the stages through which Newman has passed.
Paraphrasing the arguments of Dr. Edward de Bono's book *New
Think*, Seebohm writes:

The normal Western approach to a problem is to *fight* it. The saying "When the going gets tough, the tough get going," epitomizes this aggressive, combat-ready attitude toward problem-solving. . . . Dr. de Bono calls this *vertical* thinking; the traditional, sequential, Aristotelian thinking of logic, moving firmly from one step to the next, like toy blocks being built one on top of the other. The flaw is, of course, that if at any point one of the steps is not reached, or one of the toy blocks is incorrectly placed, then the whole structure collapses. Impasse is reached, and frustration, tension, feelings of *fight* take over.

Newman's original Wall Street consciousness is comparable to the stressful verticals of American life about which James was always apprehensive. But does James's tale of The American suggest the same alternative to Newman's feeling of frustration and fight advanced by Dr. de Bono—the alternative of "*lateral* thinking" whose "knack is making that vital shift in emphasis, that side-stepping of the problem, instead of grappling with it head-on"? Could James concur fully with the way the same solution is phrased by a professor from Columbia University, here cited by Seebohm?

It's about time we stopped fighting in order to find a solution. Let us float along with the problem so we can look at it from lateral points of view. Then we can be receptive to new ideas, renew and restimulate our senses, find a new way of living.

Certainly "lateral thinking" fits into Huck Finn's desire to float through life recumbent on the raft of the free, easy, and comfortable. Surely Newman finds relief when he is able to walk away from the dead-end streets of both Manhattan and of Paris. But Huck and Newman can never fully escape from that world through which their "frail bark" drifts, for theirs is a vertical world with little easement promised to the lateral consciousness.

Newman is himself again, a modern-day Orlando Furioso reborn from the wild-man of the forests into a man who has no harm in him. But just what *is* "himself" as he emerges from Notre Dame de Paris? Is he *new*—different from what he has ever been, or simply restored to what he had been? Which man gains ascendancy on the book's final page: the man who finds his greatest pleasure in comfort or the man who takes pleasure in pain—his own and others?

Newman often envisions his self as devoted to righteousness; therefore, to resemble himself involves the hard work of "doing what is expected of one. Doing one's duty" (p. 229). Even as he leaves the Cathedral, "Newman's last thought was that of course he would let the Bellegardes go" (p. 469). This is the thought of a man who still prides himself on having power and on being in the right, yet with the magnanimity to "let go." If Newman is a man of renewed good-nature, one who feels chagrin while "strolling soberly" away from revenge, there still lies latent within him the counter-impulse to enjoy righteous indignation and the self-justifications of vanity. He seems to be a man *restored* to what he had been when he first started on his explorations of Europe. It is inaccurate to see him as completely reborn, freed from traits that once divided his nature into the clear and the muddy streams of the Mississippi.

In the last sentences of the original 1877 version, Newman insists that he has frightened the Bellegardes badly and—since he has "all the vengeance [he] wants"—is satisfied (p. 472). But it is significant that he still can react sharply to Mrs. Tristram's observation that he "probably did not make them so very uncomfortable" (p. 473). Only at this moment does Newman come to whatever self-knowledge he gains within the story. Suddenly he realizes that that part of him which takes comfort in causing discomfort has been falsely lulled into a sense of victory, permitting his good-natured side to come to the fore. He realizes that his enemies have benefitted from the fact that that portion of his nature characterized by humor and easefulness fails in the Bellegarde world whenever he pits it, together with his own capacity for vindictiveness, against the concentrated force of their desire for self-satisfaction. One-sided people such as the Bellegardes are more indomitable in warfare than two-sided men like Newman, since the former have nothing acting from within their natures to keep them from their goals. At the shock of this realization, Newman's revived good-humor is insufficient to counter his reawakened impulse to drop back toward revenge and away from his present, perhaps always tenuous, grasp upon humor.

Because Newman as the American contains the potential for both humor and violence, James was able to write two endings for his story—each appropriate to a different aspect of the character of his hero, The American, and the country that hero represents. Newman "would obey," James wrote in his 1907 preface (included in *The Art of the Novel*, p. 22), "one of the large and easy impulses *generally* characteristic of his type." Morality of "forgiveness"— based as it is upon judgments of right and wrong—"would have, in the case, no application; he would simply turn, in the case, away. . . ." Here, then, is Newman viewed at the conclusion of James's "second go" at *The American*. This is the man whose possessions "would be therefore just the moral convenience, indeed the moral necessity, of his practical, but quite unappreciated magnanimity. . . ." James added the comment, "one's last view of him would be that of a strong man indifferent to his strength and too wrapped in fine, too wrapped above all in *other* and intenser, reflexions for the assertion of his 'rights.' "

Compare the 1907 version (the tale and the explanatory preface) to the original version of 1877. In the earlier telling, the final look discloses that Newman is anything but indifferent to his strength, once it has been called into question. Still concerned about his "rights," he wheels about to see if he might snatch back the accusatory piece of paper when he learns that the intangibles of good-nature are not enough to guarantee him victory. By comparing the Newman of 1877 with the man of 1907, we seem to see two different persons, juxtaposed one upon the other. The earlier type is a figure in a "romance" with strong melodramatic overtones. The later figure—still placed within the "romance" plot of victim-betrayed—is now a man who will at least make a try at the kind of comedy devoted to transcending worldly betrayals.

However different in degree in their commitment to humor, both "Newmans" have increasingly come to rely on what James's preface marks out as the signs of good-natured magnanimity: "moral" convenience, necessity, and practicality—that is, signs that show us humor as the most *reasonable* of human activities. Because of this insistence on the expediency of being nice, Theodore Parker might call the two Newman-figures "sensationalists." Yet they represent the initial stages of a type that presses on toward principle more than toward practicality. The "Newmans" early and late prepare the way for James's other quintessential Americans—Lambert Strether, Milly Theale, and Maggie Verver, persons who learn to deal with treachery more through the positive refusal to be vindictive than the negative reluctance to think too well of themselves.

If the Newman of 1877 comes to feel at the very end that magnanimity is a flaw—a weakness that causes a man failure in the world of the Bellegardes, the Newman of 1907 appears to believe that magnanimity is a virtue—a strength that may liberate him to find success back home in the free territory of America. America still contains both Wall Street (the "vertical" current of the Big Muddy) and Long Island (the "lateral" current that runs clear). Both are there for Newman's moral and aesthetic contemplation; both exist as reminders of his own two-sided American nature.

As for Huckleberry Finn, he is seen at the end of his book contemplating an escape into the Territory. But even he would go simply to get there "ahead of the rest." Presently he would be followed by human beings who will be "cruel to one another"; presently "conscience" will be imported and the Territory become "civilized." The necessary materials for revenge and power will soon be *out there*, impeding Huck's deepest desire to live—with some hope of satisfying permanence—the free, easy, and comfortable life. No mere hedonism, but the "good" life in its truest sense is what Huck has always wanted. It is a life overthrown, however, by the greater pleasure which others continue to find in wrath and punishment.

Huck never considers acts of vengeance as a way for himself to gain power over others, nor are acts of self-righteousness within his range of possibility. His belief in the basic "low-down and ornery" quality of his two-sided nature makes it impossible for him to put to his use methods more appropriate to people and powers superior to his own. Nor has he ever tried humor. (That was for Mark Twain to use.) Huck has, however, generally gone along with good-natured, civil, patient, and generous-minded ways. These are the particular traits found in the Americans abroad described in *The Education of Henry Adams*. They are the same traits, as well, that Adams applies to the world in which both Huck and Newman must function:

> The world is always good-natured; civil, glad to be amused; open-armed to any one who amused it; patient with everyone who did not insist on putting himself in its way, or costing it money; but this was not consideration, still less power in any of its concrete forms, and applied as well or better to a comic actor. (p. 327)

The world as Adams describes it sounds a great deal as if it were Huckleberry Finn himself, and Christopher Newman at his most amiable. But there is a catch. Characters in the narratives of Mark Twain and Henry James may share attributes with the world in which they live, but that world *contains* them, rules them; they do not—like the Transcendentalists—contain or rule it. As any Court Jester knows, his King may also be a humorist, but the underling's own comic spirit is powerless to protect him if the King is ever displeased by his japes. Revenge rigidifies and good-nature quickens. The latter quality is more advantageous to good living than the former. But the possession of a flexible, humorous nature is no guarantee of survival, especially not if the world is itself run by a comic actor whose ways are "not consideration."

In 1889 Mark Twain completed *A Connecticut Yankee in King Arthur's Court*. Through the character of Hank Morgan we can see what it might be like to have Tom Sawyer grow into an adult while elaborating his special talent for organizing the "boys" and perpetrating gaudy schemes. Hank is also Christopher Newman swaying between ease of good nature and ardor for self-righteous revenge. At the conclusion of Hank's adventures in old Europe, thousands are dead at the literal release of the electric thunderbolt which Newman had nursed only in his imagination.

In his biography of Mark Twain, Albert Bigelow Paine wrote about the shift he had detected in his subject's attitudes toward Americans in Europe between 1869 and 1880:

> In the *Innocents* the writer is the enthusiast with a sense of humor. In the *Tramp* he has still the sense of humor, but he becomes a cynic; restrained but a cynic none the less. In the *Innocents* he laughs at the delusions and fallacies—and enjoys them. In the *Tramp* he laughs at human foibles and affectations—and wants to smash them. (II, 668)

It is difficult to know just whose imagination is responsible for setting off the fuse at the end of *A Connecticut Yankee*—Hank's or Mark Twain's. Whichever, that imagination acts in the name of saving civilization under the guise of moral superiority. But from the start the liking for revenge and violent retribution has run through both Hank's tale and Mark Twain's life as a countercurrent to a fondness for relaxed amusement. By now an ending that is apocalyptic and terminal seems the best method possible for the clever American who believes he must wipe out evil in the one great and gaudy gesture permitted by the well-tested traditions of melodrama. Alas, he (Hank or Mark Twain) will find that with his success the man left most alone and dead in the universe is himself. Aggression turned outward upon the world slays many; turned inward it kills as surely.

In 1900 Henry James gave us another American in Paris in *The Ambassadors*, but Lambert Strether's reactions to the shock of being jostled into new awareness are hardly that of Christopher Newman, and certainly their expression has no resemblance to Hank Morgan's sense of style:

> That was the refinement of his supreme scruple—he wished so to leave what he had forfeited out of account. He wished not to do anything because he had missed something else, because he was sore or sorry or impoverished, because he was maltreated

or desperate; he wished to do everything because he was lucid
and quiet, just the same for himself on all essential points as he
had ever been. Thus it was that while he virtually hung about
for Chad he kept mutely putting it: "You've been chucked, old
boy; but what has that to do with it?" It would have sickened
him to feel vindictive. (xxii, 294-295)

In his essay "The Comic," Emerson pointed to what he named
"an essential element in a fine character"—"a perception of the
Comic" which acts as "a balance-wheel in our metaphysical structure." It is significant that Emerson, who said he had little interest
in either the comic or the tragic modes, speaks of the man of comic
perception as the proper companion for the "pure idealist," the
true hero. He is useful because "a man who knows the world, and
who, sympathizing with the philosopher's scrutiny, sympathizes
also with the confusion and indignation of the detected skulking
institutions." What we have in Strether is the merger within one
"fine character" of the "pure idealist," the man of comedy who has
sympathy for Woollett and Paris alike, and all the "confusion" in
between. That is, Strether takes into himself the world and two
necessary ways of perceiving that world and reacting to it.

Making further use of phrases drawn from Emerson's "The
Comic," we see that through Strether's "perception of disparity, his
eye wandering perpetually from the rule to the crooked, lying,
thieving fact," Strether, by novel's end, can make "the eyes run
over with laughter." Because he is also the idealist, there is more in
his imagination than laughter; still, laughter is the centering of the
"balance-wheel" of his "metaphysical structure," the "essential element" of his bottom being. In turn, his bottom being shares in the
bottom being of the world (both universe and society).

By 1902 yet another Jamesian male, not an American this time,
watches a precious piece of written evidence get chucked into the
grate at the close of *The Wings of the Dove*. Kate Croy "had already
turned to the fire, nearer to which she had moved, and, with a
quick gesture, had jerked the thing into the flame." At her act
Merton Densher "started—but only half—as if to undo her action:
his arrest was as prompt as the latter had been decisive. He only
watched, with her, the paper burn . . ." (xx, 386-387).

Densher is no forthright Newman, that excellent example of the
"masculine" factor. (He is portrayed throughout his novel as too
passive for that.) Nor does this scene from the closing chapter du-
plicate in detail the crisis of the final scene of *The American*. When
Christopher Newman makes his sudden decision to give over wrath

for a resigned acceptance of the way things are, it is he who throws the piece of paper into the fire. In further contrast, the paper in Newman's possession has been originally written by someone who intended after death to call down punishment upon the wicked, and he knows he can use this disclosure to advance his own desire for revenge. In *The Wings of the Dove* what Densher watches Kate destroy is the unread proof of Milly Theale's unvengeful love. Gifts of money from the dead American heiress will be sent to Densher and Kate in lieu of the revenge which this American could have taken upon learning of her love's betrayal by Old World guile and greed.

*The Wings of the Dove* has moved beyond several of the attributes of the literary mode of melodrama attached to *The American*. *The American* tends to poise itself on the single point of cultural differences and moral analogues. Once Newman recognizes he has been duped by the Old World, his methods and those of Europe meet and nearly match. James gets good marks for this. Whereas Newman is restricted to acting like the virtuous avenger in a melodrama, the author's wider "international" perspective gives us more to look at than the self-absorbed view held by Newman that narrowly limits him during those grey days of his death-watch over the Bellegarde *hôtel*. The fact of these two perspectives—the smaller one of Newman contained within the larger one of James—makes the book something more than melodrama, although less than tragedy. Still, the moral resonances remain relatively crude. In comparison, *The Wings of the Dove* takes on a similarly melodramatic plot—the life-of-the-world pitted against the life-of-the-ideal; witty betrayers and beleaguered innocents; vertical impasses and lateral thrusts. But it moves its perspectives well beyond those naively considered human responses that often threaten to invalidate the intellectual integrity of the melodramatic form. By pressing down hard on the terrible frustrations of desire characteristic of the tragedy, the novel takes its plot past any simplified portrait of sacrificed innocence (readily provided by the mode of melodrama with its relatively easy separations of pain and beauty). It comes at last to a strange, strenuous, exaltantly tragic exploration of the meaning in human terms of disinterested love and knowledge.

Jacques Barzun maintains that the only important difference between melodrama and tragedy is a matter of skill. On this score alone *Wings* has arrived at the tragic expression. But there is more involved. We see in this late James novel the essence of the meaning of failure—the hard facts of mortality and morality against which human strategies for success are essentially helpless (a matter which is discussed, brilliantly, in Kenneth Graham's book, *Henry James: The Drama of Fulfillment*). Milly wants to live and to succeed, but she must die. Densher wants "Milly" and he wants "Kate"—two unreconcilable kinds of living and being that make it impossible to choose between the valuable forms of existence represented by each girl. Either one is seen as superior to the other when evaluated according to the terms of her own nature. Each suffers dire hurt at the hands of her opponent. At the end Densher finds he has somehow "killed" them both, just as they, in turn, have irreparably wounded him to the quick and perhaps left him for "dead" at the novel's conclusion.

Novels which bear down single-mindedly upon the life-of-the-world often beguile us into viewing that life either in terms of a happy, self-engrossing hedonism or of a bleakly naturalistic treadmill existence. In the same way, stories which concentrate upon the life-of-the-ideal tend by tradition to coerce us into associating success either with heroes like the Dante-persona or Bunyan's Christian, who are lifted into magnificent visions of Paradise, or with heroines like Pollyanna or Little Eva, who are dropped into fantasies of mindless beneficence. But novels that dramatize the contending lures of both the world and the ideal can be only tragic.

Through the literary imagination we seem to be able to render successfully unto Caesar all that is his, and unto God all that He requires, but only if those antagonistic realms are kept carefully separate. Thomas Becket loved God more than his king, yet he remained on constant call to that king's love; the only end that could resolve his dilemma was a martyr's death, a kind of victory without much appeal to those who wish to stay alive and ordinary—keeping hold on what Scott Fitzgerald called the life of the "sane crook," rather than the "mad saint." Certainly, if we read existence as Herbert Spencer did, we can live well enough by the bread of physical survival, but it seems unlikely that we can, at the same time, sufficiently honor those halos described so commandingly by William James and dramatized with such poignance by his brother Henry.

In *The Wings of the Dove* Densher and Kate begin by coveting the world. To be more precise, it is Kate who wants the world she also represents (wanting its prizes, as well as wishing to be free of its controls), while Densher wants only her. Densher thinks he will find his ideal life in loving Kate, thereby avoiding the snares of the world. Kate believes she can seize what the world calls its ends and use them as the means for getting the ideal life; she tells herself she can have both loving (the ideal) and living (the world). But as events move Densher into the wake of Milly Theale's imagination (a strong tide that pulls him between contradictory longings for safety and for excitement, for death and for life), his loyalties split apart on the rocks. Like so many Jamesian "ambassadors," Densher eventually has to face the guilt of taking the sweet pay of flesh from one regal power (Kate) while doing homage to the opposing force of the remembered spirit of yet another princess (Milly).

Milly dies, free from wrath; she gives the gift of money that would allow Densher and Kate to possess the kingdoms of the earth Milly herself had once surveyed with keen interest from an Alpine ridge. It is this novel's irony, and the sense of tragedy it releases, that Densher cannot obey the *letter* of Milly's gift and take Kate; he is now compelled to exist (against the cry of his flesh) in obedience to the *spirit* of the law Milly has come to represent for him. Densher's position, which locates him betwixt and between choices, is excruciating. The ideal he obeys is splendid, and triumphant, but the cost to him of living in terms of the heart's purity is terrible and requires its own defeat.

Dorothea Krook urges us to see that in *The Golden Bowl* James at last found a way out of the tragic dilemma of the person caught between two equally compelling needs. Krook's view of Maggie Verver makes her conclude that it is possible for a human being to introduce a world-transcending happiness into worldly existence through a special kind of mortal love that goes beyond vindictiveness and self-gain. Maggie herself describes to her father what is taking place within the scope of the novel's *imagination* (though not fully within the span of its *events*). She marks the three stages (a kind of Peter Bembo's ladder) the human lover must take in ascending toward the ideal, while yet remaining fully human:

> "My idea is this, that when you only love a little you're naturally not jealous—or are only jealous also a little, so that it doesn't matter. But when you love in a deeper and intenser way, then you are, in the same proportion jealous; your jealousy has intensity and, no doubt, ferocity. When, however, you love in the most abysmal and unutterable way of all—why then you're beyond everything, and nothing can pull you down." (xxiv, 262)

In dealing with Krook's reading of Maggie's character, it can be conceded that Maggie is indeed shown as experiencing love at first only "a little" and then, later, as "intensity and, no doubt, ferocity." But Krook's confidence in the triumph of human love which she sees manifested in *The Golden Bowl* must surely be qualified by the novel's troubled ending. We simply are not completely certain whether Maggie finally comes to a love that is experienced "in the most abysmal and unutterable way of all." In *The Wings of the Dove* Milly Theale does love according to the third and highest stage. But Milly dies. By dying she avoids having to witness the tormenting effects love like hers has upon the people who must continue to live in the world where so many things "can pull you down."

At least Milly learned, magnificently, how to love, as has Maggie to some extent. Theirs is the power and the glory of the earthly Dove that "goes beyond everything." As for all the others— Densher and Kate, the Prince and Charlotte—what *they* have, together with the touch of the wings of this extravagant love, is the fact of the ominous shadow cast by those same wings.

As for us, the readers, tutored all too well by writers such as Henry James—perhaps we cannot immediately accept love (authentic though it may be) as the ultimate solution to the question of how to gain success. It is as hard to conclude that love is the answer as it is for us to acknowledge that humor and forgiveness are the resolutions we need. If our minds refuse to accept their validity and their efficacy, they have little force to save us. Perhaps, like Hawthorne's Goodman Brown, we are doomed to a lifetime in the forests of suspicion and defeat because we have lost faith in the reality of love, humor, and forgiveness: in success.

Or perhaps we have come to believe inversely that it is precisely our *faith* in impossible goodness and joy that kills us. We have come instead to believe that the idea of failure and regret is the only *fact* we have.

In his essay "On the Essence of Laughter" (included in Jonathan Mayne's edition of *The Painter of Modern Life*), Charles Baudelaire reveals he has more to say of interest to the American imagination than what he gives us in his celebrated remarks concerning Edgar Allan Poe. Baudelaire distinguishes between the world that must laugh because it is fallen and the Edenic world whose possession of joy renders laughter obsolete. Neither Christ nor the angels laugh since "the comic vanishes altogether from the point of view of absolute knowledge and power" (p. 149). Contrast this to the belief Mark Twain holds once he assumes that when we know we no longer laugh—and *what* we know is the full misery of one's fallen state. Baudelaire focuses instead upon the position claimed by *angelic* knowledge. From the vantage point of pure joy, there is no need for the ineffectual laughter of miserable and ignorant mortals.

Laughter to Baudelaire emphasizes the dual nature of mankind, which is both humble in its debasement and pridefully assertive. Laughter also has two potential uses: it announces the demonic woe of men's lives and it acts to redeem that existence. It is not surprising that Baudelaire dwells on the first—the "damnable" and "diabolic" qualities of laughter which make the comic response "one of the numerous pips contained in the symbolic apple" (p. 151). He singles out Maturin's Melmoth as the man who explodes in laughter because of "his rage and his suffering." Melmoth's laughter is "the necessary resultant of his contradictory double nature, which is infinitely great in relation to man, and infinitely vile and base in relation to Truth and Justice" (p. 151).

Baudelaire resists, however, the temptation to linger with the demonic altogether. He moves on to describe the universal progress that affects all men: the original state of childlike purity that has little need for laughter (the wise child—or Huck), the next state experienced by those who "laugh diabolically with the laughter of Melmoth" (the proud but abased man—or Newman), the last stage reached by "a bold leap towards pure poetry" with its rewards of ecstasy and the cessation of laughter (p. 154).

The final angelic state is gained only by means of the evolution of evil. "As humanity uplifts itself, it wins for evil, and for the understanding of evil, a power proportionate to that which it has won for good" (p. 154). That essential interim stage—marked by Melmothian laughter—is where men have the fullest sense of their dualism, whereas the earliest stage is the "vegetable joy" of the child who receives, breathes, contemplates, lives, and grows in almost perfect unity. But that original child is already marred by the ambitions known to "budding Satans"; he will have to pass through Satanic multiplicity before arriving at the Absolute Unity of the joy that never laughs (p. 156).

Huckleberry Finn is in many ways the Wise Child. There are signs that he has already budded into a miniature Satan in terms of his sense of self-abasement, although not as a proud diabolic egotist. By the conclusion of Huck's narrative we do not know whether he will take full possession of the second stage defined by Baudelaire's essay; if not, then he will never have a chance to burst through into the final "saved" stage of humorless joy.

Christopher Newman moves from vegetable joy into Melmothian rage and suffering. By the completion of Newman's narrative
in the 1877 version, he stands on the far side of the intermediate,
satanic stage, still caught up in his dualisms. The 1907 version
seems to indicate a Newman purified past both pain and the comic
impulse—arrived at the threshold of the third stage. But even in
James's two tellings of the Baudelarian progress of the human
condition we do not find all that much difference between the
Newman of 1907 and the man of 1877. Both of James's conclusions
give us the situation described at the end of Baudelaire's essay. The
comic, he writes, is forever opening up into its dual possibilities—
the savage and the innocent. As long as men retain any taint of
laughter, they are susceptible to the process that *may* take them on
the final leap into angelic, inhuman joy, or *may* let them fall even
farther into the humanness of impure and savage laughter.

Mark Twain and Henry James give us narratives that touch upon
the Baudelarian evolutionary triad of innocence, suffering, and
joy. But they lay most of their stress upon the passage from mirth-
less innocence to the mid-stage of comic awareness. Their novels
sketch in possibilities for escape from the dead-end of joyless
laughter when they include remembered movements away from
"Wall Street" or future hopes of going forth into "the Territory."
But just as vividly these narratives express anxiety about *not moving
past* present failure. We are made to feel unease about the fate that
befalls those who—unable to move ahead—are tempted *to fall back*
upon the "vegetable joy" of earlier Edens or anticipated Utopias.
Caught up in the middle of narrative structures, we wonder
whether it is better to stay with what we have rather than to return
to what we had. If we cannot completely escape the walled streets
by "a bold leap" into the future, will we choose to stay with a world
marred by the bad conscience and demonic laughter of Newman-
Agonistes, or will we take the step backward toward Huck's land of
Goshen—the place of silence, sleep, death, of being "very still"?

# The Drive Toward Conclusions

# ▄ CHAPTER 23 ▟

# Working Up
# the Last Effect

Clarence, that "darling" of a boy, has been the right hand of Hank Morgan, the Connecticut Yankee, The Boss of sixth-century England. Clarence possesses two kinds of laughter. One expresses itself in a "happy, thoughtless, boyish fashion"; it lets him enjoy himself "in his lighthearted way" at another's distress, easily able to make "fun of [The Boss's] sorry plight." The other laugh contains a mocking, scoffing tone of "extravagant derision"; it is "the sarcastic laugh he was born with" (pp. 23, 40, 396). Clarence has inverted the Baudelarian sequence, with the "vegetable joy" of the boy developed after his inborn "demonic" response to contemptible, corrupted things. But either laugh makes Clarence an excellent disciple of the leader who himself goes in for both play and attack, boyish funning and sarcasms of adult angers.

But it is now the final chapter of *A Connecticut Yankee in King Arthur's Court*. Clarence is setting down his record of the last moments of the stand made by The Boss and the Boys against the accumulated weight of tradition which their own training in modernity has been unable to offset. The would-be-saviors of civilization are caught fast within the inner ring of successive circles of death, surrounded by rotting corpses piled upon wires murderously charged with electricity; they are looped about by that harpooner's line of cause and effect, chance and necessity, which both Melville and Mark Twain webbed throughout their fiction.

"We were in a trap, you see," Clarence writes—"a trap of our own making. If we stayed where we were, our dead would kill us; if we moved out of our defenses, we should no longer be invincible. We had conquered; in turn we were conquered" (p. 404). There is a brief lapse of time in Clarence's record; then, *"Tomorrow*. It is here. And with it the end" (p. 404).

The end comes with the old hag who soon reveals his true form as the wizard Merlin. Superstition and magic triumph over reason and science. Merlin's laughter overwhelms whatever varied talents for laughing Clarence ever possessed. But if he who laughs last laughs best, he also, quite literally, laughs last:

> Then such a delirium of silly laughter overtook him that he reeled about like a drunken man, and presently fetched up against one of our wires. His mouth is spread open yet; apparently he is still laughing. I suppose the face will retain that petrified laugh until the corpse turns to dust. (pp. 404-405)

The Boss's gaudy mission to transform Camelot out of its stale past into the Hartford, Connecticut, U.S.A., of the future has failed. But so has Merlin's plan to transfix England within an unending, timeless Arthurian legend. Forces beyond the control of either man take over; "ends" which neither could have foretold grind the plots of men into dust. The only person to survive the debacle is the Yankee, left to sleep through the ages "like a stone" (p. 405). He is finally aroused out of his troubled sleep just long enough to work up "his last 'effect'; but he never finished it" (p. 408).

This novel of 1889 leaves these Twainian questions suspended: Will the laughter of the *best* men ever win out, and will the *right* mission to the *good* place ever succeed? Perhaps such queries, stated as they are in moral terms, are either beside the point or downright ridiculous. Nonetheless, we are still urged to ask whether the recurring patterns of victory/defeat = sleep/nightmare = beginnings/conclusions take us eventually to a "last 'effect' " which, for once and for all time, brings about *cessation*.

Death is the only solution to evil, suggests Faulkner's Horace Benbow, one of the many idealists who trail their sad and sensitive way across American writing. Try to be rid of evil, Horace advises, even if it takes dying to provide the needed sanctuary. Mark Twain considers whether death offers the most effective dream-escape. Before birth there is no guilt or anxiety; after birth that is all there is. Death is not merely the punishment for the failure of having lived but the end to failure. Henry Adams confirms that a writer can control his death by setting down his confessions in an autobiography which acts as his suicide; he thereby saves himself the shame of being murdered by the world's account of his failure. Neurosis is the tension, Freud says, that rises between the twin impulses to live and to die; one way to break out of this untenable position is to choose death and get total pleasure.

Depending on whom we overhear, and the particular moment we catch his outpourings, we can be convinced that the greatest human desire is to put an end to all tension—to every occasion for the Woollett sense of strain.

Mailer muses in *The Armies of the Night* about the reasons why so many writers in America die early. He decides that this may stem from their guilt for not having perfected America. Private failure and national debacles come together in Mailer's imagination, as they have in the minds of others since the earliest days of American settlement. Writers of this type look as if they are attempting through a final act of the imagination to destroy not only themselves but America in their regret over having failed the ideal. Their act is a gesture toward the apocalypse that is both the fact of crisis and the end of crisis. Occasionally writers dwell upon apocalyptic events which shape a redeemed and successful world into being by doing away with its present ills and current failures. But with increasing frequency we are shown the imagination at work, smashing things in the wish to annihilate them and us for all time. If the *idea* of America and the *ideas* of Americans have failed to save the world, then America's last and best gift to mankind—or so goes the plunge and drive of this particular argument—may be *to think* an end to all failing.

How easily we "poor crack-brains" take fright, Thoreau said contemptuously in his journal of September 30, 1857. "If there were a precipice at our doors, some would be jumping off to-day for fear that, if they survived, they might jump off to-morrow. . . ." Thoreau could say this since he himself realized that when fear rises within the imagination of the visionary its wealth of terror is as extravagant as any expression of hope.

Prompted by the thought of the failure to rise to the heights, Thoreau recorded a dire vision of men in the mines lost deep below the earth's surface. He calls up a scene inspired by recent accounts of the gold-madness: ". . . I had in my mind's eye, all night, the numerous valleys, with their streams, all cut up with foul pits . . . as close as they can be dug, and partly filled with water." In this vision, included in *Life Without Principle* (p. 465), Thoreau sees men "turned into demons" who dig—"regardless of each other's rights, in their thirst for riches—whole valleys, for thirty miles. . . ." In a land "suddenly honeycombed by the pits of the miners, so that even hundreds are drowned in them—standing in water, and covered with mud and clay," the men "work night and day, dying of exposure and disease."

True to his nature, Thoreau shifts from this nightmarish scene emblematic of his "own unsatisfactory life" to a new idea that perhaps mining—gone about rightly within the human heart, not *out there* in California—is the best way to hope. For "with that vision of the diggings still before me, I asked why *I* might not be washing some gold daily, though it were only the finest particles—why *I* might not sink a shaft down to the gold within me, and work that mine" (pp. 465-466).

During the presentation of this passage, Thoreau has paused for a while, in fear, over a vision of the terrible end of the failed life. Then he has quickened his pace, converting the terms of horror into a sanctified act by shifting their *place*. Once more he demonstrates that he would not have men stay fixed with failure. He does not wish them to leave off doing whatever they are doing in America; he only asks that they do it rightly and in the right location. The search for what does not exist happens to men who go *to* California and *end* in mine-shafts, drowned in the water and mud of their madness. This is their defeat: for the sake of "California" they have left the world that is real and present and filled with *their* possibilities.

The visions of terror that cause alarm to still other American imaginations than Thoreau's are characterized similarly by scenes of darkness, bestiality, blurrings, and blankness. Agitation aroused by images of darkness and beasts comes from the fear of sliding below the level of the human, of returning to chaos and old night unshaped by purpose. Blur and blankness refer to the terrible cost of going back to the unmarked start of things, the fate of having to exist before failure begins. In order to oppose the temptation to withdraw to the time-place where we need neither fail nor succeed, men's minds must provide what Christopher Ricks (in a 1973 article in *The Listener*) assigns to Robert Lowell: "the power unexpectedly to make appalling and the power unexpectedly to make not appalling."

The power of which Ricks speaks deals in *shaping*. To sustain that power, the unshaped must be resisted. But we must also control the temptation *wholly to be shaped*. Recognizing the danger of returning to first effects (that time when our minds were insufficiently exercised), we must also acknowledge the Twainian enticements of "the last 'effect' " in which the idea and the plot is all too complete.

Mark Twain's particular obsessions with despair and Henry David Thoreau's peculiar visions of hope in no way dictate the nature of the inevitable future of America or of the rest of the world.

Ends and their means can arise out of imaginations constructed along quite different lines from those of the Missouri skeptic or the Concord seer.

When survival rests upon the *"adjustment of inner to outer relations,"* as Herbert Spencer believed to be the case, the state of the organism becomes the criterion for success or failure. In his essay about Spencer, William James stated that such a situation restricts existence to "the most narrowly teleological of organisms; reacting, so far as [the organism] reacts at all, only for self-preservation." Narrowness was repugnant to James. It meant giving up rich and risky varieties of human experience in order to play it safe. It placed the same emphasis upon bodily welfare which had prompted Thoreau to see men as passing away "like vermin": to live like an organism, to die like a louse. Yet, as Robert Lowell reminds us in his sonnet from *Notebook*, "Elizabeth Schwarzkopf in New York" (perhaps with a doubling-up of irony), the edge cuts both ways. By compromising with the environment and adjusting to it on its terms, even though

> We pass up grace, our entrance free and tithe
> for dwelling in the heavenly Jerusalem—

this is

> small price for salience, and the world is here.

William James was not given to references to transcendence or grace, but his own brand of qualified idealism asserted that men's souls were something to be attended to. If the soul was lost in exchange for physical survival of the organism, what really matters might be forfeited: this was the argument central to his 1879 essay attacking Spencer's "definition of mind." Himself an agnostic, James realized that "to a Christian, or even to any believer in the simple creed . . . the deepest meaning of the world is moral." To such believers "the *failures* to 'adjust' " to "the outward actual" constitute the greatest victory even though it sends them to "the rubbish-heap, according to Spencer. . . ." Such types as the Christian reverse Lowell's stance. For them the passing up of salience and the world of here is "small price" to pay for the greater gain of grace.

William James took the middle way: between Christ and Lowell. He wondered if men might retain the world, the flesh, and the halo by their adjustment to ideals contained within a real world. He resisted both the bodily adjustment that leads one nowhere near meaning and the mind's failure to adjust that could force end-all, be-all conclusions. James (and Thoreau for that matter) would be happier with the notion of survival provided by Howard Gruber in his study, *Darwin on Man*: "... in the most general sense *survival depends on the organism remaking itself* ..." (p. 54). This is adjustment by *moving on* and *becoming new*. This is what James, and Thoreau, take as a solution that saves and does not doom.

Compare the Darwinian view of movement, adjustment, and renewal with the moon's madness as defined by the Newtonian. The moon is wild to respond to the earth's attractive force; it rushes toward the earth, but because it moves too fast it constantly misses its goal. The moon makes no adjustment in its behavior; again and again it hurtles toward and falls past the longed-for earth; its frustration is complete. The actions of the moon are somewhat comic, and also pathetic, even if it is a good thing for *us* that the moon fails so reliably. But James and Thoreau preferred not to act out of a systematic madness of desire which is unable to adjust itself away from the monotonous repetition of compulsion, pain, and distraught lunacy.

Physiologically and psychologically, anything less than complete adjustment brings pain to the organism. Accordingly, there are those whose highest aim is to adjust totally through the denial of pain, as opposed to those who gash their palms in order that the hurt will keep them alert to living. One of the uses of literature is to provide us with instances of persons who do perverse acts because they refuse to adjust themselves into nothingness. Consciousness survives by movements toward adaptation which never quite arrive at self-sufficiency. Literature helps describe what it is like to choose to live in the gap between "arrival" and "not arriving"—in that gap which is failure. Victory, rather. It is as Emerson implied. Art lasts as long as there is non-adjustment, as long as there is something to say about keeping awake, feeling pain, and going on.

There is a divergence in purpose here between the artist and the believer in spiritual worlds. Both fight for the right, and need, to feel one's lack of adjustment to this world. The believer does it for the sake of future bliss—which, by definition lies beyond life and is different from it. The artist hopes for an eternity of life as it is— which requires a continuation of the conditions that simultaneously make art possible and ask for its aid.

The psychologist B. F. Skinner stresses the selfishness of the individualist who does not gain strength "in reflecting upon any contribution which will survive him." As he puts it in *Beyond Freedom and Dignity* (p. 210), the man of total self-absorption "has refused to be concerned for the survival of his culture. . . . In the defense of his own freedom and dignity he has denied the contributions of the past and must therefore relinquish all claim upon the future." We can see that, in contrast, the artist and the believer alike resist callousness in caring about the future. The believer does this in order that he may, one day, possess intact a realm of endless joy. The artist does it to have a place in which he can always create. Well and good, since private satisfactions are gained at no expense to the world at large. But when the believer is an impatient millennialist and when the angered artist decides to concentrate his imaginative efforts upon destroying worlds, not nurturing them, we are in trouble.

Take the artist, for example. Much has been written about how powerless he is to create the good life for us all. Ironically, he seems to discover his capacity for force once he turns to demolishing bad societies. If the artist ever believes that human existence might be reduced to barren breathing in a Skinner box; if he finally comes to see the act of living as a mere attempt to survive; if his wrath mounts against uncontrollable forces hostile to human values: then he may actively image debacle as his final act of regret and revenge against a universe that shows "no consideration" to the human messiness of life and art.

The way past this dangerous situation is for the artist to struggle against both passive resignation and destructive flailings; to struggle *with* the world, not against the grain; *to struggle as the world struggles*, in resistance to and yet in league with forces which are natural and extra-human. Then the artist would be like William James— welcoming his immersion in the world because "it *feels* like a real fight." In this way his very human effort to "redeem" a universe of the "really wild" could become a form of "adjustment" taken on his own terms. Most important, he would *like* the world as an enemy which is also a friend.

It was in his essay "Is Life Worth Living?" of 1896 that William James characterized the context of the "real fight" and the kind of adjustment he favored. "For such a half-wild, half-saved universe our nature is adapted." Significantly he then turns to words descriptive of the *center* of human force—where it lies, what it is like. It is the fact of this center which converts the abyss-language of the wrathful and the despairing into words capable of portraying the salutary obstacle-course of the moral athleticism James most prized.

In the passage that follows from the same essay (excerpted in *The James Family*, p. 230) we read James's version of Thoreau's gold-mine vision:

> The deepest thing in our nature is this *Binnenleben* . . . this dumb region of the heart in which we dwell alone with our willingness and unwillingness, our faiths and fears. As through the cracks and crannies of caverns those waters exude from the earth's bosom which then form the fountain-heads of springs, so in these crepuscular depths of personality the sources of all our outer deeds and decisions take their rise.

Out of the underground caverns of James's Xanadu rises the adaptive heart-force needed to resist the adjustment that annihilates. "For here possibilities, not finished facts, are the realities with which we have actively to deal. . . ."

Men need risk, sin, tragedy, the possibility to be more. But frequently the universe acts as a conservative economist against such untidy and expensive values by permitting only the most generalized survival of the undifferentiated physical organism. In spite of this selective and leveling action, and out of spite, the incensed artist might want to work up an extravagant, gaudy, personalized "last 'effect' " even if it takes place solely within the theatre of his mind. According to William James, such "effects" can work for the greater halo-values of mankind if they serve to continue the struggle, not to end it, but too often continuation is hardly their intent.

Indians and darkness provided the aesthetic elements of contrast Thoreau required to stave off the blandness of a society complacently adjusted to itself. At the same time that he was peering into the woods and forests of Massachusetts and Maine, young Darwin in the Galapagos was noting what lack of competitiveness did to the birds and sea-creatures surviving sluggishly in that isolated region. Darwin also observed those which survived not at all when outside predators with a well-trained and aggressive intelligence penetrated the closed circle of perfect adjustment. As naturalists, Thoreau and Darwin made their observations for dissimilar purposes; the former wished the measurement of spirit and of values, and the latter the measurement of organism and of facts. But once Thoreau decided we cannot credit survival marked by the absence of struggle, and Darwin concluded we will not survive if we do not struggle, they converged at this important point: those who refuse to adjust fall to the predatory, while too complete an adjustment is its own kind of annihilation. From this it follows that since experience is pluralistic in its demands, we must be flexible if we are to last well and long enough. A richly varied natural harmony between man and environment is the *good* adjustment.

On January 4, 1857 Thoreau extolled those moments when he, the stones, and the river felt happiness in common. But even if the human body and spirit could achieve rapport with their natural envelope, this happy state would not fully satisfy the kind of artist who demands more than the bliss of earthly wholeness. When on December 16, 1850 Thoreau notes that his feet touched brute matter at the same moment he lifted his hands into the air, we see two possible responses at work. There is Thoreau the millennialist who hopes to *connect* earth and sky along the length of his body so finely that the dualities of earth and body might vanish into the oneness of sky and spirit; his pleasure comes from contentment over the completed union. And there is Thoreau the artist who insists that his position between ground and heaven confirms the *separation* of the powers of matter and of spirit; his pleasure arises from the painful impossibility of being both totally himself and totally what he is not. This artist chooses to deal endlessly with the dualities that crack open the millennialist's expectations of an eternal truce. He would stave off ending by keeping to a struggle with the complexity we've got; he would deny the millennial catastrophes that lead to the annihilation of the world as it is in the name of something too perfectly one.

To be a dualist and a realist is a guarantee against the blandishments of catastrophe, but there is as much to fear from certain kinds of yea-sayers as from the doom-sayers. The party of hope can pose a threat to life's continuation as ominous as any posed by the party of despair. The realist may be just as much an enemy of the people as the idealist. It all depends. What it depends upon will be the thread of our considerations in the pages ahead.

# ◣ CHAPTER 24 ◥
# History—as Facts
# and as Faith

Apocalypse is defined in two general senses by Meyer Abrams: sudden revelations that renew or violent upheavals that destroy. When Abrams is working in *Natural Supernaturalism* with the term as it spoke to the need of the English and Continental Romantics to revitalize decadent societies, he stresses the first of those meanings: the Biblical-historical panorama of weary, corrupt worlds which are joltingly, joyously replaced by visions of worlds freshly reborn. Those acts of the mind in America which attempt to split open the future, freeing history from its own limitations, have been informed by an urgency as great as that felt by the English and the Europeans and have resulted in similar visions. But usually the details and the emotional shadings have been characteristically American.

The writing of history has a great deal to do with assessments of success and failure. Involved in making such judgments is the author's decision to read the historical process either as God's narrative, as a man-made tale, or as nature's bagatelle. Depending upon his choice, he will select images of hope or catastrophe and draw upon the language of quasi-historical doctrines or quasi-scientific hypotheses. The man of historical bent also decides whether the process he records depicts an endless movement backward—a return in upon itself—or a projection forward in restless experimentation. He considers whether the tale he tells and the movement it takes ever halt before some kind of total conclusion, or whether they perpetuate particular, temporary terminations in order to make new beginnings.

For example, William James—whose philosophy was strongly marked by historical concerns—believed he spoke for many of his generation when he separated empiricists from scholastics according to "the way we face." In "The Will to Believe" (excerpted in *The James Family*, p. 388) James said that the scholastic dwells on "the principles, the origin, the *terminus a quo* of his thought; for us [the empiricists] the strength is in the outcome, the upshot, the *terminus*

*ad quem*. Not where it comes from but where it leads to is to decide."
In turn, that "upshot" can be looked at either as The Termination
or The Beginning. James's objections notwithstanding, "scholastic"
stress on beginnings cannot be entirely overlooked, especially in an
America where "missions"—*the idea that starts things going*—continue
to have power to effect both expectations of hope and deep chagrin
over failure. In the pluralistic American mind there abide ideas of
good beginnings and successful ends; of good starts that peter out;
of jerky openings and increasing strengths; and of failure experienced first, last, and always. For each such idea there is a theory of
history by whose method America's destiny is read.

Like her one-time teacher, William James, Gertrude Stein was
not a professional historian. But, like James, Stein claimed the right
to pronounce upon anything she turned her attention to. She knew
perfectly well, for example, that there is no real change in history.
"Slow history" she called it—history by means of accumulation. As
Harold Rosenberg pointed out, Stein shows in her writings on
Picasso that she did not associate change with evolution. She believed that one epoch simply replaces another, the later time killing
off the former time. Her brother Leo formed his collection of
paintings around the concept of the flow of developing ideas; Gertrude attested to the accumulation of separate entities that are always beginning and ending. An acorn in evolution yields Leo a
tree; an accumulation of splinters gives Gertrude many pieces of
wood. Leo's view implies ordered movements toward an end—the
perfect Tree lying behind all the trial-and-error trees; Gertrude's
stress is on things happening in no particular order and being directed to no particular conclusion. Yet history read as Gertrudian
happenings is far more open to the possibility of apocalyptic *impulses* and catastrophic terminations than history when read as an
essentially conservative evolution, a continuation that has no *reason*
to end.

Gertrude Stein's view of the leaps and bounds of history-making
was a happy one when practiced in an era of strong optimism and
self-confidence. Theodore Parker's 1848 essay "The Political Destination of America and Signs of the Times" speaks forth from
such a period (at least as many of his contemporaries liked to see it).
In his essay he characterized the American literature that emerges
from "our national intensity, our hope and fresh intuitive perceptions of truth." He made distinctions between "our permanent literature, [which] as a general thing, is superficial, tame and weak; it
is not American," and the ideas drawn from the "real national liter-

ature" that is found "almost wholly in speeches, pamphlets, and newspapers . . ." (p. 159). For Parker it was, above all, oratory that was

> pretty thoroughly American, a little turgid, hot, sometimes brilliant, hopeful, intuitive, abounding in half truths, full of great ideas; often inconsequent; sometimes coarse; patriotic, vain, self-confident, rash, strong, and youngmanish. (p. 160)

Henry Adams' jittery sense of the epochs following the Civil War differed in mood from the self-confidence Parker witnessed just before the war; but however anxiously Adams' historical sensibility responds to the situation, it still reflects an America imagination absorbed in ideas and attitudes that are thin on continuities, quick in tempo, and ever on the jump. The dates encountered in American history books do not indicate the kind of steady B.C. to A.D. movement of a purposeful narrative. To believers in epochal explosions, the end of something old and the abrupt and jarring creation of something new do not necessarily coincide with points as neatly rounded off as 1900 or 1950. To Norman Mailer in *Of a Fire on the Moon* the close of the summer of 1969 feels like finality. The moon-shot of Apollo 11 is acknowledged by the ceremonial burial of a Ford automobile, symbolically murdered in rites more than a little self-conscious. Mailer's sense of how things happen in America is reminiscent of Mark Twain's. Twain loved riverboats, but he also adored the railroad train; he had had to accept the murder of the former mistress at the insistence of the new amour. So railroads come and riverboats go. So The Great God Ford dies in 1969 while headlines declaim Long Live Apollo! If there is a kind of continuity of sovereign powers implied by such proceedings, it comes about by assassinations and palace-revolutions, not by the serene passing of the father's power into the hands of dutiful sons. You leap from Mark Twain's boats onto his trains over the tearing gap of the Civil War with its wrenching effects on transportation, economics, and social patterns; you get from the Ford to the Apollo by psychic costs almost as great.

History viewed as the act of leaping calls up images of chasms and divides with few or no bridges. If Poe is the star of the running jump over or into abysses, Henry Adams is the professional historian of the event. Adams' theory of successive phases of contraction, divided by periods of explosions, his acceptance of Clarence King's glacial theories, his insistence that science reveals that there are more gaps than links between the stages of monkey and man, his alert interest in his generation's many statements concerning epochs and catastrophes—all these elements make Adams an excellent late nineteenth-century American spokesman for apocalypse and final conclusions. But even more to the point of this entire book is his belief that *thought* is both what history sets itself to record and the material out of which history happens.

After Adams (as with Gertrude Stein) and before him (as with the Transcendentalists), it has been argued that there is a life beyond thought which thought cannot destroy. But to Adams in the essay of 1909, "The Rule of Phase Applied to History," "thought is a historical substance, analogous to an electric current, which has obeyed the laws—whatever they are,—of Phase. . . ." Call that phase Fetish or Mechanical or Electrical or Ethereal, it is ever the fact of force, and that force is an idea which both responds to historical process and directs it.

Adams' apocalyptic imagination supplied what is lacking in Gertrude Stein's subsequent notion of happenings that have no obligation to end in catastrophe and no obligations *not* to. What he added was a theory which immediately suggests an obligation to go in one particular direction—a theory of degradation by which a seemingly random accumulation of jumps, leaps, stumbles, and mistakes ultimately leads to the chill of equilibrium. According to Adams' vision of the end, we are not to be annihilated by a crescendo of noise; more likely we will be ground to bits by the silence that follows the ice-slide. Whereas the Transcendentalists urged leaps of faith marked by renewed energy and new births, Adams the degradationist indicated the very real possibility of leaps of despair. All this would be accompanied by painful contractions of the earth's surface and the solar system, leading to the labor of multiple stillbirths.

Adams believed both world and society gave signs of running down and leveling off. His imagination provided a series of appropriate images for the event: a *river* (democracy) that rushes downwards to the *ocean*, where it spreads out in stagnant equilibrium (socialism); a *ship* (sometimes Europe, sometimes Russia) that pulls the surrounding flotsam (always America) down into the still, deadly eye of the vortex; a weak *chemical solution*, whose surface can only tremble in exhaustion. These particular images all find their source in the waters of death, not the springs of life. His mind conjures up a Walden Pond that is no longer either pure in winter or capable of being revitalized by the sun in springtime.

Henry Adams' history of the world takes America and himself as its main exempla of failure; it tells of the triumph of the mediocre, who meekly inherit the fatigued earth, and the victory of the *vis inertiae*, which resists change. The buoyantly "happy mediocrity" extolled by Franklin and Crèvecœur has taken a sly twist in American affairs; it has turned out to be no more than the apathetic cessation of feelings, hopes, and endeavor. Other aspects of Adams' vision provide their own buoyancy and creative energy, but while Adams dwells on the dangers of equilibrium his moroseness is complete and his sense of defeat is final.

With its own images of water turned stiff through coldness and stagnation, Lévi-Strauss's portrait of society brought to the stage of chill crystalization by men freed from the pressure to progress is a later version of Adams' degradation theory (one to which Adams himself came fairly late). Once, Columbus could stumble into America via serendipity because the world was not flat; soon, through entropy, America and the world will be flattened out past possibilities for surprise. No more discoveries can be made, and men risk falling off the final outer edges of the world-map in fulfillment of the fear of ancient mariners. Once, the physio-theological poets of the eighteenth century said that the Fall from Paradise introduced variety into the world—fluctuations of weather and season characterizing the changeful environment in which human history took place. In contrast, Henry Adams' vision for the future suggests a return to total uniformity of temperature. From pole to pole it will not, however, be the pleasing sameness of Edenic balminess; it will be the unrelieved cold of the Old Night that preceded Paradise. The single society which antedated the confusion of languages and races after Babel will also be regained, but such equalitarianism will be no more than the monotony of socialist collectivism—a single, straight thread going nowhere, one which fate can easily cut with her scissors.

According to Henry Adams, the world, society, and the self seem likely to die of sterility if they follow the laws of equilibrium that falls in upon itself. The same will happen if Mark Twain's prediction of unrelieved repetition takes place. Flat levels must be buoyed into new heights of variety and energy, and the vicious circle broken. The only possible solution to stasis, Mark Twain implies, is for the imagination to get to work with catastrophe. To dynamite a glacier that has slid across the one road leading out of the mountains may set us free; it could also pull the landscape down around our ears in an avalanche. Those who are fearful of direct and drastic attempts to manipulate universe or society plead for gradual, possibly redemptive changes; they prefer to hold a match to the glacier, trusting that the ice will, eventually, melt. But those possessed of the instinct of dynamiters, for good or for ill, take to larger measures.

Mark Twain makes it clear enough where he stands in *A Connecticut Yankee*:

> There were two "Reigns of Terror," if we would but remember it and consider it; the one wrought murder in hot passion, the other in heartless cold blood; the one lasted mere months, the other had lasted a thousand years; the one inflicted death upon ten thousand persons, the other upon a hundred millions; but our shudders are all for the "horrors" of the minor Terror, the momentary Terror, so to speak; whereas, what is the horror of swift death by the ax, compared with lifelong death from hunger, cold, insult, cruelty, and heartbreak? What is swift death by lightning compared with death by slow fire at the stake? (p. 103)

Swift history or slow: either can bring death. For some the only choice beyond thoughts that passively record the happenings of history lies between those that shape it in hot passion or in cold blood.

Henry James wrote in *The American Scene* that that mind is endangered which insists upon comparing the actuality of America as it now is with earlier hopes for the nation's high quality of existence. "That way . . . madness may be said to lie—the way of imagining what might have been and putting it all together in the light of what so helplessly is" (p. 101). This was Henry James writing in 1907. Tocqueville had recognized by 1835 that Americans are less prone to suicide than to madness. Madmen with the imagination of disaster have not held down the whole field. Even as a noticeable shift toward pessimism enters the American mind, there are others—madmen, too, in their way—who speak out of the imagination of success.

The point to follow here is James's: that imagination which cannot accept what America is is dangerous, whether it dwells on failure or on success. The moods may be opposite, but the ends can be the same—destructive.

Let us look briefly at those who have been elated or depressed

well in excess of the immediate facts because of their responses to
the idea that America obeys a two-fold destiny—one dictated by
natural laws and by social mandate.

In 1797 *The Kentucky Gazette* printed an anonymous poem that
rhymed (and mis-rhymed) the following guarantee:

> Our soil so rich, our clime so pure,
> Sweet asylum for rich and poor—
> Poor, did I say!—recall the word,
> Here plenty spreads her gen'rous board;
> But poverty must stay behind,
> No asylum with us she'll find—
> Avaunt, fell fiend! we know thee not,
> Thy mem'ry must forever rot;
> Dame Nature, by a kind behest,
> Forbade you ever here to rest.

Even then cynics could point out that these lines appeared on the
first day of April. By October of 1819 John Keats was inspired (although with little poetic brilliance) to address a poem to Fanny
Brawne. In it is a passage that dwells on the dire fate suffered by his
brother and sister-in-law, then living in America:

> . . . that most hateful land,
> Dungeoner of my friends, that wicked strand
> Where they were wreck'd and live a wrecked life;
> That monstrous region, whose dull rivers pour,
> Ever from their sordid urns unto the shore,
> Unown'd of any weedy-hair'd gods;
> Whose winds, all zephyrless, hold scourging rods,
> Iced in the great lakes, to afflict mankind;
> Whose rank-grown forests, frosted, black, and blind,
> Would fright a Dryad; whose harsh herbag'd meads
> Make lean and lank the starv'd ox while he feeds;
> There bad flowers have no scent, birds no sweet song,
> And great unerring Nature once seems wrong.

In *Life on the Mississippi* of 1883 Mark Twain twitted geologists
who try to foretell the future when they cannot even depict the
look of the past. Have poets—whether Anon. or Keats—a surer
sense than scientists of the meaning of America's past and its
tendencies for the future? Thoreau, poet and naturalist, knew
America had a *natural destiny*. He knew, or so he said, not just by
poetic intuition but through scientific observation as well. To his

excited imagination America is nature, but even more so. Thoreau would take as particularly appropriate to the New World transformed from the dead snakeskin of the Old World the remark made by Werner von Braun (and used by Thomas Pynchon to lead off *Gravity's Rainbow*): "Nature does not know extinction; all it knows is transformation."

On March 20, 1853 Thoreau confidently stated in his journal that England is "dead." Caught in the past with little hope for renewal, England is even incapable of marking contrasts between the passing seasons in the way New England does. It is bad enough there are all those great parks lorded over by despotic kings and arrogant gentry (an idea Thoreau elaborated during his 1846 trip into the Maine woods). It is even worse that England is *always green*—a fact as distasteful to Thoreau as the vision of a world monotonously coated by ice was to Henry Adams or the sight of the Galapagos Islands covered by ashes to Melville. America might have no dryads or weedy-haired gods, but to Thoreau his country offered infinite pagan variety and the yearly resurrection to life promised by the *differences* in the landscape.

Sharing the same years of American history as Thoreau, but worlds apart in her evaluation of America's destiny, Frances Trollope set down sharp comments of the Keatsian kind. She saw Americans seizing power from both king and nature and ruining the land for purposes of commercial gain. Thoreau was hardly insensitive to the possibility of this doom, which Mrs. Trollope said was already fast upon America. In the 1853 "Chesuncook" section of *The Maine Woods* (p. 155) he noted how avid the newspapers were for "improvements." What populated Massachusetts is now, he observed, wilderness Maine will become. The liberty-poles in New England were already stripped fruitless and leafless. Men might at last be reduced to gnawing the earth in a land axed flat by tree-hating farmers (pp. 153-154). By 1857, during his third excursion into Maine, Thoreau was wondering if the natural destiny of America might not be perverted into a future of paved cities where only vermin survive and where the Indian is considered the "poorest hunter" (p. 197).

Thoreau's three forays into Maine between 1846 and 1857, and his comparisons of the "newer" land to the north with the "older" settlements of Massachusetts, demonstrate clearly his increasing fear over what America might, in bad faith, become. In 1843 when Thoreau attacked J. A. Etzler's Utopian tract, *The Paradise Within the Reach of All Men, without labor, by powers of nature and machinery*, he attested to the irony that he himself believed in "the fundamental truths" Etzler put forth. Etzler said the wind, tides, and sun were a great source of beneficent power. Thoreau agreed, but in his review of Etzler's book entitled "Paradise (To Be) Regained" he said he abhorred the attempt to commandeer natural power through mechanical means. If men try to force nature's eternal destiny into "progressive" avenues, much would be lost and America might forgo its special mission *to be everyone's*.

Nature will not be hurried into doing what it intends to bring about throughout its own "slow history." To Mark Twain the Mississippi acts as his paradigm for America's natural destiny since it can take years for its currents to heave masses of earth into the shore-shapes by which river pilots learn to read their way. To Thoreau the Concord and Merrimack Rivers also offer the river-man clues concerning the gradual but irrevocable changes, historical and spiritual, through which America has already passed—from native Indian trails, to the sites of early colonial villages, to Lowell factories ranged along the republican banksides. Rivers and men differ in the rates of their movement, and it is wrong for the latter to alter the course of nature in the name of human history, rather than allowing that history and the natural scene to move side by side—each fulfilling, not betraying, the meaning of the other.

In *The American Scene* the Hudson (which is *his* river) tells Henry James lovely things about a past hidden by the mists that rise at dawn along its shores. But once he leaves the Eastern river valleys and goes westward, the railroad invalidates the way the natural landscape suggests the vitality of a good past and a good future. Not the plains but the railroad serves as the spokesman for America's future. In James's imagination the train's cars leap contemptuously over the Mississippi like rats traversing a deep ditch that was intended to hold them back. The boast of the train is "See what I'm making of all this . . ." (p. 463). This is precisely what James feels he sees: the making of the doom of vagueness for an America that has lost whatever clear sense of natural destiny it once had along the Hudson's shores.

Thoreau wished that nature's factualness and man's imagination might work in harmony; only this mutuality would insure that America attains the noble shape commensurate with its destiny. Henry James believed that smug, jeering machines were usurping nature's power and corrupting man's spirit. Conversely to both Thoreau and James, Henry Adams viewed nature as a force stronger than man and antagonistic to human ideas; universal geography would prevail in the future, causing the collapse of civilizations. Nature eyed by Henry Adams was defined as a mechanical cosmic force, not as the soul of Walden Pond and the reflection of the human spirit. Adamsian nature would act upon America as Henry James said the mechanical force of the railroads would act upon the land, and the effects would be devastating.

In "The Rotation Method"—one of the arguments contained in Kierkegaard's 1843 study *Either/Or*—the Dane said that nature has fortunately forgotten it was once chaos; if she ever remembers that fact, mankind will be endangered in nature's attempt to fulfill her destiny through a leap of return back into her shapeless past. In Henry Adams' imagination nature is moving relentlessly forward and downward toward a future whose shape will be all too symmetrical. His is not a Kierkegaardian nightmare of unshaped chaos, but a bad dream of absolute order. If the Kierkegaardian fate would be *too natural*, man's fate imaged by Adams would *not be natural* in any sense that men can live with.

Nature was still natural in the early part of the nineteenth century. The idea of its likeness to man's better qualities helped many Americans to hope that by its example the nation could still fulfill its proper purpose. In *The House of the Seven Gables* Hawthorne's Holgrave represented the fervent young reformers of the time in the confidence with which he speaks of the goodness of the natural world whose example society will one day emulate:

> "After all, what a good world we live in! How good and beautiful! How young it is, too, with nothing really rotten or age-worn in it! . . . Could I keep the feeling that now possesses me, the garden would every day be virgin soil, with the earth's first freshness in the flavor of its beans and squashes; and the house!—it would be like a bower in Eden, blossoming with the earliest roses that God ever made. Moonlight, and the sentiment in man's heart responsive to it, are the greatest of renovators and reformers. And all other reform and renovation, I suppose, will prove to be no better than moonshine!" (p. 214)

Thoreau (like Hawthorne himself) possessed a more intricate imagination than Holgrave's (and was less given to exclamation marks). But he had his own Holgravian hopes stimulated by walks in moonlight and star-shine. He also wondered whether the ideal America was not already with us, within us at the threshold of the yet unfolded imagination. Since men are ignorant of what they are and have, perhaps the good place already exists. Undiscovered as yet, it lies just beyond the mind's eye, not in the years ahead (like the future America detailed in J. A. Etzler's tract) or over an ocean (like William Dean Howells' Altruria). "It is easier," Thoreau wrote in *A Week on the Concord and Merrimack Rivers*

> to discover another such a new world as Columbus did, than to go within one fold of this which we appear to know so well; the land is lost sight of, the compass varies, and mankind mutinies; and still history accumulates like rubbish before the portals of nature. But there is only necessary a moment's sanity and sound senses, to teach us that there is a nature behind the ordinary, in which we have only some vague preëmption right and western reserve as yet. We live on the outskirts of that region. (p. 409)

According to Thoreau, Americans live in a state of loss, though it is our spiritual destiny to gain. If value lies ready and waiting just under the surface of the Walden Pond of our consciousness, we need only to cast the double fishing-hooks that connect us to water and to sky, to the America of earthly facts and to transcendent ideas. This is Thoreau's version of the "natural" mission of Americans: to move from exile on the outskirts of nature in toward the saving center of our true home.

We sit on the outskirts of success in the "frail bark" of the world of our social and political life. Good fishing may be possible if one keeps to Thoreau's concentration on the course of nature and soul, but it is difficult to think of angling with accuracy from a leaking ship of state. Even Emerson found it hard at times to keep himself in the right mood. In his journal of 1838 Emerson recorded that he acted at times as agent of "a vixen petulance," at times as "the organ of the Holy Ghost" (vii, 9). It is characteristic of Emerson's insistence upon hope that he always has *some time* to act out of love, not hate. As William Burroughs views the situation in *Naked Lunch*, however, there never was, never is, and never will be *the right time* for that. America was "old and dirty and evil before the settlers, before the Indians. The evil is there waiting. And always cops . . ." (p. 11).

In Burroughs' imagination the Europeans piling into America merely perpetuated the already present cannibalistic culture. No corruption of innocence took place; there never was innocence. Burroughs' use of "always" concerning America's vixen petulance also blocks the chance for change. How different is Emerson, who saw to it that lacks are offset by the gains that enter through the crack of "sometimes"—all that the Holy Ghost, in whichever its forms, has ever required to intervene in human affairs.

Traditionally the Emersonian view has had more currency in America than Burroughs' belief—at least until recently, when Americans have taken a fancy to being insulted in excess of the need. But as a general rule Americans have given themselves over to an almost maniac hopefulness of the kind typified by the sign that once hung over the entrance of the old Indianapolis bus station—itself a grey coagulation of bums, perverts, pick-pockets, and plain-folk anxiously on the move; where "always cops" stood elbow to elbow to guard the stairs down to the restrooms—a sign that stated emphatically, "Through these doors pass the finest people on earth!"

Americans have tried hard to remain cheerful about their social destiny, even while watching the natural destiny being cut out from under them. Crèvecœur's early optimism about the pastoral promise of the land was kept alive as long as possible, as was the Revolutionaries' reasoned hope for a good society for true men. Well into the nineteenth century George Bancroft the historian argued that America's destiny was in God's hands and that evil could be counted on to defeat itself. Later on Mark Twain would write (with both choler and playfulness) in a fragment of the early 1900's (included in *Fables of Man*, p. 395) that "it was impossible to save the Great Republic. She was rotten to the heart." But the public consensus, almost against reason, kept to the idea of hope. Upon the death of Henry Adams a friend remarked without irony that Adams rested in peace under the protection of the Republic. In 1918 not that many people shared Adams' notion that it was a perishing republic under whose shadow he, the brave skeptic, lay. More typical of the time was the sounding of trumpets, the singing of "America the Beautiful," and the collective recitation of the Lord's Prayer when the year 1900 descended in glory.

Mark Twain exemplifies the small band of late nineteenth-century scoffers who realized that the facts did not jibe with the faith. One day in Virgina City during the Civil War he witnessed an event in which both hope and hesitation were aroused by the ambiguity of the look of things. As he describes the scene in *Roughing It*, the sun's rays rippled dramatically over the top of the mountain, centering a "little tongue of rich golden flame" around the Union flag flying in the town (VIII, 145). "It was the nation's emblem transfigured by the departing rays of a sun that was entirely palled from view; and on no other object did the glory fall." The citizens were ecstatic. "The superstition grew apace that this was a mystic courier come with great news from the war—*the poetry of the idea excusing and commending it . . .*" [italics mine] (VIII, 146).

What the crowd gathered in the streets did not know was that Vicksburg had fallen that day and the Union Army had also won at Gettysburg. Mark Twain laments there was no immediate confirmation of the people's hopes by means of facts communicated from the East. No one in Virginia City could be certain that the glory of nature and the glory of the nation were one and the same truth. If the people had had proof to substantiate the *look* of the sun and the flag, and if they had not felt restrained from acting out their joy for fear of being duped by an illusion, they would have seized the occasion and had a gaudy celebration of the kind that they (and Mark Twain) most delighted in. As Mark Twain remarks at the end of this anecdote, "Even at this distant day I cannot think of this needlessly marred supreme opportunity without regret. What a time we might have had!" (VIII, 147).

Yes, if only the American people could always get word of those facts which confirm as present truth their hopes for the national destiny, then all would be well. But either the hopes or the facts are askew in their timing; they fail to meet in the nick—with sun's rays touching the flag at the precise moment of the knowledge of victory.

In his Harvard Commemoration Speech of July 21, 1865, in "The Fortune of the Republic" of 1878, and through pronouncements in the essay "War," Emerson expressed his desire that the terrible facts of the Civil War might lead to a better society happy in its obedience to eternal law and life. But *we* know what we got. In the time just before the war's end—an end which brought severely into question all hopes for a united society based on mutual respect—Henry James was experiencing for the first time what "an American at least *was.*" Sensitive as he was to the temporal and moral distinctions implied by his constant refrain, "And there we are!" he recorded in *Notes of a Son and Brother* (p. 316) the irony that just when once we start to comprehend the good of "our national *theory* of absorption, assimilation, and conversion," that theory "appallingly breaks down" under the weight of the *facts* [italics mine].

In 1904 Henry James witnessed another such instance at Harvard, recording it in *The American Scene* (p. 259). The trustees of the university were busy furthering an extensive building program based on their awareness that in earlier years America had contained people of value who lacked the proper educational facilities for formal study. But James found the campus being crammed with expensive equipment and buildings which were having to wait for people of value to appear.

When in 1709—not yet a full century after the first settlements in the English colonies—Ebenezer Cook wrote, ". . . all Things were in such Confusion,/I thought the World at its Conclusion," we get the uncanny sense of a sacrament of baptism taking place simultaneously with a ceremony of burial. And when in our own time Saul Bellow's Augie March reports that at those moments when things are great, men are not, we ask, Will the seams never match? Can fact and hope, the fulfillment and the need, never meet at the same point and at the proper moment? Or do we have to concede to William Burroughs his dogma that "The evil is there waiting" and to Mark Twain his pronouncement, "She was rotten to the heart"? It is as if the only time that conjunctions are possible is when the beginnings of hope and the ends of despair crush together, with no space allowed for men to enjoy a good middle.

The American who retains, however faintly, the memory of the assurance that his social destiny was to have been a profound and beneficent one somehow bound up with the natural landscape—an assurance which most facts of history and personal experience seem to repudiate—is an American who feels very much out of place. He is a lost man who cannot forget that he had once been promised a splendid home and a superlative life.

Upon revisiting the American scene in 1904, Henry James said he knew what it felt like to be one of the minority groups. His America—the America of his memories—had been made totally "other" and alien to him by the great influx of new races and unfamiliar cultural habits. In his sonnet "Romanoffs" from *Notebook*, Robert Lowell suggests that White Russians and white Americans alike are in exile in a time-being perpetually "after the revolution"—a time in which "Blacks and Reds survive" and whites, by implication, fail.

James, Lowell—and Adams too—were staunch Wasps, but they were hardly as embittered over their sense of being pushed out of place as were the Nativists of the 1920s, who lamented the loss of America to a mudslide of non-Anglo-Saxon immigrants. "Americans" of the type of Adams, James, and Lowell feel their "outsidedness" in ways more complex than the mindless, vicious emotional responses limiting the Nativists. James's remarks running throughout *The American Scene* note the effects of a major cultural shift; they attempt to distinguish between those people like himself who once believed they *had already arrived* (thus *had* something even if it is just now over and done with) and those who are *always just arriving* (*not yet having* something, but with open possibilities for the future). The personal sadness James expresses in these passages from *The American Scene* also conveys his sense of what this means for his country's future. In place of promise and fulfillment in active conjunction for everyone, there will be an America divided between the haves and have-nots: those who believe they can yet come to their destined meaning, and those who have lost the ability to go through the necessary process of arriving and arrival.

Mailer finds the split James noted still active in the lives of the Wasps he views in *The Armies of the Night*, compounded by the dual responses of quiet sadness and violent rage. But frustration is hardly the exclusive property of White Anglo-Saxon Protestants. The manchild ironically displaced within the promised land lives in Harlem as well. His bitterness over the gap between fact and promises confirms the revelations of America's evil made by William Burroughs; it denies as obscene the gospel of America's goodness asserted by Ralph Waldo Emerson. Yet the American tradition contains *both* these prophecies, not just the one or the other. Which voice and whose idea we choose exclusively to listen to remains the question—and one which involves the danger of the madness that cannot accept the fact of another's faith or the denial of its own desires.

In the 1830's Tocqueville visits the brand new republic in order to learn what lessons of hope or fear it offers the rest of the world. As he moves through the forests of the supposedly raw nation, he pauses before crumbled cabins and fallen chimneys to declare, "What! Ruins so soon!" Norman Mailer considers writing a novel set in Provincetown about the beginning and the end of America. America started at that Provincetown rock in the 1620's, he says in *Of a Fire on the Moon*. It ends there, too, he sometimes feels.

Why should this be so? As Henry Adams remarked in a letter of April 28, 1894 to Charles Gaskell (included in the Ford edition), we want to know why the world at large is going to smash "without visible cause or possible advantage." We also need to be told why a country "so soon" as America must go so fast. Not surprisingly, Mailer has an opinion. In "The Third Presidential Paper" he decides the fault lies in the fact that the politics of America betrays its myths. This is the same betrayal dramatized in the savage satire by Nathanael West, *A Cool Million*. In that novel Lem Pitkin's death proves that the Alger myth of success won through virtue and good luck collides with political expediency and the cynical manipulation of events. In *Wonder-Working Providence of Sion's Savior* of 1628 Captain Edward Johnson had celebrated the approach of the New Heaven and the New Earth through the successful manifestation in time of the goodness of Providence and the virtue of the Puritans, but ever since, the Pitkinesque naïveté of this promise has been undermined.

America's sense of itself has moved from *idea* to *doctrine* to *myth* to *theory* (social, economic, political), drifting down the slope to a success so qualified that purists such as Emerson with his *there is success or there is not* could only call it a disaster. Yet idealism remains an American trait that will not be completely dislodged or denied.

In a piece for *The New York Review of Books* of February 10, 1972 Philip Rahv remarked that Henry James's snobbery was a form of idealism because it expressed his desire for a perfect society. Rahv argued that whether such snobbery (typical of all "reformers") is bad depends upon the quality of imagination and quantity of facts that accompanies it. If snobbery equals a zero and that zero equals an ideal, then the final value of the zero must be judged in terms of the numbers that come before it. Thus 999,990, rather than 10.

To pick up Rahv's suggestions, let us say, for example, that snobbery has worth when it points out the danger to American society of having as its highest aim living "for pleasure, pleasure always, pleasure alone" (an observation James made in *A Small Boy and Others*, p. 46). American histories and prophecies are also aided by such snobbery. Evaluations of the past (read as zeroes that trail off into the worthlessness of hopes without fulfillment) and anticipations of the future (envisioned as zeroes firmed to meaning by the addition of the facts) are snobberies in the act of judging the value of other snobberies, of deciding whether the country has betrayed the bright possibilities of that original zero—that perfect circle of the ideal—by turning it into the *O* of meaninglessness.

Thoreau asked on June 16, 1854, What if the people of Concord suddenly realized their village was located in Hell? Would they have as murderous ideas toward the State as he? For god-lovers are the greatest of snobs (since their zero is the ultimate value), and potentially the most wrathful. Henry Adams' friend Charles Nordhoff commented in 1883 that if the poor ever came to disbelieve in heaven they would sack Fifth Avenue. But often it is the Lord Himself whom the poor expect to serve their desires as the Holy Hun who brings affliction to the decadent city of tyrants.

James Baldwin has dramatized the kind of dénoument America can expect through the fulfillment of the words of the slave hymn, "God gave Noah the rainbow sign/No more water, the fire next time." Underdogs in any society have limited social and political means to express the refinements of their rage. Those who believe God is on their side in the battle of snobbery against the crudities of wickedness have ways to reach beyond their immediate powerlessness. By calling upon God's strength, the downtrodden elect envision catastrophes in terms more expensive than those available to the vulgar rank and file of the socially prominent. Depending on the nature of the God they think they have at their disposal, betrayed idealists project conclusions in images of power unalloyed by tenderness, though they could insist upon Last Days accompanied by love as well as energy. Because of our habit of finding paradigms for desire through the image we make of God, the basic question requires asking: "What nature of Deity have we?" Until we know this, we can hardly know what to make of the American coinage which proclaims "In God we trust"—since we do not yet fully recognize the manner of our own desiring.

The Marquis de Sade, French aristocrat, said that nature sanctions violence, not love. Norman Mailer, as a somewhat less blasphemous American prol, believes that God places His faith in courage, not charity. Caught between diverse views of the *kind* of power we may have to deal with, little wonder there are doubts whether Americans ought to follow through on instincts of love. "Love and trust in Christ," Mailer announces to the press as he leaves the Virginia jailhouse after the march on the Pentagon. His words make headline copy since they come, oddly enough, from a Jew and must, therefore, be some sort of Semitic joke. The press, indifferent to the crucial question, is incapable of defining love. But how is Mailer, who cares, to distinguish between love and the Devil's art? This is a particularly difficult problem for him since he cannot even be certain that his God rates loving very highly. Mailer's imagination must take into account that perhaps it would be best to destroy everything at once—God and Devil, nature and man—in the name of both love and hate. In that way Mailer could at least be certain of putting a clean, complete end to an endlessly botched beginning.

Saul Bellow, sometime-idealist, resists the dilemma provoked by

Mailer's idealism, which entertains destruction as a god-given possibility. Bellow is against men wearing the "livery service of St. John's horsemen." His *Herzog* denounces the *"canned sauerkraut of Spengler's 'Prussian Socialism,' the common places of the Wasteland outlook, the cheap mental stimulants of Alienation, the cant and rant of pipsqueaks about Inauthenticity and Forlornness. I can't accept this foolish dreariness. We are talking about the whole life of mankind"* (pp. 74-75).

Bellow (himself a splendid snob) further insists on hoping that sublime *thought* will outlast the worst *fact* by remaining in the possession of all men. He does not want power to go to the special few—snobs without good numbers—who expect to escape the final catastrophe that their own snobbery initiates.

Even Henry Adams, prime degradationist, frustrated idealist, and practicing elitist, suggests the possibility of hope through the agency of the same act of *thinking* that could bring about the chill stagnation of the end. However much Adams' words in "A Letter to American Teachers of History" are thicketed about by qualifications, he states his confidence in confidence:

> Granting that the intended effect of intellectual education is,—as Bacon, Descartes, and Kant began by insisting,—a habit of doubt, it is only in a very secondary sense a habit of timidity or despair. To a certain point, the more education, the more hesitation; but *beyond that point*, confidence should begin [italics mine].

The End can always be brought about by thought's wrath or mind's despair when its idea of the ideal has been betrayed. The stark possibility of the fact of this power requires that we ask about the kinds of numbers we place in front of the zero of the American ideal. We must do this in order to keep confidence going on "beyond that point" of doubt in America's value. So, anyway, urge those Americans who are fondest of success.

# CHAPTER 25

# Timing, Tact,
# and Long Views

The dawn-scenes contained within *The Hamlet* and *Walden* bring the wonder of the coming of Aurora to the idiot Ike Snopes and to Henry David Thoreau. Faulkner's dawn is a brief interlude in a narrative that soon yields to the sorrows that lie "beyond noon." Thoreau's dawn closes down his book, but even that closure is sprung open by the insistence that the joy he obliges us to feel is ours still to win in the future.

We must go past the dawn, Thoreau wrote in *A Week on the Concord and Merrimack Rivers*, else we remain there like those charming childlike poets of the morning—the Greeks and Chaucer. Go beyond noon-time as well, Thoreau argued; noon is where the philosophy of India has fixed itself. Move on toward night in order to make a new turn toward dawn since, "without doubt," night veils the creation which the next new day comes to reveal.

The dawn that marks the structural end of *Walden* is the actual beginning of the imaginative force which the entire book has tried to celebrate. The final sentences do not sound a repetition of the dawns of the previous days witnessed at Walden Pond. This is a dawn that is wholly new, the promised movement toward the discovery of a self never before known. If Robert Lowell writes of "the uncreating dawn" in the first of his sonnets from *Notebook* on "Sleep," Thoreau hymns the dawn that begins all things anew in the imagined time that lies *beyond* the final paragraph. But it is necessary to examine this contention more closely. First, because it is often argued that *Walden* is more a poem of "closure" than of "openings." Second, because an understanding of the ways in which dawn-themes may act to keep things going provides a needed contrast to the practices of the apocalyptic conclusion.

It helps to see whether Thoreau's pond serves in *Walden* to represent the impulses Emerson recorded in his journal of 1836. There Emerson urges himself to go inward in order to discover the *is* that existed before the world *was*. Emerson suggests a return that

rediscovers "Unity universal" by means of the loss of "my individuality in the waves" (v, 177). In his view wordless and timeless
selves imply absorption into the primal unity, that loss of self which
is apocalypse in a special sense because it brings to an end the bad
way things are and introduces the way things have ever been meant
to become. If *Walden* focuses its grand finale upon the pond's relation to the center of existence within the soul—if it concludes with
the image of the self's return to itself by means of immersion in the
eye/I of the inner pond—then we would indeed be witness to the
death of that self as the cost of celebrating the pond's eternal purity. We would have the end of the perception of mystery. Only
mystery (the pond) would remain; the agent of exploration and
discovery (the self) would no longer exist. The self would not be in
separation from all things that are *other*; through a final leap—not
into the chaos and madness of the Subjective—it would join the
unity and truth of the Objective.

Thoreau's approach is different from that of Emerson. The
pond in *Walden* does not draw the narrative down into its depths.
At the book's conclusion the pond is removed from the foreground
so dawn-images may take over. The pond is mentioned there only
that Thoreau's language may depict a contest between iced-surface
and sun's heat—yet more epic and more sublime than that of the
battle of the ants he recorded earlier. The sun tugs at the ice's total
adjustment and still perfection; it forces the beauty of the ice's crys-
talline symmetry toward the excitement of thaw and the challenge
of impurities.

Throughout the latter third of *Walden*, Thoreau has made several entranced pauses before the image of frozen purity. He finally
moves past them to acknowledge that (for *this* conclusion and *this*
book, at least) he rejects the pond as the final image with which to
leave us. Without this rejection we would have been given the victory of pure spirit in an eternity fixed with the chill of death. What
Thoreau does give us is sun, change, growth, and the impurities of
a dawn-world. It was a difficult choice for him of all men to make,
what with his revulsions from impurity and decay. But once chosen, dawn—not pond—graces the last pages of *Walden* with the
urgency of beginnings, not the complacency of terminations.

By giving us a review of nature's four rhythmic responses to the
ebb and pull of life, Thoreau is of course asserting that through
cyclical repetition we gain hope that the world will continue to live
even if we as individuals do not. But what if he had not selected the

hot July Day of Independence to come to Walden to experiment with life? We can see the consequences if we rearrange the narrative sequence of seasons in ways *Walden* refuses to do. If we take spring as our beginning, we circle the year and end with the closing down of the pure ice over the surface of the winter pond. If we begin, as Thoreau does not, with the delights of early morning, we sweep through the day until we come to the dead of night. What a difference it makes that Thoreau had it be otherwise! If his structural circle is the serpent that swallows its tail, that tail's tip which marks faith in commencement must be spring and dawn.

Whatever manipulations Thoreau made in the book's sequence of time, he could not guarantee that he had protected us from fixity and completion. The particulars of men's lives are not analogous to the symmetry of natural cycles, any more than to the perfect beauty of a series of mathematical progressions. Viewed as metaphors, nature and mathematics are protected from ever ending; they also go nowhere new, but only repeat rhythms once begun. Even dawn-visions like the one that ends *Walden* the book and that initiates the larger meaning of "Walden" need to break through repetitions. They must offer the possibilities of a future *better than* acquired perfection and achieved knowledge—better than, because preferring incompletion and wonder. As Thoreau suggested in his journal of June 7, 1851 the near-past is common sense and facts because it proves our limits. In contrast, the future is transcendence and faith because we do not yet know what the possibilities are for victory or defeat.

The American imagination has usually defined its epistemological mission in two ways: as the possession of perfection and the attainment of all knowledge, or as unending movements past perfection and the unfolding of further areas of things still to know. The former vision, marked by the great beauty of contentment and containment, is a vision of death as surely as those centered around holocaust and terror; the latter vision, that knows its own terrible beauty, includes the chance of life because it resists the temptations of serenity and omniscience. The former is mindless since the self loses contact with the material that creates thought; the latter vision depends upon ideas that forever birth ideas of wonder out of the world's matter. The former vision is one characteristic of Poe; the latter vision is that of William James.

In a letter of April 18, 1897 (included in Perry's study), James gives testimony to his pluralism by using language and idea in ways similar—at least in the matter of dawns—to that of Thoreau. He is heartened that there are "no grand climacteric results of being," "no finale, no one lesson to be learned. Everything happens in the middle of eternity. All days are judgment-days and creation-morns . . ." (p. 211).

Emerson had a clearer sense than William James that there is, indeed, one lesson that can be learned: it is what our fate is. But he displayed the wisdom of careful students of fairy-tales when he wrote to Carlyle on April 19, 1853. In that letter (included in Slater's collection, p. 485) Emerson observed that, although we crave to know the special secret of our fate, we ought not insist on being told. If that wish were ever granted, "the Sphinx & we are done for; and Sphinx, Oedipus, & world, ought, by good rights, to roll down the steep into the sea."

Emerson was able not only to step aside from the Poe-esque madness of Ligeia's husband with his desire to break the code of her eyes; he was also ready to say when craving is unnecessary madness. In *Nature*, and again in "Natural History of the Intellect," he asked why we seek wonder in far places or remote times when each age is wondrous and fresh as the dawn. By asking this, he presents a telling argument for the imagination of continuation. What we *know* is *verspertina cognitio*, Emerson writes. It is that remembered knowledge of the evening of the previous day. What we *might learn*—the wonder always with us—is *matutina cognitio*, the mystery of the morning that lies ahead (v, 94).

It is visions of morning we need, not dreams. Thoreau wrote on December 23, 1851 that our best visions come when we are awake. Healthy and authentic, they are unlike the stagnant dreams of our moods and humors. For Thoreau, American dreams ought to be exchanged for visions. Dreams at best are about serenity and the sterile success of complete adjustment; they kill us off inch by inch, whereas visions disturb, coerce, and propel us onward. Dreams come out of Goshen; visions arise from the inspired merger of Woollett and Paris. The people who populate the worlds of Crèvecœur, Poe, Mark Twain, and Fitzgerald are dreamers; the worlds of Thoreau, Emerson, and the Jameses take visionaries as their true heroes and heroines. Mailer, happy at his work, swings in between and Gertrude Stein seems to do nicely without either. But if the vision is more capable of dealing with existence as a continuing fact, the dream-stance in American literature gives itself over to dire endings in the name of rage, tears, and exhausted hopes; or, in ways just as insidious, ends in peaceable kingdoms where the lion, the lamb, and the child are sunk in the deep trance of the dead-to-the-world.

"Death is the mother of beauty," writes Wallace Stevens as he watches his musing lady strip down oranges on a Sunday morning. But a certain kind of beauty is also the father of death. What attracts our tastes can kill us, Thoreau warns in his journal of September 26, 1859; to eat the lovely berries hanging from certain bushes would poison us. We must be satisfied at times with merely seeing; we ought not always desire to consume what appears to us in its perfection. The natural beauty of berries, or of the newly invented machines celebrated by the artist Horatio Greenough in the 1850's, or of the symmetrical idea-structures proposed by social, political, or economic theorists should be approached with caution. All such perfection can lead to the mental impasse that, in turn, yields to the urge to destroy current systems in the name of the perfections that lie beyond.

In John Updike's novel *The Poorhouse Fair*, Conner in his puritanical atheism disdains the spiritual beliefs of Mendelssohn, his messy, drunken predecessor at the old people's home which he manages. Conner dreams a future of circles and spheres. It will be known by the absence of old age, ugliness, disease, and pain; "above all no *waste*" (p. 107). When Mrs. Mortis is informed that this pristine world will not permit her imperfect presence, the old woman says spryly, "well, then, to hell with it" (p. 108). But the Mortis-Mendelssohn position constantly has to struggle valiantly against being placed under the domination of the Conner-type.

In "The Happiness of a People," a sermon of 1676, William Hubbard stated:

> It was Order that gave Beauty to this goodly fabrick of the world, which before was but a confused Chaos, without form and void. . . . For Order is as the soul of the Universe, the life and health of things natural, the beauty and strength of things Artificial.

Hubbard tells his people that, according to the Schools, order is "Such a disposition of things in themselves equall and unequall, as gives to every one their due and proper place." He is pleased to note that seventeenth-century naturalists agree with this position. They tell us that beauty in the body arises from an exact symmetry or proportions of contrary humors, equally mixed one with another: so doth an orderly and artificial distribution of diverse materials make an comely Building, while homogeneous bodyes (as the depths of waters in the Sea, and heaps of sand on the Shore) run into confused heaps, as bodyes uncapable to maintain an order in themselves.

American dreamers often come in shapes—smooth and symmetrical—admired by Hubbard and Conner. Its visionaries are eccentrics like Thoreau (of the lop-sided jaw), who want us to give honor to the asymmetries of the slightly askew imagination. And when Emerson describes the phenomenal as matter that slips and slides under our feet, he calls on us to do balancing acts on the high-wires of the noumenal that require just as much agility of spirit. Both dreamers and visionaries may value perfection; but, according to whether the former or the latter type is at work, perfection takes on different shapes and goes through different motions. This is not to overlook the moments of anxiety Emerson and Thoreau had over asymmetry and their hours of devotion to dreams of unity, but as visionaries they are far more accommodating to the irregularities found in the structures of reality than is generally acknowledged.

That America is less than perfect is the impetus for much of the writing done about the place. Dreams of straight, broad, open roads to perfection contend with visions of pilgrims whose feet are tangled in the underbrush of the present facts. The remark made by J.R.R. Tolkien, "All's well that ends better," is a workable motto for more than dwellers of Middle Earth. It is meant for any writer who, shunning endings that settle for too little, is also wary of fulsome phrases such as "All's well that ends best."

In Howells' romance of 1894, *A Traveler from Altruria*, the visitor to America keeps repeating that most annoying of questions, "Why not?" when his hosts try to justify the country's social ills by saying there is no chance for change in human nature. The Altrurian insists upon the possibility of, and the moral necessity for, alterations in the American character. But his own nation's noble experiment—highly successful and already brought to full completion—is predicated on the cessation of the need for pushing on. The central paradoxes at the core of Howells' tale—part of which the author seems to recognize, part of which he may not have questioned directly—are these: Americans perpetuate social evils through their unflagging desire to rise; only when they come to accept a stable level of economic and social sufficiency will they do away with the enslaving greed that thwarts a free evolution into moral fitness. Altruria is the perfected society; its upward movements are completed. It is not just a dream for the future; it already exists out there as a vision for America to emulate. Only an ocean's voyage from America, it is the true land of our last chance. But that chance has already been taken by the Altrurians. Change and the possibility for change have come to a halt on the plateau of perfection. Altruria is not America as it now is: a place caught up in bad realities and false dreams. Nor is Altruria now what the Old World imagination once dreamed America of being: a faraway land which, once discovered, would furnish new ground for a better society *yet to be created*. Instead, America is what Altruria once was before it corrected itself to become what America never was and is not and never will be.

What we are given *in* Howells' telling, then, is a country that has completely fulfilled a perfect theory about itself. Unfortunately, it is Altruria's success which gives Howells a dead book. The only imaginative contrasts offered the reader are between the sterile alternatives of Altrurian "best" and America's "worst." For all its ideas about betterment, the narrative lacks insistence upon that *better* joy, wonder, and discovery which the most vital visions contain—and which rarely appear in tales restricted to the *best* of happy endings. The sense of *better* is missing from the book; all we are given is *best*, one of the unwisest gifts a story can offer.

Sorrow lets ideas spring forth; in turn, ideas, transforming sorrow, can release joy. Meyer Abrams sees this sequence as the consistent pattern in the Wordsworthian autobiography of crisis, since it places the greatest value for the imagination in a future *better*. If aesthetic problems commence whenever the writer has to deal with ideas that point toward final contentment, the writer's obstacles seem insurmountable when he chooses ideas that *begin* with peace. Ideas originating with stasis can go no farther than themselves; from their inception they have reached the limits of self-satisfaction and sufficiency. Whitman's *Democratic Vistas* is likened by Howard Mumford Jones to *Götterdammerung* with a happy conclusion. If so, it passes the test of true joy only as long as enough evidence remains in the essay of the pain out of which it was wrung, and if it offers to the imagination, through its awareness of the unperfected human condition, the chance to bring yet more joy into being.

On December 17, 1837 Thoreau wrote in his journal that during the final stage of civilization poetry, religion, and philosophy would merge into a perfect whole. If this remark arises from one of his purification moods, the transcendent gain in knowledge and unity he anticipates might presage the end of human civilization. But if Thoreau intends that the triumph of poetry, religion, and philosophy will impress upon the human imagination a sense of wonder, questioning, and joy, then there is no threat of an ending in the sense of climax. Thoreau would be saying in effect, "All's well that ends better," promising yet another dawn toward which to move.

Read the following quotations that deal with victories of "I am" and "we will," taken from the final paragraphs, respectively, of *The Clansman* and *Soul On Ice*. The first quotation, from Thomas Dixon's novel, dates from 1905; the second, from Eldridge Cleaver's book, comes out of 1968:

"Success, not failure," he answered firmly. "The Grand Dragons of six states have already wired victory. Look at our lights on the mountains! They are ablaze—range on range our signals gleam until the Fiery Cross is lost among the stars!"

"What does it mean?" she whispered.

"That I am a successful revolutionist—that Civilization has been saved, and the South redeemed from shame."

Black woman, without asking how, just say that we survived our forced march and travail through the Valley of Slavery, Suffering, and Death—there, that Valley there beneath us was hidden by that drifting mist. Ah, what sights and sounds and pain lie beneath that mist! And we had thought that our hard climb out of that cruel valley led to some cool, green and peaceful, sunlit place—but it's all jungle here, a wild and savage wilderness that's overrun with ruins.

But put on your crown, my Queen, and we will build a New City on these ruins.

The details of the apocalypses illustrated by these passages are socially antagonistic, but imaginatively similar. Their ends are to be brought about by different stage-effects, but both give us the gothic elements of night-fears, lurid flames, tottering structures, and ruins in the landscape. The final paragraphs are alike in being handed over to an image of a man and a woman, hand in hand, as survivors of a grand crisis. Like characters in *like stories*, they look out over worlds they have helped to reshape and in which they must yet live out some kind of reformed existence.

Narratives of this type are mini-apocalypses in which the virtuous outlast the general social devastation. In this sense they are only partial tales of terror and technically not "endings" at all. But because these survivors feel no less righteous in their perfect virtue than did Hank Morgan just before his end, these closing paragraphs leave the reader with the chill of actual conclusions rather than the warmth of dawn-beginnings.

Daydreams of victorious virtue are based on the imagination's seizure of present satisfaction from a past time of tears and rage. By an arbitrary act, inadequate substitutions are made for earlier inadequacies. The happy endings supplied a patient by the French psychologist Pierre Janet which William James describes in "The Hidden Self" provide a closer look at what is going on in the fictions of both Dixon and Cleaver.

Janet's patient Marie suffered various physical disabilities as the result of hysteria which had its source in terror-filled hallucinations based on childhood memories. Janet treated her by pressing her to go back over old dreams, which he then proceeded to give "a different dénoument." The past was relived but Marie was given "an entirely different result." She "substituted a comical issue for the old tragical one which had made so deep an impression." As a consequence, she was relieved of her ailments. Growing "quite stout," she was aided in her cure by the fact that the "sub-conscious Marie, passive and docile as usual, adopted these new versions of the old tale. . . ." On first response, it would be natural to applaud the success of providing substitutes for terror, of giving a good new ending for bad old beginnings. But there is something unsettling in this account. The happy endings were *given to* Marie. She accepts them in her docility, having taken no part in their creation. Marie herself seems not to be radically *transformed*; she is merely relieved of old burdens while remaining essentially the same person.

The gift of happy endings imposed upon apocalyptic narratives is soberly accepted by Dixon and Cleaver. They take literally the ironies underlined by the staging of the conclusion of Kurt Weill's and Bertolt Brecht's The Three-Penny Opera. In the original off-Broadway production the messenger from the Queen rides his hobbyhorse up the theatre aisle just in time to bring news of Macheath's reprieve from the gallows. The lovers stand hand in hand before the curtains, whose closing brings tidy settlement to a chaotic evening of unresolved social ills and human betrayals. The gifts of pardon and success parodied by The Three-Penny Opera, and accepted as dream-truth by Dixon and Cleaver, have not sprung from any act of grace, divine or secular. These gifts are handed out by a second-rate god-author—that human being who likes to manipulate scripts about the future, even though he lacks the supreme authority of imagination to bring about effective terminations or true beginnings.

There are times when we are grateful that our writers are so inept. It is better not to have a true emperor or god commandeering the right to decide the conclusions to human affairs. Perhaps hacks are needed to give us absurd pardons and mercifully impossible endings in order that things may continue to bumble along. Real and effectual power might be too ready to heed the Latin adage which commands, "Let justice be done and let the world perish."

Thoreau was contemptuous of reformers who said the world is moving promptly toward its proper final solution. To him "Presto change!" sounded like the trick of a cheap magician. Such reformers, he wrote in *A Week on the Concord and Merrimack Rivers*, are "living on anticipation."

> The derveeshes in the deserts of Bokhara and the reformers in Marlboro' Chapel sing the same song. "There's a good time coming, boys," but, asked one of the audience, in good faith, "Can you fix the date?" Said I, "Will you help it along?" (pp. 131-132)

Throughout much of the nineteenth century the artist was expected to help preserve the society and to assuage fears concerning the possible anarchy of his motives. He was supposed to "help it along," not undermine the "good time coming." In July of 1849 William Alfred Jones wrote a review of Melville's *Mardi* for *The United States Magazine and Democratic Review*. In it Jones made the unsettling observation that "With all his humanity, Mr. Melville seems to lack the absolute faith that God had a purpose in creating the world." In this passage (cited in Perry Miller's *The Raven and the Whale*, pp. 249-250) Jones then asked rhetorically, "Wherefore these baptisms by fire, if they purify us not?" And then, "For what was this MAN and this EARTH created? Will God save, or destroy his Earth-Son, and the world that he has given for his abode?"

Jones was deeply disturbed by the thought that God's universe might be shattered by any cataclysm, and however much he acted as public witness to Melville's great talent as a writer, he could not fully accept Melville's willingness to think that the world might be concluded permanently. Men in nervous watch over the strange doings of poets and scientists often find more than they can bear—especially when the world is encouraged to cease by an American compatriot, a writer meant by God to speak out for Him, for nation, and for humanity.

Melville's reviewer was troubled that the mind of the artist seemed to find no meaning as to why we live or die because of his hunch that perhaps God has never had any point to make. There were, of course, poets and scientists who resisted Melvillean notions of futility, men who in their own way furthered the imagination of continuity to which William Alfred Jones clung. For example, by the end of the nineteenth century William James had no Christian doctrine he was obliged to support, but with only his general faith in the purposefulness of human existence, he rejected Arthur James Balfour's statement that

> The energies of our system will decay, the glory of the sun will be dimmed, and the earth, tideless and inert, will no longer tolerate the race which has for a moment disturbed its solitude. Man will go down into the pit, and all thoughts will perish. The uneasy consciousness which in this obscure corner has for a brief space broken the contented silence of the universe, will be at rest.

After James cited Balfour's words in his essay of 1898, "Philosophical Conceptions and Practical Results," he proceeded to make his counter-argument. He spoke for those imaginations which insist on knowing the point of a final disaster. He proposed to head off the irresponsibility of purposelessness with the belief in a God (or god) possessed of a strong sense of the aesthetic rightness of going on. "When a play is once over," James wrote, "and the curtain down, you really make it no better by claiming an illustrious genius for its author, just as you make it no worse by calling him a common hack." James then called upon references to Dante and Wordsworth, men "who live on the conviction of . . . an order" promised by a God who defines art's action as a conserving force. Together with Dante and Wordsworth, he decided at the least to trust in the value of "the old ideals"—ideas about value and purpose and *going on*:

> A world with a God in it to say the last word, may indeed burn up or freeze, but we then think of Him as still mindful of the old ideals and sure to bring them elsewhere to fruition; so that,

where He is, tragedy is only provisional and partial, and ship-wreck and dissolution not the absolutely final things.

We may be sure that William Alfred Jones in 1849 would have been happier with this aspect of James's essay than with compara-ble elements in Melville's *Mardi*. He certainly would have wished to apply its promise that "shipwreck and dissolution [are] not the ab-solutely final things" to his reading of *Moby-Dick* in 1851.

William James wrote his brother on April 13, 1868 that Henry's work as a writer might strike some readers as "impudence" since he gave them "a story which is no story at all." In this letter (in-cluded by Perry, p. 104), William was, however, still able to praise Henry for projecting "a mysterious fulness," detectable story-plot or not. To do this was "a rather *gentlemanly* thing," and also a sensi-ble one. Henry's writing had thereby "a deep justification in nature, for we know the beginning and end of nothing" (p. 104).

In his own essay of 1910, "Is There a Life After Death?" Henry James said he liked to think of God as a gentleman. It seems as if both God and Henry James are gentlemen in these respects: both resist giving final conclusions; both are loyal to the idea of ideas; both deal with "a mysterious fulness"; both keep up human exist-ence and offer qualifications to tragedy through "tributes to the ideal."

Henry Adams also had his Jamesian moments in which he in-sisted on a world that—with or without a practical gentleman-artist as its motivating force—might support men's own stubborn insist-ence on keeping hold. As Adams wrote to Elizabeth Cameron on April 12, 1913 (in a letter included in Ford, II, 403), if the world decided to break up he would simply start afresh on his own.

Sometimes Adams was provoked by the way others insisted on living beyond the catastrophes the world may intend as final, but he kept finding his own motives for going on, however tragic the consequences. Mark Twain recognized that farce (even more than melodrama) has a bang-up, fast-paced ending, while the tragedy is a world without the benefit of apocalypse—an existence in which suffering and the exactions of patience are endless. He came in time to prefer the profits of the farce, while Adams and the Jameses chose the tragic mode with its costs.

Thoreau had a certain respect for patience, but not the kind re-quired for the endurance of unending woe. He asked rather for the ability to wait for the inevitable unfolding that reveals perfection. Advocate of neither farce nor tragedy, he defined the world-without-end as comedy—a divine one because it was staged by the consummate Dramatist whose purpose from the start was to provide the healing reconciliations and high joy characteristic of the achieved comic mode.

We cannot judge any man, Thoreau wrote on October 14, 1851, until we see the direction his particular sequence of metamorphosis is taking him toward. (Many a play we walk out on before the end of the third act might be building up to a glorious fifth act finale if only we would wait to watch it.) The weakness of too many men was the tendency to question destiny and to imagine death. In happy contrast, Thoreau noted on October 31, 1857 that the skunk cabbage thinks only of living:

> If you are afflicted with melancholy at this season go to the swamp and see the brave spears of skunk cabbage buds already advanced toward a new year. Their gravestones are not bespoken yet. . . . Is it the winter of their discontent? Do they seem to have lain down to die, despairing of skunk-cabbagedom? "Up and at 'em," "Give it to 'em," "Excelsior," "Put it through,"—these are their mottoes.

In this, Thoreau's skunk cabbage is like Robert Lowell's skunk in "Skunk-Hour" from *Life Studies*. Neither will scare, while men scare all too easily.

Compare Holden Caulfield's anxious concern in *The Catcher in the Rye* about whether ducks can survive the winter on the frozen pond in Central Park with the remarks made by Thoreau in *A Week on the Concord and Merrimack Rivers* when he reports on

> ducks by the hundred, all uneasy in the surf, in the raw wind, just ready to rise, and now going off with a clatter and a whistling like riggers straight for Labrador, flying against the stiff gale with reefed wings . . . gulls wheeling overhead, muskrats swimming for dear life, wet and cold, with no fire to warm them by that you know of . . . and countless mice and moles and winged titmice along the sunny windy shore; cranberries tossed on the waves and heaving up on the beach, their little reed skiffs beating about among the alders;—such healthy natural tumult as proves the last day is not yet at hand. (pp. 5-6)

"That ancient universe," Thoreau declares further on, is in such capital health, I think undoubtedly it will never die. . . .

I see, smell, taste, hear, feel, that everlasting Something to which we are allied, at once our maker, our abode, our destiny, our very Selves; the one historic truth. . . . I have seen how the foundations of the world are laid, and I have not the least doubt that it will stand a good while. (pp. 181-182)

Thoreau's philosophical beliefs enabled him to possess the confidence granted to spectators of the universal commedia; but it is the *imagination* of hope, not the *philosophy* of hope, he stresses. This imagination does not hover at a distance, over and above his intellectual theories; it underlies and envelops them and is *what* they are. For Thoreau to imagine well is to live with the health of good thoughts by day, not with the fever of night-fears—not with "life without principle." The imagination of hope is to live "not always as dyspeptics, to tell our bad dreams, but sometimes as *eu*peptics, to congratulate each other on the ever-glorious morning." It is to live with the challenging thrust of the concluding remark of *Life Without Principle*: "I do not make an exorbitant demand, surely" (p. 482).

Imaginations similar to Thoreau's maintain that it does not even matter if our life is not actually real as long as it is healthy. Human existence may be "this dream disturbing the sleep of the cosm," as Oliver Wendell Holmes, Junior, phrased it in a letter to William James on April 19, 1868 (included in Perry, p. 92). However, Holmes added, this life "is not the result of a dyspepsy, but is well. . . ." Robinson Jeffers took this notion and pushed it to its extreme by hoping for the annihilation of human consciousness so that the universe might dream well, undisturbed by *us*. Yet others have been anxious over what it is like *to be a dream*. For Mark Twain, that would be a terrible fate; for Holmes, it was good enough. But as Emerson stated in *Nature*, whether or not the world exists outside "the apocalypse of the mind," it is all the same—"alike useful and alike venerable."

Let us test three visions of humanity in order to know how three Americans have managed to deal with the strong images that leap into being within "the apocalypse of the mind." First, Emerson himself. Second, Robert Penn Warren. Last, William James.

Toward the closing pages of *Nature* Emerson turns to his Orphic poet to listen to the "history and prophecy" of his song about man and nature. A vision builds up around the image of what man once was, what he now is, and what he may again become:

Once he was permeated and dissolved by spirit. He filled na-

ture with his overflowing currents. Out from him sprang the
sun and moon; from man the sun, from woman the moon.
The laws of his mind, the periods of his actions externized
themselves into day and night, into the year and the seasons.
But, having made for himself this huge shell, his waters retired; he no longer fills the veins and veinlets; he is shrunk to a
drop. He sees that the structure still fits him, but fits him colos-
sally.

"R. P. W."—the narrator-witness who stands in for Robert Penn
Warren in *Brother to Dragons*—listens to the spirit-voice of Thomas
Jefferson as the President tells of the vision he once had of the
angelic colossus which "history and prophecy" promised incarnation in America. "And my heart cried out, 'Oh, this is Man!'/And
thus my minotaur." But Jefferson's "angel" is his image of "man"
which will eventually be transformed into "beast":

> . . . . But no beast then: the towering
> Definition, angelic, arrogant, abstract,
> Greaved in glory, thewed with light, the bright
> Brow tall as dawn. I could not see the eyes. (p. 9)

In his chapter "The Sick Soul" from *The Varieties of Religious Experience*, William James describes an encounter with a figure which
forces terrible self-knowledge. (Although the incident comes from
his personal experience, James alleges to have received it second-
hand from a "sufferer" from France; he allows himself only the sly
remark prefacing this passage, "I translate freely.") Within the
speaker's mind there arises

> the image of an epileptic patient whom I had seen in the
> asylum, a black-haired youth with green skin, entirely idiotic,
> who used to sit all day on one of the benches, or rather shelves
> against the wall, with his knees drawn up against his chin, and
> the coarse gray undershirt, which was his only garment, drawn
> over them inclosing his entire figure. He sat there like a sort of
> sculptured Egyptian cat or Peruvian mummy, moving nothing
> but his black eyes and looking absolutely non-human. The
> image and my fear entered into a species of combination with
> each other. *That shape am I*, I felt, potentially. Nothing that I
> possess can defend me against that fate. (p. 160)

All three visions of what the Self can be within "the apocalypse of
the mind" are given to us indirectly by means of a revelation supposedly experienced by someone else, but each is actually the reali-

zation on the part of Emerson, of Warren, and of James of what he himself is and might yet become. In Emerson, colossus man has shrunk, but there is hope; because of the fundamental health of all existence, this once-mighty form can return to his proper stature as the source of sun and moon. In Warren, angelic man looms large in a shock of light; at first it is the cause of joy, but later it will bring terror because of the dark sickness it carries within itself. In James, the form of the idiot, contracted to the width of an asylum-shelf, is a present nightmare of greenish skin, grey garment, and black eyes which promises the possibility of madness to any sane mind. Emerson's is the cosmic god-man. Warren's is the American angel-beast. James's is the general human potentiality of sickness in the midst of health.

Each of these visionaries has had to face the full implications of the shapes they see; to accept the demands for hope and courage exacted by Emerson's god and by Warren's beast, no less than by James' idiot; to be able to go on, having once acknowledged in every instance, *"That shape am I."*

Lacking in cohesion on many issues, the Transcendentalists agreed on the advantage of looking over the long sweep in order to determine meaning from the entire curve of existence. Emerson, like Thoreau, believed we need serene patience to await those future events which will disclose the pattern of meaning of all that has already taken place. In "The Method of Nature" Emerson states:

> When we are dizzied with the arithmetic of the savant toiling to compute the length of [nature's] line, the return of her curve, we are steadied by the perception that a great deal is doing; that all seems just begun; remote aims are in active accomplishment. We can point nowhere to anything final; but tendency appears on all hands: planet, system, constellation, total nature is growing like a field of maize in July; is becoming somewhat else; is in rapid metamorphosis.

For Emerson it is not a matter of lasting it out until the happy ending arrives. The Emersonian "ending" is never felt as that. "The imaginative faculty of the soul must be fed with objects immense and eternal," he continues in "The Method of Nature." "Your end should be one inapprehensible to the senses; then will it be *a god always approached, never touched*; always giving health" (italics mine). If some minds rush to end the flow of existence, Emerson's soul rushes slowly; in this way, the flow continues forever. Life is the Grecian urn set in motion; the consummation devoutly to be wished is blessedly always just beyond reach.

The imagination of the long-view furnishes the paradigm for the poetic line which refuses to arrive at its final period. "A great poem is no finish to a man or woman but rather a beginning," Whitman wrote in his 1855 Preface to *Leaves of Grass*:

> Has any one fancied he could sit at last under some due authority and rest satisfied with explanations and realize and be content and full? To no such terminus does the greatest poet bring . . . he brings neither cessation or sheltered fatness and ease. (p. 727)

In "Song of Myself," Stanza 45, Whitman celebrates the poet's resistance to endings:

> There is no stoppage and never can be stoppage,
> If I, you, and the worlds, and all beneath or upon
>     their surfaces, were this moment reduced back
>     to a pallid float, it would not avail in the
>     long run,
> We should surely bring up again where we now stand,
> And surely go as much farther, and then farther
>     and farther.

Whitman carried out his own pronouncements in the most literal typographical terms by refusing to place a period at the conclusion of the 1855 "Song of Myself." William Carlos Williams also rejected the printer's period for the non-ending of "Spring and All," concerned as he was in that poem with the awakening of life out of winter's death. Even Mailer—who lives more strenuously than Whitman or William Carlos Williams in between the imaginations of finality and of renewal—wants to hold the idea of death as new life. He believes that death takes us to the stars, that other-place described by William James which survives simply because God is there. By such mental processes death is pushed "farther and farther" into a future diagrammed as an arc made up of dots, none serving as period/full stop. But Mailer's writing style—tense, doubting, self-exaggerating, with elaborations rising out of fun and frustration—does not permit the tone of confident health and almost arrogant periodlessness appropriate to the Transcendentalists or to William James. The Mailer sentence often comes weighted by a question mark. Death as finality, or as the assurance of a future life for mankind? If an after-life, one that promises to be as existential and exciting as the one we know? If transmigration of souls takes place, how radically affected by the ill-health we suffer during our present state? Will we be done for permanently if our cancerous soul dies before the collapse of our paunchy body?

Robert Lowell gives us yet another example of how long and short views manifest themselves in the shape of the poems addressed to life. A man who worked best within the formalism of strong structures, Lowell wrote a sonnet for each point scored in the debate he carried on ceaselessly with his imagination. In the sonnet "Seal" from *Notebook* of 1970 Lowell introduces men as the sea-seals they might become; through death's metamorphosis "we'd handle ourselves better" and be "all too at home in our double elements." Another sonnet entitled "Dies Irae, *A Hope*," proposes that men shall at last be pardoned and granted continued existence. Each sonnet can defend its convictions against rebuttal by outside voices as long as those convictions stay within the "enclosed garden" of their particular sonnet-Eden. Once the mind moves beyond those fourteen lines, anything can happen, and does, when Lowell takes up yet another sonnet and launches a new attack upon his own ideas.

Mailer's prose differs in method from Lowell's sonnets. Within a single paragraph it attempts to stretch far into the future; it tries to accomplish an effect similar to the wandering, all-inclusive lines of Whitman's poetry or to the sentences of Emerson's essays that place unnumbered dots along the endless curve of the universe. Mailer, with Whitman and Emerson, strives to take the long-view. Lowell's poetry struggles for short-views. Lowell attempted to construct a "history" based on continuities from the past, but his individual poems rarely push past a look at the near future; they confirm the immediacy and limits of a mind that would not (dared not) look too far forward into time where the finite period might lie.

Lowell's method, his focus, and his time-stretch is typified by a nineteen-line prose passage from the "91 Revere Street" section of *Life Studies* (p. 45). Lowell recalls that as a boy he tried out a certain magic formula: ". . . to lean forward on my elbows, support each cheekbone with a thumb, and make my fingers meet in a clumsy Gothic arch across my forehead. I would stare through this arch and try to make life stop." Through this frame the boy looks first at three garbage cans lettered *R.T.S. Lowell—U.S.N.* They are his "father" upon which "the sun shone irreverently." He shuts his eyes "to stop the sun," but to no avail, since the sun forces upon him "the portrait of Major Myers apotheosized." This great-great grandfather skips links with the Puritan past which the boy's sense of history craves—the Salem witchcraft trials, the allegory, the *Idea*. Major Myers' scarlet waistcoat gives reference alone to "the worldly bosom" of his solidly middle-class possessions. Pressing his sight backward through the sun, the boy finds sideboard, cut-glass decanters, and celleret as "the loot" of his inheritance. Looking forward into the sun, he finds only his father's garbage cans embossed with name and rank. His own future can go no farther than the immediate present—the alleyways of the house only fifty yards away from "the Hub of the Hub of the Universe" (p. 15).

Rocking back and forth, hemmed in by obstacles in either direction, the images of this passage provide Lowell the same sense of enclosure imposed by the sonnet form. Lowell the man continued to look through Gothic arches formed by the fingers of his poetic hands at a, "history" that includes the complacent success of the Major's sensualism and the pathetic failure of his father's idea of glory. Poetic perspective tutored his imagination in just how much space he himself was allowed between the scarlet waistcoat and three garbage cans—between the Puritan Declension and the Lowell decline.

John von Neumann, mathematician, authored the book *Theory of Games and Economic Behavior*, which elicited this observation by his friend and fellow-scientist, Jacob Bronowski, in the latter's *The Ascent of Man*:

> He [von Neumann] distinguished between short-term tactics and grand, long-term strategies. Tactics can be calculated exactly, but strategies cannot. . . . As in all realistic games which contain elements of chance and guesswork, there is no method which will ensure winning. What von Neumann's theory gives is the best strategy—which, with average luck, gives the best guide to success in the long run. (p. 435)

The fact that, in the long-run, von Neumann himself failed in certain of his professional endeavors only adds fillip to Bronowski's remarks. William James would have agreed in general, but James himself chose to argue, in "Philosophical Conceptions and Practical Results," for both the near and the far view. In an attempt to distinguish between materialism, theism, and his own "practicalism," he assigns "the cutting off of ultimate hopes" to materialism and "the letting loose of hope" to theism. Materialism and theism alike take long-views; the first simply predicts disaster, and the second joy. This said, James then offers the standard objection to dealing in such breadth: "The essence of a sane mind you may say, is to take shorter views, and to feel no concern about such chimaeras as the latter end of the world." "Well," James retorts:

I can only say that if you say this, you do injustice to human nature. . . . The absolute things, the last things, the overlapping things, are the truly philosophic concern; all superior minds feel seriously about them, and the mind with the shortest view is simply the mind of the more shallow man.

William James was a supple strategist. Having cunningly argued against the detractors of long-views, he feels ready to shift into a defense of what might look like short-views. He points out that the god who adheres to this time-idea would not concentrate on "making differences in the world's latter end; he probably makes differences all along its course."

In the already cited letter of April 18, 1897 (included in Perry, p. 211), James wrote, "Everything happens in the middle of eternity. All days are judgment-days and creation-morns. . . ." A shift has been made—one that is characteristic of him. He has decided against both *shallow short-views* and *catastrophic long-views*. He has taken his position on that view which focuses upon the middle. He has chosen to go deep, and with hope, into the sense of time as continuity that renews itself without cease—that makes things happen which are different from other things, held together as they are by their placement far away from absolute starts or finishes.

Many do not want to take the middle-way. They wish to vault over time toward some kind of an ending—to the future *continuum*-comedy of the Transcendentalists or to the future *cessation*-farce of the Materialists. Anything to escape the personal sense of the *endless* tragedy of their own sense of things. In resistance to gradual spiralings toward perfection or to slow decay down to a state of rot, they like time that falls apart. One of the consequences of this preference is the interest shown in the technique of foreshortening.

Within the prefaces he contributed to the New York Edition of his novels, Henry James gave instructions in the fine art of literary foreshortening. He discussed ways to control recalcitrant moments of human time for the sake of the novel's excellence. His pleasure in this method was always aesthetic. He deplored short-cuts applied literally to events in historical time and to moral existence. In contrast, as R.W.B. Lewis comments in his essay "Days of Wrath and

Laughter," included in *Trials of the Word*, James Baldwin wants to foreshorten time for apocalyptic ends and moral purposes. Those like Baldwin who practice foreshortening out of outrage would end evil by ending everything. Only go fast enough and cut enough corners and Satan is made obsolete.

It makes a difference, then, who is doing the foreshortening: the dedicated stylist, the morally outraged mortal, or the irresponsible gods. Henry Adams the historian worried over the rapid changes that characterized American society as early as 1815; Adams the reporter of the contemporary scene in 1915 detected an increasingly killing pace. The historian had tried to calculate (thus to control) the curve along which America was moving; the reporter stated it was impossible to make such calculations since the world had spun past the mind's capacity to comprehend it. For Adams the old Euclidean rules of cause and effect, time-sequence, and concepts of measured space were upset. As he liked to phrase it, men crouched under an ominous cock-locky heaven, and a universe once controlled by Greek reason was directed from the nursery like an illogical nightmare.

Back in 1851 Adams the child was already distinguishing between Quincy's slow time and the whirl of State Street, Boston. Hawthorne the novelist was observing in *The House of the Seven Gables* that "Nothing gives a sadder sense of decay than this loss or suspension of the power to deal with unaccustomed things, and to keep up with the swiftness of the passing moment" (p. 161). Through Hawthorne's novel, the possible American fate Adams later devoted his life to examining was being foretold: "It can merely be a suspended animation; for, were the power actually to perish, there would be little use of immortality. We are less than ghosts, for the time being, whenever this calamity befalls us" (p. 161).

Clifford Pyncheon, the ghost-figure Hawthorne portrays in *The House of the Seven Gables*, is tempted to defenestrate himself from the house that has blighted his past and present, and perhaps his future as well. Whether that leap would be "impelled by the species of terror that sometimes urges its victim over the very precipice which he shrinks from, or by a natural magnetism, tending towards the great center of humanity, it were not easy to decide" (p. 166).

By the time Henry Adams reached manhood, leaping was even less motivated by humanitarian hopes. Of course, nothing kept Adams from cracking the very American joke, "United we fall" in a letter of 1911 (included in Ford's edition, 11, 570), or from embellishing (in a letter of August 11, 1905, 11, 457) the picture of men riding together in an automobile from which they dare not jump. Leapings might be done out of the brotherly desire to go down *en masse*, but they were actually deterministically compelled by terrors pushing from within and forces pulling from outside. From Hawthorne, through Adams, and on down to that latter-day New Englander, Robert Lowell, Americans have increasingly suffered the frights of speed and faster gods.

In 1848, in his address "The Political Destination of America and the Signs of the Times," Theodore Parker defined Americans as a people who cannot sit still. We "alone of all nations have added rockers to our chairs" (p. 157). By the end of the century Theodore Dreiser's Hurstwood rocks himself into apathy and death. In the late 1920's Jay Gatsby constantly taps his foot in restlessness, beckoned on by the green light that lures him toward death. In Lowell's 1970 sonnet from *Notebook*, "Bringing a Turtle Home," the speaker tells of picking up a turtle "turned to stone by fear" from "a torrent highway":

> . . . The turtle had come a long walk,
> 200 millenia understudy to dinosaurs,
> then their survivor. A god for the out-of-power. . . .
> We have our faster gods, flush yachtsmen who see
> hell as a city very much like New York,
> these gods give a bad past and worse future to men
> who never bother to set a spinnaker. . . .

For Lowell, foreshortening was in the hands of the gods. There is no sense that he—like Baldwin, say—would attempt to appropriate this particular power to his poetry (unless the tight, short form of the sonnet itself is seen as an act to arrive at final closures without further delay).

"The reader," Adams writes in the 1910 "Letter to American Teachers of History," "who marks with some nervousness that Man has certainly advanced by leaps, and that his progress seems to be irreversible, seeks at once to know whether he shows signs of reaching its limit. . . ." In 1620 John Winthrop had stood on the deck of the *Arbella*, midway in the Atlantic in a time-and-space-void between the old and new worlds; he had spoken resolutely of God and man as bound in the Covenant that would fill, before the Beast did, an erstwhile meaningless space and a yet unredeemed time.

Winthrop concluded "A Modell of Christian Charity" with an epigram that promised a good leap into and through the darkness of
the unknown territory ahead:

> Therefore lett us choose life,
> that wee, and our Seede,
> may liue; by obeyeing his
> voyce, and cleaueving to him,
> for hee is our life, and
> our prosperity.

By the middle of the nineteenth century Caroline Sturgis Tappan was writing verses (included in Miller's *The Transcendentalists*)
which indicate that leaps into the unknown still remained the constant, conscious task of the believer, even if anxiety now replaced
confidence:

> I press my hands upon my heart—
> 'Tis very cold!
> And swiftly through the forest dart
> With footsteps bold.
> What shall I seek? Where shall I go?
> Earth and ocean shudder with woe!
> Their tale is untold!

Henry Adams drew different meanings from the tales of earth
and ocean told to the late nineteenth century. Hopes that had sustained Winthrop and challenged Tappan as they leaped and darted
into that darkness were withdrawn. For Adams (and later for
Mailer) darkness is where the Beast is in control, waiting perhaps to
foreshorten time out of existence.

Orestes Brownson urged the readers of his 1840 essay, "Democracy and Liberty" that "all of us who have any just conceptions of
our manhood, and of our duty to our fellowmen . . . arrange ourselves on the side of the movement." Brownson paused to caution,
"But the movement itself is divided into two sections—one the radical section, seeking progress by destruction; the other the conservative section, seeking progress through and in obedience to existing institutions."

Those who live to conserve believe the world works by self-
protection or gradual accumulation, not by detonating accelerations. For imaginations like Emerson's and Gertrude Stein's—for
believers in "slow history"—things begin and become, even late in
life. There is always chance for life *happening*, before death *happens*.

Part of the strategy of conservation practiced by Emerson was based on his belief that the body is more cheerful than is allowed for. In contrast to those doctors who view the body as a diseased and dying thing, the body sees itself as living fully until it dies. The human organism resists taking short-cuts to the death defined by Freud in "Beyond the Pleasure Principle" as its sole aim. Requiring detours, the body is like the Mississippi River, which wanders with cunning inefficiency in order slowly to pour itself into the Delta, itself symbolic of both completion and source, death and rebirth.

In 1860 Emerson preached conservation in "Culture" through a transformation of the Furies into the Muses. By absorbing chaos into culture, he was only imitating the ways of nature. Nature acts by gradation and slowly nudges mankind from "gorilla to gentleman," Emerson observed in "The Sovereignty of Ethics" of 1878. As he had expressed it as early as "Demonology" in 1839, nature resents shock and extremes, the accidental and the contradictory. For Thoreau, as well, natural forces assure continuity, not decay or destruction. The world of *A Week on the Concord and Merrimack Rivers* is founded on a rock; air and water will not wear it away but can bring it only refreshment. In his journal of September 24, 1859 Thoreau further reported that though the earth may spin fast, the lake's surface remains unruffled.

What nature does so well, men ought to do also. Despising those "horror-mongers" who live in the shroud of the Last Days, and who cry out the rhetoric of terror, Emerson argued in "The Superlative" that—like nature—sensible people undercut fear by belittling it through the words they use. To them a spell of extreme cold is just a "cold snap." But Emerson realized that the slow history of nature takes an amount of time men may not want to give. Because impetuosity demands Presto change!—either toward blessedness or the climax of disaster—human beings can be the cause of their own hurt. They are the only living creatures, Emerson believed, who ever do this strange thing to themselves. Foxes never commit suicide, Thoreau noted in his journal of December 27, 1857. Even when faced by the facts of cold, hounds, and traps, they insist on living. Only men are so extravagantly self-indulgent that they throw away existence.

Borrowing a concept Mark Twain has given us in the form of a fictional character, let us call *Sawyerism* the curse placed upon those fascinated by the gaudy effects of crises. Sawyerism—like the Teddyism that Henry James abhorred in President Roosevelt—is very noisy. Mark Twain himself called Theodore Roosevelt "the Tom Sawyer of the political world of the twentieth century" (a remark cited by Kaplan, p. 363). In turn, Henry Adams in *The Education* said of President Roosevelt that he was "pure act"—"the similar quality that belongs to ultimate matter—the quality that mediaeval theology assigned to God . . ." (p. 417).

Emerson could never be that witty or ironic about God. He preferred to focus his slights upon those persons who are inconsequential but potentially dangerous. In "The Method of Nature" he pointed out those who—whether dealing boyishly with reform or churlishly with disaster—only scrape surfaces. Unlike true philosophers, such men fail to bore laterally through the crust of "our conventions and theories, and pierce to the core of things." They "expect to go like a thunderbolt to the centre. But the thunder is a surface phenomenon, makes a skin-deep cut. . . . The wedge turns out to be a rocket." Sawyerism (practiced by irresponsible gods of pure act and no thought) likes big comet-splashes across the sky but fails to go down to the healing core of things. Sawyerism likes "effects" so much that one day it might, like Hank Morgan—an older, more powerful Tom Sawyer—work up that final grand effect that would blow up everything in a show of might, just for the sake of the show.

Like Emerson, Thoreau, in his journal of February 26, 1840, mocked the desire for radical explosions:

> The great events to which all things consent, and for which they have prepared the way, produce no explosion, for they are gradual, and create no vacuum which requires to be suddenly filled; as a birth takes place in silence, and is whispered about the neighborhood, but an assassination, which is at war with the constitution of things, creates a tumult immediately.

Births, not assassinations, are the rule of the "constitutional" form of cosmic government upheld by the "Conservative Christian Anarchist," whether he is an Adams or a Thoreau or an Emerson.

The calming "conservation" tones of such "men" are frequently obscured by the racket made by the "boys" which fills so many pages of American writing with their angers or bragging. Some "men" try to rebuke the "boys" by the deafening crash of their own silence. Silence comes from several causes—pessimism, affirmation, or indifference. Silence can be the expression of the artist's scorn for the failures of his fellowmen, of his depression over his lack of success, or of his trust in the eternal truths which triumph over hobgoblin fears.

Yet Emerson wrote in his 1836 journal that it is the "bad man" who lives in silence. Such a man stands apart from the hum of meaning set up by the world; he exists in "A white point. And being not in the current of things [,] an outlaw, a stoppage—the wheels of God must grind him to powder in their very mission of charity" (v, 266-267). However, if Thoreau moved into silence, it was precisely for the purpose of escaping being ground in the mills of the conventional. By blocking out the world's distracting hum, his ear could better hear the mystical harp-sounds and frog-music which filled the woods around him. Silence proves an asylum in the midst of trivial words, he insists at the conclusion of *A Week on the Concord and Merrimack Rivers*. Silence is true worship, he comments in his journal of August 18, 1858. In contrast, the prattle of the Atlantic telegraph is noisy nonsense, compounded by the man who, in honor of the newly invented gadget, decked the front of his house with lights that spelled out "Glory to God in the highest." Thoreau's father lived mute in the face of the torrent of his wife's words; the father's silence could be fertile as well as sterile, creative as much as it was suicidal or judgmental.

Forty or fifty years later, those more wary of the world's void than the men of Concord had been now found other uses for silence. Whereas William James said that by 1907 Mark Twain was good only for talk, Henry Adams specifically interpreted silence as human resistance to whatever is meaningless, whether society's words or the universe's stillness. Adams, skeptic and believer, both chattered and kept still. If he spoke, he wrote in 1897, he might say something, so he shut himself up in "a sort of lockjaw." Better to "hold one's tongue, and vomit gracefully," he remarked in the same letter (included in the Ford edition, ii, 122, 123). Drawing upon the grand tradition of silent men, in *The Education* he cites Carlyle, Arnold, Swinburne, Byron (men not themselves much given to taciturnity, but those who were aware of its value). He especially approved of de Vigny's remark, "Only silence is great; all the rest is weakness" (p. 642). Silence was the true gentleman's method for dealing with the twentieth century. For the small, vain Bostonian, it certainly helped to preserve a pose of integrity, measure, and order.

But how can a man know he is a success unless he "says" it and the world hears it? Further, if the world began successfully with a Word, might it not be uncreated by silence? The question remains: is silence an act of withdrawal and rejection, or true communion?

In *The Symbolism of Evil* Paul Ricoeur observes that once the true communion of discourse ceases between men and God, myth begins. When we no longer feel free to argue against our fates, we start to tell stories, often tragic, about silent heroes who go forth to endure that fate. In *The Poetics of Reverie* Gaston Bachelard identifies silence as the feminine principle; he implies that the passive acceptance of the world has no need for the resistance effected by heroes' deeds. In *The Poetics of Space* he calls for a "good apocalypse" of calmness—the domination of destiny by means of contemplation. Bachelard's life of silence takes place in the "actual world," where neither words nor deeds are necessary; it happens wherever the mind thinks and dreams success into being; it provides a further level to the world of intense subjectivity—creative, alert, interested. But silence may be its own form of annihilation—the surest way to arrive at the end of human existence that defines itself as good talk.

# CHAPTER 26

# Opposing Perfection

To be saved by silence in order to arrive at the silence offered by total absorption into God's consciousness or the self's core: this solution to the babble of the objective world has not gone unnoticed by a number of American writers. In joy to leap away from combative individuality toward the democratic spirit held in common; to have the inferior absorbed into superior being; to replace the limitations of the phenomenal with the endless space and light of the noumenal. Any one of these acts would bring an end to the failure of being. Perhaps such attempts go counter to the intensely human, ever earthly existence of the so-called American way, but nudges toward apotheosis are essential to one strain of American thought. When Whitman envisioned the "I" meeting its splendid termination in the All-Soul through the completed "passage to India," his emotion is as native to America as are Henry Adams' fears concerning the obliteration of distinctive selves, a society sterile in its uniformity, and the dying into sameness.

When Ike McCaslin enters into the wilderness without gun, compass, or pocket-watch in Faulkner's "The Bear," he is giving up those objects by which men claim a sense of time, place, and power. He goes across the frontier without the burden of ego about which Melville had cautioned. Unlike Ahab, who destroys his quadrant but retains his rebellious ego, Ike moves in silence, without *things*, into naked silence. At the moment he sees the legendary bear fixed against the forest backdrop, he is dissolved into the dream of eternity which replaces the life of movement. Without an ego, he will not father a child or fully face what human love demands; at this cost he achieves mystic absorption into a power greater than his own ego.

Questions of the relation between soul, forms, and matter were part of the quasi-Platonism supported by Thoreau, Emerson, and the elder Henry James, not without involving paradox. Emerson suggests that we *find* the essential Is (do not escape from it) by diving deep into the unity of the God which has existed before the world of matter. He likes to think that the self discovers itself by means of self-annihilation since God is the name we give to "the last generalization to which we can arrive" (vii, 40). We see what Emerson suggests, and agree it is possible we might indeed be mirrored in that sacred name. But we also wonder whether—in the absence of any power on our part to imprint our special presence—the reflecting surface, the perfect objectiveness of the Real, might remain blank before our subjectiveness.

Thoreau also aspired at moments to this highest of successes. In his journal of February 8, 1857 he describes what it might be like to separate from all others and from himself. It would be like the silence and remoteness of a mountain lake. On July 16, 1851 he wrote out his wish to become an object to himself; but he also wanted to understand why he *as himself* was included in God's scheme and whether it was as God's partner that he existed.

As early as March 11, 1842 Thoreau was wondering if it were necessary for him to exist as conscious material which looks in detachment at God's success so that it became a success he shared in. "The unconsciousness of man is the consciousness of God," he wrote in *A Week on the Concord and Merrimack Rivers* (p. 351), but he seems also to have believed that man's consciousness is the means by which we participate in the unconsciousness of God. To Emerson the pure of heart envision God and become gods, but Thoreau required the sight of himself in the act of perceiving God.

Henry James, Senior, believed that God is our *esse*, while we are God's *existence*. God's true creation involves Him ceasing to be only Himself, pure and alone, through the act of projecting all persons outward from Himself. The primary movement initiated by God has given us the world we now possess—one tainted by our separate selfhood. The final movement toward a redeemed society will come when God absorbs Himself into us; we will go from creation (separation) to return (absorption). This does not, however, entail the reabsorption of mankind into God. Rather, it insists upon God's incarnation into mankind. The elder James's schema may twist away from the conventional mystical stress on man's return to God, but it still involves annihilation of selfhood. Absorption is the end of separate individuality, whether the movement is from man into God or God into man.

In one way or the other, and with varying amounts of emphasis, Emerson, Thoreau, and the elder James urged the disappearance of the self, as did Johathan Edwards and Walt Whitman. Edgar Allan Poe, Henry Adams, and Mark Twain also considered the consequences of such a feat, but with rather more mixed emotions. Other Americans have chosen strenuously to resist any form of absorption into the god-void, even in the name of success. Emerson had promised his American listeners the happy return of the Human Form Divine without the loss of individualism. People are not prisoners of one thought held fixed by the divine mind, he told an audience during his 1839 address on demonology. We are separate thoughts; we are like nations bound in the commonwealth of one world-mind. Notwithstanding Emerson's assurances, suspicions mount when the touch of German idealism or Eastern mysticism seems to threaten the all-American ego. For many minds the quiet reabsorption of consciousness to the inorganic world is as feared as a world of selves shattered by a bomb-blast. And so they resist even if resistance does not come easily. Not when one must try to retain identity while sponging the self free from failure—must try to be *more* than the solitary self without becoming *only everything*.

For his debut into the world of letters in 1865 as a critic for *The North American Review*, Henry James attacked the egocentricity of Walt Whitman's barbaric yawps. In the same article he complained of the bodiless vapor of Whitman's *Drum-Taps*—all those words without substance. The war poems Melville was completing at the same time James was deploring Whitman's pieces raise similar questions for later critics.

In his edition of Melville's selected poems, Robert Penn Warren asks of the Civil War how values can be found "in action desperately foredoomed to blankness" (p. 20). James placed the fault upon Whitman's verses for their absence of meaning. Warren places the fault upon the war itself. Warren wonders if the poet can uncover values only through asserting an imagination that acts "in the courage to endure, and by endurance to define its own value, outside of time . . ." (p. 20). Or perhaps he has to call upon self-denial that sinks "personal pain in a compassionate and ennobling awareness of the general human lot . . ." (p. 21).

Whether self-assertion in the name of eternal values or self-denial for the sake of universal love, such acts have to occur *in time*—in terms of particular human events and specific human consequences. They must make the sharpest of distinctions about a war that was all too vaguely alleged to have been fought in the name of American unity. "The making of distinctions," Warren writes, "—that is the very center of Melville's poetry, and of Melville's Unionism. . . . There are human values beyond mere unity by the achievement of which the Union must justify itself" (p. 29).

Through the issue of "the making of distinctions" Warren is able to compare Whitman's and Melville's responses to Union victory. Whitman understood victory "to operate by aggregation, or absorption, and to aim at the wiping out of distinction in the process. Melville would have understood it to operate by an analysis to locate first principles, and by dialectic" (p. 30). You will recall that Santayana named "clear thought" as one of the *absent* things in Whitman. According to Warren, "clear thought" lay "at the center of Melville's poetry, the effort to achieve awareness of the distinctions and paradoxes of life and to resolve them" (p. 30).

*Clear thought—first principles—awareness of distinctions*: these are the methods used by Melville, the poet of American history, whose practice runs counter to Whitman, the benign singer of American apocalypse, who would perhaps prefer to save the nation's soul by ending the world of thought, principles, and distinctions.

While visiting Germany in the 1860's, William James witnessed what it might be like to be a Whitmanian eater of strawberries (in an incident recorded in Perry's study, p. 109). Reprimanded by his hostess for taking up his berries one by one, James observed that the German way was to smash the berries with one's spoon until they made a pulp. He concluded that "the *peculiarly* German part of the occurence . . . implied a sort of religious melting of the whole emotional nature in this one small experience of the sense of taste." Ever quick to call things by names that suggest the emotions involved, James termed this "washing out of all boundary lines" *Wunderschön*. In his description (included in a letter addressed to his sister on June 4, 1868) he associates the state of "swimming in sentiment" with an absence of attention to the "original exciting cause" of that sentiment and to a lack of "the sense of form throughout." He next takes up *Wunderschön* as it applies to art, accusing the Germans of a loss of critical power when in the presence of "the divinity of *Kunst* in the abstract." By giving themselves up to wonder, they are unable to produce good art since their ability to separate performance from idea is drowned in "tender emotion."

Throughout his career William James worked, as Santayana recognized, to oppose "clear thought to *Wunderschön*. But it was his brother Henry who, even more than William, viewed the "original exciting cause" as a major source of wonder. He gave value to "the sense of form" precisely so that he might arrive at the proper effect of *Kunst*. Henry James's method of handling this sequence is similar to Henry Adams' description in *The Education* of that literary creation which moves as if with a will of its own. "The form is never arbitrary," Adams comments, "but is a sort of growth like crystallization, as any artist knows too well; for often the pencil or pen runs into side-paths and shapelessness, loses its relations, stops or is bogged" (p. 389). *Never to lose relations* even in the midst of growth was the special task of writers like Adams and James, writers who were devoted to *clear thought* with its distinctions and to *wonder* with its emotions, though they knew how hard it was to have them both as a stay against chaos.

Freud pits the ego—the container of the self—against the libido—the inner core of narcissistic sexual hunger whose will to power risks self-devouring. The ego seeks movement toward death; the libido thrusts toward life. But in the paradoxical dualisms set up by Freud, libido-life is the return to origins and the loss of distinctions, whereas ego-death permits the self to illustrate its particularities. Both sustain the other in the existence gained as a result of their mutual antagonism; each draws the other toward termination; both are needed in constant contention.

There is an analogy in the way ego and libido interact to the ideas about victory and the Union which William James proposed in 1897 during the dedication of the monument to Robert Gould Shaw on Boston Common. In his speech (treated in R. P. Warren's preface to Melville's poems, p. 30) James stated that the finest victory possible for the Union is one in which "the hour of triumph will to some degree do justice to the ideals in which the vanquished interests lay." In the same way, if the battle between ego and libido reaches the truce-stage, and if the dualisms are forced within an ostensible monism which actually serves to let one force deny the values of the other, the self would undergo the kind of mean-spirited, exclusive Union victory James believed had caused a tragic fragmentation of the national character. Whenever there is betrayal of "justice to the ideals in which the vanquished interests lay," America again suffers a fall away from the good victory experienced in Faulkner's tale "A Courtship." Once upon a time both Ikkemotubbe and David Hogganbeck won and neither lost. So it should have been with the Civil War between North and South, so it should be with the civil war between ego and libido. Otherwise, war is hell.

Ego is form. Beyond form lies the soul, madness, eternity, the void. Mailer avows this truth in *Advertisements for Myself*, that book throughout which Mailer's own ego toys, perversely, with thoughts of annihilating itself by letting the libido take over. In "On The Way Out," from the same work, he provides an apocalyptic glimpse at what seems to happen when ego moves out on its own. By means of the will, life has ascended over the centuries up from the waters onto the land. Now it probes into space. This resolute human movement corresponds to the purpose for which God created life: that His vision might be fulfilled. Mailer wants to be obedient to God's will even if it entails the end of human will, but he is equally determined to know *how* God exists, and he insists that men come to this special knowledge only by continuing to exist. Just as Ralph Touchett, dying in Henry James's *The Portrait of a Lady*, tries to stay alive as long as possible so he may watch Isabel Archer out of his love and interest, Mailer needs no other reason to resist the dying of the world and the cessation of human consciousness: *for interest*, at the least, if not whole-heartedly for love.

We see Mailer's premise worked out in detail within William James's 1884 lecture "The Dilemma of Determinism." He sets out on an arduous task: the definition of the essential difference between optimism and pessimism. During the course of his debate (which he carries out singlehandedly by representing the opinions of the several contending sides), James will argue first against, then for, subjectivism as the strategy that assures us the will to survive *in an interesting way*.

James begins by setting up a contrast between the world imagined by the advocates of classic unity and the life desired by determinists of the kind he calls "soft." (He does not bother to deal with "hard" determinism, which is "merely mechanical" and which "smiles at anyone who comes forward with a postulate of moral coherence.")

> Every one must at some time have wondered at that strange paradox of our moral nature, that, though the pursuit of outward good is the breath of its nostrils, the *attainment* of outward good would seem to be its suffocation and death. Why does the painting of any paradise or Utopia, in heaven or on earth, awaken such yawnings for Nirvana and escape? . . . . We look upon them from this delicious mess of insanities and realities, strivings and deadnesses, hopes and fears, and agonies and exultations, which forms our present state; and *tedium vitae* is the only sentiment they awaken in our breasts.

Having rejected the boredom that goes with unquestioning hope, James now tries to differentiate between the "soft" determinists whose left horn is pessimism and whose right horn is "subjectivism." Those to the left—the gnostics—look "at the goods and ills of life in a simple objective way"; those to the right—the subjectivists—regard such goods and ills "as materials, indifferent in themselves, for the product of consciousness, scientific and ethical. . . ." James starts to work up, in almost Twainian terms, an emotional "grand effect" in order to depict how the pessimistic imagination of the gnostics will not tolerate that peace which offers no contrasts:

> To our crepuscular natures, born for the conflict, the Rembrandtesque moral chiaroscuro, the shifting struggle of the sunbeam *in* the gloom, such pictures of light upon light are vacuous and expressionless, and neither to be enjoyed nor understood. If *this* be the whole fruit of the victory, we say . . . and all the sacred tears were shed for no other end than that a race of creatures of such unexampled insipidity should succeed, and protract *in saecula saeculorum* their contented and inoffensive lives,—why, at such a rate, better lose than win the battle, or at all events better ring down the curtain before the last act of the play, so that a business that began so importantly may be saved from so singularly flat a winding-up.
>
> All this is what I should instantly say, were I called on to plead for gnosticism. And its real friends, of whom you will presently perceive I am not one, would say without difficulty a great deal more.

James here takes a breath, necessary because he has been diligently propounding the cause of gnosticism and its glory-mood of defeat taken in the name of an *interesting* apocalypse. Then he readies himself to speak for the subjectivism that chooses to hope and to last, although in ways opposed to those of the classic optimists:

> Regarded as a stable finality, every outward good becomes a mere weariness to the flesh. It must be menaced, be occasionally lost, for its goodness to be fully felt as such. . . . Not the absence of vice, but vice there, and virtue holding her by the throat, seems the ideal human state. And there seems no reason to suppose it not a permanent human state.

The gnostics see life as a melodramatic war between virtue and vice; they wish a stunning end to the conflict. The subjectivists also possess the imagination of melodrama, but they prefer to keep the play going:

> Our moral horizon moves with us as we move, and never do we draw nearer to the far-off line where the black waves and the

azure meet. The final purpose of our creation seems most plausibly to be the greatest enrichment of our ethical consciousness, through the intensest play of contrasts and the widest diversity of characters. This of course obliges some of us to be vessels of wrath, whilst it calls others to be vessels of honor. But the subjectivist point of view reduces all these outward distinctions to a common denominator.

After the pause of yet another paragraph break, James plunges in once again:

> So much for subjectivism! If the dilemma of determinism be to choose between it and pessimism, I see little room for hesitation from the strictly theoretical point of view. Subjectivism seems the more rational scheme. And the world may possibly, for aught I know, be nothing else. When the healthy love of life is on one, and all its forms and its appetites seem so unutterably real: when the most brutal and the most spiritual things are lit by the same sun, and each is an integral part of the total richness,—why then, it seems a grudging and sickly way of meeting so robust a universe, to shrink from any of its facts and wish them not to be. *Rather take the strictly dramatic point of view, and treat the whole thing as a great unending romance which the spirit of the universe, striving to realize its own content, is eternally thinking out and representing to itself.* (Italics mine)

James quickly follows up his homage to the strategy for keeping things going by means of the power of the subjective mind. He details its many dangers—antinomianism, romanticism, fatalism, what we might call "Sawyerism"—before he concludes:

> the point is that, in the subjectivistic or gnostical philosophy, wild-oat-sowing becomes a systematic necessity and the chief function of life. After the pure and classic truths, the exciting and rancid ones must be experienced. . . .

Notice the progress of James's argument. He first made distinctions between the classicists and the "soft" determinists. Then he separated "soft" determinism into the gnostic who despairs and the subjectivist who hopes. He next saw that each might go too far in their common desire to do away with the deadly *tedium vitae*. Now, he turns aside to honor briefly a new group whose aid is needed to counter the most dangerous whims of these "children of light." The members of this group are the same dull types whom Norman Mailer identifies as the lords of NASA, the enemies of *his* children of light—the blacks and the hippies; enemies who, to Mailer's dismay, managed to take America's ego on further, and successful, explorations into space.

Says James

> ... and if the stupid virtues of the Philistine herd do not then come in and save society from the influence of the children of light, a sort of inward putrefaction becomes its inevitable doom.

Not that James is against "putrefaction" altogether. It depends. The "pluralistic, restless universe" which he desires is abhorred by minds possessed by "the love of unity." He reports that such a person once told him "that the thought of my universe made him sick, like the sight of the horrible motion of a mass of maggots in their carrion bed." He is quick to match this objection-by-metaphor with a counter-metaphor of his own.

From the start James has repudiated a world of stable absolutes too pure to contain carrion or maggots. He dismisses hard or mechanical determinism "with its necessary carrion . . . and with no possible maggots to eat the latter up." He also rejects "the attitude of gnostical romanticism" that "transforms life from a tragic reality into an insincere melodramatic exhibition." Gnostical romanticism, he concludes, "leaves me in presence of a sort of subjective carrion considerably more noisome than the objective carrion I called it to take away." He decides to go along with "indeterminism with its maggots"—the "free-will theory" that gives him a world of *chance*: "the chance that in moral respects the future may be other and better than the past has been."

We can look at an example of how a student (in this instance, an actual student) of William James might respond to his belief in the need to resist endings. "When I was young," writes Gertrude Stein in *Everybody's Autobiography*,

> the most awful moment of my life was when I really realized that the stars are worlds and when I really realized that there are civilizations that had completely disappeared from this earth. And now it happens again. Then I was frightened badly frightened, now well now being frightened is something less frightening than it was. . . . Now I am still out walking. I like walking. (pp. 11-12)

Walking slowly, Stein comes to this idea about walking on, and states it, appropriately, in a non-stop sentence:

There was of course science and evolution and there were of course the fact that stars were worlds and that space had no limitation and still if civilizations always come to be dead of course they had to come to be dead since the earth had no more size than it had how could other civilizations come if those that were did not come to be dead but if they did come to be dead then one was just as good as another one and so was science and progress interesting that is was it exciting but after all there was evolution and James' the Will to Live and I I had always been afraid always would be afraid but after all was that what it was to be not refusing to be dead although after all every one was refusing to be dead. (pp. 242-243)

One wonders whether Norman Mailer could be satisfied with the promise of incompleteness and chanciness given us by William James and Gertrude Stein. Theirs is the kind of existence George Santayana describes in "The Genteel Tradition in American Philosophy": "The universe is an experiment; it is unfinished. It has no ultimate or total nature, because it has no end." Mailer is fascinated by experiment, but he is also somewhat like Mark Twain's Eve, who writes in her diary that she sees herself as an experiment which is curious to find out its own results (pp. 34-35).

Twain's Eve, like Mailer, prefers experimental demonstration and practical education to theories; she, like him, believes she was created to search out the secrets of the world of wonders; she also thinks God's act of creation was hasty, too full of mistakes not to force an inevitable conclusion to all errors and temporary things (p. 35). But if Mailer—even more than Eve and rather more like Mark Twain—possesses a streak that likes to envision explosive, conclusive endings that do away with botches, he tries to restrain that tendency in order that the experiments, including the very important one which *he* is, may go on yet awhile.

We live by hazard. Hazard is what gives us our sense of aesthetic values, argues Sister Mary Slattery in her book, *Hazard, Form, and Value* (pp. 63-76). When the artist meets with risk and overcomes it, we who share this experience gain the sense of the unity which stimulates us to meaning and guards against the unity which bores us to death. In this most basic of contests order is assailed by difference. The mind is excited by the desire to see sameness restored to the tatterdemalion elements. Through its excitement the mind gets value. It is significant that Sister Mary Slattery stresses the final union of separate parts. For her it is the fact of oppositeness that promises the possibilities of assimilation. She likes to think that our final satisfaction comes when we see the superior force survive the threat caused by that particle which calls attention only to itself.

Mailer would probably go along in general with Sister Mary's formulation. He would, however, give particular honor to the self-advertised unit—the man or devil—who does the threatening and causes the menace, rather than to celebrate the act by which the Lord God finally puts the insurgents into their place. Mailer is like John Dewey in *Reconstruction in Philosophy*, where Dewey asserts that the erratic and changeful "is no longer looked upon as a fall from grace, as a lapse from reality or a sign of imperfection of Being." On the other hand, for the sake of hazard, conflict, and danger, Mailer would not choose to go along with the particulars of Dewey's optimism, which also insists that change "loses its pathos, it ceases to be haunted with melancholy through suggesting only decay and loss." Mailer cannot be as sure as Dewey that change is "associated with progress rather than with lapse and fall" and is usually "prophetic of a better future." (Besides, he rather prefers "to be haunted with melancholy.")

Mailer and William James like worlds that are uncertain of better futures (though not closing out their possibility as strict gnostic romanticists tend to do); they are somehow proud of the fallen nature of the world. They resist submission to a bad world or settling in with a cozy one. Theirs is the wild world to which they give *the full consent of their interest*.

Wildness, with its caves and gullies, peaks and ditches, is not a world of diminishment. When Henry James revisited America in 1904 he found that the consciousness of the populace matched the thin, clear, blank, flat look of the American scene. It is true that James maintained that blandness "didn't mean nothing" (p. 276). After all, he mused, it cannot be that virtue (the bland) only serves to indicate the absence of vice (the varied). Perhaps Salem's blankness had been the catalyst that, prompting Hawthorne to protest against it, thereby developed his imagination and his art. Perhaps the imagination responds through resistance to the bland as well as to merger with the wild. Still and all, a number of James's most anxious thoughts in *The American Scene* are given over to the Margin— the ambiguous "mere looming mass of the *more*, the more and more to come" which may be "a possible greater good" or "a possible greater evil" (p. 401). It is "the Margin" which surrounds America with its blankness. Out of its substance (or lack of substance) the future of American society has to be formed. What we must dread is a future of "immeasurable muchness": without ego (Mailer), without value (Sister Mary Slattery), without interest (James).

Robert Elliott's book *The Shape of Utopia* probes the question of utopian literature. Dreams of anti-utopias now replace the original hopes of utopia, he argues. Of course, from the first many Americans have followed the lead of the common-sense denunciation of the *Pays de Cocagne* Franklin included in "Information for Those Who Would Remove to America." Franklin bluntly warned about what America was not: that land where great abbeys are built of savory victuals, where geese fly roasted from the spit crying out in pleased self-advertisement, "all hot, all hot," where rivers of oil, milk, and honey flow and lusty monks chase willing nuns; a land without pain, strife, or death. It is equally true that America has been imaged by many others as the Big Rock Candy Mountain and as the diamond as big as the Ritz. But common-sense experience set up against the illusory dream-wish is not the only cause for the contemporary tendency to reject both *myth* (whose source is the ideal Golden Age which is now forever lost) and *concept* (devoted to what might yet come about through the pressure of men's reason and will).

If absorption in a mythic past is rejected by many contemporary imaginations, others also agree that the dangers of utopian futures outweigh the pleasures. Elliott maintains that in the fight of utopian writers against the historical process which acts to perpetuate social ills, they tend to freeze time. Although they wish to focus upon positive ends, their view of the way things are now is often excessively negative. By placing so much stress on *corruptio optimi pessima*—"the corruption of the best becomes the worst"—they sound that truly apocalyptic note: the worst must come before the best. Such emphasis can result in the imagination of disaster that follows itself up by ruthless acts—the acts justified by the contention that the blood being shed is a necessary prelude to the imagination of peace, as when a Robespierre declares virtue is of no value unless won by means of terror.

But let us say we have managed to get past the initial despair and the subsequent reign of terror, and that we have arrived at perfection. "Ouf! what a relief!" said William James on departing Chautauqua, that bland American middle-class utopia. Really tough imaginations like James's follow the suggestion of Thomas More in locating the *topos* (good place) in *eutopos* (no place), but soft utopians still try to fix the paradise in a particular place and time. Brook Farm, New Harmony, and Oneida were actual places *in* America where virtue was intended to reign.

That those communities failed to realize their hopes is now less a concern than the fear that eventually such a place might actually carry out the incarnation of its dream. Elliott reminds us of the Nicolas Berdiaeff epigraph used by Aldous Huxley for *Brave New World*. It warns that we must seek "*une société non utopique, moins 'parfaite' et plus libre.*" Freedom, variety, and interest are now the fancied "best." Perfection, unity, and blandness are the elements of the nightmare of utopias come true.

Elliott stresses the need for proper forms, literary as well as social, to counter the threats of perfection. It is significant that he believes that Plato shaped his idea of the Ideal Republic by means of the dialogue-form. The Socratic dialogue helps to roil the excessive smoothness of the utopian imagination; it stresses intellectual exploration and discovery; it shows the mind in the process of revealing new ideas for the human good; it dismisses the statements, pronouncements, and self-congratulating declarations of virtue which are common to less thoughtful projections of the good and happy life. The enemy of the Socratic vision, according to Elliott, is the Euclidean dream, and nowhere is that dream-shape more evident than in America:

> The euclidianism of the United States is graphically symbolized in its architecture: rectilinear glass buildings, glistening glass pavements laid out in straight lines, square harmonies endlessly repeated—a Bauhaus world gone mad, mirroring the perfect abstractness of an almost perfect life. Rebels in this brilliantly grotesque perversion of utopia adopt as their emblem$\sqrt{-1}$, thus aligning themselves with the struggles of Dostoevsky's Underground Man against the hegemony of two times two is four. (p. 94)

William James rejected the perfection of Chautauqua; his brother in turn denounced William's predelictions for the $2 + 2 = 4$ novel. (Henry took this position in a letter of November 23, 1905 in response to William's unsympathetic reaction to *The Golden Bowl*.) Give and take a few nuances, however, both Jameses reveal essentially anti-utopian imaginations. Drama requires conflict, accident, and the tragic in place of peace, order, and the idyllic. The drama found in both literature and life requires the necessary form. But theirs is not the form which enforces "an exact symmetry" upon the wildness of life; it is form that instructs us in the fine uses of hazard and surprise.

Ever like Goldilocks on the alert for the *just enough*, Henry James viewed with apprehension the excessive expanse of the Western plains whose monotony was reinforced by the horizontal thrust of the railroads. He asked in *The American Scene*:

> Is the germ of anything finely human, of anything agreeably or successfully social, supposably planted in conditions of such endless stretching and such boundless spreading as shall appear finally to minister but to the triumph of the superficial and the apotheosis of the raw? Oh for a split or a chasm, one groans . . . oh for an unbridgeable abyss or an insuperable mountain! (p. 465)

Notice that Henry James believed that Philadelphia's "admirable comprehensible flatness" is good because it precludes "the image of the porcupine," "the perpetual perpendicular" of the skyscrapers which make New York City such bad form (p. 275). The telling distinction between the flatness of the plains and railroad tracks and that of the chessboard surface of Philadelphia is a matter of *human* horizontals, which the latter has but the former lacks. The varied forms of humanity counter the killing quality of whatever "bristles" in steel verticals or lies inert along the monotonous earthern "floor." But human society must actively guard against taking on the forms—whether found in nature or the machine—that might prove deadly.

William James agreed. In his diary of 1870, he wrote out the young man's gesture of rebellion (an entry included in Perry's book, p. 121). Long before he composed "The Dilemma of Determinism," James was questioning whether he ought to reject the monotonous complacencies of both pessimism and optimism in order to accept the third alternative, "the life of moralism"—a "militant existence" whose motto is "though evil can slay me, she can't subdue me, or make me worship her."

It is one thing to resist evil. It is also necessary to escape serenity. By the 1890's William James agreed with Rudyard Kipling's judgment of the "Chautauqua 'civilization.' " It was (he wrote in a passage also included by Perry, p. 228) "the curse of America—sheer, hopeless, well-ordered boredom. . . ." The new American blandishments of niceness were to be resisted as much as the nastiness of evil.

If we follow through on the suggestions made by Robert Elliott's book on utopias and the comments provided by both the Jameses concerning America, art, and society, we arrive at this anomaly: America viewed through the eyes of her artists must answer *their* purposes, not necessarily ours. For *their* sakes America is to retain its fallen state in order to keep up the blessings of dualism, irregularity, and impossiblity.

The rest of us who are not artists may be foolish enough to yearn for "a complete *present* satisfaction" (called for by Henry James, Senior, whose mid-century socialism was later rejected by his sons for reasons more psychological and aesthetic than political). But as long as "the artists" have any power over our imaginations, we will be "saved" from happiness for the sake of the truth. Elliott flatly states, "Twentieth-century literature can no more stomach happiness as an end in life than it can accommodate a hero" (p. 152). As the gnostic romanticist who prefers the tragedy of objective truths, the Underground Man (half-brother—though not full kin—to William James) is the true enemy of the "Philistine herd," which thinks happiness is what it most wants. He will act in the name of the people's desire, but he will always oppose the tedium of perfection in order to enjoy the excitements of $\sqrt{-1}$.

The "problem of Job" is the necessity to help God win the eternal struggle against evil, at whatever costs to ourselves. We are asked to do this by opposing whatever might end that struggle and bring us rest. Under these terms, *opposition* is the value the imagination strongly instructed by Christian doctrine most wants.

There is the cruelly moralistic justification given to the opposition of our desires by Mosely, the druggist of Jefferson, Mississippi, in *As I Lay Dying*. "And then, life wasn't made to be easy on folks: they wouldn't ever have any reason to be good and die" (p. 192). There is also the more imaginative, more humanly expansive (however problematic) use named by Ike McCaslin in "Delta Autumn" (one of the stories from *Go Down, Moses*). Ike describes God's desire that men oppose His will for their ultimate gain. " 'He put them both here: man, and the game he would follow and kill, foreknowing it. . . . But He said, "I will give him his chance. I will give him warning and foreknowledge too, along with the desire to follow and the power to slay" ' " (p. 349). If ever the time comes when men's will coincides with God's will, good shall have been born out of the harsh human experience of resisting goodness. This is what Faulkner's stories try to persuade us is our goal and our impossibility.

The Christian imagination is, of course, not the only one pledged to the virtues of opposition. The humanistic imagination expressed by Gaston Bachelard insists on the will's ability to dominate matter by working through hard-fibered dreams that say "no" to whatever obstructs them. In turn, Bachelard's method is essentially the one used by Thoreau as he prepares to offer his visions for public edification.

Thoreau provides the literary form and language that inflames us with the will to arrive at goals which require us to live in opposition to our present desires, even while he taunts us to succeed now. He dares us not to keep on failing (the easiest act of all), yet sets things so afloat from their fixed points by answering question with questions that we are forced to live in the midst of opposition. Thoreau had moments (as in his journal of February 4, 1841) when he urged men to imitate the fixed stars and to forgo following the eccentric comets, whose movements against the grain of the sky endanger everything in their path. But he also left behind a trail of memoranda meant to stir the divine energy of discontent that counters the plebeian apathy of discontent he saw around him.

Why did he go into the woods, he asked himself in the journal of January 22, 1852, and why leave the pond once there? Movement possesses its own value, he realized, if the stagnation of contentment is to be avoided. He noted in *The Maine Woods* (p. 142) that "Dead Stream" was the Indians' original name for the place now settled as "Concord." Torpor is the impurity of purity, while activity is impurity struggling purely. "Most men have no inclination, no rapids, no cascades, but marshes and alligators, and miasma instead," he wrote disdainfully in *A Week on the Concord and Merrimack Rivers* (p. 137):

> Everywhere "good men" sound a retreat, and the word has gone forth to fall back on innocence. Fall forward rather on to whatever there is there. Christianity only hopes. It has hung its harp on the willows, and cannot sing a song in a strange land. It has dreamed a sad dream and does not yet welcome the morning with joy. (p. 78)

Thoreau preferred not to acknowledge the sturdy resistance to passivity native to the Christianity practiced in the original Massachusetts settlement. He makes it clear, however, that his strategy of disobedience is directed against the way men *think* things are. He does it in order to jolt them back to seeing what things actually are. His literary methods are civil only in that they avoid physical violence, not in the way they shove at the mind.

Neither Christian nor Transcendentalist, Henry Adams was far less sanguine about the ability of man's mind to put itself into successful opposition against the vast forces that oppose the human will. For Adams "the problem of Job" is the agnostic's realization of his tragic powerlessness. From his point of view the positions held within the army-of-the-right must be rearranged. No longer is it man and God arrayed in constant struggle against the foe. More often than not, it is man in pitched battle against the supersensual forces which may themselves be gods. According to Samuels (in *The Major Phase*, pp. 507-510), Adams was like others of his generation in his interest in the sacrificial roles assumed by Prometheus, Cain, Herakles, and Christ, and in the implied belief that through the ritual of sacrifice the human will, the Me, destroys itself in order to release the will-energy that liberates mankind. But however much Adams studied Eastern modes for the submission or obliteration of the self, he stayed closest to Western strategies of skepticism, argument, and resistance as part of his own tragic idealism.

Adams agreed with the Concord philosophers on one score: education is opposition to stasis. He agreed with Emerson's insistence in his 1863-1864 lectures on education that the world exists only to teach us, to stir us to activity. Adams had other companions in imagination who were as distrustful as he of dull equilibrium. We stand on a sliding, tilted surface, Emerson wrote in "The Method of Nature." Our world is a vortex, said Poe many times over. The world is the whirlpool into which the *Pequod* vanishes, suggested Melville. We must be instructed by the fish-principle, declared Thoreau in *A Week on the Concord and Merrimack Rivers*; we must mind the way the salmon fights against the down-plunging water until it mounts to a distinguished death by exhaustion.

1903 marked that stage in Adams' education when he could state, "In plain words, Chaos was the law of nature; Order was the dream of man" (*Education*, p. 451). Even if Emerson and Thoreau would disagree with him on that, for them—as well as for Adams—chaos (the basis for "the problem of Job") is preferable to stagnation. It is certainly better than the failure that comes once "the problem of Job" is resolved. Then there would be nothing left for the self to struggle against, or no self left to struggle with.

Oppositions, hazards, dilemmas, accelerations: all these help define what Norman Mailer openly celebrates in *Of a Fire on the Moon* as the romantic agony. Mailer willingly seeks out consciousness and unconsciousness alike to ask them to navigate him into trouble. The question is not so much whether he follows the Devil or God by doing so, but whether he is heeding the "boy" or the "man" in his nature, the Sawyer or the Strether.

For some time now the anti-romantics in America have been riled by the constant stress placed on questing, journey, movement. Moon-rockets likened to white whales typify exactly the kind of language and the workings of the imagination that are deplored by those wearied by Mailer's flamboyance. They wish all such romantics would go down with the *Pequod*. But so far there has always been one loquacious survivor cast up from the vortex to perpetuate the breed.

Mailer, at least, carries on an argument *against* the Ahabs who know how to oppose only by rushing leaps of defiance. If Mailer likes the romantic tradition that builds the Tower of Babel, that spins the *Pequod* away from the lee shore, and that shoots off rockets at the moon's face for more bizarre reasons than were ever dreamed of by Mission Control, he (like Henry James in *The American Scene*) questions in *Cannibals and Christians* the value of the imagination that restricts itself to the hubris of verticals and is unable to benefit from earth-loving horizontals. But, then, the best of the romantics are intensely objective about their own subjectivity. Their strength comes in countering each wild wish for self-satisfaction with the blessedly sane question, Do you really want to get *that*?

# CHAPTER 27

# The Making of
# a Good Story

The making of American narratives is the writing of a kind of history. By its means we define what America has been and where it might be going, and to what purpose, and by whose sensibility its movements have been directed. It is history as story—perhaps the ultimate record of success or failure.

What initiates our destiny? A good God, the power of evil, a wicked God, a world-soul, matter, fate or chance, Zeus or Whirl, environment, the biology of inherited genes and direct physiological impulses, male or female psychic principles? All these forces have been named the cause of the world we possess and the energy by which individual existence is sustained or concluded. However, it is the mind as First Cause that continues to fascinate and to perturb those who comment on America's wayward progress toward meaning.

Aristotle connected the world's plot with the methods of the literary plot. Both deal with potency of matter and the consciousness which wills it into being. Long after Aristotle and the qualifications made upon his aesthetics, American writers still stress the unsettling adventures of *peripeteia*. They tell us stories about consciousness as the discoverer of unknown places, the shaper of new worlds, and the seer of the ambiguous future America has yet to experience. *Peripeteia in America*: it keeps us in suspense as to the kind of climax the fundamental narrative will have and whether there will be a dénouement that revives us or whether it will be in the deepest sense "a dying fall."

The sciences make use of certain Aristotelian notions of plotting as they theorize on the ways matter and energy spin out the world's narrative. But religion keeps insisting that God is the true master of disclosures and that it is by His revelation alone we will at last be shown where we are going. Those who work with ideas concerning America have often had to choose between these two natures (physical or spiritual force) before singling out the central agent of discovery in that plot they intend to be "significant."

In *Treatise Concerning Religious Affections* of 1746 Jonathan Edwards did not ask for "mere speculative knowledge." What he
wished was "sensible knowledge, in which more than the mere intellect is concerned; the heart is the proper subject of it, or the soul
as a being that not only beholds, but has inclination, and is pleased
or displeased." One generation after Edwards, during a winter lecture series of 1790-1791, James Wilson affirmed in "The Law of
Nature" that we shall discover God's will "by our conscience, by our
reason, and by the Holy Scriptures" since the "law of nature and
the law of revelation are both divine." By 1900 George Santayana
had declined the invitation held out by both Edwards and Wilson.
In an essay of that title Santayana reassessed "the poetry of Christian dogma." He first asked whether "the spiritual experience of
man [is] the explanation of the universe," then responded: "Certainly not, if we are thinking of a scientific, not of a poetical explanation. As a matter of fact, man is a product of laws which must
also destroy him. . . ." And yet, Santayana continues,

> . . . what is false in the science of facts may be true in the sci-
> ence of values. While the existence of things must be under-
> stood by referring them to their causes, which are mechanical,
> their function can only be explained by what is interesting in
> their results, in other words, by their relation to human nature
> and to human happiness.

Like Edwards and Wilson, though for quite different ends, Santayana argues against the life devoted to pure reasoning. In *Reconstruction in Philosophy* of 1920, John Dewey agrees as he rebukes

> . . . the traditional philosophy of intellectualism—that is, of
> knowing as something self-sufficing and self-enclosed. But in
> truth, historical intellectualism, the spectator view of knowl-
> edge, is a purely compensatory doctrine which men of an intel-
> lectual turn have built up to console themselves for the actual
> and social impotency of the calling of thought to which they
> are devoted.

This "spectator view of knowledge"—defined as the "calling"
which renders its priesthood impotent—had been criticized in similarly sexual terms by Emerson in "Self-Reliance" in 1841: "The objection to conforming to usages that have become dead to you is
that it scatters your force." Emerson preferred to use the Cole-
ridgean term "Understanding" to mean the weakened faculty of

thought, whereas he gave honor to "Reason" as "the highest faculty of the soul—what we mean often by the soul itself. . . ."

Emerson explained himself further in a letter of May 31, 1834 to his brother Edward, indicating what he meant about the Reason/ Soul-force: ". . . it never *reasons*, never proves, simply perceives, it is vision" (Rusk, 1, 412-413). Since Emerson's Reason is the same for him as vision, in matters of perceiving plots (human and cosmic) Reason has an intuitive grasp of beginnings and ends; the reasoning Understanding is limited alone to the sense of middles.

In Emerson's so-called "Divinity School Address" of 1838 (where he described Reason as a force very close to that "intuition of the moral sentiment" of which Edwards and Wilson had spoken), he pointed out that the "genre" of the narrative we are living daily alters according to whether we interpret it by means of the senses or by intuitions. "Life is comic or pitiful as soon as the high ends of being fade out of sight, and man becomes near-sighted and can only attend to what addresses the senses." Joyous plots of God realized intuitively are crucially different from the tragic human narratives detected by human rationality. The former is our reality when Reason provides

> . . . an insight of the perfection of the laws of the soul. These laws execute themselves. They are out of time, out of space, and not subject to circumstance. . . . Thought may work cold and intransitive in things, and find no end or unity; but the dawn of the sentiment of virtue on the heart, gives and is the assurance that Law is sovereign over all natures; and the worlds, time, and space, eternity, do seem to break out into joy.

In 1837 Emerson defined the poet as the American Scholar—the man who knows "that nature is the opposite of the soul, answering to it part for part. One is seal and one is print. Its beauty is the beauty of his own mind. Its laws are the laws of his own mind." This assertion differs greatly from Santayana's later view that nature's laws are distinctly other than—and basically antagonistic to—the laws that appeal to the soul. But Santayana, with Emerson, spoke in praise of that mental faculty that *does not scatter force*. He also argued for that mode of interpreting revealed truths and creating values which provides a sense of living beyond an unending muddle of middles.

Henry Adams believed that, like it or not, the middle is where we live. But in *The Education of Henry Adams* he imaged society (the general "middle" we are in) as "a long, straggling caravan"—a line with a head, a middle, and an end; a line of time made up of an archaic rear-guard, an *avant-garde*, and a confused in-between Society stretches "loosely towards the prairies, its few score of leaders far in advance and its millions of immigrants, negroes, and Indians far in the rear, somewhere in archaic time" (p. 237). Those at the rear were the losers in the American historical process; those up front had the concentrated force Adams was convinced he could never share. His place—his force somewhat scattered—was in the middle of chaos; yet his need was to edge close enough to the head to avoid getting lost in helplessness altogether. "His single thought was to keep in front of the movement, and, if necessary, lead it to chaos, but never fall behind. Only the young have time to linger in the rear" (p. 403)—the young or those "so old" they are "out of it."

In 1899 André Lalande wrote, "Thought comes as a result of helplessness." Although agreeing in part, Henri Bergson hoped that thought might reveal the life-force that shares its power with the discoverer. This was the controversy out of which Henry Adams had to work. In *The Suspension of Henry Adams* (p. 211) Vern Wagner says that Hegelianism gave Adams the intellectual method that moved him toward the "larger synthesis." Still, for Adams, the last and largest synthesis would be the discovery which he recorded in *The Education*: that "order and anarchy were one, but that the unity was chaos" (p. 406). Even so, he could not lag at the rear of the caravan. He had to act with the mind, through chaos and in denial of chaos, in order to bring about the end which is chaos. The Conservative Christian Anarchist was on the move, using his force, however scattered. He was not merely given over to what he called a "spectator view of knowledge." Most importantly, he acted as the historian—the interpreter—of his own story.

Interpretation is required. For Emerson "all history is in the mind as thought long before it is executed" (v, 259). This remark from his journal of 1836 is linked with this statement from the essay "Art" of 1841: "There is but one Reason. The mind that made the world is not one mind, but *the* mind." To Emerson such acts of making—of creation—are history. Our vocation is to learn what that making is intended for. According to the tradition that places the First Cause of making elsewhere than in man or nature, the best storytellers are *the created ones*. Emerson simply adds a characteristic twist by saying, as it were, that successfully to interpret what has been written by the Law is also to create. Men's intuitive *reading* of the meaning of Creation becomes a creative *writing* of that story.

Henry James believed that history is not what *happens to* us but what we *read into* random events. James's shift away from any emphasis on the original source of the events is a gentle repudiation of the Lord God or the Over-Soul; but it continues to stress the activity of man's imagination. For Edwards the human imagination endowed by God must act for the greater glory of God; for Emerson and James it serves the glory of men in the midst of living. For all three the greatest value comes from the meaning—the revelation, the reading, the telling—not from the event alone. Henry James, as much as Edwards and Emerson, viewed history as narrative, one in which incident drops back in importance before the crucial matter of correct interpretation. Susan Sontag has offered her generation a vigorous argument against interpretation, but that imagination which is resolutely historical insists on detecting patterns in the plot it finds being enacted *upon* the self as well as *beyond* one's eyes.

The imagination can interpret history as a prayer-wheel, endlessly repetitive, turning on whichever axis—God, fate, electricity—it selects as the propulsive force; or it can diagram history as line or spiral, marking it into segments of beginning, middle, and the culmination toward which all matter, mind, and meaning move. If it is the imagination of Jonathan Edwards, it reads into history the purpose of God and the sense of Last Days. If it is like Emerson's, it escapes middles by seeing beginnings and ends that continue to expand, never resting on one moment of Genesis or of Judgment. If it is like the mind of Henry James and Henry Adams, it lives with middles, examines the past, and cares deeply about a future it intends to keep on interpreting through an unending series of experiments.

In our reading of literary works we commonly do not know what has actually happened in the story (its meaning for us) until we reach the concluding line on the final page. As we consider the task of extrapolating meaning from America's history, we might ask which of the following phrases that conclude certain famous American books best expresses America's future. Will the ending of America come with an epitaph as ambiguous as *"We shall never be again as we were!"*—as joyous as *"The kingdom of man over nature, which cometh not with observation—a dominion such as now is beyond his dream of God—he shall enter without more wonder than the blind man feels who is gradually restored to sight"*—as devastating as *"McTeague remained stupidly looking around him, now at the distant horizon, now at the ground, now at the half-dead canary chittering feebly in its little gilt prison"*—as sweetly sad as *"So we beat on, boats against the current, borne back ceaselessly into the past"*—or as teasing as *"Something further may follow of this Masquerade"?*

Imaginations that helped settle the New England colonies in the 1600s were strongly compelled by plots concerning the human fulfillment of the divinely determined End. By 1848 Theodore Parker described in "The Political Destination of America and the Signs of the Time" yet another future-feeling: "Out of new sentiments and ideas, not seen as yet, new forms of society will come, free from the antagonisms of races, classes, men—representing the American idea in its length, breadth, depth, and height, its beauty and the truth, and then the old civilization of our time shall seem barbarous and even savage" (p. 168). Theodore Dreiser's *Sister Carrie* of 1900 suggests still a third type of narrative conclusion. The story tips over the last page's white space into no true ending; the rhythms of the final sentences speak of ebb, flow, and life's restless dissatisfaction that rocks the imagination toward dreams which will never be fulfilled:

> Oh, Carrie, Carrie! Oh, blind strivings of the human heart! Onward, onward, it saith, and where beauty leads, there it follows. . . . Know, then, that for you is neither surfeit nor content. In your rocking-chair, by your window dreaming, shall you long, alone. In your rocking-chair, by your window, shall you dream such happiness as you may never feel.

There are so many conclusions to choose from in this crucial shell-game in which there is success or there is not.

In her third lecture on *Narration*, Gertrude Stein maintained that there is no longer any succession in narrative structures. Things move in every direction, anything happens, and nothing ever begins or concludes. But the imagination that plotted *Walden* insists on moving human destiny past the repetitious cycles that suffice to content nature but can hardly save men. If the world began with water, as Thoreau keeps saying it did, then the Flood promised at the conclusion of *Walden* will sweep us past our origins to something new.

If both Stein and Thoreau could manage to avoid the mythic by celebrating the new, Frank Kermode for one would be well pleased. In *The Sense of an Ending* Kermode says that the story which proceeds simply and naïvely to a predestined, "old" end is *myth*. He believes that in contrast the *novel* requires *peripeteia*—an ironic discontinuation of the expected, the skepticism which increases our sense of reality. Whether God is naïve and desires fulfillment of His expected ends as myth, or whether He (the fundamental paradigm for Mind Creating is a skilled and shrewd novelist, depends upon whether He works by both idea and ego or by ego alone. *Ego* is the self that suffices without act, or—if it acts— is governed by the desire that needs no sense of cause and effect, only self-perpetuation. *Idea*, however, makes use of ego to go somewhere, proving its value by the something it results in.

If *myth*, idea, and conclusions go together (according to the mode proposed by the New England settlers), and *novel*, ego, and continuations interconnect (in ways suggested above by Theodore Parker's essay), yet a third literary form is possible for the human narrative. Given its aesthetic analysis by Henry Adams in a letter to William James of February 17, 1908 (Ford, II, 490), this is the story whose ending is created by the ego and whose literary type is the *romance*. The God of Augustine is an Ego plotting the perfect romance in full confidence of success. Because Augustine possessed this particular sense of the God-narrator, he alone, Adams stated, had the proper sense of literary form—"a notion of writing a story with an end and object, not for the sake of the object, but for the form, like a romance." Ego is form; ego is subject; form needs no object; form's beauty is its own justification; form is God. The God of Jonathan Edwards as well as of Augustine, He creates in order to fulfill Himself—to give His self a form, not primarily to create objects.

Such a God is not available as an artistic model for Adams, nor will He serve for the patron of Adams' career as writer of the true American autobiography. Adams confesses, "I have worked ten years to satisfy myself that the thing cannot be done today." He cautions James that "you will see why I knew my *Education* to be rotten." Adams' book fails as romance because the author lacks the confidence of an ego that does not need to write to gain an object. It fails, too, as myth. It has ideas about ends but can reach no conclusions. Nor is it able to sustain itself as a novel. Certainly it contains the education of the self through endless surprise. But if it has *peripeteia* and continuation, it lacks an ego that is sufficient to itself and has no care for the causes behind effects.

Shortly after his letter to William James of the 17th of February 1908, Adams wrote another friend on the 28th in reference to the same question of the perfect literary form. In this letter (included in Cater, p. 614) he suggests that perhaps even Augustine had failed at the artist's "only serious study"—"The arrangement, the construction, the composition, the art of climax. . . ." It may be, Adams implies, that only God as artist can succeed· in perfectly identifying form with ego, thereby coming to a true climax that is no lie.

Frank Kermode's objections to grand finales in either literature or history would, however, still hold in this instance. Since the romance form Adams praises included the enactment of "the art of climax," Kermode would doubtlessly reject romance/ego as strongly as he does the combination of myth/idea. Given the premises of his objections, he is correct in doing so. God's romance is unending. Since His Ego is infinite, God has no beginning, middle, or end. But fallible and finite human imaginations, which work out of literary forms based upon their own egos, are as liable to the forcing of conclusions as are artists working with myth/idea.

The aesthetics of apocalypse put a major question to us: can America defined in terms of any one narrative form escape the dangers Kermode is so quick to point out? Richard Chase has said the true American genre is the romance; many agree, but others suggest the myth as being even more typical of American materials. Furthermore, critics like Lionel Trilling have noted that the American experience does not accommodate itself comfortably within the novelistic forms characteristic of England or the Continent. Whatever America's ideal form might be—perhaps even the epic—it is *not* the novel. If the American narrative cannot readily be the novel, and ought not be the romance, myth, or epic (since all these create master receptacles for foregone conclusions), what, then, about the essay? Would it not be the form open-ended enough to placate our fears and yet firm enough to enclose the fluidity of America without undue spillage and scattered force?

Norman Mailer maintains there are two kinds of essay collections: the one is dominated by an *idea* shared in common by all the essays in the group; the other has its fragments coerced into some sort of shape by the grandiose vision of the *ego* in charge. Mailer's own gathering of essays, *Cannibals and Christians*, uses both methods. It is jammed into whatever singleness of purpose it possesses both by the marshalling ego and by its use of section headings such as "Lambs," "Lions," "Respites," and "Arena"—ideas alternating between violence and quietude, typical of his dialectical, combat-crisis imagination. The essays in this collection, and in others put together by Mailer, generally promise, but never quite fulfill, a conclusion arrived at by means of a synthesis that would, if it could, put an end to the pendulum-swing between thesis and antithesis.

In contrast, Emerson's essays are constructed on ideas, circular movements, and the promise of good resolutions just ahead. They are excellent examples of what Kermode might call myth-essays. Mailer characteristically works best with the romance-essay. He is bored by circles because they obey only one law. He is fearful of times ahead that would be "too good." He depends on ego, not ideas, to force meaning forward. Or so it appears. Further examination of the essays of both Mailer and Emerson reveal that Mailer makes use of ideas just as much as Emerson strives to draw his loose structures together by the force of his ego. Mailer and Emerson cannot work solely with one literary form in order to express what they have to say about themselves (as idea-men or ego-types) in relation to their national destiny (as myth or romance).

As Poe would have it, the perfect plot is God's alone; as Adams implies and Augustine and Jonathan Edwards avow, only God possesses the ideal form. But men have to set up the terms of their own lives by the mix of plots and forms they concoct. There is the literary botch predicted by Kermode when artists start mixing up aesthetics with politics, philosophy, and theology. This may be better, however, than the ruined history that comes about when "America," an imagined narrative stiffening into a settled design, crowds in upon America, a reality with no discernible plot.

Mailer, Emerson, and God may be alike in agreeing with Kermode's notion that the final end will occur only when our fictions manage to coincide with reality. America as the fiction created by the mind of the God who was worshipped by the first settlers; as the plot concocted by the Over-Soul celebrated by the Transcendentalists; as the wild tales that rise from the embattled field of Mailer's imagination: in any case, only when that consummate narrative devoted to the discovery of the meaning of America passes through the eye of the needle into actuality will there be an ending. Such an ending would be too quiet and too profound to be recognizable as "wow" by Hemingway's Little Old Lady; still, it would be the most dramatic end imaginable since it would terminate the need for drama and for imagination.

The artist, rather than the social or political reformer, seems to be the one most likely to drive toward terminations, even though he may have the most to lose by his success. David L. Minter in *The Interpreted Design as a Structural Principle in American Prose* has commented concerning *The Education of Henry Adams* that its author "moves toward resolution and vision that are aesthetic, not political; the new heaven and earth are the grounds, not of life, but of art" (p. 124). What Minter detects is that Adams first formulated a philosophy of history that was conventional enough in its motivation, however eccentric in some of the particulars; then Adams began to push his quest for the meaning of history by means of a form—discovered inwardly, not out there in an America or in a universe marked by chaos. Once Adams lost Augustine and Franklin as his literary models (because he had lost their worlds), he had to depend on his own imagination. Only fictions gave him the chance to evade the chaos of incomprehensible forms and the ravages of reality. But part of "the madness of art" (to appropriate Henry James's phrase) is the hope that one day fiction and reality might coincide. To do so would be, at last, to discover the Northwest Passage, the trail to El Dorado, the route to India. That is part of the joke; the many fictions *about America* may be the facts that block the way to the reality that lies *behind America*. As Whitman realized, Columbus had to *invent* America as a fiction before the fiction could be converted into the possibility of the *discovery* of the reality of that world.

How life strikes us is a matter of syntax and style. To say, "Yes, look at the joy and beauty that can come to life, *but* . . ." tips us, through structural stress and language, toward despair. To retort, "Yes, look at the waste and pain of life and the inevitable coming of death's ending, *but* . . ." forces us to consider joy.

Even Susan Sontag, against interpretation as she is, says that the only inevitable thing about a work of art is its style. As we respond to the artist's vision, we may pay little attention to its causal parts; we are affected by the way its mass leans forward into our lives. Art, Nietzsche said, is that supplement to nature that helps us to overcome nature. Though Sontag herself shows no interest in the cosmic dimensions appropriate to the apocalyptic and reveals no anxiety over what America might mean to the imagination as idea, she agrees that art is a powerful force in reaction against all that is not art. She recognizes that it works through a style that cannot be other than what it reveals about itself.

Sontag's theories about literature coincide with others' belief in history as a made-piece that proclaims its style the moment the creator wills it to "go." Although she wants to undercut attempts to uncover values in art that encourage moral interpretations, style stubbornly remains tied to the values (concerns, interests) by which the creator seals his being. God is Love, some say, but Mailer's God, for instance, responds to courage instead. Love might want to pause in the process of existence, even to halt movement altogether in the name of order and reconciliation and in the hope of reveling in peaceful idylls. Courage, in contrast, exists only to go on resisting; it is rude enough to brush past the queue of slow waiting that is necessary to gain love's grace. Like Mailer, Thoreau also distinguishes between poets who are lovers writing *aubades* that lament the coming of the dawn because it puts an end to the ecstasy of love, and poets who cultivate courage by writing hymns of welcome to the sun. *Walden*'s conclusion denies whatever might impede unending futures of new discoveries: "Only that day dawns to which we are awake. There is more day to dawn. The sun is but a morning-star." Morning brought sorrow to Romeo and Juliet, and to Cupid and Psyche, but not to Thoreau since he had no lover to leave behind and everywhere yet to go.

In a journal entry of March 24, 1842, Thoreau noted that the progress of a narrative is the substitute for visible movement. Narrative is made by the priest-storyteller whose tale winds like "a cameltrack" among its sentences; failure lies only in the teller's fear of moving on. We can see this in Mailer's *Advertisements for Myself*. The structuring of the fragments is as "relativistic" as his stress on the existential life can make it. Yet it concludes with the impulse to ascend, not to fall away, in the piece called "On the Way Out, Prologue to a Long Novel." In a book which is a loose-knit conglomeration of brief "classified ads" and "personals" urged on by the arduous strain of its dialectics, Mailer places his final stress on the insistence to take up the strenuous option "to go —." He is as willing to follow the authority of his sentences as of his senses: he moves on, else language and its reality stagnate and stink. After all, he is not moving toward an end in sight. He is carefully providing only a "prologue" to a "Long Novel."

Critics apprehensive of art that sets up patterns that move from a beginning toward an end often fail to see how many of the "endings" which they assail have no true terminus. Kermode attacks as immature at best and "fascist" at worst the design-maker who, losing sight of "reality," falls overly in love with his "fictions." Leo Bersani has counter-attacked Kermode on this. In a *New York Times Book Review* piece of June 11, 1967, Bersani suggested that that reality Kermode is so anxious to protect from the imagination may be as much a lie as anything else. Can we ever check or qualify our fictions, he asks, except against other fictions?

We can take Leo Bersani's question and apply it to other critics who condemn the imagination for creating patterns for America's meaning that sin against reality. They may be setting up their own fictions as the truth about America. Rather than giving in to yelling-matches ("My fiction is better than your fiction"), perhaps we can give extra credit to those fictions which choose tentative conclusions marked by the "go" of further discovery. At least the poet of the New World who explores new ways to fail and who attempts excessiveness (what Thoreau praised as extravagance) does not possess the self-limitations and obsession with immediate success which the Old World has come to represent to more minds than that of Gertrude Stein.

There is an old trick used to check added columns of numbers that is called "casting out nines." If the addition is correct, you come up with a zero rather than a solid and supposedly usable number; according to this test, zero means you know exactly the reality of what you have. With this in mind, we could start to add up everyone's vision in order to arrive at the sum of the American narrative. Having included all styles (from Burroughs' bad dream of America as the cannibal isle back to Bradford's vision of America as a haven for Christian souls), we could then delete the "nines"— the expendable fictions which leave behind the zero that testifies to the accuracy of one's "casting out." But let us attend just now to the initial process of "casting in" the varied elements from which fictions and reality alike are compiled.

Style to Thoreau meant the sense of the whole. It was seizure of the essential forms of reality which reveal workable relationships, not merely believable statements. His attempt to shape "America" in terms of a written style (or multitude of styles) gives us a whole—a complex of relationships—which impresses itself upon us even when his individual statements are misleadingly orphic or overly didactic. For Mailer, style is greater than the artist, who must strain to fit himself to his prose, yet that style only exists because the self-effacing artist first sets it moving. What Thoreau and Mailer most mean by the function of style is reflected in Hugh Kenner's description of Buster Keaton's art. In *The Counterfeiters* Kenner speaks of Keaton's transcendent juggling act. Once Keaton sets his little universe in motion, the balls seem to possess a life beyond any he might endow them with. The only point of calm in the tumultuous scene is Keaton's own impervious face, but it is out of that calm—that small still point—that the energy and the style pour forth. In the various versions of the story of America provided by men like Thoreau and Mailer, believers in style as the enclosing whole, that style is Keatonian: it is greater than, but child of, its fathering intelligence.

Style is crucial, and also form.

In her book on art, hazard, and value, Sister Mary Slattery argues that we have an inborn love of forms and limits. A wished-for thing is endowed with value partially because of the *virtue* of this wish (not just "by virtue of"). Once the consciousness of our need is put into relationship with the thing's structural principle, fulfillment is easier to attain. The structure makes the value actual; it insists both upon the thing's uniqueness and its relatedness within a system which includes our ideas about it. Here is an example from *The Ambassadors*. Lambert Strether seeks the pleasure of the French countryside, which he has framed within his perception as if it were a Lambinet painting. But the raw actualities of passion and of moral complexity are forced upon his consciousness. Once the protecting aesthetic frame is removed and reality flows in, the facts of passion and complexity become part of that same lovely landscape. Or so it happens for Strether's consciousness. For us the readers, Henry James provides the framing structure of the novel that enhances the value of what we look upon even after the "inner frame" of the Lambinet conceit is removed; it lets us experience the truth of the scene as a whole we can deal with, shielding us in part from realities we might not be able to bear if assaulted by them as fragments. In the privileged position of being able to assimilate more than Strether, we are also sheltered from the devastating effects of that excessive knowledge. Is it not the same when we read narratives disclosing the meaning of America which exceed the comprehension of the characters (less-knowing and less-protected) submerged *within* those narratives?

In one of the last essays he wrote before his death, "A Pluralistic Mystic" (excerpted in Perry, p. 213), William James reiterates a phrase basic to his philosophy: "There is no conclusion." It is significant, however, that he structurally contains the supposed openness of that sentence; he sets it within the context of the words which immediately precede it: "Let *my* last word, then. . . ." An important distinction is being made here. There may be no conclusions for the world, but we each have the right to make farewell statements about life as it has finally come to be for us.

Henry James ended "The Art of Fiction" (included in *The James Family*) with the caution, "If you must indulge in conclusions, let them have the taste of a wide knowledge. Remember that your first duty is to be as complete as possible—to make as perfect a work." The brothers James would not consider that the remarks by which they concluded these essays were contradictory of their sustained belief in inconclusiveness. What mattered to them were the open possibilities for attempting completion, perfection, and conclusion; this, acting in conjunction with the saving fact of the impossibility of final achievement. It also counted heavily that they could, and must, *decide* on certain values by which to shape the tale one lives and writes about. Thus Henry James offered as *his* last word for "The Art of Fiction," "Be generous and delicate and pursue the prize."

Part of the delicacy involves the limits past which one refuses to go to pursue that prize. The Jameses would go *only so far*, not all the way to conclusion. This was as much because they believed that this is the way things ought to be (their "fictions") as it was because it is the way things are (their "reality"). But we have seen many others who—however much they prize the pursuit—covet the gaining of the prize even more.

Norman Mailer's ambition often seems to focus upon becoming the Thomas Arnold of his era; not the schoolmaster described by Henry Adams, who tells lies to little boys, but the consummate teacher-scholar Adams himself aspired to become. But will Mailer ever be serene enough to be a good influence? Richard Poirier worries about this in his book on Mailer. Mailer sees writing as warfare, and if he wants to be our teacher he also wishes to be named a commanding general, one who could direct successful attacks on the Pentagon. In *Four in America* Gertrude Stein gives us her portrait of Henry James as a general—one who knows how to win not only armies but battles and wars as well. What Stein says about James is probably closer in type to Mailer's view of himself than to James's occasional self-characterizations as a man working serenely without tension.

Let us line up Mailer with James, marking their similarities and unlikenesses, in order to see how they shape forms for the American scene that strike toward conclusions, pull back short of finality, and continue to create values.

Resistance is the main strategy of the artist-general against the forces of environment and circumstance; form is the result. To phrase it as Mailer might, form is born of the fathering soul upon the weltering fecundity of the writer's "curious" mind as it impregnates America with meaning. Mailer's style, conceived of concept and obscenity, *is* America. James possesses concept but no obscenity, even though his consciousness (to use *his* terms) is given to sexuality—to fertilizing the flowers around him in the act of deep probing.

Mailer is as fearful of formlessness as James ever was of the American Margin. Failure to Mailer means being a blob, suffering the fate of other nice Jewish boys from Brooklyn who have never licked themselves into shape through the raging need to create meaning out of chaos. James, the small boy from Manhattan, created himself out of his consciousness, once he realized he would fail at having any other kind of existence.

Mailer projects himself verbally into a future perfect condition—*I shall have written*. As Poirier notes, form for Mailer is the spiraling destiny that moves far beyond any present act. James marks a real difference on this score by continually embarking upon voyages of *I have begun*. As Stein remarked, his writing stresses the long preparations of art that provide us with as much weight of meaning *now* as any future achievement.

James's notebooks are safe-deposit vaults where interest accrues over years of patient waiting. Even though Mailer constantly works *toward* a large future work, he may not be unlike James in this. Mailer tells us he saves out good things from his current writing for later use; he wants to have just enough of the best ready if the time comes to move past the dialectics that typify his usual method.

As Poirier says it, the dialectic is the form central to Mailer's style. It is what provides him with his sanity. By means of his long sentences (upon which his form depends as much as does James's), Mailer discovers links and explodes past stalemates into oppositions. But Poirier is concerned that Mailer's dialectical method may seal him into an intellectual box too cut off from air for sustained life (the problem some critics also see as pressing down upon James's style). Poirier depicts Mailer as living on the divide between a world of recordable reality and a place of omens, a split-existence dangerous to his art (though James's 1917 letter to Adams might indicate to Poirier the advantages of life lived by the artist on the edge of abysses). Certainly Poirier's nervousness is well founded whenever Mailer indulges himself in facile remarks about the dire future of the imagination in a dread age of technology. Mailer may also have some struggling to do to get out of the closed room of his dialectical style. But to remain true to his essential devotion to dualism, he probably needs to keep on cliff-hanging between two worlds. The real risk his *style*, his *America*, takes is the temptation to give in to the word-mongering that supports the conspiratorial school of apocalypse. Yet it looks as if he might escape. There is his healthy boredom with clichés of doom-saying, his strenuous and expensive honesty, and his distaste over ever bringing things to an end.

We are still discovering how accurate Henry James was about the American scene (those aspects of it he could or would look upon in 1904). By means of *I have begun writing*, he gets us started on discovering something of what America is. Perhaps one day, through his *I shall have written*, Mailer will help move us even closer to America's reality. But even if he holds back on the synthesis of resolution, even if he keeps on delighting in complexity and refuses to choose one side of a paradox over the other, and even if he shares certain traits with the English philosopher Gregory Bateson, Mailer will probably resist Bateson's theory of detours.

As described in *Harper's* of November 1973, Gregory Bateson detests destinations, evaluations, choices, purposes. He would have us never head down the road toward paradise. Sounding like D. H. Lawrence fulminating against Walt Whitman, Bateson believes that the end of that straight and open road is death. Bateson argues that it is better to keep making detours and never to get anywhere in particular; this way we will insure that we remain *somewhere*. For all Mailer's wildness and love of intricacy, he, in contrast to Bateson, insists on direction, movements forward, declarations of intent, and statements of preference. The literary *shall have* of his heart's desire is joined to an *idea* of the self and of America, not to random, instinctive jottings.

From such urges felt by Mailer are absolutists and fanatics created. The man of ideas who insists they are only fictions likes to work with concepts because he recognizes them as mere directions; he views them as stimulating motives that never pretend fulfillment and that forever evade the perfect conclusion. But Mailer continues to imply a serious interest in the absolute. He does not seem to believe that his "fictions" are fictitious. He is working too close in to the arm-pit of God or the rear-entrance of the Devil not to believe he has had a vision of America that converts idea past whim into something approximating truth.

As for Henry James, he is to the left of Mailer on matters of believing that ideas can ever come true. But he is like Mailer (and, like Mailer, light-years away from Bateson) in *wanting* the idea to happen and in urging movements that go *toward* the heart of value. Yet both Mailer and James stay with the need to resist fulfillment.

When James writes in *The American Scene*, "Character is developed to visible fineness only by friction and discipline on a large scale, only by its having to reckon with a complexity of forces . . ." (p. 427), he wants to put that character to work *doing something fine* (a most un-Batesonian note). Mailer also feels "the Woollett strain," even as he—together with the best of the Jamesian types—moves past "the Woollett simplicity" toward the complexity that has too much of interest to act upon for him ever to wish to do it once and for all.

Norman Mailer is an improvisor. This is the point at which Mailer and James begin to diverge. James consciously works out symmetries of design in his attempt to render the random openness of life concrete and to yield glimpses of the steady value of values, whereas Mailer argues that the imagination must constantly extemporize. Style, says Poirier in his discussion of Mailer, is the way to escape the heavily deterministic hand of sociological formulas. Henry James and Mailer concur on this need; but in ways quite unlike James, Mailer wants style to be a nervous seismograph of whatever comes into the artist's head. James stands against pat endings that give out presents to everyone; Mailer goes farther in pressing for endings so unexpected they might just go off in the face of the surprised author.

Studies of the satiric mode, such as Robert Elliott's *The Power of Satire: Magic, Ritual, Art*, frequently note that the comic tradition originated in improvisations made by leaders of the Phallic songs. Once men learned to use sexual magic, they moved on to satiric critiques of the way things are, blending them with hope as to the way things might yet—wonderfully—become. This is the kind of fertile artist's act Mailer approves of, edged as it is with the phallic, the magical, and the satiric, and possessed of power to threaten corrupt leaders and to win wars interestingly.

Mailer's 1973 assessment of *Last Tango in Paris* for *The New York Review of Books* stresses that the "real problem" in this film is "to find some ending which is true to what has gone before and yet is sufficiently untrue to enable the actors to get alive." He cautions, "One does not add improvisation to a script which is already written and with an ending that is locked up," because "improvisation which is anything less than the whole of a film is next to no improvisation." If Bertolucci, the film's director, had given the story over to Marlon Brando, the film would have discovered itself in the act of creating itself. But Bertolucci kept too tight a hold and literally *directed* the *actor*. He turned Brando into what Henry James, Senior, called in his essay "Moralism and Christianity" a mere artisan—a man who is forced to record events already supplied with a priori conclusions. Only if Brando could have gone on his own would he have been the *artist* of true creation.

The aesthetic Emerson presents in his poem "Woodnotes" has the look of the god-as-Brando:

> Ever fresh the broad creation,
> A divine improvisation,
> From the heart of God proceeds. . . .

Actually, in Emerson's view the universal grows out of "A single will, a million deeds"—creation by the god-as-Bertolucci, who pushes forward "the world's incessant plan." True, that "single will" and that "incessant plan"

> Halteth never in one shape,
> But forever doth escape,
> Like wave or flame, into new forms. . . .

But to Emerson that directing will is good, the forethought plan is clear, and it is God, not man, who is the real improvisor. How different this is in kind from the improvisations urged by Mailer! He is for a myriad of amoral wills in a seemingly purposeless series of acts that lurch randomly toward ill results.

Mailer's irritation over *Last Tango in Paris* focuses on the fact that Marlon Brando was able brilliantly to improvise blasphemy and violence but was not encouraged by Bertolucci to go all the way into the forbidden and unknown. For Mailer, "A long speech can hardly be an improvisation if its line of action is able to go nowhere but back into the prearranged structures of the plot." If Brando's obvious urge to assail God is ever allowed the full power of expression, "Then we may all know a little more of what God is willing or unwilling to forgive."

As Mailer has it (and as Henry James, Senior, argued), the artist ought not simply imitate a preconceived plot out of necessity, thereby remaining "the mere artisan." The artist must test the value of the divine plan by creating on the spot that verbal resistance which God—the "film director" who is a flexible and canny thinker—then incorporates vitally into His plot. If He cannot, then this *is* as junky and meaningless a world as William Burroughs says it is. If He can, then it is a place in which the true actor can take delight—since its meanings leap out of the glorious improvisations provided by each slippery movement of lived-in time.

If plots that are too tightly controlled are a menace to vitality, what about plots that never end?

Angus Fletcher, in writing of allegory, says one weakness of that literary form is its seeming inability to conclude. Plots that imitate the perfection of perpetual motion machines become, almost literally, a deadly bore. Poe's *The Narrative of Arthur Gordon Pym*—an imperfect plot concocted by man according to Poe's own aesthetic theory—and his *Eureka*—the perfect plot of God according to the poet's testimony—must both come to their endings: the former by being arbitrarily chopped off, the latter by spinning to a massively foreordained conclusion. Franklin's *Autobiography* and Adams' *The Education*, which "allegorize" the lives of two Americans, must finally choose endings appropriate to their form and meaning. Franklin gets up from his desk, leaving his papers unfinished, in order to go on about his life, no matter how late it is in terms of the time of his life. Adams ceases to write once King and Hay have died in harness. As the last member of this triumvirate, he is already "dead"; his "posthumous report" might as well conclude. Franklin's book ends because all life needs to go on; Adams' book ends because his living is over. But both books manage to escape the terrible fate of never ending at all.

Compare Mark Twain. He often contracted with his publishers to write according to certain lengths. Linear composition gets so many dollars per written yard. Under this regime, narrative episodes can multiply until exasperation (on the part of writer or editor) forces an arbitrary cutting-off point. To borrow the metaphor his own fiction provides, Mark Twain constantly had to try not to pass by Cairo in the fog of his books. He needed to touch in on free soil as quickly as possible so as to avoid the fate of an author enslaved to unending episodes that send his narrative-craft drifting on and on down the river. Otherwise, Tom Sawyer gets called in to supply a patched-up ending based on his notion of gaudy plays-within-plays and tricky, sometimes inhumane, always protracted conclusions.

As Meyer Abrams describes it in *Natural Supernaturalism* (p. 173), Hegel's dialectical method follows a preordained plot which begins during that "moment" (out of time) when the ego sets object apart from subject. Once the pendulum starts to swing between thesis and antithesis we may feel we are caught in the tedium of a design which promises no relief (which is precisely what Poirier dislikes about Mailer's method). Abrams suggests that Hegel's version of the world-plot locates its origin just after the Fall. Its wearying subject/object movement can quite possibly go nowhere; it will continue everlastingly until, somehow, it is able to return to Eden—a beginning which would put a longed-for stop to the human narrative by bringing into blessed synthesis the radically separated positions of Ego and World.

Such a reunion of alien elements as Hegel called for is unlikely when the plot in question is the doing of several minds. Mark Twain's humorous account in *Roughing It* of the collaborative writing of a newspaper serial provides a cautionary tale about what it would be like to live in a world whose plot lacks any central artistic control or any sense of an ending.

> Mrs. F. was an able romancist of the ineffable school—I know no other name to apply to a school whose heroes are all dainty and perfect. She wrote the opening chapter, and introduced a lovely blonde simpleton who talked nothing but pearls and poetry and who was virtuous to the verge of eccentricity. She also introduced a young French duke of aggravated refinement, in love with the blonde. Mr. F. followed the next week, with a brilliant lawyer who set about getting the duke's estates into trouble. . . . Mr. D., a dark and bloody editor of one of the dailies, followed Mr. F., the third week, introducing a mysterious Roscicrucian [sic] who transmuted metals, held consultations with the devil in a cave at dead of night, and cast the horoscope of the several heroes and heroines in such a way as to provide plenty of trouble for their future careers and breed a solemn and awful public interest in the novel. (VIII, 97-98)

Contemplate the idea of America which acts according to an unfinished Hegelian plot: regulated sternly, monotonously swinging between thesis and antithesis, forever blocked from its conclusion. Then conceive of America as an absurd tale patched together by a group of Twainian authors from a meaningless hash of "troubles" who never decide on an ending and argue endlessly over plot details. We might at first think it a blessing when a new would-be author walks into the newspaper office to take over the Twainian narrative. He is a drunken poet who is more than a bit like the legendary Poe "with his imagination in a state of chaos, and that chaos in a condition of extravagant activity" (VIII, 98).

The Twain/Poe-drunk declares his intention to be "not only pleasant and plausible but instructive" (VIII, 100). Under his hands the newspaper serial (meant to stand here as one possible handling of the America-narrative) proceeds as follows:

> He scanned the chapters of his predecessor, found plenty of heroes and heroines already created, and was satisfied with them; he decided to introduce no more; with all the confidence that whiskey inspires and all the easy complacency it gives to its servant, he then launched himself lovingly into his work. (VIII, 98-99).

The drunken poet marries off or murders all the other characters; then he

> . . . opened the earth and let the Roseicrucian [sic] through, accompanied with the accustomed smoke and thunder and smell of brimstone, and finished with the promise that in the next chapter, after holding a general inquest, he would take up the surviving character of the novel and tell what became of the devil! (VIII, 99)

Hegel left incomplete, and Mark Twain winding crazily to a conclusion: these are two kinds of nightmare plottings possible for the story of America that could give anyone pause. Here is yet another, furnished by F. Scott Fitzgerald.

As Fitzgerald viewed the enclosed fictional world of Ring Lardner in his 1933 piece (included in *The Crack-Up*, p. 37) on this tale-teller of the ball-park and the boy-world of perennial athletic contests, he shuddered:

> Imagine life conceived as a business of beautiful muscular organization—an arising, an effort, a good break, a sweat, a bath, a meal, a love, a sleep—imagine it achieved; then imagine trying to apply that standard to the horribly complicated mess of living, where nothing, even the greatest conceptions and workings and achievements, is else but messy, spotty, tortuous—and then one can imagine the confusion that Ring faced on coming out of the ball park.

It is difficult to tell which Fitzgerald fears the most: the shock of life experienced by the innocent who has to follow the ball once it is knocked out of the park, or life played forever within the boundaries of the high board-fence. If America is what some imaginations take a ball-park to be, the stories about what goes on inside

this country could be as frightening in their regulations as
Abrams' version of Hegel or as the Mark Twain tales that do away
with rules, naïveté, and decisions.

"Who? Who did this?" Edward Taylor asks as he surveys the
world around him in "The Preface" to *Gods Determinations Touching
His Elect.*

> . . . Why, know
> Its onely Might Almighty this did doe.
> His hand hath made this noble worke which stands
> His Glorious Handywork not made by hands.
> Who spake all things for nothing; and with ease
> Can speake all things to nothing, if he please.

In Poe's "The Power of Words" the angel speaks new worlds
into being. In *Walden* Thoreau defines the chief duty of man as the
telling of his love for all living things in the speech natural to free
men. In contrast to these provocative theories concerning the relation of language to the idea of America, certain other analysts devoted to asking what an American is have taken a more simplistic
line. People fearful of the immigrant flood argued that merely *to
speak English* would make one a proper American. English adhered
to as the common speech would be a wall against the alienating torrents of Babel; all varieties of races might be safely assimilated into
American culture if America's speech could only be regularized
and controlled. But this is just the kind of language Mailer fears.
Betrayed by the jargon of NASA and Mission Control, the vital
language of concept and obscenity seems in danger of becoming
computerized. Once this happens, Mailer wonders, how will
Americans have the right, strong words to use against evil? He feels
at ease only when he is able to count on "The powerful language of
resistance" which Whitman praised in his 1855 Preface to *Leaves of
Grass*:

> . . . the dialect of common sense . . . the chosen tongue to ex-
> press growth faith self-esteem freedom justice equality friend-
> liness amplitude prudence decision and courage. It is the
> medium that shall well nigh express the inexpressable. (p. 728)

Even "good" language has the force to destroy as well as to
create; it can resist the world as well as act to restore it—or so poets
argue, out of the only power they possess. In "Letter to American
Teachers of History" Henry Adams uses his own versatility with

language to describe the possible end of the world in a style sufficient in felicity to suggest the strange beauty of such an important
occasion. He also pauses to chastise the cheap effects wrung out of
catastrophe by "vulgarizers of science" such as Camille Flamma-
rion, a man who speaks "with a certain sombre exaltation, like a religious prophet" armed with an array of exclamation marks. Emerson and Thoreau were also ranged against the vulgarians of the
word who are thereby corruptors of the world. Unlike Adams, they
sought to use language to remind men of the goodness of the universal laws. They kept insisting that in the beginning words were
encountered directly as signals of natural objects; in turn, words
and objects were in accord with the spiritual facts. For the Transcendentalists, men would be saved if they could relearn the proper
language and reconvert all things to strength and success. But for
Adams language could only shape with seriousness worthy
epitaphs to a dying world or wittily find fun in staving off disaster
for yet a little while.

Emerson, Thoreau—and Gertrude Stein: all three viewed facts
as living ideas that realize themselves as words. Words, Stein said in
*The Making of Americans*, control the universal fate of exciting beginnings, recircling ends, and joyously burgeoning repetitions.
Some writers seem bent on destroying words, as well as ending
worlds, but not Stein. Her own vocabulary was held down in size.
This was not because she had so little to say about how Americans
are made. She had so much to say she needed to single out those
few special words which possess weight, form, and real being.

Rhetoric, if it is viewed as the elaborate use of inflated words, is
without power to create or even to sustain life. In speaking of
Faulkner when he fails with words, Wright Morris in *The Territory
Ahead* concludes, "A rhetorical passage will neither redeem man
nor save him from himself" (p. 35). If the words "endure" and
"prevail" have no weight or form or real being, they escape into the
atmosphere like trivial gases. Faulkner himself knew this. In an
early review of 1922 for *The Mississippian* that sized up the novels of
Joseph Hergesheimer (included in Carvel Collins' collection), he
condemned the man who is enslaved by words because he is "afraid
of living." Hergesheimer wrote "flawless prose," but because he
could not bear life "he is like an emasculate priest surrounded by
puppets he has carved and clothed and painted—a terrific world
without motion or meaning."

As William James commented in rebuke of those who charged
that his writing style has many flaws (*Letters*, II, 86), "Isn't fertility

better than perfection?" It is as Sylvia Plath said (and as Arthur Oberg brought out with fine clarity in his 1972 article "The Modern British and American Lyric: What Will Suffice"), "Perfection is terrible, it cannot have children." Whether it is force scattered in disarray, or force frozen in perfection, there is no chance, either way, of going on.

In another review of 1922 (also included in Collins' edition), "American Drama: Inhibitions," Faulkner argued the old argument that in America "language is our logical savior." It may be dangerous to locate saving grace in any human skill which tempts the user to consider himself divine. But poets, and certainly those in America, often view themselves as persons who can succeed where others have failed—even God. Although many American poets possess a basic skepticism about the special power of language and self-doubts about their ability to use it well, they continue to try, through words, to discover America, not merely to reinvent it. But will those words be used by the Pharisees—the scholars; or will they be taken over by the Sadducees—the anti-intellectuals whom Faulkner scorns as word-mongers who typify America's "paucity of mental balance"?

Will the true American voice adhere to the tradition that the Scriptures—which contains all the World there is—enforces the Law of its words? Or will that true voice speak out for the American antinomianism by which free-form verbal revelations unbalance the stability of a priori word-patterns? Is the idea of God's plan and man's design for America already fixed in a written covenant that sticks to the letter—whether it follows the form of the Constitution or some other traditional document? Or is the best idea for America still to be discovered through spontaneous acts of telling tales about its spirit?

While the old man studies the Bible in the cabin of the riverboat *Fidèle* at the close of Melville's *The Confidence Man*, the Cosmopolitan undermines our faith in Holy Writ by the fact that he insists we place full confidence in it. Surely this scene forces us to reconsider the nature of the *literary* forms the Scriptures contains. Omens, truths, confessions, contradictory accounts, self-justifications, and inspired messages from God or Devil are all there. As viewed through the moted eye of *The Confidence Man* the Bible is simply a created work of art, a concept, as much and no more reliable as a revelation of the Truth than, say, *Nature* or *The Great Gatsby*; than *Divine and Supernatural Light* or *The Devil's Dictionary*; than *Uncle Tom's Cabin* or *The Invisible Man*. And when we read the narrative called "America," is it apocrypha we find, or canon law? If it is apocrypha, perhaps it is also what the querulous voice from the cabin-berth suggests when he asks, "What's this about Apocalypse?" But it is the master of the strange doings on board the *Fidèle*—Melville himself—who has the final say (the "last word" concerning the lack of conclusions of which William James has spoken): "Something further may follow. . . ."

# The Economics
# of Going On

# CHAPTER 28

# Going Up and Coming Down

Edgar Allan Poe's *Eureka* of 1848 fulfilled the dearest wishes of its author's gothic soul by cleansing the universe of all matter (that basic fact of human failure) through the return to the purity of the primal Thought. The result is an apocalypse with a happy ending—for the Poe-narrator at least, if not for the rest of us—since consciousness ends where it began: with itself alone, and all because God's plan has been carried through without a flaw.

In Poe's critical notes (edited by Robert Hough) he argued that the mortal artist forms his material by "combination." He cannot, as God can, create or destroy. "The mind of man can imagine nothing which does not exist: if it could, it would create not only ideally, but substantially—as do the thoughts of God" (p. 14). According to *Eureka* God's mind conceives a plot—a perfect arrangement of causes and effects—which will return the universe of failed matter to its original Cause, thereby providing the grandest, most successful Effect of all time. But what if the *human* mind stumbles by chance upon that same perfect combination; what if it strews just the right words across the page in just the right order that has the power to end or to create?

It is unlikely that a mind positioned in the midst of mystery can detect the key to the master code. Deciphering the puzzle of the universe might be possible, however, if the mind could place itself above and beyond what Kermode calls the hurly and the burly. Perhaps from that vantage point "the purloined letter" we all search after could be discovered.

Poe's C. A. Dupin can link words spread across maps, uncover lost correspondence, win at whist, and break the mysteries of locked rooms because his mathematical-poetical mind has no limits to its range. Dupin's mind is the same as God's; in its scope it contains what William James described as the classical-academic and the romantic-gothic capacities to deal with both theories and facts. He is of course potentially a threat to the rest of humankind. Not only can he read comic plots, he might make them up to his own satisfaction, although not to ours, since there is no guarantee that they will be safe ones. Enjoyment in the Poe-world comes only to the author; *our* feelings would be more like those of Faulkner's Joe Christmas. A man who tells himself that he is an integral part of a fated plot forcefully directed by a coldly logical God experiences terror as well as initiates terror in others; but knowingly to be *in* a plot is not the same as writing out its design for others.

One Poe-type is wild to bridge the chasms in a flawed world as yet unresponsive to the plot made by a God devoted to the perfect unity of self and universe. The other Poe-view, that of Dupin, controls things through a grasp of wholes and sees causes and entireties, not merely links and parts. The effect upon the reader of either type is frightening. The Pym-hysteric screeches as he falls toward where there is no bottom or meaning, and we fall with him. The Dupin-detective impassively makes out the whole design of the universe; it is we, not he, who feel the fear of existing in a world planned according to a divine mind as chillingly rational as Dupin's own.

Poe's own art seeks to provide that wholeness which Joseph Wood Krutch described in *Edgar Allan Poe, A Study in Genius*. The curve drawn by Poe's canon, says Krutch, "unifies all the various aspects of his life and work . . ." (p. 236). But the curve of Poe's art—unlike the circles of Emerson and Thoreau—does not bring us healing. The Poe-artist twirls on his heel in *Eureka* to create a center; but it is the violent eye of the vortex that his act discloses, not the beneficent heart of the world-soul. The Poe-mind also has the power to destroy the structure it creates whenever enraged by its imperfections. In his sonnet "The Nihilist as Hero" from *Notebook*, Robert Lowell wrote of the man who gazes "the impossible summit to rubble" so that he may "live in the world as it is." In contrast, the Poe-mind destroys out of the frustration of its ideals, not in rejection of its fantasies.

Emerson and Thoreau felt calm joy over the cosmic pattern even on days they were not directly assigning the god-role to themselves—*especially* on such days. On other days of the self-as-creator there could creep in the "noble doubt" about existence Emerson discusses candidly in *Nature*. Even so, as Emerson states in Chapter IV of that essay, "Whether nature enjoys a substantial existence without, or is only in the apocalypse of the mind, it is alike useful and venerable to me." *Simply to know* that there are external lines of benevolent force that thread through the All-Soul, the natural world, and one's own soul, joining all to the laws of the universe, is sufficient. It was when the Transcendentalists sensed that the connection between themselves and the world-soul was dropping away that fear could mount within them.

Norman Mailer is the third type of imagination which tries to survey *the whole situation* in order to see where we are being taken by the pull of time. According to Richard Poirier, Mailer wishes to write from a view so large as to be outside history. Resisting the merely local and immediate (the only range of vision available to nice boys from Brooklyn), Mailer revels in panoramas of the war of worlds—contests between imagination and technology, between cannibals and christians, between God and the Devil. The "big novel" he is currently embarked upon—as if he were Noah in the ark, put in charge by God of preserving two of everything for posterity—was once rumored to include reports on the progress of humanity from the beginnings of time on out to the moon-future. Although Mailer has denied this, something of the kind would be appropriate to his ache to know and to tell all. Impatient for answers, he looks for the patterns of causes and effects within his own imagination. Mailer can only hope that his plot has some connection with God's plot, but in the meantime he sweats to synthesize. He does not merely wait to find out. He follows pell-mell after the Navigator of his instincts, his dream, his *idea* about America and the future of the race.

Poe/the Transcendentalists/Mailer: each provides the economics of three visions of the future. Poe and the Transcendentalists are alike in permitting no waste. Poe's vision is the most spare; his perfect Unity has subtracted all matter from the universe to leave pure consciousness behind. The Transcendentalists' Oneness is inclusive of all things, phenomena and noumena alike. Mailer, who has always rather liked waste materials—even of (especially of) the excremental kind—wants a wholeness that is more bloated than lean, more liverish than ascetic. All three imaginative types want wholes, however; in this only, they agree, is there success. But what the whole consists of and how it is to be realized differs for these three essentially Romantic imaginations. Their varying methods depend upon the particular act of synthesis each performs.

Herbert Spencer's *First Principles* of 1862 stated the premise upon which the achievements of a synthesizing philosophy rest:

> At the close of a work like this, it is more than usually needful *to contemplate as a whole* that which the successive chapters have presented in parts. . . . It is requisite that we should retire a

space, and, looking at the entire structure from a distance at which details are lost to view, observe its general character. . . . [Italics mine]

Spencer seems to be one of those thinkers who yearn, as Gaston Bachelard phrases it, to stand beyond the world and weigh it on the scales of his mind. Certainly what Spencer sought as he stepped back to look was proof of the permanency of the world. What he found was "The Persistence of the Relations among Forces," ordinarily called "Uniformity of Law"—"a necessary implication of the truth that Force can neither arise out of nothing nor lapse into nothing."

John Fiske believed that many American intellectuals had taken over Spencer's perspective by 1874. When Fiske asks rhetorically in *Outlines of Cosmic Philosophy* (II, 145), "What proof have we that no force is ever created or destroyed?" he provides an image for the argument concerning the ancient necessity of stepping back to take a good look (II, 145-146). "Below the world stands the elephant on the back of the tortoise, and if under the tortoise we put the god Vishnu, where is Vishnu to get a foothold?" That is the difficulty: in order to find proof for the solidity of the universe, we must stand back far enough to see it. But how dare we if we are uncertain there will be something there to stand on?

"Logically speaking," Fiske decides about the persistence of force, "we have no proof" (II, 145). Indeed, "the proof of our fundamental axiom is not logical, but psychological" (II, 147). Rather than taking despair over this fact, he declares that "this is the strongest possible kind of proof." In fact, "our utter inability to conceive a variation in the sum total of force implies that such variation is negatived by the whole history of the intercourse between the mind and its environment. . ." (II, 147). Since human minds cannot conceive that the world will veer from creation (something made out of nothing) to destruction (the return of something into the original void), then the persistence of forces "must be an axiom necessitated by the very constitution of the thinking mind, as perennial intercourse with the environment has moulded it . . ." (II, 147-148).

The mind as Fiske defines it has its concerns determined by its environment; it also acts to maintain the existence of that environment—one of the gains of stepping out and beyond the world. This works as long as you do not fall over the edge of something into nothing—the ever-present abyss traditionally envisioned by the

American imagination at the bottom of whose bottomlessness roils that other perennial American terror: the destructive element.

Adams takes exception to Fiske's optimism when he reminds the readers of *The Education of Henry Adams* that as long ago as Lord Bacon society had been urged "to lay aside the idea of evolving the universe from a thought, and to try evolving thought from the universe" (p. 484). Adams refers to two aphorisms of Bacon—the need to obey Nature if one wishes to command her, and the necessity to strip wings from the understanding. According to Bacon, the mind ought rather be "hung with weights to keep it from leaping and flying" (p. 682). But well into the nineteenth century Lord Bacon's prudential warning against "leaping and flying" was being disregarded. What mattered was whether the anti-Baconians, as they continued to evolve "the universe from a thought," would have something solid to land on.

These days we seem to have discovered something new about the way thought is constructed which makes it still possible to contemplate leaping and flying. Insofar as Henry Adams paid most heed to the mathematics of thought, it was small wonder that he stressed *quantities* in his assessment of the world's success or failure, or that he worked with images of gain, conservation, and depletion—so much so that William James rebuked him for his excessive concern with the amounts which existence provides, not its quality. Today it is noticeably different. As Jacob Bronowski has put it in *The Ascent of Man*, "Now we see science as a description and explanation of the underlying structures of nature; and words like *structure, pattern, plan, arrangement, architecture* constantly occur in every description that we try to make . . ." (p. 112).

The angels of the Scholastics joyfully danced upon the needle's point, supported by faith in a beneficent God. The nineteenth-century mathematician felt no underlying confidence in the good that entropy with its flagging amounts of energy might do him. But the contemporary geometrician—whether chemist, physicist, or biologist—stresses the solidity of the structures at the base of the universe he creates or discloses by the energy of his thought.

This is not to overlook, however, another aspect of "modern" thought (modern since the first human being split open a solid piece of wood or stone). According to Bronowski (pp. 94-95), the hand that only molds shapes (the mud house, the clay pot) remains *with* surfaces and accepts them as all there is of interest to know about. The scientific temperament, by contrast, insists on analytic action that defies surfaces; out of a consuming need to know deep secrets, it breaks open and penetrates far in order to discover what lies within. What is crucial is *where* the mind wants to place itself—inside or outside the shapes it finds strewn about the world. Crucial, too, is its motive (love or rage) for placing itself where it does. But most crucial is what the mind plans to do with the materials it finds: to fondle American surfaces, or to pummel them; to rejoin the analyzed pieces through unceasing synthesis into interesting new combinations, or only to split apart and then refuse to put back together again.

In his essay of 1910, "Is There a Life After Death?" Henry James set himself the task of "trying to take the measure of my consciousness." For him the whole point was to increase the sense of wonder over what the consciousness can do. He made no suggestion that the consciousness can create, control, or bring the world to an end. Yet, as James said of his own consciousness in this essay (included in *The James Family*), it

> . . . at least *contained* the world, and could handle and criticise it, could play with it and deride it; it had *that* superiority: which meant, all the while, such successful living that the abode itself grew more and more interesting to me . . . that the more and more one asked of it the more and more it appeared to give. (pp. 609-610)

James admitted that the pleasures gained from a highly profitable consciousness required an "increased living in [the consciousness] by reaction against so grossly finite a world . . ." (p. 609). He became a spectator for the sake of the personal gain of wonder. To some appraisers of his fiction he became a coolly inhuman one. To those who hold this opinion James is not unlike the detached onlooker who appears to Crèvecœur's Farmer James in the midst of that poor soul's distresses as a frontier man when heaved into exile by the American Revolution. In *Letters from an American Farmer* (p. 205) Farmer James charges the "cool, the distant spectator, placed in safety," with lacking the sympathy to understand his plight. "Secure from personal danger," he views with imperturbability the turmoil taking place down below, secure in his positioning, as it were, on the serene peak of a Bierstadt mountain. Such a man, says Farmer James,

> . . . will expatiate freely on this grand question and will consider this extended field but as exhibiting the double scene of attack and defence. To him the object becomes abstracted; the

intermediate glares, the perspective distance and a variety of opinions, unimpaired by affections, present to his mind but one set of ideas.

Thoreau as spectator would not have satisfied the demands for sympathy by Farmer James any better. "Man," Thoreau wrote in his journal of April 2, 1852, "is but the place where I stand, and the prospect hence is infinite." To stand *with* Farmer James has importance for the Thoreauvian seer only if he is able to look past the person caught up in particular historical distresses. "I do not value any view of the universe into which man and the institutions of man enter very largely and absorb much of the attention." To associate with others is egotistical, Thoreau calmly replies in anticipation of any attack upon his self-centeredness. "The poet says the proper study of mankind is man. I say, study to forget all that; take wider views of the universe. That is the egotism of the race."

In our egotism the value to us of spectators like Thoreau and James remains unsettled. *They* gain the success of wonder; *they* are not dried up by the actions of their own highly conscious state. But what manner of wonder can they share with the rest of us when their wonder is won by means of withdrawal? Some say there is no wonder in Thoreau or James's vision for us to gain; others say they harbor it but we cannot get to it. Still others—more generous or adept in the ways of wondering—sense, thereby share, the wonder experienced by those two all-inclosing minds.

Whatever one decides about Thoreau and James as the source of a wonder in which others can also partake, there are men at the summit unable to imagine what it is like to live down in the midst of personal history, placed within the messy immediacy of the American experience. Emerson, for one, has been accused of bathing in the bliss of universal unity at the cost of denying the basic human sympathies. But Emerson, like Thoreau, argued that he wished to stand so high he would be raised above whatever causes distorting egotism or callousness of the heart. He maintained that he wished to share pieces of "America" in lasting freehold—something that can be done only when one is dealing with a commonwealth of ideas and not with the land itself.

On January 3, 1861 Thoreau notes in his journal that mountains ought to be made public property so that the visions seen from their summits could be shared in common. Standing high and well is also the finest act of humanity, since it will end any desire to smash the world. "For though the world is so old," Thoreau had also written in the journal of April 2, 1852, "and so many books have been written, each object appears wholly undescribed to our experience, each field of thought wholly unexplored." At this point Thoreau launches into a confident vision of the kind Mailer might like to have but cannot. Certainly Thoreau sees what Mailer is unable to as he, standing on the flatlands of Houston and Cape Kennedy, contemplates the consequences of the projection of America's ego upon a moon-terrain even more uncontrollable than the American continent. But for Thoreau

> The whole world is an America, a *New World*. The fathers lived in a dark age and throw no light on any of our subjects. . . . Astronomy, even, concerns us worldlings only, but the sun of poetry and each new child born into the planet has never been astronomized, nor brought nearer by a telescope. So it will be to the end of time. The end of the world is not yet.

Thoreau's vision here is of the proper democracy of good spectators ever on the look-out for new discoveries, freed from the self-isolation of lonely expeditions away from "America the homeland," and too interested in wonder to give in to hankerings for the end.

It is necessary not to see America as an object that is dangerously *other than* one's subject-self. It is also better not to approach it head-on or too close up. Stepping back a bit and to the side: this is Thoreau's method. He is also like Poe's Dupin in the habit of glancing lynx-eyed in order to detect all the wondrous purloined letters scattered about the world which frontal views will not show us. The difference is that the messages Poe's various intelligences make out are often frightening to men, whereas Thoreau reads mainly the good.

"I had a vision," Thoreau writes in his journal of December 11, 1855 concerning the time he had stood in the midst of a swamp in order to know it better:

> I saw this familiar—too *familiar*—fact at a different angle, and I was charmed and haunted by it. But I could only attain to be thrilled and enchanted, as by the sound of a strain of music dying away. I had seen into paradisiac regions, with their air and sky, and I was no longer wholly or merely a denizen of this vulgar earth. Yet had I hardly a foothold there. . . . It is only necessary to behold thus the least fact or phenomenon, however familiar, from a point a hair's breadth aside from our

habitual path or routine, to be overcome, enchanted by its beauty and significance. . . .

If swamps are good enough vantage points for looking well because looking indirectly, mountains are even better. Thoreau appreciates the value of zoom-lens looks: of Concord seen from the level of the jailhouse window and of ants in combat studied at eye-level, but he was by the needs of his deepest nature a climber to heights.

Perhaps the most important extended description of what Thoreau learned from a journey to the summit comes in the "Tuesday" chapter of *A Week on the Concord and Merrimack Rivers*. He tells (pp. 198-199) how he climbed Saddle-back Mountain through the valley mists to arrive at "an undulating country of clouds, answering in the varied swell of its surface to the terrestrial world it veiled. It was such a country as we might see in dreams, with all the delights of paradise." This cloud-land had "not the substance of impurity, no spot or stain." In contrast with its reality the earth below "had become such a flitting thing of lights and shadows as the clouds had been before."

As a result of the reversal caused by his ascent, the earth "had passed away like the phantom of a shadow . . . and this new platform was gained . . . the region of eternal day, beyond the tapering shadow of the earth. . . ." Paradise regained, but soon to be lost once again: ". . . alas, owing as I think, to some unworthiness in myself, my private sun did stain himself . . . [and] I sank down again into that 'forlorn world,' from which the celestial sun had hid his visage. . . ." It is with reluctance that Thoreau returns from the purity of the cloud-reality to the phantom-earth, where "the inhabitants affirmed that it had been a cloudy and drizzling day wholly."

On several occasions Herman Melville stressed the dangers involved in experiencing the high view followed by a move in for a closer look. Once the far view with its illusion of glory and meaning is exchanged for the near view, the heart's hope can be destroyed. Views from the masthead are fine if one can hang on; it is the *contrast* that kills by pulling a man down into disillusion or the drowning ocean.

And yet, Melville's sailor who mounts Rock Rodondo in the Encantadas insists his is "the very best mode of gaining a comprehensive view . . ." (p. 163). It is from such a high promontory (aided in "the elevation of his spirits" by "a dram of Peruvian pisco") that another sailor sights and rescues the forlorn Chola widow who had remained invisible to men limited to the "lower vision" (p. 181). In these sketches from "The Encandatas" (included within his *Piazza Tales*), Melville acknowledges what Thoreau insisted upon: the need to rise at times above life so not to be fixed below with those who pass from the earth "like vermin."

True, Thoreau once experienced fear on the peak of Mount Ktaadn, the highest point in New England. There in the Maine wilderness at a summit far more remote from the human world than the peak of Saddle-back Mountain, his soul was unable to detect any meaning in a universe of brute matter indifferent to the spiritual desires of men. If viewing from too close-in only encourages the Understanding in its petty interest in details, and if being placed too high up can terrify the heart through its inability to make saving connections, the best location for Thoreau—for the sake of Reason's comprehension of whole meanings—is the gentled-down Saddle-back Mountain: just high enough.

*Just enough* is not sufficient for Poe's imagination. Climbing on is his only satisfaction since it promises the purity of the heights and the pleasures of falling off. It gets colder the closer we come near heaven, Ruskin observed of the metaphysical poets, but Poe's heaven (and our probable hell) is the arctic pole of white chill. In 1905 Mark Twain wrote in his fragment "Old Age" (included in *Fables of Man*) that as we approach the end of life nothing is left but "You, centre of a snowy desolation, perched on the ice-summit," and you are only a "belated fag-end of a foolish dream. . . ." What shook Mark Twain into pessimism formed Poe's delight. The ecstatic Poe-dream is You-on-Ice, whereas the hot winds of man's earth form Poe's hellish place.

By Chapter 24 of his narrative Poe's Arthur Gordon Pym has already survived a concussion of the earth's surface that made it seem "that the whole foundation of the solid globe were suddenly rent asunder, and that the day of universal dissolution was at hand." He has undergone the terror of "being thus entombed alive"; he has for a time given up "supinely to the most intense agony and despair"; he has been "beyond the remotest confines of hope" and known "the allotted portion of the *dead*" —that "degree of appalling awe and horror not to be tolerated—never to be conceived." He has escaped all this only to come near the edge of the chasm. There Pym finds his "imagination growing terribly excited." He faces a crisis of fancy:

> . . . the crisis in which we begin to anticipate the feelings with
> which we *shall* fall—to picture to ourselves the sickness, and

dizziness, and the last struggle, and the half swoon, and the final bitterness of the rushing and headlong descent. And now I found these fancies creating their own realities, and all imagined terrors crowding upon me in fact.

Pym, "with a wild, indefinable emotion, half of horror, half of a relieved oppression," throws his "vision far down into the abyss." His "whole soul [is] pervaded with *a longing to fall*; a desire, a yearning, a passion utterly uncontrolled."

At its wildest the Poe-esque imagination craves height not for the purpose of attaining calm views out over the panorama of universal truth, but in order to fall. In *Air and Songs* (included in part in the Gaudin collection) Gaston Bachelard provides a fine insight into how Poe's writing can affect us. He says that Poe is able to render "the fundamental dream" of falling in such a way as "to make the fall *last*." "The reader can then feel such empathy that upon closing the book he still keeps the impression of not having *come back up*" (p. 15).

Pym-types, defying gravity and morality, begin to fall downward and keep on falling. But for most of us, cautioned by the combined fear of gravity and morality, when we go down it is the solid ground we most want. Too far above and too far below and one loses the right *place* (or loses all place altogether). *Place*—the right one—is where the reality of success is found; lose it, and one fails.

Faulkner illustrates the just-enough position in "The Jail." This prose selection from *Requiem for a Nun* describes how the South started to fall into its destiny of war without ever knowing it:

. . . because the first seconds of fall always seem like soar: a weightless deliberation preliminary to a rush not downward but upward, the falling body reversed during that second by transubstantiation into the upward rush of earth; a soar, an apex, the South's own apotheosis of its destiny and its pride . . . the plunging body advanced far enough now into space as to have lost all sense of motion, weightlessness and immobile upon the light pressure of invisible air, gone now all diminishment of the precipice's lip, all increment of the vast increaseless earth. . . . (p. 230)

This is a fall upwards into the events of history, back from whence no man or region can ever return to the point of departure; it is a movement as final in its consequences as the down-plunging of the Poe-esque fall. But notice a significant distinction, one which is characteristic of Faulkner and similar to the terms by

which Thoreau argues for climbing to summits. The moving body
rushes up to meet its destiny; it exceeds the mean-point, leaving the
norm of reality behind. But that body (self or nation or region) is a
trajectile which finds its mark; it fulfills its destiny by soaring,
whereas it might have missed its appointed goal if it had remained
sanely below that mark. For writers who work out of a strong sense
of destiny and of the need to encounter one's unique fate such
leaps to the height receive their Romantic justification.

Other quasi-Romanticists and part-time idealists in America have
different attitudes toward going up or falling away. If some Americans share the belief of Gaston Bachelard that the essential cosmic
daydream is the ascent of stairs winding through the ideal tower
from whose height our mind dominates the universe, others determine success by the willingness to return from the heights of
power to the plains of vulnerability.

Standing at the top of Donatello's tower, Kenyon in Hawthorne's
*The Marble Faun* gains what may be a vision of the whole design of
the universe, yet he feels relief in the act of "coming down" to ordinary life. For a character in Hawthorne's fiction to stay tucked away
like Coverdale in the tree above the riotous charades going on
below in *The Blithedale Romance* is to invite a depletion so severe it
amounts to self-annihilation. Milly Theale of *The Wings of the Dove*
"comes down" into life from her refuge on the Alpine peak and the
upper floors of the Venetian *palazzo*; she is only one of Henry
James's people who, having withdrawn into the safety of the un-
committed life, elects to return to the destructive element. Lambert
Strether of *The Ambassadors* avoids the temptation of escaping into a
"marriage" to either Woollett or Paris; he keeps free of the conventional and the abstracting wherein one is forced, as he puts it
(XXII, 82) "to be out of the question." He stays in the midst of
human questions—that place which, for James, is where life is.

For any writer concerned with the economics of art and the usefulness of memories, one good way to deal with the meaning of
America is go up and away from it for awhile, then to come back
and down. Strether has to "go out" to Paris before he can "come
back" to America well ahead of his point of departure in Woollett.
In *A Moveable Feast* Hemingway recalls that he could write best
about Michigan once he got to Paris, just as he grasped Paris best in
his imagination after going away to Switzerland or Italy. James and
Hemingway counted on going out, with return movements analogous to those in Whitman's "Passage to India," where one's origins

are finally discovered upon taking the circle-route from east to west.

There are times, certainly, when out/return and up/down are connected with east/west—the verticals of the imagination coinciding with geographical lateral movements. In *The American Scene* James's "coming down" from England after years of absence from his homeland is, he insists, the reason he is now able to see America with both clarity and renewed wonder:

> The European complexity, working clearer to one's vision, had grown usual and calculated—presenting itself, to the discouragement of wasteful emotion and of "intensity" in general, as the very stuff, the common texture, of the real world. Romance and mystery—in other words the *amusement* of interest—would have therefore at last to provide for themselves elsewhere; and what curiously befell, in time, was that the native, the foresaken scene . . . seemed more and more to appeal to the faculty of wonder. It was American civilization that had begun to spread itself thick and pile itself high . . . and to a world so amended and enriched, accordingly, the expatriated observer, with his relaxed curiosity reviving and his limp imagination once more on the stretch, couldn't fail again to address himself. (p. 366)

What we have in this passage may be the somewhat ludicrous sight of the aging roué-of-the-imagination who has been suffering from an embarrassing loss of the "sexual curiosity" James has referred to earlier in *The American Scene*; but a roué who feels his powers revive (as if by an injection of monkey glands) through contact with the "romance and mystery" of America. It is not, however, just the *amusement* of an expatriate that is at stake in this passage. The ability of the analyst of American successes and failures to judge correctly depends on the renewed vitality of his awareness. The going away and the coming back (another form of going up and coming down) has made the crucial difference.

One of the scores of examples which make up the method and the matter of *The American Scene* comes when James takes a trip to a summit located, appropriately, near the Mount Zion of the Puritans and not far from Thoreau's Saddle-back Mountain. Having "come down" to America, James now mounts to the "spacious summit of Beacon Hill" in Boston (p. 227). He wants to survey what has happened to the spirit which lay behind the original impulse to found the City on the Hill. Looking backwards and forward, as well as downwards, James sees the bullying present ("insolently safe, able to be with impunity anything [it] would") gang up on the old city, deriding its desire to be "exquisite" (pp. 235, 233). Having assessed the meaning of the scene, and his task over, James then returns to the bottom of the hill, where the sacred intentions are being mocked through the sacrilege of "the money-passion." What James finds while he is "up," he comes down to give testimony to. Because he has gone through the necessary movements, he has had a vision which marks a crisis; he is now ready to judge what it means.

In *The Sense of an Ending* Frank Kermode delineates crisis as that point in time and that position in psychological space when one *stands apart to judge* successes and failures. To take a view of history, as if from a summit, is to see eschatologically. William Faulkner sometimes reads the landscape like that, particularly if there is a human figure in it. In *As I Lay Dying* the beginnings and ends of human existence are enclosed within the scene of Jewel Bundren and Vernon Tull immersed in the flooded river (p. 156). First comes the notation of the physical facts:

> From here they do not appear to violate the surface at all; it is as though it had severed them both at a single blow, the two torsos moving with infinitesimal and ludicrous care upon the surface.

Then follows a summation of first and last things:

> As though the clotting which is you had dissolved into the myriad original motion, and seeing and hearing in themselves blind and deaf; fury in itself quiet with stagnation.

Next, coming immediately after, the scene is viewed from on high. An observing eye looks down over the landscape of a female body and sees it in the life-force that also foretells the mortal act of dying:

> Squatting, Dewey Dell's wet dress shapes for the dead eyes of three blind men those mammalian ludicrosities which are the horizons and the valleys of the earth.

Out of Faulkner's need to make these visions *significant*, their meaning is reviewed further on in the novel (p. 217) by Darl's "mad" eschatological eye:

> Life was created in the valleys. It blew up onto the hills on the

old terrors, the old lusts, the old despairs. That's why you must walk up the hills so you can ride down.

In *The Mississippian* of March 10, 1922 Faulkner presented an odd piece called "The Hill" (included in Collins' collection). Readers absorbed by Faulkner's life-work can detect—"eschatologically," as it were—the inception of certain major Faulknerian themes and descriptive mannerisms in which his "last days" as a writer already lie embedded. Significantly, "The Hill" gives us a view from a point above Yoknapatawpha County (read, for convenience, "America"). We also witness the barely articulated desires of a man who we sense might easily turn vicious out of the frustration he visits upon the valley of defeat to which he must return. This view from the hill gives us both the dream of success and the dull rage its failure arouses. It is not a summit-view that reveals for the onlooker the calming laws of life's success held by Emerson and Thoreau. It is not even the stoic vision of man's incapacities before the laws of force that centered Henry Adams' historical imagination. If it adumbrates a crisis caused by the gap between *wanting* and *not having* so prevalent in Henry James's fiction, it contains no Jamesian consciousness capable of sorting out meanings and judgments. This view provided by the early Faulkner only discloses "the old terrors, the old lusts, the old despairs." It tells what it means to have walked up the hill in order to have to come down, to have to return to a man's choice between enduring as mere "vermin" or prevailing through rage and violence:

> Before him and slightly above his head, the hill crest was clearly laid on the sky. Over it slid a sibilant invisibility of wind like a sheet of water, and it seemed to him that he might lift his feet from the road and swim upward and over the hill on this wind which filled his clothing, tightening his shirt across his chest, flapping his loose jacket and trousers above him, and which stirred the thick uncombed hair above his stubby quiet face. His long shadow legs rose perpendicularly and fell, ludicrously, as though without power of progression, as though his body had been mesmerized by a whimsical God to a futile puppet-like activity upon one spot, while time and life terrifically passed him and left him behind. At last his shadow reached the crest and fell headlong over it. . . .
>
> From the hilltop the valley was a motionless mosaic of tree and house; from the hilltop were to be seen no cluttered barren lots sodden with spring rain and churned and torn by hoof

of horse and cattle, no piles of winter ashes and rusting tin cans, no dingy hoardings covered with the tattered insanities of posted salacities and advertisements. There was no suggestion of striving, of whipped vanities, of ambition and lusts, of the drying spittle of religious controversy; he could not see that the sonorous simplicity of the court house columns was discolored and stained with casual tobacco. In the valley there was no movement save the thin spiraling of smoke and the heart-tightening grace of the poplars, no sound save the measured faint reverberation of an anvil.

Thoreau on Saddle-back Mountain is also raised above the courthouse columns "stained with casual tobacco" and "the drying spittle of religious controversy." Where Thoreau stands is the reality to him of beauty, strength, and the eternal value of the human spirit. For him to have to "come down" means the return to fantasies of ugliness, weakness, and doubt-causing events. It is not unlike this for the nameless man on Faulkner's hill, but the following portion of the passage emphasizes the anger that accompanies his instinctual recognition of the fatality of his return into failure:

The slow featureless mediocrity of his face twisted to an internal impulse: the terrific groping of his mind. . . . Behind him was a day of harsh labor with his hands, a strife against the forces of nature to gain bread and clothing and a place to sleep, a victory gotten at the price of bodily tissues and the numbered days of his existence; before him lay the hamlet which was home to him, the tieless casual; and beyond it lay waiting another day of toil to gain bread and clothing and a place to sleep: In this way he worked out the devastating unimportance of his destiny, with a mind heretofore untroubled by moral quibbles and principles, shaken at last by the faint resistless force of spring in a valley at sunset.

As long as Thoreau and the Faulknerian hill-man remain above, it is *as if* the distanced world below is the shadow—its facts for failure made unreal; it is *as if* reality is the sun:

The sun plunged silently into the liquid green of the west and the valley was abruptly in shadow. And as the sun released him, who lived and labored in the sun, his mind that troubled him for the first time, became quieted. . . . For a while he stood on one horizon and stared across at the other, far above a world of endless toil and troubled slumber; untouched, untouchable; forgetting, for a space that he must return.

But he, the nameless man, must return, and so "He slowly descended the hill." He "comes down" from "the private sun" which had fetched him a moment of glory, into the world's sun that has the power to redden the back of his toil-hard neck and to cast a glaze of blood-red wrath over the eyes by which he views the mundane life that is his only reality. His climb to the summit, and his return, have given him what he needs to hate. It could also give him the will to destroy the America that has denied the sufficiency of his view from the summit.

# CHAPTER 29

# Dealing with Dread

In "The Heritage of Henry Adams" Brooks Adams describes that heritage as it was formed by "the rise and progress of American democracy." Like many of the Adams family a comparativist, Brooks scrutinized the standard against which success is to be judged. He concluded that "the beginning of the movement as well as the form it took and the standard which must serve as the measure of its advance or recession in intellectual power, is to be computed according to the personality of George Washington, who, without doubt, stands at the apex of democratic civilization" (p. 104). In *The Education of Henry Adams*, Henry used a similar tack. Since "Any schoolboy could see that man as a force must be measured by motion, from a fixed point" (p. 434), Adams elected to measure himself in terms of twelfth-century France. Brother Brooks had measured both America and Henry by means of George Washington, "the apex of democratic civilization," while Henry used, as it were, the heights of the Gothic vault of Chartres cathedral and the tip of the sword raised in victory by the archangel Saint Michael. Measuring from the fixed point of "the best" is to measure a *coming-down*—the surest way of measuring failure.

Certain imaginations, having viewed America from the summits and finding only failure in its valleys, encourage acts of jumping into those depths. But there are leaps, and there are leaps. Henry Adams, caught up in the whirl of the laws of acceleration, wanted to jump if it meant falling forward into that *nothing* which Emerson described as all that lies between God and man. By means of the verbal paradox implied by Emerson and accepted by Adams, he had as much chance to be saved as to be lost since where there is ambiguity there may be hope.

Norman Mailer fears what can happen in America to those who deny paradox and ambiguity and thereby take the wrong way down and out. In the section "On Dread" in *The Presidential Papers* (p. 160) he foretells the special apocalyptic fate saved for us if we are afraid to die and yet want the end, even if it means *going all the way* through participation in a cosmic holocaust:

We would die with deadened minds and twilight sleep. We had turned our back on the essential terror of life. We believed in the Devil, we hated Nature.

So we watched the end approach with apathy. Because if it was God we had betrayed and the vision with which He had sent us forth, if our true terror was not of life but of what might be waiting for us in death, then how much easier we might find it to be blasted into eternity deep in the ruin of ten million others, how much better indeed if the world went with us, and death was destroyed as completely as life. Yes, how many of the millions . . . had a secret prayer; that whomever we thought of as God be exploded with us, and Judgment cease.

All minds potentially possess the imagination of disaster. But to imagine disaster does not need to be the same as its creation or as submission to its force. The vortex may image the mind, but the mind can still save itself from the vortex. The brother in Poe's "A Descent into the 'Maelström' " perishes because his frightened mind merges with the destroying whirl, but the narrator escapes. Driven toward the imagination of disaster by the way events horrendously control him, the narrator uses his dread to create the imagination of success by which he is released from the destructive waters.

However dissimilar his motives from those of the Poe-narrator, Emerson came to similar conclusions. In his journal of 1841 he describes the vertigo caused by the study of the heavens, but he promises that

> . . . soon as we have recovered ourselves from the dizziness which this immense of arithmetic gives us, (for astronomy gives us always the temptation of that dreadful GIRO at the top of the interior of the Cupola of St. Peter's where one shakes with the wish to throw himself over the balustrade onto the beautiful tesselations of the marble floor on which men are creeping below,) we are steadied by the perception that a great deal is doing [,] that indeed all seems just begun; remote aims are in active accomplishment. (VII, 427-428)

It is appropriate that William James referred to Emerson during his Gifford Lectures of 1900 concerning matters crucial to them both. There is something in the universe, James sensed, that goes beyond language, that sustains life, that provides the center and the facts necessary for success. In the following passage (included by Perry, p. 258) he insisted upon these "living moments" whose

> ... meaning seems to well up from out of their very centre, in a way impossible verbally to describe. If you take a disk painted with a concentric spiral pattern, and make it revolve, it will seem to be growing continuously and indefinitely, and yet to take in nothing from without; and to remain, if you pay attention to its actual size, always of the *same* size. Something as paradoxical as this lies in every present moment of life. Here or nowhere, as Emerson says, is the whole fact. . . . This self-sustaining in the midst of self-removal, which characterizes all reality and fact, is something absolutely foreign to the nature of language, and even to the nature of logic, commonly so-called.

While speaking of cracks, golden bowls, love, and life, Charlotte Stant in Henry James's *The Golden Bowl* responds out of her deepest wisdom when she declares to Prince Amerigo, " 'Thank goodness then that if there *be* a crack we know it! But if we may perish by cracks in things that we don't know—!' and she smiled with the sadness of it. 'We can never then give each other anything' " (XXIII, 117-118). That Charlotte is eventually lost within such a crack does not invalidate her remark. The courage of her leap into passionate commitment to the Prince is admirable, even if failure comes to her as the result of her lack of the right kind of love's faith. Maggie Verver will make a similar leap, and more nearly succeed, because her faith in *giving love* gets her over the terrible crack which opens up for those too intent only on *getting love*.

It is significant that Henry Adams' first "sensible" perception as an infant was of the color yellow—the color of sunlight, hope, and value, as well as of cowardice and putrefaction. Adams grew up swinging between optimism and pessimism, both of which are connoted by yellow. In contrast to his ambivalent stance in between, Henry James, Senior, willed himself into hope—away from the "horror of great darkness" he experienced as *his* first perception as an infant. Notwithstanding the shock of this introduction to the world (described in *The James Family*, pp. 17-18), the elder James's life became a celebration of the God-sun that never burns out or cools down in obedience to the Second Law of Thermodynamics. The sun of the elder James redeems man and society through its fertile power of love. It was the same with Thoreau, his contemporary. In his journal of February 6, 1854 he observed that "but a little colder Friday, or greater snow or more violent gale would put a period to man's existence on the globe." However, it was in that same year that *Walden* was published, the book in which Thoreau insisted on the power of the sun to strike with the force of Thor's hammer at the ice-grip of winter. The journal entry was written after the writing of *Walden*. The winning of the battle within Thoreau's imagination between sun and ice was not a finished fact, but he realized there was good chance for warmth. The imagination of success is made, not born. It must continually *keep on being made* in face of those cracks we know about, or do not.

Kierkegaard's Knight of Faith can leap and dance in mystical space because he is upheld by his confidence in the sustaining hand of a merciful God. The Knight of Infinite Resignation can do no more than swim in existence; but even if he lacks faith in the Kierkegaardian God, he can at least do *that*—swim, and keep on swimming, thereby not drowning in "the destructive element." Thoreau said that people who felt the ground quaking beneath their feet looked upon his calm saunter with astonishment. To them it seemed he was walking on air, but he (a Knight of Faith) knew he was walking safely upon the solidity of universal laws. Even on those days when he was unable to be more than the Knight of Infinite Resignation, he refused to fall down in fear of the quaking earth.

When Thoreau walked well, it was because he "knew" he walked on the water of the Law. In contrast, William James realized that his "motto for practicalism" was based on the need to act with confidence even when the facts are forever unknowable. As Perry's study of James records (p. 298), around 1876 James wrote down in his copy of John Locke's *Essay Concerning Human Understanding* that the following lines made clear the advantages of leaping as opposed to sitting. "He that will not eat till he has demonstration that it will nourish him, he that will not start till he infallibly knows the business he goes about will succeed, will have little else to do but sit still and perish."

James believed that *character*—the masterly use of energy and facts to counter the recognition of vulnerability to failure—may be all we shall ever have to help us make the good leap. In *The Literary Remains of Henry James* of 1884 he wrote:

> Well, we are all *potentially* such sick men. The sanest and best of us are of one clay with lunatics and prison-inmates. And

whenever we feel this, such a sense of the vanity of our voluntary career comes over us, that all our morality appears but as a
plaster hiding a sore it can never cure, and all our well-*being*
that our lives ought to be grounded in, but, alas! are not. (p.
118)

Sympathetic as he was to the sick-minded, William James wished
to stave off the effects of dread and despair. In a letter to Henry
Adams written on June 17, 1901 (included in James's *Letters*), he
rebuked the sickish mood emanating from Adams' essay "A Letter
to American Teachers of History":

To tell the truth, it doesn't impress me at all, save by its wit
and erudition; and I ask you whether an old man soon about
to meet his Maker can hope to save himself from the consequence of his life by pointing to the wit and learning he has
shown in treating a tragic subject. No, sir, you can't do it, can't
impress God in that way. (II, 344)

In this letter and two subsequent postcards of June 19th and
26th, 1901 (also included in *Letters*, II, 346-347), James tried to
force home his belief that what matters is how a man has made *use*
of the energy in the universe. It is of little interest how much energy there is or that it might be fast draining away. What counts
*humanly* is a proper economics of continuities. What signifies is having *"intelligent intelligence"*—mind's quality, not matter's quantity.

In "Remarks on Spencer's Definition of Mind as Correspondence," James described the power of such an intelligence to
continue existence through the sheer *idea of going on*. Even to possess "the sense of an ending" is to own to the strong likelihood of
nothingness and to make valueless all that preceded that end. Men
and the gods, together, ought to cultivate the imagination of
success—not out of stupidity, but out of fine sensibleness.

Poor Henry Adams. He had both the James brothers badgering
him to leap over, not into, the abyss. In a letter of 1914 (included in
*The James Family*, p. 669) Henry James wrote Adams to acknowledge the "melancholy outpouring" of a recent piece of correspondence. *"Of course* we are lone survivors," James agreed, "of
course that past that was our lives is at the bottom of an abyss—if
the abyss *has* any bottom. . . ." James agreed, but he resisted giving
up to that void which stands between us and value. His answer was
a variation of the pronouncement his brother William had sent
Adams four years earlier: make good use of life through *reactions*,

*having ideas*, and being *intelligently intelligent*. "It all takes doing—and I *do*," wrote Henry. "I believe I shall do yet again—it is still an act of life." This is the artist-citizen's weapon against nothingness. It is all he has, but it is enough.

Henry James detected yet another special secret power enjoyed by the artist and the citizen in America. In his little book on Hawthorne of 1879 he pointed out that fund of humor that the nation possesses to an extraordinary degree. Actually, humor was just as attractive to Henry Adams' temperament as was melancholy. Fun was one of the quirky reasons Adams manipulated the imagination of disaster; stimulating visions of crumbling worlds offset the boredom of a society or universe running down into tedium. But when the imp of the perverse tempts the imagination to blow up the world for the sake of some comic relief from ennui, it is time to shift to an excitement that, for the fun of it, energizes the imagination to sustain itself.

To point the way, we can make use of the terms employed by Rudolf Arnheim in his book *Entropy and Art, An Essay on Disorder and Order*.

According to Arnheim (pp. 27-32), "catabolism" is the tendency that smashes forms and explodes structures into chaotic bits. That is "bad," but so is the "homogeneity principle" that blurs things into intensely boring blobs. What is "good" is the "anabolic principle" at work—defying both the chaotic and the kind of orderliness that signals the end of all shape-giving tensions. Anabolism sustains shapes, distinctions, and the dynamisms of growth, even while it provides enough order to help us thread our way through the wild world.

Mark Twain, the all-American humorist, never quite solved the problems implied in having to balance "order" (humor) against "chaos" (disaster) or "orderliness" (tedium). He wrote Howells on August 16, 1898 concerning his manuscript "Which Was the Dream?" (correspondence included in the *Twain-Howells Letters*): "I feel sure that all of the first half of the story—& I hope three-fourths—will be comedy. . . . I think I can carry the reader a long way before he suspects that I am laying a tragedy-trap" (II, 675-676). One alternative to Mark Twain's strategy is to let the imagination carry us deep into the tragic vision of human existence, then to spring *the comedy-trap* that saves through its "anabolic" resistance to tragic (actually, melodramatic) "catabolic" explosions or to bathetic, boring "homogeneity."

Emerson said he felt no affinity with either comedy or tragedy. He was a scholar instead. Yet he knew that the type is not safe from threats of dread. He declared in "The American Scholar" that this hero's firm stance in the midst of the destructive element is possible only because of his faith that "The world of any moment is the merest appearance." The scholar must keep to the realities and forgo frightened submission to the shadows:

> Let him not quit his belief that a popgun is a popgun, though the ancient and honorable of the earth affirm it to be the crack of doom. In silence, in steadiness, in severe abstraction, let him hold by himself. . . . He then learns that in going down into the secrets of his own mind he has descended into the secrets of all minds. . . .

This is a descent that brings self-trust, not self-destruction; it is a journey down to the center, not to chaos.

"Free should the scholar be—free and brave." The scholar ought not look for

> . . . a temporary peace by the diversion of his thought from politics or vexed questions, hiding his head like an ostrich in the flowering bushes, peeping into microscopes, and turning rhymes, as a boy whistles to keep his courage up. So is the danger a danger still; so is the fear worse. . . . Let him look into its eye and search its nature, inspect its origin,—see the whelping of this lion—which lies no great way back; he will then find in himself a perfect comprehension of its nature and extent; he will have made his hands meet on the other side, and can henceforth defy it and pass on superior. The world is his who can see through its pretension. . . . See it to be a lie, and you have already dealt it its mortal blow.

In a college essay of 1837 (written the same year "The American Scholar" was delivered) Thoreau rebukes Edmund Burke's notion that terror and fear of death characterizes the sublime. Thoreau, with Emerson, had faith that the reality of the sublime—which is the reality of the world—is calmness and health. Daily news carted in from the realm of the mundane with its noisy dread is of little value. "We should wash ourselves clean of such news," Thoreau wrote later in "Life Without Principle":

> Of what consequence, though our planet explode, if there is no character involved in the explosion? In health we have not

the least curiosity about such events. We do not live for idle
amusement. I would not run around a corner to see the world
blow up. (p. 472)

There it is: the crucial distinction to be made between *idle amusement* that would blow up the world to save the mind from its own
fear of ennui and nothingness, and *active amusement* which the man
of character uses to interpose *value* between the self and the abyss.

Norman Mailer certainly wants to be amused; he is extravagantly
pleased by wow-endings; he confesses to being an idler. But Mailer
chooses the active amusement of leaps over the gaps that continually open between loss and gain. Unsure whether he will find God
or the Devil on the other side, he desires to risk all out of hope and
liking more than to risk all out of terror and contempt. In *Of a Fire
on the Moon* he states that each man at Mission Control must make
the decision between GO and NO GO. It is a decision that

> . . . might have to be taken in some arena of crisis where the
> answer would not be clear. So each man on that floor knew he
> could enter a stricken instant, a cauldron of adrenalin, a failure
> of nerve . . . : an order to abort the mission which later proved
> to be unnecessary, or an injunction to go ahead which resulted
> in death would have to leave an isolation of the soul. (p. 363)

Whether it is William Bradford and Edward Johnson making
calculated leaps across the Atlantic into the ambiguous wilderness
of America, or the latter-day explorers of space of whom Mailer
writes, the mission is best controlled by those who have faith in the
act of leaping. Emerson and Thoreau, Poe and Adams, the Jameses
and Mailer have very different kinds of personality and belief, but
each has character, and each possesses the faith (yes, even Poe and
Adams). They have the imagination of success that takes the facts
of failure into full consideration even as they signal GO into the
dark.

Is there a success so great that it cancels its own value? The
American devotee of victory has to be cautioned about projecting
his leap too far into the ideal, lest he fail the facts of his humanity
altogether.

As Thoreau brings *A Week on the Concord and Merrimack Rivers* to
its close (pp. 412-413), he strives to provide both the tone and the
image appropriate to his meaning. If his later book *Walden* swells
with the reviving flood-tide of primal waters, *Week* projects man's

hope into the heavens. "I am not without hope that we may, even here and now obtain some accurate information concerning the OTHER WORLD which the instinct of mankind has so long predicted." Then Thoreau asks:

> . . . why may not our speculations penetrate as far into the immaterial starry system, of which the former is but the outward and visible type? Surely, we are provided with senses as well fitted to penetrate the spaces of the real, the substantial, the eternal, as these outward are to penetrate the material universe.

For Thoreau an evolution of the senses might aid men to discover that New World which they have been made ready to perceive and rightly to possess:

> But a steep, and sudden, and by these means unaccountable transition, is that from a comparatively narrow and partial, what is called common-sense view of things, to an infinitely expanded and liberating one, from seeing things as men describe them, to see them as men cannot describe them.

In this passage we have Thoreau concentrating on the liberating sense of expanding upwards and outwards. He does not let us take our vision away from the idea which to him (at this moment, at least) is the one true reality and the only norm for success. "The roving mind impatiently bursts the fetters of astronomical orbits, like cobwebs in a corner of its universe, and launches itself to where distance fails to follow, and law, such as science has discovered, grows weak and weary." Excited himself, as he wants to excite us, Thoreau attempts to go beyond the common law, beyond policies of colonization and myths of manifest destiny that would merely betray the traveler lighting out for terrestrial territory into a repetition of old corruptions:

> I know that there are many stars, I know that they are far enough off, bright enough, steady enough in their orbits,—but what are they all worth? They are more waste lands in the West,—star territory,—to be made slave States, perchance, if we colonize them.

Thoreau pushes still farther. His imagination strains to leap across the great divide which is "the interval between that which *appears*, and that which *is*." Like Mailer, he would go "beyond NASA." Unlike Mailer, who likes to trust his senses, Thoreau wants to go beyond sensual worlds. "I have interest but for six feet of star, and that interest is transient. Then farewell to all ye bodies, such as I have known ye." Success *so complete* would lift a man past the earth and the solar system. It would involve the discovery of that "America" which is all vision, all ideal—beyond time and space, beyond all chance to fail. It is also a discovery with dangers, and one in which Thoreau did not often let himself indulge without check.

In *The Ascent of Man* Jacob Bronowski observes that the navigators of the Old World were guided by the stars, since astronomy was central to their efforts to go elsewhere. In contrast, he maintains, the early cultures of the Americas did not practice astronomy:

> And without astronomy it is really not possible to find your way over great distances, or even to have a theory about the shape of the earth and the land and sea on it. . . . It cannot be an accident that the New World never thought that the earth is round and never went out to look for the Old World. It was the Old World which set sail round the earth to discover the New.

Why was there no impulse on the part of the natives of the American continent to find a "Passage to Europe"?

> Astronomy is not the apex of science or of invention. But it is a test of the cast of temperament and mind that underlies a culture. The seafarers of the Mediterranean since Greek times had a peculiar inquisitiveness that combined adventure with logic—the empirical with the rational—into a single mode of inquiry. The New World did not. (p. 190)

The America of Thoreau's argument at the conclusion of *A Week on the Concord and Merrimack Rivers* is inhabited by the descendants of Old World believers in the stars. The land has been created by means of the force of that original belief. The issue at stake for us, even more than for Thoreau, is whether that original "peculiar inquisitiveness that combined adventures with logic" serves to send men farther than the West, farther than the stars, farther than humanity itself.

In "The Method of Nature" Emerson also urged "the ecstatical state" that points

> . . . to the whole and not to the parts; to the cause and not to the ends; to the tendency and not to the act. It respects genius

and not talent; hope, and not possession; the anticipation of all things by the intellect, and not the history itself; art, and not works of art. . . .

By "this divine method" Emerson tried to move past "gravitation and chemistry" in order to arrive at "assimilation to the object of knowledge." In opposition to the self's base possession of objects, he cites Zoroaster's belief: "Things divine are not attainable by mortals who understand sensual things, but only the light-armed arrive at the summit." According to the strict economics of the ideal, it is not merely that you are promised nothing but the best. It is that you would *have nothing*. You would *be all* because the Best would assimilate you into its own great value.

However splendid this idea is of the consummate, all-consuming Success, most of us cannot define success as a movement beyond desire. We see it as *having something* and having it here. Even if it costs us success, we could not give ourselves wholly to the star-territories of Thoreau's vision. We want knowledge that grabs the *thing* and gives us power in the flesh. We cannot be content with a wonder that would absorb us into its being. The Concordians would go to the moon to receive the prize of manna only by becoming manna—by *becoming force*. We wish the moon in order to annex it as a new real-estate venture. We want moon-rocks for the force we could convert into scientific or sensual knowledge-power.

The problem here is that both we and the Transcendentalists are partially right and partially wrong. Our stress on total possessiveness of a world of things is questionable; in contrast, their act of total communion with the universal being is far more defensible. But even if their imagination gives us the signs of the ultimate success, it is difficult to desire the chill of ecstasy which moves beyond the warmth of the senses and the community of men.

That chill, moreover, may be proof of the loss of ecstasy, not of its attainment. Hawthorne in his flawed and unfinished romance *Septimus Felton* suggests just this possibility through his hero who yearns for the liberation promised by the elixir of immortality. Upon discovering the secret of the magic potion, Felton sees that the draught has taken the coldness of the chaste moon quite literally into itself, and also a terrible sense of solitude. Failures of mortality are gotten rid of through the drinking of the potion, but also human life and love. What is gained is immortality; what is lost are occasions for ecstasy and wonder.

Fitzgerald's *The Great Gatsby* is also about what Hawthorne was fumbling toward in *Septimus Felton*. If Jay Gatsby had ever made it *all the way* either to the stars above the trees (where he was headed before he met Daisy) or to the green light across the bay (his goal after meeting her), then the "America" of his existence which made Gatsby's life a strange and wondrous fact, as well as a dark and painful one, would vanish.

It seems as if the seizure of the final wonder of the god-state will lead inevitably to the loss of wonder. The heart turns to the stars, longing to possess their mystery, but if those stars are reached—the projection completed and the discovery fulfilled—the heart (as defined by Hawthorne, by Fitzgerald, and by Faulkner, whose words here are taken from the final page of *The Mansion*) would know only "Helen and the bishops, the kings and the unhomed angels, the scornful and graceless seraphim."

The world E. E. Cummings images in *The Enormous Room* as he sits in his prison cell singing of the moon, friends, and privies may be just too cozy, literally, for words. Faulkner's earth as described at the conclusion of *The Mansion* (p. 398) seems at first glance to be the better place both for language and for life:

> . . . all the little grass blades and tiny roots, the little holes the worms made, down and down into the ground already full of the folks that had the trouble but were free now, so that it was just the ground and the dirt that had to bother and worry and anguish with the passions and hopes and skeers, the justice and the injustice and the griefs. . . .

This is the all-absorbing earth. It is like Huck Finn's dream of Goshen—a free-floating raft, easy and comfortable. It is a barrel of good things all sloshed around, not unlike the Germanic *Wunderschön*-mash of strawberries reported by William James and poeticized by Walt Whitman. Specifically, it is Mink Snopes's vision of a place where

> . . . the folks themselves [are] easy now, all mixed and jumbled up comfortable and easy so wouldn't nobody even know or even care who was which any more, himself among them, equal to any, good as any, brave as any, being inextricable from, anonymous with all of them. . . .

Hope gained by going deep down into the free, proud, warm soil is too much like that other Faulknerian dream of freedom experienced by leaping up to the free, proud, cold stars. Through the cessation of consciousness, both earth and stars promise immortality, anonymity, eternal solitude, and the end of love and wonder. If this could come about, Robinson Jeffers would have his desire that there be an end to human consciousness so that the soulless sun can be free of its own worst nightmare—the presence of mankind in the world. What would survive in Jeffers' universe would be Truth—the success of eternal laws replacing the failures of the petty and transitory. But that Truth lies beyond human existence. As John Updike's Mrs. Mortis says out of her right to reject perfection won by a hard life of full living, "Well, then, to hell with it."

In her *Domestic Manners of the Americans* Frances Trollope describes a debate of 1829 that went on for eight days between Robert Owen, skeptic, and the Reverend Alexander Campbell in an attempt to settle the issue of the reality of religious truths; but eight days are hardly enough. Septimus Felton drives himself (and perhaps Hawthorne) to an early grave by his obsession to discover the Truth through an occult formula that promises to reveal all. The poor lad whom Mark Twain tells us about in *Roughing It* (VIII, 265-272)—the one who *must* know how to turn turnips into climbing vines—is kept from success and joy because of an undecipherable formula sent him by Horace Greeley; he, comically, dies of despair, just as Felton, tragically, expires. But we keep on asking. If Arthur Gordon Pym could only decipher the code marked on the walls of the cave on the island of the Tsalalians, and if Ishmael could but understand the meaning of the marks tattooed upon Queequeg's body: *then* we might indeed possess the Law. And if we possessed *that*, it might be that even as we die we will endure because the Law lasts, and will succeed because the Law is success.

The Puritan Nathaniel Ward believed that his fellows in the Church possessed that single truth. Its possession was the firm and lasting foundation upon which the New England settlements could erect their success. Ward wrote in "The Simple Cobler of Aggawam" that God's truth is "the Parent of all Liberty" and "better than any creat' *Ens* or *Bonum*" since "there is nothing in the world any further than Truth makes it so." Ward felt no anxiety about deciphering the truth of the Scriptures. He was only concerned about its possible loss:

... the least Truth of Gods Kingdome, doth in its place, uphold the whole kingdome of his Truths; Take away the least *vericulum* out of the world, and it unworlds all, potentially, and may unravell the whole texture actually. ...

Some two hundred years later, Theodore Parker still pointed to the *vericulum* in his 1841 "Discourse of the Transient and Permanent in Christianity" when he used Luke 21:33, as his epigram: "Heaven and earth shall pass away; but my words shall not pass away." Truth, wrote Thoreau in a fiercely anti-Manichean entry of February 12, 1840, has no foe. A man is "on his way to all that is great & good" even in a brothel, declared Emerson (see Slater, p. 39), thereby implying that not only does such a man find in truth satisfactions beyond those of the flesh, but that he can find that truth surely. Hemingway believed success comes to the writer who creates the one true sentence. Mailer irritates his interviewer in the "Arena" section of *Cannibals and Christians* by insisting on the right "to get away with anything if you tell the truth about yourself" (p. 249).

Whitman (practicing the heresies of inclusiveness Nathaniel Ward most hated) believed that the poem was the gospel, not the Scriptures. The Whitmanian poet of the Preface to *Leaves of Grass* recognizes "no particular sabbath or judgment day" and divides "not the living from the dead or the righteous from the unrighteous" (p. 725). Still, Whitman, like Ward, rested all the weight of his faith upon the *vericulum* of the truth. Ward insisted that God's truth satisfies the soul, while Whitman reversed the order in the statement from his 1855 Preface to *Leaves of Grass*: "Whatever satisfies the soul is truth" (p. 725). The difference made by such a reversal and such inclusiveness is crucial, but it does not disallow Whitman's focus on truth as satisfaction and satisfaction as the success upon which all else rests.

Ends come and go, but truth survives. But what truth? Ward's *something in particular*? Or Whitman's *everything*? Emerson's "When all forms vanish what is left is the Law of Law"? Or Adams' "All is running down even though men resist accepting this truth as their fate"? It is hard, if not impossible, to decide which goes straightest to the mark. Let us for the moment argue that through intelligent explorations it would be possible for us to arrive at the perception of eternal truth. Even so, the attainment of perfect success could seem cold if we, with our warmth and sweat, are told that we must be absent while the Law remains. Let us say that we, like Melville's Billy Budd, are granted an ascension at the instant of our death which blooms into "the full rose of the dawn." However, the day which remains—whose "clearness" and "serenity" is likened to "smooth white marble in the polished block not yet removed from the marble-dealer's yards"—would be a day *without us* (p. 401).

Characteristically, Mailer worries that God may be forced to betray His truth in order to help the world survive. Mailer's stance is a variation of the age-old belief that God's truth is the only thing worth saving, else mere survival be all we have left us. This is in more or less agreement with Paul Ricoeur that we ought to be glad for the residue in historical events of what he calls the *undeviating scrupulousness*. But here is the dilemma which has been underlying the many questions of success or failure this book has been tracing from its start until now, the near-finish: Which do we most prefer—the chance to survive by means of compromises with the truth, or the triumph of scrupulosity at the cost of the annihilation of our own unscrupulous existence? Might there be a way past either dilemma? Is there another way by which we could arrive at a balancing between survival and perfection—a way to continue our being with enough success to make it worth the while, a way to deal sufficiently with our failures that gives some worth to the bluntest facts of our lack?

# ◣ CHAPTER 30 ◢

# Sufficiency

The answer to more than survival and less than perfection proposed by many of the writers we have been listening to is simplicity itself: *find sufficiency*. What keeps us still failing is the fact incarnated by Norman Mailer—he who is like God and like us, only more so. It is, as he constantly shows us, the fact of bad timing and wrong positioning. When we are not where our destiny requires us to be, frustration mounts. When we have "found life too brief for perfection and long for comfort," we fit these words of Robert Lowell's sonnet from *Notebook*, "Henry and Waldo." We cannot be certain whether Lowell's "long" means *length* or *to yearn*—both, probably. Either meaning is appropriate to the condition of insufficiency wherein we have failed to go the needed distance and therefore experience the desire for whatever we so desperately lack.

If a man chances to be a genius, then he possesses "all." He must still produce a work of genius, else he be "nothing." Under the heading "Genius," Poe noted in 1845 a brief definition of the type (included in the Hough edition of Poe's critical essays). Few geniuses are capable of "the constructive ability," he said. This ability is partially "the faculty of analysis" but largely comes from "properties strictly moral"—that is, the properties of "energy or industry." It is, Poe declares, "chiefly because this quality [of *doing*] and genius [of *being*] are nearly incompatible that 'works of genius' are few, while mere men of genius are, as I say, abundant." According to this criterion, agreed to by both Poe and William James, sufficiency must include what one does together with the right amount one has. That is plain enough, especially in a country which has always put so much stress on doing, but it is the contemplation of the nature of *amount* which concerns us just now.

In *The Making of Americans* Gertrude Stein says some people do not fill up their space. She seems to mean by this what Henry James did when he spoke in *The American Scene* of The Margin—that blank waste of unused human consciousness surrounding America which might prove the nation's doom. Books, too, must fill their implied sufficiency. As the writer of a novel devoted to the greatest success story she knew how to tell, Stein was anxious to fill its space with portraits that would depict the full human history of *everyone*—all the lesses and the mores and the enoughs—in America.

One of the families Stein chooses to show in the making is the Schilling family. Their name is money, but their habitual practice of robbing Peter to pay Paul is poor economics; none of their transactions brings them enough good. In happy contrast, there is David Hersland, who is filled up; he has a bigness inside himself that opposes the threats of nothingness that loom inside and out. Stein, once a model student of William James, is in agreement with James's words (included in *The James Family*, p. 673), "There is very little difference between one man and another, but what little there is, *is very important*."

Ernest Hemingway preferred not to think of himself as the model student of Stein. But he also had a strong bent for the higher economics of successful being. Within *A Moveable Feast* alone there are many incidents that illustrate this. Irritated by a chimney that wastes heat and loses money; buying clothes for comfort and wear, not for style; reading when hungry so he will not care too much about the inner ache of his stomach; being content without plumbing or hot water because the flat has a fine view: Hemingway is unbothered by poverty just then because he is a man doing his work well with all he's got.

For Hemingway, you never win if you fight futilely against poverty. Instead, spend just enough to eat and drink cheaply (as Thoreau did), and sleep warmly (as Thoreau could not) by bedding with your wife. Of course, temptations come to the young ascetic from the Michigan woods, but he learns to curb his yearnings to bet lucky on the horses by filling the emptiness caused by that denied desire with the substitute of work—what psychologists call sublimation, what others call smart economy.

Then the big disaster. A suitcase full of writing—all the manuscripts he had completed up to that time, the ones which would have proved to the world the success of his life—lost, irretrievable. Hemingway never tells us what he did in the night after that terrible loss. (Was it what Thoreau did that time when the night and the pond's stillness pressed in on him?) Yet Hemingway's economics for the good life worked for him as long as it kept him solvent. He always worked very close to the margin, though. Not much of a gambler on conventional luck, he took risks when it came to the sufficiency of work and talent. Stein, who was more bourgeois than Hemingway with her artistic frugalities, commented on his sudden splurges and quick depletions. When the time came that Hemingway no longer had enough, he acted out his acknowledgement of his failure. He admitted the killing emptiness of insufficiency by giving himself over to death.

The Puritans came to America with the idea of doing God's bidding in His land, as well as to bring off a commercially profitable venture in colonization. However much they might fall short as deeply flawed humans, they knew what Thomas Hooker told them was true: "There's a sufficiency of God to content and satisfy us." In the land represented in *Letters from an American Farmer* in the late eighteenth century such ideas were secularized mightily. But Crèvecœur's good American was, like the Puritan God, characterized by self-sufficiency and sound land-holdings. In the next century Henry James, Senior, extended the moral economics of self-sufficiency through revolutionary proclamations that would have made conservatives like Hooker and Crèvecœur wince. According to his son Henry's recollection in *Notes of a Son and Brother*, the elder James viewed "the idea of the Revolution" as

. . . a single turn of the inward wheel, one real response to pressure of the spiritual spring, [which] would bridge the chasms, straighten the distortions, rectify the relations and, in a word, redeem and vivify the whole mass. . . . It was of course the old story that we had only to *be* with more intelligence and faith. . . . (p. 225)

The elder James had the solution: *to be, with more*—not with too much or too little—in order fully to possess the New Heaven on Earth through the manifestation of the Divine-Natural-Humanity that would so fill the corners of life that evils would be squeezed out of existence and failure would find no place.

Faulkner's Lucas Beauchamp thinks that matters are a bit more complicated down in Mississippi by the twentieth century. Still, "That money's there." In "The Fire and the Hearth" (included in *Go Down, Moses*), Lucas' need is not the having to know where to dig deep, but *when*:

Man has got three score and ten years on this earth, the Book says. He can want a heap in that time and a heap of what he can want is due to come to him, if he just starts in soon enough. I done waited too long to start. (p. 131)

In "The Old People" (still another of the stories from *Go Down,*

*Moses* deeply involved with questions of gain and loss, wrong possession and right-giving), McCaslin Edmonds and young Ike
McCaslin lie in the cold night under body-warmed sheets. There
Edmonds attempts to tell the boy about the soundness of the
earth's basic economy, saying, "And the earth dont want to just
keep things, hoard them; it wants to use them again" (p. 186). In
"Delta Autumn" (next to the last story in this related grouping of
stories by Faulkner), Ike McCaslin—now an old man—still holds to
the faith learned that long-ago night about the perfect natural
economy which urges each man to do the best by the earth:

> Because it was his land, although he had never owned a foot of
> it. He had never wanted to, not even after he saw plain its ul-
> timate doom . . . because it belonged to no man. It belonged to
> all; they had only to use it well, humbly and with pride. . . . It
> was because there was just exactly enough of it. (pp. 353-354)

In that centerpiece of *Go Down, Moses*, "The Bear," the truth
Faulkner images as Keats's ode-urn is very beautiful. But the pure
economics of love about which the urn speaks is of a kind devastating to life. It tells "*about a young man and a girl he would never need to
grieve over because he could never approach any nearer and would never
have to get any further away*" (p. 297). Ike himself lives with fine
economy in his relation to the land; he lives with rare and too inhuman an economy in his relation to people. However successful
he is in terms of "America," he is a failure as an "American."

If it has always been difficult in this nation to practice the economy of "just enough" toward the land, it is even harder to treat it in
matters of private love and public citizenship. Admirable land
economists like Ike McCaslin and Henry David Thoreau tend to
avoid the expenditures which come with human contact. They
seem incapable of converting the fact of *other people* into spiritual
gain—especially the gain of giving. And once they have "waited too
long to start," even America will not yield them a second chance.

In 1905 Henry James wrote that the only success men and
women ever know derives from true relationships. This in turn is
dependent quite directly upon the language they use. Success is,
indeed, "The Question of Our Speech," the title of an address he
gave that year at Bryn Mawr College. Speech must be used with
what his brother William called "intelligent intelligence," else it will
fail to convey the right ideas out of which success may come. If
America *is* the sufficiency of its ideas, success in America and as an

American requires the best language to present those ideas. The crucial study of the economic theories of success could well start, and proceed, with language. Out of language are created concepts of time, the land, and human beings in relationship with one another. In Henry James's mind these creations are not trivial illusions, since language, rightly used, is life as we as human beings most deeply experience it.

William James, in contrast, wrote of that central area of fact where all is non-verbal. But Henry James would contend that such a center is too abstract a realm for human beings to live in since they must *speak*. Of course, Henry's people often speak without words (with silences, eye-glances, psychic intuitions almost occult in their power), but it is *language* in whatever form which he insists is *the* center and *the* fact of life.

Perhaps ideas are not the origin of language; perhaps it is the other way around. The Norsemen and Columbus may have discovered the new continent geographically, but they failed to pronounce the right word that would give it, by the force of a name, the historical and human substance it needed; only with that name could all the possible ideas about the place's meaning come into play. In *The Golden Bowl* Fanny Assingham observes to Colonel Bob that it was Amerigo Vespucci, "the pushing man who followed, across the sea, in the wake of Columbus and succeeded, where Columbus had failed, in becoming godfather, or name-father, to the new Continent . . ." (xxiii, 78).

It may have been the same at the very beginning of all things. Perhaps God did not know what universe to create until He said the Word. Perhaps this world was mere undifferentiated mass until Adam the man set to work to name things into distinctive being and purpose. What could the world mean to the human imagination until Adam made it ready for aesthetic contemplation by distinguishing all there is to wonder over and to desire? As for America, our own garden of creation, it is significant that men of authenticity failed to articulate the new continent into reality. It took upstarts like Amerigo to supply the word that instigated our sense of place and destiny. "America" is the word we still use to expropriate things in questionable ways (including Canada and the lands south of Texas in the greedy, sweeping looseness of our all-inclusive sense of things). But since, as James has told us, language changes according to how human beings choose to alter it, we could still use the word "America" to speak good visions and to intonate actualities into existence.

Once words get started they tend to keep on going. Gertrude Stein wrote in *Everybody's Autobiography* of what artists and words can do together:

> . . . it makes it do what they never did do, this time it made them do as if the last word had heard the next word and the next word had heard not the last word but the next word.
> After all why not.
> I like anything that a word can do. And words can do do all they do and then they can do what they never do do. (p. 317)

Energy abounding within them, and constant interest about them: there is no endingness about words. Perhaps the sun is cooling down in obedience to the Second Law of Thermodynamics as Henry Adams warned, but the law of the dynamics of speech rushes in to fill the cold void with the generating heat of tongues.

When, in an earlier section of this book, the matter of silence came up, reference was made to Paul Ricoeur's notion that *myth* begins with silence. If one keeps in mind Frank Kermode's own association of myth with *lie*, it is intriguing to encounter Kermode's attitude toward language as it is colored in his mind by the attitudes he says are held by Jean-Paul Sartre and Iris Murdoch. In speaking of the plight of the novel in *The Sense of an Ending* Kermode states bluntly enough, "It has to lie. Words, thoughts, patterns of word and thought, are enemies of truth, if you identify that with what may be had by phenomenological reductions." Under such conditions, "truth would be found only in a silent poem or a silent novel. As soon as it speaks, begins to be a novel, it imposes causality and concordance, development, character, a past which matters and a future within certain broad limits determined by the project of the author rather than that of the characters" (p. 140).

We could come back at Kermode with the retort that Gertrude Stein's *Everybody's Autobiography* and her novel *The Making of Americans* are not silent, or as lyingly "deterministic" as the words which Murdoch or Sartre put to the cause of truth. We can go further still—not to settle this debate conclusively, but to indicate a way past Kermode's unease when he looks at the relations between thought as the determining agent and the words imposed upon the randomness of reality.

Coached by Sartre, Kermode sees thought as the cause that comes before words. This is not the way it is according to Gaston Bachelard. In speaking of what language is like in *Air and Songs* (in the portion included in the Gaudin collection, p. 30), Bachelard says it "is always somewhat ahead of our thoughts, somewhat more seething than our love." Language "is the beautiful function of human rashness, the dynamic boast of the will; it is what exaggerates power."

This pull of exaggeration of which Bachelard speaks causes good arrears, not bad economics. He argues, "Without this exaggeration, life cannot develop. In all circumstances, life takes *too much* in order that thought may have *enough*. The will must imagine *too much* in order to realize enough" (italics mine).

Bachelard believes in an economics of language that is based on the idea of yea-saying. In seeming contrast, Paul Ricoeur presses the importance of No. In his view No creates the affirmations which contain dissonance and mark off the boundaries necessary to give us, by opposition, our sense of freedom. Without the contrast of the world's No, Ricoeur says, we would be doomed to nothingness; once all is Yes success loses its meaning. If ever success requires meaninglessness, failure would be what we have got. It is only vanity which reads No as the lord which forbids and destroys our happiness. No is the blessing that aids us in creating what we most want.

Freud said that dreams contain no No. Freud and Ricoeur might both be right if we can envision the world as being where No is and dreams as being where No is absent. If this is true, we need to consider an America that is No: a place largely free of those dreams that could destroy us. It would be a place admirably suited to *visions*—not dreams—of joy and freedom. But would there be wonder in America if there were no dreams? Of course, since with the fact of No's limitations there are always those areas we cannot see into—the space beyond which we know we *could yet discover* if we *thought* to do it.

It is as Bachelard suggests: by our conscious will we are able continually to imagine the excess which life constantly acts to subtract. We have "cast in" meaning, while the world is at work "casting out" its nines. What is left is the correctly added sum, its accuracy signaled by the good zero which is the snobbery of our hope and our ideals. The balance (verified by that hope and those ideals) is our thought. Thought can just as well lead back to the reality of conscious, spoken experience as to the vanity of inarticulated dreams. With the economics of "just enough," *thought* is what suffices as *vision*, even though it lies alongside the *dream* of "more" (the will's imagination) and the *facts* of "less" (the circumstances of our lives).

It is unlikely that Frank Kermode would ever be placated by the sum total of these suggestions. But if he were, perhaps he could find a way past words like "desolately" and "painfully" by which he describes his awareness that "None of our fictions is a supreme fiction" and that ours is "the condition Sartre calls 'need' and Stevens' 'poverty' " (pp. 155-156). This other way past defeat would not involve an evasion of the blunt obstacle which reality is. It would simply, but not too simply, suggest that the fictions (what this book has continually dealt with as the *ideas*) of good success and good failure *actually do suffice*; they need not be feared as being too much or lamented as being too little.

In America we are often urged to live with the language of the *superlative*—what Bachelard describes in *The Poetics of Space* as *so much more than*. This is the language which comes from the region of the hidden and the infinite; it has the power to drive the Poemind mad with desire. But we can also choose to live at ease with the language of the *comparative*—defined by Bachelard as that which is always *held in relation to the finite*; this is the region in which the mind of Benjamin Franklin finds it success. We might also elect to keep on moving through that ever interesting space which spreads out between the superlative and the comparative—to be, thereby, like Henry James, like Thoreau and Emerson, like Mailer, like Faulkner, like the America of their ideas: not concluding with more, certainly not ending with less, but going on with *just enough*.

# Selected
# Bibliography

# SELECTED BIBLIOGRAPHY

Titles which the text cites in terms of quotations and/or page references.

Abrams, Meyer. *Natural Supernaturalism: Tradition and Revolution in Romantic Literature*. New York: Norton, 1971.

Adams, Brooks. "The Heritage of Henry Adams." Introduction to *The Degradation of the Democratic Dogma*. New York: Macmillan, 1919.

Adams, Henry. "Captain John Smith." *The North American Review*, 104 (January 1867), pp. 1-30.

———. "The Tendency of History" (1894); "The Rule of Phase Applied to History" (1909); "A Letter to American Teachers of History" (1910). *The Degradation of the Democratic Dogma*. New York: Macmillan, 1919.

———. *The Education of Henry Adams. An Autobiography*. Boston: Houghton Mifflin, 1918.

———. "Prayer to the Virgin of Chartres." From Mabel LaFarge's *Letters to a Niece and Prayer to the Virgin of Chartres, by Henry Adams, with a niece's memories*. Boston: Houghton Mifflin, 1920.

Allen, Gay Wilson. *William James Reader*. New York: Houghton Mifflin (Riverside Edition), 1972.

Arnheim, Rudolf. *Entropy and Art: An Essay on Disorder and Order*. Berkeley: University of California, 1971.

Bachelard, Gaston. *Air and Songs, Lautréamont*, and *Water and Dreams*. Translated in part from the French by Colette Gaudin. Included in *On Poetic Imagination and Reverie: Selections from the Works of Gaston Bachelard*. Indianapolis: The Library of Liberal Arts, Bobbs-Merrill, 1971.

———. *The Poetics of Reverie, Childhood, Language, and the Cosmos*. Translated from the French by Daniel Russell. Boston: Beacon, 1969.

———. *The Poetics of Space*. Translated from the French by Maria Jolas. New York: Orion, 1964.

———. *The Psychoanalysis of Fire*. Translated from the French by Alan C. M. Ross. Boston: Beacon, 1964.

Bakan, David. *Disease, Pain, and Sacrifice: Toward a Psychology of Suffering*. Chicago: University of Chicago, 1968.

Bakan, David. *The Duality of Human Existence: An Essay on Psychology and Religion*. Chicago: Rand McNally, 1966.

Barlow, Captain Arthur. Included in *Richard Hakluyt, Principle Navigations Voyages Traffiques & Discoveries of the English Nation*. Vol. VII, 298. Glasgow: Hakluyt Society, 1903-1905.

Baudelaire, Charles. "On the Essence of Laughter and, in General, on the Comic in the Plastic Arts." *The Painter of Modern Life and Other Essays*. Translated and edited by Jonathan Mayne. Greenwich, Conn.: Phaidon, 1964.

Bellow, Saul. *Herzog*. New York: Viking, 1964.

Bentley, Eric. *The Life of the Drama*. New York: Atheneum, 1964.

Beveridge, Albert J. *Americans of To-Day and To-morrow*. Philadelphia: Altemus, 1908.

Blair, Walter. *Mark Twain and Huck Finn*. Berkeley: University of California, 1960.

Bradford, William. *Of Plymouth Plantation*. (Published in 1856 as "History of Plymouth Plantation.") Included in *The Puritans*, ed. P. Miller and T. H. Johnson, Vol. I, 91-117.

Branch, Edgar L. *The Literary Apprenticeship of Mark Twain*. Urbana, Ill.: University of Illinois, 1950.

Bronowski, Jacob. *The Ascent of Man*. Boston: Little, Brown, 1973.

Brownson, Orestes. "Democracy and Liberty." Vol. XII. *The Works of Orestes A. Brownson*. Ed. Henry F. Brownson. Detroit: Thorndike Nourse, 1882-1887.

Burroughs, William. *Naked Lunch*. New York: Grove, 1959.

Carlyle, Thomas. *Latter-Day Pamphlets*. (First published in 1850.) Vol. XX. *Works*. Centenary Edition. London: Chapman and Hall, 1898.

Cater, Harold D., ed. *Henry Adams and His Friends: A Collection of His Unpublished Letters, Compiled with a Biographical Introduction*. . . . New York: Octagon, 1970.

Cawelti, John G. *Apostles of the Self-Made Man*. Chicago: University of Chicago, 1965.

Cleaver, Eldridge. *Soul on Ice*. New York: McGraw-Hill, 1968.

Clemens, Samuel L. [Mark Twain]. *Adventures of Huckleberry Finn*. (First published by Webster, New York, 1885.) Vol. XIII. *Writings of Mark Twain*. Authors National Edition. New York: Harper, 1912.

———. *The Autobiography of Mark Twain*. Arranged and edited by Charles Neider. New York: Harper and Row, 1959.

———. *A Connecticut Yankee in King Arthur's Court*. (First published by Webster, New York, 1889.) Vol. XVI. *Writings of Mark Twain*. Authors National Edition. New York: Harper, 1917.

————. *The Diaries of Adam and Eve*. New York: American Heritage, 1971.

————. *Life on the Mississippi*. (First published by Osgood, Boston, 1883.) Vol. IX. *Writings of Mark Twain*. Authors National Edition. New York: Harper, 1903.

————. *Mark Twain's Fables of Man*. Ed. John S. Tuckey. Berkeley: University of California, 1972.

————. *Mark Twain-Howells Letters, The Correspondence of Samuel L. Clemens and William D. Howells, 1872-1910*. Ed. H. N. Smith and William Gibson. Cambridge, Mass.: Belknap Press, 1960.

————. *Roughing It*. (First published by American Publishing Co., Hartford, Conn., 1872.) Vols. VII-VIII. *Writings of Mark Twain*. Authors National Edition. New York: Harper, 1899.

————. *Which Was the Dream? and Other Writings of the Later Years*. Ed. John S. Tuckey. Berkeley: University of California, 1968.

Cotton, John. From "Christian Calling." (First published in *The Way of Life*, Fawne and Gellibrand, London, 1641.) Included in *The Puritans*, ed. P. Miller and T. H. Johnson. Vol. I, 319-327.

Crèvecœur, Michel Guillaume St. Jean de (called Saint John de Crèvecœur). *Letters From an American Farmer. . . .* (First published by Davies, London, 1782.) London: Dent (Everyman's Library Series), 1912.

Crews, Frederick C. "Love in the Western World." *Partisan Review*, Special Issue, 34 (Spring 1967), pp. 272-287.

Cummings, Edward Estlin. *I: Six Nonlectures*. Cambridge, Mass.: Harvard University, 1953.

————. *The Enormous Room*. New York: Boni and Liveright, 1922.

Danforth, Samuel. From *Records of the First Church in Roxbury, Mass., 1664-1667*. Included in *America Begins*, ed. R. M. Dorson, pp. 164-166.

Dewey, John. From *Reconstruction in Philosophy*. (First published by Holt, New York, 1920.) Included in *Documents in the History of American Philosophy*, ed. M. G. White, pp. 446-479.

Dickens, Charles. *The Life and Adventures of Martin Chuzzlewit*. London: Macmillan, 1954. (Reprint of first edition, 1844.)

Dickinson, Emily. *The Poems of Emily Dickinson*. Ed. Thomas H. Johnson. Cambridge, Mass.: Belknap Press, 1958.

Dixon, Thomas, Jr. *The Clansman: An Historical Romance of the Ku Klux Klan*. New York: Doubleday, Page, 1905.

Dorson, Richard M., ed. *America Begins, Early American Writings*. New York: Pantheon, 1950.

Dreiser, Theodore. *Sister Carrie*. (First published by Doubleday, New York, 1900.) Ed. Donald Pizer. New York: Norton, 1970.

Edwards, Jonathan. From *A Treatise Concerning Religious Affections*. (First published in Boston, 1746.) Included in *Documents in the History of American Philosophy*, ed. M. G. White, pp. 42-50.

Einstein, Albert. "Autobiographical Notes." Vol. 1. *Albert Einstein: Philosopher-Scientist*. Translated from the German and edited by Paul Arthur Schilpp. La Salle, Ill.: The Library of Living Philosophers, 1949.

Eliot, T. S. "Little Gidding" from *Four Quartets*. Included in *Collected Poems, 1909-1962*. London: Faber and Faber; New York: Harcourt, Brace, 1963.

Elliott, Robert C. *The Shape of Utopia: Studies in a Literary Genre*. Chicago, Ill.: University of Chicago, 1970.

Emerson, Ralph Waldo. From *Complete Works*. Centenary Edition. Boston: Houghton, Mifflin, 1903-1904.

    "An Address Delivered Before the Senior Class in Divinity College, Cambridge," Vol. 1; "The American Scholar," Vol. 1; "Art," Vol. vii; "Aristocracy," Vol. x; "Character," Vol. iii; "The Comic," Vol. xiii; "Culture," Vol. vi; "Demonology," Vol. x; "Destiny," Vol. ix; "Fate," Vol. vi; "The Fortune of the Republic," Vol. xi; "Historic Notes of Life and Letters in New England," Vol. iv; "Immortality," Vol. viii; "The Method of Nature," Vol. 1; "Nature," Vol. 1; "Perpetual Forces," Vol. x; "Poetry and Imagination," Vol. viii; "Power," Vol. vi; "Progress of Culture," Vol. viii; "The Scholar," Vol. x; "Self-Reliance," Vol. ii; "Society and Solitude," Vol. vii; "The Sovereignty of Ethics," Vol. x; "Success," Vol. vii; "The Superlative," Vol. x; "Thoreau," Vol. x; "Woodnotes," Vol. ix.

————. *Journals and Miscellaneous Notebooks*. Ed. William H. Gilman and others. 10 vols. Cambridge, Mass.: Belknap Press, 1960-c 1973.

————. *The Letters of Ralph Waldo Emerson, in Six Volumes*, Ed. Ralph L. Rusk. New York: Columbia University, 1939.

Faulkner, William. *Absalom, Absalom!* New York: Random House, 1936.

————. *As I Lay Dying*. New York: Cape and Smith, 1930.

————. "A Courtship." (First published in *Sewanee Review*, 1948.) Included in *Collected Stories of William Faulkner*. New York: Random House, 1950.

————. "A Note on Sherwood Anderson." *Essays, Speeches & Public Letters*. Ed. James B. Meriwether. New York: Random House, 1965.

————. "Foreword" to *The Faulkner Reader*. New York: Modern Library, 1954.

————. *Go Down, Moses and Other Stories*. New York: Random House, 1942.

————. *The Hamlet*. New York: Random House, 1940.

————. *Intruder in the Dust*. New York: Random House, 1948.

————. *Light in August*. New York: Harrison Smith and Robert Hass, 1932.

————. *The Mansion*. New York: Random House, 1959.

————. *Requiem for A Nun*. New York: Random House, 1951.

————. *The Town*. New York: Random House, 1957.

————. "Books and Things" (Review of Joseph Hergesheimer); "Books & Things. American Drama: Inhibitions"; "The Hill." From *William Faulkner: Early Prose and Poetry*. Ed. Carvel Collins. Boston: Little, Brown, 1962.

Fiske, John. From *Outlines of Cosmic Philosophy, Based on the Doctrine of Evolution, with Criticisms on the Positive Philosophy*. 4 vols. (First published in 1874). Boston: Houghton Mifflin, 1916.

Fitzgerald, F. Scott. *The Crack-Up*. New York: New Directions, 1945.

————. *The Great Gatsby*. New York: Scribner's, 1925.

————. *Tender Is the Night*. New York: Scribner's, 1934.

Flaubert, Gustave. *Flaubert in Egypt; A Sensibility on Tour; A Narrative Drawn from Gustave Flaubert's Travel Notes & Letters*. Translated from the French and edited by Francis Steegmuller. London: Bodley Head, 1972.

Fletcher, Angus. *Allegory: The Theory of a Symbolic Mode*. Ithaca, New York: Cornell University 1964.

Ford, W. C., ed. *Letters of Henry Adams, 1858-1891*. 2 vols. Boston: Houghton Mifflin, 1930-1938.

Franklin, Benjamin. "The Autobiography." Vol I. *Works*. Ed. John Bigelow. Federal Edition. New York: Putnam's, 1904.

Fuller, Margaret. "American Literature: Its Position in the Present Time and Prospects for the Future," pp. 358-374, *The Writings of Margaret Fuller*. Ed. Mason Wade. New York: Viking, 1941.

————. "Conversation in Boston." Vol. 1. *Memoirs*. Ed. Ralph Waldo Emerson, James Freeman Clarke, and William Ellery Channing. Boston: Phillips, Sampson, 1852.

Gaudin, Colette. Introduction to *On Poetic Imagination and Reverie: Selections from the Works of Gaston Bachelard*. Indianapolis: The Library of Liberal Arts, Bobbs-Merrill, 1971.

Gruber, Howard E. *Darwin on Man: A Psychological Study of Scientific Creativity, Together with Darwin's Early and Unpublished Notebooks, transcribed and annotated by Paul H. Barrett*. New York: Dutton, 1974.

Harper, Ralph. *Nostalgia: An Existential Exploration of Longing and Fulfillment in the Modern Age*. Cleveland: Western Reserve University, 1966.

Hartshorne, Thomas L. *The Distorted Image: Changing Conceptions of American Character Since Turner*. Cleveland: Case Western University, 1968.

Hawthorne, Nathaniel. *The House of the Seven Gables*. (First published by Ticknor, Reed, and Fields, Boston, 1851.) Ed. Fredson Bowers. Vol. ii. *Works*. Centenary Edition. Columbus, Ohio: Ohio State University, 1965.

Hemingway, Ernest. *A Moveable Feast*. New York: Scribner's, 1964.

Hubbard, William. From *The Happiness of a People in the Wisdome of Their Rulers Directing*. . . . (First published by Foster, Boston, 1676.) Included in *The Puritans*, ed. P. Miller and T. H. Johnson, Vol. i, 247-250.

James, Henry, Senior. "Autobiography" and "Socialism and Civilization." Included in *The James Family*, ed. F. O. Matthiessen, pp. 17-38; 45-58.

James, Henry. *The Ambassadors*. (First published by Harper, New York, 1903). Vols. xxi-xxii. *Novels and Tales*. New York: Scribner's, 1909.

——. *The American*. Boston: Osgood, 1877.

——. *The American Scene*. New York and London: Harper, 1907.

——. *The Art of Fiction*. With Walter Besant. (First published by DeWolfe, Fiske, Boston [1884?].) Included in *The James Family*, ed. F. O. Matthiessen, pp. 353-370.

——. *The Art of the Novel: Critical Prefaces by Henry James; with an introduction by Richard P. Blackmur*. New York: Scribner's 1934.

——. *The Golden Bowl*. (First published by Scribner's, New York, 1904.) Vols. xxii-xxiv. *Novels and Tales*. New York: Scribner's, 1909.

——. *Henry James Letters*. Ed. Leon Edel. 2 vols. Cambridge, Mass.: Belknap Press, 1975.

——. "Is There a Life After Death?" from *In After Days. Thoughts On a Future Life*. (First published by Harper, New York, 1910.) Included in *The James Family*, ed. F. O. Matthiessen, pp. 602-614.

——. *The Notebooks of Henry James*. Ed. F. O. Matthiessen and Kenneth B. Murdock. New York: Braziller, 1947.

——. *Notes of a Son and Brother*. New York: Scribner's, 1914.

——. *The Question of Our Speech: The Lesson of Balzac: two lectures, by Henry James*. Boston: Houghton, Mifflin, 1905.

——. *A Small Boy and Others*. New York: Scribner's, 1913.

————. *The Wings of the Dove.* (First published by Scribner's, New York, 1902.) Vols. XIX-XX. *Novels and Tales.* New York: Scribner's, 1909.

James, William. "The Dilemma of Determinism." (First published in *Unitarian Review and Religious Magazine*, 1884.) Included in *William James Reader*, ed. G. W. Allen, pp. 16-40.

————. "The Hidden Self." (First published in *Scribner's Magazine*, 1890.) Included in *William James Reader*, ed. G. W. Allen, pp. 90-108.

————. *The Letters of William James.* Ed. by his son Henry James. 2 vols. Boston: Atlantic Monthly, 1920.

————. *The Literary Remains of the Late Henry James.* Ed. with an Introduction by William James. Boston: Houghton, 1884.

————. "The Moral Equivalent of War." (First published in *McClure's Magazine*, 1910.) Included in *William James Reader*, ed. G. W. Allen, pp. 211-221.

————. "Philosophical Conceptions and Practical Results." (First published in *University of California Chronicle*, 1898.) Included in *William James Reader*, ed. G. W. Allen, pp. 138-154.

————. "The Stream of Thought," Chapter IX, pp. 224-290, and "The Theory of the Soul" (from "The Consciousness of Self"), Chapter X, pp. 342-350. Vol. I. *Principles of Psychology.* New York, Holt, 1890.

————. "Remarks at the Peace Banquet." (First published in *Atlantic Monthly*, 1904.) Included in *William James Reader*, ed. G. W. Allen, pp. 182-184.

————. "Remarks on Spencer's Definition of Mind as Correspondence." (First published in *The Journal of Speculative Philosophy*, 1878.) Included in *William James Reader*, ed. G. W. Allen, pp. 3-15.

————. "Gospel of Relaxation." *Talks to Teachers and Students on Psychology: and to Students on Some of Life's Ideals.* New York: Holt, 1899.

————. From "The Sick Soul." *The Varieties of Religious Experience: A Study in Human Nature.* . . . New York: Longmans, Green, 1902.

————. "What The Will Effects." (First published in *Scribner's Magazine*, 1888.) Included in *William James Reader*, ed. G. W. Allen, pp. 74-89.

Jones, Howard Mumford. *The Age of Energy: Varieties of American Experience, 1865-1915.* New York: Viking, 1971.

Josselyn, John. From *An Account of Two Voyages.* (Published by Widdows, London, 1674.) Included in *America Begins*, ed. R. M. Dorson, pp. 21-32.

Kaplan, Justin. *Mr. Clemens and Mark Twain*. New York: Simon and Schuster, 1966.

Kermode, Frank. *The Sense of An Ending: Studies in the Theory of Fiction*. New York: Oxford University, 1967.

Kolodny, Annette. *The Lay of the Land, Metaphor as Experience and History in American Life and Letters*. Chapel Hill: University of North Carolina, 1975.

Krook, Dorothea. *The Ordeal of Consciousness in Henry James*. London: Cambridge University, 1962.

Krutch, Joseph Wood. *Edgar Allan Poe: A Study in Genius*. New York: Russell & Russell, 1926.

Lawrence, David Herbert. "The Evening Land." Vol. 1. *Complete Poems*. New York: Viking, 1964.

Levett, Christopher. From *A Voyage Into New England: begun in 1623 and ended in 1624*. (First published in London, 1628.) Included in *America Begins*, ed. R. M. Dorson, pp. 102-103.

Levy, Leo Ben. *Versions of Melodrama: A Study of the Fiction and Drama of Henry James, 1865-1897*. Berkeley: University of California, 1957.

Lowell, Robert. "91 Revere Street," "Terminal Days at Beverly Farms," and "Commander Lowell." From *Life Studies*. New York: Farrar, Straus and Cudahy, 1959.

————. *Notebook*. 3rd edition, revised and expanded. New York: Farrar, Straus and Giroux, 1970.

Lubbock, Percy, ed. *The Letters of Henry James*. 2 vols. New York: Scribner's, 1920.

Mailer, Norman. *Advertisements for Myself*. New York: Putnam's, 1959.

————. *An American Dream*. New York: Dial, 1965.

————. *The Armies of the Night*. New York: New American Library, 1968.

————. *Cannibals and Christians*. New York: Dial, 1966.

————. *Miami and the Siege of Chicago*. New York: New American Library, 1968.

————. *Of a Fire on the Moon*. Boston: Little, Brown, 1970.

————. *The Presidential Papers*. New York: Putnam's, 1963.

————. *The Prisoner of Sex*. Boston: Little, Brown, 1971.

————. "A Transit to Narcissus." *New York Review of Books*, May 17, 1973, pp. 3-10. [Review of "Last Tango in Paris."]

————. *Why Are We in Vietnam?: A Novel*. New York: Putnam's, 1967.

Mather, Cotton. From "A General Introduction." *Magnalia Christi Americana. . . .* (Published by Parkhurst, London, 1702.) Included in *The Puritans*, ed. P. Miller and T. H. Johnson. Vol. I, 163-179.

Mather, Increase. From *The Life and Death of that Reverend Man of God, Mr. Richard Mather*. (Published by Green and Johnson, Cambridge, Mass.; 1670.) Included in *The Puritans*, ed. P. Miller and T. H. Johnson. Vol. II, 489-496.

Matthiessen, Francis O. *The James Family: Including Selections from the Writings of Henry James, Senior, William, Henry & Alice James*. New York: Knopf, 1947.

McAleer, John J. *Theodore Dreiser: An Introduction and Interpretation*. Chicago, Ill.: Holt, Rinehart, Winston (American Authors and Critics Series), 1968.

Melville, Herman. *Billy Budd, Sailor*. (First published 1924.) Ed. Harrison Hayford and Merton M. Sealts, Jr. Chicago: University of Chicago, 1962.

———. *The Confidence-Man: His Masquerade*. (First published by Dix, Edward, New York, 1857.) Ed. Hershel Parker. New York: Norton, 1971.

———. "The Encantadas: or Enchanted Islands." From *The Piazza Tales*. (First published by Dix, Edward, New York, 1856.) Ed. Egbert S. Oliver. New York: Hendricks House, 1948.

———. *Moby-Dick: or, The Whale*. (First published by Harper, New York, 1851.) Ed. Harrison Hayford and Hershel Parker. New York: Norton, 1967.

———. *Typee: A Peep at Polynesian Life During a Four Months' Residence in A Valley of the Marquesas*. (First published by Wiley and Putnam, New York, 1846.) Ed. Harrison Hayford, Hershel Parker and G. Thomas Tanselle. Evanston, Ill.: Northwestern University, 1968.

Miller, Perry. *Consciousness in Concord: The Text of Thoreau's Hitherto "Lost Journals," 1840-1841*.... Boston: Houghton, Mifflin, 1958.

———. "Errand Into the Wilderness," "The Marrow of Puritan Divinity," "Religion and Society in the Early Literature of Virginia." From *Errand Into the Wilderness*. Cambridge, Mass.: Belknap Press, 1956.

———. *The Puritans*, ed. with Thomas H. Johnson. 2 vols. Revised Edition. New York: Harper Torchbooks, 1963.

———. *The Raven and the Whale: The War of Words and Wits in the Era of Poe and Melville*. New York: Harcourt Brace & World, 1956.

———. *The Transcendentalists*. Cambridge, Mass.: Harvard University, 1960.

Minter, David L. *The Interpreted Design as a Structural Principle in American Prose*. New Haven, Conn.: Yale University, 1969.

Montanus, Arnoldus. From *Description of New Netherland*. (First published in translation, Albany, New York, 1851.) Included in *America Begins*, ed. R. M. Dorson, pp. 94-96.

Morison, Samuel Eliot. *The European Discovery of America: The Northern Voyages, 500-1600.* New York: Oxford University, 1971.

Morris, Wright. *The Territory Ahead.* New York: Harcourt, Brace, 1958.

Novak, Barbara. *American Painting of the Nineteenth Century, Realism, Idealism, and the American Experience.* New York: Praeger, 1969.

Oakes, Urian. From *The Sovereign Efficacy of Divine Providence.* . . . (Published by Sewall, Boston, 1682.) Included in *The Puritans*, ed. P. Miller and T. H. Johnson. Vol. 1, 350-367.

Paine, Albert Bigelow. *Mark Twain: A Biography.* 4 vols. New York: Harper, 1912.

Parker, Theodore. "The Political Destination of America and the Signs of the Times"; "Transcendentalism." From Robert E. Collins' *Theodore Parker: American Transcendentalist: A Critical Essay and a Collection of His Writings.* Metuchen, N.J.: Scarecrow Press, 1973.

Peirce, Charles Sanders. From "How To Make Our Ideas Clear." (First published by *Popular Science Monthly*, 1878.) Included in *Documents in the History of American Philosophy*, ed. M. G. White, pp. 291-318.

Perry, Ralph Barton. *The Thought and Character of William James: Briefer Version.* Cambridge, Mass.: Harvard University, 1948.

Poe, Edgar Allan. "Genius"; "N. P. Willis" [concerning "arrangement" vs. "creation"]. From *Literary Criticism of Edgar Allan Poe.* Ed. Robert L. Hough. Lincoln, Neb.: University of Nebraska Press (Regents Critics Series), 1965.

———. *The Narrative of Arthur Gordon Pym of Nantucket.* (First published by Harper, New York, 1838.) Ed. Sidney Kaplan. New York: Hill and Wang, 1960.

Poirier, William Richard. *Norman Mailer.* New York: Viking, 1972.

———. *A World Elsewhere: The Place of Style in American Literature.* New York: Oxford University, 1966.

Pynchon, Thomas. *Gravity's Rainbow.* New York: Viking, 1972.

Quam, Alvina, trans. *The Zunis: Self-Portrayals by the Zuni People.* Albuquerque: University of New Mexico, 1972.

Ricks, Christopher. "Profile. The Poet Robert Lowell—seen by Christopher Ricks." *The Listener*, June 21, 1973, pp. 830-832.

Ricoeur, Paul. *The Symbolism of Evil.* Translated from the French by Emerson Buchanan. Boston: Beacon, 1969.

Rieff, Philip. *Freud: The Mind of the Moralist.* New York: Viking, 1959.

Robb, John S. *Streaks of Squatter Life and Far-West Scenes*. Philadelphia: Carey and Hart, 1847.

Rosenberg, Harold. *Barnett Newman: Broken Obelisk and Other Sculptures*. Seattle: Index of Art in the Pacific Northwest, No. 2: University of Washington, 1971.

Royce, Josiah. From *The Conception of God: A Philosophical Discussion Concerning the Nature of the Divine Idea as a Demonstrable Reality*. With Joseph Le Conte, G. H. Howison, and Sidney E. Mezes. (First published by Macmillan, New York, 1897.) Included in *Documents in the History of American Philosophy*, ed. M. G. White, pp. 373-399.

Rush, Benjamin. "Lectures on Animal Life." *The Selected Writings of Benjamin Rush*. Ed. Dagobert D. Runes. New York: Philosophical Library, 1947.

Samuels, Ernest. *Henry Adams: The Major Phase*. Cambridge, Mass.: Belknap Press of Harvard University, 1964.

———. *Henry Adams: The Middle Years*. Cambridge, Mass.: Belknap Press of Harvard University, 1956.

———. *The Young Henry Adams*. Cambridge, Mass.: Harvard University, 1948.

Santayana, George. From "The Genteel Tradition in American Philosophy." (First published in *University of California Chronicle*, 1911.) Included in *Documents in the History of American Philosophy*, ed. M. G. White, pp. 404-428.

———. From "The Poetry of Christian Dogma." (Published in *Interpretations of Poetry and Religion*, Scribner's, New York, 1900.) Included in *Documents in the History of American Philosophy*, pp. 428-442.

Seebohm, Caroline. "How to Change Your Point of View." *House and Garden*, April 1974, pp. 90-91.

Skinner, Burrhus Frederic. *Beyond Freedom and Dignity*. New York: Knopf, 1971.

Slater, Joseph, ed. *The Correspondence of Emerson and Carlyle*. New York: Columbia University, 1964.

Slattery, Sister Mary. *Hazard, Form, and Value*. Detroit, Mich.: Wayne State University, 1971.

Smith, Henry Nash. *Mark Twain: The Development of A Writer*. Cambridge, Mass.: Harvard University, 1962.

Smith, Martha L. *Going to God's Country*. Boston: Christopher, 1941.

Spencer, Herbert. From *First Principles*. (First published by Williams and Norgate, London, 1862.) Included in *Documents in the History of American Philosophy*, ed. M. G. White, pp. 195-211.

Stein, Gertrude. *Everybody's Autobiography*. New York: Random House, 1937.
————. "Henry James." *Four in America*. New Haven, Conn.: Yale University, 1947.
————. "Portraits and Repetition"; "What Is English Literature." *Lectures in America*. New York: Random House, 1935.
————. *The Making of Americans, The Hersland Family*. Abridged Edition. New York: Harcourt, Brace, 1934.
Stone, Albert E., Jr. *The Innocent Eye: Childhood in Mark Twain's Imagination*. New Haven, Conn.: Yale University, 1961.
Styron, William. *The Confessions of Nat Turner*. New York: Random House, 1966.
Taylor, Edward. Prologue and Preface to *Gods Determinations Touching His Elect*. From *Poems*. Ed. Donald E. Stanford. New Haven, Conn.: Yale University, 1960.
Thoreau, Henry David. "Sir Walter Raleigh." *Early Essays and Miscellanies*. Ed. Joseph J. Moldenhauer and Edwin Moser. *Writings*. Princeton, N.J.: Princeton University, 1975.
————. *Journals*,Vols. vii-xx. *Writings*. Walden Edition. Boston: Houghton Mifflin, 1906.
————. *Life Without Principle*. Vol. iv. *Writings*. Walden Edition. Boston: Houghton Mifflin, 1906.
————. *The Maine Woods*. Ed. Joseph J. Moldenhauer. *Writings*. Princeton, N.J.: Princeton University, 1973.
————. *Walden*. Ed. J. Lyndon Shanley. *Writings*. Princeton, N.J.: Princeton University, 1971.
————. *Walking*. Vol. v. *Writings*. Walden Edition. Boston: Houghton Mifflin, 1906.
————. *A Week on the Concord and Merrimack Rivers*. Vol. i. *Writings*. Walden Edition. Boston: Houghton Mifflin, 1906.
Tocqueville, Alexis de. *Democracy in America*. Translated from the French by George Lawrence; edited by J. P. Mayer and Max Lerner. New York: Harper, Row, 1966.
Tomkins, Calvin. *Living Well Is the Best Revenge*. New York: Viking, 1971.
Trilling, Lionel. *E. M. Forster, A Study*. London: Hogarth Press, 1944.
Trollope, Frances. *Domestic Manners of the Americans: Edited with a History of Mrs. Trollope's Adventures in America by Donald Smalley*. (First published by Whittaker, Treacher, 1832.) New York: Knopf, 1949.
Updike, John. *The Poorhouse Fair*. New York: Knopf, 1958.

Wagner, Vern. *The Suspension of Henry Adams: A Study of Manner and Matter*. Detroit, Mich.: Wayne State University, 1969.

Ward, Nathaniel. From *The Simple Cobler of Aggawam in America*. . . . (Published by Bowtell, London, 1647.) Included in *The Puritans*, ed. P. Miller and T. H. Johnson, I, pp. 226-236.

Warren, Robert Penn. *Brother to Dragons: A Tale in Verse and Voices*. New York: Random House, 1953.

————, ed. *Selected Poems of Herman Melville: A Reader's Edition, with an Introduction*. . . . New York: Random House, 1967.

Wharton, Edith. *The Age of Innocence*. New York: Appleton, 1920.

White, Morton G., ed. *Documents in the History of American Philosophy*. New York: Oxford University, 1972.

Whitman, Walt. *Leaves of Grass*. Ed. Harold W. Blodgett and Sculley Bradley. New York: New York University, 1965.

Whorf, Benjamin. "Time, Space, and Language." Included in *Culture in Crisis*, pp. 152-172. Ed. Laura Thompson. New York: Harper, 1950.

Wilkins, Burleigh T. *Hegel's Philosophy of History*. Ithaca, New York: Cornell University, 1974.

Wilson, James. From "The Law of Nature" (part of his 1790-1791 lectures on the law). Included in *Documents in the History of American Philosophy*, ed. M. G. White, pp. 80-94.

Winthrop, John. From "A Modell of Christian Charity." Included in *The Puritans*, ed. P. Miller and T. H. Johnson. Vol. I, 195-199.

# INDEX

**Library of Congress Cataloging in Publication Data**

Banta, Martha.
    Failure and success in America.

    Bibliography: p.
    Includes index.
        1.    American literature—History and criticism.
    2.    Failure (Psychology) in literature.
    3.    Success in literature.        I.    Title.
    PS169.F34F3        810'.9'353        78-51156
    ISBN 0-691-06366-4
    ISBN 0-691-10070-5 pbk.